RHETORICAL CRITICISM

Second Edition

RHETORICAL CRITICISM
Exploration & Practice

Second Edition

Sonja K. Foss

WAVELAND

PRESS, INC.

Prospect Heights, Illinois

For information about this book, write or call:
Waveland Press, Inc.
P.O. Box 400
Prospect Heights, Illinois 60070
(847) 634-0081

Printed in the United States of America

7   6   5   4   3   2

Contents

Part II
CRITICAL APPROACHES   61

Preface

Rhetorical criticism is not a process confined to a few assignments in a rhetorical or media criticism course; it is an everyday activity we can use to understand our responses to symbols of all kinds in our environment, to reject those with negative impacts, and to create symbols of our own that generate the kinds of responses we intend. I hope this book will convey the excitement and significance of rhetorical criticism while providing clear guidelines for understanding and practicing critical analysis.

I am grateful to a number of people who have assisted me throughout my work on this project. Ernest G. Bormann, Cindy L. Griffin, D. Lynn O'Brien Hallstein, Kellie Hay, and Debian L. Marty read portions of the manuscript and provided invaluable suggestions that significantly improved the work. A. Susan Owen generously shared materials from her criticism courses that contributed in significant ways to my conception of the chapter on ideological criticism. Karen A. Foss, Robert Trapp, and Richard L. Johannesen read the entire manuscript of the first edition, which formed the basis for this version. Their gifts of time, energy, and support are particularly appreciated. Diana Brown Sheridan, Xing Lu, Laura K. Hahn, and Michelle A. Holling provided research support and assistance with bibliographies with competence, care, and efficiency. My publishers, Carol Rowe and Neil Rowe, provided their usual enthusiastic support, freedom to develop this book as I deemed best, and just the right amount of prodding to produce this revision. I also appreciate the willingness of the scholars whose work I have reprinted here to share their work; their excellent models of criticism both enrich and clarify the approaches they illustrate. Finally, this book is also a product of the questions, insights, and essays of criticism of the students in my rhetorical criticism courses at the University of Denver, the University of Oregon, and Ohio State University.

Special thanks go to my mother, Hazel M. Foss, for her continuing love and support, and to my husband, Anthony J. Radich, who is himself a superb rhetorical critic. He contributed to this project entertaining antics, constant good humor, and love.

PART I

Introduction

The Nature of Rhetorical Criticism

We live our lives enveloped in symbols. How we perceive, what we know, what we experience, and how we act are the results of our own symbol use and that of those around us. We distinguish between good and bad professors because one keeps us awake and interested in the subject, and another does not. We see a movie and urge our friends to see it. We listen to a speech by a political candidate and find ourselves supporting her because of the humor and grace with which she presents her arguments and the compassion they reveal. We choose posters, prints, and paintings to decorate our homes that give us new ways of seeing. These are but a few examples of the symbols we encounter every day. As we do, we engage in a process of thinking about symbols, discovering how they work, why they affect us, and choosing to communicate in particular ways as a result of the options they present. This process is called *rhetorical criticism*, and this book is designed to provide the opportunity to explore the theory of and to develop skills in this process.

Rhetoric

A useful place to start in the study of rhetorical criticism is with an understanding of what rhetoric is. Many of the common uses of the word, *rhetoric*, have negative connotations. *Rhetoric* is commonly used to mean empty, bombastic language that has no substance. Political candidates and governmental officials often call for "action, not rhetoric," from their opponents or the leaders of other nations. In other instances, *rhetoric* is used to mean flowery, ornamental speech that contains an abundance of metaphors and other figures of speech. These conceptions are not how rhetoric will be viewed in this book.

Here, *rhetoric* means the action humans perform when they use symbols for the purpose of communicating with one another. This definition suggests that four dimensions are of particular importance in conceptualizing rhetoric: (1) rhetoric is an *action*; (2) rhetoric is a *symbolic* action; (3) rhetoric is a *human* action; and (4) rhetoric functions to *enable us to communicate* with one another.

Action. When we engage in action, we are making conscious decisions about what to do. When we engage in rhetorical action, not only do we make conscious decisions to communicate, but we also make conscious choices from among our communicative options. The distinction between rhetorical and non-rhetorical action can be clarified with an example of someone who does not exercise regularly and who plays tennis for the first time in many years. Following the match, he tells his partner that he is out of shape and doesn't have much stamina. This is rhetorical activity because he selects symbolic strategies in an effort to explain to his partner how he is feeling, to suggest the source of his discomfort, and perhaps to rationalize his poor performance. The man also experiences an increased heart rate, a red face, and shortness of breath, but these changes in his bodily condition are not conscious choices. They communicate to his partner, just as his words do, but they are not actions he consciously wills and thus are not rhetorical.

Symbolic Action. Rhetoric is accomplished through a system of signs. In the simplest sense, a sign communicates when it is connected to another object. A distorted heart rhythm is connected to a heart attack. The freezing of water in winter is connected to a change in temperature. The word *chair* is connected to an object on which to sit. Some signs are symbolic; others are not. A non-symbolic sign is inherently connected to its physical referent in the way that changes in heart rate and rhythm are connected to a heart attack and the freezing of water is connected to a low temperature. All of these events are communication, but they are not rhetorical. A symbolic sign, in contrast, is only indirectly connected to its referent and is a human creation. The word *chair* has no natural relationship to an object for sitting; it was invented by someone who needed to refer to such an object. Rhetoric involves the kinds of signs that are symbolic; it is the use of arbitrary symbols to communicate with other people.

Human Action. The symbols we study in rhetorical criticism are those that are created by human beings or are products of the human imagination. Natural objects and events are not appropriate objects of analysis because they are independent of human invention, will, and control. Thus, we do not criticize the Grand Canyon or anthuriums, even though we may judge them to be grand or beautiful and recognize that they do affect our thought and actions. People can use natural phenomena, however, as part of rhetorical action—they can use them in symbolic ways. The Sierra Club, for example, may use a photograph of the Grand Canyon in a membership-recruitment brochure, and a bouquet of anthuriums placed in the center of a table may be used to create a particular kind of decor; these constitute symbolic uses. Humans, then, use all sorts of non-rhetorical objects in rhetorical ways.

Likewise, communication among animals is not considered to constitute rhetoric. Some people debate whether or not symbol use is a characteristic that distinguishes humans from all other species of animals, pointing to recent research with chimpanzees and gorillas in which these animals have been taught to communicate using American Sign Language or other kinds of signs. The debate about whether symbols are uniquely human is unresolved and perhaps unresolvable. Such communication, however, involves such a *difference in degree* that whether or not it is also a *difference in kind* is largely irrelevant to the position that the human is the symbol-using animal. Furthermore, even if certain primates can be taught signs that operate in some fundamentally symbolic ways, these species do not create any substantial part of their reality through their use of symbols. Accordingly, humans are animals who engage in action and who use rhetoric. Birds, bees, and dolphins communicate, but they do not communicate rhetorically. The term, *rhetor*, then, as used here, is a human designer, creator, or producer of rhetoric such as a speaker, a writer, an architect, or a filmmaker.

Enables Communication. Rhetoric functions in a variety of ways to allow humans to communicate among themselves, and they do so for a variety of reasons. In some cases, we use rhetoric in an effort to persuade others—to encourage others to change in some way. In other instances, rhetoric is an invitation to understanding—we offer our perspective and invite others to enter our world and to see it as we do, not in the hope that they will adopt our perspective but so they can understand us and our perspective better. Sometimes, we use rhetoric simply as a means of self-discovery or for coming to self-knowledge.

We may articulate thoughts or feelings out loud to ourselves or in a journal or diary and, in doing so, come to know ourselves and perhaps come to new perspectives on or make new decisions about our lives.

As we communicate with one another for these various reasons, we are creating, to some extent, a common world. Rhetoric is not simply the translation of some knowledge that we acquired somewhere else into a communicable form. It is the process by which our reality or our world comes into being; reality or knowledge of what is in the world is the result of communicating about it.

The notion that reality is created through rhetoric means that reality is not fixed. It changes according to the symbols we use to talk about it. What we count as "real" or as "knowledge" about the world depends on how we choose to label and talk about things. One example is in our use of terms to describe love. We commonly describe love as madness ("I'm *crazy* about him," "She *drives me out of my mind*," "He's gone *mad* over her," "I'm just *wild* about Harry") or as magic ("She *cast her spell* over me," "The *magic* is gone," "I was *entranced* by him," "She is *bewitching*").[1] Because we communicate about love using a vocabulary connected with madness and magic, we conceive of and experience love as a condition in which we are slightly out of control and in an abnormal state of some sort. The labels we use for love, then, suggest particular ways of believing about, acting toward, and knowing love. The labels focus our attention on certain features, exhibit an evaluation or attitude toward those features, and thus encourage us to experience the concept in a particular way. Labels affect our experience of empirical phenomena, as well. To call a police officer a *pig* rather than, for example, a *security officer*, suggests that we will view, interact with, and experience that individual in a particular way.

As its definition suggests, the scope of rhetoric is broad. Rhetoric is not limited to written and spoken discourse; indeed, speaking and writing make up only a small part of our total rhetorical environment. Symbols assume a variety of forms; any message, regardless of the form it takes or the channel of communication it uses, is rhetoric and is appropriate to study in rhetorical criticism. Rhetoric includes, then, nondiscursive or nonverbal symbols as well as discursive or verbal ones. Speeches, essays, conversations, poetry, novels, stories, television programs, films, art, architecture, plays, music, dance, advertisements, furniture, public demonstrations, and dress are all forms of rhetoric.

Rhetorical Criticism

Rhetorical criticism is the process of systematically investigating and explaining symbolic acts and artifacts for the purpose of understanding rhetorical processes. This definition includes three primary dimensions: (1) systematic analysis; (2) symbols as the objects of analysis; and (3) a purpose of understanding rhetorical processes.

Systematic Analysis. We all respond to symbols constantly, and as we encounter symbols, we try to figure out how they are working and why they have the impacts on us they do. The process of rhetorical criticism simply involves engaging in this natural process in a more systematic and focused way. Through the study and practice of rhetorical criticism, we can become more sophisticated and discriminating in explaining, investigating, and understanding symbols and our responses to them.

Symbolic Acts and Artifacts. The objects of study in rhetorical criticism are symbolic acts and artifacts. An *act* is executed in the presence of the rhetor's intended audience—a speech or a musical performance presented to a live audience, for example. Because an act tends to be fleeting and ephemeral, making its analysis difficult, many rhetorical critics prefer to study the artifact of an act—the text, trace, or tangible evidence of the act. When a rhetorical act is transcribed and printed, recorded on film, or preserved on canvas, it becomes a rhetorical artifact, which then is accessible to a wider audience than the one that witnessed the rhetorical act. Both acts and artifacts are objects of rhetorical criticism. But since most critics use the tangible product as the basis for criticism—a speech text, a building, a sculpture, a recorded song, for example—the term *rhetorical artifact* will be used in this book to refer to the object of study. The use of the term is not meant to exclude acts from the critic's investigation but rather to provide a consistent and convenient way to talk about the object of criticism.[2]

Understanding Rhetorical Processes. One reason to engage in criticism is to understand particular symbols and how they operate. A critic is interested in a particular kind of symbol use or a particular rhetorical artifact—the Vietnam Veterans Memorial in Washington, D.C., for example—and engages in criticism to deepen the appreciation and understanding of that artifact. But criticism undertaken only to comment on a particular artifact tends not to be "enduring; its importance and its functions are immediate and ephemeral."[3] Once the historical situation has been forgotten or the rhetor is no longer the center of the public's attention, such criticism no longer serves a useful purpose if it has been devoted exclusively to an understanding of a particular artifact.

The critic, then, does not study a rhetorical artifact for its qualities alone. Instead, the critic is interested in discovering what the artifact teaches about the nature of rhetoric. The critic moves beyond the particularities of the artifact under study to discover what it suggests about symbolic processes in general. Rhetorical criticism provides an initial general understanding of some aspect of rhetoric on the basis of the necessarily limited evidence available in the artifact.

The critic engages in rhetorical criticism to make a contribution to rhetorical theory.[4] *Theory* means a tentative answer to a question posed by someone seeking to understand the world. A theory is a set of general clues, generalizations, or principles that explain a process or phenomenon and thus help to answer the question asked. We are all theorists in our everyday lives, developing explanations for what is happening in our worlds based on our experiences and observations. If a friend never returns your phone calls, for example, you might come to the conclusion—or develop the theory—that the friendship is over. You have asked yourself a question about the state of the friendship, collected some evidence (made phone calls and observed that they were not returned), and reached a tentative conclusion (that the other person no longer wishes to be your friend).

In rhetorical criticism, the theorizing that is done deals with explanations about how rhetoric works. The critic asks a question about a rhetorical process or phenomenon and how it works, analyzes an artifact or artifacts that might offer some general clues about that process, and provides a tentative answer to the question. This answer does not have to be fancy, formal, or complicated. It simply involves identifying some of the basic concepts involved in a rhetorical phenomenon or process and how they work. Theorizing, then, is a process of stepping back from the myriad details of a phenomenon or process to take a broader view of it and to draw some conclusions about what it suggests for some aspect of rhetoric. The outcome should be a better understanding of rhetoric.

But the process of rhetorical criticism does not end with a contribution to theory. Its final outcome is a contribution to the improvement of our abilities as communicators and consumers of symbols. Rhetorical critics implicitly suggest how more effective symbol use may be accomplished. In suggesting some theoretical principles about how rhetoric operates, the critic is providing principles or guidelines for those of us who want to communicate in more self-reflective ways and to construct and employ rhetorical structures that best accomplish our goals.[5] As a result of our study of these principles, we should be more skilled, discriminating, and sophisticated in our efforts to communicate—in talk with our friends and family, in the design of persuasive messages for political and advertising campaigns, and in the decoration of our homes, for example.

Knowledge of the operation of rhetoric also can help make us more sophisticated audience members for messages. When we understand the various options available to rhetors in the construction of messages and how they work together to create the effects they produce, we are able to question the choices made in the construction of rhetorical artifacts because we see possibilities other than those selected. We are less inclined to accept existing rhetorical practices and to respond uncritically to the messages we encounter. As a result, our participation in the shaping of our culture is less reactive and more proactive.

Notes

[1]George Lakoff and Mark Johnson, *Metaphors We Live By* (Chicago: University of Chicago Press, 1980), p. 49.

[2]This distinction is suggested by Kathleen G. Campbell, "Enactment as a Rhetorical Strategy/Form in Rhetorical Acts and Artifacts," Diss. University of Denver 1988, pp. 25–29.

[3]Karlyn Kohrs Campbell, "Criticism: Ephemeral and Enduring," *Speech Teacher*, 23 (January 1974), p. 11.

[4]More elaborate discussions of rhetorical criticism as theory building can be found in: Roderick P. Hart, "Forum: Theory-Building and Rhetorical Criticism: An Informal Statement of Opinion," *Central States Speech Journal*, 27 (Spring 1976), 70–77; Richard B. Gregg, "The Criticism of Symbolic Inducement: A Critical-Theoretical Connection," in *Speech Communication in the 20th Century*, ed. Thomas W. Benson (Carbondale: Southern Illinois University Press, 1985), pp. 42–43; and Campbell, "Criticism," pp. 11–14.

[5]Discussions of rhetorical criticism to increase the effectiveness of communication can be found in: Robert Cathcart, *Post Communication: Criticism and Evaluation* (Indianapolis: Bobbs-Merrill, 1966), pp. 3, 6–7, 12; and Edwin Black, *Rhetorical Criticism: A Study in Method* (Madison: University of Wisconsin Press, 1978), p. 9.

Doing Rhetorical Criticism

The definitions of *rhetoric* and *rhetorical criticism* in chapter 1 have provided a starting place for understanding rhetorical criticism. Knowledge about what rhetorical criticism is does not automatically translate into the ability to *do* criticism, however. This chapter is designed to provide a practical supplement to chapter 1 by focusing on the actual process of producing an essay of criticism. It provides guidelines for the critic concerning how to proceed in the four steps involved in the process of rhetorical criticism: (1) formulating a research question and selecting an artifact; (2) selecting a unit of analysis; (3) analyzing the artifact; and (4) writing the critical essay.

Formulating a Research Question and Selecting an Artifact

The first step in the process of rhetorical criticism is to select a rhetorical artifact to criticize and a research question to answer through the criticism of the artifact. The artifact is the data for the study—the rhetorical act, event, or product that the critic analyzes. It may be any instance of symbol use that is of interest to the critic and seems capable of generating insights about rhetorical processes. It may be discursive—written or spoken language, such as a speech or an essay—or non-discursive—involving nonverbal symbols, such as a painting, a building, or a film. The research question is what the critic wants to find out about rhetoric by studying the artifact. The question guides the critic's analysis so that, at the end of the study, the critic is able to contribute to our understanding of how rhetorical processes work. Research questions are questions such as, "How does an ambiguous rhetorical artifact persuade?," "What strategies can an individual or an organization use to regain credibility after it has been lost?," or "What are the strategies used by subordinate groups to achieve legitimacy for their own perspective?"

Research questions contribute to the development of rhetorical theory in different ways. Some questions may suggest further elaboration of an existing theory about some aspect of rhetoric. The critic may notice contradictions in the artifact, for example, suggesting that a question about the nature and function of paradox may be appropriate. Research questions also may generate new theories about how rhetoric operates—they may bring the rhetor into territory that has not been studied by rhetoricians before. The critic may be interested in works of visual art, for example, and generate a question about what constitutes argumentation in visual artifacts. Visual argumentation has not been an area of study for rhetoricians, so, in asking and answering this question, the critic will be involved in the development of a new area of theory.

The process of formulating a research question and selecting an artifact to use as data for answering the question operates in one of three ways: (1) the critic discovers the artifact and research question simultaneously; (2) the critic formulates a research question first and then searches for data or a rhetorical artifact that will answer it; or (3) the critic encounters a rhetorical artifact of interest and then formulates a research question to ask about it.

Artifact and Question as Impetus

The impetus for a critical study may be that the critic encounters a rhetorical artifact and a question to ask about it simultaneously. In other words, the critic experiences an artifact, which itself seems to suggest a question. For example, visiting Elvis Presley's home, Graceland, could be such an impetus for a critic. A critic who was not very familiar with Elvis's music or perhaps did not like it prior to visiting Graceland may find that the tour of the home "converted" her into an Elvis fan.

Reflecting, as she leaves Graceland, on the change in attitude that the mansion and the artifacts displayed there seem to have evoked in her, she may ask herself how they were able to change her mind about the man to whom they belonged. This is a case where the rhetorical artifact—Graceland—and the question to be answered—"How do personal artifacts construct appeal for and impute value to their owner?"—are generated together.

Question as Impetus

A second stimulus for criticism is a question the critic wants to answer. The critic is interested in finding out about a particular aspect of a rhetorical process and has in mind a specific question that inquires into that process. The critic may be interested, for example, in how rhetors design messages for audiences they know will be hostile. Or, a critic may wonder if strategies used in the civil rights movement have changed since its inception in the 1950s, suggesting a contribution to rhetorical theory in the area of how movements change over time.

If the impetus for the critical study is a question, the critic next must discover a rhetorical artifact that will provide an answer to the question. Generally, locating an artifact is easy, for the question directs the critic to an appropriate artifact or artifacts for study. For a study of rhetors facing hostile audiences, the critic can choose an artifact from an almost infinite selection, ranging from a speech by the Pope to a group of American nuns who want to be priests to the screening of a pro-union film for an anti-union audience. The critic who wants to study changes in civil rights rhetoric can select speeches, essays, and books by civil rights leaders from both the 1950s and the 1990s as the artifacts for study. Another option for the same critic is to narrow the focus of the analysis and to look at the changes over time in the discourse of one civil rights leader—perhaps Jesse Jackson.

Artifact as Impetus

In many instances, a rhetorical artifact is of interest to the critic but does not immediately suggest a particular question that the critic wants to answer. The critic simply knows that the artifact is appealing, generates a sense of uneasiness or amazement, or seems unusual in some way. In this third approach to discovering the artifact and question, the critic has selected the artifact but has not yet formulated a question to ask about it. In this case, the impulse for criticism might originate from listening to a Supreme Court nominee withdraw from consideration and finding the speech interesting. Or it might result from viewing and being fascinated by the Norwegian artist Edvard Munch's paintings in a museum.

Once the artifact is selected, the critic turns to the task of generating a research question to ask about it. To develop a question from and about an artifact, the critic engages in a close examination of the artifact. The critic studies the artifact in detail over and over again, viewing the artifact from different perspectives and attending to different features each time. Each examination produces more information about the artifact's constituent elements, how they change over the course of the artifact, the relationships among the elements, patterns in the elements that comprise the artifact, and oppositions or contradictions, to name but a few. When the research question is generated from an artifact, the process of developing an appropriate research question often is difficult, frustrating, and time consuming. The critic knows something of rhetorical significance is occurring in the artifact but is not yet able to articulate it in a question. Sufficient time and energy spent exploring the artifact eventually will yield a question that will enable the critic to understand the particular artifact better and also make a contribution to rhetorical theory.

The critic who wants to analyze the NAMES Project AIDS Memorial Quilt, for example, might pay attention to features of the Quilt such as the size and shape of the blocks; the various media used, their colors and textures; the ways in which the individuals commemorated are presented; contradictions in these presentations; the specificity or ambiguity of the presentations; the themes depicted; the metaphors in the Quilt; the function the Quilt seems to serve for those who create the panels and those who view the Quilt; and the political assumptions and values suggested by the Quilt. As a result of such observations, the critic might develop as a research question, "What strategies are used by stigmatized groups in an effort to secure the support and acceptance of those who stigmatize them?"

The first step in the process of rhetorical criticism is the formulation of a question to ask that relates to rhetorical theory and selection of an artifact that can be investigated in order to provide at least a partial answer to the question. The artifact and the question may be formulated together in the critic's mind, or the question or the artifact may be generated first. Once both are selected, the critic moves to the second step of the process.

Selecting a Unit of Analysis

The second step in the process of rhetorical criticism is to select a unit of analysis that will be used to answer the research question. At this stage, the critic must decide on the aspects of the artifact to which to attend in order to answer the research question. The critic cannot possibly examine all of the rhetorical features of any artifact, so a unit of analysis on which to focus must be selected. The unit of analysis serves as a vehicle or lens for the critic to use to examine the artifact in order to answer the research question. It is a scanning device for picking up particular kinds of information about the artifact, and whichever one is selected will direct and narrow the analysis and thus the answer in particular ways, revealing some things and concealing others about the artifact. Units of analysis may be broad, such as strategies, types of evidence, implicit values, or components of an argument, or they may be more narrow, such as word choice, figures of speech, or metaphors.

The unit of analysis selected will depend on the research question the critic asks. The unit selected should be the one the critic believes best illuminates the significant features of the artifact and allows the question being asked about it to be answered. In some cases, more than one unit of analysis is needed to allow a research question to be answered. The critic may find, for example, that both the units of analysis of metaphors and fantasy themes are needed to explain the artifact and to answer the research question.

In many cases, the research question itself will suggest the unit of analysis that is most likely to answer the research question. A critic, for example, may notice that visual, aesthetic artifacts such as flowers, dress, jewelry, and other decoration seem to be a prominent part of the communication in traditional women's cultures such as sororities, Mary Kay Cosmetics, and the Junior League. From such an observation, the critic might develop as a research question, "How does aesthetic communication function in traditional women's cultures?" The units of analysis the critic chooses to use to answer this question would be the various aesthetic artifacts in the cultures and the functions they seem to perform.

In other instances, the critic will have more choice about the unit of analysis to use in analyzing the artifact to answer the research question. Many different kinds of units may seem to be appropriate and useful, particularly if the research question is broad. For example, if the research question deals with the strategies used to regain credibility, units of analysis could be metaphors, word choice, evidence, or strategies, to name but a few; rhetorical theory provides an infinite number of constructs that may function as units of analysis. The development of units of analysis from the research question, concepts, and theories is the subject of chapter 12.

Yet another source for units of analysis are those suggested in formal methods of criticism developed and used by rhetorical critics and theorists. Chapters 3 through 11 provide some samples of such methods, with each featuring a different unit or units of analysis. Simply because they are the focus of chapters in the book is not meant to suggest that the units of analysis included in formal methods of criticism should be privileged as units of analysis or that they are superior to any others. The critic should construct or select whatever unit of analysis best enables the research question to be answered. The units of analysis explained and illustrated in the chapters that follow should serve only as starting points for practicing criticism and for becoming accustomed to working with different kinds of units of analysis.

Analyzing the Artifact

At this point in the process of doing rhetorical criticism, the critic has an artifact to study, a question to ask about it that will elicit a contribution to rhetorical theory, and a unit of analysis that will allow the question to be answered. The critic's next task is to analyze the artifact using the unit of analysis selected or created. If the critic has selected metaphors as the unit of analysis, for example, the critic now identifies the metaphors in the artifact. If the critic has selected key terms as the unit of analysis, the terms are identified, and their meaning and function are explored. This is, then, a stage in which the critic engages in a close analysis of the artifact and becomes thoroughly familiar with whatever dimensions the selected unit of analysis features.

Writing the Critical Essay

Following the analysis of the artifact, the critic writes up the results or findings in an essay. An essay of criticism should include five major components: (1) an introduction; (2) description of the artifact and its context; (3) description of the unit of analysis; (4) report of the findings of the analysis; and (5) discussion of the contribution the analysis makes to answering the research question. These components do not need to be discussed in separate sections or identified with headings, but in some way they should be included in the essay.

Introduction.   The critic's task in the introduction to the essay is essentially the task of the introduction to any paper. It orients the reader to the topic and presents a clear statement of purpose that organizes the essay. The critic, in the introduction, says what artifact is being analyzed, the research question that is the impetus for the analysis, and the contribution to rhetorical theory that will result from the analysis. The critic also discusses why knowledge of the rhetorical process to which a contribution will be made is important—the "so what?" question. Why should the reader care about the topic and continue to read the essay? In an analysis of a speech in which a rhetor attempts to synthesize two polarized positions, for example, the critic may argue that this artifact is a model of how rhetors can create identification between opposing positions and suggest that knowledge about such a model is important for managing conflict effectively between any opposing factions.

Description of the Artifact. In order for those reading the essay to understand the analysis of the artifact, they must be somewhat familiar with the artifact itself. To acquaint readers with the artifact, the critic gives a brief overview or summary of the artifact near the beginning of the essay. If the critic is analyzing a film, for example, the critic provides an overview of the plot, the major characters, and significant technical features. If a speech is being analyzed, the description of the artifact contains the major arguments presented by the rhetor and any significant particularities of the rhetor's delivery, the occasion, and the response of the audience. The critic also needs to provide the context for the artifact, locating it within the social, political, and economic arrangements of which it is a part. If, for example, the critic is analyzing the anti-abortion film, *The Silent Scream*, the critic may want to give a brief history of the abortion controversy in the United States, name the groups and individuals who have figured prominently in the campaigns on both sides, and mention the Supreme Court decisions concerned with abortion.

The description of the artifact is, to some extent, an interpretation of the artifact. The critic cannot tell the reader everything about the artifact; decisions must be made about what to feature in the description. In this process, the critic chooses to describe and thus to highlight aspects of the artifact that are most important for and relevant to the analysis that will follow.

In the description of the artifact, the critic also provides a justification for why that artifact is a particularly appropriate or useful one to analyze in order to answer the research question. Many different artifacts often can be used for answering the critic's research question, so an explanation needs to be provided as to why the critic chose to analyze this particular artifact.

Description of the Unit of Analysis. The critic needs to cover one more topic to complete the reader's understanding of what will happen in the essay—a description of the unit of analysis to be used to analyze the artifact. If the unit of analysis derives from a formal method of criticism, this description references the method, defines its key concepts, and briefly lays out its basic tenets or procedures. If the unit of analysis chosen by the critic derives from the fantasy-theme method of criticism, for example, such a description might include a mention of its creator, Ernest Bormann; a definition of its basic terms, *fantasy theme* and *rhetorical vision*; and a brief explanation of the method's assumptions. The critic also justifies the selection of this method for the analysis, answering the question of why it provides the best unit of analysis for answering the research question.

If the unit of analysis was created by the critic from the research question, the unit of analysis is described by establishing links between the unit of analysis and the question; the critic explains why a particular unit of analysis is appropriate for the question. If the research question clearly calls for a particular unit of analysis, this description will be very short. A justification for its selection may not even be required if the link between the research question and the unit of analysis is obvious. A critic may choose to analyze Garrison Keillor's radio monologues on *A Prairie Home Companion*, for example, to discover the nature of spectatorship in the monologues; spectatorship is a preferred viewpoint from which to view the world of the text. In this case, a description of the unit of analysis (means of creating spectatorship) probably would consist of little more than an initial overview of the major ways in which Keillor creates such spectatorship.

Report of the Findings of the Analysis. The report of the findings of the analysis constitutes the bulk of the essay. In this section, the critic lays out for the reader the results of the analysis of the artifact. The critic tells what has been discovered from an application of the unit of analysis to the artifact and provides support for the discoveries from the data of the artifact. If the critic uses terms of the pentad as the unit of analysis (a unit derived from the pentadic method developed by Kenneth Burke), for example, the pentadic terms of act, purpose, agent, agency, and scene of the artifact are identified. If the critic has analyzed the artifact according to the ways in which the form enacts the rhetor's argument, the various means by which the message is or is not enacted are described.

The critic's task, in reporting the findings, is not to provide the one correct interpretation of the artifact or to uncover the truth about it. The artifact does not constitute a reality that can be known and proved—the critic never can know what the artifact "really" is. Objectivity and impartiality also are impossible in reporting the findings because the critic can know the artifact only through a personal interpretation of it. The critic brings to the critical task particular values and experiences, and these are reflected in how the critic sees and writes about the artifact. Thus, two critics may analyze the same artifact, ask the same question, use the same unit of analysis, and come up with different conclusions about the artifact. The critic's task is simply to offer one perspective on the artifact—one possible way of viewing the artifact and what is happening rhetorically in it.[1]

Because the critic cannot verify the various dimensions and qualities of an artifact objectively, the critic's task in reporting the findings is to offer reasons for or argue in support of the claims made.[2] The critic does this by presenting samples of the data of the artifact—actual quotations from a speech, descriptions of specific scenes in a film, or descriptions of the forms in a painting, for example. The critic then shows how these data led to a particular conclusion about them—the relationship the critic sees between the data and the conclusion or what in the artifact led to the claim the critic is making about it. The critic will not always be successful in convincing the reader to accept the claim being made about the artifact, but the reader should be able to see how the critic arrives at a particular view of and conclusions about the artifact.

Contribution to Answering the Research Question.   The critic ends the essay with a discussion of the contribution the analysis makes to answering the research question that generated the analysis. Here, the critic answers the research question to the extent possible and uses the answer to make a contribution to our understanding of the rhetorical processes with which the question deals. At the end of this section, the critic discusses the implications or expands on the significance of the contribution mentioned in the introduction. As a result of the new theoretical understanding of some rhetorical process provided, the critic suggests what that understanding means and why it is important.

Conclusion

The process of doing rhetorical criticism includes four major steps: (1) formulating a research question and selecting an artifact; (2) selecting a unit of analysis; (3) analyzing the artifact; and (4) writing the critical essay. Five components should be included in the completed essay: (1) an introduction, in which the research question, its contribution to rhetorical theory, and its significance are discussed; (2) description of the artifact and its context; (3) description of the unit of analysis; (4) report of the findings of the analysis; and (5) discussion of the contribution the analysis makes to answering the research question. These steps in the process of rhetorical criticism are repeated in each of the following chapters to provide a basic framework for criticism that remains constant regardless of the critic's research question, artifact, or unit of analysis.

The guidelines suggested for what is included in an essay of criticism and how it should be written point to the essence of rhetorical criticism as an art, not a science. Artifacts are dealt with more as the artist deals with experience than as the scientist does. A rhetorical critic, then, needs to bring a variety of creative abilities to bear throughout the process of rhetorical criticism—writing in a way that is not dull, helping the reader envision and experience an artifact in the way the critic does and conveying the critic's passion for and interest in the artifact; persuading the reader to view the artifact's contribution to rhetorical theory as the critic does; and offering a compelling invitation to readers to experience the world in a new way or to transform their lives as a result of contact with the artifact and the critical essay.[3]

The chapters that follow are designed to provide additional guidelines for the rhetorical critic. They provide samples for using formal methods of rhetorical criticism as the source for units of analysis. Each of the chapters features a critical method devised by a theorist or critic that may be useful if the research question being asked is one for which the method features an appropriate unit of analysis.

The chapters discussing formal methods of criticism are organized alphabetically: cluster, fantasy-theme, feminist, generic, ideological, metaphoric, narrative, and pentadic criticism. Because a critic might find any unit of analysis to be useful in answering a research question, I chose not to impose an order on them that might restrict the way in which they are used by critics. The exceptions to this organizational schema are the chapters on neo-Aristotelian criticism and generative criticism. Neo-Aristotelian criticism is the first of the chapters on formal methods because it was the first method of criticism developed in the communication field and the one to which other formal methods responded. It differs from the others in that it dictates a particular end for criticism. The chapter on generative criticism concludes the book because it involves a different source for units of analysis than do the types of criticism in the other chapters. Generative criticism also is an advanced approach to criticism that not all students will be ready to try.

Remember that the ten chapters that deal with various critical methods do not constitute all of the critical methods that have been or could be developed; the units of analysis they suggest, then, are not the only ones available to the critic. The units of analysis available to critics are infinite and limited only by the critic's imagination. The best criticism is done not by imposing a critical method with its unit of data on an artifact but by developing a unit of analysis that best suits the research question and the artifact. The chapters on various methods of criticism, then, are provided only as samples to acquaint critics with some of the previous thinking that has been done on what constitutes useful units of analysis in criticism and to provide practice in some of the basic procedures of rhetorical criticism. These methods are not to be viewed as the only sources for units of analysis or as the only legitimate ones to be applied to any and all rhetorical artifacts.

To help the critic become comfortable with the critical process and to learn to produce excellent criticism, I have included in each chapter four components, each offering a different opportunity for exploring the method and the kinds of insights its units of analysis produce. Each chapter begins with a theoretical overview of the critical method, including a discussion of its origins, assumptions, and the units of analysis the method offers. The second part of each chapter details the procedures or steps the critic goes through to use the unit of analysis provided by the method to do rhetorical criticism. This is followed by sample essays in which the unit of analysis offered by the method has been used; these are designed to show beginning critics how the unit of analysis offered in the method is used in a critical essay. Some of the sample essays were written by students, and some were written by professional rhetorical critics. Beginning critics with no experience in rhetorical criticism probably will find the essays by the students shorter, simpler, and more accessible, but all of the essays were selected because they model the use of a unit of analysis in criticism with particular clarity. (Many of the essays, however, exemplify more than one critical approach.) Each chapter ends with a list of additional samples of essays in which the unit of analysis that is the subject of the chapter has been used. These bibliographies are not exhaustive; they are designed simply to serve as places to start for critics who wish to locate other samples of the various critical methods.

I hope these different kinds of opportunities for learning about, exploring, and actually using various critical methods will make them accessible and understandable to anyone who is interested in practicing rhetorical criticism. I hope, too, that they will make the process of learning about and using criticism an enjoyable one. For while the process of rhetorical criticism is demanding and difficult, it is also very exciting and, quite simply, fun.

Notes

[1] Standards for adequacy in rhetorical criticism are discussed more fully in Sonja K. Foss, "Criteria for Adequacy in Rhetorical Criticism," *Southern Speech Communication Journal*, 48 (Spring 1983), 283–95.

[2] A good discussion of the role of argument in rhetorical criticism is provided by Wayne Brockriede, "Rhetorical Criticism as Argument," *Quarterly Journal of Speech*, 60 (April 1974), 165–74. Barbara A. Larson suggests that Stephen Toulmin's model of argument can be used to connect data and claims in rhetorical criticism. See "Method in Rhetorical Criticism: A Pedagogical Approach and Proposal," *Central States Speech Journal*, 27 (Winter 1976), 297–301.

[3] This notion was suggested in Philip Wander and Steven Jenkins, "Rhetoric, Society, and the Critical Response," *Quarterly Journal of Speech*, 58 (December 1972), 446.

Neo-Aristotelian Criticism
Beginnings of Rhetorical Criticism

The first formal method of rhetorical criticism developed in the communication field came to be called the *neo-classical, neo-Aristotelian,* or *traditional* method of criticism. The central features of the neo-Aristotelian method first were suggested in 1925 by Herbert A. Wichelns in "The Literary Criticism of Oratory."[1] Until Wichelns' essay, no specific guidelines for criticism were used by critics, nor was there even a clear understanding of what rhetorical criticism was. Because Wichelns' essay provided "substance and structure to a study which heretofore had been formless and ephemeral, . . . it literally *created* the modern discipline of rhetorical criticism."[2] Donald C. Bryant elaborated on the impact Wichelns' essay had on the practice of rhetorical criticism, asserting that it "set the pattern and determined the direction of rhetorical criticism for more than a quarter of a century and has had a greater and more continuous influence upon the development of the scholarship of rhetoric and public address than any other single work published in this century."[3]

In his essay, Wichelns began by distinguishing literary criticism from rhetorical criticism, asserting that rhetorical criticism "is not concerned with permanence, nor yet with beauty," as is literary criticism. Rather, it "is concerned with effect. It regards a speech as a communication to a specific audience, and holds its business to be the analysis and appreciation of the orator's method of imparting his ideas to his hearers."[4] Wichelns' concern with this distinction reflects the origins of the communication discipline in departments of English; early theorists in communication wanted to develop their field as a separate and legitimate discipline.

But Wichelns' major contribution to the development of neo-Aristotelianism was that he listed the topics that should be covered in the study of a speech. The critic, he suggested, should deal with these elements: the speaker's personality, the public character of the speaker or the public's perception of the speaker, the audience, the major ideas presented in the speech, the motives to which the speaker appealed, the nature of the speaker's proofs, the speaker's judgment of human nature in the audience, the arrangement of the speech, the speaker's mode of expression, the speaker's method of speech preparation, the manner of delivery, and the effect of the discourse on the immediate audience and its long-term effects.[5]

Although Wichelns did not discuss *how* the critic should analyze these topics, they were many of the same topics discussed by Aristotle in the *Rhetoric* and by other classical rhetoricians such as Cicero and Quintilian. Thus, critics turned to classical sources for elaboration of Wichelns' guidelines and began to use as units of analysis the classical canons of rhetoric—invention, arrangement, style, delivery, and memory. They used as their framework for criticism the topics covered and the perspectives taken on them by the ancient rhetorical theorists.

Wichelns' suggested approach to rhetorical criticism was solidified in numerous critical studies that followed. The widespread use of neo-Aristotelianism was particularly evident in the two-volume *A History and Criticism of American Public Address*, edited by William Norwood Brigance and published in 1943.[6] In the studies included in this work, authors used either the Aristotelian pattern alone or in combination with those of other classical rhetoricians to guide their critical efforts. Wichelns' method became more firmly fixed in 1948 with the publication of *Speech Criticism*, in which Lester Thonssen and A. Craig Baird presented an elaborated system for the practice of rhetorical criticism based on the topics suggested by Wichelns and the writings of classical rhetoricians.[7]

As a consequence of the adoption of neo-Aristotelianism as virtually *the* method of rhetorical criticism in the early years of the communication field, the practice of rhetorical criticism was limited in subject matter and purpose. Rhetorical criticism became the study of speeches, since the approach required that the critic determine the effect of the rhetoric on the immediate audience; thus, neo-Aristotelianism was not used to study written discourse or non-discursive rhetoric. Neo-Aristotelianism also led to the study of single speakers because the sheer number of topics to cover relating to the rhetor and the speech made dealing with more than a single speaker virtually impossible. Thus, various speeches by different rhetors related by form or topic were not included in the scope of rhetorical criticism.[8]

The single speakers who were the focus of study were limited further in that they tended to be individuals of the past—generally, white men—who had made significant contributions in a particular area of public affairs. The critic was required to determine a number of details about the speaker's life, public character, and the audience for the speech at the time. Such data were only available for famous people and usually more readily available after their deaths.

Neo-Aristotelian criticism was virtually unchallenged as the method to use in rhetorical criticism until the 1960s, when the orthodoxy that had developed in rhetorical criticism began to be criticized on a number of grounds. One criticism was that the work on which neo-Aristotelianism is based, Aristotle's *Rhetoric*, was not intended as a guide for critics. The *Rhetoric* and other classical works that were being used to guide the critic were designed to teach others how to speak well; nothing in them suggested they were to be used to appraise discourse.[9]

The use of classical works as the basis for criticism was the result, suggested Mark Klyn, of an erroneous view of the proper role of the critic. The rhetorical critic was being imagined primarily in the role of a teacher, concerned less with the illumination of particular works of rhetoric than with using insights gained from criticism to help others speak effectively. Thus, the role of the critic had been designed to be useful to the practitioner. In order to be useful in this way, the critic was required to produce criticism concerned "with the intricacies of rhetorical strategies and the 'effects' they are thought to have produced."[10] Klyn argued that the absurdity of this notion can be seen if a parallel argument is made in the areas of fiction and film. The task of the critic of fiction is not considered to be to teach readers to write their own stories or of the film critic to teach readers how to make their own films.[11] Yet, the rhetorical critic is required to be concerned with teaching the art of speaking. As a result, Klyn argued, "the practical has become the mundane, the technical, the arid."[12]

The concern with effects that derived, in part, from an emphasis on teaching effective speech led to another problem with the singular approach to rhetorical criticism embodied in neo-Aristotelianism. An exclusive concern with effects does not always produce significant criticism, critics of neo-Aristotelianism argued. "Did the speech evoke the intended response from the immediate audience?" and "Did the rhetor use the available means of persuasion to achieve the desired response?" are not always the most appropriate questions to ask about a rhetorical artifact, do not always produce significant insights into it, and sometimes are simply not worth asking. As Otis M. Walter pointed out, the critic who is studying Jesus' Sermon on the Mount using the neo-Aristotelian approach asks whether Jesus used the means of persuasion available to him. But this question may not produce a significant answer. More interesting might be questions such as, "Were Jesus' means of persuasion consistent with his ethical doctrines?" or "What changes in Old Testament morality did Jesus present?"[13] But neo-Aristotelian criticism does not allow the critic to explore these questions. As Karlyn Kohrs Campbell explained, neo-Aristotelianism "excludes all *evaluations* other than the speech's potential for evoking intended response from an immediate, specified audience."[14]

Still others objected to neo-Aristotelianism on the grounds that the works on which it was based—Aristotle's *Rhetoric* and other classical writings—were written at a time and in the context of cultures that were different in values, orientation, and knowledge from ours. Yet, critics using the neo-Aristotelian mode of criticism assumed that what were believed to be ideal rhetorical principles in ancient Greek and Roman cultures are the same today. In other words, critics of this approach suggested that rhetorical principles have undergone change since their formulation in classical Greek and Roman times, and later cultures have modified or elaborated those principles.[15] To use only classical tenets of rhetoric as units of analysis in criticism was to ignore a large body of new scholarship in and thinking about rhetorical principles.

Yet another criticism of neo-Aristotelianism concerned its rational bias. As Campbell explained, a basic assumption of the approach is that our unique attribute is the capacity to be rational, and humans are able to engage in persuasion and be subject to it only because they are rational beings. Thus, rhetoric is seen as the art of reasoned discourse or argumentation. Emotional and psychological appeals exist and affect persuasion, the neo-Aristotelian view holds, but they are secondary to judgments resulting from rational means of persuasion. One consequence, explained Campbell, is that " 'true' or 'genuine' rhetoric becomes the art by which men are induced to act in obedience to reason in contrast to 'false' or 'sophistic' rhetoric which uses any and all means to produce acquiesence."[16] Critics and theorists operating out of this approach either must denigrate or ignore nonrational appeals and attempt, generally fruitlessly, to distinguish between rational and nonrational appeals.

Another major criticism of neo-Aristotelianism as the presiding method of criticism was that it encouraged the mechanical application of categories to rhetoric, with the result that critics were sometimes unimaginative and self-fulfilling. Critics set out to find the particular rhetorical techniques suggested by classical rhetoricians, such as logical argument and emotional appeals, and, indeed, did find them being used in the speech under study. But rather than helping the critic understand and illuminate the speeches using these units of analysis, neo-Aristotelianism sometimes became "a mechanical accounting or summing up of how well the speech fits an *a priori* mold."[17]

These criticisms and others of how the neo-Aristotelian framework for criticism limited the potential of criticism led, in the 1960s, to pluralism in approaches taken to rhetorical criticism. As evident in the remaining chapters of this book, a wide variety of approaches now are being used in rhetorical criticism. Today, critics who use the neo-Aristotelian approach to analyze rhetoric are few, and essays that feature the method rarely find their way into the journals and convention programs of the communication field. Discussions and defenses of neo-Aristotelianism ended largely in the early 1970s.[18]

As the first critical approach developed in the communication field, neo-Aristotelianism served to differentiate the discipline from literature and literary criticism and helped to legitimize it by focusing on its classical roots. While the critic may not choose to use this approach in critical essays, understanding its basic components will facilitate the critic's understanding of the approaches discussed in the remainder of the book, for they were developed largely in response to both the strengths and limitations of neo-Aristotelian criticism.

Procedures

The neo-Aristotelian approach to criticism involves three major tasks: (1) reconstructing the context in which the rhetorical artifact occurred; (2) analyzing the artifact itself; and (3) assessing the impact of the artifact on the audience in light of the various options available to the rhetor. The summaries of these three procedures in the following sections are brief; much more detail about them is available in *Speech Criticism*.[19]

Reconstruction of Context

Connecting the rhetorical artifact with its context helps the critic discover how various components of the context affected the rhetoric that was formulated. To understand this context, the critic investigates three major components of it—the rhetor, the occasion, and the audience.

First, the critic discovers information about the rhetor. The aim of this inquiry, however, is not to develop a typical biography of the individual's life. Rather, the purpose is to study the individual as a rhetor and to discover links between the rhetor's history, experience, and character and the rhetorical efforts of the rhetor. The critic, for example, may want to seek information about early environmental influences on the rhetor's attitudes, motivation, and communication skills. Other areas to investigate include whether the rhetor had formal training in the rhetorical medium selected for expression, the rhetor's previous experience with the subject and the medium, the rhetor's rhetorical philosophy or principles, and methods of rhetorical preparation. Finally, the critic seeks to discover the motivating forces of the rhetor—why the rhetor chose to produce this rhetoric on this particular occasion and what the rhetor sought to accomplish.

After investigating the background of the rhetor to ascertain any effects on the rhetorical artifact, the critic turns to an examination of the occasion on which the rhetoric was presented. The rhetorical act is affected by factors in the occasion, so the critic attempts to determine the elements in the occasion that influenced the rhetor in choice of subject and approach or the peculiar demands of the time and the place of the rhetoric. The critic tries to discover the historical antecedents of the rhetoric, the specific events that gave rise to and followed it, and the social and cultural attitudes toward the topic of the rhetoric.

The critic completes the examination of the context by looking at the audience for the rhetoric. The rhetor constructs rhetoric to accomplish a particular goal for a specific individual or group. Knowing about the audience, then, helps the critic understand why the rhetor selected particular strategies. The same forces that helped to shape the occasion for the rhetor also affect the audience, so the critic probably already knows something about the audience through investigating the occasion. Additional lines of inquiry are the composition of the audience, the rhetor's reputation for this audience, and the listeners' knowledge about and attitudes toward the rhetor's subject.

Analysis of the Rhetorical Artifact

The second component of neo-Aristotelian criticism is the actual analysis of the rhetorical artifact itself. This analysis is done according to the five canons of classical rhetoric. In classical Greek and Roman times when the study of rhetoric began, rhetoric was divided into five parts—the canons of rhetoric. They involved all the steps that go into the process of public speaking.[20] The canons are: (1) invention, the location and creation of ideas and materials for the speech; (2) organization, the structure or arrangement of the speech; (3) style, the language of the speech; (4) memory (mastery of the subject matter), which may include the actual memorizing of the speech; and (5) delivery, management of the voice and gestures in the presentation of the speech.

Invention.   The critic's concern in applying the canon of invention is with the speaker's major ideas, lines of argument, or content. Invention is based on two major forms of proof. External or inartistic proofs are those the author uses from other sources but does not create, including the testimony of witnesses or documents such as contracts and letters. Internal or artistic proofs, those that the rhetor creates, fall into three categories: (1) *logos*, or logical argument; (2) *ethos*, or the appeal of the rhetor's character; and (3) *pathos*, or emotional appeal.

Logos deals with the logical or rational elements of the rhetoric and with the effect of these elements on the audience. In discovering the rhetor's use of logical appeals, the critic identifies the argument or thesis the rhetor is presenting and determines how that thesis is developed and supported. The evidence presented to enforce or support the point is evaluated in terms of the beliefs of the audience and the context of the rhetoric. Whether the evidence is the quoting of experts, statistical summaries, personal experience, or some other form, the critic examines it to see whether it is relevant to the thesis being developed, whether the evidence is consistent, and whether sufficient evidence has been supplied to make the point.

But a rhetor cannot simply present evidence to the audience and leave it; something has to be done with the evidence to encourage the audience to come to some conclusion based on it. This is the process of reasoning, which assumes two major forms—inductive and deductive. In inductive reasoning, a series of specific examples is used to draw a general conclusion. Six cases in which individuals who drove cars after they had been drinking alcohol were involved in serious accidents could be used by a rhetor to make the point, for example, that people should not drink and drive. Deductive reasoning, in contrast, begins with a generalization that is acceptable to the audience, and the rhetor then applies the generalization to a specific case. A rhetor who begins with the generalization that smoking and lung cancer are linked may conclude, using deductive reasoning, that those in the audience who smoke are in danger of developing the disease. The critic, then, assesses both the evidence and the reasoning used by the rhetor to develop the thesis.

The second form of artistic proof, *ethos*, is what we today call *credibility*; it deals with the effect or appeal of the speaker's character on the audience. The critic's concern in analyzing *ethos* is with determining how the rhetor's character, as known to the audience prior to the speech and as presented to the audience through the rhetorical act or artifact, facilitates the acceptance of belief on the part of the audience. Credibility is demonstrated by a rhetor largely through the display of three qualities in the rhetorical act: (1) moral character or integrity, demonstrated through linking the message and rhetor with what the audience considers virtuous; (2) intelligence, demonstrated through a display of common sense, good taste, and familiarity with current topics and interests; and (3) good will, or the establishment of rapport with the audience. Good will is created through identification of the rhetor with the listeners, straightforwardness, and praise of the audience.

The third form of artistic proof, *pathos*, concerns appeals designed to generate emotions in the audience. Here, the critic tries to discover what emotions were generated by the speech—perhaps fear or shame or pity—and how those emotions put the listeners in a frame of mind so they will react favorably to the rhetor's purpose.

Organization. The second major area of the rhetorical artifact the critic analyzes using the neo-Aristotelian method is the arrangement or structure of the rhetoric. The critic's task here is to determine the general pattern of arrangement adopted for the rhetoric—for example, a chronological order, where material is divided into time units, or a problem-solution order, where a discussion of a problem is followed by suggested solutions to it. The critic also determines which aspects of the content are given emphasis by the rhetoric through the structure and the various functions the parts of the artifact perform. Emphasis can be determined by discovering which parts of the rhetoric are given greater stress through their placement at the beginning or end, the topic on which the rhetor spends the most time, and the ideas that are repeated. Finally, the critic assesses the results of the arrangement of the discourse in its entirety and wants to know if the organization of the speech is consistent with the subject and purpose of the discourse and is appropriate for the audience.

Style. The canon of style deals with the language used by the rhetor. The critic assesses how particular kinds of words or other symbols are used by the rhetor to create varying effects and how the symbols are arranged to form larger units such as sentences. The critic makes a determination of the general effect that results—whether common and ordinary, forceful and robust, or stately and ornate. In general, the critic's concern in examining style is with whether the language style contributes to the accomplishment of the rhetor's goal—assists in the development of the thesis, facilitates the communication of ideas, and thus helps to create the intended response.

Delivery.   The canon of delivery is concerned with the speaker's manner of presentation. In the application of this canon, the critic investigates the influence of delivery on the success of the rhetorical artifact. In a public speech, delivery involves the rhetor's mode of presentation—whether the speech is delivered impromptu, from memory, by reading from a manuscript, or extemporaneously. The critic examines the bodily action of the rhetor while delivering the rhetoric— posture, movement, gestures, and eye contact, as well as how the appearance and physical characteristics of the rhetor affected the audience. Finally, the critic assesses the vocal skill of the rhetor, including how articulation, pronunciation, rate of speech, and pitch contributed to the audience's acceptance of the message.

Memory.   While memory also is among the five classical canons of rhetoric, it was not dealt with systematically by Aristotle. Partly for this reason and also because few speeches are memorized today (and memory is irrelevant to most non-discursive forms of rhetoric), this canon often is not applied by the neo-Aristotelian critic. When it is, it deals with the rhetor's control of the materials of the rhetorical artifact, the relation of memory to the mode of presentation selected, and methods for improving memory.

Assessment of Effects

At the conclusion of criticism using neo-Aristotelianism, the critic judges the effects of the rhetoric. Because the rhetoric was designed to accomplish some goal—the rhetor sought a response of some kind—the critic determines whether or not this goal was met or what happened as a result of the rhetoric. There is no single measure of effectiveness, however, and how the critic chooses to assess the effects depends on the characteristics of a rhetorical artifact itself, the rhetor's intention, the audience to which the rhetoric is addressed, and the context in which the rhetoric is presented. The effectiveness of a speech frequently is judged by the immediate and/or long-term response of the audience— either those changes immediately visible in the audience or that emerge at a later time.

The process of neo-Aristotelian criticism, then, involves a recon- struction of the context in which the rhetoric occurred, including attention to the rhetor, the occasion, and the nature of the audience. The second part of the criticism involves the analysis of the rhetorical artifact itself, in which the critic uses the canons of classical rhetoric to assess the invention, organization, style, and delivery of the artifact. Finally, the critic judges the rhetorical artifact's effects according to the rhetor's purpose.

Sample Essays

The two essays that follow demonstrate the neo-Aristotelian approach to criticism. Forbes Hill's essay on a speech by Richard Nixon not only provides an illustration of neo-Aristotelian criticism but also an assessment of the value of this critical approach. Gary W. Brown uses neo-Aristotelian criticism to analyze the rhetoric of Saddam Hussein during the Persian Gulf War.

Notes

[1]Herbert A. Wichelns, "The Literary Criticism of Oratory," in Studies in Rhetoric and Public Speaking in Honor of James A. Winans, ed. A. M. Drummond (New York: Century, 1925), pp. 181–216. A more accessible source for the essay is Herbert A. Wichelns, "The Literary Criticism of Oratory," in Methods of Rhetorical Criticism: A Twentieth-Century Perspective, ed. Bernard L. Brock and Robert L. Scott, 2nd ed. (Detroit: Wayne State University Press, 1980), pp. 40–73.

[2]Mark S. Klyn, "Toward a Pluralistic Rhetorical Criticism," in Essays on Rhetorical Criticism, ed. Thomas R. Nilsen (New York: Random House, 1968), p. 154.

[3]Donald C. Bryant, ed., The Rhetorical Idiom: Essays in Rhetoric, Oratory, Language, and Drama (Ithaca: Cornell University Press, 1958), p. 5.

[4]Wichelns, in Brock and Scott, p. 67.

[5]Wichelns, in Brock and Scott, pp. 69–70.

[6]William Norwood Brigance, ed., A History and Criticism of American Public Address, 2 vols. (New York: McGraw-Hill, 1943). A third volume was published in 1955: Marie Kathryn Hochmuth, ed., A History and Criticism of American Public Address, III (New York: Longmans, Green, 1955).

[7]Lester Thonssen and A. Craig Baird, Speech Criticism (New York: Ronald, 1948). In the second edition of the book, a third author was added: Lester Thonssen, A. Craig Baird, and Waldo W. Braden, Speech Criticism, 2nd ed. (New York: Ronald, 1970).

[8]Mohrmann and Leff point out that neo-Aristotelianism itself does not preclude the study of discourse larger than a single speech; in fact, Aristotle discusses oratorical genres— deliberative or political speaking, forensic or legal speaking, and epideictic or ceremonial speaking. The notion of genres was not incorporated into the neo-Aristotelian approach because of Wichelns' determination that the purpose of rhetorical criticism is to uncover effects on the specific audience. See G. P. Mohrmann and Michael C. Leff, "Lincoln at Cooper Union: A Rationale for Neo-Classical Criticism," Quarterly Journal of Speech, 60 (December 1974), 463.

[9]Edwin Black, Rhetorical Criticism: A Study in Method (Madison: University of Wisconsin Press, 1978), p. 33; and Otis M. Walter, "On the Varieties of Rhetorical Criticism," in Essays in Rhetorical Criticism, ed. Thomas R. Nilsen (New York: Random House, 1968), p. 162.

[10]Klyn, p. 150.

[11]Klyn, pp. 150–51.

[12]Klyn, p. 155.

[13]Walter, pp. 162–65.

[14]Karlyn Kohrs Campbell, "The Forum: 'Conventional Wisdom—Traditional Form': A Rejoinder," Quarterly Journal of Speech, 58 (December 1972), 454.

[15]Black, p. 124.

[16]Karlyn Kohrs Campbell, "The Ontological Foundations of Rhetorical Theory," *Philosophy and Rhetoric*, 3 (Spring 1970), 98.

[17]Douglas Ehninger, "Rhetoric and the Critic," *Western Speech*, 29 (Fall 1965), 230.

[18]See, for example: J. A. Hendrix, "In Defense of Neo-Aristotelian Rhetorical Criticism," *Western Speech*, 32 (Fall 1968), 216-52; Forbes I. Hill, "Conventional Wisdom—Traditional Form: The President's Message of November 3, 1969," *Quarterly Journal of Speech*, 58 (December 1972), 373-86; Campbell, "The Forum," pp. 451-54; Forbes I. Hill, "The Forum: Reply to Professor Campbell," *Quarterly Journal of Speech*, 58 (December 1972), 454-60; and Mohrmann and Leff, pp. 459-67.

[19]Thonssen, Baird, and Braden.

[20]Although these canons were formulated to apply to public speaking and neo-Aristotelian criticism originally was applied to speeches, the canons can be applied to rhetorical acts and artifacts of various kinds. Admittedly, in such an application, the canons and neo-Aristotelian criticism must be stretched. For an excellent example of this kind of expansion of the scope of the canons, see Nancy Harper, *Human Communication Theory: The History of a Paradigm* (Rochelle Park, NJ: Hayden, 1979), pp. 181-261.

Conventional Wisdom—
Traditional Form—
The President's Message of
November 3, 1969

Forbes Hill

More than one critique of President Nixon's address to the nation on November 3, 1969 has appeared,[1] which is not remarkable, since it was the most obvious feature of the public relations machine that appears to have dammed back the flood of sentiment for quick withdrawal of American forces from Southeast Asia. To be sure, the dike built by this machine hardly endured forever, but some time was gained—an important achievement. It seems natural, then, that we should want to examine this obvious feature from more than one angle.

Preceding critiques have looked at Nixon's message from notably non-traditional perspectives. Stelzner magnified it in the lens of archetypal criticism, which reveals a non-literary version of the quest story archetype, but he concluded that the President's is an incomplete telling of the story that does not adequately interact with the listeners' subjective experiences. Newman condemned the message as "shoddy rhetoric" because its tough stance and false dilemmas are directed to white, urban, uptight voters. Campbell condemned it on the basis of intrinsic criticism because though its stated purposes are to tell the truth, increase credibility, promote unity, and affirm moral responsibility, its rhetoric conceals truth, decreases credibility, promotes division, and dodges moral responsibility. Then, stepping outside the intrinsic framework, she makes her most significant criticism: the message perpetuates myths about American values instead of scrutinizing the real values of America.

I propose to juxtapose these examinations with a strict neo-Aristotelian analysis. If it differs slightly from analyses that follow Wichelns[2] and Hochmuth-Nichols,[3] that is because it attempts a critique that re-interprets neo-Aristotelianism slightly—a critique guided by the spirit and usually the letter of the Aristotelian text as I understand it. What

From *Quarterly Journal of Speech*, 58 (December 1972), 373–86. Used by permission of the Speech Communication Association and the author.

the neo-Aristotelian method can and should do will be demonstrated, I hope, by this juxtaposition.

Neo-Aristotelian criticism compares the means of persuasion used by a speaker with a comprehensive inventory given in Aristotle's *Rhetoric*. Its end is to discover whether the speaker makes the best choices from the inventory to get a favorable decision from a specified group of auditors in a specific situation. It does not, of course, aim to discover whether or not the speaker actually gets his favorable decision; decisions in practice are often upset by chance factors.[4] First the neo-Aristotelian critic must outline the situation, then specify the group of auditors and define the kind of decision they are to make. Finally he must reveal the choice and disposition of three intertwined persuasive factors—logical, psychological, and characterological—and evaluate this choice and disposition against the standard of the *Rhetoric*.

The Situation

The state of affairs for the Nixon Administration in the fall of 1969 is well known. The United States had been fighting a stalemated war for several years. The cost in lives and money was immense. The goal of the war was not clear; presumably the United States wanted South Viet Nam as a stable non-Communist buffer state between Communist areas and the rest of Southeast Asia. To the extent that this goal was understood, it seemed as far from being realized in 1969 as it had been in 1964. In the meantime, a large and vocal movement had grown up, particularly among the young, of people who held that there should have been no intervention in Viet Nam in the first place and that it would never be possible to realize any conceivable goal of intervention. The movement was especially dangerous to the Administration because it numbered among its supporters many of the elements of the population who were most interested in foreign policy and best informed about it. There were variations of position within the peace movement, but on one point all its members were agreed: the United States should commit itself immediately to withdraw its forces from Viet Nam.

The policy of the Nixon Administration, like that of the Johnson Administration before it, was limited war to gain a position of strength from which to negotiate. By fall 1969 the Administration was willing to make any concessions that did not jeopardize a fifty-fifty chance of achieving the goal, but it was not willing to make concessions that amounted to sure abandonment of the goal. A premature withdrawal amounted to public abandonment and was to be avoided at all costs. When the major organizations of the peace movement announced the first Moratorium Day for October 15 and organized school and work stoppages, demonstrations, and a great "March on Washington" to dramatize the demand for immediate withdrawal from Viet Nam, the Administration launched a counterattack. The President announced that he would make a major address on Viet Nam November 3. This announcement seems to have moderated the force of the October moratorium, but plans were soon laid for a second moratorium on November 15. Nixon's counterattack aimed at rallying the mass of the people to disregard the vocal minority and oppose immediate withdrawal; it aimed to get support for a modified version of the old strategy: limited war followed by negotiated peace. The address was broadcast the evening of November 3 over the national radio and television networks.

The Auditors and the Kind of Decision

An American President having a monopoly of the media at prime time potentially reaches an audience of upwards of a hundred million adults of heterogeneous backgrounds and opinions. Obviously it is impossible to design a message to move every segment of this audience, let alone the international audience. The speaker must choose his targets. An examination of the texts shows us which groups were eliminated as targets, which were made secondary targets, and which were primary. The speaker did not address himself to certain fanatical opponents of the war: the ones who hoped that the Viet Cong would gain a signal victory over the Americans and their South Vietnamese allies, or those who denied that Communist advances were threats to non-Communist countries, or those against any war for any reason. These were the groups the President sought to isolate and stigmatize. On the other hand, there was a large group of Americans who would be willing to give their all to fight any kind of Communist expansion anywhere at any time. These people also were not a target group: their support could be counted on in any case.

The speaker did show himself aware that the Viet Cong and other Communist decision-makers were listening in. He represented himself to them as willing and anxious to negotiate and warned them that escalation of the war would be followed by effective retaliation. The Communists constituted a secondary target audience, but the analysis that follows will make plain that the message was not primarily intended for them.

The primary target was those Americans not driven by a clearly defined ideological commitment to oppose or support the war at any cost. Resentment of the sacrifice in money and lives, bewilderment at the stalemate, longing for some movement in a clearly marked direction—these were the principal aspects of their state of mind assumed by Nixon. He solicited them saying "tonight—to you, the great silent majority of my fellow Americans—I ask for your support."[5]

His address asks the target group of auditors to make a decision to support a policy to be continued in the future. In traditional terms, then, it is primarily a deliberative speech. Those who receive the message are decision-makers, and they are concerned with the past only as it serves as analogy to future decisions. The subjects treated are usual ones for deliberation: war and peace.[6]

Disposition and Synopsis

The address begins with an enthymeme that attacks the credibility gap.[7] Those who decide on war and peace must know the truth about these policies, and the conclusion is implied that the President is going to tell the truth. The rest of the proem is taken up by a series of questions constructing a formal partition of the subjects to be covered. The partition stops short of revealing the nature of the modification in policy that constitutes the Nixon plan. The message fits almost perfectly into the Aristotelian pattern of proem, narrative, proofs both constructive and refutative, and epilogue. Just as proem has served as a general heading for a synoptic statement of what was done in the first few sentences, so the other four parts will serve us as analytical headings for a synopsis of the rest.

The narrative commences with Nixon's statement of the situation as he saw it on taking office. He could have ordered immediate withdrawal of American forces, but he decided to fulfill "a greater obligation . . . to think of the effect" of his decision "on the next generation, and on the future of peace and freedom in America, and in the world." Applicable here is the precept: the better the moral end that the speaker can in his narrative be seen consciously choosing, the better the ethos he reveals.[8] An end can hardly be better than "the future of peace and freedom in America, and in the world." The narrative goes on to explain why and how the United States became involved in Viet Nam in the first place. This explanation masquerades as a simple chronological statement—"Fifteen years ago . . ." but thinly disguised in the chronology lie two propositions: first, that the leaders of America were right in intervening on behalf of the government of South Viet Nam; second, that the great mistake in their conduct of the war was over-reliance on American combat forces. Some doubt has been cast on the wisdom of Nixon's choice among the means of persuasion here. The history, writes one critic, "is a surprising candidate for priority in any discussion today. . . . The President's chief foreign policy advisors, his allies on Capitol Hill, and the memorandum he got from the Cabinet bureaucracy all urged him to skip discussions of the causes and manner of our involvement. Yet history comes out with top billing."[9] This criticism fails to conceive the rhetorical function of the narrative: in the two propositions the whole content of the proofs that follow is foreshadowed, and foreshadowed in the guise of a non-controversial statement about the historical facts. Among traditional orators this use of the narrative to foreshadow proofs is common, but it has seldom been handled with more artistry than here.

Constructive proofs are not opened with an analytical partition but with a general question: what is the best way to end the war? The answer is structured as a long argument from logical division: there are four plans to end American involvement; three should be rejected so that the listener is left with no alternative within the structure but to accept the fourth.[10] The four plans are: immediate withdrawal, the consequences of which are shown at some length to be bad; negotiated settlement, shown to be impossible in the near future because the enemy will not negotiate in earnest; shifting the burden of the war to the Vietnamese with American withdrawal on a fixed timetable, also argued to have bad consequences; and shifting the burden of the war to the Vietnamese with American withdrawal on a flexible schedule, said to have good consequences, since it will eventually bring "the complete withdrawal of all United States *combat ground* forces," whether earnest negotiations become possible or not. Constructive proofs close with one last evil consequence of immediate withdrawal: that it would lead eventually to Americans' loss of confidence in themselves and divisive recrimination that "would scar our spirit as a people."

As refutative proof is introduced, opponents of the Administration are characterized by a demonstrator carrying a sign, "Lose in Viet Nam"; they are an irrational minority who want to decide policy in the streets, as opposed to the elected officials—Congress and the President—who will decide policy by Constitutional and orderly means. This attack on his presumed opponents leads to a passage which reassures the majority of young people that the President really wants peace as much as they do. Reassuring ends with the statement of Nixon's personal belief that his plan will succeed; this statement may be taken as transitional to the epilogue.

The epilogue reiterates the bad consequences of immediate withdrawal—loss of confidence and loss of other nations to totalitarianism—it exhorts the silent majority to support the plan, predicting its success; it evokes the memory of Woodrow Wilson; then it closes with the President's pledge to meet his responsibilities to lead the nation with strength and wisdom. Recapitulation, building of ethos, and reinforcing the right climate of feeling—these are what a traditional rhetorician would advise that the epilogue do,[11] and these are what Nixon's epilogue does.

Indeed, this was our jumping-off place for the synopsis of the message: it falls into the traditional paradigm; each frame of the paradigm contains the lines of argument conventional for that frame. The two unconventional elements in the paradigm—the unusual placement of the last evil consequence of immediate withdrawal and the use of the frame by logical division for the constructive proofs—are there for good rhetorical reasons. That last consequence, loss of confidence and divisive recrimination, serves to lead into the refutation which opens with the demonstrator and his sign. It is as if the demonstrator were being made an example in advance of just this evil consequence. The auditor is brought into precisely the right set for a refutation section that does not so much argue with opponents as it pushes them into an isolated, unpopular position.

Because of the residues-like structure, the message creates the illusion of proving that Vietnamization and flexible withdrawal constitute the best policy. By process of elimination it is the only policy available, and even a somewhat skeptical listener is less likely to question the only policy available. Approaching the proposal with skepticism dulled, he perhaps does not so much miss a development of the plan. In particular, he might not ask the crucial question: does the plan actually provide for complete American withdrawal? The answer to this question is contained in the single phrase, "complete withdrawal of all United States combat ground forces." It is fairly clear, in retrospect, that this phrase concealed the intention to keep in Viet Nam for several years a large contingent of air and support forces. Nixon treats the difference between plan three, Vietnamization and withdrawal on a fixed schedule, and plan four, Vietnamization and withdrawal on a flexible schedule, as a matter of whether or not the schedule is announced in advance. But the crucial difference is really that plan three was understood by its advocates as a plan for quick, complete withdrawal; plan four was a plan for partial withdrawal. The strategic reason for not announcing a fixed schedule was that the announcement would give away this fact. The residues structure concealed the lack of development of the plan; the lack of development of the plan suppressed the critical fact that Nixon did not propose complete withdrawal. Although Nixon's message shows traditionally conventional structure, these variations from the traditional show a remarkable ability at designing the best adaptations to the specific rhetorical situation.

Logical and Psychological Persuasive Factors

Central to an Aristotelian assessment of the means of persuasion is an account of two interdependent factors: (1) the choice of major premises on which enthymemes[12] that form "the body of the proof" are based, and (2) the means whereby auditors are brought into states of feeling favorable to accepting these premises and the conclusions following from them. Premises important here are of two kinds: predictions and values. Both kinds as they relate to good and evil consequences of the four plans to end American involvement, will be assessed. The first enthymeme involving prediction is that immediate withdrawal followed by a Communist takeover would lead to murder and imprisonment of innocent civilians. This conclusion follows from the general predictive rule: the future will resemble the past.[13] Since the Communists murdered and imprisoned opponents on taking over North Viet Nam in 1954 and murdered opponents in the city of Hue in 1968, they will do the same when they take over South Viet Nam. Implied also is an enthymeme based on the value premise that security of life and freedom from bondage are primary goods for men;[14] a Communist takeover would destroy life and freedom and therefore destroy primary goods for men.

Presumably no one would try to refute this complex of enthymemes by saying that life and freedom are not primary goods, though he might argue from more and less;[15] more life is lost by continuing the war than would be lost by a Communist takeover, or American-South Vietnamese political structures allow for even less political freedom than the Communist alternatives. Nixon buries these questions far enough beneath the surface of the message that probably auditors in the target group are not encouraged to raise them. One could also attack the predictive premise: after all, the future is not always the past writ over again. But this kind of refutation is merely irritating; we know that the premise is not universally true, yet everyone finds it necessary to operate in ordinary life as if it were. People on the left of the target group, of course, reject the evidence—North Viet Nam and Hue.

A related prediction is that immediate withdrawal would result in a collapse of confidence in American leadership. It rests on the premise that allies only have confidence in those who both have power and will act in their support.[16] If the United States shows it lacks power and will in Viet Nam, there will be a collapse of confidence, which entails further consequences: it would "promote recklessness" on the part of enemies everywhere else the country has commitments, i.e., as a general premise, when one party to a power struggle loses the confidence of its allies, its enemies grow bolder.[17] The conclusion is bolstered by citations from former presidents Eisenhower, Johnson, and Kennedy: the statement of the "liberal saint," Kennedy, is featured.

It is difficult to attack the related premises of these tandem arguments. They rest on what experience from the sandbox up shows to be probable. The target group consists of people with the usual American upbringing and experience. Someone will question the premises only if he questions the worldview out of which they develop. That view structures the world into Communist powers—actual or potential enemies—and non-Communist powers—allies. America is the leader of the allies, referred to elsewhere as the forces of "peace and freedom" opposed by "the forces of totalitarianism." Because of its association with freedom, American leadership is indisputably good, and whatever weakens confidence in it helps the enemies. Only a few people on the far left would categorically reject this structure.

The foregoing premises and the worldview fundamental to them are even more likely to be accepted if the auditors are in a state of fear. Fear may be defined as distress caused by a vision of impending evil of the destructive or painful kind.[18] This message promotes a state of fear by the nature of the evil consequences developed—murder and imprisonment of innocents, collapse of leadership in the free world, and reckless aggressiveness of implacable enemies. America is the prototype of a nation that is fearful; her enemies are watching their opportunities all over the globe, from Berlin to the Middle East, yes even in the Western Hemisphere itself. The enemies are cruel and opposed to American ideals. They are strong on the battlefield and intransigent in negotiations. Conditions are such that America's allies may lose confidence in her and leave her to fight these enemies alone. But these circumstances are not too much amplified: only enough to create a state of feeling favorable to rejecting immediate withdrawal, not so much as to create the disposition for escalation.

Nixon claims to have tried hard to make a negotiated settlement, but he could not make one because the Communists refused to compromise. The evidence that they would not compromise is developed at length: public initiatives through the peace conference in Paris are cited, terms for participation of the Communist forces in internationally supervised elections offered, and promises made to negotiate on any of these terms. Then there were private initiatives through the Soviet Union and directly by letter to the leaders of North Viet Nam, as well as private efforts by the United States ambassador to the Paris talks. These efforts brought only demands for the equivalent of unconditional surrender. The citation of evidence is impressive and destroys the credibility of the position that negotiations can bring a quick end to the war.

Nixon does not explicitly predict that the plan for negotiated settlement will not work ever; on the contrary, he says that he will keep trying. But if the auditor believes the evidence, he finds it difficult to avoid making his own enthymeme with the conclusion that negotiated settlement will never work; the major premise is the same old rule, the future will be like the past. Nixon gives another reason, too: it will not work while the opposite side "is convinced that all it has to do is to wait for our next concession, and our next concession after that one, until it gets everything it wants." The major premise—no power convinced that victory is probable by forcing repeated concessions will ever compromise—constitutes a commonplace of bargaining for virtually everyone.

Peace is seen in these arguments as almost an unqualified good. Although compromise through bargaining is the fastest way to peace, the other side must make concessions to assure compromise. Reasons for continuing the war, such as an ideological commitment, are evil. There is no glory in war and prolonging it is not justified by political gains made but only by a commitment to higher values like saving lives and preserving freedom. Prolonging the war is also justified as avoiding future wars by not losing Southeast Asia altogether and not promoting the spirit of recklessness in the enemies. "I want," states Nixon, "to end it [the war] in a way which will increase the chance that their [the soldiers'] younger brothers and their sons will not have to fight in some future Vietnam. . . ."

A listener is prone to reject the likelihood of a negotiated peace if he is angry with his opponents. Anger is a painful desire for revenge and arises from an evident, unjustified slight to a person or his friends.[19] People visualizing revenge ordinarily refuse compromise except as a temporary tactic. Nixon presents the American people as having been slighted: they value peace, and their leaders have with humility taken every peace initiative possible: public, private, and secret. The Communist powers wish to gain politically from the war; they have rebuffed with spite all initiatives and frustrated our good intentions by demanding the equivalent of unconditional surrender. Frustration is, of course, a necessary condition of anger.[20] Again, Nixon does not go too far—not far enough to create a psychological climate out of which a demand for escalation would grow.

Nixon announces that his plan for Vietnamization and American withdrawal on a flexible timetable is in effect already. Its consequences: American men coming home, South Vietnamese forces gaining in strength, enemy infiltration measurably reduced, and United States' casualties also reduced. He predicts: policies that have had such consequences in the past will have them in the future, i.e., the future will be like the past. Again, the undisputed value that saving lives is good is assumed. But in this case the argument, while resting on an acceptable premise, was, at the time of this speech, somewhat more doubtful of acceptance by the target group. The evidence constitutes the problem: obviously the sample of the past since the policy of Vietnamization commenced was so short that no one could really judge the alleged consequences to be correlated with the change in policy, let alone caused by it. There is, then, little reason why that audience should have believed the minor premise—that the consequences of Vietnamization were good.

A temporizing and moderate policy is best presented to auditors who while temporarily fearful are basically confident. Nothing saps the will to accept such a proposal as does the opposite state, basically fearful and only temporarily confident. Confidence is the other side of the coin from fear: it is pleasure because destructive and painful evils seem far away and sources of aid near at hand.[21] The sources of aid here are the forces of the Republic of South Viet Nam. They have continued to gain in strength and as a result have been able to take over combat responsibilities from American forces. In contrast, danger from the enemy is receding—"enemy infiltration . . . over the last three months is less than 20 per cent of what it was over the same period last year." Nixon assures his auditors that he has confidence the plan will succeed. America is the "strongest and richest nation in the world"; it can afford the level of aid that needs to be continued in Viet Nam. It will show the moral stamina to meet the challenge of free world leadership.

For some time rumors about gradual American withdrawal from Viet Nam had been discounted by the peace movement. The only acceptable proof of American intentions would be a timetable showing withdrawal to be accomplished soon. Thus the third plan: withdrawal on a fixed timetable. Nixon predicts that announcing of a timetable would remove the incentive to negotiate and reduce flexibility of response. The general premise behind the first is a commonplace of bargaining: negotiations never take place without a *quid pro quo*; a promise to remove American forces by a certain date gives away the *quid pro quo*. For most Americans, who are used to getting things by bargaining, this premise is unquestionable. Only those few who think that the country can gain no vestige of the objective of the war are willing to throw away the incentive. The premises behind the notion of flexibility—that any workable plan is adaptable to changes in the situation—is a commonplace of legislation and not likely to be questioned by anyone. Nixon adds to this generally acceptable premise a specific incentive. Since withdrawal will occur more rapidly if enemy military activity decreases and the South Vietnamese forces become stronger, there is a possibility that forces can be withdrawn even sooner than would be predicted by a timetable. This specific incentive is illusory, since it is obvious that one can always

withdraw sooner than the timetable says, even if he has one; it is hard
to see how a timetable actually reduces flexibility. Everyone makes
timetables, of course, and having to re-make them when conditions
change is a familiar experience. But the average man who works from
nine to five probably thinks that the government should be different:
when it announces a timetable it must stick to it; otherwise nothing is
secure. This argument may seem weak to the critic, but it is probably
well directed to the target group. The real reason for not announcing
a timetable has already been noted.[22]

One final prediction is founded on the preceding predictions—
whenever a policy leads to such evil consequences as movement of
Southeast Asia into alliance with the enemy and a new recklessness on
the part of enemies everywhere, it will eventually result in remorse and
divisive recrimination which will, in turn, result in a loss of self-
confidence. Guiltlessness and internal unity, the opposites of remorse
and recrimination, are here assumed as secondary goods leading to self-
confidence, a primary good. The enthymeme predicting loss of self-
confidence consequent on immediate withdrawal is summary in
position: it seems to tie together all previous arguments. It comes right
after a particularly effective effort at *ethos* building—the series of
statements developed in parallel construction about not having chosen
the easy way (immediate withdrawal) but the right way. However, it rests
on the assumption that the long term mood of confidence in the country
depends on the future of Southeast Asia and the recklessness of our
enemies. Since these two factors are only an aspect of a larger picture
in which many other events play their parts, it is surely not true that
they alone will produce a loss of confidence. The enthymeme based on
this assumption, placed where it is, however, does not invite questioning
by the target group. Doubtful though it may look under searching
scrutiny, it has an important function for the structure of psychological
proof in this message. It reinforces the vague image of the danger of
facing a stronger enemy in a weakened condition: America itself would
be less united, less confident, and less able to fight in the future if this
consequence of immediate withdrawal were realized.

Other things being equal, the more commonplace and universally
accepted the premises of prediction in a deliberative speech, the more
effective the speech. This is especially true if they are set in a frame that
prepares the auditor psychologically for their acceptance. There is almost
no doubt that given the policy of the Nixon Administration—
Vietnamization and partial withdrawal on a flexible schedule not
announced in advance—the message shows a potentially effective choice
of premises. In some cases it is almost the only possible choice. Likewise
the value structure of the message is wisely chosen from materials

familiar to any observer of the American scene: it could be duplicated in hundreds of other messages from recent American history.

Several additional value assumptions are equally commonplace. Betraying allies and letting down friends is assumed to be an evil, and its opposite, loyalty to friends and allies the virtue of a great nation. This premise equates personal loyalty, like that a man feels for his friend, with what the people of the whole nation should feel for an allied nation. Many people think this way about international relations, and the good citizens of the target group can be presumed to be among them.

Policies endorsed by the people they are supposed to help are said to be better policies than those not endorsed by them. This statement undoubtedly makes a good political rule if one expects participation in the execution of policy of those to be helped. Policies that result from the operation of representative government are good, whereas those made on the streets are bad. This value is, of course, an essential of republican government: only the most radical, even of those outside the target group, would question it. Finally, Nixon assumes that the right thing is usually the opposite of the easy thing, and, of course, he chooses to do the right thing. Such a value premise does not occur in rhetorics by Aristotle or even George Campbell; it is probably a peculiar product of Protestant-American-on-the-frontier thinking. Its drawing power for twentieth-century urban youngsters is negligible, but the bulk of the target group probably is made up of suburbanites in the 30–50 category who still have some affinity for this kind of thinking.

Some shift from the traditional values of American culture can be seen in the tone of Nixon's dealing with the war: the lack of indication that it is glorious, the muted appeal to patriotism (only one brief reference to the first defeat in America's history), the lack of complete victory as a goal. But nowhere else does the culture of the post-atomic age show through: by and large the speech would have been applauded if delivered in the nineteenth century. That there has been a radical revolution of values among the young does not affect the message, and one might predict that Nixon is right in deciding that the revolution in values has not yet significantly infected the target group.

Characterological and Stylistic Factors

Nixon's choice of value premises is, of course, closely related to his *ethos* as conveyed by the speech. He promises to tell the truth before he asks the American people to support a policy which involves the overriding issues of war and peace—phraseology that echoes previous Nixonian messages. He refrains from harsh criticism of the previous administration; he is more interested in the future America than in political gains: such an avowal of disinterestedness is the commonest topic for self-character building.

Nixon is against political murders and imprisonments and active pushing initiatives for peace. He is flexible and compromising, unlike the negotiators for the enemy. He chooses the right way and not the easy way. He is the champion of policy made by constitutional processes; his opponents conduct unruly demonstrations in the streets. But he has healthy respect for the idealism and commitment of the young; he pledges himself in the tradition of Woodrow Wilson to win a peace that will avoid future wars. He has the courage to make a tasteful appeal to patriotism even when it's unpopular. Such is the character portrait drawn for us by Richard Nixon: restrained not hawkish, hard-working and active, flexible, yet firm where he needs to be. He seems an American style democrat, a moral but also a practical and sensitive man. The message is crowded with these overt clues from which we infer the good ethos of political figures in situations like this. Any more intensive development of the means of persuasion derived from the character of the speaker would surely have been counter-productive.

The language of Nixon's message helps to reinforce his ethos. His tone is unbrokenly serious. The first two-thirds of the message is in a self-consciously plain style—the effort is clearly made to give the impression of bluntness and forthrightness. This bluntness of tone correlates with the style of deliberative argumentation:[23] few epideictic elements are present in the first part of the speech. Everything seems to be adjusted to making the structure of residues exceedingly clear.

About two-thirds of the way through, the message shifts to a more impassioned tone. The alternative plans are collapsed into two, thus polarizing the situation: either immediate withdrawal or Nixon's plan for Vietnamization and unscheduled withdrawal. From here on parallel repetitions are persistent, and they serve no obvious logical function, but rather function to deepen the serious tone. There is, in short, an attempt to rise to a peroration of real eloquence. The qualities aimed at in the last third of the message seem to be gravity and impressiveness more than clarity and forthrightness. The effort seems to tax the speechwriter's literary skill to the limit, and the only new phrases he comes up with are the "silent majority" and the description of the energies of the young as "too often directed to bitter hatred against those they think are responsible for the war." All else is a moderately skillful pastiche of familiar phrases.

General Assessment

A summary answer can now be given to the question, how well did Nixon and his advisors choose among the available means of persuasion for this situation? The message was designed for those not ideologically overcommitted either to victory over Communism or to peace in any case while frustrated by the prolonged war. It operates from the most universally accepted premises of value and prediction; it buries deep in its texture most premises not likely to be immediately accepted. Enough of the means for bringing auditors into states of fear, anger, and confidence are used to create a psychological climate unfavorable to immediate withdrawal and favorable to Vietnamization. The goals—life, political freedom, peace, and self-confidence—are those shared by nearly all Americans, and connections of policies to them are tactfully handled for the target group. The structure is largely according to tradition: it can best be seen as falling into the four parts, and the right elements are contained in each of the parts. Two minor variations from the traditional are artfully designed to realize evident psychological ends. Conventional wisdom and conventional value judgments come dressed in conventional structure. The style of the narrative and proofs reflects adequately Nixon's .reliance on clearly developed arguments from accepted premises; the style of the latter part of the message shows a moderately successful attempt at grandeur. In choice and arrangement of the means of persuasion for this situation this message is by and large a considerable success.

Neo-Aristotelian criticism tells a great deal about Nixon's message. It reveals the speech writer as a superior technician. It permits us to predict that given this target group the message should be successful in leading to a decision to support the Administration's policies. It brings into sharp focus the speechwriter's greatest technical successes: the choice of the right premises to make a version of the domino theory plausible for these auditors and the creation of a controlled atmosphere of fear in which the theory is more likely to be accepted. Likewise, the choice of the right means of making success for peace negotiations seems impossible and the building of a controlled state of anger in which a pessimistic estimate of the chances for success seems plausible. Also the finely crafted structure that conceals exactly what needs to be concealed while revealing the favored plan in a context most favorable to its being chosen.

What neo-Aristotelianism does not attempt to account for are some basic and long-run questions. For instance, it does not assess the wisdom of the speaker's choice of target audience as does Newman, who wanted the President to alleviate the fears of the doves. All critics observe that Nixon excludes the radical opponent of the war from his audience. Not only is this opponent excluded by his choice of policy but even by the choice of premises from which he argues: premises such as that the Government of South Viet Nam is freer than that of North Viet Nam, or that the right course is the opposite of the easy one. Radical opponents of the war were mostly young—often college students. The obvious cliché, "they are the political leadership of tomorrow," should have applied. Was it in the long run a wise choice to exclude them from the target? An important question, but a neo-Aristotelian approach does not warrant us to ask it. There is a gain, though, from this limitation. If the critic questions the President's choice of policy and premises, he is forced to examine systematically all the political factors involved in this choice. Neither Newman nor Campbell do this in the objective and systematic fashion required by the magnitude of the subject. Indeed, would they not be better off with a kind of criticism that does not require them to do it?

Nor does the neo-Aristotelian approach predict whether a policy will remain rhetorically viable. If the critic assumes as given the Nixon Administration's choice of policy from among the options available, he will no doubt judge this choice of value and predictive premises likely to effect the decision wanted. To put it another way, Nixon's policy was then most defensible by arguing from the kinds of premises Nixon used. It seems less defensible at this writing, and in time may come to seem indefensible even to people like those in the target group. Why the same arguments for the same policy should be predictably less effective to people so little removed in time is a special case of the question, why do some policies remain rhetorically viable for decades while others do not. This question might in part be answered by pointing, as was done before, to the maturing of the students into political leadership. But however the question might be answered, neo-Aristotelianism does not encourage us to ask it. As Black truly said, the neo-Aristotelian comprehends "the rhetorical discourse as tactically designed to achieve certain results with a specific audience on a specific occasion"[24] in this case that audience Nixon aimed at on the night of November 3, 1969.

Finally, neo-Aristotelian criticism does not warrant us to estimate the truth of Nixon's statements or the reality of the values he assumes as aspects of American life. When Nixon finds the origin of the war in a North Vietnamese "campaign to impose a Communist government on South Vietnam by instigating and supporting a revolution," Campbell takes him to task for not telling the truth. This criticism raises a serious question: are we sure that Nixon is not telling the truth? We know, of course, that Nixon oversimplifies a complex series of events—any speaker in his situation necessarily does that. But will the scholar of tomorrow with the perspective of history judge his account totally false? Campbell endorses the view that basically this is a civil war resulting from the failure of the Diem government backed by the United States to hold elections under the Geneva Agreements of 1954. But her view and Nixon's are not mutually exclusive: it seems evident to me that both the United States and Communist powers involved themselves from the first to the extent they thought necessary to force an outcome in their favor in Viet Nam. If a scientific historian of the future had to pick one view of the conflict or the other, he would probably pick Nixon's because it more clearly recognizes the power politics behind the struggle. But I am not really intending to press the point that Campbell commits herself to a wrong view, or even a superficially partial one. The point is that she espouses here a theory of criticism that requires her to commit herself at all. If anyone writing in a scholarly journal seeks to assess the truth of Nixon's statements, he must be willing to assume the burden of proving them evidently false. This cannot be done by appealing to the wisdom of the liberal intellectuals of today.[25] If the essential task were accomplished, would the result be called a *rhetorical* critique? By Aristotle's standards it would not, and for my part I think we will write more significant criticism if we follow Aristotle in this case. To generalize, I submit that the limitations of neo-Aristotelian criticism are like the metrical conventions of the poet—limitations that make true significance possible.

Notes

[1]Robert P. Newman, "Under the Veneer: Nixon's Vietnam Speech of November 3, 1969," *QJS*, 56 (Apr. 1970), 168–178; Hermann G. Stelzner, "The Quest Story and Nixon's November 3, 1969 Address," *QJS*, 57 (Apr. 1971), 163–172; Karlyn Kohrs Campbell, "An Exercise in the Rhetoric of Mythical America," in *Critiques of Contemporary Rhetoric* (Belmont, CA: Wadsworth, 1972), pp. 50–58.

[2]Herbert A. Wichelns, "The Literary Criticism of Oratory," in Donald C. Bryant, ed., *The Rhetorical Idiom: Essays in Rhetoric, Oratory, Language, and Drama* (1925; rpt. Ithaca: Cornell Univ. Press, 1958), pp. 5–42.

[3]Marie Hochmuth [Nichols], "The Criticism of Rhetoric," in *A History and Criticism of American Public Address* (New York: Longmans, Green, 1955) III, 1–23.

[4]Aristotle, *Rhetoric* I. 1. 1355b 10–14. "To persuade is not the function of rhetoric but to investigate the persuasive factors inherent in the particular case. It is just the same as in all other arts; for example, it is not the function of medicine to bring health, rather to bring the patient as near to health as is possible in his case. Indeed, there are some patients who cannot be changed to healthfulness; nevertheless, they can be given the right therapy." (Translation mine.) I understand the medical analogy to mean that even if auditors chance to be proof against any of the means of persuasion, the persuader has functioned adequately as a rhetorician if he has investigated these means so that he has in effect "given the right therapy."

[5]Text as printed in *Vital Speeches*, 36 (15 Nov. 1969), 69.

[6]Aristotle *Rhetoric* I. 4. 1359b 33–1360a 5.

[7]Aristotle *Rhetoric* III. 14. 1415a 29–33. Here Nixon functions like a defendant in a forensic speech. "When defending he will first deal with any prejudicial insinuation against him . . . it is necessary that the defendant when he steps forward first reduce the obstacles, so he must immediately dissolve prejudice."

[8]See Aristotle *Rhetoric* III. 16. 1417a 16–36.

[9]Newman, p. 173.

[10]See Aristotle *Rhetoric* II. 23. 1398a 30–31. This basic structure is called method of residues in most modern argumentation textbooks.

[11]Aristotle *Rhetoric* III. 19. 1419b 10–1420a 8.

[12]For the purpose of this paper the term enthymeme is taken to mean any deductive argument. Aristotle gives a more technical definition of enthymeme that fits into the total design of his organon; in my opinion it is not useful for neo-Aristotelian criticism.

[13]Remarkably enough Aristotle does not state this general rule, though it clearly underlies his treatment of the historical example, *Rhetoric* II. 20.

[14]See Aristotle *Rhetoric* I. 6. 1362b 26–27 for life as a good; I. 8. 1366a for freedom as the object of choice for the citizens of a democracy.

[15]The subject of *Rhetoric* I. 7. Chaim Perelman and L. Olbrechts-Tyteca, commenting on this chapter, indicate that there is usually a consensus on such statements as 'life is good'; the dispute is over whether life is a greater good than honor in this particular situation. See *The New Rhetoric: A Treatise on Argumentation*, trans. John Wilkinson and Purcell Weaver (Notre Dame: Univ. of Notre Dame Press, 1969), pp. 81–82.

[16]See Aristotle *Rhetoric* II. 19. 1393a 1–3.

[17]This principle follows from *Rhetoric* II. 5. 1383a 24–25.

[18]Aristotle *Rhetoric* II. 5. 1382a 21–22. Aristotle treated the *pathe* as states of feeling that a man enters into because he draws certain inferences from the situation around him: he sees, for example, that he is the type of man who experiences pity when faced with this type of victim in these circumstances. The means of getting a man to draw inferences are themselves logical proofs; hence *pathos* does not work apart from the logical proofs in a message but through them. See Aristotle *Rhetoric* II. 1. 1378a 19–28 and my explication in James J. Murphy, ed. *A Synoptic History of Classical Rhetoric* (New York: Random House, 1972).

[19]Aristotle *Rhetoric* II. 2. 1378a 30–32.

[20]Aristotle *Rhetoric* II. 2. 1379a 10–18.

[21]Aristotle *Rhetoric* II. 5. 1383a 16–19.

[22]Since he gave this speech Nixon has made a general timetable for American withdrawal, thus, presumably, showing that he was not utterly convinced by his own argument. But he has never quite fixed a date for complete withdrawal of all American support forces from Viet Nam; he has been consistent in maintaining that withdrawal as a bargaining point for negotiation with the Viet Cong and North Vietnamese.

[23]See Aristotle *Rhetoric* III. 12. 1414a 8–19.

[24]Edwin Black, *Rhetorical Criticism: A Study in Method* (New York: Macmillan, 1965), p. 33.

[25]Richard H. Kendall, writing a reply to Newman, "The Forum," *QJS*, 56 (Dec. 1970), 432, makes this same point, particularly in connection with Newman's implication that ex-President Johnson was a fraud. "If so, let us have some evidence of his fraudulent actions. If there is no evidence, or if there is evidence, but an essay on the rhetoric of President Nixon does not provide proper scope for a presentation of such evidence, then it seems to me inclusion of such a charge (or judgment) may fall into the category of gratuitous." Newman in rejoinder asks, "Should such summary judgments be left out of an article in a scholarly journal because space prohibits extensively supporting them? Omission might contribute to a sterile academic purity, but it would improve neither cogency nor understanding." I would certainly answer Newman's rhetorical question, yes, and I would go on to judge that view of criticism which encourages such summary judgments not to be a useful one.

The Power of Saddam Hussein's War Rhetoric

Gary W. Brown

In January, 1991, the United States and its allies, Great Britain, France, and Saudi Arabia, initiated a war with Iraq in response to Iraq's invasion of Kuwait in August of that year. Although the United States and its allies won the war quickly, another less destructive—yet equally important—war was being fought while the air and ground campaigns occurred. This was a war of words that involved campaigns by the two sides to instill public support for the war and their respective causes. In sharp contrast to the clear victory that the United States and its allies obtained as a result of the air and ground campaign, the outcome of the war of the rhetoric that occurred during the conflict proved to be less decisive.

From a Western perspective, Saddam Hussein was a ruthless tyrant who would stop at nothing to conquer the world and to eliminate any opposition to him. His rhetoric during the war, usually disseminated through radio addresses, often was discredited by the Western listener. Yet, how was Hussein's rhetoric viewed from the perspective of his own people or of the people of Iraq's neighboring nations? That is the question I wish to address in this essay.

Using neo-Aristotelian criticism, I will examine how influential Saddam Hussein's war rhetoric was for those in his own country and neighboring countries using as my artifact five daily radio addresses Hussein presented during February, 1991. The tapes of the short-wave radio addresses used for my analysis were obtained by a classmate whose boyfriend was stationed in Saudi Arabia during the war. These tapes contained Hussein's speeches in Arabic, which I translated into English. I lived in Kuwait and had taken two years of intensive Arabic language classes as a requirement for graduating from the American School of Kuwait, the high school I attended. I will proceed, in my analysis, by examining the context in which the speeches were presented, analyzing the speeches by applying the five canons of rhetoric, and assessing the success of Hussein's rhetoric for its intended audience.

This essay was written while Gary W. Brown was a student in Karen A. Foss' rhetorical criticism class at Humboldt State University in 1991. Used by permission of the author.

Context

I will examine three areas that will help provide the context for the artifact: Hussein as a rhetor, the occasions on which the rhetoric was presented, and the audience to whom the rhetoric was addressed.

Information about Hussein's background helps to explain the motives for and nature of his war rhetoric. First, Hussein is Muslim, and his rhetoric was directed at a Muslim audience, which means his rhetoric was not typical of rhetorics that embody Western ideologies. Rather, his speeches deal with philosophies and background experiences that are completely foreign to us. In most of his speeches, he devoted a great deal of time to praising Allah, for example. Thus, in order to criticize the war rhetoric of Hussein effectively, my examination of the artifact must take place, as far as is possible, through the eyes of a Muslim rather than those of a Westerner.

At the time he gave the speeches, Hussein was the political as well as the military leader of Iraq. This position had an impact on the way he addressed his people as well as on the flavor and tone of his rhetoric. Hussein was interested in maintaining his power and prestige, and his rhetoric reflected a desire for dominance and authority.

Although Hussein was the military leader of Iraq as well as its political leader, curiously, he never served in the military. Not until he became the leader of Iraq did he have any extensive training in military strategy and tactics. This factor may have affected audiences' assessment of his war rhetoric. Military leaders both from his and other countries may not have responded favorably to his war rhetoric simply because of his lack of a military background. This lack of military experience, however, may have been of less importance to the average listener with little or no military background. Thus, Hussein's rhetoric probably was targeted to the untrained military public rather than to the trained military.

In terms of the occasion for the radio addresses, an all-out confrontation between the United States and its allied forces and Iraq was underway. Baghdad, Iraqi military targets, and Iraqi troops constantly were being bombed by the allies. Because of this heavy air assault, I assume that morale in Iraq was low. In an attempt to increase morale and public support for Iraq, Hussein made irregularly timed addresses over short-wave radio to inform his people of war-worthy news such as allied "defeats." These radio addresses came at a time when the leader of Iraq was under severe criticism by both his own people and many other nations around the world.

The intended audiences for these radio broadcasts consisted primarily of the people of Iraq and the neighboring "friendly" nations that border Iraq. Evidence for these as his intended audience comes first from the fact that the addresses were spoken in the Arabic language. In addition, the common, ordinary words and phrases he used seemed to be directed at the average Arab citizen. Very little effort was made to discuss sophisticated and technical specifications about war strategies or the like. In fact, very little, if any, time was spent by Hussein in dealing with such topics. Rather, he chose to read scriptures from the Koran and to denounce the evil Western societies, strategies that seemed designed to motivate and strengthen general Arab public opinion in support of Hussein.

The Arabic audiences to which Hussein's speeches were addressed were, like Hussein, Muslim. They shared the same background philosophies and ideologies as Hussein, and they all possessed a certain amount of national and racial pride about their heritage. There also existed a high degree of tension and animosity toward Western societies, especially the United States, which probably heightened the Arab audiences' national pride.

Another hidden audience that could have been a target audience that Hussein was trying to reach was the Western societies themselves. Such descriptions as "the allies will drown in their own pools of blood" or "the holy mother war to end all wars and bring the downfall of Western societies" were presented with a possible intent to scare Western audiences and encourage the allied forces to move back due to a lack of Western public support.

Analysis of Hussein's Rhetoric

I now will examine Hussein's rhetoric itself by applying the five canons of rhetoric to the radio addresses. I will examine how Hussein used (1) invention; (2) organization; (3) style; (4) memory; and (5) delivery in order to create a rhetoric that was effective for his audience.

Invention

In terms of invention, the major sources on which Hussein depended for logical proof was the Koran, the holy book of Muslims; traditional Arab tribal laws; and Arab unity against evil Western societies. In his speeches, every movement he made, such as the initial attack on Kuwait, was justified by the Koran and Allah. In Arab society and culture, if an individual is able to perform an action with little or no opposition, then, in God's eyes, that person is assumed to be correct and that individual's action is justified by Allah. Because Hussein's military was successful in conquering Kuwait in a matter of days with very little resistance, Arab logic dictated that Hussein must have been right in Allah's eyes.

Using this logic, Hussein was able to justify his action to the Arab people. In all five radio broadcasts I analyzed, Hussein justified his right to take over Kuwait. In his first public radio announcement shortly after the air raids began, for example, he stated, "God has given us the strength and power to rid Kuwait of its corrupt and sinful leaders." Thus, Hussein used the logic that Allah had given him the power to conquer Kuwait to set it straight; he removed the responsibility for the action from himself and attributed it to God. In this way, Hussein tried to establish his *ethos* among the people of his nation and those of other neighboring Arab countries.

In addition, Kuwait always has been considered part of Iraq by the Iraqis. This idea can be traced back to tribal conflicts, when the Bedouins migrated around the Middle East during the different seasons. Part of the land now found in Kuwait, as far as the Iraqis are concerned, belongs to members of tribes whose descendants currently inhabit Iraq. Thus, in their minds, Kuwait actually belongs to Iraq, a belief that aided Hussein in justifying his conquering of Kuwait.

Hussein's third major argument, which remained consistent throughout the radio addresses, was the appeal to other Arabic nations to help Iraq fight off the "evil" Western societies that interfered with Arab business. He developed this argument in two ways: (1) He sought to instill or reinforce a sense of racial prejudice; and (2) He sought to draw attention away from the Kuwait issue by trying to involve Israel in the conflict.

In several radio addresses before and during the air and ground campaign, Hussein called upon other "Arab brothers" to help Iraq "conquer and humiliate" the United States and its allies. Hussein developed this argument by employing *logos*, *ethos*, and *pathos*. He relied on the logic that Arab "brothers must stick together to fight off the evil Bush and his minions." The logic assumed that all Arab brothers would converge together regardless of past conflicts that may have occurred: "You are all, in the eyes of Allah, Arab brothers. We all need to come together to rid ourselves of the evil menace that infects our lands."

Hussein also was trying to establish his *ethos* in the speeches. He accomplished this by indicating repeatedly that all the Arab people were "brothers" as well as Muslims who must fight together for a common cause. By referencing his identity as a Muslim as well as an Arab and by showing that the majority of the inhabitants of the allied nations were neither, he provided a reason to support his war efforts. This argument also showed signs of *pathos* for similar reasons. Because Hussein and the residents of Iraq were both Muslim and Arab, he hoped to stir up emotions to sway other Muslims and Arabs to help Iraq fight.

Hussein also developed his appeal to fight evil Western societies by taking the focus off of the Kuwait conflict and placing it on the Palestinian issue. He tried to pull other Arab nations into the conflict by addressing an issue that was a political "hot potato" in the Arab culture's eyes. Perhaps Hussein realized the reservations that other nations possessed about entering into his "holy war." Bringing up Iraq's commitment to help the Palestinians regain the land from Israel that was "rightfully theirs" was a means Hussein used to encourage other Arab nations to fight on the side of Iraq in the war. As a consequence of this argument, Hussein could be seen as a leader who was attempting to settle the Palestinian dispute, thus contributing to his ethos. He could be perceived as a leader who was fighting for the good of all Arab people because he was addressing an issue close to the hearts of all Arabs.

Organization

An examination of the organization of Hussein's radio addresses reveals a consistent pattern. Each speech began with a quote or paraphrase from the Koran, the holy book of the Muslim faith. This was followed by praise for the strength and courage of the Iraqi citizens who were enduring constant air raids by allied forces. He also reassured his people that Iraq would prevail and would be victorious in the war. Hussein concluded the speeches by criticizing the Western allied nations. He used such descriptive terms as "evil corrupt society" or "evil President Bush" to help instill emotional hatred of the allies. Finally, he again appealed to other Arabs to join the fight that Iraq entered in order to help the Palestinian cause.

Style

The style of speech Hussein used during his addresses also played a critical role in their effectiveness. Hussein used the classical Arabic dialect rather than any other dialect of Arabic, a style that helped give him authority. Classical Arabic is used as both the diplomatic and religious languages of Iraq. Thus, simply using classical Arabic promotes an image of prestige and grace. To use an example of how effective this style of Arabic is, let me use an example of how this dialect might apply to Western languages. The President of the United States, when addressing the nation, would not use slang terms. Rather, he or she purposely would use a somewhat formal style because it would be appropriate for a leadership role. The same argument can be made for the use of classical Arabic. In the minds of Arabs, a leader who uses this dialect of the language is both eloquent and appropriate.

By using classical Arabic, Hussein also was assured that every Arab citizen was able to understand his speech. Many different dialects exist in the Arab language, and I know from my own experience in Kuwait that if I attempted to speak a different dialect of Arabic to an individual unfamiliar with it, that person would have no idea what I was saying. Because classical Arabic is the dialect taught in the schools of Arab nations, however, all Arabs would have been able to understand the words of Hussein regardless of their local dialects.

Because the classical Arabic style is used as the written language of the Koran, Hussein's use of this form also contributed to his credibility as a religious authority. Hussein had declared this war a holy war, and by using the holy language, Hussein reinforced this image. In essence, Hussein used the classical Arabic to establish himself as a religious leader protected by Allah.

Delivery

The delivery of Hussein's addresses also helped to promote a sense of authority and control for his listeners. Hussein's style of delivery was dynamic and energetic, particularly when he read from the Koran. His delivery style, in fact, helped to create the impression that he was passionate about the cause.

I believe that Hussein's speeches were prepared much earlier than the dates on which they were delivered. Most of the wording in the speech was carefully chosen so as not to insult any potential allies of Iraq. Also, the vividness of the descriptive language used to condemn the United States (such as ''let them lie drowning in their own pools of blood for their persistence'' or ''Allah sheds the dust upon the evil machines [the war machines used by the allies] to protect the true followers of Muhammad'') suggests that much preparation went into the speeches before they were delivered.

Memory

The last canon I will use to analyze the effectiveness of Hussein's radio addresses is memory. As I have suggested, I believe the speeches were prepared prior to their delivery. I also believe the speeches were written in manuscript form and read over the radio. On occasion, Hussein seemed to stumble on certain words, after which he quickly corrected himself. I suspect this was due to misreading his script.

Assessment of Effects

The creation of memorable speeches constituted only part of the purpose of Hussein's rhetoric. The other part is how effective the rhetoric was in meeting its objectives. In spite of the outcome of the military campaign, I argue that his rhetoric was successful. Although many Arab nations did not go to the aid of Iraq, Hussein was successful in obtaining some sympathy from Muslim nations as well as other nations around the world. The most memorable example of such a case occurred when the United States bombed a "public residence." When Hussein sharply accused the United States of intentionally killing innocent citizens, many Arab nations announced their agreement with his position and suggested their disgust with the United States' action. Hussein's attempts to address the Palestinian issue as well as Iraq's attempt to sign a peace treaty with Russia also contributed to the speeches' effectiveness. All these attempts by Iraq to address political problems and peaceful solutions to issues concerning the Arab community helped create a feeling of sympathy for Iraq.

Hussein's speeches did help to promote Arab pride. As reports from CNN and other network news stations illustrated, many Arabs felt that the Iraqi leader's attempt to address the Palestinian issue, as well as to fight the allies for the good "of the Arab people," was a valiant attempt on Hussein's part. They argued that the Palestinian issue had become public once again and had helped to establish a sense of Arab "brotherhood" and unity. If the military campaign had not been so one-sided in favor of the allies, I believe that stronger Arab unity eventually would have created problems for the allied forces.

Finally, Hussein was successful in reaching his intended audience, evidenced in the fact that many Arabs from nations other than Iraq were willing to join the Iraqi army and fight for Hussein. Once again, the concept of Arab "brotherhood" was a strong political theme that Hussein used to his advantage.

The allied nations may have won the military campaign, but I am less sure that they achieved such a decisive victory from a rhetorical standpoint. If the Iraqi forces had been more successful in fighting off the allies, I believe that, given time, Hussein would have proved to be a deadly rhetorical weapon by influencing other Arab nations to fight for his cause. In fact, Hussein was successful in achieving many of the goals he set out to accomplish through the use of his rhetoric. In addition, after the victory by the allied nations, Hussein remained in power. Potentially, Hussein could have suffered defeat and been forced to resign as the Iraqis' leader, but this did not occur. This may not have been the case had he not used rhetoric effectively to bring Arabs together in a spirit of unity and pride.

Additional Samples
Neo-Aristotelian Criticism

Anderson, Jeanette. "Man of the Hour or Man of the Ages? The Honorable Stephen A. Douglas." *Quarterly Journal of Speech*, 25 (February 1939), 75–93.

Bauer, Marvin G. "Persuasive Methods in the Lincoln-Douglas Debates." *Quarterly Journal of Speech*, 13 (February 1927), 29–39.

Brigance, William Norwood, ed. *A History and Criticism of American Public Address.* Vol. I. New York: McGraw-Hill, 1943, numerous essays, pp. 213–500.

Brigance, William Norwood, ed. *A History and Criticism of American Public Address.* Vol. II. New York: McGraw-Hill, 1943, numerous essays, pp. 501–992.

Casmir, Fred L. "An Analysis of Hitler's January 30, 1941 Speech." *Western Speech*, 30 (Spring 1966), 96–106.

Dell, George W. "The Republican Nominee: Barry M. Goldwater." *Quarterly Journal of Speech*, 50 (December 1964), 399–404.

Hochmuth, Marie Kathryn, ed. *A History and Criticism of American Public Address.* Vol. III. New York: Longmans, 1955, numerous essays, pp. 24–530.

McCall, Roy C. "Harry Emerson Fosdick: Paragon and Paradox." *Quarterly Journal of Speech*, 39 (October 1953), 283–90.

Miller, Joseph W. "Winston Churchill, Spokesman for Democracy." *Quarterly Journal of Speech*, 28 (April 1942), 131–38.

Mohrmann, G. P., and Michael C. Leff. "Lincoln at Cooper Union: A Rationale for Neo-Classical Criticism." *Quarterly Journal of Speech*, 60 (December 1974), 459–67.

Peterson, Owen. "Keir Hardie: The Absolutely Independent M. P." *Quarterly Journal of Speech*, 55 (April 1969), 142–50.

Reid, Ronald F. "Edward Everett: Rhetorician of Nationalism, 1824–1855." *Quarterly Journal of Speech*, 42 (October 1956), 273–82.

Stelzner, Hermann G. "The British Orators, VII: John Morley's Speechmaking." *Quarterly Journal of Speech*, 45 (April 1959), 171–81.

Thomas, Gordon L. "Aaron Burr's Farewell Address." *Quarterly Journal of Speech*, 39 (October 1953), 273–82.

Thomas, Gordon L. "Benjamin F. Butler, Prosecutor." *Quarterly Journal of Speech*, 45 (October 1959), 288–98.

Wills, John W. "Benjamin's Ethical Strategy in the New Almaden Case." *Quarterly Journal of Speech*, 50 (October 1964), 259–65.

Wilson, John F. "Harding's Rhetoric of Normalcy, 1920–1923." *Quarterly Journal of Speech*, 48 (December 1962), 406–11.

Critical Approaches

Cluster Criticism

4

A review of tools that critics may use to provide insights into rhetorical artifacts is not complete without an acknowledgment of the contributions of Kenneth Burke to the study of rhetoric.[1] Burke's elaborate theory of rhetoric is too extensive to detail here, nor can all of the critical approaches he suggested for investigating the use of rhetoric be covered. His notions of identification,[2] representative anecdote,[3] perspective by incongruity,[4] motivational orders,[5] form,[6] and redemption,[7] to name only a few, have been used as units of analysis by critics. Although a combination of Burkean tools for analyzing rhetoric is likely to produce the greatest insight into a rhetorical artifact,[8] the use of just one Burkean notion or method produces useful knowledge about an artifact. Two samples of Burkean approaches to criticism are included in this book to illustrate the kinds of perspectives Burkean criticism may produce. Cluster criticism is the focus of this chapter, and pentadic criticism is the subject of a later chapter.

Cluster criticism is a method developed by Burke to help the critic discover a rhetor's worldview. In this method, the meanings that key symbols have for the rhetor are discovered by charting the symbols that cluster around those key symbols in the rhetorical artifact. Burke explained the central idea of cluster analysis: "Now, the work of every writer [rhetor] contains a set of implicit equations. He uses 'associated clusters.' And you may, by examining his work, find 'what goes with what' in these clusters—what kinds of acts and images and personalities and situations go with his notions of heroism, villainy, consolation, despair, etc."[9] In other words, the task of the critic using this method is to note "what subjects cluster about other subjects (what images b, c, d the poet [rhetor] introduces whenever he talks with engrossment of subject a)."[10]

The equations or clusters that the critic discovers in a rhetor's artifact generally will not be conscious to the rhetor: "And though he be perfectly conscious of the act of writing, conscious of selecting a certain kind of imagery to reinforce a certain kind of mood, etc., he cannot possibly be conscious of the interrelationships among all these equations."[11] In essence, a cluster analysis provides "a survey of the hills and valleys of the [rhetor's] mind,"[12] resulting in insights that may not even be known to or conscious for the rhetor.

Procedures

Using clusters as units of analysis, the critic analyzes an artifact in a four-step process: (1) formulating a research question and selecting an artifact; (2) selecting a unit of analysis; (3) analyzing the artifact; and (4) writing the critical essay.

Formulating a Research Question and Selecting an Artifact

The first step in the process of rhetorical criticism is to develop a research question to ask about rhetoric and to select a rhetorical artifact to analyze that will provide an initial answer to the question.

Selecting a Unit of Analysis

The critic's next step is to select a unit of analysis that can help the critic answer the research question. The unit of analysis is that aspect of the artifact to which the critic attends in the analysis. The units of analysis provided by cluster criticism are key terms and the terms that cluster around them.

Analyzing the Artifact

In criticism in which key terms and the terms associated with them are used as units of analysis, the critic analyzes an artifact in three steps:

(1) identification of key terms in the rhetorical artifact; (2) charting of terms that cluster around the key terms; and (3) discovery of patterns in the clusters around the key terms to determine meanings of the key terms for the rhetor.

Identification of Key Terms. The first step in cluster criticism is to select the key terms or the most important terms used in the rhetorical artifact. Generally, no more than five or six terms should be picked that appear to be the most significant for the rhetor. The task of analysis becomes more complex with each term added.

Significance of terms is determined on the basis of frequency or intensity. A term that is used over and over again by a rhetor is likely to be a key term in that person's thought and rhetoric, so if one term frequently appears in the artifact, that term probably should be selected as one of the rhetor's key terms. In Martin Luther King, Jr.'s speech, "I Have a Dream," for example, *dream* is such a term. A second criterion to use in selecting the rhetor's key terms is intensity. A term may not appear very often in a rhetor's work, but it may be extreme in degree, size, strength, or depth of feeling conveyed. It may be a term, for example, that refers to a major turning point in the plot of a film or a poem that expresses a particularly strong feeling. In many of Bill Clinton's speeches on health-care reform, *fairness* was a key term because it was used as the starting point for many of his arguments and was the focus of the conclusions of many of his speeches. Its intensity, then, suggests that *fairness* was a key term for him.

Often, the terms selected as key terms are *god* and *devil* terms. God terms are ultimate terms that represent the ideal for the rhetor—the rhetor's view of what is best or perfect. Devil terms are the counterparts of god terms and represent the ultimate negative or evil for the rhetor.[13] In the speeches of many politicians, for example, *crime* constitutes a devil term, and *prison* constitutes a god term, with both probably functioning as key terms.

If the rhetorical artifact is non-discursive, such as a work of art, the key terms are not words but visual elements. A particular color, shape, image, or placement, for example, may be seen as a key term. An analysis of the Vietnam Veterans Memorial in Washington, D.C., may suggest that its key terms are its black color, its V shape, and its listing of the names of those who died in Vietnam in chronological order by date of death.

Charting of Clusters. After the key terms have been identified in the rhetorical artifact, the critic charts the clusters around those key terms. This involves a close examination of the rhetoric to identify every occurrence of each key term. The terms that cluster around each key term, and the context in which they appear, are noted. Terms may cluster around the key terms in various ways. They simply may appear in close proximity to the term, or a conjunction such as *and* may connect a term to the key term. The rhetor also may suggest a cause-and-effect relationship between the key term and another term, suggesting that the one depends on the other or that one is the cause of the other.

Discovery of Patterns in the Clusters. At this step of the process, the critic attempts to find patterns in the associations or linkages discovered in the previous charting of the clusters as a way of charting the worldview the rhetor has constructed. If a rhetor often or always associates a particular word or image with a key term, that linkage suggests that the key term's meaning for the rhetor is modified or influenced by that associated term. If the term *freedom*, for example, usually appears with *security*, the critic may speculate that the rhetor's view of freedom is constrained by the notion of security. The critic may come to believe that, for the rhetor, freedom is more a feeling of security or freedom from threat than it is a feeling of being unbound and unrestrained.

At this point, an agon analysis may help the critic discover patterns in the clusters that have been identified. In agon analysisis, the examination of opposing terms, the critic discovers what terms oppose or contradict other terms in the rhetoric. In the contexts surrounding the key terms, then, the critic thinks about the terms that the key terms seem to oppose, suggesting what is not a part of the meaning of the key term. The critic also looks for actual opposing terms that cluster around a key term—perhaps suggesting some confusion or ambiguity on the part of the rhetor about that term. In addition, the critic notes whether key terms emerge in opposition to other key terms, suggesting a conflict or tension in the rhetor's worldview that must be resolved.

Writing the Critical Essay

After completion of the analysis, the critic writes an essay that includes five major components: (1) an introduction, in which the research question, its contribution to rhetorical theory, and its significance are discussed; (2) description of the artifact and its context; (3) description of the units of analysis—in this case, key terms and the terms associated with them; (4) report of the findings of the analysis, in which the critic reveals the key terms, the terms that cluster around them, and the meanings for the key terms suggested by the clustered terms; and (5) discussion of the contribution the analysis makes to answering the research question.

Sample Essays

In the sample essays that follow, clusters of terms, suggesting particular meanings, are used as units of analysis to answer various research questions. Peter J. Marston and Bambi Rockwell examine Charlotte Perkins Gilman's short story, "The Yellow Wallpaper," as a way to begin to answer the question, "How does a text function to subvert a dominant ideology?" Kathaleen Reid analyzes a non-discursive text, a painting by Hieronymus Bosch, as a way to answer a question that interests her, "How do viewers establish the meanings of ambiguous messages?" Sonja K. Foss analyzes the controversy over women priests in the Episcopal Church to answer the question, "What rhetorical strategies do institutions use to respond to challenges to their ideologies?"

Notes

[1]For an overview of Burke's rhetorical theory, see Sonja K. Foss, Karen A. Foss, and Robert Trapp, *Contemporary Perspectives on Rhetoric*, 2nd ed., (Prospect Heights, IL: Waveland, 1991), pp. 169–207.

[2]See, for example, Chester Gibson, "Eugene Talmadge's Use of Identification During the 1934 Gubernatorial Campaign in Georgia," *Southern Speech Journal*, 35 (Summer 1970), 342–49.

[3]Barry Brummett explores this notion as a critical tool in "Burke's Representative Anecdote as a Method in Media Criticism," *Critical Studies in Mass Communication*, 1 (June 1984), 161–76.

[4]An example is James L. Hoban, Jr., "Solzhenitsyn on Detente: A Study of Perspective by Incongruity," *Southern Speech Communication Journal*, 42 (Winter 1977), 163–77.

[5]See, for example, Karen A. Foss, "Singing the Rhythm Blues: An Argumentative Analysis of the Birth-Control Debate in the Catholic Church," *Western Journal of Speech Communication*, 47 (Winter 1983), 29–44.

[6]One critical essay that focuses on form is Jane Blankenship and Barbara Sweeney, "The 'Energy' of Form," *Central States Speech Journal*, 31 (Fall 1980), 172–83.

[7]For an example, see Barry Brummett, "Burkean Scapegoating, Mortification, and Transcendence in Presidential Campaign Rhetoric," *Central States Speech Journal*, 32 (Winter 1981), 254–64.

[8]Charles Conrad argues for using Burke's methods together in "Phrases, Pentads, and Dramatistic Critical Process," *Central States Speech Journal*, 35 (Summer 1984), 94–104.

[9]Kenneth Burke, *The Philosophy of Literary Form* (1941; rpt. Berkeley: University of California Press, 1973), p. 20.

[10]Kenneth Burke, *Attitudes Toward History* (1937; rpt. Berkeley: University of California Press, 1984), p. 232.

[11]Burke, *The Philosophy of Literary Form*, p. 20.

[12]Burke, *Attitudes Toward History*, pp. 232–33.

[13]Kenneth Burke, *A Grammar of Motives* (1945; rpt. Berkeley: University of California Press, 1969), p. 74; Kenneth Burke, *A Rhetoric of Motives* (1950; rpt. Berkeley: University of California Press, 1969), pp. 298–301; and Richard M. Weaver, *The Ethics of Rhetoric* (South Bend, IN: Regnery/Gateway, 1953); pp. 211–32.

Charlotte Perkins Gilman's
"The Yellow Wallpaper"
Rhetorical Subversion in Feminist Literature

Peter J. Marston
Bambi Rockwell

"When a doe wishes to run far and fast, she is not making a buck of herself—it is because she is a deer, just as much of a deer as he is" (Gilman, cited in Boxer, 1982, pp. 141–142). These words, written by turn-of-the-century feminist, historian, and social analyst Charlotte Perkins Gilman, express a sentiment that continues to resound in contemporary feminist thought: namely that women may establish their humanity without sacrificing their identity as women. During her lifetime, Gilman was a key voice of the feminist movement; in both her fiction and sociological writings, she radically confronted androcentric attitudes that constrained women and were perpetuated to the detriment of both sexes.

Her works include a number of significant sociological treatises examining the role of women in her time (including *Man-Made World: Our Androcentric Culture, Women and Economics,* and *The Home and Its Influence*) as well as hundreds of essays and short stories. She is, however, best known for her haunting short story, "The Yellow Wallpaper," a work that has been heralded as a masterpiece of feminist literature, and which continues to stand as a staple of courses in both feminist literature and women's studies (Hedges, 1973).

Whereas previous critical readings of "The Yellow Wallpaper" have focused upon its feminist underpinnings and literary qualities (e.g., Fetterley, 1986; Hill, 1980; MacPike, 1975; Schopp-Schilling, 1975; Treichler, 1984), the present study seeks to examine the *rhetorical* functions of this remarkable short story. Given the traditional distinctions between rhetoric and poetic, the selection of a rhetorical perspective for an analysis of a literary work may appear incongruous. However, we would argue that such a perspective is justified in two ways. First, the very phrase "feminist literature" implies a rhetorical purpose: the

From *Women's Studies in Communication*, 14 (Fall 1991), 58–72. Used by permission of the Organization for Research on Women and Communication and the authors.

presentation of a particular ideological view of society and human relations as salient, and indeed, preferable. Thus, by its very nature, feminist literature invites and merits rhetorical analysis. Second, a rhetorical approach is consistent with the movement away from foundationalism and toward interdisciplinary studies in feminist criticism. As Carolyn Allen (1987) argues, if feminist criticism is to advance its concerns successfully, it must address the full range of signifying practices and symbolic forms that are manifest in feminist discourse. This study is one attempt to examine a function of significa-tion, rhetoric, and a symbolic form, literature, that, in conjunction, have been largely neglected in contemporary feminist criticism.

Our general thesis is that "The Yellow Wallpaper" functions to subvert a dominant patriarchal ideology through the development and presenta-tion of what Kenneth Burke (1941) has termed "associational clusters": implicit equations between terms within discourse that reveal and, indeed, recommend an author's attitudes to his or her audience. Accordingly, in this essay we will: (a) provide a brief summary of "The Yellow Wallpaper" and describe its rhetorical functions; (b) present an overview of Burke's conception of associational clusters and its appli-cation in rhetorical criticism; (c) report the findings of our cluster analysis of "The Yellow Wallpaper" and discuss the ways in which these clusters function rhetorically; and (d) present our conclusions concerning the rhetorical effectiveness and limitations of associational clusters in feminist discourse.

"The Yellow Wallpaper"

"The Yellow Wallpaper" was first published in *The New England Magazine* in 1892. The work bears a remarkable resemblance to bio-graphical details of Gilman's own life, but is presented as a work of fiction. The story's narrator is a woman writer who has retreated to a colonial mansion for the summer with her husband, a physician, in order to remedy a "nervous condition." Her husband prescribes phosphates and bedrest and forbids her to continue with her writing until she recovers. The story centers around the narrator's response to the wallpaper in her bedroom, which she detests. Eventually, she resolves her hatred of the wallpaper, but only at the expense of her sanity and her humanity. At the end, she "creeps" around the room, compulsively peeling the wallpaper off the wall, convinced that she herself is a figure in the wallpaper's disturbing pattern.

The rhetorical function of "The Yellow Wallpaper" is to subvert the dominant patriarchal ideology: to undermine the salience, appeal, and/or coherence of that ideology in the mind of the reader. Indeed, one of the most notable characteristics of "The Yellow Wallpaper" is that it is so thoroughly subversive, with no corresponding affirmation of an alternative ideology to replace the dominant patriarchy. As Judith Fetterley (1986) observes, the story exposes how men may drive women to insanity through control and calls for women to escape this fate, but the narrator's "escape"—into madness—clearly is no solution, as it denies the narrator both an identity and a place within humanity.

Previous feminist criticisms of "The Yellow Wallpaper" have focused primarily upon the ideological functions of the story: that is, the ways in which the story reveals hegemonic structures perceived by Gilman. For example, Paula Treichler (1984) maintains that the prohibition against writing that is imposed upon the narrator by her husband reveals the conflict between a patriarchal ideology and women's expression through discourse. Similarly, Fetterley (1986) writes that "The Yellow Wallpaper" is, in fact, "an analysis of why who gets to tell the story and what story one is required, allowed, or encouraged to tell matter so much, and therefore, why in a sexist culture the practice of reading" is controlled by men (p. 159).

The present analysis, however, focuses not upon the relationship between Gilman's story and society, but rather upon the relationship between the story and the attitudes it may induce in the reader. It is this emphasis upon inducement that characterizes such an analysis as rhetorical, even though the object of analysis is literary.

It is important to note that our claim that "The Yellow Wallpaper" functions as a rhetorical act of subversion does not require an explicit or intentional rhetorical purpose to Gilman's story. Indeed, it is always problematic to attribute such an intention to literary authors. On the one hand, literary authors rarely seem to have as their primary concern the immediate practical rhetorical effects of their discourse (Burke, 1966, pp. 296, 303–305). On the other hand, to attribute an explicitly rhetorical purpose is often taken as a denigration of the literature as "mere" rhetoric.

In light of Gilman's later works, however, she was undoubtedly concerned with the feminist attitudes her story might induce in her audience—an audience that was plainly "women," specifically the women who were avid readers of short fiction during the period in which "The Yellow Wallpaper" appeared. Further, given the constraints upon women writing in nonfictive genres at the time, it seems likely that writing in a literary form was itself a rhetorical strategy for Gilman, a way of reaching her audience and advancing her ideology in an effective and appropriate manner, for in the early twentieth century, one of the only forums available to women was short fiction for women readers.

As Burke has argued in both *The Philosophy of Literary Form* (1941) and *A Rhetoric of Motives* (1950), the rhetorical function of inducement lurks in modes of expression that are both explicitly and implicitly suasory, affecting attitudes that are both manifest and latent in the minds of the author and reader. The problem of establishing an explicit and intentional rhetorical purpose need not be resolved in order to warrant the rhetorical analysis of literary texts, and, as our analysis reveals, "The Yellow Wallpaper" does indeed imply a viable rhetorical function: it serves to create a feeling of "dis-ease" within readers, leading them to question the acceptability of a dominant social order in which women's roles are circumscribed and submissive.

Kenneth Burke's Associational Clusters

Due largely to the efforts of rhetorical theorists such as Wayne Booth (1961) and Kenneth Burke (1941), the proposition that poetic works may function rhetorically is generally accepted. As a result, a number of methods for analyzing the rhetorical functions of literature, drama, and even poetry have emerged over the last several decades. One of these is Burke's technique of analyzing associational clusters, an approach that is particularly well-suited to an analysis of "The Yellow Wallpaper." Burke explicates this concept most clearly in *The Philosophy of Literary Form* (1941):

> The work of every writer contains a set of implicit equations [or] "associational clusters." And you may, in examining [a] work, find "what goes with what" in these clusters—what kinds of images and personalities and situations go with [the author's] notions of heroism, villainy, isolation and despair, etc. And though [the author may] be perfectly conscious of the act of writing, conscious of selecting a certain kind of imagery to reinforce a certain kind of mood, [he or she] cannot possibly be conscious of the interrelationships among all these equations. (p. 20)

Burke (1941) goes on to provide a relatively simple sample of this type of analysis: "If you kept a list of subjects, noting what was said [every time someone with a tic blinked] you would find out what the tic was symbolic of" (p. 20).

Although Burke focuses upon the usefulness of this method in understanding an author's attitudes and motives in creating a particular work, it is clear that such clusters also function to encourage similar attitudes and motives in the reader. George Lakoff and Mark Johnson (1980) note that, syntactically, "closeness is the strength of effect" (p. 128). In other words, the strength of the effect one term has upon another in an utterance depends, in part, upon how close the terms are structurally. Thus, terms that cluster together in discourse will have a stronger effect on one another than terms that appear in separation. As Lakoff and Johnson (1980) maintain, the "strength of effect" gives rise to metaphorical meaning by implicitly encouraging the reader to view one term in relation to other terms that appear near it. Whenever we have metaphorical meaning, we have rhetoric, for metaphors urge us to view an object, idea, or sentiment from one particular perspective rather than another (Burke, 1945).

In her discussion of Burke's concept of association, Christine Oravec (1989) draws a similar conclusion: "to effect the transfer of motives from the substructural to the superstructural level, a transfer of motives occurs in language" (p. 188). The substructural association of terms within a text "articulates, or 'bodies forth,' a strategy which encompasses its author's motivations" (Oravec, 1989, p. 188), thereby recommending the author's motivations to the reader on a superstructural level, the level of attitudes and ideas in the minds of the audience. As Oravec (1989) observes, an analysis of associational clusters in discourse may therefore reveal "the power of the text in constructing [the author's] identity, and possibly that of his [or her] audience" (p. 188).

The application of this method to "The Yellow Wallpaper" has two major advantages. First, whereas other methods for uncovering the rhetorical functions of poetic works emphasize characterization and plot (e.g., Booth, 1961; Fisher, 1987), these elements are less prominent in an analysis of a work's associational clusters. As even a cursory reading reveals, "The Yellow Wallpaper" is much more a work of images and perceptions than characters and actions. Second, as both Burke and Oravec observe, an analysis of associational clusters is demonstrable through citation: the critic can identify the clusters in the language of the discourse itself (Burke, 1941; Oravec, 1989).

Our analysis of associational clusters in "The Yellow Wallpaper" focuses upon the narrator's descriptions of the wallpaper that dominate the story. Although other elements in the story are relevant to Gilman's feminist perspective (e.g., the narrator's relationship with her husband, the "prescription" she is given for her ailment, etc.), the wallpaper itself is clearly the central focus of the narrative, and further, has been the main object of literary and feminist criticisms of the story to date. These previous readings have suggested that the wallpaper is a symbol representing the narrator's mind, the narrator's unconscious, the hegemonic structures that disenfranchise women, or women's discourse, among others (see Treichler, 1984, for overview). Our purpose is not to argue that the wallpaper represents a particular object or phenomenon, but rather to reveal the variety of terms and meanings that cluster around the narrator's description of the wallpaper in order to explicate the rhetorical effect such clusters may have on the reader.

Associational Clusters in "The Yellow Wallpaper"

Clusters in "The Yellow Wallpaper" were derived through a method almost identical to that suggested by Burke's example of the person with a "symbolic" tic—every time the narrator mentioned the wallpaper in the story, a list of associated descriptions was recorded and later categorized.[1] Our analysis reveals four associational clusters manifest in the narrator's descriptions of the wallpaper. These clusters are organized around three different characteristics the wallpaper: the wallpaper's color, the overall pattern or design of the wallpaper, and a figure the narrator perceives within this larger pattern.

The color of the wallpaper is associated with nausea and disgust. The narrator describes it as "repellent, almost revolting," an "unclean yellow"—"dull, yet lurid orange in some places, a sickly sulphur tint in others" (p. 13). She characterizes the color as "hideous" (p. 25), writing that the color reminds her of "all the yellow things I ever saw— not beautiful ones like buttercups, but old foul, bad yellow things" (p. 28). At one point, the narrator describes an unsettling odor that lingers in the house. As she attempts to identify the smell, she exclaims, "The only thing I can think of is that it is like the *color* of the paper! A yellow smell" (p. 29).

The overall pattern of the wallpaper is associated with two related but distinct sets of meanings. First, the pattern is associated with disorder and chaos. Indeed, the narrator's first description of the pattern is that it is "sprawling, . . . committing every artistic sin" (p. 13). She observes "lame, uncertain curves" that "destroy themselves in unheard of contradictions" (p. 13). Later, she notes that the pattern is "pointless" and arranged against any "principle of design" (pp. 19–20). Each breadth of the paper "stands alone, the bloated curves and flourishes . . . waddling up and down in isolated columns of fatuity" (p. 20). In fact, the pattern is so chaotic that the narrator becomes exhausted in "trying to distinguish [its] order" (p. 20).

The second set of meanings associated with the pattern of the wallpaper relate to death and horror. The narrator writes, "There is a recurrent spot where the pattern lolls like a broken neck and two bulbous eyes stare at you upside down" (p. 16). These eyes, she continues, are "unblinking," and "everywhere," crawling "up and down and sideways" (p. 16). At another point in the story, she describes the pattern as "a bad dream," resembling "an interminable string of toadstools, budding and sprouting in endless convolutions'' (p. 25). These images persist throughout the story, for as she is tearing the paper off the walls, she imagines that ''all those strangled heads and bulbous eyes and waddling fungus growths just shriek with derision!'' (p. 34).

The final cluster is organized around a shape or figure that the narrator perceives within the overall pattern of the wallpaper. While scrutinizing this pattern, the narrator detects ''dim shapes . . . like a woman stooping down and creeping about'' (p. 22). As the story progresses, the shapes become less dim and she becomes certain that this figure is, in fact, a woman, ''plain as can be'' (p. 26). Eventually, the narrator identifies so closely with this figure that she becomes convinced that she is herself a figure in the wallpaper.

This figure in the wallpaper is associated with images of both constraint and resistance. The narrator writes that ''by day, she is subdued, quiet,'' and further, speculates that it is the pattern of the wallpaper that ''keeps her so still'' (p. 26). As night falls, however, the figure begins to ''shake the pattern, just as if she wanted to get out'' (p. 23). The image of the figure shaking the pattern is repeated twice more in the story. While watching the wallpaper one night, the narrator detects a movement in the wallpaper and is surprised to discover that ''the front pattern *does* move—and no wonder! The woman behind shakes it!'' (p. 30). A few nights later, the figure once again begins to ''crawl and shake the pattern'' (p. 32). That this shaking represents an act of resistance is evidenced by the fact that at night the pattern of the wallpaper ''becomes bars'' with the womanlike figure held within (p. 26).

These four clusters constitute the core of the narrator's descriptions of the wallpaper, and further, provide an explanation of the rhetorical functions of Gilman's short story. As noted above, associational clusters function rhetorically by suggesting particular metaphorical views of objects, ideas, or sentiments—views that entail corresponding attitudes towards the central terms or meanings in the clusters.

Note that the various characteristics of the wallpaper that form the organization of the clusters are arranged hierarchically: its color, its overall pattern, and the figure inside the pattern. The color of the wallpaper is the most immediate and most general characteristic, while the figure in the pattern is the least immediate and most interior characteristic. Thus, these characteristics establish a chain of contexts: the color is the context for the pattern, and the pattern is the context for the figure. In describing the various clusters, we began with the most general characteristic, the color of the wallpaper, and follow the order in which the clusters are revealed in the story itself. In describing the metaphors established by these clusters, however, we will move in the opposite direction, beginning with the womanlike figure within the pattern. This is consistent with both the general feminist concerns of Gilman's story and with the nature of the metaphors themselves, fundamentally organized around the role of women in a patriarchal society.

The associational clusters manifest in "The Yellow Wallpaper" suggest a series of three interrelated metaphors which are consistent with Gilman's ideological concerns. Each of these metaphors reveals how Gilman views the situation of women in society, and further invites and encourages the reader to share in this view, thereby giving rise to a rhetorical effect. The first metaphor is established through Gilman's repeated associations of the feminine figure in the wallpaper with images of constraint and resistance. These associations suggest to the reader a view of women as subjects of oppression.

The clusters surrounding the pattern of the wallpaper characterize Gilman's view of the cause and "context" of women's oppression, for, in the story, it is the pattern of the wallpaper that subdues the figure during the day and which the figure resists at night. The pattern is associated with images of both disorder and horror, which implies a metaphorical view of the "oppressor" of women as a *monster*: an unnatural and destructive force.

The association of the color of the wallpaper with nausea provides a more general contextual metaphor for the oppression of women, inviting the reader to see such oppression as a sickness. This metaphor is more general, extending to both the oppression of women (as represented by the figure within the pattern) and the cause of this oppression (as represented by the pattern itself). Perhaps it is significant that this metaphor is the result of a cluster of terms organized around the *color* of the wallpaper: The term color itself means, in one of its senses, to characterize generally, as in "to color a situation." Certainly, color is a suitable metaphor for ideological oppression in that color is both pervasive and yet, in and of itself, intangible. One cannot, for example, point to "yellow" as a particular object or entity; one can only point to a yellow *something*. Like ideological oppression, color is always "hiding" in something else, be it the wallpaper in Gilman's story or the social, political, and economic structures that characterize a patriarchal society.

These metaphors, and the corresponding attitudes they suggest, can be summarized in the following manner: Women are oppressed by a monster; the whole situation is a sickness. The nature of these metaphors reveals the essential rhetorical character of Gilman's story as an act of subversion. Each of these metaphors seeks not to advance or affirm an image, but rather, to disturb an image, to undermine its salience or appeal in the mind of the reader.

Conclusions

In the previous sections of this essay, we have sought to describe and explain the rhetorical function of "The Yellow Wallpaper." In this closing section, we will evaluate this rhetorical function and, in so doing, discuss some general implications concerning the rhetorical effectiveness and limitations of feminist literature.

Typically, rhetorical artifacts are evaluated against standards of aesthetics, ethics, truth, and/or results. In assessing "The Yellow Wallpaper," we have adopted the results criterion. This criterion is consistent with the ideological agenda associated with feminist literature: by its very nature it is driven by ideological concerns and, accordingly, the rhetorical success or failure of such literature may appropriately be assessed by its effect upon the attitudes and ideologies of its readers. Of course, assessing the rhetorical effectiveness of "The Yellow Wallpaper" is somewhat problematic in that the story is not addressed to any concrete, practical exigence, but rather to an exigence that is enduring and pervasive. Nonetheless, it is possible to offer some general conclusions concerning its rhetorical power and limitations in relation to effecting attitude change.

The rhetorical strengths and weaknesses of "The Yellow Wallpaper" both derive from the subliminal nature of associational clusters. Subliminal modes of persuasion, such as the associational clusters manifest in Gilman's story, may have an effect that more explicit modes do not precisely *because* they address the reader's unconscious. Burke (1966) himself notes the subliminal power of associational clusters in his essay, "Mind, Body, and the Unconscious":

> A rhetorician . . . may deliberately identify certain acts with courage, cowardice, negligence and so on. Or such equations may be but implicit in a work (as when the poet, or the neurotic, spontaneously attitudinizes towards persons and things, thereby in effect pronouncing them admirable, despicable, consoling, fearsome, and the like). And however unconscious such equations may happen to be, the critic or the analyst can make all such associations as explicit as though they had been deliberately intended. The more "unconscious" such equations are (in the minds of an audience), the greater their effectiveness is likely to be as "stimuli" that provoke "responses." (p. 74; see also, Oravec, 1989, p. 188)

Of course, the "response" elicited by the associational clusters (or equations) in "The Yellow Wallpaper" may not be sympathetic to the feminist ideology that informs Gilman's story. A reader may respond negatively to associational clusters, just as he or she might respond negatively to the explicit associations advanced in argumentative forms of discourse.

At least for those potentially persuadable, however, the subliminal effects of associational clusters may be significant.

Another way of viewing the rhetorical power of associational clusters is suggested by Michael McGee in his essay "Text, Context, and the Fragmentation of Contemporary Culture" (1990). McGee (1990) argues that contemporary discourse is best conceived in terms of fragments that imply a larger "text" than the discourse itself:

> Critical rhetoric does not begin with a finished text in need of interpretation; rather, texts are understood to be larger than the apparently finished discourse that presents itself as transparent. The apparently finished discourse is . . . fashioned from what we call "fragments" [and as such, the discourse] is only a featured part of an arrangement that includes all facts, events, texts, and stylized expressions deemed useful in explaining its influence and exposing its meaning. (p. 279)

For McGee (1990), the only way to address an issue in contemporary culture is to "provide readers/audiences with dense, truncated fragments which cue them to produce a finished discourse in their minds. In short *text construction is now something done more by the consumers than by the producers of discourse*" (p. 288).

From this perspective, "The Yellow Wallpaper" is a fragment that invites readers to "complete" the text by drawing associations between elements of the discourse (such as those highlighted in the present analysis) and other facts, events, and situations. The rhetorical effect of the associational clusters in "The Yellow Wallpaper" derives from the reader's construction of a "text" from not only the clusters in the story, but also from other sources, including the lives of the readers themselves. This construction, of course, need not be deliberate or conscious, and in the mind of a naive reader the construction is more likely to occur as a series of implicit "snap judgments" made about the story's salience and meaning (McGee, 1990). From this view, whether "The Yellow Wallpaper" induces feminist attitudes depends upon the types of constructions made by readers, which in turn depend upon other discourse and experiences that the readers are familiar with. Thus, it is not surprising that the story should be most effective for audiences of women and perhaps others who are sensitive to women's concerns.

The subliminal nature of associational clusters also reveals certain limitations of "The Yellow Wallpaper" as a rhetorical artifact. As an implicit mode of persuasion, associational clusters are typically ambiguous. As Burke (1941) notes, associational clusters lead to "hunches" rather than neatly circumscribed definitions or statements. Although "The Yellow Wallpaper" may induce a disturbing feeling or attitude, especially for a naive reader precisely *what* should be found disturbing about the narrator's situation may remain ambiguous. The reading we have advanced is in part grounded in an understanding of Gilman's work as a feminist, and therefore, we conclude that Gilman intends to disturb or subvert the prevailing patriarchal ideology. However, a naive reader might attribute the disturbing attitude aroused by the associational clusters to either: (a) the woman's alleged insanity; (b) her own doubts and inhibitions; or (c) the dominance of her husband.

Although the first of these alternative interpretations has no feminist implications, the other two interpretations are at least compatible with a feminist view of society, in that they reflect more specific problems that are often associated with an oppressive patriarchy. Of four possible interpretations, three may advance, at least to some extent, a feminist perspective in the mind of the reader. There is no guarantee that a given reader will be induced toward one interpretation rather than another, but in those cases where readers *are* induced towards a feminist perspective an analysis of the associational clusters implicit in the text provides a basis for understanding the story's rhetorical effect.

In addition to the limitations associated with the ambiguity of associational clusters, there are also limitations of exposure and reader ideology. Exposure to "The Yellow Wallpaper" is largely a matter of choice, and it is perhaps unlikely that the audiences most resistant to feminine discourse (e.g., those adherent to a sexist ideology) would read a short story written by a woman author, especially if she were known to be a feminist activist. Further, such audiences, by virtue of their sexist ideology, may be most likely to "read" the cause of the woman's oppression as her own madness, an interpretation that is likely to preclude the inducement of a feminist perspective or attitude.

Each of these limitations suggests the same general conclusion concerning the rhetorical effectiveness of associational clusters in feminist literature: such clusters may be persuasive only to those already persuaded or potentially persuadable. Although this may seem a harsh evaluation of an entire genre of rhetorical discourse, it is important to note that in the arena of public discourse ideological battles are rarely if ever won by converting the opposition; rather, success comes by sustaining the converted and converting the uncommitted or the ambivalent. Those who are already persuaded or potentially persuadable are perhaps the most suitable audiences, from a purely rhetorical perspective, for feminist literature.

As with any particular rhetorical strategy, the use of associational clusters cannot ensure adherence or conversion to a particular ideological perspective. As our analysis has sought to demonstrate, however, associational clusters in feminist literature may be a liberating resource for advancing feminist concerns: they invite identification with women's experiences of oppression at the level of attitude and feeling, and they may, by virtue of their implicit nature, circumvent attitudinal resistance in readers who are ambivalent or uncommitted toward a feminist ideology. To the extent that the audience for feminist literature most likely is women, such clusters may be a highly effective strategy, for the reasons suggested by Burke (1941) and McGee (1990). Clearly, from a rhetorical perspective, feminist literature deserves a respected place among the various forms of feminist discourse, as well as further critical attention. It is hoped that the present analysis will serve to reaffirm this claim and to persuade other critics of feminist literature to consider carefully not only the ideological functions of such discourse, but also its *rhetorical* function—a function that is absolutely necessary in the real-world struggle against sexism.

Note

[1]The edition of "The Yellow Wallpaper" used in this analysis is published by the Feminist Press (Old Westbury, NY: 1973). All page citations are from this edition.

References

Allen, C. J. (1987). Feminist criticism and postmodernism. In J. Natoli (Ed.), *Tracing literary theory* (pp. 273-290). Champaign-Urbana: University of Illinois Press.

Booth, W. C. (1961). *The rhetoric of fiction*. Chicago: University of Chicago Press.

Boxer, M. J. (1982). Are women human beings? Androcentricity as a barrier to intercultural communication. In L. Samovar & R. Porter (Eds.), *Intercultural communication: A reader* (141-150). Belmont, CA: Wadsworth.

Burke, K. (1941). *The philosophy of literary form*. Baton Rouge: Louisiana State University Press.

Burke, K. (1945). *A grammar of motives*. New York: Prentice-Hall.

Burke, K. (1950). *A rhetoric of motives*. New York: Prentice-Hall.

Burke, K. (1966). *Language as symbolic action*. Los Angeles: University of California Press.

Fetterley, J. (1986). Reading about reading: "A Jury of Her Peers," "The Murders in the Rue Morgue," and "The Yellow Wallpaper." In E. A. Flynn & P. F. Schweickart (Eds.), *Gender and reading: Essays on readers, texts, and contexts* (pp. 147-164). Baltimore: Johns Hopkins University Press.

Fisher, W. R. (1987). *Human communication as narration: Toward a philosophy of reason, value, and action*. Columbia: University of South Carolina Press.

Hedges, E. R. (1973). Afterword. In C. P. Gilman. *The Yellow Wallpaper* (pp. 37-63). Old Westbury, NY: The Feminist Press.

Hill, M. A. (1980). Charlotte Perkins Gilman: A feminist's struggle with womanhood. *Massachusetts Review, 21*, 503-626.

Lakoff, G., & Johnson, M. (1980). *Metaphors we live by*. Chicago: University of Chicago Press.

MacPike, L. (1975). Environment as psychopathological symbolism in "The Yellow Wallpaper." *American Literary Realism 1870-1910, 8*, 286-288.

McGee, M. C. (1990). Text, context, and the fragmentation of contemporary culture. *Western Journal of Speech Communication* 54:274–289.

Oravec, C. (1989). Kenneth Burke's concept of association and the complexity of identity. In H. W. Simons & T. Melia (Eds.), *The Legacy of Kenneth Burke* (pp. 174–195). Madison: University of Wisconsin Press.

Schopp-Schilling, B. (1975). "The Yellow Wallpaper": A rediscovered "realistic" story. *American Literary Realism 1870–1910*, 8, 284–286.

Treichler, P. A. (1984). Escaping the sentence: Diagnosis and discourse in "The Yellow Wallpaper." *Tulsa Studies in Women's Literature*, 13, 61–77.

The Hay-Wain
Cluster Analysis in Visual Communication

Kathaleen Reid

The popularity of the fifteenth-century painter Hieronymus Bosch has fluctuated dramatically over the last five centuries. This fluctuation is due, in part, to his surrealistic style; his paintings are executed in brilliant colors and with bold presentation, which was a major deviation from the style typical of the fifteenth century. Also contributing to his on-again, off-again popularity were his apparently mystical statements about humanity's plight here on earth. The paintings depict torment, suffering and unearthly terrors.

Art historians have debated the meaning behind Bosch's visions, but few of their methods have unraveled successfully the cloud of mystery that still envelops his work. What is of concern in this paper is how a rhetorical methodology can be used to understand forms of visual communication such as the painting of Bosch. Also of concern are further issues that apply both to traditional visual media (such as painting) and to modern technological media (such as photography and video): the fixed versus fleeting nature of visual communication (e.g., photographs versus film) and the transition of meaning (including shifts of meaning that occur within a culture as a result of time) through visual images.

The Hay-Wain by Bosch is an example of medieval visual communication designed specifically for use by the public, functioning in ways similar to contemporary mass communication. Originally a triptych, a three-part altar piece, this painting depicts the medieval story of the creation, the fall, and the potential redemption or destruction of humankind. Placed in a cathedral where the populace would have congregated on a regular basis, the triptych would have been viewed simultaneously by all individuals attending worship services. The audience would have been composed of rich and poor, noble and simple, scholars and tradesmen, clergy and laymen. In this way, the painting would function as a form of public visual communication for a diverse audience; therefore, such a painting as this might be considered a predecessor of contemporary mass communication.[1]

From Journal of Communication Inquiry, 14 (Summer, 1990), 40–54. Used by permission of the Iowa Center for Communication Study and the author.

The *Hay-Wain* and other such paintings designed specifically for public audiences provide contemporary public communication scholars with an opportunity to examine early forms of visual communication in which the author of the work presents a narrative through full control over the manipulation of the materials, the ideas, and the representations of objects found within the work. Thus, these early paintings like contemporary narrative film can present stories that may have highly subjective simultaneous representations of natural, supernatural and ideological worlds.

This juxtaposition of the natural and supernatural may result in potentially more ambiguous, difficult messages in both film and traditional media. A rhetorical methodology such as Burke's cluster analysis may aid viewers in establishing the meanings of ambiguous messages. Applying the methodology to a piece of visual communication such as The *Hay-Wain* simplifies the task of attributing meaning, since the static nature of the painting eliminates the dimensions of movement and time that add complexities to study of film and video.

In this paper, the visual communication of Bosch's painting—The *Hay-Wain*—has been analyzed in order to: 1) test the applicability of a rhetorical methodology to visual communication and 2) demonstrate how such a methodology can help the audience derive meaning from a highly subjective visual communication such as The *Hay-Wain*, which is often assessed as being so idiosyncratic that its meaning must remain a mystery.

Background

Hieronymus Bosch Van Aeken was born around 1450 in southern Holland. His family originally may have been from Aachen, but Bosch was born in a quiet town in the central lowlands called 's Hertogenbosch, which was less than two days' journey from the Dutch artistic capitals of Haarlem and Delft. Bosch was a member of a highly puritanical, nonclerical organization called the Brotherhood of Our Lady, whose staunch religious *Weltanschauung* may have influenced Bosch's artistic visions. He married into a wealthy family, and he had no children. Little else is known of his personal life, except that he died in 1516.

Several attempts have been made to understand Bosch's work, efforts made particularly difficult because of the lack of information about Bosch. Charles de Tolnay (1965) has made the most complete catalog of Bosch's work, dividing it into three major periods (early, middle, and late). Bosch became more esoteric throughout his career, de Tolnay asserts, moving from traditional approaches to Biblical topics to a more introspective view of creation, redemption, and damnation.

Another of Bosch's chroniclers, Max Friedlander (1969), has sought to find explanations of the artist's unique style and themes in his personal characteristics. He attempts to link what was known about Bosch as a person with the subject matter and themes of his work and suggests that Bosch's idiosyncratic personality explains his divergence from the mainstream of art during the fifteenth century. Friedlander never explains fully, however, what impact Bosch's personality might have had on his individual works.

Still other theories exist to explain why Bosch painted as he did. Cuttler (1968) and Combe (1946) have suggested that belief in alchemy and superstition could have influenced the artistry of someone like Bosch. Bax (1979) suggests that popular folklore and contemporary prose seem an integral part of Bosch's work.

A Rhetorical Perspective

As the above scholarship indicates, Bosch's paintings have been interpreted most often from one of two perspectives: 1) as a product of his personality, or 2) as a product of his environment. Since neither of these deductive methods seems to explain satisfactorily his motive and uniqueness, another approach that may be more adequate is the analysis of a single work without allowing either his personality or history to overshadow its content. Thus, the critic could move from the painting to the man rather than moving from the man to the communication.

One potentially useful perspective for analyzing the meaning behind a form of visual communication, especially work as complex as that of Bosch, is derived from rhetoric. In the past, rhetoric was limited to the study of discursive communication, but, recently, a broader definition has expanded the arena for rhetorical criticism to include non-discursive communication. These non-discursive forms of communication function in a way that is similar to discourse in that they transmit information and evoke some response from the audience. Here the non-discursive form being examined is visual communication, defined as communication through visual forms such as painting, photography, videography, and film.

That such human activity is within the purview of rhetorical criticism was suggested by the Committee on the Advancement and Refinement of Rhetorical Criticism (Sharf, 1979), which reported that the rhetorical critic "studies his subject in terms of its suasory potential or persuasive effect. So identified, rhetorical criticism may be applied to any human act, process, product or artifact" (Sharf 1979, p. 21). Karlyn Kohrs Campbell echoed this sentiment by asserting that "if criticism is to fulfill its function, the rhetorical critic must proclaim: Nothing that is human symbolization is alien to me" (1974, p. 14).

Foss and Radich suggest that art is a form of visual communication that is within the scope of rhetoric because it is a "conscious production to evoke a response" (1980, p. 47). Burke lends further credence to the view that a painting is a visual communicative act when he states:

> For when an art object engages our attention, by the sheer nature of the case we are involved in at least as much of a communicative relationship as prevails between a pitchman and a prospective customer (1964, p. 106).

Thus, visual communication such as painting can be defined in a way that is similar to verbal communication based on its ability to engage our attention to evoke responses.

This basic parallel between visual and verbal rhetoric—that both convey information and evoke some response from an audience—can be found in the aesthetics studies of art history. Egbert notes that the artist "is intent on expressing something which he feels can best be said through the medium of his art . . ." (1944, p. 99). Gombrich stresses the importance of good articulation in the rhetorical process. When commenting on the works of artists like Constable, he says, "All human communication is through symbols, through the medium of a language [he includes the visual arts in his notion of language] and the more articulate that language the greater the chance for the message to get through" (1960, p. 385).

Just as others use words to describe things, "the artist uses his categories of shapes and color to capture something universally significant in the particular" (Arnheim, 1971, p. vi). Kleinbauer states that "an artist may deliberately or even unconsciously conceal or transfigure his intention, thoughts and experience in his work" (1971, p. 68). These and other theorists indicate that the artist uses his or her techniques as a medium of rhetoric for expressing ideas and experiences just as verbal rhetoric functions to express the experiences of the speaker.

Schools such as the Prague Structuralists reinforce the phenomenological position that both verbal and visual rhetoric function as social artifacts in the communication process. They study how the relationships between creator of the artifact and the interpreter function in forming our society. Their work, especially that of Lotman and Mukarovsky, presents both verbal and visual communication as part of the communication process that constitutes our entire social system (Lotman 1976; Mukarovsky 1977; Morawsky 1974; Lucid 1977; Bailey, Matejka, and Steiner 1980).

Methodology for the Analysis of Bosch's Works

Perhaps one key to unraveling the mystery of Bosch lies in his use of symbolic counterpoint—the juxtaposition of various elements within a single setting.

> Simultaneously attracted by the joys of the flesh and seduced by the promises of asceticism, too much a believer to fall into heresy, but too clear-sighted not to see through the short-comings of the clergy and the evils of the world, dazzled by the beauty and wonders of nature and unwilling to recognize their divine or human value, contenting himself with the *docta ignorantia*, Bosch lays bare the contradictions of his age and makes them the subject of his artistic production (De Tolnay, 1965, p. 49).

If the juxtaposition of elements is viewed as basic to the structure of his works, then a method to describe this structure may be of value in understanding Bosch.

Burke contends that a communicator consciously or unconsciously juxtaposes ideas within a communication act, showing how he or she sees the meaning of terms. This process of clustering of ideas gives evidence of the communicator's motive for the rhetorical act or work. Burke asserts that the motive and the form of a rhetorical act are inseparable.

In *A Grammar of Motives*, Burke states, "There must . . . be some respect in which the act is a *causa sui* a motive in itself" (1945, p. 66) and that when one is searching for motives of the communicator, "the thinker will in effect locate the motive under the head of the Act itself' (1945, p. 69). So each act has within it some measure of motive directing the communicator. Duncan clarifies Burke's position: ". . . as we think about human motives, it becomes increasingly obvious that they depend on the forms of communication available to us . . ." (1954, p. xvii).

In order to reveal this motive, Burke develops, in *Attitudes Toward History*, a methodology for discovering what elements are associated with what other elements in the mind of the communicator (1937, p. 233). This methodology is called "cluster analysis," which he clarifies in later essays (Burke, 1954, 1957). Cluster analysis asks "what follows what?" and is concerned with the examination of elements that are linked together by the communicator.

The methodology consists of three steps. The first is the selection of key terms, or the important elements used in the rhetoric. The key terms are selected because of their high frequency and/or high intensity of use (Rueckert 1963, p. 84). Frequency refers to how often the term is repeated, and intensity refers to how significant the term appears to be in the work. Wong (1972) discusses principles of design and notes that the main elements of design in a painting consist of color, line, form, value, texture, rhythm, balance, repetition, similarity, and other design elements. These are used as key terms in this analysis.

The second step is to identify what clusters around each key term each time it appears in painting. This is a description of what elements are adjacent to or in close radius to each key term.

The third step is interpretation of the clusters. In this step, each cluster is analyzed to reveal what potential messages are being presented by the communicator. The interpretations revealed then are examined as a whole to determine an overall interpretation of the painting and a possible explanation of the communicator's motive for creating the work.

While cluster analysis generally has been applied to written discourse, such as Berthold's (1976) analysis of Kennedy's Presidential speeches, it also should provide valuable insights into visual communication.

The Hay-Wain

One aspect of Burke's method of cluster analysis is that each communication act is in itself a microcosm of an individual's motives. Thus, to assess these motives, the critic can survey, in detail, a single communicative act to derive understanding of motive. Because Bosch's paintings universally contain contradictory elements I have narrowed the scope of this investigation to a single work—*The Hay-Wain*. Not only is it one of Bosch's most recognizable works, but many art historians have selected it as highly representative of his paintings in general. The work is a triptych—composed of three panels—and is attributed to the start of Bosch's middle period, painted sometime around 1485–1490.

The central panel of the painting shows a hay wagon overflowing with hay and drawn by a team of minotaur-like creatures. The wagon is surrounded by peasants clamoring to grab pieces of hay, while other peasants are crushed beneath the wheels. Common interpretation suggests that this scene was taken from a Flemish proverb that says that the world is a haystack from which each person plucks what he or she can. Behind the wagon is a procession headed by clerical figures who look down upon the melee from horseback with stoic aloofness. On top of the hay are lovers, flanked by an angel and a demon. This central, frantic scene is counterpointed by the depiction of everyday activities— such as a woman changing a baby's diaper, another cooking food, and a patient being tended by a medieval physician in the foreground. Above hovers a large cloud containing the Christ figure, with His hands raised in a blessing.

The left panel is a traditional visualization of the story of creation and follows Adam and Eve from their "birth" to their expulsion from the Garden. Executed mainly in tranquil blues and greens, this panel portrays a peaceful environment except for three elements: rebellious angels being cast from the heavens, the serpent tempting the couple inside the Garden, and the archangel with drawn sword guarding the entrance to the Garden.

In stark contrast to the left panel, the right panel is a scene of unearthly horrors, with demons attacking naked humans in front of a tower. The whole panel is crowned with violent reds and oranges, representing fire and smoke. Colors are flat and bold. The figures seem to bathe in the light, turning them shades of pink and orange, totally different from the jaundiced skin of those in the center panel and from the skin tones provided by the blues and greens of the left panel.

Key Elements

The figures in this painting appear small and somewhat weightless as they engage in numerous activities. Still dominant is Bosch's concern with color. The golden mass of hay on the wagon is the central focus and part of the first and most striking key term—gold color. In The Hay-Wain, the use of the bright golden color dominating the central panel is a significant design element. By its dominance—via size and intensity or brightness—it attracts the eye more rapidly than other important, yet less significant design elements. By its eminence and brightness, the gold color shows high intensity; therefore, it is considered a major key term.

While the golden color was the most dominant and intense design element, repetition and similarity were the major criteria for choosing the other key terms. These were the arch shape, ladders, clerics, couples, fish, and the boar. Similarity was a strong criterion for choosing the two arches as key elements. They are of the same elongated form and both serve the same function as portals or entry ways. The same is true of the ladders. Two ladders are parallel in structure, length, and usage.

The other key terms—clerics, couples, fish, and boars—were chosen because of frequency; they each occur in the painting three or more times. Clerics are presented in three places. Four couples—as prototypes of the original Adam and Eve—appear. The fish or variations of the fish appear three times and the same is true for the boar. Because the image of the boar is connected to that of the fish in two places, the boar and the fish are treated as one unit.

Clusters around Key Elements

Gold Color. The golden-yellow color that pervades the painting is one of its most striking elements. The two golden clouds that float in the blue sky contain the figure of God as Judge and the figure of Christ. The God-Judge figure is surrounded by the rebellious angels who are being cast from heaven. Their blue and light-red tones contrast with the bright yellow of the cloud in which they are placed. The golden cloud is matched by a similar one in the upper portion of the center panel. Within this cloud, Christ is isolated from others. His hands, with their bleeding wounds, are raised as if in blessing, and the light-red drapery surrounding His pierced body is similar in color to the clothing of the God-Judge figure.

Most of the gold color is found in the central panel. Creating a large golden triangle, the large patch of color includes the majority of the center ground and has as its central focus the hay wagon. Within this golden triangle are many scenarios: people fighting, others scrambling to grab a piece of hay, a woman tending an injured man, peasants being crushed by the wagon, a boar's head and a fish roasting over a fire, and anthropomorphic creatures such as the boar-like demonic figure pulling the wagon toward hell. At the apex of the triangle is a soberly clad pilgrim. Standing with his staff, he carries a small child on his shoulders and is accompanied by an adolescent. The small trio seems separated from the crowd; yet, they are a part of life on earth as they stand adjacent to women involved in everyday activities.

Ladders. Bosch has incorporated two similar ladders in *The Hay-Wain.* These are parallel in design and structure, one resting against the wagon in the center panel and the other leaning against the tower in the right panel. The ladder of the center panel is held by a member of the crowd, apparently attempting to climb toward the couple on top. The ladder of the right panel holds a demon who is climbing it in order to work on building the tower. Members of the clergy and nobility are next to the center ladder. At the base of the ladder in the right panel, a group of demons in animalistic form leads a naked human toward the tower.

Arches. Two arches are significant elements. These two key terms are similar not only in size and shape but also similar in function and location within the painting. The similar function is that they are both entry ways, one in the left panel and one in the right. The left-panel arch is the entrance into the pastoral Garden of Eden, which is barred by the archangel who threatens the now-guilty Adam and Eve. The other arch symmetrically positioned in the right panel is filled with blackness. Before it cowers a figure reminiscent of Adam, who is being pushed toward the portal by a demon with a staff.

Couples. Bosch has included several couples in *The Hay-Wain*, all of whom have either a good or evil supernatural figure near them. Adam and Eve are shown in a number of vignettes: in one, depicting the creation, God as creator is standing with them; the fall of humankind is depicted in the vignette containing the couple and the serpent. The most prominent pair are being thrown out of the Garden by the archangel, and their flight leads the viewer directly into the center panel with all of its banality and travail. The second prominent couple sits on top of the hay wagon, flanked by an angel and a demon. This pair enjoys the music of a lute player, and they are oblivious to the turmoil just below their feet. They do not display the anguish of those who struggle to attain the heights of the wagon, but they are equally unaware that the wagon is being dragged toward damnation.

Fish and Boar. A fish appears on the spit by the fire in the center panel, waiting to serve as nourishment for the humans around it. The immediate environment suggests the humdrum of everyday life, with the fish being just one more artifact of human existence. In the same panel, however, the fish symbol begins to change. It becomes a demonic half-fish, half-human creature that is helping pull the wagon into hell. In the right panel, the fish symbol is perverted even more, so that now the fish feeds upon the human rather than the opposite. This scene also is surrounded by activities, but these are the activities of hell, such as an emaciated black-hooded demonic priest carrying a human on a spit, animals attacking men, and other grotesque torture of humans.

Because of the similarity of their treatment, the boar is placed in the same cluster as the fish. The boar's head, along with the fish, is being roasted over the open fire. It, too, will serve as part of a meal for the women around the fire. Boar-headed creatures also are found pulling the wagon toward hell. Unlike the fish, the boar is not as clearly found in the right panel—though some demonic faces are reminiscent of a boar.

Clerics. Church figures appear in opposite corners of the center panel. In the upper left, prelates mounted on horses observe the anguish of the peasants as they fight around the wagon. In the lower right corner, nuns carry hay to a priest who calmly sits oblivious to what is happening around him. These people are outside the flow of action but have potentially significant positions. In the right panel, directly across from the black-hooded priest located in the central panel, is a black-hooded demonic priest who carries a human thrust upon a spit-like staff. This demonic cleric is a mocking replica of the priest sitting amongst the nuns in the center panel.

Interpretation of Clusters

Examination of the clusters in *The Hay-Wain* reveals a common theme—that of transition. Whether the symbols in each cluster reveal a physical transition such as the moving hay wagon or a more esoteric transition such as the moral transition of Adam and Eve, this theme is suggested in each cluster.

Gold Color. While the golden-color cluster is the most dominant key term and gives an underlying commonality to the diverse elements contained within the cluster, it is also the most confusing. Contained within this large cluster are terms of both good and evil. Because it represents warmth, prosperity, and power in most cultures, it lends a positive atmosphere to the cluster. This positiveness is offset somewhat by such negative elements as greed and conflict as people struggle for handfuls of hay.

The God-Judge figure in the gold cluster immediately and visually transmits the concept of transition as the rebellious angels are forced to leave the heavens. The second element, Christ with hands raised, does not indicate transition visually; yet, traditionally in the Christian religion, Christ represents the greatest of all transitions. He descends from heaven to earth and ascends back to heaven. He was God who became human and the One who moved from life to death, from immortal to mortal and from temporal to eternal. Via Him, humans also may attain these characteristics, thereby moving the individual past human limitations.

With the hay wagon in the gold-color cluster, Bosch presents the viewer with both a physical transition—the journey along the earthly trail—and an esoteric transition—the journey of greed that takes a person from life on earth to life in hell. The pilgrim shares this same duality, both a physical and an esoteric transition. Physically, the pilgrim is on a journey through the plane containing the mob surrounding the hay wagon. Also, by definition, a pilgrim refers to a wayfarer on a spiritual journey as he or she seeks to make the transition from a mundane plateau to a more holy place.

Ladders. The first prominent ladder in this painting speaks of an important transition, for the individual may follow the ladder in the central panel to the false plateau atop the hay wagon, or he or she may continue in an upward direction toward Christ. The parallel ladder in the right panel allows the person ascending to reach the top of the tower, while the viewer's eye again allows for a transition from the bottom of the ladder to the ladder's ultimate direction—into the depths of hell where the fire burns the brightest.

Arches. The two major arches function as portals, openings leading from one setting to another. The concept of transition is found in the left panel, as the arch is the doorway from earthly life to paradise. The interior side of the portal is smooth and straight, seemingly indicating an easy movement from paradise to outside, while movement in the opposite direction is much more difficult because of the archangel guarding the rough-hewn facade on the outer side of the portal. Although some light flows through the archway, the rocky exterior, irregular and rugged, seems to denote this as a portal from God's grace into the travails of humanity. In contrast, the corresponding archway in the right panel is smooth and sleek. This architecturally precise portal makes entrance into the black interior easy, while the demon holding a wooden beam seems to block anything trying to exit the interior of the tower. The darkness of the interior of a building that has no roof speaks of a transition into an unnatural, black void.

Couples. Major transitional aspects can be noted among the couples. In the left panel, Adam and Eve make both moral and immortal-mortal transitions as they succumb to the temptation presented by the serpent in the garden. The transition from one life to another is presented in the couple's removal from a perfect garden, which required no work, to a life of toil outside the gates of paradise. Both physical and spiritual journeys are presented in the couple on the wagon in the center panel. Physically, they are being transported, while spiritually they are continuing in a destructive, even if entertaining, direction. Thus, when the couples are followed through the narrative via the composition leading from one vignette to the next, we can note the idea of transition on both physical and metaphoric levels.

Fish and Boar. Both the fish and boar representations suggest a transition of power. Both are presented in a traditional fashion such as food being prepared for a household. The next appearance of a fish and boar is in anthropomorphic form, human legs with either a boar or fish head, and they are part of the power that pulls the loaded wagon toward hell. The right panel, while not clearly presenting the boar, does present the fish in its final form—a red-eyed monster that has human legs instead of fins. But more grotesque than its form is its action: it is swallowing a human being. This is the ultimate transition in power. Instead of the fish functioning as nourishment for the humans who control the animals, the fish now feasts upon the humans whom they now control.

Clerics. Even if it has not actually occurred yet, the prelates astride their horses seem to present the transition of the church from an organization that is deeply involved in the concerns of the people to an organization of clerics who merely observe, not prevent, the people moving in the direction of damnation. The group of nuns is located at the entrance of hell, and although they are not as compositionally active in carrying the eye from the center panel to the right as are the half-humans pulling the wagon, they are still part of the visual transition into hell. That they are part of the transition seems incongruous with their role as representatives of religion. Perhaps more fascinating is Bosch's placement of the black-hooded demon immediately adjacent to the black-hooded priest. Though located in separate panels, their physical proximity causes the viewer to recognize immediately the similarity between the two figures. This presents the illusion of a transition from an easy-going priest to a sadistic ogre.

In summary, the two major themes derived from this interpretation center around transition. The first theme deals with the transition of life from that which is good and innocent to that which eventually may be and most often is destructive. Only two of the transitions are positive: the Christ figure, who offers salvation through a transition from mortal to immortal life, and the pilgrim, who seeks to attain a higher spiritual being. Except for the pilgrim, no other human on earth seems exempt from a destructive transition, and even the success of the pilgrim is questioned since the path appears difficult to follow. The second theme is the transition of power from the humans to outside forces, whether they are supernatural animals that become masters of human beings or the Christ figure as master when the individual chooses the difficult route along with the pilgrim.

In numerous ways the transitions suggest the loss of the "autonomous" individual. In each vignette of couples, supernatural figures such as imps and angels can be found, and power over the individual shifts to those beings. The center panel demonstrates the loss of power as individuals strive to control each other as they fight one another for the hay. The major and final transition of power to others outside of the self is shown in the right panel. While the center panel shows that humans have delusions of power in their attempts to control each other and the animals (roasting the fish and boar, prelates riding on horses), the right panel illustrates the final, most tragic transition of power: the animals mutilate and torture the humans, who had controlled them in the center panel.

Bosch seems to be motivated in The Hay-Wain by an over-riding pessimism that indicates that all the world is doomed for destruction. He does provide a limited amount of optimism by placing the Christ figure and the pilgrim within the gold cluster suggesting warmth, prosperity, power and security. That touch of optimism, however, seems largely overshadowed by the sweeping movement of the entire painting toward hell. Thus, Bosch seems motivated to shove people out of their complacent acceptance of life viewed only from a single perspective, although he seems to doubt his ability to produce change in the perspectives and direction of most individuals.

Also revealed in the analysis were four important presuppositions. These reinforce Bosch's motive for persuading individuals to consider the transitions of their lives. As the painting indicates, he is predominantly concerned with the spiritual and moral transitions, not the physical.

The Ambiguity of Human Existence. Ambiguity, uncertainty of a symbol's meaning, is one of the first presuppositions generally noted about the paintings of Bosch. In one place, a symbol has one meaning and in another place, its counterpart has an opposite meaning. This is demonstrated, for example, by his use of the arch shape, where one arch leads into a beautiful garden and the other into a tower of punishment for humans. Duality also is seen in the ladder symbol, where one ladder leads to Christ and salvation, and the other points toward blackness, fire, and eternal torture.

Such contradictions with their resulting ambiguity suggest that Bosch understood the reflexive nature of symbols. The reflexivity that he demonstrated using the arch, ladder, and fish illustrates his consciousness of the complexity of the many facets of life. As a result, Bosch perceived life as being ambiguous, with the artifacts of life drawing meaning from their surroundings; their meanings are not fixed. These artifacts can fall on the side of good or evil, and Bosch's placement of elements seems to state his recognition of right and wrong. He seems to believe that anything can be an instrument of salvation or perdition.

Demonstration of the Reality of the Supernatural. The supernatural elements are not treated as dreams or figments of the imaginations of the individuals within the painting; rather, they are treated the same way as the human, earthly figures. This can be seen with clusters surrounding the couples and, in particular, with the archangel guarding the entrance to the garden. The archangel with drawn sword is truly there, as he refuses to allow Adam and Eve to reenter the garden. The couples in the garden also are in a pastoral setting that is treated as natural and real. One couple is seated above the hay wagon happily singing with the angel and demon perched near their shoulders being as clearly and naturally depicted as the couple.

Further evidence of this treatment of the supernatural as the natural can be seen in the gold-color cluster. The Christ figure's physical portrayal is as accurate as the painting of the pilgrim at the apex of the golden triangle. Also within the golden cluster are the anthropomorphic figures that are pulling the wagon. In particular, the boar-headed creatures are as real as the boar's head roasting over the fire near the everyday activities of the women in the foreground. This portrayal of anthropomorphic creatures as being as real as the people in the crowd makes this painting gruesome. The strife and death shown in the golden triangle are mere forerunners of that which follows in the right panel, where humans suffer eternal torture.

Bosch shows the viewer a hideousness that is a tangible, real entity. His view of hell is as real in his mind and in this painting as is the common daily life portrayed in the center panel. This is indeed *no dream*, but rather a *wakeful reality* in which humans must overcome depravity just as surely as they must overcome the trials of earthly existence.

Choice in Life. Bosch made clear that one must select a path of salvation or destruction and that one must seek guidance in order to complete the journey successfully. He depicts the people with decisions to be made; decisions that have direct impact upon their current lives. They choose to fight or not fight for the hay, for example, and for their eternal destiny. These are illustrated by the clusters around the gold color. Only the pilgrim seems to have the strength to make the difficult choice. At the apex of the triangle, he must choose one of two paths. One of those paths is difficult; it goes against the cultural customs and norms such as grabbing pieces of the hay. The pilgrim must traverse through the crowd and climb higher than those around him. He must not stop on the false plateau atop the hay wagon, where the couple sits. Rather, he must continue toward the next golden cloud of color—toward Christ, who acts as intercessor for the pilgrim on the long, difficult journey.

Questioning the Role of the Church. In this painting, the clergy are not acting in their traditional role of "priests for confession"; instead, Church officials are following the wagon of destruction. The other members of the Church are now nuns, whose interaction with people outside the Church is limited to the one playing cat's cradle. This lack of interaction seems to indicate more concern with internal problems than with caring for those around them in dire need of help. Bosch does not want to exclude the Church from the life drama of salvation, but he has difficulty justifying the excesses of the clergy that infected the Church of the fifteenth century. He could not bring himself to give the clergy a key role, but neither could he bring himself to exclude them, depicting them as he viewed their lack of effectiveness in aiding humanity.

On the basis of these four indicators, the basic motive of *The Hay-Wain* is reinforced. It seems to be that Bosch had a high level of concern for his fellow human beings who cannot act alone and who must eventually face the reality of perdition if they continue in their current direction.

This motive is enhanced further by noting the relationships of the indicators to each other. The high levels of ambiguity in the painting generally confuse viewers and lead them to conclude that Bosch is either inconsistent or a mystic who follows his own rules of logic. However, if we take that ambiguity as simply an indicator of his recognition that things are not always as they first appear, and that there are two sides to a coin, then internal consistency demands that Bosch note both sides and that he question whether or not something is always as good as it first seems.

The second indicator, demonstration of the supernatural as real, takes this ambiguity into a level that incorporates the earthly and the supernatural. It explains why so many seemingly harmless things on earth can have a flip side that is detrimental for people. For example, a common wagon becomes an instrument of destruction for the people snatching at the hay. It suggests the potential of a greed that can destroy totally and the supernatural forces that affect the individual's decisions.

If Bosch held these presuppositions, as *The Hay-Wain* indicates, then he would be highly concerned about the plight of those around him. He deals with these presuppositions by illustrating the difficulty of choosing the right path. This is accomplished by placing the pilgrim at a distance from the Christ-figure, who can provide salvation. Yet he gives hope by placing Christ in a bright golden cloud that the pilgrim can keep in sight as he traverses the tumultuous path on earth.

Another way in which Bosch acts upon these presuppositions is to question the role of the Church. This questioning is natural since traditionally the Church's major responsibility is for the spiritual and physical lives of the people. Therefore, Bosch would seek to evaluate how well the Church's representatives were performing, since failure on their part could have severe consequences for individuals.

The basic motivation of concern for others, which I have derived, may seem too simple and too obvious. However, Bosch's complexity of design and his mixing of cues (i.e., a nun playing cat's cradle instead of binding the wounds of the injured) confuses the casual observer who then questions what his true stance and motive might have been. This cluster analysis, which began by examining clusters of elements around key symbols of the painting, shows that Bosch indeed did hold and express a consistent perspective regarding human life on earth.

Conclusion

The purposes of this paper were to: 1) discover whether highly subjective visual communication such as the work of Bosch can be deciphered; and 2) to test whether a rhetorical methodology such as Burke's cluster analysis can be applied to visual communication. Although, by its nature, cluster analysis permits the discovery and analysis of the structure of a form of visual communication first and foremost, it also suggests dimensions of the communicator's character. This methodology has revealed enough insights to affirm that Bosch was not so idiosyncratic that he cannot be understood.

The cluster analysis reveals repeated patterns of elements within the painting that had high levels of consistency. While the consistency found may be the result of the critic's biases, I propose that enough clarity exists to suggest that Bosch, though intricate and complex, is not as bewildering as many observers assume. The consistencies found through cluster analysis support the idea that this work is not simply a private language of a communicator who cannot be understood except by his contemporaries. For through an analysis such as this, the critic can examine the underlying framework of the paintings, ''what goes with what,'' and determine what synonyms and metaphors Bosch has expressed in his communication.

The cluster analysis reveals one of the major conflicts in Bosch's work that accounts for much of the confusion surrounding his work regarding intended meaning. The conflict is defined as the point at which traditional cultural images such as the figure of Christ meet and clash with incongruities. Such conflict is found in the distant figure of Christ, seemingly isolated from others, in *The Hay-Wain*. Bosch takes the traditional and places it in a context that at first is confusing: Why is the figure of Christ so distant? Why is Christ not interacting with those in the groups around Him? Perhaps, Bosch is asking the viewer, as well as himself, to contemplate the role of traditional Christian spirituality in the midst of the fluctuating Western world of the fifteenth and early sixteenth centuries.

Whether this questioning reflects Bosch's own private skepticism and doubt or whether it is a rhetorical tool to push viewers to face issues regarding their psychological and physical destiny cannot be determined by this study. Whichever is the case, this painting by Bosch has continued through the years as a rhetorical device that challenges the observer to question his or her own understanding of the issues portrayed in the process of trying to understand Bosch.

The primary purpose of the paper, to test whether a rhetorical methodology can be applied to visual communication, however, raises a number of issues that should be considered. Cluster analysis is based on the assumption that the connotative meaning of a term can be known by examining the context of that element. Questions arise as to how those connotative meanings are derived and interpreted when cluster analysis is applied to visual communication.

One area of concern is with the data—the paintings by Bosch. The nature of this form of communication is fixed rather than fleeting. An important distinction between visual communication such as painting and photography and other types of communication is that the forms within painting and photography are "fixed."[2] The advantage is that there is no need to halt a process as when "freezing" a frame in film or when using recordings. While cluster analysis could be applied to fleeting communication (incorporating paralinguistics and other aspects of the spoken word) perhaps it is most easily applied to fixed data where the structure and context of elements can be more easily examined, collected, and interpreted.

Another issue is to what extent we should treat the visual communication as a language. If, in using cluster analysis, we do indeed treat visual images as language, we ignore differences between the images and full language systems. In other words, we need to examine to what extent Burke's methodological procedures are grounded in his understanding of language systems and are at least partially ruled by those presuppositions.

Like other forms of nonverbal communication that are not full language systems, some basic questions may need to be asked: 1) Is there a given rule structure governing how visual symbols should he put together, just as there is a full rule structure for use of verbal language? 2) Based on Burke's ideas of the distinction between verbal and nonverbal communication, can visual communication reference the negative (communicate absence of joy, absence of pain)? 3) Can the visual communications be self-reflective—talk about themselves as in verbal language, when Mary says that Joe says that Bill says that Janie says? 4) We know that visual communication is not time bound in the sense that it can depict events of yesterday and today as well as project scenes into the future. But does visual communication have full ability to indicate past, present, and future tense? Can it depict present perfect, past perfect, or future perfect tense? What about the subjunctive mood?[3] Perhaps these four areas are not crucial for the use of cluster analysis and interpretation; however, these are ways in which visual communication may differ from verbal communication that could present potential problems if we treat the two in the same manner.

Still another issue revealed in this application of cluster analysis to visual communication concerns methodology. A major drawback to examining a painting or photograph rather than discourse is that the critic is presented with a more limited number of symbols. A comparison to clarify my point would be to look at the difference between a short poem by e. e. cummings as compared to a lengthy address by President J. F. Kennedy. Social artifacts such as paintings, photographs, and poems that contain fewer elements may create problems in generating sufficient material to study when using the methodology of cluster analysis.

A final issue in this kind of application involves interpretation. A major problem here concerns the high level of reflexivity found in visual communication. While written and spoken language is reflexive, it expresses as much by what is between words as by the words themselves, there is even more reflexivity in visual communication, since elements such as those found in paintings are not always as specific as words for describing the communicator's intentions. This high level of reflexivity allows for more multiple realities than do words. The extent to which the visual communicator and viewer have similar interpretations is based on the extent of their shared knowledge and understanding of the elements (Merleau-Ponty 1964, 1968).

Despite these issues that arise from the application of cluster analysis, the rhetorical perspective helps open the door for more research regarding visual communication. However, further research needs to be done in order to establish more clearly the boundaries of cluster analysis and how it might relate to contemporary media such as film and video that have a fleeting rather than fixed nature. I hope this application of cluster analysis can challenge and encourage others within the field of communication to apply this method to "fleeting" communication and to explore further the issues raised.

Notes

[1]The distinction that often is made between fine arts, mass mediated and applied arts is subject to much debate. Dondis (1973), for instance, suggests that the dichotomy between fine and applied arts is false. He notes the varying historical perspectives, emphasizing that groups such as the Bauhaus made no distinctions. Painting, architecture, photography. all were assumed to have similar communicative functions.

Dondis further emphasizes his point by noting that "The idea of a 'work of art' [fine art] is a modern one, reinforced by the concept of the museum as the ultimate repository of the beautiful. . . . This attitude removes art from the mainstream, gives it an aura of being special and petty, reserves it for an elite, and so negates the true fact of how it is struck through our lives and our world. If we accept this point of view, we abdicate a valuable part of our human potential. We not only become consumers with not very sharp criteria, but we deny the essential importance of visual communication both historically and in our own lives" (1973, p. 6). Contemporary critics who view Bosch's *Hay-Wain* in the art museum must remember that the current setting was not its original. It was not designed with the purpose of being simply a work of fine art, rather its form and function was one of public communication.

[2]This characteristic is based on Ricoeur's (1971, p. 528) notion of fleeting versus fixed communication. He notes that spoken language is fleeting, and the written text is fixed. The major distinction between them is their temporal aspects. Fleeting communication is the "instance of discourse," while fixed communication exists and continues over time in the form originally intended by the communicator.

[3]For further elaboration of these concepts see Burgoon and Saine (1978, pp. 18-20). In addition to these four questions by Burgoon and Saine, other works that question similarities and differences among visual art and other forms of rhetoric include Barthes (1977, pp. 32-51) and Eco (1976, pp. 190-216).

References

Arnheim, R. (1971). *Art and Visual Perception*. Berkeley: University of California.

Bailey, R. W., Matejka, L., and Steiner, P. ([1978] 1980). *The Sign: Semiotics around the World*. Reprint. Ann Arbor, MI: Slavic Publications.

Barthes, R. (1977). *Image Music Text*. New York: Hill and Wang.

Bax, D. (1979). *Hieronymus Bosch: His Picture-Writing Deciphered*. Montclair, NJ: Abner Schram.

Berthold, C. A. (1976). "Kenneth Burke's Cluster-Agon Method: Its Development and an Application." *Central States Speech Journal*, 27, 302–09.

Burgoon, J. K. and Saine, T. (1978). *The Unspoken Dialogue*. Boston: Houghton Mifflin.

Burke, K. (1945). *A Grammar of Motives*. New York: Prentice-Hall.

Burke, K. (1954). "Fact, Inference, and Proof in the Analysis of Literary Symbolism" in Bryson, L. (ed.), *Symbols and Values: An Initial Study* (pp. 283–306). New York: Harper and Brothers.

Burke, K. (1957). *Philosophy of Literary Form*. rev. ed. New York: Vintage.

Burke, K. ([1937] 1961). *Attitudes Toward History*. Reprint. Boston: Beacon Press.

Burke, K. (1964). On Form. *Hudson Review*, 17, 106.

Campbell, K. K. (1974). Criticism: Ephemeral and Enduring. *Speech Teacher*, 23, 14.

Combe, J. (1946). *Jheronimus Bosch*. Paris, France: Pierre Tisne.

Cuttler, C. D. (1968). *Northern Painting from Puccelle to Bruegel/Fourteenth, Fifteenth, and Sixteenth Centuries*. New York: Holt, Rinehart and Winston.

De Tolany, C. (1965). *Hieronymus Bosch*. New York: Reynal.

Dondis, D. A. (1974). *A Primer of Visual Literacy*. Cambridge: Massachusetts Institute of Technology.

Duncan, H. D. (1954). Introduction to *Performance and Change*, by K. Burke. Indianapolis: Bobbs-Merrill.

Eco, U. (1976). *A Theory of Semiotics*. Bloomington: Indiana University Press.

Egbert, D. D. (1944). Foreign Influences in American Art, in Bowers, D. F. (ed.), *Foreign Influences in American Life: Essays and Critical Bibliographies* (pp. 99–126). Princeton: Princeton University Press.

Foss, S. K. and Radich, A. J. (1980). The Aesthetic Response to Nonrepresentational Art: A Suggested Model. *Review of Research in Visual Arts Education*, 12(4), 40–49.

Friedlander, M. J. ([1937] 1969). *Early Netherlandish Painting*. Vol. 5, *Geertgen tot Sint Jans and Jerome Bosch*. Reprint, with translation by H. Norden. New York: Frederick Praeger.

Gombrich, E. H. (1960). *Art and Illusion: A Study in the Psychology of Pictorial Representation*. New York: Pantheon Books.

Guillaud, J. and M. (in collaboration with Isabel Matco Gomez) (1989). *Hieronymus Bosch: The Garden of Earthly Delights*. Ian Robson, Translator. New York: Clarkson N. Potter.

Kleinbauer, W. E. (1971). *Modern Perspectives in Western Art History*. New York: Holt, Rinehart and Winston.

Lotman, Y. (1976). *Analysis of the Poetic Text*. Ed. D. B. Johnson. Ann Arbor: Ardis.

Lucid, D. P., ed. (1977). *Soviet Semiotics*. Baltimore: Johns-Hopkins University Press.

Merleau-Ponty, M. (1964). *Signs*. Evanston: Northwestern University Press.

Merleau-Ponty, M. (1968). *The Visible and the Invisible*. Ed. C. Lefort. Evanston: Northwestern University Press.

Morawsky, S. (1974). *Inquiries into the Fundamentals of Aesthetics*. Cambridge: Massachusetts Institute of Technology.

Mukarovsky, J. (1977). *The Word and Verbal Art*. Ed. J. Burbank and P. Steiner. New Haven: Yale University Press.

Reid-Nash, K. (1984). *Rhetorical Analysis of the Paintings of Hieronymus Bosch*. University of Denver.

Ricoeur, P. (1971). The Model of the Text: Meaningful Action Considered as a Text. *Social Research*, 38, 529–62.

Rueckert, W. H. (1963). *Kenneth Burke and the Drama of Human Relations*. Minneapolis: University of Minnesota Press.

Sharf, B. F. (1979). Rhetorical Analysis of Nonpublic Discourse. *Communication Quarterly*, 21(3), 21–30.

Wong, W. (1972). *Principles of Two-dimensional Design*. New York: Van Nostrand Reinold.

Women Priests in the Episcopal Church
A Cluster Analysis of Establishment Rhetoric

Sonja K. Foss

> Incomplete, they call us,
> unrecognizable.
> Because we are eleven
> and not the Magic Twelve
> of your chosen few?
> Because we are female
> (nigger-women)
> and not important enough
> to mention in Matthew,
> Mark, Luke or John,
> our Hebrew sisters present
> at your First Feast?[1]

This portion of a poem by Alla Bozarth-Campbell, written after her "irregular ordination" as a priest in the Episcopal Church on July 29, 1974, summarizes the challenge to the Church and its response concerning a major tenet of its belief system—that women should not be priests. The irregular ordination of eleven women on that date marked a turning point in a conflict within the Church over whether or not to allow women to be priests. A challenge to a tenet of a religious system has the potential to weaken or even destroy the entire system—a system that is often one of the strongest and most influential belief systems that human beings have. Thus, an examination of the Church's response to the conflict perhaps can reveal general strategies for coping with conflict in other contexts.

Background of the Conflict

A clear understanding of the history of the issue of women priests must begin with a basic knowledge of the structure of the Episcopal Church in the United States and the means through which change occurs in that

From *Religious Communication Today*, 7 (September 1984), 1-11. Used by permission of the Religious Speech Communication Association and the author.

structure. The Protestant Episcopal Church in the United States of America (PECUSA) is part of the Anglican Communion, a voluntary association of national churches originally established in England. Every ten years, bishops from all of the churches in the Communion meet in convocation at Lambeth, England. More frequent meetings are held by the Anglican Consultative Council, an organization of elected bishops, priests, and laity that meets every two years in a different country. Both of these bodies are consultative; they do not make decisions on doctrine or practice that bind the Episcopal Churches.

Establishment of policy and enactment of legislation for PECUSA is accomplished through the General Convention, which is held every three years. The General Convention is comprised of two bodies: the House of Bishops, composed of approximately 200 bishops, and the House of Deputies, composed of more than 1,000 clergy and lay representatives elected from each diocese.

Voting in the House of Deputies at a General Convention may be done by a simple majority of all present or by orders in which the clergy and the laity vote separately; the latter process generally is used for controversial issues. In this case, the majority of votes within each delegation representing a diocese must be affirmative in order for the delegation to cast an affirmative vote. When the four members of a delegation are divided two and two, all four votes are considered negative, and the delegation registers a negative vote. As a result, a minority can overrule a majority vote, and as much as an 89 percent majority may be needed to pass a resolution.[2]

While the possibility of allowing women to be ordained clergy first arose in the Episcopal Church in 1920 at a Lambeth conference, the contemporary debate on the issue began in 1970. Meeting in Houston, the General Convention voted to allow women to be ordained as deacons on the same basis as men. The Houston convention also saw the first vote on the issue of women priests. A commission appointed to study the position of women in the ministry presented a resolution that would have interpreted "bishop," "priest," and "deacon" as including both males and females. The resolution lost in a close vote by orders.[3] At their meeting in October 1971, the bishops appointed a committee to study the issue further. In response, several women organized the Episcopal Women's Caucus, declared their refusal to participate in any more studies, and urged women to "make no peace with oppression."[4]

A year later, in November 1972, the House of Bishops, meeting in New Orleans, voted to approve the ordination of women as priests and bishops. At the 1973 General Convention in Louisville, however, the resolution lost in a vote by orders. As at the Houston convention, a majority of the voters supported the resolution.

In 1974, women deacons wanting ordination to the priesthood began to protest their exclusion during ordination ceremonies of men. They read statements of protest when the congregation was asked if there were any objections to the ordination of the men, stood behind the male candidates and answered with them the questions of the examination, and received the laying on of hands—which is given by the bishop to the individual receiving ordination—by groups of women supporters.[5]

The impetus for immediate action on the part of the Church regarding women priests came on July 29, 1974. Eleven women deacons were ordained to the priesthood in the Church of the Advocate in Philadelphia. Although no canon specifically prohibited the ordination of women, canons did state that a deacon must be recommended by the standing committee of the diocese before ordination to the priesthood; none of the women met this requirement. In an open letter to their supporters, the new priests declared: "We know this ordination to be irregular. We believe it to be valid and right. . . . Our primary motivation is to begin to free priesthood from the bondage it suffers as long as it is characterized by categorical exclusion on the basis of sex."[6]

Two days later, Presiding Bishop John M. Allin called an emergency meeting of the House of Bishops in Chicago. There the members passed a resolution invalidating the ordination of the women on the grounds that the necessary conditions for valid ordination had not been fulfilled and censuring the bishops who had performed the ordinations. In response, Charles Willie, who had preached the sermon at the irregular ordination ceremony, resigned his position as vice-president of the House of Deputies, calling the actions a "blatant exercise of male arrogance."[7]

At the regular meeting of the House of Bishops in October 1974, in Oaxtepec, Mexico, a resolution was passed stating that the irregularly ordained women were "not recognizable but not incompletable" and reaffirmed support for the principle of the ordination of women to the priesthood. That same month, the eleven irregularly ordained women began to celebrate communion, and they continued to do so in Episcopal and nondenominational churches throughout the country into 1976. Among them were the churches of William Wendt in Washington, D.C., and L. Peter Beebe in Oberlin, Ohio. As a result of their invitations to the women to celebrate communion, Wendt and Beebe were tried in ecclesiastical courts and found guilty for disobeying their bishops' orders.

On September 7, 1975, four more women deacons were ordained to the priesthood at the Church of St. Stephen and Incarnation in Washington, D.C. In April 1975, one of the eleven irregularly ordained women, Merrill Bittner, left the Church with this declaration: "The journey I am on is one of affirming life. I now find that it is impossible for me personally to be about that task within the Episcopal Church, because of the pain I have suffered from a brutally negligent institution in its refusal to fully accept and affirm the women in its midst."[8] She was the second of the eleven to leave the Church; Marie Moorefield had quit to join the United Methodist Church.

September 16, 1976, marked formal approval for the ordination of women to the priesthood by the Church. The House of Deputies, at the General Convention in Minneapolis, approved a resolution that ordination to the three orders of bishops, priests, and deacons be equally applicable to men and women. The House of Bishops had approved the resolution a day earlier. The House of Bishops then adopted a resolution describing the process for the regularization of the irregularly ordained women—a public event at which communion would be celebrated and at which the women would recite an oath of loyalty to the Church. The last of the "completion" ceremonies for the irregularly ordained women was held in November 1977.

Cluster Analysis

To gain insights into the process of and motivation for the events and actions that occurred in the development of this controversy, Kenneth Burke's method of cluster analysis will be used to examine the discourse of the establishment concerning the question of women priests in the Episcopal Church. Cluster analysis is a method of "noting what subjects cluster about other subjects"[9] in an effort to discover what goes with what and why.

The method involves selecting the key terms in the discourse, using as criteria high frequency and high intensity. Terms of high frequency are simply terms that frequently are repeated in the discourse, while terms of high intensity are those that are naturally charged or that are particularly significant in the works being studied. The next step is an examination of each context in which those key terms implicitly or explicitly appear. By discovering what is repeatedly associated with these key terms in various contexts, the critic is able to formulate an equation to help explain the meanings of the key terms. As Rueckert explains, cluster analysis "is a way of finding out what the term is associated with in the poet's [or rhetor's] mind."[10] As a result of cluster analysis, the critic is able to locate the conflict or opposition in the principles and images of the discourse. Agon analysis, then, allows the critic to interpret the results of the cluster analysis in order to discover how the symbols function for the rhetor.[11]

In an attempt to understand the response of the Episcopal Church to those who wanted to see women become priests, that is, the challengers, I examined samples of discourse of the establishment, or those who did not want to see women priests,[12] prior to the resolution of the issue in September 1976. I looked for terms that clustered around four key terms, identified as such because of their intensity and frequency of appearance: "Church," "priest," "male," and "female." The clusters that emerged around these terms then were used as the basis for an attempt to understand the conflict from the establishment's perspective and the functions of the discourse for it. The clusters of terms around each key term will be examined in turn.

"Church"

A major group of terms that formed around the idea of the Church concerned the Church as authority because of its connection with the highest possible authorities—God and Christ and their various manifestations. The Church is the "Body and Bride" of Christ[13] and has "divine authority in Christ."[14] The authority is revealed through the "holy Gospel,"[15] "the Bible,"[16] or "that Holy Scripture."[17] "Canon" seemed to be a synonymous term with the authority derived from God and the Bible; it was broad enough, too, in its clustering around the concept of the Church to encompass theological thinking and documents based on these two sources of supreme authority. The Church, then, was seen as based on a "canonical structure,"[18] and "these canons can only be altered by . . . all the Catholic Churches."[19]

A cluster of terms that directly opposed this authority of God, Christ, the Bible, and the canons emphasized the essential connection of the Church with this authority. Terms such as the "rejection of the authority of Scripture" in the Church,[20] the Church as "formed or reformed by majority votes and decisions,"[21] the Church as "a parliamentary democracy,"[22] or "the vote of a church legislature,"[23] when used as the basis for Church authority, were viewed with dismay because opponents saw authority as deriving only from God.

Also closely associated with the Church in the establishment's rhetoric were terms dealing with tradition and history. To members of the establishment, the Church was an institution with a long history and well-established patterns and practices. The "long life"[24] and the "irreversible history"[25] of the Church emphasized the importance of the past and the notion that the past must be retained currently in "agelong practice"[26] that is "unvarying"[27] and "governed by . . . tradition."[28] Once again, we find that negatives that opposed tradition were used to link the Church more firmly to this tradition, and practices and principles that run counter to the nature of the Church were portrayed vividly as undesirable. Being "modern,"[29] following "every wind of doctrine," "following fashion,"[30] and accommodating "changes taking place in the world"[31] were seen to introduce into the Church "idols,"[32] to dilute "in tepid and polluted waters the ever-fresh mainspring of Christianity" (the Church),[33] and to result in "a loss of power"[34] for the Church.

As a result of connection with tradition, the Church became closely aligned with the concept of order. The "ordered life of the Church"[35] could be seen in all aspects of the life of the Church, including "the temporal order;" "the hierarchical order,"[36] and "the supernatural order."[37] This order, of course, was viewed as a "good order"[38] and a "divine order."[39]

Unity was closely associated with the Church in the discourse of the establishment, but there was some confusion about the nature of that unity. For some, the identification of the Church with unity meant unity within the Episcopal Church, exemplified in linkages such as "the Church as unity in diversity,"[40] "the unity of the Church,"[41] and the Church acting "with a common mind."[42] Others saw unity in connection with the Church as a much broader concept that included unity with the Catholic Church. In these instances, the Episcopal Church was shown as "part of the whole Catholic Church,"[43] and the Episcopal Church had to be concerned that it maintained the "right to be called Catholic."[44]

Still another sense of unity in this view of the Church was seen in the descriptions of the Episcopal Church as "a bridge-Church between two poles"[45]—between Protestant and Catholic churches—because its heritage is rooted in both. In this meaning of unity, the Episcopal Church was seen unifying all churches because of the special role it could play as a "mediator between the Catholic and Protestant Ways."[46] The Church as "divided,"[47] "fractured,"[48] or "acting separately from the Orthodox and Roman Catholic Church"[49] was a strong negative image that suggested the breaking of an essential association between the Church and unity.

The last major group of terms that clustered around the "Church" equated the Church with the feminine; members of the establishment often formulated images that suggested that the Church is female. One writer suggested a physical basis for the image because the Church congregation is "preponderantly feminine."[50] In most instances, however, the image was a metaphoric one. The Church was seen as "the Bride," in relation to the priest as bridegroom, making the Church "feminine towards" the priest.[51] Others connected the two terms by suggesting that "woman is [a symbol] of the Church,"[52] while others did so simply by referring to the Church with feminine pronouns, as in "what she is doing" and "what she understands."[53]

"Priest"

Around the term "priest" clustered several terms that operationalized the term for the establishment. One such cluster concerned the exclusiveness of the priesthood; it was viewed as a select group to which only some could be admitted. This notion of an elite group emerged from a juxtaposition of the priesthood with "divine choice,"[54] "inherent character," and a vocation that "is more than a profession";[55] as a result, not everyone "has a right to be a priest."[56] Further evidence of the select nature of the priesthood came from its differentiation from "other forms of Christian ministry." As one writer explained: "The congregationally oriented ministry in Protestant denominational churches is, therefore, something quite different from the priesthood."[57] The essential nature of the priesthood as "exclusive"[58] was developed further as the opponents created negative images of a ministry that was not characterized by elitism. "Religious professionals,"[59] for example, were not seen as the same as Episcopal priests.

The exclusiveness of the priesthood derived in part from a view of the priest as a symbol of God and Christ. The discourse of the establishment included a conception of the priest as a "God symbol,"[60] "the steward of God's symbols," " 'an earthenware pot' containing the transcendent power of God,"[61] and a "copy of God."[62] The priest's relationship to God was considered analogous to that of Jesus to God; thus, the priest also became linked with Christ. In "the priesthood of Christ,"[63] the priest was "the symbol of Christ's presence among the flock,'[64] "*Alter Christus,*"[65] "the commissioned agent of Christ,"[66] or an "icon of Christ."[67] Simply, then, the priest represented "Christ to the Church."[68]

A third cluster of terms around "priest" created a clear view of the priest as male. "Male priesthood," "masculine priesthood,"[69] "priesthood of men,"[70] and "the priesthood . . . as a male vocation"[71] are statements that did not leave room for conceptions of priests as women. The definition of a priest as male was developed further when the possibility of a female priesthood was seen only in the context of heresy: "The only examples of a female priesthood in ancient times are those found in heretical sects."[72]

Descriptions of the priest's activities tended to emphasize qualities that traditionally have been regarded as appropriate male behaviors, thus further cementing the priesthood to maleness. The priesthood, the establishment argued, is an expression of "the rites of initiation and direction";[73] it is "generative, initiating, giving"[74] as the priest "sows the seed of the Word into the earthed community."[75] Supplementing the allusions to the male role in the sex act were descriptions of the priest's characteristics that conformed to the stereotyped male role. The priest "guards the temple"[76] and has "vigour," "energy," "aggression," and "objectivity."[77] Although these qualities certainly could be used to describe many women, the establishment saw them as male characteristics only, furthering the development of their view that priests are male.

"Male"

Not only the clusters surrounding the term "priest" pointed to maleness as an essential nature of the priest, those surrounding the terms "male" and "man" reinforced that definition of the priest. Definite ideas of what a man is emerged from three basic clusters that connected the man with God, superiority, and bold activity, and thus ultimately with the priesthood.

Many images were developed in the rhetoric of the establishment that portrayed an essential linkage between God and the male. The masculinity of God was shown as having "matched and mastered the compulsive and seductive qualities of the Great Mother."[78] That God is male (which gives special respect for the male) could be seen in the facts that "God taught us to call Him . . . Father" and that "God . . . thought it best to become a man."[79]

The man derived authority from his special connection with God, making him superior to the woman, according to the second cluster of terms that developed around "male." The man was seen "to represent . . . the Head";[80] in other words, "the 'authority' . . . is normally understood to be that of the man."[81] Because "supreme authority in both Church and home has been divinely vested in the male,"[82] masculinity "rules"[83] and demonstrates "powerfulness, domination, and control."[84]

Finally, we see a cluster in which the male was identified with bold activity—the same type of activity we saw as essential to the priest role. The male, of course, "has the initiative in creation,"[85] which made "initiative . . . a male rather than a female attribute"[86] and made "the conscious, active pole" that of the male.[87] Images associated with masculinity included "assertiveness,"[88] "aggression and ruthlessness,"[89] qualities that put the man on the "cutting edge"[90] of "social, cultural, and religious advance."[91] Concomitant with these qualities was responsibility for the "protection and guardianship of the family and home,"[92] in which the man protected the family "from the fiery dragon,"[93] slew "dragons" and cast out "devils," and generally played the role of "the saviour-figure."[94]

"Female"

The images that clustered around the term "female" tended to be negative ones. One such cluster focused on woman as defined by "the body,"[95] which made sexuality central in this view of the woman. "The feminine, as woman, . . . receives and *actively* holds within itself whatever of the masculine is poured in—ideas, words, man's lower animal nature";[96] thus, woman represented "*eros, physical love*."[97]

Woman's association with physical love generally was not positive. She was seen as nudging us "into world, flesh, and even, sometimes, the territory of the devil."[98] In this context, the woman was associated with "prostitute,"[99] a "charming, seductive" exterior,[100] and "adultery and 'adulteration.'"[101] To step out of the feminine sphere in which woman is essentially sexual, however, was far worse in its consequences for her sexuality. For in a masculine role, woman "will become incurably frigid, . . . incurably promiscuous, . . . or destructive."[102] Woman's sexuality made her a "feared female,"[103] someone who could "bedevil"[104] and who was "experienced as a threat."[105]

Other negative terms clustered around the image of the woman to create an unflattering view of the female. Linked to woman were qualities such as "bitchy and greedy,"[106] violent,[107] and an association with "disease."[108] Women were portrayed as being primarily interested in "play,"[109] as "dithering" and causing "real confusions,"[110] as "vehicles for guilt and disillusionment,"[111] and as causing an abundance of troubles associated with "Pandora's Box."[112] And, of course, women were viewed as emotional. In one such description, "the archetypal mermaid" was seen "slipping through the stone and deepening it with emotion."[113] Other descriptions pointed to emotionality as essential to motherhood, associating woman with the "flood tide of maternal emotion,"[114] with being "equipped emotionally . . . to nurture and shape children's lives,"[115] and "to mediate to the child/man all those emotions which will energize him into mature manhood."[116] On the whole, women's emotions were not viewed as positive. The opposition maintained: "Emotions are apt to rule" the direction of their discussions,[117] making women "unpredictable,"[118] "compulsive,"[119] and apt to "meet any attempt at sober argument by leaving the room in a temper, often slamming the door for emphasis."[120]

A less negative quality connected with women—but still one that was portrayed as less effective than men's qualities—was that women rely on intuition as a major source of their knowledge. Women were considered "more in tune than men with these inner dimensions":[121] "to feel something in one's bones . . . is profoundly feminine."[122] Their tendency to "listen to the world of dream and nature and to follow such personal instincts"[123] meant that they were "not clothed with institutional authority"[124] and represented "the unconscious . . . *pole of mankind.*"[125]

The most positive portrayal of the female came in her association with motherhood, which also was the strongest image to cluster around the woman. She was associated with "the mother of Messiah,"[126] the "mother-archetype,"[127] "motherhood,"[128] "a potential mother,"[129] "maternal function," "maternal instinct,"[130] and "maternal rhythm."[131] Terms that associated the woman with children and the process of child bearing further developed this view of woman. She "carries these embryos,"[132] waits "nine months for a child to come,"[133] "bears a child,"[134] and then finds her "energies are largely absorbed in nourishing and tending."[135] Woman's role as a mother—in particular her fertility—linked her to the earth, a connection that was developed in the opposition's rhetoric. Because "all life depended upon her bounty"[136] and her "fecundity," the "cult of fertility and the feminine" became linked with "woman and earth."[137] When the "earth divinity is feminine," any symbolic interaction of a woman with the process of burial in the earth—the "earth-tomb-womb equation"[138]—was viewed as "cosmic Lesbianism,"[139] a strong image that conveyed not only a connection with the earth but also a focus again on woman's sexuality.

But even the motherhood cluster around "woman" sometimes was seen as negative, for there is a "dark side of the Mother . . . which is, in the last analysis, hostile to growth."[140] Here we see the mother as "devouring or destructive"[141] and connected with "domination"[142] and "tyranny."[143] In fact, in this cluster, "a good mother, like a bad mother, must in the end be 'bad' for her child."[144]

The wide array of generally negative characteristics associated with the female led naturally to the final cluster around this term—that of "the inferiority of woman,"[145] the "subjection of women,"[146] or "female subordination."[147] This definition of woman as inferior meant that "femininity . . . submits";[148] "the wife must 'reverence' her husband, placing herself in subjection to him"; and "woman must place a greater or lesser dependence upon the man."[149] Such is the proper natural order since "the image of God is in man directly, but in woman indirectly."[150]

Conclusion

A cluster analysis of the rhetoric of the establishment concerning the issue of women priests reveals that in the minds of the establishment, the Episcopal Church was a traditional, orderly, and unified structure based on the highest possible authority, God. It was a feminine structure in its proper relation to the priest who, because he symbolized God and Christ, belonged to an exclusive male group. Men were defined by a special connection to God and energetic activity, both of which made them superior to women. Women's inferiority resulted from a focus on their bodies and sexuality as a central feature of their being. The negative qualities that they were seen to possess included their emotionality and their reliance on intuition as a source of knowledge. Their potential as mothers, because it could be negative as well as positive and required women to focus their attention on child rearing, provided further support for their inferiority.

A structure that emerges from the clusters established around the key terms suggests that the rhetoric of the opposition revolved around a system of polarities. While formal Episcopal theology recognizes God and the potential for good in all of its members, the rhetoric of the opponents seemed to ignore this shared substance and established in its place a series of oppositions, with one set valued as positive and the other rejected as negative.

We find, then, that the clusters around the Church were good, while their opposites were evil:

View of Church revealed in cluster analysis	Opposites
institutional authority	personal authority
tradition	modernity
order	chaos
unity	dissension
feminine	masculine

The concepts viewed as negative—those in opposition to the establishment's view—were precisely the concepts introduced into it by the women who wanted to be priests and their supporters. They argued that they were called to the priesthood by their own consciences—their own source of authority—that challenged the institutional authority of the Church. Their demands also introduced modernity, chaos, and dissension into a Church that was supposed to be the epitome of history, order, and unity. In essence, the women stated that through their demand to be priests, the Church was something very different from what the establishment believed it was.

In contrast to the other oppositions established, "masculine" as the opposite of the feminine was not viewed as a negative. As we have seen in the clustering of terms around "priest" and "male," the masculine was highly valued by the establishment. The masculine was negative in the sense that a male-male relationship between the Church and the priest would be improper.

By operationalizing the definition of "priest" through the clusters selected, the establishment again posited a duality in which its terms were positive and the opposites introduced by the challengers were negative:

View of priest revealed in cluster analysis	Opposites
exclusive	popular
symbolic of God and Christ through maleness	symbolic of God and Christ through humanness
male	female

Again we see that the women who believed that they should be allowed to be priests contradicted the very notion of what a priest was in the minds of the establishment. To allow women priests would be an action approaching heresy, for anyone then could claim the right to be a priest, even though that individual was a woman who could not represent properly "God the Father" and "Christ the Son."

The positive and negative implications of the polarity organized in the rhetoric of the opponents became even more clear in the clusters that defined male and female and their opposites. The characteristics of men were seen as positive; their opposites were qualities that made their possessors less valuable:

View of male revealed in cluster analysis	Opposites
God	void
superior	inferior
active	passive

What comes through clearly was that women were seen as endowed with less God spirit and as less capable than were men. Women's negative qualities continued to add up when they were viewed in terms of the clusters around "female" and their opposites:

View of female revealed in cluster analysis	Opposites
body	mind
intuition	rational knowledge
mother	father
inferior	superior

Now we begin to see the entire framework that the rhetoric of the establishment constructed. The qualities opposite those that defined the female were precisely those that defined the male and, more important, corresponded closely to the qualities that defined the priest. The priesthood was considered exclusive or superior and emphasized a rational manifestation of the authority of the Church and its basis in God and Christ. Even the term "father" was more highly valued than "mother" in that it is used as a name for God and for priests and is not limited in its application only to the biological father.

The polarities and the values evident in the clusters around the terms "Church," "priest," "male," and "female" were used as the basis for an entire ideology or worldview that was constructed by the establishment. This worldview took the form of a hierarchy based on the degree to which entities possessed what were considered to be positively valued qualities. Thus we find that the Church held the top position in the hierarchy because it had the most direct link to the source of the most positive quality possible: God. This association gave the Church the right and the responsibility to manifest God through tradition, order, and unity. At the second level of the hierarchy was the priest, who also possessed several positive traits—a connection with God, a special nature that set him apart, and maleness. The priest ranked below the Church because the Church provided the larger structure in which the priest functioned and from which he derived authority.

Maleness was higher on the hierarchy than femaleness, not only because of the interrelationship between the male and the priesthood but because of man's special connection to God and his active, assertive nature. At the lowest level on this hierarchy was the woman, who earned her inferior position because she was seen as having fewer of those qualities that were regarded as important. Her concerns, the opposition believed, were with her body and motherhood, and her source of knowledge was intuition, none of which were traits positively valued in this particular hierarchy.

The challenge to the Episcopal Church concerning women priests, then, really was about the legitimacy of the established hierarchy and the authority on which it rested. Although there was an unequal distribution of power and resources within the hierarchy because all entities did not share the valued properties to the same degree, it was viewed as legitimate and was maintained as long as it served the needs of the entities. When, however, members of the system—in this case, women—felt their needs were not being met and wanted the same rewards accorded to members higher up in the system, the legitimacy of the hierarchy was questioned. The women who challenged the Episcopal Church on the issue of women priests were demanding an alternative hierarchy or authority based on new definitions of what is positive, valuable, and worthwhile, that is, qualities seen as exact opposites of those presented as such on the old hierarchy.

In response to the challenge, the Episcopal Church continued to argue out of a context of the traditional hierarchy and tried to maintain what Burke would call the mystery[151] within the hierarchy. In this case, the mystery not only was serving spiritual needs but also was helping to hide the inequalities of the hierarchy in terms of resources and respect accorded individual members. When the discourse of the challengers exposed the great differences between the classes on the hierarchy, destroying the mystery, change became possible in the system.

The Episcopal Church, upon seeing its worldview shattered through the demand for change, continued to support for a time the original hierarchy, trying to maintain the orientation it offered and reaffirming belief in it. Such action, Burke says, is motivated by "piety" or "the yearning to conform to the 'sources of one's being.'"[152] Through the selection of particular clusters to group around its key terms and thus define them, the establishment attempted to hold the Church within the context of the hierarchy of Church-priest-male-female.

Once the challengers' rhetoric opened up an alternative world view with a new hierarchy, however, the arguments against women priests based on the original hierarchy no longer were accepted as the only possibility; other views became possible and thus legitimate. These views generated movement within the Church and an eventual reorganization of the old hierarchy as a result of the successful challenge to the establishment. Although there are some members of the Episcopal Church who have not accepted the new hierarchy, in which male and female are viewed as equally positive and personal authority based on God's direction is as valid as institutional authority derived from God, the Church no longer can remain pious to its original hierarchy. Instead, it has had to fit the pieces of its world together in new, more adaptive, and more egalitarian ways.

Not every established institution or belief system that is so challenged, of course, will adopt a new hierarchy, with new definitions for its key terms. It may decide to retain its old hierarchy and make no changes. A number of factors appear to be influential in whether a change is made or not, factors such as the strategies of the challengers, the establishment's need for external support and its perception of the amount of external support it has, precedents in the history of the establishment for the types of changes being urged, and the strength of the meanings of the clusters around key terms in the rhetoric of the establishment. Further investigation into these types of variables should clarify the type of resolution that is likely to occur in a conflict such as the one examined here. But whether or not any overt change in the hierarchy occurs, small increments in growth are likely that make the next challenge more apt to succeed. One of the eleven irregularly ordained women priests summarized well this growth process:

> Because I never left the institutional Church through this process, it's been forced to deal with me, to redefine itself in relationship to me, as I have had to redefine myself in relationship to it. We— the institutional Church and I—have helped each other to grow by standing with and against one another at the same time.[153]

Notes

[1] Alla Bozarth-Campbell, *Womanpriest: A Personal Odyssey* (New York: Paulist Press, 1978), pp. 125–26.

[2] Ibid., p. 112.

[3] Shirley Sartori, "Conflict and Institutional Change: The Ordination of Women in the Episcopal Church (Ph.D. dissertation, State University of New York at Albany, 1978), p. 55.

[4] Ibid., p. 62.

[5]A description of one such "nonordination" ceremony is contained in Ibid., pp. 95–100.

[6]Ibid., p. 124.

[7]Cheryl Forbes, "The Episcopal Church: When Is a Priest Not a Priest?" *Christianity Today*, 13 September 1974, p. 70.

[8]"Briefs: 2d Women Priest Quits Church," *Chicago Tribune*, 3 April 1976, sec. 1, p. 14.

[9]Kenneth Burke, *Attitudes Toward History*, 2 vols. (New York: New Republic, 1937), 2:76.

[10]William H. Rueckert, *Kenneth Burke and the Drama of Human Relations* (Minneapolis: University of Minnesota Press, 1963), p. 86.

[11]More detailed explanations of the method of cluster analysis can be found in Ibid., pp. 83–111; Burke, 2:76–78; and Carol A. Berthold, "Kenneth Burke's Cluster-Agon Method: Its Development and an Application," *Central States Speech Journal*, 27 (Winter 1976): 302–309.

[12]The discourse examined through cluster analysis came from religious journals, including *Anglican Theological Review, Theology, Journal of Dharma, The Ecumenical Review, The Modern Churchman, Journal of Ecumenical Studies, Churchman: A Quarterly Journal of Anglican Theology, Nashotah Review*, and *Communio*; religious magazines and newspapers, including *Christianity Today, The Christian Century, Christianity and Crisis*, and *The Episcopalian*; books by women and bishops involved in the controversy; and collections of essays in support of or against women priests. A complete list of the sources considered in the analysis is available from the author.

[13]E. L. Mascall, "Some Basic Considerations," in *Man, Woman, and Priesthood*, ed. Peter Moore (London: SPCK, 1978), p. 26.

[14]Peter Moore, p. 167.

[15]Ibid., p. 164.

[16]Harold Riley, "Women as Priests?" in *Sexuality-Theology-Priesthood: Reflections on the Ordination of Women to the Priesthood*, ed. H. Karl Lutge (San Gabriel, CA: Concerned Fellow Episcopalians, n. d.), p. 8.

[17]John Paul Boyer, "The 'Open Mind' and the Mind of Christ," in Lutge, p. 55.

[18]Robert E. Terwilliger, "A Fractured Church," in Peter Moore, p. 142.

[19]George William Rutler, "Speech to the Convention of the Diocese of Pennsylvania," in Lutge, p. 59.

[20]Roger Beckwith, "The Bearing of Holy Scripture," in Peter Moore, p. 62.

[21]Peter Moore, p. 164.

[22]Mascall, p. 18.

[23]Robert E. Terwilliger, "Foreword," in Lutge, p. 5.

[24]Albert J. duBois, "Why I Am Against the Ordination of Women," *The Episcopalian*, July 1972, p. 21.

[25]Susannah Herzel, "The Body is the Book," in Peter Moore, p. 102.

[26]Riley, p. 8.

[27]Kallistos Ware, "Man, Woman, and the Priesthood of Christ," in Peter Moore, p. 22.

[28]Paul Moore, Jr., *Take a Bishop Like Me* (New York: Harper & Row, 1979), p. 22.

[29]Louis Bouyer, "Christian Priesthood and Women," in Peter Moore, p. 66.

[30]Rutler, p. 59.

[31]Elisabeth Elliot, "Why I Oppose the Ordination of Women," *Christianity Today*, 6 June 1975, p. 12.

[32]Bouyer, p. 66.

[33]Ibid.

[34]Elliot, p. 12.

[35]Paul Moore, p. 25.

[36]Elliot, p. 14.

[37]Peter Moore, p. 166.

[38]Edwin G. Wappler, "Theological Reasons Against the Ordination of Women to the Priesthood and Episcopate," *Nashotah Review*, 15 (Fall 1975): 323. Joint issue with *Saint Luke's Journal of Theology*, 18 (September 1975): 461.

[39]Peter Moore, p. 165.

[40]Ware, p. 85.

[41]Terwilliger, "A Fractured Church," p. 150.

[42]John MacQuarrie, "Women and Ordination: A Mediating View," in Lutge, p. 45.

[43]Riley, p. 8.

[44]Rutler, p. 57.

[45]Peter Moore, p. 1.

[46]Herzel, p. 107.

[47]Terwilliger, "A Fractured Church," p. 151.

[48]Ibid., p. 160.

[49]Paul Moore, p. 90.

[50]Elizabeth R. Noice, "Priesthood and Women: A Lay View," *Anglican Theological Review*, 55 (January 1973): 53.

[51]Gilbert Russell and Margaret Dewey, "Psychological Aspects," in Peter Moore, p. 96.

[52]Boyer, p. 55.

[53]Urban T. Holmes, III, "Priesthood and Sexuality: A Caveat Only Dimly Perceived," *Anglican Theological Review*, 55 (January 1973): 64.

[54]C. Kilmer Myers, "Should Women be Ordained?" *The Episcopalian*, February 1972, p. 8.

[55]Riley, p. 8.

[56]Rutler, p. 58.

[57]duBois, p. 22.

[58]Herzel, p. 102.

[59]Boyer, p. 55.

[60]Myers, p. 8.

[61]Holmes, p. 64.

[62]duBois, p. 23.

[63]O. C. Edwards, Jr., "The Failure of the Anti-Nicene Church to Ordain Women and Its Significance Today," *Nashotah Review*, 15 (Fall 1975): 212. Joint issue with *Saint Luke's Journal of Theology*, 18 (September 1975): 350.

[64]John R. Sheets, "The Ordination of Women," *Communio*, 3 (1976): 12.

[65]duBois, p. 23.

[66]Myers, p. 8.

[67]Russell and Dewey, p. 96.

[68]Boyer, p. 53.

[69]Wappler, p. 322 [460].

[70]duBois, p. 30.

[71]Terwilliger, "Foreward," p. 5.

[72]Riley, p. 9.

[73]Herzel, p. 101.

[74]Myers, p. 8.

[75]Herzel, p. 101.

[76]duBois, p. 22.

[77]Herzel, p. 101.

[78]Russell and Dewey, p. 95.

[79]Rutler, p. 58.

[80]Bouyer, p. 65.

[81]Beckwith, pp. 51–52.

[82]Elliot, p. 14.

[83] Ibid., p. 16.
[84] David H. Fisher, "Symbol, Myth, and Parable," *Nashotah Review*, 15 (Fall 1975): 291. Joint issue with *Saint Luke's Journal of Theology*, 18 (September 1975): 429.
[85] duBois, p. 22.
[86] Myers, p. 8.
[87] Holmes, p. 66.
[88] Fisher, p. 291 [429].
[89] Russell and Dewey, p. 95.
[90] Herzel, p. 119.
[91] Russell and Dewey, p. 95.
[92] duBois, p. 22.
[93] Herzel, p. 121.
[94] Russell and Dewey, p. 98.
[95] Herzel, p. 120.
[96] Ibid.
[97] Ibid., p. 113.
[98] Ibid., p. 116.
[99] Ibid., p. 120.
[100] Russell and Dewey, p. 92.
[101] Herzel, p. 119.
[102] Ibid., p. 120.
[103] Ibid., p. 112.
[104] Russell and Dewey, p. 97.
[105] Ibid.
[106] Herzel, p. 103.
[107] Holmes, p. 66.
[108] Russell and Dewey, p. 100.
[109] Herzel, p. 114.
[110] Ibid., p. 106.
[111] Ibid., p. 103.
[112] Ibid., p. 116.
[113] Ibid.
[114] Russell and Dewey, p. 93.
[115] duBois, p. 21.
[116] Herzel, p. 121.
[117] duBois, p. 21.
[118] Herzel, p. 118.
[119] Russell and Dewey, p. 95.
[120] duBois, p. 21.
[121] Herzel, p. 105.
[122] Ibid., p. 111.
[123] Ibid., p. 117.
[124] Russell and Dewey, p. 97.
[125] Holmes, p. 66.
[126] Elliot, p. 13.
[127] Russell and Dewey, p. 92.
[128] Mascall, p. 24.
[129] M. E. Thrall, *The Ordination of Women to the Priesthood: A Study of the Biblical Evidence* (London: SCM Press, 1958), p. 102.
[130] Ibid., p. 103.
[131] Ibid., p. 102.
[132] Herzel, p. 120.

[133] Ibid., p. 106.

[134] Thrall, p. 105.

[135] duBois, p. 23.

[136] Russell and Dewey, p. 95.

[137] Ibid., p. 94.

[138] Holmes, p. 66.

[139] Ibid., p. 65.

[140] Russell and Dewey, p. 98.

[141] Ibid., p. 92.

[142] Herzel, p. 119.

[143] Russell and Dewey, p. 93.

[144] Ibid., p. 94.

[145] duBois, p. 23.

[146] Elliot, p. 14.

[147] Thrall, p. 17.

[148] Elliot, p. 16.

[149] duBois, p. 23.

[150] Beckwith, p. 57.

[151] For an explanation of Burke's notion of mystery, see Kenneth Burke, *A Rhetoric of Motives* (New York: Prentice-Hall, 1950; reprint ed., Berkeley: University of California Press, 1962), pp. 114–24, 176–80.

[152] Kenneth Burke, *Permanence and Change: An Anatomy of Purpose* (New York: New Republic, 1935; reprint ed., Indianapolis: Bobbs-Merrill, 1965), p. 69.

[153] Bozarth-Campbell, p. 222.

Additional Samples
Cluster Criticism

Avalos, Elizabeth Riley. "Concepts of *Power* in Betty Friedan's Rhetoric: An Application of Burke's Cluster-Agon Method." Diss. University of Denver 1983.

Berthold, Carol A. "Kenneth Burke's Cluster-Agon Method: Its Development and an Application." *Central States Speech Journal*, 27 (Winter 1976), 302–09.

Cooks, Leda, and David Descutner. "Different Paths from Powerlessness to Empowerment: A Dramatistic Analysis of Two Eating Disorder Therapies." *Western Journal of Communication*, 57 (Fall 1993), 494–514.

Corcoran, Farrel. "The Bear in the Back Yard: Myth, Ideology, and Victimage Ritual in Soviet Funerals." *Communication Monographs*, 50 (December 1983), 305–20.

Crowell, Laura. "Three Sheers for Kenneth Burke." *Quarterly Journal of Speech*, 63 (April 1977), 152–67.

Fritz, Paul Alvin. "A Cluster Analysis of the Hippocratic Oath." Diss. Bowling Green State University 1978.

Lee, Sang-Chul, and Karlyn Kohrs Campbell. "Korean President Roh Tae-Woo's 1988 Inaugural Address: Campaigning for Investiture." *Quarterly Journal of Speech*, 80 (February 1994), 37–52.

Mechling, Elizabeth Walker, and Jay Mechling. "Sweet Talk: The Moral Rhetoric Against Sugar." *Central States Speech Journal*, 34 (Spring 1983), 19–32.

5

Fantasy-Theme Criticism

The fantasy-theme method of rhetorical criticism, created by Ernest G. Bormann, is designed to provide insights into the shared worldview of groups of rhetors.[1] Impetus for the method came from the work of Robert Bales and his associates in their study of communication in small groups. Bales discovered the process of group fantasizing or dramatizing as a type of communication that occurs in small groups.[2] This communication is characterized in this way: "The tempo of the conversation would pick up. People would grow excited, interrupt one another, blush, laugh, forget their self-consciousness. The tone of the meeting, often quiet and tense immediately prior to the dramatizing, would become lively, animated, and boisterous, the chaining process, involving both verbal and nonverbal communication, indicating participation in the drama."[3] Bormann extended the notion of fantasizing discovered by Bales into a theory (symbolic convergence theory) and a method (fantasy-theme criticism) that can be applied not only to the study of small groups but to the communication of social movements, political campaigns, organizational communication, and other kinds of rhetoric as well.

Symbolic convergence theory is based on two major assumptions. One is that communication creates reality. Ernst Cassirer has offered a useful explanation of how this process occurs. To say that rhetoric creates reality means that "symbolic forms are not imitations, but *organs* of reality, since it is solely by their agency that anything real becomes an object for intellectual apprehension, and as such is made visible to us."[4] Symbols create reality because of their capacity to introduce form and law into a disordered sensory experience. The chaotic and disorderly sensory world is organized and made manageable by the symbols that are devised to dominate it: "The process of language formation shows for example how the chaos of immediate impressions takes on order and clarity for us only when we 'name' it and so permeate it with the function of linguistic thought and expression."[5] Language or rhetoric is a force through which the essence of a substance or an idea becomes known or "real" to us because it halts the constant flux of the contents of consciousness by fixing a substance with a linguistic symbol.

In the field of communication, the idea that rhetoric creates reality is known as the notion that rhetoric is epistemic, which simply means that rhetoric creates knowledge; *epistemology* is the study of the origin and nature of knowledge. Robert L. Scott started the debate in the field in 1967 over exactly how rhetoric functions in this manner: "Insofar as we can say that there is truth in human affairs, it . . . [is] the result of a process of interaction at a given moment. Thus rhetoric may be viewed not as a matter of giving effectiveness to truth but of creating truth."[6] Scott's essay spawned numerous essays debating the process by which and degree to which rhetoric creates reality, knowledge, and truth,[7] but all of the scholars involved agree that there is a connection between the symbols we use and the reality we experience or the knowledge we have of the world.

A second assumption on which symbolic convergence theory is based is that symbols not only create reality for individuals but that individuals' meanings for symbols can converge to create a *shared* reality for participants. *Convergence*, in the theory, refers "to the way two or more private symbolic worlds incline toward each other, come more closely together, or even overlap during certain processes of communication." It also might be thought of as shared meaning, consensus, or general agreement on subjective meanings. Bormann elaborates: "If several or many people develop portions of their private symbolic worlds that overlap as a result of symbolic convergence, they share a common consciousness and have the basis for communicating with one another to create community, to discuss their common experiences, and to achieve mutual understanding."[8]

Such convergence results, Bormann explains, in a number of consequences: "[The individuals] have jointly experienced the same emotions;

they have developed the same attitudes and emotional responses to the personae of the drama; and they have interpreted some aspect of their experience in the same way. They have thus achieved symbolic convergence about their common experiences."[9] The notion of convergence emphasizes the audience as a critical element in the rhetorical process. The message itself is important, but the *sharing* of the message is seen as even more significant in the symbolic convergence theory.

The basic unit of analysis of symbolic convergence theory and fantasy-theme criticism is the *fantasy theme*. *Fantasy*, in the context of symbolic convergence theory, is not used in its popular sense—something imaginary and not grounded in reality. Instead, *fantasy* is "the creative and imaginative interpretation of events,"[10] and a *fantasy theme* is the means through which the interpretation is accomplished in communication. It is a word, phrase, or statement that interprets events in the past, envisions events in the future, or depicts current events that are removed in time and/or space from the actual activities of the group. Fantasy themes tell a story that accounts for the group's experience and that *is* the reality of the participants.

The fantasy themes that describe the world from the group's perspective are of three types, corresponding to the elements necessary to create a drama: setting, characters, and actions. A statement that depicts where the action is taking place or the place where the characters act out their roles is called a *setting theme*. Setting themes not only name the scene of the action but also may describe the characteristics of that scene. *Character themes* describe the agents or actors in the drama, ascribe qualities to them, assign motives to them, and portray them as having certain characteristics. Often, some characters are portrayed as heroes, while others are villains; some are major characters, while others are supporting players. *Action themes*, which also can be called *plotlines*, deal with the action of the drama. The actions in which the characters engage comprise action themes.

The notion of *dramatizing* helps clarify the definition of *fantasy* as it is used by Bormann. A fantasy theme depicts characters, actions, and settings that are removed from the actual current group situation in time and place. Bormann distinguishes between a dramatic situation that takes place in the immediate context of the group and a dramatized communication shared by the group: "If, in the middle of a group discussion, several members come into conflict, the situation would be dramatic, but because the action is unfolding in the immediate experience of the group it would not qualify as a basis for the sharing of a group fantasy. If, however, the group members begin talking about a conflict some of them had in the past or if they envision a future conflict, these comments would be dramatizing messages."[11]

In addition to their dramatic nature, fantasies are characterized by their artistic and organized quality. While experience itself is often chaotic and confusing, fantasy themes are organized and artistic. They are designed to create the most credible interpretation of experience or the most comprehensible forms for making sense out of experience. Thus, fantasy themes are always slanted and ordered in particular ways to provide compelling explanations for experiences. While all fantasy themes involve the creative interpretation of events, the artistry with which the fantasies are presented varies. Some groups construct fantasies "in which cardboard characters enact stereotyped melodramas," while others participate in "a social reality of complexity peopled with characters of stature enacting high tragedies."[12] But regardless of the qualities of the fantasies, they always present an interpretation or a bias and attempt to persuade others of the correctness of that perspective.

A close relationship exists between fantasies and argumentation in that shared fantasies are a necessary and prior condition for arguments. They provide the ground for arguments or establish the assumptive system that is the basis for arguments. Argumentation requires a common set of assumptions about good reasons and the nature of proof or the proper way to provide good reasons for arguments for belief and action, and fantasy themes provide these assumptions. Bormann provides an example of the connection between fantasy themes and arguments:

> For instance, the Puritan vision gave highest place to evidence not of the senses but to revelations, from God. The assumptive system undergirding the Puritan arguments was a grand fantasy type in which a god persona revealed the ultimate truth by inspiring humans to write a sacred text. Supplementing this core drama was the fantasy type in which the god persona inspired ministers to speak the truth when preaching and teaching. These fantasy types provided the ultimate legitimization for the Bible as a source of revealed knowledge and for the ministers as the proper teachers of biblical truths.[13]

Other shared fantasies provide different kinds of assumptions for argumentation—scientists assume that argument is based on the careful observation of facts, for example, while lawyers assume precedent or past experience is the basis for argument.

When similar scenarios involving the same scenes, characters, and settings have been shared by members of a community, they form a rhetorical vision known as a *fantasy type*. A fantasy type is a stock rhetorical vision that appears repeatedly in the rhetoric of a group. Once a fantasy type has developed, rhetors do not need to provide the audience with details about the specific characters engaging in actions in particular settings. They simply state the general story line of the fantasy type, and the audience is able to call up the other details of the entire scenario.

If a fantasy type has formed, a student in a university community might say, "Students are fed up with professors who are so busy with their own research that they don't have time for students," and an entire rhetorical vision is called up by most members of the audience. The success of the vision shows that audience members have shared specific fantasies about teachers who are unprepared for class, who do not hold office hours, and who return exams and papers late or perhaps not at all.

Fantasy types allow a group to fit new events or experiences into familiar patterns. If a new experience can be portrayed as an instance of a familiar fantasy type, the new experience is brought into line with the group's values and emotions. If the members of a university community, for example, share a fantasy type that the State Board of Higher Education does not support the university, the forced retirement of the university's president by the Board may be interpreted as a continued lack of support for the school. The creation of the terms *Billygate* to describe Jimmy Carter's brother's Middle-Eastern affairs, *Irangate* to describe the Iran-contra affair during Ronald Reagan's administration, and *Whitewater* to describe Bill Clinton's involvement in a failed real-estate venture are other examples. All three situations were interpreted by fitting them into the fantasy type of the Watergate scenario of Richard Nixon's administration.

The term, *rhetorical vision*, also constitutes a unit of analysis in the fantasy-theme approach to criticism. *Rhetorical vision* is a "unified putting together of the various shared fantasies"[14] or a swirling together of fantasy themes to provide a credible interpretation of reality. It contains fantasy themes relating to setting, characters, and actions that together form a symbolic drama or a coherent interpretation of reality. In the debate on the Equal Rights Amendment (ERA), the proposed Constitutional amendment that would have prohibited discrimination on the basis of sex, one rhetorical vision of the opponents centered around the battlefield. Women were subject to the draft and were depicted in military service fighting along with men, dodging bombs, bullets, grenades, and mines. Another rhetorical vision was centered in the home; the major characters were women who remained home to care for their husbands and children. Opposition discourse to the ERA, then, included at least two different rhetorical visions.[15]

The presence of a rhetorical vision suggests that a rhetorical community has been formed consisting of participants in the vision or members who have shared the fantasy themes.[16] The people who participate in a rhetorical vision, then, constitute a rhetorical community. They share common symbolic ground and respond to messages in ways that are in tune with their rhetorical vision: "They will cheer references to the heroic persona in their rhetorical vision. They will respond with antipathy to allusions to the villains. They will have agreed-upon procedures for problem-solving communication. They will share the same vision of what counts as evidence, how to build a case, and how to refute an argument."[17]

The motives for action for a rhetorical community reside in its rhetorical vision. Each rhetorical vision contains as part of its substance the motive that will impel the participants. As Bormann explains: "Motives do not exist to be expressed in communication but rather arise in the expression itself and come to be embedded in the drama of the fantasy themes that generated and serve to sustain them."[18] Bormann provides some examples of how participation in a particular rhetorical vision motivates individuals to particular action: "The born-again Christian is baptized and adopts a life-style and behavior modeled after the heroes of the dramas that sustain that vision. . . . Likewise the convert to one of the countercultures in the 1960s would let his hair and beard grow, change his style of dress, and his method of work, and so forth."[19]

Actions that make little sense to someone outside of a rhetorical vision make perfect sense when viewed in the context of that vision, for the vision provides the motive for action. The willingness of martyrs and terrorists to die in support of a cause, for example, may seem absurd to most of us. Once we discover the rhetorical vision in which the martyrs or terrorists participated, however, we have a much better idea of why they were motivated to sacrifice their lives.

Procedures

The critic who chooses to focus on rhetorical visions and fantasy themes proceeds, as all critics do, through four steps: (1) formulating a research question and selecting an artifact; (2) selecting a unit of analysis; (3) analyzing the artifact; and (4) writing the critical essay.

Formulating a Research Question and Selecting an Artifact

The first step in the process of rhetorical criticism is to develop a research question to ask about rhetoric and to select a rhetorical artifact to analyze that will provide an initial answer to the question.

Selecting a Unit of Analysis

The second step in the process of rhetorical criticism is to select a unit of analysis that can help the critic answer the research question. The unit of analysis is that aspect of the artifact to which the critic attends in the analysis. The fantasy-theme method offers the critic two units of analysis. One is the fantasy theme, which is a word, phrase, or statement that interprets the world in a particular way. Fantasy themes deal with settings, characters, and the characters' actions. A second unit of analysis available is the rhetorical vision, a combination of fantasy themes into a coherent worldview.

Analyzing the Artifact

Analysis of an artifact using fantasy themes and rhetorical visions as units of analysis involves three steps: (1) finding evidence of the sharing of fantasy themes or a rhetorical vision; (2) coding the rhetorical artifact for setting, character, and action themes; and (3) *construction* of the rhetorical vision(s) on the basis of the fantasy themes.

Finding Evidence of Shared Fantasies. The critic's first task in fantasy-theme criticism is to find evidence that symbolic convergence has taken place—that people have shared fantasy themes and a rhetorical vision. If the critic is observing or listening to group members talk, the chaining out or sharing of fantasy themes is evident when a dramatizing message is picked up and elaborated on by others, who add new dramatizations to the original comment. A group member, for example, may tell a story in which the characters enact a particular dramatic scenario. One or more of the others will be caught up in the narrative and begin to add to it. In such instances, a number of people become deeply involved in the discussion, excitedly adding their input and playing with ideas and themes. The members' participation in a fantasy also may be communicated nonverbally. Facial expression, bodily posture, and sounds such as laughter and moaning all indicate such participation.

Other evidence of the sharing of fantasies includes cryptic allusions to symbolic common ground. When people have shared a fantasy theme, they have charged that theme with meanings and emotions that can be set off by an agreed-upon cryptic symbolic cue. This may be a code word, phrase, slogan, or nonverbal sign or gesture. These serve as allusions to a previously shared fantasy and arouse the emotions associated with that fantasy. Among a group of college students who lived together in a dorm, for example, *sweet red grape* serves as a symbolic cue that evokes fond memories of dorm parties where they drank cheap, red wine. *Remember the Alamo*; the peace sign of the late Sixties; and "we believe her," referring to Anita Hill's charges of sexual harassment against Supreme Court Justice Clarence Thomas, served as similar symbolic triggers for groups of people.

Evidence of shared fantasies can be located even when we are not actual observers of or participants in the process by which the fantasy is created. Frequent mention of a theme, a narrative, or an analogy in a variety of messages in different contexts by public officials, for example, may signal the existence of a theme that has caught on among the public. The war on drugs discussed by many politicians exemplifies such a theme. Widespread appeal of a theme also may indicate its nature as a fantasy theme. The themes and style of the television program, *thirtysomething*, for example, caught the imagination of a segment of the American public and thus may be viewed as a set of fantasy themes that chained out through a variety of forms. George Bush referred to the show in a campaign speech, Jif peanut butter and Kool Aid created ads that had a *thirtysomething* feel, and the male contestants on *The New Dating Game* were described as having a "real clean-cut 'thirtysomething' look."[20]

Coding for Fantasy Themes.   The second step in the use of fantasy themes as units of analysis is to code the rhetorical artifact for fantasy themes. This involves a careful examination of the artifact, sentence by sentence in a verbal text or image by image in a visual artifact. The critic picks out each reference to settings, characters, and actions and notes each as a possible fantasy theme. This coding process can be illustrated in a verse from Don McLean's song, "American Pie":

> Helter-skelter in the summer swelter the birds flew off with a fallout shelter
> Eight miles high and fallin' fast, it landed foul on the grass
> The players tried for a forward pass, with the jester on the sidelines in a cast
> Now the half-time air was sweet perfume while the sergeants played a marching tune
> We all got up to dance but we never got the chance
> 'Cause the players tried to take the field, the marching band refused to yield
> Do you recall what was revealed
> The day the music died
> We started singin' . . .[21]

The settings the critic would code are: *summer, swelter, grass, sidelines, half-time, field,* and *day the music died;* they all suggest where the action takes place or characteristics of the places in which the action occurs. Characters coded include: *birds, players, jester, sergeants, we, marching band, you,* and *music.* In this case, two non-human entities are coded as characters—*birds* and *music;* any person or object shown engaging in human-like action should be coded as a character. The actions in which the characters are shown engaging are coded as action themes, with the critic also noting the character to whom the action is linked: *flew off* (birds), *tried for a forward pass* (players), *played a marching tune* (sergeants), *got up to dance* (we), *tried to take the field* (players), *refused to yield* (marching band), *recall* (you), *started singin'* (we), and *died* (music). If more than one setting is presented, the critic also notes which characters appear in which settings. At this preliminary stage of the coding, the critic may not always be sure if a theme belongs in one category or another—setting, characters, or action. A word such as *oppression*, for example, may be seen as both an element of a scene and as an action. If the appropriate category is unclear, the critic initially should code it in both; decisions made in the next step of looking for patterns will determine in which category the phrase best belongs.

Construction of Rhetorical Vision. The third step is to look for patterns in the fantasy themes and to construct the rhetorical vision from the patterns. This involves determining which of the fantasy themes appear to be major and minor themes. Those that appear most frequently are major themes that become the subject of the analysis, and those that appear only once or infrequently are discarded as not important parts of the rhetorical vision. In "American Pie," for example, the birds may appear only once, while the jester may appear several times. The jester would be considered a character in the vision, but the birds would not.

The critic then constructs the rhetorical vision from the patterns of fantasy themes discovered. This involves looking at the major setting themes identified and linking them with the characters who are shown depicted in those settings and the actions those characters are shown performing. There may be more than one rhetorical vision in the rhetoric under study. Some rhetorical communities participate in numerous dramas, with each one developed around a different topic. By linking setting themes with the appropriate characters and actions, the critic can discover if more than one rhetorical vision exists in the rhetoric. If two setting themes appear in the rhetoric—a battlefield and the home, for example, as was the case in the opponents' discourse around the Equal Rights Amendment, the characters of soldiers engaged in the act of fighting obviously would be combined with the battlefield setting to create one rhetorical vision. Characters of husbands, wives, and children engaged in family activities would combine with the home setting to form another.

Writing the Critical Essay

After completion of the analysis, the critic writes an essay that includes five major components: (1) an introduction, in which the research question, its contribution to rhetorical theory, and its significance are discussed; (2) description of the artifact and its context; (3) description of the unit of analysis, the fantasy theme and the rhetorical vision; (4) report of the findings of the analysis, in which the critic reveals the fantasy themes and rhetorical vision(s) identified in the analysis; and (5) discussion of the contribution the analysis makes to answering the research question.

Sample Essays

The sample essays that follow illustrate various uses that critics may make of fantasy themes and rhetorical visions as units of analysis. In Sonja K. Foss' study of the debate on the Equal Rights Amendment, fantasy-theme criticism is used to answer the research question, "What rhetorical factors, other than arguments, affect the nature and outcome of public controversies?" Diana Brown Sheridan analyzes the "Unity Statement" of the Women's Pentagon Action in an effort to answer the research question, "What are the rhetorical characteristics of artifacts that are able to unite diverse audiences?" The research question that guides Robert Huesca's analysis of African Americans' use of the "In Memoriam" section of the newspaper is, "What strategies can minority or submerged groups use to empower themselves in the face of oppression or discrimination?"

Notes

[1] Overviews of fantasy-theme criticism are provided by Bormann in: Ernest G. Bormann, "Fantasy and Rhetorical Vision: The Rhetorical Criticism of Social Reality," *Quarterly Journal of Speech*, 58 (December 1972), 396-407; Ernest G. Bormann, "Symbolic Convergence Theory: A Communication Formulation," *Journal of Communication*, 35 (Autumn 1985), 128-38; and Ernest G. Bormann, John F. Cragan, and Donald C. Shields, "In Defense of Symbolic Convergence Theory: A Look at the Theory and Its Criticisms After Two Decades," *Communication Theory*, 4 (November 1994), 259-94. For other information on and samples of the fantasy-theme approach, see John F. Cragan and Donald C. Shields, *Applied Communication Research: A Dramatistic Approach* (Prospect Heights, IL: Waveland, 1981). For an attack on and a defense of the usefulness of fantasy-theme criticism, see: G. P. Mohrmann, "An Essay on Fantasy Theme Criticism," *Quarterly Journal of Speech*, 68 (May 1982), 109-32; Ernest G. Bormann, "Fantasy and Rhetorical Vision: Ten Years Later," *Quarterly Journal of Speech*, 68 (August 1982), 288-305; and G. P. Mohrmann, "Fantasy Theme Criticism: A Peroration," *Quarterly Journal of Speech*, 68 (August 1982), 306-13. Additional critiques of fantasy-theme analysis include: Stephen E. Lucas, rev. of *The Force of Fantasy: Restoring the American Dream*, by Ernest G. Bormann, *Rhetoric Society Quarterly*, 16 (Summer 1986), 199-205; and Charles E. Williams, "Fantasy Theme Analysis: Theory vs. Practice," *Rhetoric Society Quarterly*, 17 (Winter 1987), 11-20.

[2] Robert Freed Bales, *Personality and Interpersonal Behavior* (New York: Holt, Rinehart and Winston, 1970), pp. 136-55.

[3] Bormann, "Fantasy and Rhetorical Vision," p. 397.

[4]Ernst Cassirer, *Language and Myth*, trans. Susanne K. Langer (New York: Harper, 1946), p. 8.

[5]Ernst Cassirer, *The Philosophy of Symbolic Forms*, I, trans. Ralph Manheim (New Haven: Yale University Press, 1953), p. 87.

[6]Robert L. Scott, "On Viewing Rhetoric as Epistemic," *Central States Speech Journal*, 18 (February 1967), 9–17.

[7]Contributions to the debate on rhetoric as epistemic include: Barry Brummett, "Some Implications of 'Process' or 'Intersubjectivity': Postmodern Rhetoric," *Philosophy and Rhetoric*, 9 (Winter 1976), 21–51; Thomas B. Farrell, "Knowledge, Consensus, and Rhetorical Theory," *Quarterly Journal of Speech*, 62 (February 1976), 1–14; Robert L. Scott, "On Viewing Rhetoric as Epistemic: Ten Years Later," *Central States Speech Journal*, 27 (Winter 1976), 258–66; Richard A. Cherwitz, "Rhetoric as a 'Way of Knowing': An Attenuation of the Epistemological Claims of the 'New Rhetoric,'" *Southern Speech Communication Journal*, 42 (Spring 1977), 207–19; Michael C. Leff, "In Search of Ariadne's Thread: A Review of the Recent Literature on Rhetorical Theory," *Central States Speech Journal*, 29 (Summer 1978), 73–91; Walter M. Carleton, "What is Rhetorical Knowledge? A Response to Farrell—and More," *Quarterly Journal of Speech*, 64 (October 1978), 313–28; Thomas B. Farrell, "Social Knowledge II," *Quarterly Journal of Speech*, 64 (October 1978), 329–34; Richard A. Cherwitz and James W. Hikins, "John Stuart Mill's *On Liberty*: Implications for the Epistemology of the New Rhetoric," *Quarterly Journal of Speech*, 65 (February 1979), 12–24; Richard B. Gregg, *Symbolic Inducement and Knowing: A Study in the Foundations of Rhetoric* (Columbia: University of South Carolina Press, 1981); Barry Brummett, "On to Rhetorical Relativism," *Quarterly Journal of Speech*, 68 ((November 1982), 425–37; Earl Croasmun and Richard A. Cherwitz, "Beyond Rhetorical Relativism," *Quarterly Journal of Speech*, 68 (February 1982), 1–16; Richard A. Cherwitz and James W. Hikins, "Toward a Rhetorical Epistemology," *Southern Speech Communication Journal*, 47 (Winter 1982), 135–62; Richard A. Cherwitz and James W. Hikins, "Rhetorical Perspectivism," *Quarterly Journal of Speech*, 69 (August 1983), 249–66; Celeste Condit Railsback, "Beyond Rhetorical Relativism: A Structural-Material Model of Truth and Objective Reality," *Quarterly Journal of Speech*, 69 (November 1983), 351–63; Richard A. Cherwitz and James W. Hikins, *Communication and Knowledge: An Investigation in Rhetorical Epistemology* (Columbia: University of South Carolina Press, 1986); Barry Brummett, "A Eulogy for Epistemic Rhetoric," *Quarterly Journal of Speech*, 76 (February 1990), 69–72; Richard A. Cherwitz and James W. Hikins, "Burying the Undertaker: A Eulogy for the Eulogists of Rhetorical Epistemology," *Quarterly Journal of Speech*, 76 (February 1990), 73–77; Thomas B. Farrell, "From the Parthenon to the Bassinet: Death and Rebirth Along the Epistemic Trail," *Quarterly Journal of Speech*, 76 (February 1990), 78–84; and Steve Whitson and John Poulakos, "Nietzsche and the Aesthetics of Rhetoric," *Quarterly Journal of Speech*, 79 (May 1993), 131–45.

[8]Ernest G. Bormann, "Symbolic Convergence: Organizational Communication and Culture," in *Communication and Organizations: An Interpretive Approach*, ed. Linda L. Putnam and Michael E. Pacanowsky (Beverly Hills: Sage, 1983), p. 102.

[9]Bormann, "Symbolic Convergence Theory," p. 104.

[10]Ernest G. Bormann, "How to Make a Fantasy Theme Analysis," unpublished essay, p. 4.

[11]Ernest G. Bormann, *The Force of Fantasy: Restoring the American Dream* (Carbondale: Southern Illinois University Press, 1985), pp. 4–5.

[12]Bormann, *The Force of Fantasy*, p. 10.

[13]Bormann, *The Force of Fantasy*, pp. 16–17.

[14]Bormann, "Symbolic Convergence Theory," p. 114.

[15]Sonja K. Foss, "Equal Rights Amendment Controversy: Two Worlds in Conflict," *Quarterly Journal of Speech*, 65 (October 1979), 275–88.

[16]Bormann, *The Force of Fantasy,* p. 8.

[17]Bormann, "Symbolic Convergence Theory," p. 115.

[18]Bormann, "Fantasy and Rhetorical Vision," p. 406.

[19]Bormann, "Fantasy and Rhetorical Vision," pp. 406–07.

[20]Susan Faludi, *Backlash: The Undeclared War Against American Women* (New York: Crown, 1991), p. 161.

[21]Don McLean, "American Pie," (Mayday Music, Inc. and The Benny Bird Co., 1971, 1972).

Equal Rights Amendment Controversy
Two Worlds in Conflict

Sonja K. Foss

Twenty-four words have triggered a debate in the United States between those who would persuade citizens to accept equality for women and those who desire to save traditional womanhood. The issue at stake is the proposed Equal Rights Amendment (ERA) to the Constitution, which was passed by Congress and is currently before the states for ratification. Three more states must approve the amendment by June 1982 if it is to become law. The refusal of many organizations to hold conventions in states that have not ratified the amendment and suits by Nevada and Missouri to end the convention boycotts illustrate the volatile nature of the issue and its impact on various segments of society.

Method of Analysis

Many rhetorical critics have attempted to understand the progress of the debate on the ERA through an argumentative perspective in which the various issues discussed in the controversy are examined—issues such as whether women will be drafted under the ERA, whether women actually face discrimination, and whether the ERA will nullify protective labor laws for women. But this argumentative approach does not explain the vehemence with which the debate is conducted and the emotional response elicited by the amendment, and it appears to ignore some rhetorical factors that affect the controversy and that perhaps are more significant than the arguments themselves. Blahna, who uses an argumentative analysis to examine the ERA, recognizes at the end of her study that nonargumentative factors do affect the debate and therefore need to be studied: "This history of the amendment's travel through Congress indicates that many factors other than the arguments played an important role in the amendment's progress. Except for a few years

From *Quarterly Journal of Speech*, 65 (October 1979), 275–88. Used by permission of the Speech Communication Association and the author.

after the birth of the equal rights controversy these other factors outweighed the arguments in determining the fate of the amendment."[1]

One means of discovering and studying "these other factors" is through the perspective that the ERA involves a conflict between two worldviews that are created by the rhetoric generated by each side. That is, the discourse formulated and presented by proponents and opponents of the ERA may create perceptions that—whether they correspond to reality or not—are more influential than the arguments presented to the public. But the rationale for such a perspective lies not only in its focus on rhetorical elements beyond arguments. It also represents a rhetorical approach to the study of movements that has been called for by numerous rhetorical critics.[2]

A methodological approach for studying how rhetoric creates particular realities was suggested by Bormann[3] and is based on the process of fantasizing that occurs in small groups.[4] The concept of fantasy central to this approach is defined as the dramatization of a hypothetical or actual situation in the rhetoric generated by the group's participants. A fantasy chain in a group is established when a participant communicates symbols that relate either to the group's here-and-now problems or to the individual psychodynamics of the participants. Such communications—that cause the members of a group to empathize, to improvise on the same theme, or to respond emotionally—form fantasies that tend to be played out in a more and more complete way until they reflect the members' common preoccupations and serve to make those commonalities public.

The concept of rhetorical vision, introduced by Bormann, extends the fantasy chain to the level of social movements. Rhetorical vision refers to the composite dramas which catch up large groups of people in a symbolic reality. Just as fantasy chains create a unique culture within a small group, so the fantasy themes of campaigns and movements chain out in public audiences to form rhetorical visions. When group members wish to convert others to their position, they will begin to create messages for public speeches, the media, and literature, shaping the fantasy themes that excited them in their original discussions into suitable form for various public audiences. The dramas of this public rhetoric draw in members of the audience, transporting them to the symbolic reality held by the smaller group. The audience members then take up the dramas in small groups of their acquaintances, and some of these dramas chain out as fantasy themes in the new groups. The process continues to reach a larger public audience until a rhetorical movement emerges.

If the rhetorical worlds or visions of the proponents and opponents of the ERA are to provide a clue to the essence or motivation inherent in the debate, the rhetoric produced by the two sides must be examined to determine the nature of their rhetorical worlds or, in Goffman's term, their "frames" or ways in which they organize experience.[5] A dramatistic approach will be used to examine these worlds, an approach which assumes, with Goffman, that the means speakers employ as they talk are intrinsically theatrical, that they undertake not so much to provide information to a recipient as to "present dramas to an audience."[6] Burke's suggestion that a rounded statement about motives consists of an investigation of act, scene, agent, agency, and purpose[7] confirms the usefulness of the theatrical metaphor here since the attempt is to determine the nature and motivations of a rhetorical world with a particular setting in which some action occurs, characters attempt to carry out the action, and other characters attempt to prevent its completion. This dramatistic approach is appropriate, too, for an examination of rhetorical worlds because both Burke and Bormann build their systems on a view of language and thought as primarily "modes of action."[8]

Proponents' World

Fundamental to the world that the proponents of the ERA have created through their rhetoric is a grassroots scene in which the common, undistinguished majority is supporting the ERA. References abound in the proponents' rhetoric to "grass roots effort,"[9] "grass roots education campaign,"[10] and "grass-roots people."[11] The grassroots scene is explained more fully in a publication of the National Federation of Business and Professional Women's Clubs: "Because ERA will touch everyone, it is only natural that support for the Amendment is wide-ranging and comes from all segments of society."[12] This grassroots support for the ERA demands an accompanying tenet in the proponents' world that demonstrates why this support is widespread: More people are realizing that women are excluded from full participation with men in the nation's life. That is, many people are aware that women stand at, rather than within, the gates of the democracy. Senator George McGovern sets such a scene: "The barrier that restricts a woman's life is invisible, based on unspoken assumptions. It is like a glass wall."[13] The analogy of the closed door is prevalent in the proponents' rhetoric, furthering this image: "An open society cannot close the doors of opportunity to half its citizens."[14]

If proponents view women as standing at the gates of democracy, they also hold a view of the nature of the world from which women are excluded. For the proponents, this world is the wide world of abundant opportunities outside of the home. Possibilities for women are limitless in this expanded sphere of experience. Gladys O'Donnell, president of the National Federation of Republican Women, explains: "We have expanded beyond the four walls and roof that once defined our province."[15] To support their view that woman's place is in the outside world, proponents cite statistics about how much time women now spend outside of the home: "Today more than half of all women between 18 and 64 years of age are in the labor force, where they are making a substantial contribution to the Nation's economy. Studies show that 9 out of 10 girls will work outside the home at some time in their lives."[16]

For the proponents, then, widespread support for the ERA results as more people come to believe that women are denied entrance to a limitless world that extends far beyond the confines of the home. The formulation of these scenes by the proponents enables them to establish sacred and profane spaces in their world. The sacred ground is the new, ready-to-be-explored world, a world which gives rise to the opening of gates to women and to grassroots support for participation in this world. The profane ground, of course, is the home, symbolic of entrapment and imprisonment. When reality for the proponents is created according to this system, the arguments employed by the proponents fall into place. Their arguments that women want to and should engage in all activities of the world, including military service, for example, are consistent with the sacred setting of the world rather than the home.

Because they see women as excluded from a desirable world, the proponents build into their reality the notion that women are taking specific steps to gain entrance into this world. The proponents' rhetoric shows women struggling for their rights against discrimination, exemplified in a statement by Mary Jean Tully of the Legal Defense and Education Fund of the National Organization for Women: "But this is only one skirmish in a long war. The hard-fought gains which women have won for the right to control their own lives and for the chance to participate equally in American society are under attack from many directions. We must have the tools for this fight! ERA is one of them."[17] According to this view, however, women are not content simply to struggle against injustice. They also are participating as much as possible in the world, often breaking sex-role stereotypes in the process by engaging in a wide variety of activities: "There has been a marked increase in the number of women seeking and getting credentials in previously all-male fields. Women . . . have departed from the traditional sex-related academic choices. A study of women political scientists in one region showed the younger women moving into more fields in the discipline and pursuing their careers ambitiously."[18]

The actions that the proponents see occurring in their world function to magnify the importance of the ERA controversy for the participants. The notion that women are struggling against discrimination enlarges the battle into a struggle of justice and equality against tyranny and oppression. When the proponents' cause thus is aligned with notions of justice and equality—democratic ideals—the participants can view themselves as sacrificing and working for a vital cause of freedom and liberty.

Characterizations of the types of people involved in the ERA battle—both the proponents and their opponents—are included in the world constructed by the proponents' rhetoric. The opponents are villains with a variety of negative traits. Primarily, they are persons or businesses in opposition to the ERA because its passage would harm their profits or influence. Proponents, for example, accuse Phyllis Schlafly, leader of the opposition, of receiving money from organizations such as the Roman Catholic Church and the Ku Klux Klan.[19] They also charge that the insurance industry is a key funding source for the ERA opposition, since the ERA would prohibit insurance practices that discriminate against women and decrease insurance companies' profits.[20] Schlafly often is accused of using the ERA simply to promote her own interests: "What is important to Phyllis Schlafly is the ERA, because she needs it for the national exposure she craves. Ever since she wrote her first book, she has needed national attention to feed her ego and ambition. For ten years she tried anti-communism and other ultra-conservative issues without much success."[21]

In addition to viewing their enemies as parties of self-motivated interests, proponents see them as right-wing radicals who are using the ERA as an organizing tool. Irwin Suall of B'nai Brith explains this theme: "The right is always looking for issues of this kind that have some popular appeal and that will bring them into contact with segments of opinion in the mainstream. Then, within that broad context, they try to press their own personal point of view on other issues. There is no doubt that the John Birch Society latched onto ERA because they sensed an issue they could exploit. . . . They saw it as an avenue to expand their influence."[22]

Those who oppose the ERA out of selfish interests are seen as oppressors. In this view, applied most often to male opponents, members of the opposition are tyrannical monsters who consciously and deliberately turn their backs on women and their rights. A statement by Florida state senator Lori Wilson exemplifies this characterization:

> . . . the Good Ole Boys in the Southern legislatures traditionally do not consider people issues, like ERA, on their merit.
>
> They consider only what it might do to their own manpower—their manliness, or their moneyness.
>
> The Good Ole Boys in Southern politics refused to give up their slaves . . . until the rest of the nation whipped them on the battlefields.

The Good Ole Boys refused to approve the 19th amendment, granting women the right to vote . . . until the rest of this nation whipped them in the courtrooms, and on the streets, and at the polls . . .

And now, on the last remaining issue of human rights, civil rights, people rights and equal rights, the Good Ole Boys are summoning all their remaining, but weakening power, for one last hurrah.

The Good Ole Boys are trying desperately to hold on to the power they have given each other, or taken from each other.[23]

Proponents often explain men's opposition to the ERA as the result of socialization processes. They believe that these men generally are not motivated by desires to be deliberately unjust or discriminatory. Rather, they always have enjoyed and have become accustomed to holding superior positions. Should women assume positions of equality, these men would feel threatened. Newspaper columnist Joan Beck presents such a picture of these male opponents: "Men who oppose E.R.A. aren't concerned about keeping women on pedestals—but in having women around to dust the pedestals they build for themselves. They want women in relationships dedicated to making them look good (cheerleader-football player, secretary-boss, homemaker wife-dominant husband, patient mistress-potent lover). The doll's house women who oppose E.R.A.—women who have yielded to the cultural brain-washing to be compliant and ego-massaging in every male-female relationship from bedroom to board room—provide just the excuse a male legislator needs to vote no."[24]

Intertwined with the theme that male opponents are insecure men who feel threatened by women is the more complimentary view that they are simply uninformed. Although these men presently oppose the ERA, they do so, this view suggests, because they are novices who are just starting down the road to an awareness of the rights that women deserve. This notion is exemplified in the rhetoric of Virginia V. Chanda of the National Organization for Women: "We believe that, while most of the opponents of ERA are sincere, they are sadly, even dangerously, misinformed."[25] Jacqueline Gutwillig of the Citizen's Advisory Council on the Status of Women agrees: "Men generally are not antiwomen—I say this hopefully—and may not consciously discriminate, but also may not be mindful of the effects on women of outmoded attitudes and pressures. The biggest obstacle to improvement in the status of women is lack of knowledge."[26]

Although proponents can excuse opponents for their lack of knowledge, they are less able to understand what they view as the opponents' dirty and unfair campaign tactics. Columnist Ellen Goodman explains: "While the pro-ERA forces have been playing chess, their opposite numbers have been playing rugby."[27] In this characterization of the opponents, the proponents return once more to their view of the opponents as villains with no understandable motive for opposing the amendment. They point to the opponents' attempts to link the ERA with abortion as one example of this type of campaign tactic. They accuse the opponents of distorting facts, of accepting pro-ERA contributions with no intention of supporting the ERA, and of resorting to "shabby legislative maneuvers to keep the issue of equal rights for women from full legislative consideration."[28]

Although opposition to the ERA among women themselves often has been a source of surprise for many ERA proponents, they do include in their rhetoric the notion that the women who oppose the amendment are a middle-class, white minority. This characterization is negative not only because it excludes large populations of women, but also because of unfavorable characteristics associated with these types of women. They are totally dependent on their husbands for support and the fulfillment of their needs and thus have no idea of the nature of life for a woman who must work to survive. They are not representative of the majority of women: "Phyllis Schlafly is a most eloquent spokesperson for the middle-class, infantile, white woman. The many prerogatives that she lists as the right of the American woman when she marries are unknown to the poor, the black, and the chicano—many of whom expect to work after marriage and do not, realistically, expect such an uxorious husband."[29] In an attempt to understand and explain opposition to the ERA among women, proponents label them an unaware minority.

The proponents' views of themselves differ drastically from their views of the opponents. The qualities they ascribe to themselves are positive; thus, they become the heroes of their world. Primarily, they see women who support the ERA as capable contributors—talented and willing to participate in the formulation of solutions to the nation's problems: "Half of the brightest people in our country—half of the most talented people with the potential for the highest intellectual endeavor are women."[30]

ERA supporters are viewed as representing all women, a label summarized in a statement by Ms. magazine editor Gloria Steinem: "I hope this committee [Senate Subcommittee hearings on the ERA] will hear the personal, daily injustices suffered by many women—professionals and day laborers, women housebound by welfare as well as by suburbia. . . . We may appear before you as white radicals or the middleaged middleclass or black soul sisters, but we are all sisters in fighting against . . . outdated myths."[31] In their unity, the proponents become the majority. A pamphlet published by the U.S. Commission on Civil Rights, for example, focuses on the margin by which the ERA passed Congress as evidence of this majority support: "The Equal Rights Amendment passed the 92nd Congress by an overwhelming margin."[32] ERAmerica spokespersons assert that this majority is evident not only in Congress, but also among the people: "The Harris poll shows that 65% of the American people *want* the Amendment ratified. Only 27% actually oppose it."[33] Along with a portrayal of the opponents as actively seeking to prevent women from attaining their rights, then, the proponents develop images that portray themselves as worthy of such rights and as a united majority working toward their attainment.

Consistency in their characterizations is a problem for the proponents. They are unable to develop a cohesive view of their opponents because of their diverse statures and sexes. Because the opponents include Congressional senators and representatives as well as housewives, and men as well as women, the proponents cannot characterize the opponents with one label. As a result, a focus on character does little to unify the proponents' own forces or to damage the public's view of the opposition. Thus, when ERA supporters suggest that their opponents are middle-class white women, the theme cannot unify supporters who are aware of opposition to the ERA by men in status positions. Similarly, if proponents characterize opponents as males who feel threatened or who deliberately are oppressing women, the theme cannot be applied to female opponents who are housewives.

Two major dramas operate in the world of the proponents as a result of their rhetoric. In one drama, women stand at the gates of democracy and struggle against oppression to win the equal rights of the world to which they are denied access. In this scenario, the act is the struggle against oppression, the scene is the total physical and psychological environment of exclusion from democratic practices and equal treatment, and the characters include all women regardless of class. In this drama, the scene—an oppressive, limiting, unequal state—determines and in fact almost creates the other elements of the world. The scene is fertile ground from which a struggle against oppression might arise and demands characters who will struggle for full equality.

In the second major drama developed in the world of the proponents, women are seen as capable contributors fully participating in the world to achieve self-fulfillment. In this drama, the act is full participation in activities and tasks, the scene is the world with its limitless opportunities, and the characters are capable contributors. Once again, the focus is on scene. The fact that the scene represents limitless and abundant activities as well as justice and knowledge requires that the characters live up to the fullness of the world and take advantage of its opportunities. A wide world in which to participate automatically allows for a wider degree of participation in that world. At the same time, the scene generates a particular type of character. Because the environment is viewed as the wide world, the personae must be capable of handling its possibilities and be able to contribute to that world in a meaningful way. This scene, then, demands competence from its participants.

Opponents' World

The world created by the rhetoric of the opponents of the ERA centers around the home and contrasts with the notion in the proponents' world that the domain of the ERA is not the home, but rather the world outside of it. Thomas G. Abernethy, Representative from Mississippi, provides an example of this scene in his statement that his wife instructed him to vote against the ERA "because she doesn't want to lose her home."[34] Schlafly also contributes to the development of the home as a scene envisioned by the opponents: "The world has not devised . . . a better place to bring up children than the home. No more radical piece of legislation [than the ERA] could have been devised to force women outside of the home."[35]

Women who remain in their proper sphere of the home and perform their wifely duties well are glorified by the opponents and are placed on pedestals. Statements that establish the pedestal as a scene in the world of the opponents include "I'll be darned if I appreciate a bunch of . . . malcontents badgering legislators into trading the lofty pedestal on which men have held me, and which I try to deserve, for mere equality!"[36]

From the home and the pedestal settings, the opponents digress to predict a future world filled with horrors if the ERA is adopted. "Horrible places" encompasses this setting; in contrast to the seclusion and safety of the home and pedestal, it deals with the hardships and dangers to which women will be subjected under the ERA. The most common horrible place cited is the battlefield: There is the possibility that women could be drafted into military service under the ERA. Senator Sam J. Ervin, Jr., of North Carolina, provides an example of this scene. In Senate debate, he described a world in which women "will be slaughtered or maimed by the bayonets, the bombs, the bullets, the grenades, the mines, the napalm, the poison gas, or the shells of the enemy."[37]

In another version of this horrible places theme, women are shown in sweatshops and factories, driven to perilous labors on unending assembly lines and deprived of all protections. This scene develops in argumentation about the effect of the ERA on protective labor laws for women. Senator John C. Stennis, of Mississippi, for example, sets such a scene: "I have visited in countries where I saw gangs of women laborers out there in the street with pick and shovel, repairing the streets, with blacktop, hot, boiling, creosote material, laboring hour upon hour."[38]

Finally, opponents envision women in the desegregated public restroom as a result of the ERA. Bette Jean Jarboe, founder of the International Anti-Women's Liberation League, focuses on this scene:

"Do you know what kind of horrible things the loose wording of that amendment could produce? It could lead to such things as communal bathrooms."[39]

For the opponents, then, the sacred ground in their world is the home. As a result of the performance of women in the homemaker role, they are placed on pedestals and do not have to endure the horrors of the world as do men. Profane ground for the opponents, of course, is the man's world outside of the home, including the battlefield and factories in which women work as hard and as long as men. The opponents' reality depends on the home; thus, they employ tactics to oppose the ERA that can be engaged in while remaining in the home, including writing letters and baking pies to serve as symbols for their campaign.

The home and the pedestal are traditional settings for women; similarly, the opponents' rhetoric creates a world in which actions are taken to preserve tradition. Opponents see themselves as attempting to maintain established and traditional social customs and institutions against the onslaught of reform. Newspaper columnist Patrick Buchanan, for example, asserts: "Yet, if embraced by 38 states, that innocuous-sounding amendment would trigger a social revolution in this country, sweeping away like so much debris state laws, local traditions, and national customs."[40] ERA opponents specifically detail customs and institutions they are fighting to maintain: the family, marriage, financial support of women by men, chivalry, and religious practices that designate certain restricted roles for women.

Because the opponents assume that the old is better than the new and that tradition is a greater good than change, they include in their world the idea that the ERA is being passed hastily without sufficient consideration. Legislation such as the ERA, that would cause changes in the status quo, requires much more debate than the ERA is receiving, according to the opponents. This notion frequently appeared in the rhetoric of the opposition during congressional debate, as exemplified in the statement of William M. McCulloch, member of the House of Representatives from Ohio: "To adopt this constitutional amendment without adequate hearings and debate would raise more questions than it would answer, and would be a most irresponsible act by this great legislative body."[41]

When the ERA had passed in both houses of Congress, the idea of hasty passage was applied to the passage of the ERA in individual states. Since the recision of ratification votes on the ERA in two states—Nebraska and Tennessee—opponents have delighted in pointing to the recisions as fulfillment of their warnings about passing the amendment too quickly. An editorial in the *New Orleans Times-Picayune* commented on Nebraska's recision: "Symptomatic of the faddist approach to constitutional revision that many otherwise levelheaded lawmakers have taken,

Nebraska 'rushed the amendment through its unicameral legislature last March,' notes The Associated Press, 'in hopes of becoming the first state to approve the ERA.' . . . This month the Nebraska legislature repented of that hasty action by a decisive 31–17 vote. . . . The Nebraska lesson could prove a pivotal influence for the rest of the states against a frivolous flip of the lid of that Pandora's Box.''[42]

As a result of the actions that they see themselves undertaking, the opponents are able to expand the world created by their rhetoric. For them, the battle against the ERA is not simply a battle against one particular amendment to the Constitution, but is instead a crucial battle in the war to save a great nation that is wavering on the verge of destruction. Both of the opponents' action themes contribute to this intensified view of the controversy since they show the opponents working to defend an old, superior tradition and trying to prevent the disastrous consequences that would result should this tradition be disregarded. In addition, the attempt to prevent hasty passage of the ERA is particularly effective in terms of its capacity for preventing the opponents from being viewed as anti-democratic. By maintaining that the ERA is being passed without sufficient consideration, opponents can argue against the ERA without appearing to be opposed to the basic ideas of equality and justice.

The characters who act in the world created by the opposition are consistent with the opponents' view of the traditional as good and the new or different as potentially evil. Opponents see supporters of the ERA, who deviate from the traditional woman's role, as "libbers" who support the feminist movement. They often suggest that anyone who supports the ERA is a libber, as Schlafly does when she urges, "Don't you boys give in to those libbers."[43]

Opponents ascribe a variety of negative characteristics to libbers. Proponents are portrayed as "straggly-haired"[44] people engaged in "bra-burning and other freak antics,"[45] "scolding, marching."[46] Some opponents accuse advocates of being masculine and homosexual. Others believe that they have personal problems that cause them to agitate for the ERA, although few of the opponents agree on the exact nature of these problems. Joyce Gage, an opponent from Illinois, wonders, "Why must nonfeminists suffer because some loud-mouth females wish they were born male?"[47] Other opponents, feeling that housework must be frustrating these women, call them a "bunch of disgruntled eccentrics with a phobia about dishpan hands."[48] Regardless of the nature of the problem ascribed to them, proponents are viewed by opponents as deviates from the traditional feminine woman.

According to the opponents, supporters of the ERA are different from the majority of women in yet another way: They are executive and professional women insensitive to the needs of housewives or factory workers. Emanuel Cellar of New York developed this theme in debate in the House of Representatives: "Some feminists casually say—We do not want protection, we want liberation. Will you tell that to the female factory worker and to the female farmworker and get their reply?"[49]

Finally, ERA opponents portray supporters as proponents of un-American ideals. This theme generally begins with the idea that ERA supporters are against marriage, motherhood, and children—elements held by opponents to be essential ingredients of the American way of life. Schlafly, for instance, asserts that advocates are "antichildren, antimen and antifamily."[50] She elaborates on the connection between the ERA and un-American ideals: "Women's libbers are promoting free sex instead of the 'slavery of marriage.' . . . They are promoting abortions instead of families."[51]

A variation of the image of ERA advocates as un-American is the association of the ERA with Communism. Despite the fact that the Communist Party of the United States opposes the ERA, many opponents claim that the amendment is Communist-inspired. Literature circulated in the ERA campaign in California contained such a reference, stating the Communists "are drawing in support from thousands of misguided women and even men who do not know that this is all part of the Communist plan."[52] Opponents believe that if the ERA supporters advocate the adoption of such un-American reforms as legalized abortion, lesbianism, the drafting of women, childless marriages, and Communism, the ERA also must be un-American.

In contrast to their views of the proponents, the opponents characterize themselves as "real" women—wives and mothers, feminine women who stay at home and love their husbands and rear their children. Carol Joyce, an opponent from Illinois, expresses this theme: "What's happened to the concept of 'woman,' which meant strength, courage and love? The woman was the center of the family, the heart of the home. It takes all the energy and creativity one can muster to be teacher, mother, wife, mistress, and lover. And I'll use all the gifts God has given me to fulfill those roles. That'll take a lifetime."[53]

The world of the ERA opponents includes the idea that they are dependent and require protection. According to the opponents, because women have been homemakers throughout the years, they are helpless and incapable of functioning outside of the home, as they claim they would be forced to do under the ERA. Schlafly contributes to the development of this theme when she states that elderly women, in particular, "made their career a lifetime in the home. They don't have their education and won't be able to take care of themselves."[54] Intertwined with the opponents' view of themselves as homemakers who have had little experience in the outside world, then, is the view of themselves as incapable of autonomy and independence outside of the home. The possible negative effects of the incorporation of this self-denigrating theme in the opponents' world is mitigated by the strength of their descriptions of the proponents as abnormal and almost evil—feminist, deviant, and un-American.

As wives and mothers who prefer to remain in the home, the opponents see themselves representing the majority of women. Schlafly claims that opponents represent "about 95 percent of Illinois voters,"[55] and Happiness of Womanhood claims to represent 97 percent of American women—"all those not represented by Women's Lib."[56] The opponents become, as a New Orleans Times-Picayune editorial points out, a "Silent Majority."[57]

Opponents have the advantage over the supporters of the ERA in that all of their character themes unite around the common persona of the ERA supporter as a deviate of some type. Proponents are radical, militant libbers (rather than feminine women); professional and executive women (rather than wives and mothers); masculine, aggressive women with personal problems (rather than feminine women who are content with their roles); and represent un-American values such as Communism and a hatred of children (rather than freedom and a love of children). Although men also are ERA supporters, opponents can dismiss their support for the amendment by further continuing the characterization: They, too, are deviates because they do not prefer feminine, protected females as their mothers, girl friends, wives, or daughters. This singular characterization of ERA supporters can not only unify opponents, but can also effectively discourage legislators and members of the public audience from joining the supporters. For when ERA proponents and those who join them are labeled weird or abnormal, the focus of the conflict shifts so that the supporters must defend themselves as legitimate persons rather than concentrate on issues directly relevant to the battle over the ERA.

The world of the opponents, however, includes one major inconsistency in the development of its characterizations. Schlafly, the leader of the opponents, is not herself a true representative of the woman that ERA opponents claim women are and should be. Although she dresses and acts like the opponents' "lady," is married, and has six children, her activities are not limited to those of a homemaker. She worked her way through college as a gunner and ballistics technician at an ammunition plant and graduated from Radcliffe with a master's degree in political science. She co-authored four books, ran unsuccessfully for Congress three times, started her own newspaper, and founded a conservative women's group called The Eagles Are Flying. She admits the inconsistency between her actual activities and her image and explains: "It's obvious that I'm fully liberated. And that irritates some people. . . . If a woman can work and still make her husband think he's the greatest . . . and be able to keep the kids happy, then it's OK. It's fine. But I believe the most fulfilling role for a woman is that of a wife and mother."[58]

Although some proponents do not find this explanation of the inconsistency totally satisfactory, opponents can incorporate Schlafly's image and activities into their characterization of themselves by viewing her as a martyr. She is sacrificing herself and the fulfillment she could receive from the traditional female role to fight to preserve this type of womanhood for other women: "We are busy with our homes and families, but she has taken her time and efforts and given us a voice."[59]

The opponents, like the proponents, develop two major dramas in their rhetorical world, but each one is motivated by a different element. The opponents' major scenario is one in which individuals seek to defend tradition in order to maintain the life style they now enjoy. The women remain in the home, dependent on men for support; thus, they deserve positions on pedestals. In this drama, the act is the defense of tradition, the scene is the home and the pedestal, and the characters are dependent, real women. The primary motivating force in this drama appears to come from the nature of the characters involved. The women participating are seen as dependent, helpless, weak, and centered in the home. Thus, they must act to ensure that they be allowed to remain in the home, leading lives that are consistent with the traditional feminine nature.

In their second drama, the opponents attempt to keep the ERA from being passed hastily in order to prevent catastrophic consequences. In this drama, the act becomes the blocking of the hasty passage of the ERA, the scene is the composite of horrible places in which women could find themselves under the ERA, and the characters are individuals who believe in traditional womanhood. In this drama, the focus is on the act itself. In the very act of blocking the passage of the ERA, the consequences of passage must be considered. This process leads to an envisioning of horrible scenes in which women may be involved if the ERA is adopted.

Conclusion

Different elements motivate the proponents and opponents to create their particular worlds. For the proponents, the scene is of primary importance as the persons, events, and ideas that exist in the characters' environment combine to create a scene of oppression. The opponents, however, depend on the agent, or a particular view of women, as their primary motivation. From the debate on the ERA, then, emerges a conflict in motivation between oppressive conditions and a particular view of womanhood.

The differences between the motives of the two sides can be seen further in the philosophical distinctions implied by the two motives.[60] For the proponents, with scene as a primary motivation, the corresponding philosophic terminology is materialism,[61] in which the physical universe or the natural order is the context in which concepts are formed. Proponents see the natural order as a free state in which all people are able to develop fully their own potentials uninhibited by synthetic restraints. But some kind of social organization is needed to maintain harmony and prevent chaos. Proponents acknowledge this fact by willingly participating in the social and political systems, but they urge that these be changed to accord with the ideal natural order.

In their emphasis upon the agent, the opponents adhere to the framework of idealism.[62] This terminology establishes two major demands on the opponents. First, because the universal essence is defined as personal—composed of the same stuff as the self—opponents attribute to the world their own particular view of reality. Because they view the essential role of woman as wife, mother, and homemaker, they must extend this individual perception to the larger world and all women, believing that this role is the natural and proper one for them. The concept of agent or woman thus is universalized. As Burke explains: "We can say that such a way of seeing is not the property of just *your* understanding or *my* understanding but of '*the* understanding' in general."[63] Second, because the individual is viewed as a part and not the whole of reality, opponents view each individual as entitled to a *proper* share or portion of the universe. To dispute or complain about the portion one has been given is to refuse to conform to the ways of the cosmos, which operates for the welfare of the whole. A particular role for women, the opponents believe, best enables all individuals within the society to operate in harmony, and the limitations imposed on individuals merely maintain an order that is consistent with reality.

Horror at an oppressive scene and a glorification of the nature of woman serve functions other than to motivate each side in the controversy. These motivating forces are used as a rationale to keep the participants of each group from being influenced by or being forced to pay attention to the arguments and themes presented by its opposition. By focusing on the scene, the proponents deflect attention from the criticism of personal motives on their part. Because they derive their acts and attitudes from the nature of the situation rather than from the agents, they can ignore the criticism by the opponents that they are unfeminine, that they do not measure up to the criteria established by society for acceptable behavior by women, and that they are deviant and abnormal. Similarly, by situating the motives for their acts in the agent, the opponents can deflect attention from scenic matters—from the conditions of unequal treatment and oppression of women—and can focus their attention on the nature of womanhood alone.

The creation of two conflicting rhetorical worlds by the proponents and opponents of the ERA leaves little or no common ground on which argumentation can occur or through which an understanding of the opposing viewpoint can be reached. Each side's rhetoric is not only a threat to the other's way of making sense of the world, but also is a reason to defend strongly its particular world. Once the two sides in a controversy have developed worlds that are in total conflict—with different notions of the settings, characters, and acts in these worlds— the traditional modes of argumentation and persuasion are not likely to be effective in dissuading participants from their worlds.

Notes

[1]Loretta J. Blahna, "The Rhetoric of the Equal Rights Amendment," Diss. Kansas 1973, p. 315.

[2]See, for example, Robert S. Cathcart, "New Approaches to the Study of Movements: Defining Movements Rhetorically," *Western Speech*, 36 (1972), 83; and Karlyn Kohrs Campbell, "The Rhetoric of Women's Liberation: An Oxymoron," *Quarterly Journal of Speech*, 59 (1973), 74.

[3]Ernest G. Bormann, "Fantasy and Rhetorical Vision: The Rhetorical Criticism of Social Reality," *Quarterly Journal of Speech*, 58 (1972), 396–407.

[4]Robert Freed Bales, *Personality and Interpersonal Behavior* (New York: Holt, Rinehart and Winston, 1970), pp. 136–55.

[5]Erving Goffman, *Frame Analysis: An Essay on the Organization of Experience* (Cambridge: Harvard Univ. Press, 1974), pp. 10–11.

[6]Ibid., p. 508.

[7]Kenneth Burke, *A Grammar of Motives* (1945; rpt. Berkeley: Univ. of California Press, 1969), p. xv.

[8]Ibid., p. xxii.

[9]Karen DeCrow, Letter to National Organization for Women members, Chicago, Summer 1975, p. 2.

[10]"NOW Claims Election Victories for the Equal Rights Amendment!!!!" *Do It NOW*, Dec. 1974, p. 7.

[11]Margaret Ellen Traxler, "Statement in Favor of Equal Rights Amendment," Catholic Women for the E.R.A., Cincinnati, Ohio, n.d., p. 1.

[12]National Federation of Business and Professional Women's Clubs, *Equal Rights Amendment: Background Material*, Washington, D.C., n.d., p. 28.

[13]U.S., Congress, Senate, 92nd Cong., 1st sess., *Congressional Record*, 117 (15 July 1971), 25349.

[14]Edmund S. Muskie, *Muskie News*, Washington, D.C., 26 Aug. 1971, p. 2.

[15]U.S., Congress, Senate, 91st Cong., 2nd sess., *Congressional Record*, 116 (22 June 1970), 20728.

[16]U.S. Dept. of Labor, Employment Standards Administration. Women's Bureau, *The Myth and the Reality* (Washington, D.C.: U.S. Govt. Printing Office, 1974), p. 1.

[17]Mary Jean Tully, Letter to National Organization for Women members, New York, New York, 1976, p. 2.

[18]"Higher Education and the Equal Rights Amendment," *Equal Rights Monitor*, March/April 1977, p. 10.

[19]Dale Wittner, "All Women's Liberationists Hate Men and Children," *Chicago Tribune*, 20 May 1973, sec. 9, p. 12.

[20]Ann K. Justice, ed., *The Insurance Connection with Stop ERA Forces*, National Organization for Women, Lincoln, Nebraska, 1974.

[21]Doug Thompson, "Phyllis Schlafly," *New Orleans ERA Coalition Newsletter*, New Orleans, n.d., National Organization for Women Legislative Office, Washington, D.C., p. 1.

[22]Lisa Cronin Wohl, "Phyllis Schlafly: 'The Sweetheart of the Silent Majority,'" *Ms.*, Mar. 1974, p. 86.

[23]Lori Wilson, "Florida State Senator Lori Wilson: 'Y'all Took the Wrong Turn Again,'" *Equal Rights Monitor*, May/June 1977, p. 12.

[24]Joan Beck, "E.R.A. Scores Illinois Gain, but Lags in U.S.," *Chicago Tribune*, 2 May 1975, sec. 2, p. 2.

[25]Virginia V. Chanda, Letter to church leaders, National Organization for Women, Springfield, Illinois, n.d., p. 1.

[26]Catharine Stimpson, ed., *Women and the "Equal Rights" Amendment: Senate Subcommittee Hearings on the Constitutional Amendment, 91st Congress* (New York: R. R. Bowker, 1972), p. 121.

[27]Ellen Goodman, "The Name of the (ERA) Game Is Politics," *The Washington Post*, 31 Jan. 1978, sec. A, p. 19.

[28]League of Women Voters, *ERA YES!*, Washington, D.C., Aug. 1974, p. 1.

[29]Fay Ruth, "Letters: Schlafly Pro and Con," *Chicago Tribune*, 24 June 1973, sec. 9, p. 7.

[30]Stimpson, p. 125.

[31]Ibid., p. 103.

[32]U.S. Commission on Civil Rights, *Statement of U.S. Commission on Civil Rights on the Equal Rights Amendment*, Washington, D.C., July 1973, p. 1.

[33]ERAmerica, *200 Years is Long Enough . . . For Your Rights to be Denied*, Washington, D.C., n.d., p. 4.

[34]Eileen Shanahan, "Equal Rights Amendment Passed by House, 354–23," *New York Times*, 13 Oct. 1971, p. 20.

[35]Thompson, p. 1.

[36]Betty 'Laine Larsen, "Voice of the People: She Prefers a Pedestal," *Chicago Tribune*, 19 Mar. 1975, sec. 2, p. 2.

[37]U.S., Congress, Senate, 92nd Cong., 2d sess., *Congressional Record*, 118 (21 Mar. 1972), 9333.

[38]Ibid., p. 9318.

[39]Rick Soll, "New Gals Group Sees Lib as One Big Mistake," *Chicago Tribune*, 3 Aug. 1972, sec. N4A, p. 3.

[40]Patrick Buchanan, "ERA Could Force Social Revolution," *Chicago Tribune*, 6 Apr. 1975, sec. 2, p. 6.

[41]U.S., Congress, House, 91st Cong., 2d sess., *Congressional Record*, 116 (10 Aug. 1970), 28006.

[42]"Nebraska ERA Vote Salutary Lesson," *New Orleans Times-Picayune*, 30 Mar. 1973, sec. 1, p. 10.

[43]Michael Sneed, "Ms. Nemesis Hits Equal Rights Bill," *Chicago Tribune*, 19 Aug. 1974, sec. 1, p. 5.

[44]Phyllis Schlafly, "What's Wrong With 'Equal Rights' for Women?" *The Phyllis Schlafly Report*, Alton, Illinois, Feb. 1972, p. 2.

[45]U.S., Congress, Senate, Committee on the Judiciary, *Equal Rights 1970*, 91st Cong., 2d sess., 1970, p. 29. Testimony of Myra Wolfgang.

[46]Elsieliese Thrope, "But Women Are the Favored Sex," *Reader's Digest*, May 1972, p. 82.

[47]Joyce Gage, "Voice of the People: E.R.A. Hurts Women," *Chicago Tribune*, 28 May 1975, sec. 3, p. 2.

[48]Thrope, p. 82.

[49]U.S., Congress, House, 91st Cong., 2d sess., *Congressional Record*, 116 (10 Aug. 1970), 28001.

[50]"Women's Rights: Why the Struggle Still Goes On," *U.S. News & World Report*, 27 May 1974, p. 41.

[51]Margaret I. Miller and Helene Linker, "State Politics and Public Interests," *Society*, 11 (May/June 1974), 49.

[52]Ibid., p. 50.

[53]Carol Joyce, "Voice of the People: 'Full-Time' Woman," *Chicago Tribune*, 20 May 1975, sec. 2, p. 2.

[54]"ERA to Illinois Senate," *Compass* [Hammond, Indiana], 5 Feb. 1975, p. 8.

[55]Carol Kleiman, "A New Savvy Fuels the Drive for Equal Rights Passage," *Chicago Tribune*, 12 Feb. 1975, sec. 3, p. 6.

[56]Gayle White, "Here's HOW," *Atlanta Journal and Constitution Magazine*, 17 Mar. 1974, p. 57.

[57]"Lib Amendment—or Volstead Anew," *New Orleans Times-Picayune*, 27 Mar. 1972, sec. 1, p. 10.

[58]Sally Quinn, "Mrs. Schlafly: View From Pedestal," *Los Angeles Times*, 10 Dec. 1974, sec. 4, p. 10.

[59]Mary Hollis, "Letters: Schlafly Pro and Con," *Chicago Tribune*, 24 June 1973, sec. 9, p. 7.

[60]Burke, p. 128.

[61]Materialism is the philosophic system that regards all facts and reality as explainable in terms of matter and motion or physical laws. It is represented by philosophers such as Hobbes, Spencer, and Marx.

[62]Idealism is the philosophic system that views the mind or spirit as each person experiences it as fundamentally real. The totality of the universe is believed to be mind or spirit in its essence. Kant, Hegel, and Berkeley are regarded as idealistic philosophers.

[63]Burke, p. 187.

Inclusiveness in Rhetorical Visions
Unity Statement of the Women's Pentagon Action

Diana Brown Sheridan

In response to the Pentagon's escalating commitment to the development and placement of nuclear weapons around the world, the Women's Pentagon Action was formed in 1971 as a means of protesting the Pentagon's threat to the survival of the entire earth. By 1980, women in numerous peace, environmental, and feminist movements were becoming increasingly distressed by America's new first-strike capability, which meant that if the United States first deployed weapons on Soviet cities and missile sites, the Soviet Union would be forced to adopt a "launch on warning policy"—launching its weapons immediately without checking for computer error. The nuclear catastrophes of Three Mile Island and Love Canal gave further impetus to the women for another action at the Pentagon to protest America's relentless commitment to militarism.

On a chilly day in November, 1980, large numbers of women surged forward to block all of the entrances of the Pentagon. One of their primary organizing tools was a "Unity Statement" that had been worked on collectively in the months preceding the protest action. Over the intervening years, the "Unity Statement" has circulated among a variety of peace and feminist organizations.

In this essay, I will attempt to discover the rhetorical characteristics of artifacts that are able to unite diverse audiences by analyzing the "Unity Statement." The unit of analysis in my essay will be the fantasy theme, derived from Bormann's fantasy-theme criticism.

The analysis of the 1400-word "Unity Statement" results in a number of fantasy themes divided among the categories of character, setting, and action. Two rhetorical visions emerge from the analysis of the discourse. One vision, located in the present, focuses on the Pentagon and the patriarchal men within the institution who are implicated, along with all men, in the "atrocities" committed against humanity. The second vision, located in the present and future of women's lives,

This essay was written while Diana Brown Sheridan was a student in Sonja K. Foss' rhetorical criticism class at the University of Oregon in 1988. Used by permission of the author.

emphasizes the oppressive conditions exerted on women by the first vision and looks toward an idealized world free of the suffocating constraints imposed by those who control the Pentagon vision.

Rhetorical Vision of the Pentagon

In the [present] vision of the Pentagon, the fantasy themes of character and setting are subordinate to the actions of those operating inside the Pentagon. Essentially, there are two *characters*—the key character, consisting of the men who occupy the Pentagon and design military strategies, and a secondary character, the Pentagon itself, portrayed as a living entity. The men become the nameless "they" and the faceless "these men . . . with coldness of heart," undifferentiated from one another. They also are described in anonymous military terms as "colonels and generals who are planning our annihilation." With the overwhelming power of military technology at their command, however, these men are not just ordinary military officers but "industrial militarists" cast as technocrats of the highest order that the patriarchy produces. Also evident in the "Unity Statement" is a portrayal of the Pentagon as a character, which acts on its own accord as it "extracts" huge amounts of money for its "sickness." In a sense, the Pentagon becomes a diseased organism in need of sustenance from those citizens who constantly are called on "to feed the Pentagon [dollars] . . . for its murderous health."

The Pentagon, as a *setting* for the vision, has significance, for it is the place in which the men undertake actions that reach out to the bucolic heartland of America and to countries far beyond our shores. Within its walls, plans for the "MX missile and its billion-dollar subway system" or "warheads with the power of 750 Hiroshimas" move from the embryonic stage to full implementation. The edifice of the Pentagon itself becomes a symbol of "that dominance which is exploitive and murderous."

The *action* themes provide the core of this vision by articulating how and what the Pentagon does. The men of the Pentagon engage in an array of activities that "have separated them from the reality of daily life and from the imagination." The men "produce" bombs that "kill people but leave property and buildings . . . intact," "proclaim" directives, "destroy" cities and children, and "revive the killer nerve gas." Outside the Pentagon, the men "draft" minority youth to be "cannon fodder," cause our lands to be marked by "scars[s]," turn "our cities" into "ruins," and "deprive" our hospitals and schools of vital resources. Within the Pentagon, action is what creates a reality that, for these women, dominates nearly every other action occurring across the American landscape.

The rhetorical vision of the Pentagon that emerges is one that accentuates action more than character or setting. The data suggest that these actions are performed by impersonal male perpetrators who plan and execute them, creating victims in their wake. Although character and setting are important, the actions themselves enable the Pentagon (setting) and its resident staff of industrial-militarists (characters) to extend their tentacles throughout the web of present-day society. With action themes receiving the emphasis, the rhetorical vision is rooted in the male ego's self-centered desire to control the world by dominating the forces of nature that surround him. He becomes a participant through his actions in the ultra-scientific technology of control.

Rhetorical Vision of the Women's Changed World

Part of the rhetorical vision of the women is rooted in the present, but most of it is grounded in a future ideal of a changed reality. The fantasy themes in this vision, unlike those in the Pentagon vision, equally emphasize character, setting, and action.

The *character* of the women is personified in the present as the collective "we" made out of common "blood and bone," with multiple characteristics that, in essence, define much of the American character. They represent all types of women—"city women"; "country women"; "young and older" women; "married, single, lesbian" women; and "daughters and sisters." As professionals, they are "teachers factory workers office workers lawyers farmers doctors builders waitresses weavers engineers homemakers electricians artists and horseloggers." Note that, in describing who they are, no punctuation is used to separate the women's respective professions. They appear to be recognizing the differences of their public images but celebrating their private-becoming-public unity. This perspective of unity further is enhanced by the constant use of "we"—reiterated 71 times throughout the "Unity Statement," in contrast to the 10 times the term "they" is used to describe the men of the Pentagon.

Another character takes an important place in the women's visionary ideal—"the children who are our human future." Mentioned 11 times, the children represent those who are the inheritors of the earth, the recipients of the fantasized benefits that will result from the women's present struggle.

The *setting* for the women's vision of the present is an "intolerable precipice" on a "poisoned Earth." This precipice on which they live their "ordinary lives" is described as the "wreckage . . . of city streets," lost "small farms," lands turned into "radioactive rubble," "dark country roads and city alleys," "woods containing missile silos," and the "stolen night." The ideal setting of the future, for these women, is a restored and balanced "earth, as our home to be cherished, to be fed as well as harvested." The terrain of tomorrow's earth will include "new nations and colonies free of exploitation," "the light of the moon . . . the stars and the gaiety of city streets," "resources left in the earth or replaced," and "decommissioned nuclear plants."

The women's *actions* focus both on the present opposition to the Pentagon's constructed reality that envelopes all women and on future actions that create a narrative of a changed world. They begin their "Unity Statement" with a clear assertion of their actions by claiming, "We are gathering at the Pentagon . . . because we fear for our lives . . . for the life of this planet, our Earth." The women continue by describing the momentum of the present with blunt statements that indicate who they "are," where they "live," and how they "work." They expand their actions to be inclusive of the sufferings of those who are the poor, the ill, the uneducated, and the minorities, all of whom "fear" they are a part of the "end of human time." For these women, poised on "the precipice," the act of knowing and understanding becomes an extremely important action for themselves and those for whom they speak. They demand "to know what anger in these men . . . drives their days" and "to understand all is connectedness." For their future vision to become a reality, they insist that in today's present time, "we will not allow these violent games to continue."

After describing the woeful and oppressive conditions of the present, the women turn to a futuristic vision in which they repeatedly insist on the changes necessary for an earth that "nourishes us as our bodies will eventually feed it." To reach this vision, the women "will certainly return in the thousands and hundreds of thousands in the months and years to come." Sentence after sentence begins with the words, "We want," followed by a litany of goals they believe are achievable once the Pentagon ceases to "play its games." Their repetitious reiteration of the act of wanting focuses on good food, work, housing, child care, health care, education, safe streets, reproductive rights, open sexual expression, elimination of the draft, an end to racism, a renewable environment, and "an end to the arms race." These actions will result, they maintain, in a deep sense of "connectedness," just as "our mothers connected the human past to the human future."

In the rhetorical vision of the women, the characters are innocent women and other oppressed people going about their lives, the settings are the common locales where people live out their lives, and the actions are those of victims striving to right the injustices done to them since military might gained preeminence over human life. This vision features character, setting, and action in equal proportion in the present and ideal realities. Consequently, those who participate in this vision seek to enact righteousness in all aspects of their lives. By giving equal credence to each theme and offering a voluminous number of fantasy themes within each, the vision focuses on repetitive righteousness in daily living.

Uniting Diverse Audiences

In the "Unity Statement," the rhetors establish two rhetorical visions. One vision portrays the men in the Pentagon as wreaking havoc on the world, motivated by a self-centered desire for mastery and control. In the other vision, diverse women are working to right the injustices done in the world, motivated by the desire to enact righteousness in all areas of their lives. I suggest that the nature of these two visions and the way in which they are juxtaposed account for the statement's capacity to unify women, the purpose for which the statement was written.

The unifying properties of the statement derive from four characteristics of the rhetorical visions presented. The first is that the rhetorical vision the women create for themselves is one that reflects women's lived experiences—it is one with which most women can identify. Its potential for identification is evident in its focus on the many aspects of oppression women and minorities experience. It also is evident in its focus on the character theme of children, who are likely to be an important and cherished part of many women's lives.

The rhetorical vision of the women is built on values the potential audience members share; these values constitute a second building block toward unity. Rather than focusing on specific proposed policies the women should support or particular activities in which they should engage, the rhetorical vision is built on abstract values to which many women likely would adhere. The rhetorical vision presented embodies values such as empathy and a concern for others, interconnection, self-determination, and concern for the future. The vagueness and abstractness of these values allow women of diverse viewpoints to come together and to establish common ground.

The statement also contributes to the creation of the unification of women in its depiction of a common enemy. The juxtaposition of the two rhetorical visions clearly establishes the men of the Pentagon as the enemy; the women thus can unite on the basis of a threat to their own safety. The nature of the enemy selected to be featured in the rhetorical vision of the Pentagon also is significant. They are depersonalized, abstract, faceless, and nameless; they are not specific men who might be known and loved by the women. Thus, the enemies depicted are easy to dislike because they are an abstract construction and not real men in the women's lives.

Finally, the "Unity Statement" successfully draws women together because of its depiction of women themselves—the women who are to be unified by the statement. The equitable balancing of the themes of setting, character, and action within the rhetorical vision in which they portray themselves suggests that the women are levelheaded and balanced human beings, not radical fanatics obsessed with one trivial concern. They are able to see the whole picture and are broad in their thinking, this even-handed rhetorical vision suggests.

The rhetorical visions embedded in the "Unity Statement" help to account for the statement's potential capacity for unifying women of diverse backgrounds and perspectives. Its focus on dimensions of women's experiences, values rather than policies, a common enemy, and a balanced depiction of women all contribute to the unifying potential of the statement. These features very well might be characteristics of rhetorical unification in general and deserve further exploration in other artifacts.

Dying to Make the Paper

Robert Huesca

Nearly 25 percent of the population of Columbus, Ohio, is made up of African-American residents. That such a large minority group exists is not evident, however, in the area's only daily newspaper, *The Columbus Dispatch*. The minimal coverage accorded African Americans in the newspaper reflects the thinking, concerns, values, and worldview of the newspaper's predominantly conservative, middle-aged, white staff; of the top 10 editors at the paper, all are white. These leaders set the tone of the newspaper as they control story assignments and placement of news and direct approximately 65 reporters, 4 of whom are black and the rest white.

African Americans are not proportionately represented at the newspaper either in staffing or content. The only exception to their absence is the content in the "Deaths and Funerals" section—the only section of the newspaper where African Americans appear both regularly and in high proportions. In fact, blacks outnumber whites in appearances on this page, where space is sold to readers much like space is sold in the classified-advertising section. For $2.21 a line on weekdays and $3.24 a line on Sundays, readers can place a photo and a message about a loved one in this section.

Most of the death notices are formal announcements of funerals and are written in a conventional manner. But in a portion of the page headlined "In Memoriam," families show more diversity and self-expression in the messages they place with the pictures of their loved ones. While death notices placed by funeral homes generally list the date of death, survivors, and time and place of burial, "In Memoriam" announcements usually include heartfelt expressions of grief, loss, and pain written in prose and verse. Remembrances of loved ones often include testimonies of physical traits and personality characteristics such as the shape of one's face, appearance of a smile, and degree of love and devotion. In addition, the accompanying pictures include both conventional head-and-shoulders snapshots as well as more descriptive environmental portraits: a man dressed in a favorite hat, a woman tending her garden, a youth arm in arm with a companion.

This essay was written while Robert Huesca was a student in Sonja K. Foss' rhetorical criticism class at Ohio State University in 1991. Used by permission of the author.

In the two years I worked for *The Columbus Dispatch*, I always was puzzled by the way African Americans dominated the page of death announcements in the newspaper. No employees I questioned seemed to have any idea of why African Americans were drawn to the page or how long they had been using the section. Apparently, no one had given the matter much thought; the predominance of black faces on that page seemed as normal as their absence in all the other sections.

In this essay, I will analyze the messages written by families and individuals during a one-week period in February, 1991, in the "In Memoriam" section. Because this study is specific to race, I coded only those messages accompanied by a photograph where race was discernable. Using fantasy themes and rhetorical visions as my units of analysis, I hope to discover the rhetorical functions this section serves for this minority community with an eye toward discovering strategies minority and oppressed groups may use to empower themselves.

That a shared vision does exist is an initial assumption I am making, regardless of the content of the messages. Because of the dominant, white structure of the newspaper and its content, I am assuming that the African Americans carving out this space in the newspaper are drawn there based on a shared vision. This position is supported by a sorting of content by setting, character, and action.

Fantasy Themes

Six messages were coded during the week, with the settings, characters, and actions reported in table 1. The similar themes I discovered are grouped and labeled to suggest the settings, characters, and actions of the rhetorical vision. Elements reported more than once have the number of repetitions recorded in parentheses following the theme.

Setting is the category with the least important themes. The most frequently mentioned time setting involves anniversaries of either birth or death of the person being remembered. Because this is an external exigence of sorts, I do not consider it germane to the rhetorical vision I am trying to explicate.

Beyond time settings, actual places rarely are noted in the newspaper passages. Of those places that are mentioned, most are not concrete places but conceptual locations such as "in memory," "in our hearts," an "empty place," or "up there." The only concrete place mentioned is "home," which is mentioned only once.

Within character, two major themes emerged: family and body parts. The vast majority of references in the texts are to family members and

Table 1.

Settings

Conceptual locations
- in memory
- in loving memory (5)
- empty place
- in our hearts (2)
- down here
- up there
- our side

Time
- every day
- today
- 7 years ago
- 1 year ago (2)
- birthday (2)
- forever

Concrete locations
- home

Characters

Family
- our (2)
- I (5)
- me
- we (2)
- you (3)
- her
- husband and son
- mother (2)

- family (2)
- families by proper name (4)
- proper name of individual (4)

Body parts
- lips
- face
- memory
- hearts
- smile

Actions

Timeless endurance
- missed (7)
- remembered
- can't take away
- [no one] could fill
- cannot tell
- knows (2)
- love[d] (2)
- will remember (2)
- stay

Mournful effusion
- am longing to hear
- is haunting
- is lonesome
- try to hold [tears]

Transcendence
- passed away (2)
- left us

relationships. Sometimes, the relationship is clear, as with "mother," "husband," "family," or "son." In other cases, the pronouns "we," "I," "our," and "you" refer to individuals, but they always are used in the context of family relationships. Occasionally, families list members by name and relationship, such as "stepfather, mother and sisters,

Carlos, Sharon, Natasha and Shalonda." A second major character theme is body parts—body parts belonging either to the loved one who has died or the one who is grieving; they serve as a synecdoche for the whole person. References to "face," "lips," "hearts," and "memory" contribute to this theme.

Within the action category, two major themes emerged that overlap somewhat: timeless endurance and mournful effusion. For example, the words "missed," "love[d]," "can't take away," and "could [not] fill" express both timelessness or endurance as well as effusion. The remainder of the words in this theme cluster speak exclusively to matters of endurance. The second cluster, comprised of the words "is lonesome," "is haunting," "longing to hear," and "try to hold [tears]," fits into the major theme of mournful effusion, although it also expresses notions of endurance. One minor theme emerges from the announcements: The theme of transcendence is expressed in the actions "left us" and "passed away."

Rhetorical Vision

From the data, setting—a conceptual location—appears to be of little importance, while two major themes emerge from both the characters and actions. Under characters, I have identified both family and body parts. Under action, I have identified endurance and effusion. Because of the overlap in the action categories, matching one set of dominant characters to one set of actions is difficult. Family members are involved in the enduring actions of missing, remembering, and enduring as well as in the effusive actions of trying to hold back tears and longing to hear. Likewise, body parts may be linked with both the endurance and effusion themes. Lips cannot tell, face is haunting, and hearts are lonesome. Nevertheless, the body-parts category seems to be more closely aligned with the effusion theme than with the endurance theme.

The theme receiving most of the attention and driving the remainder of the vision is the action theme of timeless endurance. Missing; remembering; and not being able to take away, to tell, or to fill are necessary for this rhetorical vision to take place. The daily repetition of black endurance in the pages of The Columbus Dispatch functions to counterbalance the white-normed portrayal of urban life displayed in the non-paid news and features sections of the paper. Through the "In Memoriam" columns, African Americans undermine the symbolic annihilation of black culture by attaching themselves to a very powerful instrument of aggression against them and their culture—the newspaper.

In addition, the emphasis on families, personal names, and body parts suggests that the columns do not merely interact on a symbolic level but function within the social body as well. By including the names of living relatives, these columns stress the importance of survivors and the maintenance of relations. They suggest that these clippings are embodied and used in social settings and family gatherings as a means of validation and preservation of the African-American culture. Once fixed in cold type and half-tones on the printed page, the names and photographs of the living and dead become locked onto microfilm in area libraries and probably are clipped from the newspaper, pasted into albums, and handed down for generations.

Remarkably absent from the text is mention of details about where and how the people died or about what work they did and the things they accomplished in life. Of only passing attention are mentions of God and allusions to an afterlife. These omissions, while seemingly glaring in the context of an obituary or memorial, are quite explicable in the context of the rhetorical vision centered on endurance. Including such details about the relative would detract, in fact, from the task.

Functions of the Vision

This limited review of newspaper text contains enormous implications regarding minority people and how they maneuver within dominant institutions to create community, to challenge hegemonic assumptions, and to cope with unjust physical and social conditions. That a high proportion of black faces appears daily on the pay-to-display pages of the deaths and funerals section indicates that the community of participants extends beyond those directly involved. Behind the scenes of the printed page is a much larger community participating in the immortalization of its members. As evidenced by the regularity and vitality of African Americans' contributions to this page, community members read the pages not only out of the need to recognize and validate their own experiences vicariously but to accumulate fantasy themes that they eventually may tap when participating directly. The "In Memoriam" section is a forum of exchange, where participants not only bring conceptualizations to the task but take fantasy themes away, only to return them at some later date. Implicating the larger community in this column functions to reinforce and extend the principal theme of these texts: timeless endurance.

The major themes in this analysis also demonstrate that the minority culture is challenging some of the hegemonic assumptions concerning black culture. Although the state, media, and academy seem fixated on underscoring the disintegration of the black family, the community under study here does not lend support to that notion. As illustrated in the dominant character theme, African Americans, in their use of this section of the newspaper, emphasize the importance of family structure. These community members simply do not believe the hegemonic reading of their domestic structure. In instances where the fractures in families appear in the text, such as in the message signed, "Stepfather, mother and sisters, Carlos, Sharon, Natasha and Shalonda," African Americans appear to be piecing together structures from the remnants of broken families. Whether intact or recycled, the family structure emerges as solid and significant in this text.

Perhaps most remarkable is how this disenfranchised group creates a space for self-expression within a white structure. Although The Columbus Dispatch virtually ignores the African-American community, members of this group have created a niche within the publication, despite the closed nature of the newspaper. In doing so, they advance a rhetorical vision of endurance that can be read as an empowering strategy by constituents feeling fatigued in their struggle for equality. This group not only creates a community in a repressive environment but advances a strategy for coping with that environment. Although this achievement is attained within the perimeters of a media institution, the technique can be adapted to the development of shared visions and strategies for change by minority communities in general.

Additional Samples

Fantasy-Theme Criticism

Bormann, Ernest G. "A Fantasy Theme Analysis of the Television Coverage of the Hostage Release and the Reagan Inaugural." *Quarterly Journal of Speech,* 68 (May 1982), 133–45.

Bormann, Ernest G. "Fetching Good Out of Evil: A Rhetorical Use of Calamity." *Quarterly Journal of Speech,* 63 (April 1977), 130–39.

Bormann, Ernest G. "The Eagleton Affair: A Fantasy Theme Analysis." *Quarterly Journal of Speech,* 59 (April 1973), 143–59.

Bormann, Ernest G. *The Force of Fantasy: Restoring the American Dream.* Carbondale: Southern Illinois University Press, 1985.

Brown, William R. "The Prime-Time Television Environment and Emerging Rhetorical Visions." *Quarterly Journal of Speech,* 62 (December 1976), 389–99.

Cragan, John F. "Rhetorical Strategy: A Dramatistic Interpretation and Application." *Central States Speech Journal,* 26 (Spring 1975), 4–11.

Cragan, John F., and Donald C. Shields. *Applied Communication Research: A Dramatistic Approach.* Prospect Heights, IL: Waveland, 1981, several essays.

Doyle, Marsha Vanderford. "The Rhetoric of Romance: A Fantasy Theme Analysis of Barbara Cartland Novels." *Southern Speech Communication Journal,* 51 (Fall 1985), 24–48.

Endres, Thomas G. "Rhetorical Visions of Unmarried Mothers." *Communication Quarterly,* 37 (Spring 1989), 134–50.

Foss, Karen A., and Stephen W. Littlejohn. "*The Day After:* Rhetorical Vision in an Ironic Frame." *Critical Studies in Mass Communication,* 3 (September 1986), 317–36.

Glaser, Susan R., and David A. Frank. "Rhetorical Criticism of Interpersonal Discourse: An Exploratory Study." *Communication Quarterly,* 30 (Fall 1982), 353–58.

Haskins, William A. "Rhetorical Vision of Equality: Analysis of the Rhetoric of the Southern Black Press During Reconstruction." *Communication Quarterly,* 29 (Spring 1981), 116–22.

Hensley, Carl Wayne. "Rhetorical Vision and the Persuasion of a Historical Movement: The Disciples of Christ in Nineteenth Century American Culture." *Quarterly Journal of Speech,* 61 (October 1975), 250–64.

Hubbard, Rita C. "Relationship Styles in Popular Romance Novels, 1950 to 1983." *Communication Quarterly,* 33 (Spring 1985), 113–25.

Ilkka, Richard J. "Rhetorical Dramatization in the Development of American Communism." *Quarterly Journal of Speech,* 63 (December 1977), 413–27.

Kidd, Virginia. "Happily Ever After and Other Relationship Styles: Advice on Interpersonal Relations in Popular Magazines, 1951–1973." *Quarterly Journal of Speech,* 61 (February 1975), 31–39.

King, Andrew A. "Booker T. Washington and the Myth of Heroic Materialism." *Quarterly Journal of Speech,* 60 (October 1974), 323–27.

Koester, Jolene. "The Machiavellian Princess: Rhetorical Dramas for Women Managers." *Communication Quarterly,* 30 (Summer 1982), 165–72.

Kroll, Becky Swanson. "From Small Group to Public View: Mainstreaming the Women's Movement." *Communication Quarterly,* 31 (Spring 1983), 139–47.

Nimmo, Dan, and James E. Combs. "Fantasies and Melodramas in Television Network News: The Case of Three Mile Island." *Western Journal of Speech Communication,* 46 (Winter 1982), 45–55.

Porter, Laurinda W. "The White House Transcripts: Group Fantasy Events Concerning the Mass Media." *Central States Speech Journal,* 27 (Winter 1976), 272–79.

Putnam, Linda L., Shirley A. Van Hoeven, and Connie A. Bullis. "The Role of Rituals and Fantasy Themes in Teachers' Bargaining." *Western Journal of Speech Communication,* 55 (Winter 1991), 85–103.

6

Feminist Criticism

Feminist criticism has its roots in a social and political movement, the feminist or women's liberation movement, aimed at improving conditions for women. Definitions of *feminism* vary, ranging from "the belief that women and men should have equal opportunities for self-expression"[1] to "movement towards creating a society where women can live a full, self-determined life"[2] to "an active commitment to equality and respect for life."[3] What these various definitions of feminism have in common is "the struggle to end sexist oppression"—to change existing power relations between women and men.[4]

The diversity that characterizes the definition of *feminism* also marks the goals and methods of feminists. A variety of perspectives exist within feminism, exemplified in just a few samples of different kinds of feminism. Liberal-humanist feminists, for example, aim to extend to women the rights already possessed by men; they work for equality within the present system. Radical feminists, in contrast, advocate the revolutionary transformation of society and the development of alternative social arrangements to those currently in place. Marxist or socialist feminists see the capitalist economic structures as at the root of women's oppression, while lesbian feminists see heterosexuality as a primary cornerstone of male supremacy. Women do not need to define themselves by their relation to a male world, these feminists suggest, and they point to various kinds of identifications women can make with each other, ranging from giving support to one another to sexual relationships.

Although diversity characterizes feminism, most feminists agree on at least three basic principles. First, women are oppressed by patriarchy. *Patriarchy* is a system of power relations in which men dominate women so that women's interests are subordinated to those of men, and women are seen as inferior to men. In a patriarchal society, relations of domination between women and men exist in all institutions and social practices, so we all learn patriarchal values and modes of operation as appropriate and natural and thus help to perpetuate them. Feminists not only recognize the oppression of women under patriarchy, but they seek to change it. They seek to disrupt the patriarchal hegemony of our current culture and to transform it into one that offers more enriching, humane ways to live.

A second principle on which feminists generally agree is that women's experiences are different from men's. Women are biologically different from men in ways that influence, to some degree, their life experiences. Women are biologically different from men in that they menstruate, have the capacity to bear children, and experience and express themselves sexually in particular ways. The point is not that anatomy is destiny but that women's biological characteristics affect the kinds of experiences they have.

Men and women also have different experiences as a result of sex-role or gender socialization, the process by which children identify as girls or boys and learn what society considers appropriate behavior for them because of their sex. The different expectations that society has for women, embodied and disseminated through practices of sex-role socialization, create different lives for women and men. Socializing agents include parents, who typically respond differently to their children according to their sex. To cite but a few examples, they tend to talk more to girls than to boys and to allow girls to express a wider range of emotions than boys. They give different toys, decorate rooms in different colors, and assign different household chores according to the sex of their children. The different ways in which the two sexes live also are taught by the mass media and educational, social, and religious institutions that reinforce society's representations of the ideal woman and man. The ideals are different for the sexes; thus, from earliest childhood, women and men are exposed to systematically different treatment and experience the world in dissimilar ways.[5]

A third principle on which most feminists agree is that women's perspectives are not now incorporated into our culture. Our cultural forms and expressions rarely reflect women's experiences, perspectives, and meanings, for in a patriarchal culture, men are the ones who have the greatest opportunity to create culture. Those who create culture and its various manifestations naturally do so from their own point of view, putting themselves at the center. Thus, culture features men's perspectives and devalues and silences those of women. Feminist Sonia Johnson describes the moment, in St. Patrick's Cathedral in New York City, when she realized the extent to which women are excluded from the creation of culture:

> None of this has ever really belonged to women. All the great church architecture, the religious art, music, poetry—Michelangelo, Mozart, Gerard Manley Hopkins—none of this has ever really belonged to us. As far back as we can see clearly into the past, the church has belonged to men. The worship, the music, the art, the poetry, the architecture—it was all *by* men *for* men. I thought it was for me, mine, this heritage, this precious thing we call "Western civilization." I thought I had a part in it, that it represented me. I have loved it so and been so proud.
>
> But the fact is that I have always been excluded from it, always outside it, always, as all women have. I have no history. I have no heritage, no civilization. Women have not left our mark on this at all; we have never really participated in it, been a part of it. It is as if we have never lived, millions of us, for thousands of years."[6]

Women's lack of input into patriarchal culture also can be seen in the nature of our language. Women's perspectives are missing from language, which centers on men and their experiences. This feature of language is evident, for example, in words that indicate that men are the standard and that women are somehow different—generic terms such as *mankind* or *chairman* and terms in which a suffix must be added before they apply to women, such as *actress, waitress,* and *majorette.* Women's exclusion from language also can be seen in the negative connotations that words associated with women tend to acquire, thus denying visibility to women's positive attributes.[7] The numerous words that describe women in non-human terms (*bitch, chick, dish*) and the use of negative labels for women and positive ones for men to describe the same quality (*bachelor/spinster, grandfatherly advice/old wives' tales*) are examples.

The silencing of women in language is most apparent in the incapacity of language to express women's perceptions and meanings. Women often have experiences for which there are no terms in the language. The term *sexual harassment,* for example, was created to name an experience

women often have and for which there previously was no term—being
fired from or quitting a job because they have been made uncomfortable
by the behavior of men.[8] Language is one example, then, of how a
patriarchal culture tends not to incorporate women's perspectives.

Despite its origin in a movement designed to transform the patriarchy
to allow the contributions of women to be visible and valued, feminism
is much larger than a commitment to achieve equality for women. A
society that names white, heterosexual men as superior not only
oppresses women but everyone else who does not fit into the category
of white, male, and heterosexual. Thus, feminists are committed to
eliminating relations of oppression and domination in general, whether
of women, African Americans, old people, lesbians, gay men, or others.
Feminists do not believe that oppression and domination are worthy
human values and seek to eradicate the ideology of domination that
permeates Western culture. They want to transform relationships and
the larger culture so that the patriarchal values and traits of alienation,
competition, imperialism, elitism, control, and dehumanization that
characterize interaction under an ideology of domination are disrupted.
They seek instead to contribute to relationships and cultures characterized by self-determination, equality, fairness, responsibility, affirmation,
a valuing of others, acknowledgment of the interdependence of all life
forms, and respect for others.[9]

Feminist criticism is rooted in the same commitment to the elimination
of oppression that characterizes feminism, but its focus is on the
rhetorical forms and processes through which oppression is maintained
and transformed. Feminist criticism is the analysis of rhetoric to discover
how the rhetorical construction of gender is used as a means for
oppression and how that process can be challenged and resisted. Gender
is a culture's conception of the qualities considered desirable for women
and men, a construction created and maintained through various forms
of rhetoric. In feminist criticism, then, the focus is on the rhetorical
process by which these qualities come to seem natural and ways in which
that naturalness can be called into question.

Because the concern of feminist critics is with oppressive relationships
of all kinds, not simply those based on gender, feminist criticism can
be used to analyze the construction of oppression based on race, class,
sexual orientation, or any other dimension of identity. I have chosen
to call this criticism *feminist* because oppression on the basis of sex,
as bell hooks explains, "is the practice of domination most people
experience, whether their role be that of discriminator or discriminated
against, exploiter or exploited. It is the practice of domination most
people are socialized to accept before they even know that other forms
of group oppression exist."[10] Although the procedures outlined in the
following sections are discussed in terms of gender and women, then,

they could be used as well in the analysis of artifacts where the concern is primarily with race, class, or another variable on which oppression is based.

Procedures

The feminist critic approaches an artifact, as all critics do, through a four-step process: (1) formulating a research question and selecting an artifact; (2) selecting a unit of analysis; (3) analyzing the artifact; and (4) writing the critical essay.

Formulating a Research Question and Selecting an Artifact

The first step in the process of rhetorical criticism is to develop a research question to ask about rhetoric and to select a rhetorical artifact to analyze that provides an initial answer to the question. Because, in feminist criticism, the critic's primary interest is in the construction of oppression and its elimination, often as it relates to gender, the research questions asked by feminist critics are likely to deal with how, through rhetorical means, gender is constructed, oppression related to gender is constructed and maintained, and patriarchy can be challenged and transformed. Many feminist critics also are interested in reconceptualizing rhetorical theory and ask research questions with a focus in this area. Because most existing rhetorical constructs and theories reflect the patriarchal values and structures from which they originated, feminist critics often ask whether constructs and theories incorporate women's perspectives and feminist values and, if they do not, they engage in criticism to revise or reconceptualize them to eliminate that bias.[11]

Selecting a Unit of Analysis

The second step in the process of rhetorical criticism is to select a unit of analysis that can help the critic answer the research question. The unit of analysis is that aspect of the artifact to which the critic attends in the analysis. The unit of analysis in feminist criticism is those aspects of the artifact that depict a particular construction of gender.

Analyzing the Artifact

Feminist criticism involves two basic steps: (1) analysis of the construction of gender in the artifact studied; and (2) exploration of what the artifact suggests about how the patriarchy is constructed and maintained or how it can be challenged and transformed.

Analysis of Gender. Feminist criticism begins with an analysis of how women and men, femininity and masculinity, are depicted in the artifact, using as units of analysis ones drawn from the artifact itself, ones discussed in other chapters in this book, or any that provide clues to the construction of gender in an artifact. The critic's concern is with discovering what the artifact presents as standard, normal, desirable, and appropriate behavior for women and men. Women and men are constructed in particular ways through rhetorical artifacts, and the critic's task is to discover the particular nature of the construction in the artifact under investigation. The critic may discover that women are portrayed in an artifact in ways that accord with particular forms of male interest—they are depicted, for example, as sexual objects for men; as primarily responsible for housework, childrearing, and caregiving; and as weaker or secondary to men. Alternatively, women may be absent from texts except as necessary devices to support the depiction of masculinity in artifacts, as in conventional Western and horror films.

The critic also may gain information about the construction of gender by identifying how the artifact positions its audience. An artifact provides a preferred viewpoint from which to view the world of the artifact. This is the position the audience member must occupy in order to participate in the pleasures and meaning of the text. This position requires a particular cultural experience in order to make sense of the artifact and is the result of the structures of characters, meanings, aesthetic codes, attitudes, norms, and values the rhetor projects into the text.

In many cases, the subject position offered to the audience is a gendered one—feminine or masculine—that describes how the world looks and feels to women or to men, a sense of self and ways of understanding typically associated with women or men.[12] In many popular artifacts, a masculine position is structured for the subject—audience members are asked to identify with a male protagonist who controls events and conveys a sense of omnipotence. Men's experiences are universalized so that the masculine is aligned with the universal; what happens to men or what men find desirable and appropriate is seen as applying to women. The female subject in such texts, in contrast, usually is positioned as the object rather than the subject of the action; she is displayed for the gaze and enjoyment of men.

In artifacts in which the subject position is a masculine one, women are asked to identify with a male point of view, to think as men, and to accept as normal and legitimate a system of patriarchal values. Consequently, women as audience members for such texts are accorded a position of powerlessness because they do not see their experiences articulated and legitimized. When women and women's perspectives are excluded from the experience of the story, women must adopt a masculine viewpoint in order to be included.

As a result of exploring the construction of gender in an artifact, the critic makes a judgment about the conceptions of femininity and masculinity in it and whose interests the conceptions seem to serve: Does the conception affirm and support the patriarchy or seek to transform it? At this point, the critic has two options. If the analysis of the artifact reveals that it depicts a patriarchal view of the world and confirms the status quo's oppressive structures, the critic's next step is to use the analysis to help discover how oppression is constructed and maintained through rhetoric. If the analysis of the artifact reveals that it departs from a patriarchal perspective and challenges the status quo, the critic uses the analysis to contribute to our understanding of how rhetoric can be used to challenge or transform patriarchy.

Contribution to Understanding Patriarchy. When the critic discovers a text in which men's experiences are central and perhaps universalized, in which women are not taken into account, or in which patriarchal values such as hierarchy are featured, the critic has an opportunity to use the artifact as a vehicle to study the patriarchal ideology and the rhetorical processes that create and sustain it. The critic uses the analysis to contribute to the description of rhetorical practices through which the existing patriarchal system is constructed and maintained—to understand how patriarchal relations happen through rhetoric. Such a description may include analyzing how power is exercised in the system through rhetoric and how the hegemony or dominance of particular groups is constructed and maintained in patriarchy. *Hegemony* is the imposition of the ideology of one group on other groups—it is the power to describe reality and to have that description accepted. It expresses the advantaged position of white, heterosexual men in a patriarchal system, and the critic can describe how that advantaged position is maintained through particular rhetorical strategies. Other directions the critic might pursue are whose interests are marginalized, silenced, or excluded and how the patriarchal structures of the artifact are able to draw audience members into its designs, providing satisfaction and pleasure to audiences, even to women.

If the critic's artifact is one that affirms and reinforces patriarchal structures, the critic uses it to contribute to our understanding of how those structures are constructed and maintained through rhetoric. Such an analysis provides a critical distance on existing gender relations, clearing a space in which existing gender arrangements can be evaluated.

By describing patriarchal relations, it calls them into question, opening the way for change and for new kinds of relations.

Contribution to the Transformation of Patriarchy. As a result of the analysis of gender in an artifact, the critic may find that the conception of gender encoded in the artifact suggests ways in which patriarchy can be transformed or offers imaginative alternatives to existing patriarchal structures and relations. In such a case, the critic's next step is to discuss how the artifact resists, challenges, or transforms the patriarchy.

The critic may find that a text provides an opening for transformation by describing experiences of oppression in a patriarchal system. With such descriptions, in which the effects and consequences of patriarchy are made visible, experiences of oppression can be felt by those who usually do not have such experiences. Those for whom experiences of oppression are common can discover that others have the same experiences they do, a process that validates their experiences and confirms their doubts about the patriarchy. Such texts, then, may provide a glimpse into the experiences of women in patriarchal institutions, the nature and feel of subordinate positions, and the communication options available to individuals in such positions.

The critic may find that the artifact being analyzed challenges the patriarchy in yet another way: It may provide evidence of ways in which women can resist patriarchy. An artifact, for example, may provide models for the ways in which women have managed to articulate their perspectives and have them heard in spite of the formidable forces that have attempted to silence and exclude them. It may provide role models of those who have resisted the patriarchy. It may highlight women's acts of re-naming or re-definition, the creation of subject positions for women, or women's skills at coping with patriarchy.

Another focus the critic may discover in an artifact that challenges patriarchy is a presentation of women's experiences as positive, valuable, and worthy of emulation. Some artifacts suggest that women's ways of communicating can be used as the basis for creating non-patriarchal structures and relationships. As a result of their particular experiences and treatment, many women have developed alternative ways of communicating and espouse values that are different from those typically held by men. Women often are taught to be nurturing, affiliative, and cooperative, for example—qualities that are contrary to patriarchal values of competition, domination, and hierarchy. If women's values were incorporated into general cultural structures, they probably would produce more humane ways of living. An artifact, then, may offer themes, styles, values, forms of communication, and kinds of relationships that can serve as models for alternatives to the patriarchy.

These are just a few of the ways in which an artifact may challenge and seek to transform patriarchy or provide openings for its transformation. By describing the experiences of women, ways in which their subordinate position is resisted, and ways in which their communication and values can serve as models for alternatives to patriarchy, artifacts can contribute to an understanding of how the description or transformation of patriarchy can occur through rhetorical means.

Writing the Critical Essay

After completion of the analysis, the critic writes an essay that includes five major components: (1) an introduction, in which the research question, its contribution to rhetorical theory, and its significance are discussed; (2) description of the artifact and its context; (3) description of the unit of analysis, the construction of gender as revealed in rhetoric; (4) report of the findings of the analysis, in which the critic suggests the conception of gender in the artifact and contributes to an understanding of how patriarchy is constructed and maintained or how it can be transformed; and (5) discussion of the contribution the analysis makes to answering the research question.

Sample Essays

The essays that follow provide examples of different kinds of feminist criticism. The first two essays exemplify criticism in which the analysis of gender in an artifact contributes to an understanding of patriarchy. James Fredal analyzes a song from Sesame Street to answer the question, "How are patriarchal attitudes and beliefs engendered in artifacts directed at children?" Nick Trujillo focuses on the construction of masculinity in patriarchy in his analysis of the media representation of a baseball pitcher; his analysis is guided by the research question, "How do mediated sports function to perpetuate a patriarchal definition of masculinity?" Sonja K. Foss' analysis of a work of art by Judy Chicago exemplifies criticism in which the analysis of gender in an artifact leads to contributions to the transformation of patriarchy. She seeks to answer the question, "What strategies do submerged groups use to legitimize their own perspectives?"

Notes

[1] Sonja K. Foss, Karen A. Foss, and Robert Trapp, Contemporary Perspectives on Rhetoric, 2nd ed. (Prospect Heights, IL: Waveland, 1991), p. 275.

[2] Mary MacNamara, "What Is Feminism? Another View . . .," Wicca: "Wise Woman" Irish Feminist Magazine, 21 (c. 1982), 6–7, qtd. in Cheris Kramarae, Paula A. Treichler, and Ann Russo, A Feminist Dictionary (Boston: Pandora, 1985), p. 159.

³Julia T. Wood, *Gendered Lives: Communication, Gender, and Culture* (Belmont, California: Wadsworth, 1994), p. 4.

⁴bell hooks, *Feminist Theory: From Margin to Center* (Boston: South End, 1984), p. 26.

⁵For an excellent summary of sex-role-socialization practices in American culture, see Letty Cottin Pogrebin, *Growing Up Free: Raising Your Child in the 80's* (New York: Bantam, 1980).

⁶Sonia Johnson, *From Housewife to Heretic* (1981; rpt. Albuquerque, New Mexico: Wildfire, 1989), pp. 314-15. The notion that women are a muted group is discussed in detail in: Cheris Kramarae, *Women and Men Speaking: Frameworks for Analysis* (Rowley, Massachusetts: Newbury, 1981), pp. 1-32; and Dale Spender, *Man Made Language* (Boston: Routledge & Kegan Paul, 1980), pp. 76-105.

⁷For more on the semantic derogation of women, see Spender, pp. 16-19.

⁸Spender, pp. 182-90.

⁹hooks, p. 24; Wood, p. 4; and Sonja K. Foss and Cindy L. Griffin, "Beyond Persuasion: A Proposal for an Invitational Rhetoric," *Communication Monographs*, 62 (March 1995), 2-18.

¹⁰hooks, p. 36.

¹¹Samples of such feminist reconceptualizations include: Mary Rose Williams, "A Reconceptualization of Protest Rhetoric: Women's Quilts as Rhetorical Forms," *Women's Studies in Communication*, 17 (Fall 1994), 20-44; Foss and Griffin; Candace West, "Women's Competence in Conversation," *Discourse and Society*, 6 (January 1995), 107-31; and Elizabeth J. DeGroot, "A Reconceptualization of the Enthymeme from a Feminist Perspective," Diss. University of Oregon 1990.

¹²Laura Mulvey, *Visual and Other Pleasures* (Bloomington: Indiana University Press, 1989). For an example of such an analysis, see Sonja K. Foss and Karen A. Foss, "The Construction of Feminine Spectatorship in Garrison Keillor's Radio Monologues," *Quarterly Journal of Speech*, 80 (November 1994), 410-26.

"Ladybug Picnic"
Engendering Pyrophobia and Promethean Desire

James Fredal

Patriarchy is not a monolith, nor is it ever finished. Like other ideologies and practices of domination, patriarchy constantly must be reproduced and maintained rhetorically. Those engaged in this maintenance rarely perceive themselves as reproducing the cultural forms that allow patriarchy to exist. More often, cultural products are seen simply as enacting what they proclaim for themselves: news programs simply report the news, advertisements simply sell, songs simply entertain. Rhetorical critics who question these ostensible functions, as feminist critics do, are said to be reading too much into an artifact or to be finding things that aren't really there. In fact, hegemonic practices rely on this resistance to criticism in order to maintain the appearance of naturalness that they construct.

The resistance is particularly noticeable and especially important in those arenas where the construction and maintenance of dominant ideologies, like patriarchy, are most needed. The substance of children's television programming, for example, resists serious critical attention as a relatively unimportant cultural activity at the same time that it is crucial for engendering in young girls and boys the attitudes and beliefs on which patriarchy relies for its survival. In this essay, I will examine one song from a children's program that is particularly adept at resisting serious attention in order to discover the ways in which it portrays and reinforces the attitudes and values characteristic of patriarchy.

"Ladybug Picnic" is a short, animated counting song on a *Sesame Street* video called *Silly Songs*. The song features twelve identical ladybugs in identical pink bonnets who engage in various picnicking activities. They run sack races, play jump rope, tell jokes, and finally sit around a campfire and talk while roasting marshmallows. Each refrain begins with the singer rhythmically counting up to twelve in groups of three as the ladybugs appear to enjoy their next game. The song is short, only one minute and fifteen seconds. It immediately follows the opening song on the video, "Honker Duckie Dinger Jamboree" and precedes the ever-popular "Jellyman Kelly." *Silly Songs* is just one of

This essay was written while James Fredal was a student in Sonja K. Foss' rhetorical criticism class at Ohio State University in 1994. Used by permission of the author.

many *Sesame Street* videos, most of which are arranged thematically. Other videos include *Rock and Roll* and an animal-songs video called *Sing, Hoot and Howl*.

Sesame Street has been around for over twenty years. Its residents—Big Bird, Bert and Ernie, Oscar the Grouch, and Cookie Monster, among others—are some of the best-known television personages for children and adults alike. As a program broadcast by public television, *Sesame Street* enjoys a trust increasingly withheld from the networks. Thus, the many caveats about television sex and violence and the need for parents to "screen" shows not intended for young audiences typically are not applied to shows like *Sesame Street*. In this negative sense, then, it has earned the right to be overlooked by adults even more than network children's shows. *Sesame Street* is overlooked by children as well. Lewis Lapham's article in the December, 1993, issue of *Harper's*, "Adieu, Big Bird: On the Terminal Irrelevance of Public Television," argues that public broadcasts continue to lose audience share because they do nothing that cable channels and the networks don't do, only public television does it on a tighter budget. "Instead of offering an alternative to the Roman circus of commercial television," argues Lapham, public television "presents a show of slightly less expensive lions" (35). As more cable channels offer more sophisticated, action-oriented, high-tech entertainment, *Sesame Street* goes the way of other public television broadcasts: toward increasing marginalization.

Silly Songs is interesting because its very title further resists serious attention even by those children who do watch. In the unique parlance of parenting toddlers, *silly* is a useful term rich in meaning. More commonly used than in standard English, *silly* refers to the non-serious and nonsensical, unreal, or pretend and frequently inappropriate behavior of children. In the never-ending battle to teach, model, and reinforce socially appropriate behavior, *silly* usually refers to the uninhibited, make-believe play that seems always on the verge of getting out of hand, especially in public. Thus, the term implies actions that are pretend, non-serious, or inconsequential (Lapham might call public television *silly*) as well as actions that are unethical, inappropriate, or incorrect (actions such as interrupting a group activity that does not include the child). *Silly Songs* thus announces itself to children and parents as a program that does not merit serious attention. The songs will not deal with "real" or socially appropriate behaviors or with serious content. As such, the video explicitly invites a sort of benign neglect. "You needn't pay attention too closely," the viewer is told, "we're just being silly."

Analysis of Gender

"Ladybug Picnic," paradoxically, *is* an educational song and, to that extent, does have a serious message. The song teaches children their numbers, in this case the number twelve. The silliness of the song lies rather in its narrative content, the details that fill out the number. These are, of course, the twelve ladybugs engaged in a thoroughly non-serious activity: a picnic. The ladybugs are indeed silly, finding themselves unable to engage in any activity to completion, much less any serious activity. Their first game, the sack race, is both competitive and active, requiring agility and strenuous effort. The race ends prematurely as the ladybugs all "fall on their backs and they fall on their faces." Wobbly but undaunted, the ladybugs proceed to a less demanding activity, jumping rope. More traditionally a "girl's game," jumping rope is non-competitive but still requires substantial agility and energy to do well. Here, the ladybugs' failure is not one of physical ability (perhaps because this is what females are supposed to do well); rather, the rope breaks. Baffled by even this rudimentary mechanical problem (retying the rope), they opt for a game that is entirely non-competitive and non-active: telling knock-knock jokes.

Curiously, the ladybugs play this game by knocking their heads together, which is not the typical way that knock-knock jokes are told but perhaps appropriate to this silly song. Head knocking often signifies stupidity or ineptitude and is often signified by knocking the head with the knuckles. This would be the equivalent of calling someone a *blockhead* or *thick headed*. Perhaps this is the best way to portray this silly bunch of bugs. Their doltishness matches their clumsy ineptitude well.

We are not told why they quit the joke telling, but they very quickly retire to the campfire, around which they begin to "chatter away." Maybe "chattering" is just what they enjoy. This is, after all, the traditional female pastime *par excellence*, a communal version of the back-fence gossip, where the ladybugs reach the pinnacle of silliness. As their heads turn this way and that, their mouths are all going at once. We can't hear the chatter over the song lyrics, but it's just as well since none of them seems to be listening, either. Their inconsequential, meaningless, and unceasing talk or "chatter," as the lyrics label it, revolves around such trivia as "the high price of furniture and rugs," typical domestic-commodity concerns. Unfortunately, the bugs' chatter is soon to be interrupted by their campfire, which is steadily growing out of control. As the topic turns from furniture and rugs to the high price of "fire insurance for ladybugs," the fire threatens their circle. They all (finally!) stop talking and jump back away from the fire.

The topic of fire insurance is an important one for this group since, as the traditional nursery rhyme tells us ("Ladybug, ladybug, fly away home/Your house is on fire, and your children have flown"), house fires are common for ladybugs, frequently resulting in the loss of their children. Such criminal neglect—mothers away from home while the house burns and the children flee—is to be expected from bugs as silly as these ladies. It plays upon the deepest of a mother's fears: the loss or death of her children, especially in her absence or because of her neglect. Curious, then, that this endemic specter, filial loss, and the attendant guilt, should spill into discourse just as the ladybugs' campfire roars larger without their noticing. Most likely, they were distracted by their own chatter. Their discussion of their fear concerning a topic of unanimous import (understandable, given how often the disastrous nursery rhyme is recited to them), their consequent guilt and self-deprecation, and their difficulty in purchasing insurance for their families prevents them from attending to the fire, which then proceeds, as though on purpose, to break out of its appointed bounds.

Language itself, then, seems to be the culprit responsible for the fire. But not just any language. Specifically, the discourse of ladybugs when they are together, especially when this language turns to serious topics, is to blame. Perhaps, in fact, the nursery rhyme got its start because of this calamitous tendency of ladybugs to chatter among themselves, as they might at a picnic. Discourse as picnic chatter leads ladybugs to ignore their domestic responsibilities and brings about familial ruin. As though to remind them of the dangers of ladybug chatter, the campfire re-enacts the very concern that they begin to discuss. Just as they become engrossed in ladybug talk, the fire threatens to engulf them, overtaking their discursive space even as it signifies the danger of their inflammatory chatter. Like a fire that breaks out of its bounds, ladybug chatter can become dangerous when it goes on too long, even or especially when it turns to topics of serious concern to the ladies themselves. Chatter may turn to commiseration and commiseration to resolve. Like fire for ladybugs is women's talk for men: something to be always feared and controlled.

Unable to control the fire themselves, these ladybugs are fortunate to have a firefighter show up just in time. He pulls out his firehose and douses the fire. The ladybugs cheer, saved from destruction. With the fire out, the picnic is over, and the ladybugs can return to their homes.

Understanding Patriarchy

The task of cataloguing all video recordings that featured men or the relationships between men and women would be rather simple, since the deletions would be so few. The relationships that women share with each other probably have been overlooked more systematically than any other type of human relationship. What *Sesame Street* calls *silly* we might call *neglected, marginalized,* or *suppressed.* Films that do feature women's relationships with each other tend to do so along a very few lines. They compete with each other for a man, they share their attempts to win a man, or they are just silly. Women who attempt to build relationships outside the world of men typically either fail (as does the ladybugs' chatter) or die (as do Thelma and Louise).

The only masculine figure in this video is a dog dressed in a firefighter's hat and wielding a rather phallic-looking firehose. This unmarked dog might not be male, but the role the dog plays has been a traditionally male one. This dog controls fire. Like a modern Prometheus, the firefighting dog controls technology (such as fire trucks) as much as fire, representing exactly what it did for Hesiod, Aeschylus, and Shelley: the domination of nature, including human nature. Mary Shelley observed, in her retelling of the Prometheus myth, that technological, scientific control over human nature was the modern equivalent of controlling fire, the ultimate goal of man's Promethean desire. In "Ladybug Picnic," the control over human nature takes a gender-specific turn. As an insect, she is an embodiment of nature, but, by nature, she is female. Ladybugs thus physically coalesce what men always have desired to control the most: wilderness and women.

We then might read the growth of the fire as the assertion of male prerogatives for dominance over the other. In the ladybugs, this other is both nature and woman. As the firedog arrives, we see the fire as man's best friend, breaking up the ladybugs' chatter before it leads to anything serious and then responding obediently to the master's tool. By controlling fire, this dog symbolically controls the ladybugs as well, since bug and flame are connected with each other through the fire-centered discourse. Both fire and women are of great domestic use when kept under control at home, yet both become dangerously inflammatory when unleashed, as at this picnic. As a fire's heat aids its own spread, so women's chatter feeds off itself, becomes all consuming and dangerous.

Of course, boys and girls watching "Ladybug Picnic" don't know Prometheus and wouldn't be likely to see in ladybugs a symbolic conflation of nature and the female. In an apparently innocuous song, however, one that resists serious attention (by being *silly* and by calling attention to ladybugs as sheer numbers), the story can so boldly be told about women failing in competitive and physical activities, about women's inability to play together, about women's attempts to talk together outside the world of men, and about the consequences of such attempts. Curious, too, is that such an apparently silly song can be so doubly damning of women's talk. The ladybugs' chatter about fire insurance was itself engendered by a children's rhyme that reproduced for them the tragic consequences of their being away from home, yet their attempts to discuss this concern are themselves out-shouted by the roar of the growing fire. As their fear of fire pushed its way into discourse, the fire pushed the words back into their mouths and sent them back home. These ladybugs could not keep quiet yet could not speak. The panoptic fire guarded them.

The silly stories we tell recreate for us a reality, a reality into which we are forced to fit ourselves. As a nursery rhyme constructed the ladybugs' fire-fear for them, shaping their emotional reality, their insurance bills, and their discourse, just so we would have to suppose that this silly song could narrate itself into real lives of the children who watch the video on which it is featured. We would have to find it warning young girls about what is inappropriate for them (mechanical prowess and exclusive girl-talk about serious matters), while it conscripts young boys to their roles as fire-masters (even if they prefer chatter).

Feminist critiques of rhetorical artifacts are important as clues to the ways in which women and men have been shaped by the largely male language with which we speak and important to overcoming those often invisible shaping forces. This song alerts us to the powerful messages that shape our conceptions of gender—of what is appropriate and what isn't—and suggests that we begin to take very seriously indeed artifacts that are seen to be, or claim themselves to be, unserious, inconsequential, and silly. This is particularly true of the discourse about, by, and for children. Because children are most open to the messages they see and hear, children's books, songs, and television shows deserve our close attention, the better to understand the places at which gender constructions begin and the better to resist the confines that children's texts construct.

Hegemonic Masculinity on the Mound
Media Representations of Nolan Ryan and American Sports Culture
Nick Trujillo

Baseball pitcher Nolan Ryan, in his mid-forties, has become a national phenomenon. Although his major league baseball career spans over twenty-five years, he has received considerable publicity in the last few years following his seventh no-hitter in 1991, his 300th victory in 1990, and his 5,000th strikeout in 1989. With national endorsements for Advil, Bic, Nike, Wrangler Jeans, and Major League Baseball itself, he also has become a prominent sports celebrity. Sportswriters have called him "the ageless wonder," "a living legend," "miracle man," and "the last real sports hero."

This article examines print and television representations of Nolan Ryan as an illustration of how images of male athletes are reproduced in American culture. Specifically, I argue that the media have functioned hegemonically by personifying Ryan as an archetypal male athletic hero. In the next section, I present five distinguishing features of hegemonic masculinity and discuss the general role of mediated sport in reinforcing these features. Following this, the mass media's role in reproducing these features is analyzed.

Hegemonic Masculinity and American Sports Culture

As Connell (1990) defined it, *hegemonic masculinity* is "the culturally idealized form of masculine character" (p. 83) which emphasizes "the connecting of masculinity to toughness and competitiveness" as well as "the subordination of women" and "the marginalization of gay men" (p. 94). Connell argued that such an idealized form of masculinity becomes hegemonic when it is widely accepted in a culture and when

From *Critical Studies in Mass Communication*, 8 (September 1991), 290–308. Used by permission of the Speech Communication Association and the author.

that acceptance reinforces the dominant gender ideology of the culture. "Hegemonic masculinity," concluded Hanke (1990), "refers to the social ascendancy of a particular version or model of masculinity that, operating on the terrain of 'common sense' and conventional morality, defines 'what it means to be a man'" (p. 232).

Distinguishing Features of Hegemonic Masculinity

Media critics and scholars of gender ideology have described at least five features of hegemonic masculinity in American culture: (1) physical force and control, (2) occupational achievement, (3) familial patriarchy, (4) frontiersmanship, and (5) heterosexuality (see Brod, 1987; Connell, 1990; Jeffords, 1989; Kaufman, 1987; Kimmel, 1987a).

First, masculinity is hegemonic when power is defined in terms of physical force and control. According to Connell (1983), "force and competence are . . . translations into the language of the body of the social relations which define men as holders of power, women as subordinate [and] this is one of the main ways in which the superiority of men becomes 'naturalized'" (p. 28). In this way, the male body comes to represent power, and power itself is masculinized as physical strength, force, speed, control, toughness, and domination (Komisar, 1980; Messner, 1988, 1990).

Second, masculinity is hegemonic when it is defined through occupational achievement in an industrial capitalistic society (Ochberg, 1987; Tolson, 1977; Whyte, 1956). Work itself can become defined along gender lines. "Hegemony closely involves the division of labor," wrote Carrigan, Connell, and Lee (1987), "the social definition of tasks as either 'men's work' or 'women's work,' and the definition of some kinds of work as more masculine than others" (p. 94).

Third, masculinity is also hegemonic as patriarchy—"the manifestation and institutionalization of male dominance over women and children in the family and the extension of male dominance over women in society in general" (Lerner, 1986, p. 239). Traditionally, such patriarchal representations include males as "breadwinners," "family protectors," and "strong father figures" whereas females are "housewives," "sexual objects," and "nurturing mothers." In fact, Segal (1990) argued that modern representations of the so-called "sensitive father" have remained hegemonic insofar as "the contemporary revalorization of fatherhood has enabled many men to have the best of both worlds" because "they are more involved in what was once the exclusive domain of women but, especially in relation to children, they are sharing its pleasures more than its pains" (p. 58). (See also Hearn, 1987; Pleck, 1987).

Fourth, masculinity is hegemonic as symbolized by the daring, romantic frontiersman of yesteryear and of the present-day outdoorsman. Frederick Jackson Turner's so-called "frontier thesis" (Berquist, 1971; Billington, 1971; Carpenter, 1977) argues that the general U.S. image is so defined. In this context, the *cowboy* stands very tall as an archetypal image reproduced and exploited in literature, film and advertising (Cawelti, 1976; Kimmel, 1987b; Maynard, 1974; Rushing, 1983). As reconstructed in media representations of the western genre, the cowboy is a *white* male with working-class values (see Wright, 1975).

Finally, masculinity is hegemonic when heterosexually defined. Rubin (1985) refers to the "sex hierarchy" and predictably, the type of sexuality that rules "is 'good', 'normal', and 'natural' " . . . "heterosexual, marital, monogamous, reproductive, and non-commercial" (p. 280). Thus, hegemonic *male* sexuality "embodies personal characteristics [which] are manifest by adult males through exclusively social relationships with men and primarily sexual relationships with women" and it "requires not being effeminate (a 'sissy') in physical appearance or mannerisms; not having relationships with men that are sexual or overly intimate; and not failing in sexual relationships with women" (Herek, 1987, pp. 72–73).

Symbolism of male sexuality has received considerable attention from media critics (see Duncan, 1990; Dyer, 1985; Fiske, 1987; Segal, 1990) and not surprisingly, much of this symbolism is thought to center on the penis as "the symbol of male potency . . . that appears to legitimate male power" (Dyer, 1985, p. 31). As Fiske (1987) argued, "the phallus is a cultural construct: it bears a culture's meanings of masculinity and attempts to naturalize them by locating them in the physical sign of maleness—the penis" (p. 210).

Mediated Sport and Hegemonic Masculinity

Perhaps no single institution in American culture has influenced our sense of masculinity more than sport. Throughout our history, dominant groups have successfully persuaded many Americans to believe that sport builds manly character, develops physical fitness, realizes order, promotes justice, and even prepares young men for war (see Dubbert, 1979). More recently, American football's hostile takeover of the more pastoral baseball as our "national pastime" has reinforced a form of masculinity which emphasizes sanctioned aggression, (para)militarism, the technology of violence, and other patriarchal values (Real, 1975; Real, 1989). The corporatization of sports also has provided far more opportunities for male participants than for female participants and has placed far more emphasis on marginalizing women as cheerleaders, spectators, and advertising images. Indeed, Naison's (1972) conclusion twenty years ago still applies: "as long as the social relations of contemporary capitalism generate a need for violent outlets and a vicarious experience of mastery in American men, the corporations will be glad to finance the sports industry and mold it in their own image" (p. 115).

The mass media, as key benefactors of institutionalized sports (see Jhally, 1989), have thus been a powerful site for fashioning hegemony. "Sports tend to be presented in the media," wrote Hargreaves (1982), "as symbolic representations of a particular kind of social order, so that in effect they become modern morality plays, serving to justify and uphold dominant values and ideas" (p. 128). For example, scholars have demonstrated that mediated sports reaffirm mainstream values such as teamwork, competition, individualism, nationalism, achievement, and others (see Duncan, 1983; Real, 1989; Trujillo & Ekdom, 1985).

Media representations of sport reproduce and reaffirm the features of hegemonic masculinity described earlier in important ways. Media representations of sport privilege these features of masculinity when they emphasize these features or link them positively with cultural values and when they ignore and/or condemn alternative features of opposing gender ideologies on preferences such as feminism or homosexuality (see Bennett, Whitaker, Woolley Smith & Sablove, 1987; Bryson, 1987). Media representations of sport naturalize hegemonic masculinity when they depict its features as conventional or acceptable and depict alternatives to it as unconventional or deviant (see Nelson, 1980; Wernick, 1987; Whitson, 1990). Finally, media representations of sport personalize hegemonic masculinity when they elevate individuals who embody its features as role models or heroes worthy of adoration and emulation and when they castigate individuals who do not (see Hargreaves, 1982, 1986). "To be culturally exalted, the pattern of masculinity must have exemplars who are celebrated as heroes" (Connell, 1990, p. 94). In Texas Ranger pitcher Nolan Ryan, the mass media have found an exemplar to celebrate as a hero and they have reinforced hegemonic masculinity through him in several ways.

Reproducing Hegemonic Masculinity Through Nolan Ryan

Nolan Ryan's major league baseball career has spanned over 25 years as he has played for the New York Mets (1966–1971), the California Angels (1972–1979), the Houston Astros (1980–1988), and the Texas

Rangers (1989–present). Although Ryan was publicized throughout his career, he became a mediated hero and celebrity in recent years; he also has become a striking image of American masculinity as well.

This analysis is based on an examination of over 250 articles in popular print media including newspapers (e.g., *The New York Times*, *Los Angeles Times*, *The Houston Post*, *The Dallas Morning News*, and others) and magazines (general ones such as *Life*, *Time*, and *Gentlemen's Quarterly*, and sports-oriented ones such as *Sport*, *Sports Illustrated*, and *The Sporting News*). The dates of these print materials span the period from 1965, the year before Ryan made his major league debut with the Mets, to 1991, the year Ryan pitched his seventh no-hitter at the age of forty-four. I also examined over 100 local (Dallas, Texas) and national television news reports, videotaped during the time Ryan first signed with the Texas Rangers until the summer of 1990. Finally, I examined over 30 print and television advertisements featuring Ryan, most of which appeared in the last few years.

Pitching with Power:
Ryan as the Embodiment of Male Athleticism

Media representations of Nolan Ryan have reaffirmed the power of the male body. Throughout his career, Ryan has been described as a "power pitcher." Early media coverage during Ryan's career with the Mets focused on his unique ability to throw the ball with force. *The New York Times* characterized him as "the rookie pitcher with the cannonball serve" (Durso, 1968, p. 24) while *The Sporting News* labeled him the "Texas flame-thrower" (Lang, 1968, p. 26). A *Life* magazine article revealed that Ryan had "a fast ball that has been described as faster than Bob Feller's (98.6 mph)—the fastest ever timed" ("Brine for Nolan Ryan," 1968, p. 78). These early articles suggest that Ryan embodied the *force* of male athletic power.

However, although Ryan had the force, he did not have control. [See Connell's (1983) distinction.] He was described in *The New York Times* as the "tall, slim Texan . . . who has not yet mastered control and consistency" ("These are the Mets," 1969, p. 57) and "as wild as the spinning Black Dragon ride at Astroworld" (Chass, 1970, p. 59). Reporters presented this lack of control as a challenge to Ryan's athletic success. If Ryan could not control his ability, his "heat" would be just a "flash in the pan" and he would fail as many fastball pitchers had failed before him.

Ryan, though, would not achieve success with the Mets. On December 10, 1971, he was traded to the California Angels. In a *Los Angeles Times* report, Angel general manager Harry Dalton used synecdoche to emphasize Ryan's promise: "We've obtained the best arm in the National League and one of the best in baseball. We know Ryan has had control problems, but at 24 he may be ready to come into his own" (Newhan, 1971, p. 3, part III). At this point, Ryan was disembodied power; he was "the best arm" in baseball who might develop into someone complete.

With the Angels, Ryan developed enough control to win and set several pitching records. With success, his status as power pitcher was embellished by the sports media. One feature in *Sports Illustrated* documented that a group of Rockwell scientists timed his pitches during a game at speeds of 100.8 and 100.9 miles per hour, the fastest pitches *ever* recorded (Fimrite, 1974). His dominance over batters was ritualized in sportspage cliches, as when power-hitter Reggie Jackson said this about Ryan: "He's faster than instant coffee. He's faster than a speeding bullet and more powerful than a locomotive. He throws wall-to-wall heat" (Newhan, 1972, p. 1, part III). And stories about Ryan's power took on a mythological significance as well, as when a feature in *The Saturday Evening Post*, titled "Nolan Ryan: Whoosh!" made a direct case: "All the while he was leaving a trail of incidents that formed a legend—or myth. The day he tried out with the Mets before signing, his fastball broke through the hands of catcher John Stephenson and broke his collarbone. At Williamsport, Pennsylvania, he bounced a warmup pitch in front of the plate and gave catcher Duffy Dyer a concussion. Not with a fastball, but with a changeup" (Jacobson, 1974, p. 16). Ryan's power—manifested in his force and, in part, in his ability to hurt people—was celebrated as baseball mythology.

In his later years with the Astros and Rangers, Ryan still was portrayed as a fast, power pitcher. One feature in *Gentlemen's Quarterly* put it this way: Ryan "is grateful he can remain true to his singular purpose, which is to rear back, show his numbers and throw a baseball that becomes, in its flight, the approximate size of a ball bearing" (Hoffer, 1988, p. 292).

With age also came media reconstructions of other features of Ryan's masculinity. One article in *The Dallas Morning News*, titled "Pitching with pain not new to Ryan," told readers that Ryan had pitched his sixth no-hitter with a stress fracture in his back but that because of his "will power" he was able to "block it out" (Fraley, 1990, p. 6B). A feature in *Sport* magazine even reconstructed his toughness as a child, quoting his mother: "'I remember when we first came to Alvin, this young wife, a friend of ours, kept pestering me to take Nolan to the doctor,' says his mother, 'because he didn't cry enough'" (Furlong, 1980, p. 68).

Although he came to be portrayed as a complete pitcher, some writers continued to disembody his power. Features in *Gentlemen's Quarterly* (Hoffer, 1988) and *Life* (Brewster, 1989) presented photographs of Ryan's disembodied right arm; in the former feature, past Dodger pitcher Don

Sutton described Ryan's arm as a weapon, as "a howitzer" (Hoffer, 1988, p. 292). Correspondent Dick Schaap concluded his *ABC Evening News* report about Ryan's 5,000th strikeout on August 23, 1989 by providing the length of the appendage: "Nolan Ryan's arm is 35 inches long. It will fit perfectly in the Hall of Fame." An article in the *New York Post* noted that Ryan was "blessed with the most remarkable arm in the history of the game" but it cut off his legs as well: "Ryan has a pair of treetrunk legs that supply a great deal of the power behind his fastball" (Hecht, 1983, p. 102). Even in the end, the force—the essence—of Ryan's power remained disembodied.

Pitching Records and Pitching Products: Ryan as Capitalist Worker

If sport and work independently play a role in producing hegemonic masculinity as some have suggested (Fiske, 1987), then the construction of sport as *work* is even more powerful. The mass media represent sport as work in at least three ways. First, mediated sport reaffirms the Protestant work ethic. "Athletes," wrote Sadler (1976), "often are aware that what they do is not play. Their practice sessions are workouts; and to win the game they have to work harder" (p. 245). Second, as in American society, there is in sport an overemphasis on success as occupational achievement, defined (and quantified) in terms of team victories and individual records. If "achievement and successful performance (the primary definers of masculinity) are the fundamental requirements of capitalism," as Fiske (1987, p. 210) argued, then sport is a key arena for displaying exemplars of successful and unsuccessful men in a capitalist society. Finally, sport is commodified inasmuch as leagues, teams, and individual athletes are sold as commodities in a competitive marketplace (see Brohm, 1978; Jhally, 1989; Rigauer, 1981).

Media coverage of Nolan Ryan has reinforced all of these features and, as such, he has been reproduced as a successful male worker in an industrial capitalist society. First, Ryan's work ethic has been exalted throughout his career. When he enjoyed early success with the Angels, one *Sports Illustrated* story quoted former player and then coach, John Roseboro, as saying: "There is no pitcher in baseball today who is in better shape than Nolan Ryan. He knows what work is, and he works" (Leggett, 1973, p. 27). Then, as he continued to achieve success as a power pitcher in his later years, his work ethic was reified in vivid detail when publications such as *Newsweek* and *The Dallas Morning News* printed his entire "rigid workout routine" (see Givens, 1989; Ringolsby, 1990). Ryan's commitment to this workout was described as so regimented that a *USA Today* reporter wrote that even after throwing his sixth no-hitter, "Ryan was riding the stationary bicycle in the middle of the Rangers' clubhouse" as "his teammates were either fastening their ties, drinking another beer or driving back to the hotel. . . . 'You don't deviate from your routine,' he said" (Shea, 1990, p. 8C).

Second, Ryan's success has been quantified in records of individual achievement. The Texas Rangers 1991 Media Guide states that Ryan has set or tied 48 major league records (see Texas Rangers, 1991, pp. 71–91). Most of these records involve two categories of athletic dominance: no-hitters and strikeouts.

The no-hitter is one of the most dominating forms of pitching performance over athletic opponents. Ryan achieved his record seventh no-hitter in 1991 at the age of 44; Sandy Koufax is second on the list with four. Ryan's no-hitters were celebrated in media accounts and, with each one, the lore of previous no-hitters grew in significance. One sportswriter for *The New York Times* retold the story of his second no-hitter—against the Tigers in 1973—on the occasion of his fourth one—against the Orioles in 1975: "With two outs in the ninth, Norm Cash of the Detroit Tigers strolled up to the plate in surrender. Instead of a bat, he was carrying a broken-off piano leg. He even got into the batter's box with it before glancing back at Ron Luciano, the umpire" (Anderson, 1975, p. 39). Through coverage of Ryan's no-hitters, the media defined complete dominance over others as ultimate occupational success.

Ryan's strikeout achievements also were praised as records of dominance, especially his record 5,000th strikeout on August 21, 1989 against Rickie Henderson of the Oakland Athletics. Stories about this milestone appeared on national news broadcasts and in major daily newspapers across the country while Texas papers published separate sections with stories, color posters, and "K" sign inserts; *Sports Illustrated* even ran a complete list of Ryan's 1,061 separate strikeout victims ("K," 1989). Reporters used testimony from baseball luminaries as well as unknown fans in attendance to corroborate the historic nature of the 5,000th strikeout; for example, the front page of the *Dallas Times Herald* quoted a nine-year-old boy who said "I'll probably tell my grandchildren it was the most exciting thing that ever happened in my life" (Henderson, 1989, p. A-1). A report in the *Fort Worth Star-Telegram* indicated that President Bush, father of Ranger owner George W. Bush, watched the game on television and it published the full text of Bush's brief epideictic address which was played on the ballpark's Diamond Vision screen after the milestone strikeout (and which represented state support of Ryan's domination): "Congratulations Nolan Ryan. What an amazing achievement. Indeed, everybody that loves baseball pays tribute to you on this very special record-breaking occasion. Well done, my friend. Well done, my noble friend" ("President's Message," 1989, p. 6, section 3).

Although all of Ryan's milestone achievements of domination were exalted, some sportswriters still charged that he was mediocre in terms of the occupational bottom line—the won-loss column. For example, Ryan's career record after the 1979 season with the Angels was 167–159; when Ryan became a free agent that year after he and Angel general manager Buzzi Bavasi failed to agree on a new contract, Bavasi told *Los Angeles Times* reporters that he could replace Ryan "with two 8–7 pitchers," a sarcastic reference to Ryan's 16–14 record in 1979 (Littwin, 1980, p. 1, part III); in the same article, the reporter himself critiqued Ryan with the statement, "He's won numerous battles but he keeps losing the war" (Littwin, 1980, p. 1, part III).

In fact, ultimate occupational achievement eluded Ryan until late in his career when, on July 31, 1990, at age 43, he won his 300th game, becoming only the 20th pitcher in history to do so. The Associated Press story on Ryan's victory over the Milwaukee Brewers began with this lead: "Nolan Ryan, a pitcher defined by great numbers, finally got the number that defines great pitchers" (see "No. 300," 1990, p. E1). A reporter for *The Dallas Morning News*, commenting on Ryan's critics, wrote that "No. 300 cuts their vocal chords" (Horn, 1990, p. 2H); a columnist for the same newspaper wrote that Ryan's 300th win "represents a triumphant and unarguable validation of the man and his heroic career" (Casstevens, 1990, p. 2B); another columnist for the same newspaper went even further: "God is good. But Nolan Ryan may be better" (Galloway, 1990b, p. 1B). His status as a successful male achiever at last was confirmed. Even so, Ryan's life-long quest for success epitomized the paradox of masculinity in a capitalist society that Fiske (1987) described when he wrote that "men are cast into ceaseless work and action to prove their worth" such that "masculinity becomes almost a definition of the superhuman, so it becomes that which can never [at least rarely] be achieved" (p. 210).

Finally, Ryan has been represented as a valuable commodity with instrumental impacts on his teams. A *Sports Illustrated* feature on Ryan called him "an Angel who makes turnstiles sing" (Leggett, 1973, p. 26).[1] Yankee-owner George Steinbrenner, quoted in *Sports Illustrated*, called Ryan "one of the most desirable quantities in baseball" (Keith, 1979, p. 34). Reporters then bragged for Ryan when he signed with the Astros as the first million dollar free agent to become "not only the best-paid player in the history of baseball but one of the best paid players in the history of team sports"—at least in 1980 (Furlong, 1980, p. 66).

Reporters bragged for Ryan and his earning power in part because they represented him as a humble, honest man who was not preoccupied with money, unlike many other athletes who have been depicted as greedy, selfish men. One article in *The Sporting News*, titled "Ryan raps pay preoccupation," quoted Ryan, who then was making $125,000, as saying that he had "never seen a ballplayer worth even $250,000" and that he himself was "not bugged over money" because "I feel I have all I can do to keep my mind on conditioning and on pitching" (Durslag, 1976, p. 12). Years later when the Rangers exercised their option to keep Ryan for the 1990 season at an under-market-value of $1.4 million, reporters commended Ryan's refusal to renegotiate as other athletes would have done; as he was quoted in one newspaper report: "That signature on your contract is the same as your word" (Galloway, 1990a, p. 1B). Reporters also reinforced Ryan's commodification of himself as an endorser and entrepreneur when they wrote that he was "a good spokesman" because "he uses the products he talks about" (Baldwin, 1990, p. 1A) and that he was a smart businessman who recently bought a bank and then "sat in on loan meetings" and "formulated bank policy" (Montville, 1991, p. 124).

In sum, as the media juxtaposed Ryan's values of hard work and modesty with his achievements and his earning power, they reaffirmed his identity as a successful businessman and reinforced the Protestant Ethic and system of American capitalism itself. Ryan has been represented as one who proves the system does work, at least for hard-working men.

Father Throws Best:
Ryan as Family Patriarch

The media have reaffirmed hegemonic representations of male-female relations in the family as they have described the relationship between, and respective roles of, Nolan and Ruth Ryan. Predictably, the media chose to present Nolan as the breadwinner. One story in *The Saturday Evening Post* told of the struggles of Nolan early in his career to support the family: "The first year they were married [in 1967], Nolan made $1,200 a month for six months and worked in an air-conditioning shop the other six" (Jacobson, 1974, p. 124). Ryan also has been portrayed as the protecting husband; one reporter for the *New York Daily News* even reconstructed the Mets' trade that sent Ryan to California as motivated by the "fact" that "Ryan personally requested a trade because—says a Mets insider—he feared for the safety of his lovely wife in New York" (Lang, 1984, p. C26).

In contrast, reporters have chosen to cast Ruth Ryan as the attractive woman *behind* the man. Reporters wrote that Ruth chose not to (or failed to) develop her own career interests; one article in *The Dallas Morning News* quoted Ruth's own admission: "I tried to go to college. I tried to keep up with my tennis and my ballet at first. . . . Some of the other wives I knew in baseball tried, but it just didn't work" (Harasta, 1990, p. 17H). Reporters objectified her as the beautiful wife. Finally, reporters wrote that Ruth has experienced satisfaction through Nolan's pitching; one columnist for The Houston Post also suggested that she would be lost without Nolan's baseball: "'At times I get really tired of the hectic pace,' Ruth admits. 'Then I think about how much I would miss it, if he retired, and what I would do when spring training rolls around'" (Herskowitz, 1990, p. B-15).

In these ways, the media reaffirmed the gender-based divisions of labor in the traditional American family through Nolan and Ruth Ryan and they naturalized this division of labor by presenting Nolan and Ruth as the ideal couple. "After 23 years, the man is still married to his high school sweetheart," confirmed a Sports Illustrated reporter, who then spoke for them when he wrote: "The idea of staying married never came to debate. Why not? Isn't that what you're supposed to do? The idea of raising a family was ingrained. Wasn't that what our parents did?" (Montville, 1991, p. 128).

Additionally, the media reaffirmed the hegemony of family patriarchy by glorifying Nolan's role as actual and symbolic father. The media have emphasized Ryan's relationships with his two sons while they have deemphasized his relationship with his daughter. Dallas station KTVT's live television coverage of Ryan's sixth no-hitter against Oakland on June 11, 1990 focused in as the youngest son Reese, in a little Ranger uniform, sat next to Nolan in the dugout, rubbing his dad's back, which, as later was reported, had a stress fracture. During the 1991 pre-season, Ryan pitched against his eldest son Reid, who then was a freshman for the University of Texas, in an exhibition game. One article in the sportspages of Austin American-Statesman, subtitled "Father throws best," noted that "mom Ruth threw out the ceremonial first pitch, her 'nervous fastball'" (Wangrin, 1991, p. C7); however, another article on the front page of the same newspaper deified father Nolan's relationship with his eldest son: "The serious baseball crowd sat huddled against an intermittent evening breeze, watching father and son, concentrating, straining to see if they could detect the signs of greatness passing from the right hand of the father to that of his son" (Johnson, 1991, p. A12).

Ryan also has been represented as the symbolic father. "Ryan is providing stability and quiet leadership" to the "young, home-produced talent" of the Angels, wrote one reporter in Newsweek (Axthelm, 1975, p. 59). Years later, a report in Time extended the father metaphor more specifically: "His second family is the Ranger teammates, who mobbed him after the [sixth] no-hitter. Because some of them were barely in Pampers when Ryan first pitched for the Mets in 1966, the scene also suggested a Father's Day celebration—a bunch of baseball's children swarming around the grandest old man in the game" (Corliss, 1990, p. 68). One *Sports Illustrated* feature revealed that former Astro teammate Harry Spilman "is one of 10 current or former teammates who have named a son after Nolan" (Montville, 1991, p. 127); on Father's Day (June 16), 1991, ESPN "SportsCenter" aired a report which offered video proof of these little Ryans. In these and other ways, the media have reproduced Nolan Ryan as the archetypal husband and father and, in so doing, they have reaffirmed the hegemony of patriarchy.

Castrating Steers in the Off-Season: Ryan as Baseball Cowboy

Throughout his career, Nolan Ryan has been portrayed as a rural cowboy who symbolizes the frontiersmen of American history. According to many reports, he grew up and still lives in rural Alvin, Texas (Jacobson, 1974; Montville, 1991). One feature in the society pages of *The Dallas Morning News* regaled viewers with Ryan's predictable favorites: his favorite music ("country-western"), his personal transportation ("a pickup"), and his hero ("John Wayne") (Jennings, 1989, p. 2E).

Given Ryan's rural Texas roots, the mythic West gave reporters grist for coverage and colorization. The day that Ryan had his first match-up against fastball pitcher and native Texan Roger Clemens of the Boston Red Sox on April 30, 1991, a CNN "SportsNight" sportscaster described the game in his aired report as "the Shootout at the O.K. Corral in the lone star state" where "a native Texan who had taken his blazing arm to New England" was "back in town to face the fastest draw the game has ever known, also a native son." The night that Ryan achieved his seventh no-hitter on May 1, 1991, an ESPN sportscaster described Ryan in this way in his aired report: "He's John Wayne." Of course, as a recent *Sports Illustrated* feature quoted Ryan's longtime friend and business partner, "in Texas he is bigger than John Wayne right now" (Montville, 1991, p. 124).

Advertisers, too, have cashed in on the Western motif. One advertisement for Wrangler Jeans pictures Ryan on the mound, holding a baseball in his right hand and wearing a baseball glove on his left hand, but he is wearing a cowboy hat and Wrangler Jeans; the caption reads: "A Western original wears a Western original" (*Dallas Times Herald*, August 23, 1989, p. C10).

However, Ryan is not merely a metaphorical cowboy for stories and advertising: he has been described as a "real cowboy" who owns and works three cattle ranches with hundreds of registered "Beefmaster" cattle. "Ryan is no gentleman rancher," wrote one reporter in a *Sports*

Illustrated feature, accompanied by several pictures of Ryan riding horseback on his ranch. "In the off-season, he's on horseback, riding herd, 'getting kicked, stomped, and hooked'" (Fimrite, 1986, p. 92). His ranch manager gave more impressive testimony in another *Sports Illustrated* feature, again accompanied by color photos of Ryan in chaps and on horseback: "He helps us castrate the steers, dehorn 'em, everything. Nothing fazes him. I'll see him reach into the chute with that million dollar right arm and I'll say to myself, 'Are you sure you want to do that?' But he'll never buckle" (Montville, 1991, p. 124).

Reporters have used Ryan's status as real and metaphorical cowboy to represent his commitment to several mainstream values of rural America. Unlike another image of the cowboy who, as Kimmel (1987b) wrote, "must move on, . . . unhampered by clinging women and whining children" (p. 239), Ryan has been the devoted husband and father, as described in the last section. Representations of his toughness, his hard work ethic, and his fairness also were described earlier. In addition, reporters have written that he is *unassuming*: "As we say in Texas, he is as common as dirt," said his high school principal in a *USA Today* article (Tom, 1985, p. 2C). They have written that he is *loyal*: "Has anyone ever heard him knock a manager, a teammate, an owner, anyone?" asked a columnist from *The Houston Post* (Herskowitz, 1988, p. C-1). And they have written that he is *wholesome*: After his fourth no-hitter, a reporter for the *Los Angeles Times* revealed that "Ryan, who seldom drinks, turned down a glass [of champagne] and said he would celebrate by taking Ruth out for a quiet dinner" (Newhan, 1975, p. 6, part III). In a rare sports-related editorial, *The Dallas Morning News* published this tribute the day of Ryan's 5,000th strikeout:

> Unfortunately, in these times of pill poppers and gamblers, the private lives of too many ballplayers in all sports are hardly fit for prime time. A towering exception is Mr. Ryan. From work habits that have kept his middle-aged muscles fighting trim, to a clean-cut personal life straight out of the rural Texas he loves, Mr. Ryan is a hero for all ages ("Striking example," 1989, p. 14A).

In short, Ryan has been reproduced as the American hero who embodies the values of our frontier past. This reproduction may perform a bardic function by giving these idealized values a manifest form (Fiske & Hartley, 1978) and may perform a compensatory function by helping audiences compensate "for the passing of the traditional dream of success" (Rader, 1983, p. 11).

Finally, the rural cowboy of our frontier past usually is presented as a *white* male. Ryan's identity as a white male athlete was reaffirmed in a powerful, if indirect, way on the recent occasion of his seventh no-hitter on May 1, 1991. Earlier that day, Rickie Henderson of the Oakland

Athletics broke Lou Brock's record for career stolen bases. Henderson, who epitomizes the "cool pose" of the inner-city black athlete (see Majors, 1986) with his brash, display-oriented demeanor, pumped his fists above his head and, as play was interrupted, told the crowd over a microphone: "Lou Brock was a symbol of great basestealing. But today, I am the greatest of all time" ("A day when," 1991, p. 6).

Later that same night, Ryan achieved his seventh no-hitter then told reporters: "This no-hitter is the most rewarding because it was in front of these hometown fans who have supported me since I have been here. This one was for them" ("A day when," 1991, p. 6).

In the days following these two milestones, sportswriters—most of whom are middle-class, white men (see Edwards, 1976; Johnston, 1979; McCleneghan, 1990)—focused their attention on how the two star athletes handled their achievements (see Bodley, 1991; Boswell, 1991; Lopresti, 1991). The Sporting News presented the most revealing critique in an editorial ("A day when," 1991). "Too bad Henderson couldn't have handled his moment of renown with similar decorum," read the editorial. "It was a day when Henderson and Ryan displayed two forms of speed, but only one man exhibited class" (p. 6). Although writers of this editorial and of the other stories did not ever mention the race of the two athletes and probably did not intend such metacommentary, they presented an implicit reaffirmation that the hegemonic masculinity embodied by Ryan's white, rural, mainstream values is preferable to the masculinity represented by the counterculture "cool pose" of the black, inner-city athlete. Simply stated, when white reporters exalt white athletes and castigate black athletes, they reinforce racial hegemony whether they intend to or not.

Wearing Balls in His Holster: Ryan as a (Hetero)sexual Being

In general, "sport," Segal (1990) argued, "provides the commonest contemporary source of male imagery" inasmuch as "the acceptable male image suggests—in its body's pose, its clothes and general paraphernalia—muscles, hardness, action" (p. 89). In particular, Nolan Ryan has been reproduced as an acceptable image of male sexuality.

Throughout his career, some sports reporters have commented directly on Ryan's physical attractiveness. Early in Ryan's career, sportswriter Ron Fimrite of Sports Illustrated described him in this way: "Ryan is tall, slender, deceptively strong, and certainly one of the handsomest men in sports—a natural born hero" (1974, p. 100). One year later, Fimrite (1975) was even more specific: "Ryan wears his hair short and neatly trimmed and is a tidy, unflashy dresser, unlike the many peacocks in modern sports. He is an uncommonly handsome young man with near-perfect features and a long, lean physique. With his good looks, lanky build and Texas drawl, he would seem a natural for Western roles in Hollywood" (p. 36). Ten years later, the same writer included Ryan's high school picture with the caption: "Most Handsome Senior" (Fimrite, 1986, p. 94). In these descriptions and images, this white, middle-aged sportswriter directly reaffirmed an image of hegemonic male sexuality, positioning it against other nontraditional images of male sexuality embodied by flashier sports "peacocks."

Dave Anderson (1978), another white, middle-aged sportswriter, disclosed this telling revelation when he described Ryan's unnoticed appearance at a restaurant early in his career with the Angels: "'Table for Ryan,' he told the hostess. 'Oh, yes, Mr. Ryan,' the hostess, a young brunette, replied with hardly a glance at the man who is surely one of the most handsome in baseball. 'Right this way, please.' The waitress, a young blonde, did not seem to recognize him either. Neither did anybody at the other tables, not even any of the dozen teenage girls enjoying a birthday party" (1978, p. 69).

In this example, the white, middle-aged sportswriter presented a preferred image of male sexuality; however, he revealed unwittingly that the preference was *his own*. Ryan's physical attractiveness is seen *only* by this male sportswriter, not by the young blonde or brunette women or by the teenage girls.

The homoerotic (and narcissistic) implications of these examples notwithstanding, it is unusual for male sportswriters to comment directly on the physical attractiveness of most male athletes (though they often comment on the attractiveness of many female athletes; see Duncan, 1990). However, in his representation as a wholesome, monogamous, heterosexual, white man, Ryan serves as an acceptable sexual image whose physical attractiveness can be discussed by white male reporters without much risk. Stated differently, Nolan Ryan is a *safe sex symbol*, one that is much safer for white male sportswriters to comment on directly than are white playboys, black beasts, gay blades, and other alternative images (see Hoch, 1979; Segal, 1990).

As they are wont to do, advertisers have capitalized on Ryan's image of safe sexuality. Some print and television advertisements, including those for Advil, Duracell Batteries, Southwest Airlines, Starter Apparel, and Whataburger, are relatively asexual insofar as they simply show Ryan in his baseball uniform and make reference to his status and athleticism as a major league pitcher. However, other advertisements seem more sexual in their orientation. For example, Ryan wore a fine tailored suit in the BizMart print advertisements (see Baldwin, 1990), while he wore a *tuxedo* in the Bic network television advertisements. In the Wrangler Jeans print advertisements, he wears tight-fitting jeans, a cowboy shirt, a cowboy hat, and cowboy boots. Most strikingly, a recent print advertisement for Nike Air in *Sports Illustrated* presents a close-up of Ryan's face and pitching hand, but the top of his balding head is cut out of the picture and his face and hands are moistened so that they glisten in the sepia tones used to color the image. Although these and other images are not overtly sexual, they do reveal the choices that advertisers have made in an effort to exploit Ryan's physical appearance to sell their products.

Perhaps the most intriguing use of sexual imagery can be found in a poster, titled "Texas Ranger," distributed by Nike (see MacCormack, 1989). The poster shows Ryan standing in the middle of a dirt street on a Western set: a saddled horse is behind him on his right and a wooden derrick for a water or oil well is behind him on his left, near a sign which reads "Pride, Texas." Ryan is dressed in a white Ranger baseball uniform and his feet are safely on a pitching "rubber." However, Ryan is wearing a long leather overcoat over his uniform and instead of a baseball cap, he is wearing a cowboy hat. Most impressively, Ryan is wearing a holster below his baseball uniform belt; but instead of wearing guns in this holster, he is wearing baseballs, one on each side, though they are not quite symmetrically hung.

For those who are inclined to interpret phallic symbolism, Ryan's "Texas Ranger" poster is fertile with possibilities. Some could interpret the long derrick at Ryan's left, placed next to the "Pride, Texas" sign, as a fairly obvious phallic symbol. Others might see Ryan's hat, especially the longer cowboy hat, as another. Others could see the not-quite symmetrical baseballs placed in Ryan's holster as symbolic of testicles. Conspicuously absent from the holster is the gun, another phallic symbol, or "penile extender" as Fiske (1987, p. 210) called it (see also Dyer, 1985; Shadoian, 1977). But with a (base)ball on each side of his body and a rounded tip on the top of his head, the image is striking, even to those not seduced by psychoanalytic theory. Ryan is the gun; Ryan is the phallus.

"The promise of phallic power," argued Segal (1990), "is precisely this guarantee of total inner coherence, of an unbroken and unbreakable, an unquestioned and unquestionable masculinity" (p. 102). Ryan is the hard phallus, conditioned by years of rigorous exercise. He is a true phallus offered only to one woman, his beautiful and devoted wife. Perhaps most importantly, he is the middle-aged phallus with the power still to explode. As another Wrangler Jeans advertisement put it: "300 wins and he still hasn't lost the crease [or, by extension, the bulge] in his jeans" (*The Dallas Morning News*, August 2, 1990, p. 18H). No small wonder that on the day after Ryan threw his sixth no-hitter at age 43,

USA Today ran the front-page headline, "Great Day to Be 43," and celebrated the fact that "nearly 4 million 43-year-olds woke up feeling young" (see Greene, 1990).

In the final analysis, Nolan Ryan represents a white, middle-aged, upper-class, banker-athlete, with working-class cowboy values, who was raised by a middle-class family in a small rural town, and who is a strong father and devoted heterosexual husband. For white, middle-aged, middle-class, beer-drinking scribes interested in maintaining hegemonic masculinity, at least in mediated sports, it doesn't get any better than this.

Concluding Remarks

In professional sport, some challenges have been made to the dominant image of masculinity, e.g., women's sports (especially women's tennis), the public presentation of gays and lesbians, e.g., tennis star Martina Navratilova and umpire Dave Pallone (Pallone, 1990), and charges of racism in sport such as those by former baseball star Henry Aaron (Aaron, 1991). In addition, we have witnessed the demise of the homogeneous mass audience in recent decades and the rise of a fragmented audience composed of heterogenous groups with diverse values and media consumption habits. To the extent that hegemonic masculinity in sport and in other arenas of society continues to be contested by various groups, and to the extent that these various groups continue to constitute fragmented audiences, media critics should study the attempts made in reporting, broadcasting, and advertising to maintain hegemony.

The study of mediated sport should not be taken lightly as a category of academic trivial pursuit. As Bryson (1987) argued, feminists who ignore sport do so at their own peril because "sport is a powerful institution through which male hegemony is constructed and reconstructed and it is only through understanding and confronting these processes that we can hope to break this domination" (p. 349); in fact, Bryson went so far as to say that "sport needs to be analyzed along with rape, pornography, and domestic violence as one of the means through which men monopolize physical force" (p. 357).

Hegemonic masculinity in mediated sport also has negative consequences for men which should be analyzed and critiqued. As Sabo and Runfola (1980) advised, "in a world sadly consistent with the Hobbesian legacy, sports encourage men to forever compete with one another, never trusting and never feeling, and to regard women as frail underlings who are far removed from the panoply of patriarchical pugnacity and privilege" (pp. 334–335). Critics should continue to examine how the mass media aid in reproducing these and other values.

Notes

[1]The media reported that Ryan generated additional revenues for baseball-related businesses inside and outside the stadium as well. To take a few reported examples the day after Ryan's 5,000th strikeout: ARA Services, the company which runs concessions at Arlington Stadium, was said to have sold a record 6,000 commemorative shirts at $15 each; scalpers were getting several hundred dollars for unauthorized ticket sales; and the value of his rookie baseball card went from $225 to $450 in one day (Tomaso, 1989). In a more recent report, Ryan's rookie card was said to have been auctioned off for $5,000 ("Ryan Rookie Card," 1991).

References

A day when crass gave way to class. (1991, May 13). [Editorial]. *The Sporting News*, p. 6.

Aaron, H., with Wheeler, L. (1991). *I had a hammer: The Hank Aaron story*. New York: Harper Collins.

Anderson, D. (1975, June 3). For a change, another Ryan no-hitter. *The New York Times*, p. 39.

Anderson, D. (1978, August). The Ryan Express races for the records. *Sport*, pp. 67–71.

Axthelm, P. (1975, June 16). Fastest arm in the West. *Newsweek*, pp. 56–60.

Baldwin, P. (1990, July 10). Pitch man. *The Dallas Morning News*, pp. 1A, 6A.

Bennett, R. S., Whitaker, K. G., Woolley Smith, N. J., & Sablove, A. (1987). Changing the rules of the game: Reflections toward a feminist analysis of sport. *Women's Studies International Forum, 10*, 369–379.

Berquist, G. F. (1971). The rhetorical heritage of Frederick Jackson Turner. *Transactions of the Wisconsin Academy of Sciences, Arts, and Letters, 59*, 23–32.

Billington, R. A. (1971). *The genesis of the frontier thesis*. San Marina, CA: Huntington Library.

Bodley, H. (1991, May 3). Ryan: Oasis from off-field turmoil. *USA Today*, p. 5C.

Boswell, T. (1991, May 3). Ryan wears age and success with equal grace. *The Sacramento Bee*, pp. C1, C4.

Brewster, T. (1989, May). The care and feeding of baseball's greatest arm. *Life*, pp. 86–87.

Brine for Nolan Ryan. (1968, May 31). *Life*, pp. 77–78.

Brod, H. (Ed.), (1987). *The making of masculinities: The new men's studies*. Boston: Unwin Hyman.

Brohm, J-M. (1978). *Sport—A prison of measured time*. (I. Fraser, Trans.). London: Ink Links.

Bryson, L. (1987). Sport and the maintenance of masculine hegemony. *Women's Studies International Forum, 10*, 349–360.

Carpenter, R. (1977). Frederick Jackson Turner and the rhetorical impact of the frontier thesis. *Quarterly Journal of Speech, 63*, 117–129.

Carrigan, T., Connell, B., & Lee, L. (1987). Toward a new sociology of masculinity. In H. Brod (Ed.), *The making of masculinities: The new men's studies* (pp. 63–100). Boston: Unwin Hyman.

Casstevens, D. (1990, July 25). 300th will be Ryan's reply to his critics. *The Dallas Morning News*, p. 1B.

Cawelti, J. (1976). *Adventure, mystery, and romance*. Chicago: University of Chicago Press.

Chass, M. (1970, June 11). Pepitone clouts four-run homer. *The New York Times*, p. 59.

Connell, R. W. (1983). *Which way is up? Essays on sex, class, and culture*. Sydney: George Allen & Unwin.

Connell, R. W. (1990). An iron man: The body and some contradictions of hegemonic masculinity. In M. A. Messner & D. F. Sabo (Eds.), *Sport, men and the gender order: Critical feminist perspectives* (pp. 83–95). Champaign, IL: Human Kinetics.

Corliss, R. (1990, June 25). An old-timer for all seasons: For Nolan Ryan, 43, it's no hits, no runs—and no peers. *Time*, p. 68.

Dubbert, J. (1979). *A man's place: Masculinity in transition*. Englewood Cliffs, NJ: Prentice Hall.

Duncan, M. C. (1983). The symbolic dimensions of spectator sport. *Quest, 35*, 29–36.

Duncan, M. C. (1990). Sports photographs and sexual difference: Images of women and men in the 1984 Olympic Games. *Sociology of Sport Journal, 7*, 22–43.

Durslag, M. (1976, April 24). Ryan raps pay preoccupation. *The Sporting News*, p. 12.

Durso, J. (1968, July 4). Pirates shell Ryan and rout Mets, 8–1. *The New York Times*, p. 24.

Dyer, R. (1985). Male sexuality in the media. In A. Metcalf & M. Humphries (Eds.), *The sexuality of men* (pp. 28–43). London: Pluto.

Edwards, H. (1976). Race in contemporary American sports. In A. Yiannakis, T. D. McIntyre, M. J. Melnick, & D. P. Hart (Eds.), *Sport sociology: Contemporary themes* (pp. 194–196). Dubuque, IA: Kendall/Hunt.

Fimrite, R. (1974, September 16). Speed trap for an Angel. *Sports Illustrated*, pp. 98, 100.

Fimrite, R. (1975, June 16). The bringer of the heat. *Sports Illustrated*, pp. 33, 35–39.

Fimrite, R. (1986, September 29). A great hand with the old cowhide. *Sports Illustrated*, pp. 84–88, 90–94, 96.

Fiske, J. (1987). *Television culture*. London: Methuen.

Fiske, J., & Hartley, J. (1978). *Reading television*. New York: Methuen.

Fraley, G. (1990, June 16). Pitching with pain not new to Ryan. *The Dallas Morning News*, p. 6B.

Furlong, B. W. (1980, April). Baseball's best paid pitcher comes home. *Sport*, pp. 66–70.

Galloway, R. (1990a, March 29). At all cost, Ryan must be paid to stay. *The Dallas Morning News*, p. 1B.

Galloway, R. (1990b, August 1). Ryan's greatness affirmed. *The Dallas Morning News*, p. 1B.

Givens, R. (1989, August 28). Throwing old gracefully: The workout behind the Ryan strikeouts. *Newsweek*, p. 65.

Greene, B. (1990, June 24). Nolan Ryan is newest star of the baby boom set. *The Dallas Morning News*, p. 50.

Hanke, R. (1990). Hegemonic masculinity in thirtysomething. *Critical Studies in Mass Communication, 7*, 231-248.

Harasta, C. (1990, August 2). Married to a legend, Ruth Ryan understands sacrifices. *The Dallas Morning News*, p. 17H.

Hargreaves, J. (1982). Sport and hegemony: Some theoretical problems. In H. Cantelon & R. Gruneau (Eds.), *Sport, culture, and the modern state* (pp. 103-140). Toronto: University of Toronto Press.

Hargreaves, J. A. (1986). Where's the virtue? Where's the grace? A discussion of the social production of gender relations in and through sport. *Theory, Culture, and Society, 3*, 109-121.

Hearn, J. (1987). *The gender of oppression: Men, masculinity, and the critique of Marxism.* New York: St. Martin's Press.

Hecht, H. (1983, April 29). Whatever Ryan does, it never quiets critics. *New York Post*, p. 102.

Henderson, J. (1989, August 23). 5-oh!-oh!-oh!: Heroic Ryan finishes quest for historic K. *Dallas Times Herald*, pp. A-1, A-15.

Herek, G. M. (1987). On heterosexual masculinity: Some psychical consequences of the social construction of gender and sexuality. In M. S. Kimmel (Ed.), *Changing men: New directions in research on men and masculinity* (pp. 68-82). Newbury Park, CA: Sage.

Herskowitz, M. (1988, October 28). Ryan's loyalty isn't the issue. *The Houston Post*, p. C-1.

Herskowitz, M. (1990, April 1). A Ruth-less spring training doesn't suit Mrs. Ryan. *The Houston Post*, B-15.

Hoch, P. (1979). *White hero, black beast.* London: Pluto.

Hoffer, R. (1988, May). Armed and still dangerous. *Gentlemen's Quarterly*, pp. 245-248, 292-294.

Horn, B. (1990, August 2). Expressly Ryan: In honor of 300. *The Dallas Morning News*, pp. 1H-2H.

Jacobson, S. (1974, June/July). Nolan Ryan: Whoosh! *The Saturday Evening Post*, pp. 14-16, 124.

Jeffords, S. (1989). *The remasculinization of America: Gender and the Vietnam War.* Bloomington: Indiana University Press.

Jennings, D. (1989, March 26). Nolan Ryan. *The Dallas Morning News*, pp. 1E-3E.

Jhally, S. (1989). Cultural studies and the sports/media complex. In L. A. Wenner (Ed.), *Media, sport, and society* (pp. 70-95). Newbury Park, CA: Sage.

Johnson, M. T. (1991, April 3). Dueling Ryans throw fans a curve on loyalty. *Austin American-Statesman*, pp. A1, A12.

Johnston, D. H. (1979) *Journalism and the media: An introduction to mass communications.* New York: Barnes & Noble.

K. (1989, August 28). *Sports Illustrated*, pp. 30-32.

Kaufman, M. (Ed.). (1987). *Beyond patriarchy: Essays by men on pleasure, power, and change.* Toronto: Oxford University Press.

Keith, L. (1979, November 19). It's fishing season for Nolan Ryan. *Sports Illustrated*, pp. 34–35.

Kimmel, M. S. (1987a). Rethinking 'masculinity': New directions in research. In M. S. Kimmel (Ed.), *Changing men: New directions in research on men and masculinity* (pp. 9–24). Newbury Park, CA: Sage.

Kimmel, M. (1987b). The cult of masculinity: American social character and the legacy of the cowboy. In M. Kaufman (Ed.), *Beyond patriarchy: Essays by men on pleasure, power, and change* (pp. 235–249). Toronto: Oxford University Press.

Komisar, L. (1980). Violence and the masculine mystique. In D. F. Sabo & R. Runfola (Eds.), *Jock: Sports and male identity* (pp. 131–157). Englewood Cliffs, NJ: Prentice-Hall.

Lang, J. (1968, March 30). Ryan whiff saga a fable? Mets wonder. *The Sporting News*, p. 26.

Lang, J. (1984, May 1). What drove Ryan from N.Y.: Concern for wife led to trade-me-or-I'll-quit demand. *New York Daily News*, p. C26.

Leggett, W. (1973, May 14). An Angel who makes turnstiles sing. *Sports Illustrated*, pp. 26–27.

Lerner, G. (1986). *The creation of patriarchy*. New York: Oxford University Press.

Littwin, M. (1980, April 17). Nolan Ryan: Fastest (and richest?) gun in Alvin. *Los Angeles Times*, pp. 1, 10, part III.

Lopresti, M. (1991, May 3–5). Texas Ranger rides very tall in the saddle. *USA Today*, pp. 1A–2A.

MacCormack, J. (1989, August 22). Alvin's uniform anxiety. *Dallas Times Herald*, pp. A-1, A-10.

McCleneghan, J. S. (1990). Sportswriters talk about themselves: An attitude study. *Journalism Quarterly*, 67, 114–118.

Majors, R. (1986). Cool pose: The proud signature of black survival. *Changing Men: Issues in Gender, Sex and Politics*, 17, 5–6.

Maynard, R. M. (1974). *The American west on film: Myth and reality*. Rochelle Park, NJ: Hayden Book Co.

Messner, M. A. (1988). Sports and male domination: The female athlete as contested ideological terrain. *Sociology of Sport Journal*, 5, 197–211.

Messner, M. A. (1990). Masculinities and athletic careers: Bonding and status differences. In M. A. Messner & D. F. Sabo (Eds.), *Sport, men, and the gender order: Critical feminist perspectives* (pp. 97–108). Champaign, IL: Human Kinetics.

Montville, L. (1991, April 15). Citizen Ryan. *Sports Illustrated*, pp. 120–129, 131.

Naison, M. (1972). Sports and the American empire. *Radical America* (July–August), pp. 95–120.

Nelson, M. (1980). Feminism, the jockocracy, and men's liberation: Crying all the way to the bank. In D. F. Sabo & R. Runfola (Eds.), *Jock: Sports and male identity* (pp. 239–248). Englewood Cliffs, NJ: Prentice-Hall.

Newhan, R. (1971, December 11). Fregosi 'thrilled' by trade to Mets. *Los Angeles Times*, pp. 1, 3, part III.

Newhan, R. (1972, May 23). Homer lucky blow says Jackson as A's top Angels, 6–3. *Los Angeles Times*, pp. 1, 6, part III.

Newhan, R. (1975, June 2). Ryan: A hitless wonder for the 4th time. *Los Angeles Times*, pp. 1, 6, part III.

No. 300: Ryan puts final touch on application to Hall. (1990, August 1). *The Bakersfield Californian*, pp. E1, E6.

Ochberg, R. L. (1987). The male career code and the ideology of role. In H. Brod (Ed.), *The making of masculinities: The new men's studies* (pp. 173–192). Boston: Unwin Hyman.

Pallone, D., with Steinberg, A. (1990). *Behind the mask: My double life in baseball*. New York: Signet.

Pleck, J. H. (1987). American fathering in historical perspective. In M. S. Kimmel (Ed.), *Changing men: New directions in research on men and masculinity* (pp. 83–97). Newbury Park, CA: Sage.

President's message. (1989, August 23). *Fort Worth Star-Telegram*, p. 6, sec. 3.

Rader, B. G. (1983). Compensatory sports heroes: Ruth, Grange, and Dempsey. *Journal of Popular Culture*, 16, 11–22.

Real, M. R. (1975). Super Bowl: Mythic spectacle. *Journal of Communication*, 25, 1975, 31–43.

Real, M. R. (1989). Super Bowl football versus World Cup soccer: A cultural-structural comparison. In L. A. Wenner (Ed.), *Media, sports, and society* (pp. 180–203). Newbury Park, CA: Sage.

Rigauer, B. (1981). *Sport and work*. (A. Guttmann, Trans.) New York: Columbia University Press.

Ringolsby, T. (1990, July 30). Ryan says arm, back recuperated from tiring effort against Yankees. *The Dallas Morning News*, p. 5B.

Rubin, G. (1985). Thinking sex: Notes for a radical theory of the politics of sexuality. In C. Vance (Ed.), *Pleasure and danger: Exploring female sexuality* (pp. 267–319). Boston: Routledge & Kegan Paul.

Rushing, J. H. (1983). The rhetoric of the American western myth. *Communication Monographs*, 50, 14–32.

Ryan rookie card goes for $5,000. (1991, June 22). *The Sacramento Bee*, p. D2.

Sabo, D. F., & Runfola, R. (Eds.). (1980). *Jock: Sports and male identity*. Englewood Clills, NJ: Prentice-Hall.

Sadler, W. A., Jr. (1976). Competition out of bounds: Sport in American life. In A. Yiannakis, T. D. McIntyre, M. J. Melnick, & D. P. Hart (Eds.), *Sport sociology: Contemporary themes* (pp. 253–261). Dubuque, IA: Kendall/Hunt.

Segal, L. (1990). *Slow motion: Changing masculinities, changing men*. New Brunswick, NJ: Rutgers University Press.

Shadoian, J. (1977). *Dreams and dead ends: The American gangster/crime film*. Cambridge, MA: MIT Press.

Shea, J. (1990, June 13). Ryan celebrates with bike workout. *USA Today*, p. 8C.

Striking example: Tonight's the night for Ryan to make history. (1989, August 22). [Editorial]. *The Dallas Morning News*, p. 14A.

Texas Rangers. (1991). *Texas Rangers 1991 media guide*. Arlington: Texas Rangers Baseball Club.

These are the Mets, champions all. (1969, October 17). *The New York Times*, p. 57.

Tolson, A. (1977). *The limits of masculinity: Male identity and women's liberation.* New York: Harper & Row.

Tom, D. (1985, July 10). Nolan Ryan smokes only his pitches. *USA Today,* pp. 1C–2C.

Tomaso, B. (1989, August 22). Making a fast buck off Ryan: Tickets to witness pitcher's quest are costly and scarce. *The Dallas Morning News,* pp. 1A, 11A.

Trujillo, N., & Ekdom, L. R. (1985). Sportswriting and American cultural values: The 1984 Chicago Cubs. *Critical Studies in Mass Communication, 2,* 262–281.

Wangrin, M. (1991, April 3). Big hit: Father throws best. *Austin American-Statesman,* pp. C1, C7.

Wernick, A. (1987). From voyeur to narcissist: Imaging men in contemporary advertising. In M. Kaufman (Ed.), *Beyond patriarchy: Essays by men on pleasure, power, and change* (pp. 277–297). Toronto: Oxford University Press.

Whitson, D. (1990). Sport in the social construction of masculinity. In M. A. Messner & D. F. Sabo (Eds.), *Sport, men, and the gender order: Critical feminist perspectives* (pp. 19–29). Champaign, IL: Human Kinetics.

Whyte, W. H. (1956). *The organization man.* New York: Simon and Schuster.

Wright, W. (1975). *Sixguns and society: A structural study of the Western.* Berkeley: University of California Press.

Judy Chicago's *The Dinner Party*
Empowering of Women's Voice in Visual Art

Sonja K. Foss

With his notion of the discursive formation, Michel Foucault has focused attention on the lack of input into mainstream discourse by subordinate groups on the periphery of society. A discursive formation is the code of a culture that governs "its language, its schemas of perception, its exchanges, its techniques, its values, the hierarchy of its practices" (Foucault, 1970, p. xx). It is the characteristic system, structure, or network that defines the conditions for the possibility of knowledge or for the worldview of an age. Various rules govern who is allowed to speak and be heard in a discursive formation, the conditions under which they are allowed to speak, and the content and form their discourse must assume (Foucault, 1972, pp. 41–44, 56–67, 68, 224–225). Knowledge is generated by the discursive practices of a discursive formation so that those individuals who are not "heard" or allowed to participate in the dominant discourse do not have their knowledge incorporated into the common cultural knowledge.

Kramarae (1981) arrives at similar conclusions about the role of a submerged group's discourse in a culture in her discussion of the minority perspective on language. Minority groups in a culture, she asserts, tend to have little power because they have little control over their economic fortunes or social status. Consequently, they find that their speech is not evaluated highly by those in the predominant culture, they generally are not represented in decision-making or policy-making processes of that culture, and they thus are denied a voice in it. Samuel Beckett (1958) explained this inability to be heard particularly well: "I am walled round with their vociferations, none will ever know what I am, none will ever hear me say it, I won't say it, I can't say it, I have no language but theirs, . . ." (p. 52).

A prerequisite to having their voices heard in a discursive formation or the dominant culture is that members of a submerged group must develop their own authentic voice. They must develop knowledge and discourse out of their own experiences and interpret and label these experiences in their own terms. Perhaps even more important, they must

From *Women Communicating: Studies of Women's Talk*, ed. Barbara Bate and Anita Taylor (Norwood, New Jersey: Ablex, 1988), pp. 9–26. Used by permission of Ablex Publishing Corporation and the author.

come to see their experiences and discourse as legitimate and valuable. Developing this authenticity and attributing power to it are difficult for a submerged group, however, because their experience has been interpreted for them for so long by others and devalued by those others. The submerged group has been trained to see itself as represented in the dominant discourse of the culture and has come to subordinate even its authentic and potentially powerful voice to that culture (Schulz, 1984). Certainly, the submerged group faces difficulties following development and empowerment of its authentic voice—it must secure acknowledgment of its authority to speak by the dominant group. But empowerment cannot happen without a strong sense of identity within the submerged group apart from the dominant culture. Group members first must possess the "courage to be and to speak. . . . the Courage to Blaspheme" (Daly, 1978, p. 264) the definitions of themselves as powerless that have been established by the dominant discourse.

My purpose in this essay is to identify some of the strategies that submerged groups use to empower their own perspective or to develop legitimacy for the knowledge and discourse that are available to them. I have chosen to examine the discourse of women as a case study of this process. In a male-dominated culture where "[p]atriarchy is itself the prevailing religion" (Daly, 1978, p. 39), women constitute a marginal group. They have been excluded in many ways from public life, and they occupy largely peripheral and powerless positions when they do enter that realm. Because of their different positions from men, women have experience that "is institutionally and linguistically structured in a way that is different from that of men" (Ferguson, 1984, p. 23). Yet, this experience, along with the knowledge and discourse it generates, is submerged, devalued, and generally not heard in the male-dominated culture. As Daly (1978) explains, "It is when women speak our own truth that incredulity comes from all sides" (p. 91). Women's words, because they do not conform to the rules of the dominant discursive formation, are treated as "officially worthless" (Daly, p. 92).

While numerous scholars have attempted to identify the characteristic qualities of women's perspective or voice as a result of their different experiences in the culture, I do not want to make a case either for or against particular qualities as representative of the female voice. Instead, my focus in this essay is on the process by which women come to see their symbols, rituals, and regular practices—the *content* of their experiences that tends to be overlooked in the male worldview—as legitimate.

I have selected for the study of strategies used to empower women's voice a work of visual art, Judy Chicago's *The Dinner Party* (a detailed description and photographs of the work can be found in Chicago, 1979). I chose this work for my object of study because of its richness of data. Because it incorporates both discursive and nondiscursive data—words, colors, lines, textures, and images—it may reveal strategies that would not be apparent in a work of discursive rhetoric alone. In addition, if, in fact, women's perspective is submerged in our culture, a work that is free to go beyond the bounds of the conventional language system, which gives voice largely to men, might demonstrate more clearly strategies used to empower that alternative perspective.

In selecting *The Dinner Party* as the data for my study, I am aware of a number of assumptions I require the reader to accept if this study is to be seen as capable of contributing to theory development in communication. First, of course, I am assuming that visual images are included in the scope of rhetoric or communication. As the conscious production or arrangement of colors, forms, images, textures, and other elements in a manner that affects or evokes a response, I see visual images as forms of rhetoric that attempt, as does discursive rhetoric, to influence others' "thinking and behavior through the strategic use of symbols" (Ehninger, 1972, p. 3).

I also recognize that works of art contain both rhetorical and aesthetic qualities. Experience of a work at an aesthetic level is the apprehension or perception of the sensory elements of the object—enjoyment of its colors or the valuing of its texture, for example. But when a viewer attributes meaning to those sensory elements and they begin to refer to images, emotions, and ideas beyond themselves, the response has become a rhetorical one—that with which I will be concerned here.

No one true meaning or interpretation can be made of an art object's function as a rhetorical symbol. To say that an art object has meaning for a viewer does not suggest that it signifies some fixed referent. Rather, meaning results from and requires a viewer's creation of an interpretation of the visual object. Different meanings are attributed to a work of art, then, by different viewers as a result of the differing endowments and experiences brought to the work.

The predominant role of the viewer in the establishment of the meaning for a work of art, however, does not mean that a viewer has total freedom to attribute any meaning at all to the work. A viewer's interpretation is limited by the actual object itself. Although that meaning is not an inherent part of the object, the solid physical presence of a work of art makes possible the work's aesthetic and rhetorical effects. More important, the physical characteristics render one rhetorical interpretation more likely to occur than another.

In my analysis of *The Dinner Party*, I will identify the physical or material properties of the work that a viewer is likely to use as the basis for attribution of meanings to it. While my description may seem anthropomorphic in that I will use phrases such as, "*The Dinner Party* provides" or "the work generates," this style was selected simply as a matter of convenience. I do not intend to suggest that the meaning of the work lies in these physical attributes or that *The Dinner Party* itself is a rhetor capable of producing purposive communication. Rather, I am suggesting that as the physical embodiment of its creator's intention, the work can be examined as containing particular characteristics that are likely to guide the viewer's interpretation in particular directions. The viewer is free to interpret *The Dinner Party* or create meaning for it according to her own experiences, as long as the meaning attributed is grounded somehow in the material form of the art object.

The Dinner Party

The Dinner Party opened on March 14, 1979, at the San Francisco Museum of Modern Art. The show next traveled to the University of Houston in Clear Lake City, Texas, opening there on March 9, 1980.

Credit: © Judy Chicago, 1979. Photograph by Michael Alexander.

It was shown at the Boston Center for the Arts in July and August of 1980 and at the Brooklyn Museum in New York from October, 1980, through January, 1981. In July and August of 1981, *The Dinner Party* was on display in Cleveland Heights, Ohio, followed by its exhibition in Chicago from September, 1981, through February, 1982. It now is in storage until a permanent gallery space can be located for it.

The work itself is a room-size installation piece whose primary element is an open-centered, triangular table approximately 48 feet long on each side and 26 inches wide. Resting on the table are 39 sculptured plates, each representing a woman from history—from the mythical past through the present. The first wing of the table represents women from prehistory to the decline of Greco-Roman culture and includes plates representing women such as the Primordial Goddess; Kali, an ancient Indian goddess; Hatshepsut, an Egyptian pharoah of the eighteenth dynasty; and Sappho, a Greek poet of about 600 B.C. The second wing of the table represents women from the period of Christianity to the Reformation and includes plates for such figures as Saint Bridget, a sixth-century Irish saint; Eleanor of Aquitaine, a French queen of the thirteenth century; and Petronilla de Meath, a woman who was burned as a witch in Ireland. The third wing represents the seventeenth through the twentieth centuries and includes plates for Anne Hutchinson, a seventeenth-century American Puritan and reformer; Caroline Herschel, a nineteenth-century German scientist; Sojourner Truth, an American abolitionist and feminist; and English writer Virginia Woolf.

Each place setting includes a ceramic or painted china plate, a gold-lined ceramic goblet, lustre flatware, a gold-edged napkin, and an elaborate needlework runner that contains the name of the woman represented in gold script. The goblets, napkins, and flatware are the same for all the place settings, but each of the plates and runners is different.

The place setting representing Emily Dickinson, for example, contains a very feminine, pink plate with a vulva-like center surrounded by six rows of real lace that were dipped in liquid ceramic and then fired. The plate rests on a round pink-and-white lace "collar" or placemat, and the gold runner beneath it is edged in the same pink lace of the plate.

The plate that represents Susan B. Anthony also contains a center vaginal form—this time in a deep red color, edged by a fold of lighter red. Four molded, draped "wings" spread out from this center and curl up at the edges of the plate, suggesting a butterfly rising from the plate. The butterfly form is a luminescent red, which seems to vibrate against a beige background. The plate rests on a bright red triangle of sturdy woven fabric edged with fringe. Streaming out from behind this triangle are strips of white and black fabric, representing a "Memory Quilt" for Anthony. Embroidered on each white strip is the name of a suffragist from Anthony's period, including Anna Howard Shaw, Harriot Stanton Blatch, and Paulina Wright Davis.

In the plate of Theodora, a Byzantine empress of the sixth century, the illusion of separate mosaic tiles in green, pink, and gold is created through a series of lines etched into the plate. While this plate is flat, in contrast to Dickinson's and Anthony's, it again features a butterfly form. The butterfly image is composed of circles, diamonds, and other forms that suggest traditional designs of stained-glass windows. Theodora's plate rests on a round, braided gold placemat on top of a gold satin runner. At the front of the runner, below Theodora's name, is a strip of purple satin edged with purple and gold lace and ribbon.

The table, containing 39 such place settings, rests on a raised triangular platform called the Heritage Floor. It is composed of more than 2,300 hand-cast white pearlescent triangular tiles. Written across the tiles in gold script are the names of 999 women, grouped by historical period around the woman's place at the table who represents that particular period.

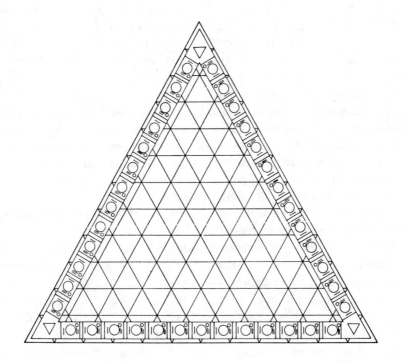

Credit: © Judy Chicago, 1979.

The Dinner Party was the creation of artist Judy Chicago, born Judy Cohen in Chicago in 1939. She studied art at the University of California at Los Angeles, where the sexually feminine images she employed in her work were ridiculed by her male professors. She began to realize the need for more support for women artists and for recognition that the images produced by women artists would be different from those produced by men. She became known as a feminist artist and in 1969 renounced "all names imposed upon her through male social dominance" (Chicago, 1977, p. 63) and chose her own name: Judy Chicago.

While teaching at Fresno State, Chicago organized an art class for women. With the members of the class, she founded Womanspace, an exhibition space for women housed in an old mansion in Los Angeles. She went on to develop a Feminist Art Program at the California Institute of the Arts in Valencia, which led her to conclude that women artists need an entirely independent structure in which to work. She then organized the Feminist Studio Workshop in Los Angeles. In 1973, the Workshop, Womanspace, and other feminist galleries and organizations were incorporated into the Woman's Building in Los Angeles, which was designed to provide a feminist context for women artists.

Chicago worked on the execution of The Dinner Party by herself for three years, studying ceramics and china painting in order to learn the techniques necessary for the execution of the piece. In October, 1975, faced with the growing awareness that she could not complete a work of this magnitude alone, Chicago began taking on help. She obtained the assistance of a graduate student with experience in porcelain to work on the execution of the plates, an assistant to supervise the needlework on the runners, researchers to compile the biographies of the 3,000 women from which the names for the floor tiles were selected, and an assistant to supervise the casting and sanding of the floor tiles. Diane Gelon, an art historian, was added to coordinate the entire project and to serve as second-in-command to Chicago.

In addition to the five or six individuals who fully participated during the three-year cooperative period of the project, about 125 individuals were considered "members of the project," and another 300 assisted with smaller contributions of both work and ideas to the execution of the piece. The work was carried out in Chicago's Santa Monica studio, which had been remodeled with the assistance of a grant from the National Endowment for the Arts to include a ceramics studio, an electric kiln, a needlework loft, and a dust-free china painting room. Thus, although the piece was conceived and directed by Chicago, it incorporated the work and ideas of many others as well.

Strategies of Empowerment

Analysis of *The Dinner Party* reveals three primary strategies used in the work as means to empower and legitimize women's authentic voice: (a) The work is independent from male-created reality; (b) it creates new standards for evaluation of its own rhetoric; and (c) women are clearly labeled as agents.

Independence from Male-Created Reality

In *The Dinner Party*, the presentation of women's culture occurs entirely apart from the male-dominated world outside the setting of the exhibition. It is a separatist piece not only because it deals exclusively with women's culture but also because it lacks reference to anything male. Women's achievements are the sole focus of the work, and men are not referred to in any way in it. The work is formed entirely from women's traditional arts such as china painting and needlework, art forms not recognized as having value in the male-dominated art world. Further, female imagery predominates. The triangular shape of the table is a primitive symbol of the feminine; vaginal images appear in the centers of many plates; and the dinner-table setting suggests women's traditional concerns. *The Dinner Party*, then, encourages the viewer to focus only on women, a stance that has two consequences.

First, the work's independence from male culture defines women's culture as derived from women's positive experiences rather than in opposition to men's culture. It presents the creation or formation of a new, separate symbolic order for women that "does not essentially depend upon an enemy for its existence/becoming" (Daly, 1978, p. 320). Refusal to create in opposition to a male enemy allows the formulation of positive, affirming discourse in contrast to that created from a sense of inferiority.

The danger of focusing on an enemy as the basis for creation and empowerment of an authentic voice, explains Daly (1978), is that it does not allow that voice to grow and develop. It remains at the level of attacking the enemy. The individual who defines herself and her voice only in opposition "may become fixated upon the atrocities of androcracy, 'spinning her wheels' instead of spinning on her heel and facing in Other directions" (p. 320). Betty Friedan (1981) makes the same point, asserting that there is value in a fight "within, and against, and defined by that old structure of unequal, polarized male and female sex roles. But to continue reacting against that structure is still to be defined and limited by its terms" (p. 40). In contrast, in *The Dinner Party*, women's culture by itself is portrayed as rich, abundant, self-sufficient, and positive, with energy and worth arising from its own special qualities. It is seen as having authentic qualities that constitute a significant and valuable perspective in and of themselves.

Definition of women's culture totally apart from men's also enables *The Dinner Party* to present an alternative to the male-dominated view of the world more effectively. It creates this view not by comparing the female perspective to that of men but through presentation of an alternative vision on its own terms. Ferguson (1984) makes a strong case as to why empowerment of a dissenting voice will not result from the integration of the subordinate group into the existing structure. When members of a submerged group attack the system from within by integrating themselves into the system, climbing to the top, and then attempting to change it, they are doomed to fail. As Ferguson asks, after "internalizing and acting on the rules of [the dominant system] for most of their adult lives, how many . . . will be *able* to change? After succeeding .in the system by using those rules, how many would be *willing* to change?" (p. 192). She continues: "It is hard to be a 'closet radical' when an inspection of the closets is part of the organization's daily routine" (p. 193). The dominant system, then, cannot be resisted on its own terms, since they are terms that render opposition invisible.

Ferguson (1984) explains how discourses of opposition must function in order to be effective: they must present their visions in terms other than those of the dominant structure. This task is accomplished by "unearthing/creating the specific language of women, and comprehending women's experience in terms of that linguistic framework rather than in terms of the dominant discourse" (p. 154). By creating a rhetoric in terms other than those of the dominant discourse, Ferguson explains, experiences are changed:

> Just as our experience is defined by the intuitive and reflective awareness that our language makes available, our language in turn is circumscribed by our experience; to alter the terms of public discourse one must change the experiences people have, and to restructure experiences one must change the language available for making sense of those experiences. (p. 154)

The Dinner Party, then, frames a world and uses images and forms rooted in the female experience. Thus, it poses an alternative to the dominant discourse, the "old molds/models . . . by being itself an Other way of thinking/speaking" (Daly, 1978, p. xiii). *The Dinner Party*, through its presentation of women alone and lack of reference to men, suggests that women "eject, banish, depose the possessing language— spoken and written words, body language, architectural language, technological language, the language of symbols and of institutional structures" (Daly, 1978, p. 345), inspiriting and empowering their own vision of the world.

Creation of New Standards for Evaluation of Rhetoric

A second strategy used in The Dinner Party to authenticate the female experience is the development of new standards for judging women's rhetoric. Just as viewers are led, in The Dinner Party, to reject the male-dominated perspective as the only reality, so they are encouraged to develop new means of evaluating women's discourse. Rejection of male domination and focus on the creation of an independent women's reality frees participants from dependence on, as Daly (1978) names it, "Male Approval Desire" (p. 69)—male standards of evaluation. Thus, participants are able to construct their own expectations and criteria for evaluation derived from the authentic experiences of women's culture: "Depending less and less upon male approval, recognizing that such approval is more often than not a reward for weakness, we approve of our Selves. We prove our Selves" (Daly, 1978, pp. 341–342).

The evaluation typically accorded the discourse of a submerged group such as women tends to be negative. One of the earliest to express this view formally was Otto Jespersen in 1922, who described women's speech as an aberration of men's. He said women use less complex sentences, talk faster and with less thought, and have less extensive vocabularies than men. Studies that revealed that women's speech contained more hedges and qualifiers frequently were interpreted as suggesting women's lack of certainty and confidence, while nonverbal gestures sometimes described as characteristic of women, such as more frequent smiling and eye contact, were seen as suggesting powerlessness and submissiveness. These kinds of conclusions illustrate a view of women's speech as a deviation from "real speech." It is "non-standard" because it is different from the speech of men and does not conform to the norms of male speech; consequently, it is inferior. When women's rhetoric is judged negatively according to the standard of conformity to male rhetoric, it is accorded little status and is unable to affect, in any significant way, the dominant discourse (Kramarae, 1981, pp. 95–97).

In The Dinner Party, viewers are able to see a number of possibilities for new standards for judgment of women's discourse. They center not around the impact of women's rhetoric on the dominant discourse but rather around the effects of women's rhetoric on themselves. One standard that emerges is the degree to which the rhetoric corresponds to women's experiences, suggested from the focus in The Dinner Party on the dinner-table setting. The dinner-party setting is a traditional one for women. It points to the domestic role usually assumed by women, which includes setting tables, preparing meals, and giving dinner parties. The traditional art forms of needlework and china painting used in the work—traditional art forms for women—also are derived from women's experiences, as are the vaginally suggestive images of many of the plates, corresponding to women's biological and physical experiences.

A second standard suggested by *The Dinner Party* to use in assessing women's rhetoric is whether female imagery is presented as positive and valuable. Application of this standard suggests that images unique to or at least typical of the submerged group must not be demeaned, as they might be outside of the culture. In *The Dinner Party*, Chicago almost makes the feminine holy by elevating and celebrating female imagery and traditionally female arts to provide affirmative symbols for women. Because each woman represented at the table stands for one or more aspects of women's experiences and achievements, the viewer is led to see that women have achieved in many areas throughout history, which also points to the notion that the feminine is valuable. The idea is repeated in the sophistication and excellent craftsmanship of the plates and runners, suggesting that women's creations and women as creators are outstanding and certainly deserving of positive evaluations. The 13 place settings on each side of the table, which suggest the 13 individuals seated at the Last Supper, encourage the conclusion that this is a gathering of particular worth and significance, again suggesting the value of the female.

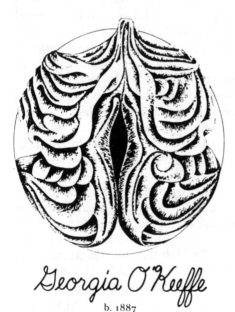

Georgia O'Keeffe
b. 1887

The Dinner Party has the potential capacity to evoke a number of strong emotions in its viewers, suggesting yet another standard by which to judge women's rhetoric—its capacity to evoke emotions. A submerged group develops authenticity and legitimacy only when its users are excited by that discourse and thus have strong desires to use and maintain it. One emotion evoked by *The Dinner Party* is hope or optimism, which is generated by the work's presentation of steady progress in women's status and condition. This progress is suggested by the gradual rising of the butterfly images of the plates as they move from historical to

contemporary times. The
plates representing the contemporary women appear as
though they may fly off the
plates, suggesting continued
growth and movement for
women in their accomplishments and achievements.
Viewers also are encouraged
to feel the emotion of pride in
the accomplishments of
women through the numer-
ous women represented in
the work as well as anger that
the many achievements of
women presented in the
piece have been ignored for
so long. The variety and the
brightness of the colors used
in *The Dinner Party* also
function to induce qualities
of joy, celebration, and excitement in the female experience.

Elizabeth Blackwell

1821–1910

© Judy Chicago, 1979

A fourth criterion offered in *The Dinner Party* by which women's
rhetoric might be judged is whether or not the rhetoric provides a context
in which it should be viewed. When rhetoric is presented apart from
the dominant culture, it may appear disconnected, irrelevant, and
perhaps even a bit absurd simply because it does not conform to the
standards established in the dominant discourse. To avoid these negative
perceptions, a new context is needed so that the users of the rhetoric
understand it in a context in which it is significant and legitimate.

The provision of context can assume many forms. In *The Dinner Party*,
context is provided for women's voice through a presentation of the
history of that voice. Of particular importance to a submerged group is
the need for knowledge of its history—usually a history that has been
forgotten or suppressed by the dominant group. The recapturing of that
history provides a basis for constructing current culture and generates
a sense of pride in it. In *The Dinner Party*, women's history is re-created
for viewers through the traditional women's art forms of needlework
and china painting. It is also shown in the presentation of women's
accomplishments from the past, both in the plates representing women
and in the names of women on the Heritage Floor.

A second way in which context can be provided for a submerged group's discourse and knowledge is through presentation of a vision for that group in the future. Such a vision suggests to members of the group that their rhetoric will survive and that it will continue to create a version of reality that is authentic and strong. *The Dinner Party* helps viewers envision the future of women's culture, discourse, and knowledge in a number of ways. The butterfly image of many of the plates is a conventional symbol of flight and growth. As the butterflies lift farther off the plates as they progress through time, they indicate that women currently are capable of flying much farther than they have in numerous realms of endeavor. The table setting itself creates expectancy and anticipation in the viewer that women will continue to achieve and make valuable contributions. The table is ready, and food presumably has been prepared; the hosts now await the arrival of the guests, just as the viewer awaits further contributions by women.

The rhetoric of *The Dinner Party*, then, standing apart from the dominant discourse and the usual context it provides, creates its own context with a past and a future. Thus, the female voice gains greater authenticity as a legitimate alternative to that dominant discourse.

A final criterion for evaluation that emerges from *The Dinner Party* concerns a work's accessibility. If discourse is to have sufficient impact on its users to be given legitimacy as an authentic and powerful voice, it must be accessible to them. This requirement does not mean that all symbols used must be conventional and concrete and that nothing abstract or ambiguous can be included in the rhetoric of a submerged group. But major aspects of the rhetoric must be available to all participants—regardless of their stage of development as participants in their own culture. *The Dinner Party* exemplifies this accessibility in that it is a work of art that almost any viewer can understand. It relies heavily on conventional form—an everyday, familiar dinner-table setting—that is easily understood and accessible in its meaning. This form evokes expectations that have been learned from past experience with the dinner-table form and that the viewer brings with her to the work of art. Experience with the form, then, makes the image and thus the voice represented comfortable and familiar; the reactions of bewilderment and puzzlement that many viewers may have to contemporary art are not those accorded *The Dinner Party*.

Just as *The Dinner Party* rejects the view that male culture is normative by creating a culture apart from it and refusing interaction with it, so are male standards of the dominant discourse rejected for judging women's discourse. Instead, *The Dinner Party* suggests a new set of standards by which to judge rhetoric derived from the culture of a submerged group: The goodness of fit with the experiences of the submerged group; the degree to which the images of the submerged group are presented as positive; the rhetoric's capacity to evoke emotions; the capacity of the rhetoric to provide a context in which it is seen as appropriate and significant; and the degree to which the rhetoric is accessible to members of the submerged group.

Labeling of Agents

A prominent feature of *The Dinner Party* is that it specifically and clearly names who the agents are in the rhetoric it presents—who has the power and authority to act in the world presented. In contrast to rhetoric in which the agent who is communicating is not revealed, subjects of the rhetoric are clearly named in *The Dinner Party*. The women represented at the table and those whose names appear on the Heritage Floor are described in biographies available to viewers and in the images used to depict them in the plates and the runners. Viewers can learn a great deal about the women who serve as the subjects of *The Dinner Party*.

Simply viewing the place setting of Theodora, for example, tells a great deal about who she was. The tiny squares on her plate that create the illusion of mosaic work suggest her connection with churches. The placemat of gold embroidery that surrounds her plate suggests a gold halo and thus rule in the religious realm. The runner of gold and purple satin suggests royalty, as does the illuminated capital letter of her name on the runner. Thus, viewers of *The Dinner Party* leave the work with a sense of the individuality of these distinctive women's experiences and qualities.

Two consequences arise from this specific labeling of agents in *The Dinner Party*. First, it shows women how they can create and control the discourse and knowledge of their world. Total lack of control and responsibility is the result of rhetoric that mystifies, deletes, or hides the agents involved (Daly, 1978, pp. 120, 123–124). In such rhetoric, women are not able to control the world because that control belongs to some unknown authority that cannot be questioned and challenged simply because it is unknown.

In contrast, when agents are specifically named and described, as they are in *The Dinner Party*, women are able to question old authority and control structures. They are allowed to see that women have been and are active agents who have the capacity to control their lives; this control is not exerted by some unknown source. Thus, clear labeling of who the agents are and the nature of their qualities enables the viewers of *The Dinner Party* to begin to conceptualize about themselves as controllers in relation to one another and to the world.

A second consequence of the labeling of agents in *The Dinner Party* is that it allows and encourages a relationship to develop between the viewers and the subjects of the work. It suggests a reciprocity between the viewers and the women who are the subjects of the work by providing points of identification between the two parties. The agents, because they are made known in such detail, then, may begin to have an impact on the viewers and affect their existence so that viewers' and agents' lives become related. As the viewers investigate and analyze why the subjects made the decisions they did to follow particular paths, the women who are the subjects of The Dinner Party may perform the role of guides.

Viewers thus may find in the lives of these women qualities and models to make their own lives whole or more meaningful. A viewer of a place setting representing a woman who clearly was the architect of her own choices, for example, might experience confidence or uncertainty about her own choices or lack of them. Personal identifications may develop between subjects and viewers of The Dinner Party as the subjects offer their stories, encourage, and suggest new options for the viewers in their own lives. By understanding better the sources of their respective positions in the world and gaining a clearer sense of themselves from the subjects of The Dinner Party, viewers may become better able to see the legitimacy and value of their own discourse and knowledge.

The Dinner Party avoids naming the enemy in order that undue attention is not given to responding and reacting to that enemy. Instead, the focus of the work is on women themselves as subjects. These agents are specific women with concrete stories and personal qualities much like those of the work's viewers. The Dinner Party thus creates a strong sense of who women are and of their potential to control that definition, meeting a criterion essential to the development of a powerful and legitimate voice for women.

Implications for Generative Theory

Investigation of the strategies used by submerged groups to develop an authentic voice and legitimize that voice in the face of a dominant discourse yields findings relevant to a number of research areas. One is the possibility it raises for the development of generative theory. A generative theory "is one that unsettles common assumptions within the culture and thereby opens new vistas for action" (Gergen, 1982, p. 133). It is a theory that has "the capacity to challenge the guiding assumptions of the culture, to raise fundamental questions regarding contemporary social life, to foster reconsideration of that which is 'taken for granted,' and thereby to generate fresh alternatives for social action"

(Gergen, p. 109). A generative theory may accomplish these tasks by instigating doubt, generating doubt and implying alternative courses of action, or fully articulating alternatives to current investments (Gergen, p. 169). Certainly, some research in gender and communication already is contributing to the development of generative theory, but other research is done within the framework of the dominant discourse. What I am advocating is the development of theories about gender and communication that challenge that framework systematically, comprehensively, and consistently.

An investigation of the efforts of a submerged group to develop its own authentic discourse encourages the construction of generative theory in two ways. First, it provides a new set of data or "facts" from which to develop theory. While most researchers generally hold that theory should be premised on sound facts, what counts as a fact is determined by the theoretical framework in which the researcher is operating. When an investigator begins with the facts of how rhetoric operates in the dominant discourse, he or she already has incorporated the consensus of that framework, and "the potential for a generative outcome is thereby reduced" (Gergen, 1982, p. 135). But when an investigator views and collects as data the rhetoric of a submerged group that is not valued by or given input into the dominant discourse, a new theory of communication or implications for current theories may be discovered that encourage us to invent and study "new modes of Being/Speaking" (Daly, 1978, p. 33).

A second way in which this type of investigation may result in generative theory is through an examination of theory in its linguistic aspects. The chief products of research and inquiry are essentially word systems, and the theoretical language selected determines the function the language and thus the inquiry plays in the culture (Gergen, 1982, pp. 95, 98). Every theory or form of interpretation can be viewed as a potential form of social control, legitimizing and victimizing various groups by the conceptions expressed in the language of that theory. By formulating theory in the language of a submerged group, the linguistic context of research can be critically examined, suggesting new theoretical conceptions as a result.

When we develop generative theory, as the study of submerged rhetoric encourages, we will have the satisfaction of knowing that we have not necessarily or unjustly constricted our inquiry by neglecting alternative views of understanding, and we will not "place a range of significant restrictions over the kinds of theories that are likely to be developed and sustained" (Gergen, 1982, p. 133). Our central product of research, then, will not be simply an elaboration and extension of a singular worldview. Instead, we will have a clearer picture of the production and maintenance of the dominant order from which some of our biases about women's communication and their associated ideologies are derived and clear the air of "the conventions of the powerful solidified into universal truths" (Ascher, 1984, p. 101).

References

Ascher, C. (1984). On "clearing the air": My letter to Simone de Beauvoir. In C. Ascher, L. DeSalvo, & S. Ruddick, (Eds.), *Between women* (pp. 84–103). Boston: Beacon.

Beckett, S. (1958). *The unnamable.* New York: Grove.

Chicago, J. (1977). *Through the flower: My struggle as a woman artist.* Garden City, NY: Anchor/Doubleday.

Chicago, J. (1979). *The Dinner Party: A symbol of our heritage.* Garden City, NY: Anchor/Doubleday.

Daly, M. (1978). *Gyn/ecology: The metaethics of radical feminism.* Boston: Beacon.

Ehninger, D. (Ed.). (1972). *Contemporary rhetoric: A reader's coursebook.* Glenview, IL: Scott, Foresman.

Ferguson, K. E. (1984). *The feminist case against bureaucracy.* Philadelphia: Temple University Press.

Foucault, M. (1970). *The order of things: An archaeology of the human sciences.* New York: Pantheon.

Foucault, M. (1972). *The archaeology of knowledge* (A. M. S. Smith, Trans.). New York: Pantheon.

Friedan, B. (1981). *The second stage.* New York: Summit.

Gergen, K. J. (1982). *Toward transformation in social knowledge.* New York: Springer-Verlag.

Jespersen, O. (1922). *Language: Its nature, development and origin.* London: George Allen & Unwin.

Kramarae, C. (1981). *Women and men speaking: Frameworks for analysis.* Rowley, MA: Newbury House.

Schulz, M. (1984). Minority writers: The struggle for authenticity and authority. In C. Kramarae, M. Schulz, & W. M. O'Barr, (Eds.), *Language and power* (pp. 206–217). Beverly Hills: Sage.

Additional Samples
Feminist Criticism

Altman, Karen E. "Consuming Ideology: The Better Homes in America Campaign." *Critical Studies in Mass Communication*, 7 (September 1990), 286–307.

Biesecker, Barbara A. "Towards a Transactional View of Rhetorical and Feminist Theory: Rereading Helene Cixous's *The Laugh of the Medusa*." *Southern Communication Journal*, 57 (Winter 1992), 86–96.

Bineham, Jeffery L. "Theological Hegemony and Oppositional Interpretive Codes: The Case of Evangelical Christian Feminism." *Western Journal of Communication*, 57 (Fall 1993), 515–29.

Borisoff, Deborah, and Dan F. Hahn. "Thinking with the Body: Sexual Metaphors." *Communication Quarterly*, 41 (Summer 1993), 253–60.

Bostdorff, Denise M. "Vice-Presidential Comedy and the Traditional Female Role: An Examination of the Rhetorical Characteristics of the Vice Presidency." *Western Journal of Speech Communication*, 55 (Winter 1991), 1–27.

Brinson, Susan L. "TV Rape: Television's Communication of Cultural Attitudes Toward Rape." *Women's Studies in Communication*, 12 (Fall 1989), 23–36.

Brummett, Barry, and Margaret Carlisle Duncan. "Toward a Discursive Ontology of Media." *Critical Studies in Mass Communication*, 9 (September 1992), 229–49.

Bybee, Carl R. "Constructing Women as Authorities: Local Journalism and the Microphysics of Power." *Critical Studies in Mass Communication*, 7 (September 1990), 197–214.

Cantor, Muriel G. "Prime-Time Fathers: A Study in Continuity and Change." *Critical Studies in Mass Communication*, 7 (September 1990), 275–85.

Carlson, A. Cheree. "Creative Casuistry and Feminist Consciousness: The Rhetoric of Moral Reform." *Quarterly Journal of Speech*, 78 (February 1992), 16–32.

Carlson, A. Cheree. "Defining Womanhood: Lucretia Coffin Mott and the Transformation of Femininity." *Western Journal of Communication*, 58 (Spring 1994), 85–97.

Carlson, A. Cheree. "Limitations on the Comic Frame: Some Witty American Women of the Nineteenth Century." *Quarterly Journal of Speech*, 74 (August 1988), 310–22.

Cooks, Leda M., Mark P. Orbe, and Carol S. Bruess. "The Fairy Tale Theme in Popular Culture: A Semiotic Analysis of *Pretty Woman*." *Women's Studies in Communication*, 16 (Fall 1993), 86–104.

Daughton, Suzanne M. "Women's Issues, Women's Place: Gender-Related Problems in Presidential Campaigns." *Communication Quarterly*, 42 (Spring 1994), 106–119.

Dow, Bonnie J. "Femininity and Feminism in *Murphy Brown*." *Southern Communication Journal*, 57 (Winter 1992), 143–55.

Dow, Bonnie J. "Hegemony, Feminist Criticism and *The Mary Tyler Moore Show*." *Critical Studies in Mass Communication*, 7 (September 1990), 261–74.

Dow, Bonnie J., and Mari Boor Tonn. "'Feminine Style' and Political Judgment in the Rhetoric of Ann Richards." *Quarterly Journal of Speech*, 79 (August 1993), 286–302.

Downey, Sharon D., and Karen Rasmussen. "The Irony of *Sophie's Choice*." *Women's Studies in Communication*, 14 (Fall 1991), 1–23.

Fabj, Valeria. "Motherhood as Political Voice: The Rhetoric of the Mothers of Plaza de Mayo." *Communication Studies*, 44 (Spring 1993), 1–18.

Foss, Sonja K., and Karen A. Foss. "The Construction of Feminine Spectatorship in Garrison Keillor's Radio Monologues." *Quarterly Journal of Speech*, 80 (November 1994), 410–26.

Goldman, Robert, Deborah Heath, and Sharon L. Smith. "Commodity Feminism." *Critical Studies in Mass Communication*, 8 (September 1991), 333–51.

Griffin, Cindy L. "A Feminist Perspective on Age: Anne Noggle's Photographs of Women and Aging." *Women's Studies in Communication*, 16 (Fall 1993), 1–26.

Griffin, Cindy L. "Rhetoricizing Alienation: Mary Wollstonecraft and the Rhetorical Construction of Women's Oppression." *Quarterly Journal of Speech*, 80 (August 1994), 293–312.

Haaland, Bonnie A. "The Decontextualization of Abortion: An Analysis of 'The Silent Scream.'" *Women's Studies in Communication*, 12 (Fall 1989), 59–76.

Hanke, Robert. "Hegemonic Masculinity in *thirtysomething*." *Critical Studies in Mass Communication*, 7 (September 1990), 231–48.

Illouz, Eva. "Reason Within Passion: Love in Women's Magazines." *Critical Studies in Mass Communication*, 8 (September 1991), 231–48.

Jablonski, Carol J. "Rhetoric, Paradox, and the Movement for Women's Ordination in the Roman Catholic Church." *Quarterly Journal of Speech*, 74 (May 1988), 164–83.

Japp, Phyllis M. "Gender and Work in the 1980s: Television's Working Women as Displaced Persons." *Women's Studies in Communication*, 14 (Spring 1991), 49–74.

Jasinski, James. "The Feminization of Liberty, Domesticated Virtue, and the Reconstitution of Power and Authority in Early American Political Discourse." *Quarterly Journal of Speech*, 79 (May 1993), 146–64.

Jorgensen-Earp, Cheryl R. "The Lady, the Whore, and the Spinster: The Rhetorical Use of Victorian Images of Women." *Western Journal of Speech Communication*, 54 (Winter 1990), 82–98.

King, Janis L. "Justificatory Rhetoric for a Female Political Candidate: A Case Study of Wilma Mankiller." *Women's Studies in Communication*, 13 (Fall 1990), 21–38.

Kray, Susan. "Orientalization of an "Almost White" Woman: The Interlocking Effects of Race, Class, Gender, and Ethnicity in American Mass Media." *Critical Studies in Mass Communication*, 10 (December 1993), 349–66.

Loeb, Jane Connelly. "Rhetorical and Ideological Conservatism in *thirtysomething*." *Critical Studies in Mass Communication*, 7 (September 1990), 249–60.

Lutfiyya, M. Nawal. "Critical Street Theorizing: A Case Study of Ladies Against Women, or, Comedy as Political Policy Development." *Women's Studies in Communication*, 15 (Spring 1992), 25–48.

Marston, Peter J., and Bambi Rockwell. "Charlotte Perkins Gilman's 'The Yellow Wallpaper': Rhetorical Subversion in Feminist Literature." *Women's Studies in Communication*, 14 (Fall 1991), 58–72.

Mattina, Anne F. "'Rights as Well as Duties': The Rhetoric of Leonora O'Reilly." *Communication Quarterly*, 42 (Spring 1994), 196–205.

McLaughlin, Lisa. "Discourses of Prostitution/Discourses of Sexuality." *Critical Studies in Mass Communication*, 8 (September 1991), 249–72.

McMullen, Wayne J., and Martha Solomon. "The Politics of Adaptation: Steven Spielberg's Appropriation of *The Color Purple*." *Text and Performance Quarterly*, 14 (April 1994), 158–74.

Perkins, Sally J. "The Dilemma of Identity: Theatrical Portrayals of a 16th Century Feminist." *Southern Communication Journal*, 59 (Spring 1994), 205–14.

Perkins, Sally J. "The Myth of the Matriarchy: Annulling Patriarchy through the Regeneration of Time." *Communication Studies*, 42 (Winter 1991), 371–82.

Perkins, Sally J. "The Rhetoric of Androgyny as Revealed in *The Feminine Mystique*." *Communication Studies*, 40 (Summer 1989), 69–80.

Perkins, Sally J. "*The Singular Life of Albert Nobbs*: Subversive Rhetoric and Feminist Ideology." *Women's Studies in Communication*, 16 (Spring 1993), 34–54.

Procter, David E., Roger C. Aden, and Phyllis Japp. "Gender/Issue Interaction in Political Identity Making: Nebraska's Woman vs. Woman Gubernatorial Campaign." *Central States Speech Journal*, 39 (Fall/Winter 1988), 190–203.

Ragan, Sandra L., and Victoria Aarons. "Women's Response to Men's Silence: A Fictional Analysis." *Women's Studies in Communication*, 9 (Fall 1986), 67–75.

Rasmussen, Karen. "*China Beach* and American Mythology of War." *Women's Studies in Communication*, 15 (Fall 1992), 22–50.

Rogers, Richard A. "Pleasure, Power and Consent: The Interplay of Race and Gender." *Women's Studies in Communication*, 16 (Fall 1993), 62–85.

Rushing, Janice Hocker. "Evolution of 'The New Frontier' in *Alien* and *Aliens*: Patriarchal Co-optation of the Feminine Archetype." *Quarterly Journal of Speech*, 75 (February 1989), 1–24.

Rushing, Janice Hocker, and Thomas S. Frentz. "The Frankenstein Myth in Contemporary Cinema." *Critical Studies in Mass Communication*, 6 (March 1989), 61–80.

Schwichtenberg, Cathy. "Madonna's Postmodern Feminism: Bringing the Margins to the Center." *Southern Communication Journal*, 57 (Winter 1992), 120–31.

Sheckels, Jr., Theodore F. "Mikulski vs. Chavez for the Senate from Maryland in 1986 and the 'Rules' for Attack Politics." *Communication Quarterly*, 42 (Summer 1994), 311–26.

Stearney, Lynn M. "Feminism, Ecofeminism, and the Maternal Archetype: Motherhood as a Feminine Universal." *Communication Quarterly*, 42 (Spring 1994), 145–59.

Sullivan, Patricia A. "Women's Discourse and Political Communication: A Case Study of Congressperson Patricia Schroeder." *Western Journal of Communication*, 57 (Fall 1993), 530–45.

Sutton, Jane. "The Taming of *Polos/Polis*: Rhetoric as an Achievement Without Woman." *Southern Communication Journal*, 57 (Winter 1992), 97–119.

Taylor, Bryan C. "Register of the Repressed: Women's Voice and Body in the Nuclear Weapons Organization." *Quarterly Journal of Speech*, 79 (August 1993), 267–85.

Vande Berg, Leah R. "*China Beach*, Prime Time War in the Postfeminist Age: An Example of Patriarchy in a Different Voice." *Western Journal of Communication*, 57 (Summer 1993), 349–66.

White, Cindy L., and Catherine A. Dobris. "A Chorus of Discordant Voices: Radical Feminist Confrontations with Patriarchal Religion." *Southern Communication Journal*, 58 (Spring 1993), 239–46.

Williams, Mary Rose. "A Reconceptualization of Protest Rhetoric: Women's Quilts as Rhetorical Forms." *Women's Studies in Communication*, 17 (Fall 1994), 20–44.

7

Generic Criticism

Generic criticism is rooted in the assumption that certain types of situations provoke similar needs and expectations among audiences and thus call for particular kinds of rhetoric. Rather than seeking to discover how one situation affects one particular rhetorical act, the generic critic seeks to discover commonalities in rhetorical patterns across recurring situations. The generic critic attempts to understand rhetorical practices in different time periods and in different places by discerning the similarities in rhetorical situations and the rhetoric constructed in response to them.

The generic critic may study, for example, public proceedings—a trial, the monthly meeting of a board of education, the debate of a state legislative body, and the convention of a political party. These situations are seen as sharing certain features and eliciting common rhetorical responses—the conducting of the proceeding in the name of a larger community, for example, and the inability of the observers to the proceeding to effect change in it.[1] Generic criticism, then, enables the critic to view rhetoric "panoramically rather than as a series of snapshots of discrete moments."[2]

Generic criticism investigates rhetoric across situations through a process of categorization. In generic criticism, rhetorical artifacts are grouped according to similarities; one group is seen as sharing some important characteristics that differentiate it from other groups. The French word, *genre*, is the term used to refer to such a distinct group, type, class, or category. Certainly, aspects of genres or categories are involved in all rhetorical criticism because criticism of any kind involves classification, but generic criticism makes the process of classification central.

A rhetorical genre is a constellation, fusion, or clustering of three different kinds of elements so that a unique kind of rhetorical artifact is created. One element is *situational requirements,* or the perception of conditions in a situation that call forth particular kinds of rhetorical responses. A genre also contains *substantive and stylistic characteristics* of the rhetoric—features of the rhetoric chosen by the rhetor to respond to the perceived requirements of particular situations. Substantive characteristics are those that constitute the content of the rhetoric; stylistic characteristics constitute the form of the rhetoric.[3] The third element of a rhetorical genre, the *organizing principle,* is the root term or the notion that serves as an umbrella term for the various characteristic features of the rhetoric. It is the label for the internal dynamic of the constellation that is formed by the substantive, stylistic, and situational features of the genre.[4]

If there is a genre of eulogistic discourse, for example, then speeches of eulogy for Martin Luther King, Jr., John Lennon, and Georgia O'Keeffe should be similar in significant aspects. They should share characteristics in stylistic and substantive strategies and in the organizing principle that binds them together. While strategic responses and stylistic choices, in isolation, may appear in other rhetorical forms, what is distinctive about a genre of rhetoric is the recurrence of the forms together, unified by the same organizing principle. A genre, then, is not simply a set of features that characterize various rhetorical acts; it is a set of interdependent features.

Critics are interested in the relationship between recurring situations and the rhetoric developed in response to them for a number of reasons. The study of genres enables critics to understand social reality and its relationship to rhetoric. Because genres represent conventionalized patterns for thought or structures for meaning, they can serve as an index to the social reality in which they figure. The rhetorical forms that constitute genres not only structure the meanings of a particular social reality, but they also reflect beliefs, attitudes, and values and thus arise out of that reality. Bruce E. Gronbeck explains this connection between genres and social reality: "A 'tragedy,' a 'sonnet,' and a 'chronologically ordered speech' are not natural objects; rather, they are quasi-linguistic cells for cerebration provided by cultures for their members. . . . Such forms, therefore, are more than literary constructs, for they are grounded, not merely upon technical plot devices, rhyme schemes, and textbook pedagogy, but upon culturally imposed criteria for thinking.''[5]

Not only can generic criticism help the critic discover the nature of the social reality created by and reflected in genres, but it also allows critics to study how rhetorical acts influence each other and how rhetoric is shaped by prior rhetoric.[6] Generic criticism, as Kathleen Hall Jamieson explains, enables the critic to explore ''the continuity and discontinuity of rhetorical forms''[7] or how rhetorical forms have developed, changed, and degenerated. Critics thus are able to secure a fuller picture of the evolution of rhetoric in a culture and of the threads that unite the rhetoric of a culture across seemingly diverse time periods and settings.

Finally, generic criticism is useful because it heightens awareness of the way in which classification operates in any critical approach. It encourages critics to recognize that numerous and divergent systems of classification are possible, to examine and regard as problematic the classification system they are imposing on a rhetorical artifact, and to consider how that system affects perceptions of the artifact. Consequently, it encourages the critic to bring alternative classifications to the artifact. The result may be insights into the work that may not have been possible using other classification systems.[8]

The roots of the notion of genre and of generic criticism can be traced to the writings of Aristotle and other classical rhetoricians. Much of classical rhetorical theory is based on the assumption that situations fall into general types, depending on the goal of the rhetoric. Poetic discourse, for example, is seen as different from rhetorical discourse because the end of poetic discourse is imitation, while rhetoric is designed to persuade. In a similar fashion, rhetoric is divided into three types of discourse—deliberative or political, forensic or legal, and epideictic or ceremonial. Each of these types has distinctive aims— expedience for deliberative, justice for forensic, and honor for epideictic speaking. They have distinctive strategies as well—exhortation and dissuasion for deliberative, accusation and defense for forensic, and praise and blame for epideictic speaking.[9] Thus, classification of discourse on the basis of similar characteristics and situations has been part of the tradition of the communication field since its inception.

The first person to use the term, *generic criticism*, in the communication discipline was Edwin Black in 1965, as part of his criticism of neo-Aristotelianism. He proposed as an alternative to the traditional method of criticism a generic frame of reference that included these tenets: (1) ''there is a limited number of situations in which a rhetor can find himself''; (2) ''there is a limited number of ways in which a rhetor can and will respond rhetorically to any given situational type''; and (3) ''the recurrence of a given situational type through history will provide the critic with information on the rhetorical responses available in that situation.''[10]

Lloyd F. Bitzer's notion of the rhetorical situation, presented in 1968, also contributed to the development of generic criticism. Bitzer's notion of recurring situations was particularly significant for generic criticism: "From day to day, year to year, comparable situations occur, prompting comparable responses; hence rhetorical forms are born and a special vocabulary, grammar, and style are established.''[11] Although his notion of the rhetorical situation has generated controversy,[12] it further developed the theoretical base for generic criticism.

Yet another contribution to the development of generic criticism was a conference held in 1976 at Lawrence, Kansas, called "'Significant Form' in Rhetorical Criticism." Sponsored by the Speech Communication Association and the University of Kansas, the conference was organized around a notion of "significant form" as genre: "The phrase 'significant form' is intended to refer to recurring patterns in discourse or action including, among others, the repeated use of images, metaphors, arguments, structural arrangements, configurations of language or a combination of such elements into what critics have termed 'genres' or 'rhetorics.'"[13] The result of the conference was a book, *Form and Genre: Shaping Rhetorical Action,* edited by Karlyn Kohrs Campbell and Kathleen Hall Jamieson. It provided theoretical discussions of the concept of genre in criticism and included samples of generic criticism. Thus, it brought into one volume the best thinking that had been done on generic criticism and served as a catalyst for further work in the area.[14]

Procedures

Four steps are involved in a generic critic's analysis of an artifact: (1) formulating a research question and selecting artifacts; (2) selecting a unit of analysis; (3) analyzing the artifacts; and (4) writing the critical essay.

Formulating a Research Question and Selecting an Artifact

The first step in the process of rhetorical criticism is to develop a research question to ask about rhetoric and to select rhetorical artifacts to analyze that will provide an initial answer to the question.

Selecting a Unit of Analysis

The critic's next step is to select a unit of analysis that can help the critic answer the research question. The unit of analysis is that aspect of the artifact to which the critic attends in the analysis. The units of analysis provided by generic criticism are the three primary elements of a genre—situational requirements, substantive and stylistic characteristics, and the organizing principle.

Analyzing the Artifact

Generic criticism involves three different options for the critic, with each leading to a different contribution to the understanding of genres—generic description, generic participation, and generic application.[15] The first option available in generic criticism is *generic description*, where the critic examines several rhetorical artifacts to determine if a genre exists. This is an inductive operation; the critic begins with a consideration of specific features of rhetorical artifacts and moves to a generalization about them in the naming of a genre. The second option, *generic participation*, is a deductive procedure in which the critic moves from consideration of a general class of rhetoric to consideration of a specific rhetorical artifact. Here, a specific rhetorical artifact is tested against a genre to discover if it participates in that genre. The third option is *generic application*; it also is a deductive procedure and involves application of a generic model to particular rhetorical artifacts in order to assess them.

Generic Description. In the attempt to describe a genre, the critic examines various rhetorical artifacts to see if a genre exists. The point is for the critic to define a genre and formulate theoretical constructs about its characteristics. Generic description involves four steps: (1) observation of similarities in rhetorical responses to particular situations; (2) collection of rhetorical artifacts occurring in similar situations; (3) analysis of the artifacts to discover if they share characteristics; and (4) formulation of the organizing principle of the genre.

The first step of generic description is the observation by the critic that similar situations, removed from each other in time and place, seem to generate similar rhetorical responses. The critic speculates that a genre of rhetoric may exist. The critic's suspicion of the presence of a genre is not to be confused with a preconceived framework that predicts or limits the defining characteristics of the genre. Rather, the hunch simply serves as a prod to the critic to begin an investigation to see if a genre exists and, if so, what elements characterize it. If a critic begins with the idea that the messages produced in situations when someone announces the intention to run for public office seem to share characteristics, that idea does not dictate that certain characteristics will be discovered. All the critic knows at this point is that the situations seem similar, and the rhetoric in these situations also may share commonalities.

The second step is the collection of a varied sample of rhetorical artifacts that may represent the genre. The critic identifies rhetorical acts in which the perceived rhetorical situation appears similar or searches out contexts, preferably from various historical periods, that seem to be characterized by similar constraints of situation. If the critic suspects a genre of rhetoric may exist in which individuals announce their candidacy for office, for example, the critic collects instances where individuals have announced their intention to run for office. A study by James S. Measell began in a similar fashion. He noticed that similar rhetorical situations were faced by Abraham Lincoln and William Pitt, Prime Minister of England during the French Revolution: both Lincoln and Pitt needed to justify "their administrative policy to withhold the privileges of habeas corpus."[16] The rhetoric of Lincoln and Pitt on the topic became the data for his study, and he well might have found other such instances to study had he wanted to expand his sample.

The third step in the process is close analysis of the rhetorical artifacts collected to discover if there are substantive or stylistic features shared in the various rhetorical artifacts that were collected. Here the critic seeks commonalities in how the rhetors dealt with the perceived problem in the situation.

In the process of discovering similarities and differences among the rhetorical acts under study, the critic is not confined to looking for particular kinds of strategies or to using one critical methodology. Ideally, the critic allows the rhetorical artifacts being studied to "suggest" the important similarities and differences; those elements that stand out as most critical are the ones on which the critic focuses. These might be metaphors, images, sentence structure, failure to enact arguments, or an infinite variety of other elements. The critic may discover, for example, substantive strategies—those that deal primarily with content—such as use of metaphors dealing with family or the expression of self-sacrifice. Stylistic strategies—those that deal largely with form—may include elements such as adoption of a belligerent tone or use of ambiguous terminology.

The critic may choose to focus, however, on units of analysis suggested in particular critical methods such as neo-Aristotelianism or fantasy-theme analysis. Neo-Aristotelian criticism could be used at this stage of generic description to discover similarities among the various rhetorical artifacts in use of emotional appeals, for example. Using fantasy-theme criticism, the critic could search for commonalities in depictions of characters, settings, or actions.

In the process of textual analysis to discover rhetorical strategies, the critic may want to perform subsample comparisons of the rhetorical artifacts being investigated to identify subclasses of a genre. The critic may seek to determine, for example, if a genre of resignation rhetoric exists and, in the process, discover variants of resignation rhetoric, each characterized by a somewhat different set of rhetorical strategies. The critic may need to distinguish, then, among various characteristics, seeing some as paradigm cases of a genre, some as borderline cases, and some as characteristics of a subgenre.[17] B. L. Ware and Wil A. Linkugel's essay on speeches of apology is an example of the delineation of subgenres; they identify four different subgenres of apologetic discourse: absolutive, vindicative, explanative, and justificative.[18]

If sufficient similarities are noted to continue the search for a genre, the fourth step for the critic in the process of generic description is to formulate the organizing principle that captures the essence of the strategies common to the sample collected. In his study of the sentimental style, for example, Black identified such common elements in rhetorical artifacts as evasiveness and refusal to apprehend the ugly and the corrupt. He then named as the core of the sentimental genre "the manifestation of a disposition to subordinate all values to aesthetic values in order, essentially, to escape a burden of moral responsibility."[19] This act of labeling the organizing principle actually may occur simultaneously with the delineation of substantive and stylistic strategies since the elements identified may come to the critic's attention grouped around an obvious core or principle. Regardless of the order in which the steps occur, at the end of this process, the critic has formulated a list of rhetorical characteristics that appear to define the genre and an organizing principle that unites them.

In attempting to determine the distinguishing features of a genre, the critic sometimes has difficulty deciding whether or not a particular characteristic appears to be such a feature. In such instances, the following questions may be useful in helping the critic determine if a characteristic is one that contributes to a distinct genre:

1. Can rules be identified with which other critics or observers can concur in identifying characteristics of rhetorical practice when confronted with the same examples of rhetorical practice? The distinguishing features of a genre must not only be namable but so must the rules that are serving as guides for the critic in making such distinctions among characteristics in different rhetorical artifacts. These rules, of course, do not specify precisely how the rhetorical act is to be performed. A genre is not formulaic; there is always another strategy that a rhetor can use to meet the requirements of the situation. But a genre establishes bounded options for rhetors in situations, and naming the rules that define those options can help clarify if a characteristic is part of a genre or not.[20]

2. Are the similarities in substantive and stylistic strategies clearly rooted in the situations in which they were generated? In other words, does the way in which the situation is defined require the inclusion of an element like this in the rhetorical artifact? Simply the appearance of one characteristic in several rhetorical artifacts does not mean it was devised to deal with the same perceived situational constraints. The critic needs to refer frequently to the description of the perceived situation to establish that the similarities are not simply coincidental but have a relationship to the perceived situation. This is not to say that a situation demands one particular response, for rhetors are engaged in action and not reaction. Rhetors have great latitude in responding to situations, and the strategies they select to fit a situation are varied. Still, the critic must be able to ground the strategy in some aspect of the perceived situation.[21]

3. Would the absence of the characteristic in question alter the nature of the rhetorical artifact? A genre is created from a fusion of characteristics, and all are critical in the dynamic of that fusion. Simply saying that a certain element appears in all the artifacts under study is not enough; a genre exists only if each element is fused to the other elements so its absence would alter the organizing principle. A genre is given its character by a fusion of forms, not by its individual elements.[22]

4. Does the characteristic contribute to insight about a type of rhetoric or simply lead to the development of a classification scheme? The test of a genre is the degree of understanding it provides of the rhetorical artifacts; the point of classification is the critical illumination it produces. Insight, and not neatness of a classification scheme, is the critic's goal in generic description. If the discovery of similarities among rhetorical artifacts classifies but does not clarify, it may not be particularly useful.[23]

Description of a genre, then, is one option for the critic who engages in generic criticism; various rhetorical artifacts are examined to see if a genre exists. This procedure involves examining a variety of rhetorical artifacts that seem to be generated in similar situations to discover if they have in common substantive and stylistic strategies and an organizing principle that fuses those strategies. If, in fact, they do, the critic has developed a theory of the existence of a genre. This theory then may be used in a second option called *generic participation*.

Generic Participation. The critic who engages in generic participation determines which rhetorical artifacts participate in which genres. This involves a deductive process in which the critic tests an instance of rhetoric against the characteristics of a genre. Generic participation as a critical operation involves three steps: (1) description of the perceived situational requirements, substantive and stylistic strategies, and organizing principle of a genre; (2) description of the situational requirements, substantive and stylistic strategies, and organizing principle of a rhetorical artifact; and (3) comparison of the characteristics of the rhetorical artifact with those of the genre to discover if the artifact belongs in that genre. The critic then uses the findings to confirm or suggest modifications in the rhetorical genre.

As an example of this process, the critic may be interested in discovering if the campaign rhetoric of Marian Barry constitutes a rhetoric of apology. Barry, formerly the mayor of Washington, D.C., ran again for the office in 1994 after serving a prison term for possession of crack cocaine; his campaign was successful, and he was re-elected. In his campaign speeches, he emphasized the "god force" that helped him recover from his drug and alcohol addictions and asked for voters' forgiveness. For a study of generic participation, the critic first would turn to earlier studies in which the characeristics of apologetic rhetoric are delineated and then would see what elements characterize Barry's speeches. Comparison of the two sets of features would enable the critic to discover if Barry's speeches participate in the genre of apologetic discourse.

Generic Application. Yet a third option is open to the critic who is interested in studying genres—generic application. Rather than simply determining if a particular rhetorical artifact belongs in a particular genre, the critic uses the description of the genre to evaluate particular instances of rhetoric. The situational, stylistic, and substantive elements that characterize a genre are applied to a specific rhetorical artifact that has been defined as participating in that genre in order to assess it. On the basis of the application of the generic characteristics to the specific model, the critic is able to determine if the artifact is a good or poor exemplar of the genre.

Four basic steps are involved in generic application (the first three are the same as the ones for generic participation): (1) description of the perceived situational requirements, substantive and stylistic strategies, and organizing principle of a genre; (2) identification of the perceived situational requirements, substantive and stylistic strategies, and organizing principle of the rhetorical artifact representative of that genre; (3) comparison of the characteristics of the rhetorical artifact with those of the genre; and (4) evaluation of the rhetorical artifact according to its success in fulfilling the required characteristics of the genre.

In using generic features to evaluate a rhetorical artifact, the critic draws critical insights about the effectiveness of a particular rhetorical artifact in fulfilling perceived situational demands. When a generic form is used by a rhetor, it creates expectations in the audience members, who perceive and evaluate rhetoric in terms of generic classifications and expect a particular style and certain types of content from particular types of rhetoric. If the rhetoric does not fulfill these expectations, the audience tends to be confused and to react negatively. Such violations of expectations tend to occur, for example, with viewers who encounter works of art known as *body art* in an art gallery. Visitors to the gallery expect to see art framed and hanging on walls—the generic form of visual art. Instead, they encounter works such as *Transfixed*, in which body artist Chris Burden nailed himself to the roof of a Volkswagen bug and had the engine run at full speed for two minutes. While viewers may come to realize that the breaking of the generic frame is done intentionally by the artist/rhetor to encourage viewers to question the definition of art, simply the violation of generic expectations initially may create confusion, frustration, and rejection for viewers.[24]

The critic also may discover that generic violations increase the rhetorical artifact's effectiveness, as is the case with Sergio Leone's film, *Once Upon a Time in the West*. Viewers expect a film in the genre of the Western tradition but find many violations of the genre—in unusual costumes worn by the cowboys; comic characters; the slow, unfolding of scenes; and difficulty telling the heroes from the villains—but these violations create an experience for the viewer that is positive rather than negative. The critic's evaluation, whether positive or negative, is made on the basis of the suasory impact of the rhetoric that results from its fulfillment or violation of generic expectations.

Writing the Critical Essay

After completion of the analysis, the critic writes an essay that includes five major components: (1) an introduction, in which the research question, its contribution to rhetorical theory, and its significance are discussed; (2) description of the artifacts and their contexts; (3) description of the units of analysis, either the characteristics of the genre (in generic description) or the characteristics of the genre and the rhetorical artifacts under investigation (in generic participation and generic application); (4) report of the findings of the analysis, in which the critic reveals the findings of the generic description, participation, or application; and (5) discussion of the contribution the analysis makes to answering the research question.

Sample Essays

The three sample essays that follow illustrate some of the options open to the critic who engages in generic criticism. Leah R. Ekdom Vande Berg's essay on the television program, *Moonlighting*, exemplifies the process of generic description. She seeks to discover the characteristics of the new genre to which the television program belongs in order to answer the research question, "How do artistic texts impede the assumptions encouraged by generic conventions?" Sharon M. Varallo's essay also is an example of generic description. She is interested in discovering if a genre of family photographs exists and is guided by the research question, "What rhetorical means do families use to construct themselves as a unit?" John M. Murphy's essay on Robert Kennedy's speeches following the death of Martin Luther King, Jr. is a sample of both generic participation and generic application. He establishes that Kennedy's speeches fit the characteristics of the genre of the jeremiad, and he then uses the description of that genre to evaluate Kennedy's rhetoric. His research question is, "How does the jeremiad function in times of crisis?"

Notes

[1]Michael Halloran, "Doing Public Business in Public," in *Form and Genre: Shaping Rhetorical Action*, ed. Karlyn Kohrs Campbell and Kathleen Hall Jamieson (Falls Church, VA: Speech Communication Association, [1978]), p. 121.

[2]Karlyn Kohrs Campbell and Kathleen Hall Jamieson, "Introduction," *Southern Speech Communication Journal*, 51 (Summer 1986), 296.

[3]For a useful description of substance and form as they relate to genre, see Carolyn R. Miller, "Genre as Social Action," *Quarterly Journal of Speech*, 70 (May 1984), 159.

[4]For a discussion of strategies and organizing principle, see: Karlyn Kohrs Campbell and Kathleen Hall Jamieson, "Form and Genre in Rhetorical Criticism: An Introduction," in *Form and Genre: Shaping Rhetorical Action*, ed. Karlyn Kohrs Campbell and Kathleen Hall Jamieson (Falls Church, VA: Speech Communication Association, [1978]), pp. 18, 21, 25; Karlyn Kohrs Campbell and Kathleen Hall Jamieson, "Rhetorical Hybrids: Fusion of Generic Elements," *Quarterly Journal of Speech*, 68 (May 1982), 146; Jackson Harrell and Wil A. Linkugel, "On Rhetorical Genre: An Organizing Perspective," *Philosophy and Rhetoric*, 11 (Fall 1978), 263–64; and Robert L. Ivie, "Images of Savagery in American Justifications for War," *Communication Monographs*, 47 (November 1980), 282.

[5]Bruce E. Gronbeck, "Celluloid Rhetoric: On Genres of Documentary," in *Form and Genre: Shaping Rhetorical Action*, ed. Karlyn Kohrs Campbell and Kathleen Hall Jamieson (Falls Church, VA: Speech Communication Association, [1978]), p. 141.

[6]Campbell and Jamieson, "Form and Genre in Rhetorical Criticism," p. 27.

[7]Kathleen M. Hall Jamieson, "Generic Constraints and the Rhetorical Situation," *Philosophy and Rhetoric*, 6 (Summer 1973), 168.

[8]Jamieson, p. 169.

[9]Aristotle, *Rhetoric*, 1.5–10. For a more elaborate discussion of genre in the *Rhetoric*, see G. P. Mohrmann and Michael C. Leff, "Lincoln at Cooper Union: A Rationale for Neo-Classical Criticism," *Quarterly Journal of Speech*, 60 (December 1974), 463. For a discussion of differences between contemporary notions and Aristotle's notion of genre,

see Thomas M. Conley, "Ancient Rhetoric and Modern Genre Criticism," *Communication Quarterly*, 27 (Fall 1979), 47-48.

[10]Edwin Black, *Rhetorical Criticism: A Study in Method* (Madison: University of Wisconsin Press, 1978), p. 133.

[11]Lloyd F. Bitzer, "The Rhetorical Situation," *Philosophy and Rhetoric*, 1 (Winter 1968), 13.

[12]Among the essays that deal with Bitzer's notion of the rhetorical situation are: Lloyd F. Bitzer, "The Rhetorical Situation," *Philosophy and Rhetoric*, 1 (Winter 1968), 1-14; Richard L. Larson, "Lloyd Bitzer's 'Rhetorical Situation' and the Classification of Discourse: Problems and Implications," *Philosophy and Rhetoric*, 3 (Summer 1970), 165-68; Arthur B. Miller, "Rhetorical Exigence," *Philosophy and Rhetoric*, 5 (Spring 1972), 111-18; Richard E. Vatz, "The Myth of the Rhetorical Situation," *Philosophy and Rhetoric*, 6 (Summer 1973), 154-61; Scott Consigny, "Rhetoric and Its Situations," *Philosophy and Rhetoric*, 7 (Summer 1974), 175-86; Barry Brummett, "Some Implications of 'Process' or 'Intersubjectivity': Postmodern Rhetoric," *Philosophy and Rhetoric*, 9 (Winter 1976), 21-51; David M. Hunsaker and Craig R. Smith, "The Nature of Issues: A Constructive Approach to Situational Rhetoric," *Western Speech Communication*, 40 (Summer 1976), 144-56; Lloyd F. Bitzer, "Functional Communication: A Situational Perspective," in *Rhetoric in Transition: Studies in the Nature and Uses of Rhetoric*, ed. Eugene E. White (University Park: Pennsylvania State University Press, 1980), pp. 21-38; and Richard A. Cherwitz and James W. Hikins, *Communication and Knowledge: An Investigation in Rhetorical Epistemology* (Columbia: University of South Carolina Press, 1986).

[13]Karlyn Kohrs Campbell and Kathleen Hall Jamieson, "Acknowledgements," in *Form and Genre: Shaping Rhetorical Action*, ed. Karlyn Kohrs Campbell and Kathleen Hall Jamieson (Falls Church, VA: Speech Communication Association, [1978]), p. 3.

[14]Current work on genre continues to raise questions about and refine its application in rhetorical criticism. See, for example, Herbert W. Simons and Aram A. Aghazarian, *Form, Genre, and the Study of Political Discourse* (Columbia: University of South Carolina Press, 1986). For a good discussion of some of the problems with generic criticism, see Thomas Conley's essay in this volume: "The Linnaean Blues: Thoughts on the Genre Approach," pp. 59-78.

[15]These three options were suggested by Harrell and Linkugel, pp. 274-77.

[16]James S. Measell, "A Comparative Study of Prime Minister William Pitt and President Abraham Lincoln on Suspension of Habeas Corpus," in *Form and Genre: Shaping Rhetorical Action*, ed. Karlyn Kohrs Campbell and Kathleen Hall Jamieson (Falls Church, VA: Speech Communication Association, [1978]), p. 87.

[17]For more discussion of this process, see Herbert W. Simons, " 'Genre-alizing' About Rhetoric: A Scientific Approach," in *Form and Genre: Shaping Rhetorical Action*, ed. Karlyn Kohrs Campbell and Kathleen Hall Jamieson (Falls Church, VA: Speech Communication Association, [1978]), p. 41.

[18]B. L. Ware and Wil A. Linkugel, "They Spoke in Defense of Themselves: On the Generic Criticism of Apologia," *Quarterly Journal of Speech*, 59 (October 1973), 282-83.

[19]Edwin Black, "The Sentimental Style as Escapism, or the Devil with Dan'l Webster," in *Form and Genre: Shaping Rhetorical Action*, ed. Karlyn Kohrs Campbell and Kathleen Hall Jamieson (Falls Church, VA: Speech Communication Association, [1978]), p. 83.

[20]For more on the notion of rules, see: Campbell and Jamieson, "Introduction," pp. 295-96; and Simons, p. 37.

[21]This notion receives some treatment in: Stephen E. Lucas, "Genre Criticism and Historical Context: The Case of George Washington's First Inaugural Address," *Southern Speech Communication Journal*, 51 (Summer 1986), 356-57; and Campbell and Jamieson, "Form and Genre in Rhetorical Criticism," p. 22.

[22]Campbell and Jamieson, "Form and Genre in Rhetorical Criticism," pp. 23-24.

[23]This notion was suggested by: Campbell and Jamieson, "Form and Genre in Rhetorical Criticism," p. 18; Walter R. Fisher, "Genre: Concepts and Applications in Rhetorical Criticism," *Western Journal of Speech Communication*, 44 (Fall 1980), 291; and Roderick P. Hart, "Contemporary Scholarship in Public Address: A Research Editorial," *Western Journal of Speech Communication*, 50 (Summer 1986), 292.

[24]For a discussion of body art and its function for an audience, see Sonja K. Foss, "Body Art: Insanity as Communication," *Central States Speech Journal*, 38 (Summer 1987), 122–31. For more discussion and examples of the impact of genres on audience expectations, see Jamieson, pp. 166–67.

Dramedy
Moonlighting as an Emergent Generic Hybrid

Leah R. Ekdom Vande Berg

And the nominee for best drama is . . . *Moonlighting.*
And the nominee for best comedy is . . . *Moonlighting.*
—Hollywood, Directors Guild of America (1985–86)

Newcomb (1978) has suggested that we can enhance our understanding of the significance of television for American culture by "concentrat[ing] on those crucial moments when whole sets of meaning change, for here we gather the meaning of television and of culture as they are reorganized" (p. 13). Among such moments are the appearances of televisual forms which do not fit conventional genre categories—moments when an evolving formula takes a significant step beyond invention within the conventional genre. At such moments, audiences' expectations are disrupted, recontextualized, and defamiliarized; that is, viewers "see" these television texts, as well as their expectations about "types" of televisual texts, in new ways. As a consequence of this defamiliarizing experience, viewers are invited, perhaps even compelled, to renegotiate their understandings of the text, the genre and the medium of television (see Shklovsky, 1965).

This essay examines one such moment. The "moment" was signified publicly by the nomination of the same television series, *Moonlighting,* for both best drama and best comedy awards: an unprecedented event in the 50-year history of the Directors Guild of America (Horowitz, 1986). Although thus far *Moonlighting* alone has stymied established genre schema, a number of other recent first-run network and cable series also have blurred certain generic conventions (e.g., *The Days and Nights of Molly Dodd,* NBC; *Frank's Place,* CBS; *Diamonds,* CBS Late Night; *Hooperman,* ABC; *1st and Ten,* HBO). This essay uses *Moonlighting* to examine the blurring of television genre distinctions between comedy and drama and the emergence of "dramedy" as a generic hybrid.

The essay begins with an overview of the notion of genre on television and a discussion of the usefulness of television genre studies. A newly formulated framework for genre study, Altman's (1986) semantic/syntactic approach, then is introduced and used to analyze the creative fusion of television drama and comedy genre elements in the recent

From *Communication Studies,* 40 (Spring 1989), 13–28. Used by permission of the Central States Communication Association and the author.

popular television series, *Moonlighting*. The analysis supports the argument that the self-conscious questioning of generic features effected through creative generic fusion is a reflexive technique which defamiliarizes the viewing experience, disrupts automatic conventional perceptions, and thus empowers viewers to see fresh generic features and expectations. The essay further argues, in accord with formalist critical theory, that in doing this the dramedy *Moonlighting* establishes itself as an artistic text. The essay concludes that the presence and popularity on prime time television of such a self-consciously artistic text suggests that the medium of television has come of age. Additionally, the essay concludes that Altman's approach also can be applied usefully to help explain how television genres and artistic texts emerge.

Genre Study and Television

Popular culture forms, including American television series and Hollywood films, are strongly generic. Audiences of these popular texts come to their viewing experiences with definite expectations. They welcome originality, as Warshow (1964) notes, "only in the degree that it intensifies the expected experience without fundamentally altering it" (p. 85). Most literary, television, film, and rhetorical critics agree that audiences develop genre expectations and employ them in understanding and evaluating popular art forms (e.g., Altman, 1986; Campbell & Jamieson, 1976; Cawelti, 1976, 1986; Jamieson, 1973; Jamieson & Campbell, 1982; Neale, 1981; Newcomb, 1974; Rose, 1985). However, scholars vary greatly in their approbation of popular generic texts. Thus, some critics have focused on the negative and hegemonic dimensions of popular generic forms, while others have highlighted the positive and pleasurable dimensions of genericity.

These latter critics (e.g., Warshow, 1964; Cawelti, 1976; Newcomb, 1974) theorize that original elements in popular culture texts are most enjoyable when audiences read these new elements as innovations—that is, as new variations of extant generic conventions. Thus, while new and original elements in popular culture texts can confuse, disorient, and frustrate audiences, popular texts with innovations appearing *qua* innovations (i.e., against the backdrop of generic conventions and expectations), are experienced as pleasurably rather than confusingly new. From this theoretical perspective, genre conventions such as familiar types of characters, settings, narrative structures, conflicts and dialectical tensions enhance viewers' viewing pleasure by fulfilling their expectations and enabling them to feel knowledgeable as they see familiar conventions played out.

The major American television networks are commercial endeavors which benefit economically when viewers derive pleasure from their television viewing experiences and which suffer when viewers are confused, frustrated, or offended by televisual texts and cease viewing them. As a result, it is not surprising that most American television programs are highly predictable and strongly generic. However, from time to time televisual texts which do not fit conventional generic categories appear. Such disruptions of generic expectations constitute "defamiliarizing" experiences which, according to certain formalist critical theories, epitomize the experience and purpose of art: They jar viewers into conscious awareness of previously taken-for-granted perceptual patterns (Shklovsky, 1965). For these critics, genre conventions are a means not to see because they encourage automatic, formulaic perceptions rather than conscious awareness and appreciation. From this perspective, highly generic texts would be narcotizing and inartistic texts. "Artistic" texts, on the other hand, would utilize various techniques to impede the automatic assumptions encouraged by generic conventions. One critical approach which we can use to examine both the genericity and the artistry of popular texts is genre criticism.

Genre criticism provides insights into the "psychology of forms" (Burke, 1957). That is, genre analysis produces enhanced understanding of particular texts, and cumulatively genre studies provide the basis for theories of "how a text works to achieve its ends," including theories about the power of conventions to create and satisfy audience expectations and thereby constrain the construction as well as the interpretation of texts. Genre studies, therefore, constitute a "mechanism through which both theory and practice can be modified and improved" (Campbell & Jamieson, 1976, pp. 19, 13).[1]

Genre studies also provide historical and cultural insights. According to Campbell and Jamieson (1976), "the critic who classifies a rhetorical artifact as generically akin to a class of similar artifacts has identified an undercurrent of history rather than comprehended an act isolated in time . . . [and] the existence of the recurrent provides insight into the human condition" (pp. 26–27). Cultural insights are also the basis of Newcomb's (1978) justification of television genre studies:

> When we have overcome the naive vision of television, we begin to understand the history of television as a tool with which to approach other questions. . . . We should carefully chronicle the changes in television in order to move toward those larger questions, and. . . . a history of formulas or larger patterns of action . . . provides the major services of establishing the appropriate field of reference. . . . An appropriate history of television, then, would be a history of those major stylistic shifts that are also shifts in meaning, and

would lead toward a very different conception of the medium and its role in American culture (pp. 12–13).

Genre studies of television provide critical, historical and theoretical contributions to our understanding of both specific texts and television's cultural role. Thus, the study of a generically problematic text such as *Moonlighting* enables us to trace the evolution of artistic forms and aesthetic values and to identify undercurrents of television and cultural history. Specifically, this genre study of *Moonlighting* examines an historically significant moment in television programming history and concomitantly enhances our theoretical understanding of how new television genres and artistic texts emerge.

A Semantic/Syntactic Approach to Genre Study

Two disparate approaches have dominated genre studies of popular texts—semantic approaches and syntactic approaches. Semantic approaches to genre theory and criticism, according to Altman (1986), stress "the genre's building blocks" and depend for genre definitions upon lists of recurrent semantic elements such as stock characters, common traits, attitudes, technical features such as locations and typical shots. Syntactic approaches to genre studies privilege the "constitutive relationships between undesignated and variable placeholders," including narrative structures, the dialectics in westerns between nature and culture, community and the individual, and the future and the past.

The distinction between semantic and syntactic textual features, according to Altman, "corresponds to a distinction between the primary, linguistic elements of which all texts are made and the secondary, textual meanings that are sometimes constructed by virtue of the syntactic bonds established between primary elements" (1986, p. 37).[2] Having discussed those distinctions, Altman offers an alternative by utilizing a combined semantic/syntactic approach in genre studies which can be used to explain how new genres emerge. As Altman argues in regard to popular cinema:

> I suggest that genres arise in one of two fundamental ways: either
> [a] relatively stable set of semantic givens is developed through
> syntactic experimentation into a coherent and durable syntax, or an
> already existing syntax adopts a new set of semantic elements. . . .
> A measure of continuity is thus developed between the task of the
> historian and that of the theoretician, for the tasks of both are now
> redefined as the study of the interrelationships between semantic
> elements and syntactic bonds (1986, p. 34).

Altman's theory, thus, suggests an explanation for the Directors Guild's dilemma concerning *Moonlighting*'s generic identity. Specifically, application of this theory suggests that *Moonlighting* is emblematic of an emergent genre (dramedy) which is developing by combining the semantic elements of one genre (drama) within the syntax of another genre (comedy). Additionally, Altman's semantic/syntactic approach to genre theory helps explain why *Moonlighting* is simultaneously a popularly successful and an artistic television text.

Moonlighting, Dramedy, and Generic Fusion

Dramedy, as the neologism implies, asserts a fusion of the television genres of drama and comedy into a generic hybrid. In Altman's terms, dramedy is an emergent genre which is evolving by combining semantic elements conventionally constitutive of one television genre within a syntax conventionally characteristic of another television genre. Thus an important difference exists between the generic hybrid dramedy and dramas or comedies with some cross-genre features. All three exhibit some features of both drama and comedy; however, in dramedy the anomalous generic features are not mere flickers in otherwise quite stolidly conventional generic forms. Rather, in dramedy, there is a sustained fusion of elements characteristically associated with two relatively distinct genres. In the dramedy *Moonlighting*, for example, semantic features constitutive of television drama and the organizing principles of comedy fuse throughout each episode to create a generic hybrid. The summary description of the premiere episode of *Moonlighting*, titled "The Lady in the Iron Mask," will serve as a starting point for discussing this generic fusion.

"The Lady in the Iron Mask"

—*Moonlighting*, ABC, 1 October 1985

The episode opens with a scene evocative of the movie *Psycho*: Through a glass shower door we watch as an opaque figure except for nails (unidentifiable as male or female) shaves both legs in the shower and subsequently (with only hands and legs in the frame) puts on hose and heels. Next, at the Blue Moon Detective Agency Office, owner and former model Madeline—Maddie—Hayes arrives at work and discovers her detective partner David Addison, secretary Agnes Dipesto, and other office workers simulating a fight to fill their time at this over-staffed and under-worked agency.

Into these less-than-cheerfully busy environs a client, still a once-in-a-blue-moon phenomenon, arrives. The client, who is wearing a black mask and black dress, identifies herself as Mrs. Barbara Wylie and tells a strange story. Ten years ago on the eve of her wedding, a young man named Frank Harbort, who was not her fiancé, professed his love for Barbara. Then, unable to bear the thought of Barbara marrying someone else, Harbort threw acid at Barbara Wylie's face, forever disfiguring her. Barbara and her fiancé, Benjamin, married anyway and Frank Harbort went to prison. Now, a decade later, this person claiming to be Barbara Wylie (and wearing a black mask to hide her disfigured face) wants to hire the Blue Moon agency to locate Frank Harbort—who has served his sentence and been released from prison. Further, she wants this message delivered to Harbort: Barbara forgives him, she has always loved him, and if he will still have her, she will divorce her husband and marry him.

After this potential client leaves, Maddie and David argue over the ethics of taking this case and finally decide to do so. They locate Harbort's work address and drive out to speak to him at his current job as tour guide at an historical mission. They deliver Barbara's message. Harbort responds by asking them to tell Barbara that they never found him. However, they disregard his request; instead, Maddie and David stop on their drive back to the city and telephone the day's events to their client.

Several hours later, David and Maddie leave the restaurant at which they have dined and saunter by a shop window with a television set tuned to the news. Their attention is arrested by a late breaking news story about the murder of recently released parolee Frank Harbort. Shocked and angry, they drive to Wylie's suite and accuse Barbara of using them to find Frank so she could murder him. Barbara denies hiring them or even having seen them before. They leave promising that she will not get away with this.

Back in the office, Maddie informs David that they should go to the police and tell them that their client committed a murder. David responds that they can't do that because they have no proof. What they need, David tells Maddie, is "evidence . . . the kind that stands up in court, sits down in jail." In pursuit of such evidence Maddie and David stake out the lobby of the hotel in which the Wylies are staying. They trail a masked lady whom they presume is Barbara Wylie to a park where she walks to a secluded gazebo overlooking a large pond and drops a gun—presumably the murder weapon— into the water.

Maddie and David then follow the masked lady back to the hotel. However, they are astonished when almost immediately after she enters the hotel the masked lady reemerges—sans the characteristic wiggle they had noticed previously—and reenters the hotel through a service entrance. Their suspicions aroused, they climb to the roof of a building opposite the Wylies' room. Their window peeking surveillance pays off: They observe the masked lady they trailed to the park peel off her mask to reveal that "she" is Benjamin, not Barbara, Wylie.

Back in the office David and Maddie argue about how to proceed. David suggests that Maddie should don a Barbara Wylie costume, gain a key, and search the Wylie suite for evidence. Maddie rejects that idea as risky and hare-brained and adds that she would be better off in business by herself. This comment injures David's feelings. Nonetheless, in the next scene, first Maddie and then David, each wearing a black dress and mask, unbeknownst to each other acquire keys and enter the Wylie suite. They meet in the Wylies' hall closet where first Maddie and then David takes refuge when their search is interrupted by the entrance of a masked lady.

When this third masked lady opens the closet, David and Maddie assume it is Barbara Wylie and begin to explain what they have discovered. However, their report is interrupted by the arrival of a fourth masked lady. The third masked lady then pulls out a gun and reveals "herself" to be Benjamin Wylie. Benjamin then confesses that he murdered Frank Harbort and framed Barbara because he could no longer live with a woman who for ten years had refused to allow him to get close enough to her to see her face.

However, this time Benjamin can't bring himself to pull the trigger. He runs out. Maddie, David, and Barbara—all wearing black dresses and masks—chase Benjamin (also in a black dress) through the hotel kitchen, dining room and lobby. One after another these masked ladies burst through the hotel dining room door and knock down the same waiter while throughout the chase scene the musical soundtrack plays the theme song from *The Lone Ranger*.

This humorously melodramatic pursuit reaches a climax when Benjamin is chased by the other three masked ladies into the hotel lobby. There, one after another, each of the four masked ladies slips on the newly mopped sudsy floor and slides across the lobby into the waiting, pistol-poised hands of the police. The scene ends with David pulling up his mask and yelling, "Anyone want to play twister?"

In the epilogue a pensive rendition of the series theme song plays in the background while the camera alternates shots of David in his office and Maddie in her office. Both are writing at their desks. Ms. Dipesto is called into David's office. She asks if he is planning to leave. However, before David can respond, Maddie appears in the doorway and interjects, "I hope not." Maddie then obliquely apologizes for hurting David's feelings by commenting, "I never had a man put on a dress for me before." David equally obliquely accepts the apology and continues to undercut the seriousness of the scene with his retort, "And you say you've been around."

The Semantic Features of the Dramedy *Moonlighting*

Three of the central semantic features of the dramedy *Moonlighting*, are conventionally constitutive of television drama and not television comedy. These characteristically dramatic features include the following: (1) subject matter that is serious; that, as Abrams (1971) notes, "has magnitude" and "pertains to incidents arousing pity and fear" (p. 174); (2) protagonists who are rounded, not flat, characters (Forster, 1927); that is, characters who are neither thoroughly good nor thoroughly evil but rather a complex mixture of both and who tend to manifest power, benevolence, courage and resourcefulness in the face of personal and professional crises; (3) the use of textured lighting such as *chiaroscuro* lighting to create shadows, depth, and a sense of dangerous and mysterious suspense; and soft, diffused lighting (accompanied by soft focus) to create an aura of romantic dreaminess (Monaco, 1977). Less important semantic features typical of the dramedy *Moonlighting* and of television drama in general include the frequent use of outdoor location scenes as backdrops for the narrative events and single camera shooting on film. We turn now to a brief discussion of these core semantic features shared by dramedy and drama.

Serious Subject Matter. First, and most important, the subject matter of dramedy, like that of drama, is serious. Traditionally, the subject matter of drama has concerned a conflict between individuals, between an individual and "society," between individuals and nature, or within an individual (i.e., between the individual's warring selves). However, a central element of all types of drama is a serious conflict. Furthermore, as Burke (1969) notes, a conflict between particular characters is always also a conflict between social types of characters and the principles they represent.

In the dramedy *Moonlighting*, as in most detective dramas, the central, serious subject matter concerns conflicts among characters over the acquisition or loss of such things as money, power, love or sex. Thus, *Moonlighting* episodes typically feature detective protagonists Maddie and David solving crimes resulting from these conflicts. "The Lady in the Iron Mask" episode summarized above concerned the serious matters of revenge, callous insensitivity, vicious jealousy, and murder. Many other *Moonlighting* episodes also have dealt with the serious subject of murder. For example, " 'Twas the Episode Before Christmas" (12/17/85) concerned the murder of a federal organized crime witness and the threatened murder of his wife and infant son; "The Dream Sequence Always Rings Twice" (10/15/85) concerned the unsolved 1940s murder of a jazz musician; "In God We Strongly Suspect" (2/4/86) concerned the mysterious death of a magician. Other *Moonlighting* episodes featured the equally serious subjects of adultery ("Every Father's Daughter is a Virgin," 2/18/86), bank robbery ("Somewhere Under the Rainbow," 11/19/85), and blackmail ("Camille," 5/13/86).

The centrality of serious, often deadly, conflicts typifies television dramatic narratives and distinguishes them from television comedies, which conventionally feature less weighty interpersonal and organizational matters (see Newcomb, 1974, pp. 53, 57). However, in the dramedy *Moonlighting* these generic distinctions are fused. The somberness, suspense, and pathos typically engendered by drama's grave subject matter and serious actions (e.g., the discovery and investigation of murder, blackmail, bank robbery or adultery) are mitigated in the dramedy *Moonlighting* through the comedic syntax within which the serious dramatic narrative is enacted. As a result, dramedy's viewers are encouraged to feel the compassionate understanding and empathy which are characteristic responses to tragicomedy and melodrama rather than the conventional pity and fear responses invited by drama (see Newcomb, 1974, pp. 38–42, 55; Abrams, 1974, pp. 175–76). In the "Lady in the Iron Mask" episode, for example, the viewer is reminded repeatedly that the common motive behind Harbort's jealousy-enraged acid throwing, Benjamin Wylie's murder of Frank Harbort, and David's near-resignation from the Blue Moon Detective agency was the callous insensitivity of one person to another. These reminders encourage viewers to recognize that Frank Harbort and Benjamin Wylie were victims as well as perpetrators and, therefore, to feel compassionate understanding. The fusing of the serious subject matter and comedic syntax is reinforced visually by having the murderer's chase scene end with all four major characters, wearing nearly identical black dresses and masks, sliding through cleansing white soapy suds into the arms of justice.

Round Central Characters. The second core semantic feature of the dramedy *Moonlighting* and drama is the multi-dimensional nature of its central characters. Dramedy's protagonists and antagonists are neither thoroughly heroic nor entirely evil. In Forster's (1927) terms, they are "rounded" rather than flat characters; that is, they are temperamentally and motivationally complex, capable of change and of surprising the viewer. *Moonlighting* features two "round" protagonists—private detective David Addison (Bruce Willis) and private detective agency owner and former model Maddie Hayes (Cybil Shepard). David Addison is a smart, slovenly, perpetually tardy party animal and womanizer whose life motto is "Live fast. Die young. Leave clean underwear." David is also loyal, as evinced in the "Lady in the Iron Mask" episode when he dons a dress and mask in order to help Maddie complete the Wylie investigation even though Maddie has injured his personal and professional feelings (by telling him she doesn't need him and clearly implying that she fervently regrets keeping the detective agency and him as one of its employees). Furthermore, despite his cynical manner and caustic repartee, David is a generous, empathic person who displays his concern for others in various ways. For example, he volunteers to forego his salary to avoid laying off members of the office staff when the agency fails to gain any new clients ("Camille," 5/13/86). And although he is deeply in love with Maddie Hayes, David demonstrates that he values her happiness as much as his own by accepting Maddie's relational and lifestyle choices: choices which relegate him to the role of colleague, friend, and unstinting supporter through Maddie's brief "marriage" to Walter and her pregnancy. In sum, central character David Addison is neither an unremittingly heroic nor an unrelentingly offensive character; rather, he is a "rounded" character.

David's detective partner and the owner of the Blue Moon Detective Agency is the beautiful, haute couture-attired Maddie Hayes. Maddie is snobbish, spoiled, selfish and insensitive, as illustrated by her previously discussed callous comments to David. Yet, she also has a strong sense of justice, fair play and empathy. She displays all these contradictory characteristIcs in "The Lady in the Iron Mask." Maddie's initial empathy for Barbara Wylie's disfigurement—"Oh, that poor woman"—is replaced by a burning commitment to ensure that justice is done when she believes Barbara has used the Blue Moon agency to wreak vengeance on Frank Harbort. This commitment does not waver even after Maddie and David discover that Benjamin Wylie framed his wife Barbara for the murder, a discovery which means that the agency has no paying client underwriting this investigation. In the episode titled "Big Man on Mulberry Street" (11/18/86), Maddie again displays the warm, empathic dimension of her character. She flies to New York and takes a hotel room next to David's just in case he needs a friendly shoulder to cry on after he attends the funeral of his youthful friend and ex-brother-in-law. And in the episode "Knowing Her" (11/12/85), when David telephones, Maddie comes to the police station in the middle of the night to help David and his recently resurfaced old flame, despite Maddie's own growing romantic attraction to David. Clearly Maddie Hayes is also a multi-dimensional, "round" central character.

Many of the dramedy *Moonlighting*'s guest central characters including villains and clients also display moral and dispositional complexity. In the "Lady in the Iron Mask" episode, for example, both Benjamin Wylie and Barbara Wylie are portrayed as partly evil and partly noble people. There is palpable pain in Benjamin Wylie's voice as he confesses that he framed his wife for Harbort's murder because after ten years of patiently, futilely waiting to see the face of the lady behind the mask, his wife, he could endure no more. His confession suggests that for ten years Barbara Wylie has been a self-indulgent martyr, either oblivious or insensitive to others, including her husband and his need to "know" her, disfigurement and all. While that motive is not presented as justification for Benjamin's murder of Harbort, its disclosure does invite viewers to see Benjamin Wylie as a man pushed beyond his limit of endurance and not as a flat, unidimensional evil character. Concomitantly, viewers are encouraged to regard Benjamin and Barbara Wylie as both victims and perpetrators.

Textured Lighting. In contrast to the bright, flat lighting of most television comedies (Newcomb, 1974), most scenes in the dramedy *Moonlighting* feature either the soft lighting and focus characteristic of Hollywood's romantic dramas or the dark, shadowy *chiaroscuro* lighting typical of Hollywood's *film noir* dramas.

The opening scene in "The Lady in the Iron Mask," for example, features shadowed, opaque lighting which in combination with the shower setting metonymically evokes viewers' memories of the suspenseful, terror-filled shower scene in Hitchcock's dramatic film *Psycho*. However, the soft focus and diffused lighting characteristic of such Hollywood romantic dramas as *Easter Parade* and *Singin' in the Rain* also are used often in the dramedy *Moonlighting*. For example, the opening scene of "Knowing Her" overtly, intertextually references the Hollywood film *Singin' in the Rain* with soft focus and accompanying extradiegetic music. The epilogue of "The Lady in the Iron Mask" also illustrates the dramatic use of textured lighting. There the soft focus and diffused lighting which visually frame Maddie's face as she obliquely apologizes to David signify metonymically the softening and resolution of tension between these work partners and incipient lovers.

Other episodes of this dramedy use soft focus and diffused lighting to evoke a dream-like atmosphere as well. For example, "Every Daughter's Father Is a Virgin" (2/18/86) opens with this impressionistic style of lighting framing Maddie, who is in bed asleep. As she slowly awakens, the softly focused camera tracks her glance over to a framed picture of her smiling, apparently happily married parents. The combination of the dreamy soft lighting and focus with the gentle tracking of her gaze suggests that Maddie was dreaming about her happily married parents who would be arriving that day to attend a wedding. However, in a subsequent brightly lit, sharply focused scene, harsh reality destroys the dreamy illusion for Maddie and the viewer when Maddie's mother tearfully confesses that she fears that Maddie's father is having an affair, a fear David's subsequent investigation proves valid.

Another type of textured lighting which differentiates the dramedy *Moonlighting* from television comedy and links it to Hollywood drama is the expressionistic technique of *chiaroscuro* or *film noir* lighting. For example, most of the scenes in the *Moonlighting* episode, "The Dream Sequence Always Rings Twice" (10/15/85), are filled with shadows, lit for night with oblique, vertical lines of light, and shot on black and white film. In other episodes such as "Knowing Her" (11/12/85) and "The Next Murder You Hear" (1/7/86), the dramedy *Moonlighting* displays other semantic features characteristic of Hollywood *film noir* dramas and such "telenoir" dramas as *Baretta*, *Miami Vice*, and *Wise Guy* (e.g., scenes filled with rain, water, and other reflective surfaces, compositional tension equal or preferable to physical action). As one critic has noted, *Moonlighting* is "edged by its creator with a dark border that is evocative of the *film-noir* genre of the 40s" (Horowitz, 1986, p. 5-C). In sum, in its use of the semantic element of highly textured lighting, the dramedy *Moonlighting* again displays characteristics of Hollywood film and television drama.

Multiple Exterior and Interior Settings. Television dramas usually feature multiple interior and exterior action locales while television comedies typically depend almost exclusively on a few interior settings with neat, middle-class surroundings (Newcomb, 1974, pp. 28–31). The dramedy *Moonlighting*, like most television detective dramas, typically features both exterior and interior location settings. Among those exterior settings used in the "Lady in the Iron Mask" episode were the park, the mission at which Frank Harbort worked as a tour guide, the roof of the building opposite the Wylies' hotel, and the sidewalk from which Maddie and David observed the newscast about Harbort's murder through a store window. Interior settings in this episode included the Blue Moon Detective Agency office reception area, Maddie's office, David's office, the Wylies' suite foyer, and the kitchen, dining room, and lobby of the Wylies' hotel. Thus, while *Moonlighting*'s use of multiple exterior and interior scenes is a subordinate semantic element of this dramedy, it constitutes yet another feature typical of both dramedy and television drama.

Syntactic Features of the Dramedy *Moonlighting*

That the dramedy *Moonlighting* is indeed a generic hybrid which fuses television drama and comedy generic conventions becomes evident when one examines the comedic syntax within which its dramatic detective plot premise is enacted. Three characteristic dimensions of television comedy syntax central to the structuring of *Moonlighting*'s semantic features are: (1) a four-act narrative structure typical of television situation and domestic comedies; (2) the metatextual practices of verbal and musical self-reflexivity and ironic intertextuality; and (3) the syntactic organizing devices of repetition and witty repartee.

Narrative Structure. According to Newcomb (1974), the syntactic arrangement characteristic of television situation and domestic comedy is a four-act narrative structure: the situation (the special humorous problem that happens this week in the lives of a group of characters), the complication (the conundrum that results from human failure or misunderstandings of the situation), the confusion (layers of humorous complications resulting from further, often repeated, misunderstandings and mistakes) and the resolution (a restoration of order and normalcy). Although dramedy's central problematic situations involve serious matters, the humorous dimensions of these situations are heralded in Act I by the office persiflage and droll asides David often makes during and immediately after the initial client interview. For example, in "The Lady in the Iron Mask," the problematic situation is introduced in Act I (Scenes 3–6) when a masked lady client hires Maddie and David to locate ex-convict Frank Harbort and deliver a proposition. Here, as is often the case, a secondary problematic situation also is introduced. These subplots usually involve professional and personal conflicts between the protagonists or other office staff and usually thematically parallel the central plot. In this episode, the subplot concerns Maddie's insensitivity to David's feelings, her apparent lack of appreciation for David's detective competence and contributions to the agency, and her selfish martyrdom over having lost all her investments except this detective agency.

Complications arise in Act II. In the "Lady in the Iron Mask" episode, these complications occur in scenes 7–11. First, Frank Harbort suspiciously dies shortly after Maddie and David notify their client of Harbort's whereabouts. Further complications arise when Maddie and David tail their client and observe "Ms. Wylie" dispose of a gun in the park pond.

In Act III (scenes 12–16) confusion mounts when the masked lady Maddie and David tailed to the park pagoda and back to the hotel re-emerges from the main hotel entrance wing and enters a side door of another wing—sans distinctive wiggle. After further tailing and surveillance, Maddie and David discover that they have been duped; they learn that their client's husband, dressed as his wife, killed Harbort and deliberately deceived them to "prove" that his wife had committed the murder by hiring them to locate Harbort. By this time (the third narrative act) dramedy's comedic syntax is evident; the syntactic features have cohered to clearly locate the serious problem in a comic frame. For example, when David and Maddie discover from window peeking that their masked lady is a man, David's humorous response, "Ooooh! I feel so-oo used!" clearly establishes that this subject is being enacted in a comedic context.

Confusion continues when, late at night back in the office, Maddie and David disagree over how to gather proof of this frame-up. A tired, frustrated Maddie cuts David to the quick with insensitive, impulsive and martyred comments. They part angrily, neither one knowing what the other intends to do.

In Act IV (scene 17), the narrative reaches a climax. Detective protagonists Maddie and David again briefly and humorously further complicate the situation by mistakenly reporting their findings to the wrong masked lady, Benjamin Wylie. However, the chase scene finale, which includes a repeated slapstick sight gag and a slide through suds into the waiting arms of the police, humorously resolves the central problematic situation. As this example illustrates, the dramedy *Moonlighting* does indeed display the narrative structure Newcomb (1974) argues is characteristic of television comedies.

Metatextual Practices. The syntax of the dramedy *Moonlighting* features three metatextual practices through which the generic features of drama and comedy are questioned humorously and fused. These include verbal self-reflexivity, musical self-reflexivity, and intertextuality.

Self-reflexivity. According to Neale (1981), some level of self-referentiality is an integral dimension of comedic syntax. "Comedy," he notes, "always and above all depends upon an awareness that it is fictional. What comedy does, in its various forms and guises, is to set in motion a narrative process in which various languages, logics, discourses and codes are, at one point or another—at precisely the points of comedy itself—revealed to the audience as fictions" (p. 23). Such comic revelations occur, Neale suggests, in two basic ways: either the "comic text itself periodically stresses its own artifice" (p. 23) or "comedy plays on verbal 'wit' . . . or disjunctions between discourses, modes of dress, behavior, etc." (p. 24). The dramedy *Moonlighting* uses both of these syntactic strategies to fuse drama with comedy and thereby to invite viewers to call into question the taken-for-granted genericity of these features.

Verbal self-reflexivity is the deliberate verbal referencing of the material or technical aspects of the television medium or genre conventions in order to highlight humorously the text's artifice (deLauretis, 1979). *Moonlighting*'s central protagonists Maddie and David often break the theatrical "fourth wall" convention with self-reflexive references to themselves as actors in a television program. For example, in the *Moonlighting* episode titled " 'Twas the Episode Before Christmas" (12/17/85), detectives David and Maddie arrive at their secretary's apartment, hoping to find her and the baby she is guarding for its missing mother, who is being pursued by the mob hitmen. Instead of Ms. Dipesto and the baby, they find a cryptic note on the refrigerator. As they study the note, Maddie comments, "You know what we're going to have to do." David self-reflexively replies, "Wrap this up in the next twelve minutes—there's another show coming on the air!" Viewers, thus, are reminded of the commercial nature of the television medium and the comedic syntax of this dramedy.

The above example illustrates how verbal self-reflexivity on the dramedy *Moonlighting* functions to locate serious subject matter and actions within a comedic frame. The resultant fusion of drama and comedy genres provides a jarring awareness of the constraints of taken-for-granted generic expectations. Moreover, this artistic experience of self-conscious awareness enhances rather than diminishes the program's popularity with viewers, as Williams' (1988) preliminary audience response analysis indicates. According to Williams, "this use of self-reflexivity at once breaks up the audience's willing suspension of disbelief by reminding them that they are watching television and reinforces their connection with the show through the feeling that this is a joke being shared by audience and character" (p. 92).

Musical Self-reflexivity. The dramedy *Moonlighting* also employs music to self-reflexively jar viewers out of their willing suspension of disbelief through the incongruous juxtaposition of the musical soundtrack and the narrative action. This syntactic technique provides perspective by incongruity on the narrative action; it humorously alerts viewers to the constructed nature of this detective drama. One example of such humorous musical self-referentiality occurred in the narrative climax of "The Lady in the Iron Mask" episode summarized earlier. There, as David Addison, Maddie Hayes, and Barbara Wylie all ran through the halls, kitchen, and dining room of a hotel in pursuit of Benjamin Wylie, the confessed murderer, the musical soundtrack played the theme song from the 1950s western *The Lone Ranger* (ABC). The musical theme from the serious old western drama series *The Lone Ranger* (which featured a hero who always wore a black mask) is mixed with a chase scene through a fancy hotel involving two men and two women, all wearing black dresses and black masks. This incongruous mixture signals to viewers that the preferred interpretation of this scene is not as a serious, life-threatening detective drama pursuit that might have a deadly outcome, but rather as a comedic finale replete with slapstick sight gags and repetition. A serious situation, the pursuit and capture of a murderer, is reframed here as a humorous event by the musical soundtrack's self-referential and intertextual commentary. Such incongruous reframing simultaneously fuses drama and comedy and calls into question generic expectations.

Intertextuality. According to Fiske (1987), "The theory of intertextuality proposes that any one text is necessarily read in relationship to others and that a range of textual knowledges is brought to bear upon it" (p. 108). In Fiske's view genre is the preeminent expression of horizontal intertextuality because genre references all other texts possessing that common cluster of features which identifies them as having a similar type of structure. The dramedy *Moonlighting* plays with generic boundaries, referencing connections between itself and two genres. In so doing, *Moonlighting* questions rather than reinforces viewers' notions of genericity.

Moonlighting typically intertextually references the narrative premises of other texts (films, songs, novels) through episode titles and visual techniques. For example, the episode "It's a Wonderful Job" (12/16/86) intertextually references the 1946 film *It's a Wonderful Life*, the "The Dream Sequence Always Rings Twice" episode (10/15/85) references the 1944 black and white *noir* film *The Postman Always Rings Twice*, and "Atlas Belched" (12/10/85) references Ayn Rand's novel *Atlas Shrugged*. Such intertextuality, as deLauretis (1979) explains, involves "showing the connections between two or more different texts . . . recalling in one text other familiar messages not just by 'quoting' them, but by integrating them in the present message as a legitimate part of it" (p. 108). However, many of *Moonlighting*'s intertextual references are clearly intentionally fractured (e.g., "Somewhere Under the Rainbow" 11/19/85, "The Bride of Tupperman" 1/14/86, "Brother Can You Spare a Blonde" 9/24/85). Such referential twists again signify the fusion of serious subject matter and comedic syntax in the dramedy *Moonlighting*'s enactment of the referenced narrative premises.

Repetition.   Another comedic organizing device dramedy recurrently employs is repetition—the doubling, tripling, general repeating and compounding of the same action or incident until the repetition itself becomes humorous. For example, in the conclusion of the "Lady in the Iron Mask" episode, four characters successively barge through a swinging door between the hotel kitchen and the dining room; each knocks the same waiter and his tray into the same couple who are seated at a table near the door. By the third repetition, the audience can anticipate the coming action and can begin laughing before the action is repeated. Such repetition is rarely seen in television drama; however, this syntactic technique frequently is used to organize television comedies and the dramedy *Moonlighting*.

Witty Repartee.   Dramedy's comedic syntax is evident also in the witty dialogue and sparkling repartee characteristic of its pair of protagonists. The verbal duels in which *Moonlighting*'s Maddie and David engage are reminiscent of the banter and ripostes exchanged by such classic comedy pairs as Beatrice and Benedick and Mirabell and Millamant. In *Moonlighting* the witty repartee of these mismatched work partners and incipient lovers from different social words is one of the syntactic devices through which the fusion of comedy and drama are effected. For instance, in the episode "Knowing Her" David's mention to Maddie that he "ran into" their new client and his former flame, Gillian, the previous night generates these witty rejoinders from Maddie:

> Maddie: Oh, yeah, where?
> David: Her hotel room.
> Maddie: Talk about the hand of fate. . . . Old Gillian sure knows how to fan a flame.
> David: My interest is strictly professional.
> Maddie: As opposed to amateur?

The tone of Maddie's retorts here is one of studied sarcasm, but her ripostes convey a serious undercurrent of professional and personal unease. In the dramedy *Moonlighting*, such witty repartee typically comedically articulates serious personal and professional issues, thereby fusing these life spheres as well as these comedic and dramatic genre features.

The dramedy *Moonlighting* incorporates other characteristics typical of television comedy as well, including hyperbolic coincidence. For example, in the 1985 *Moonlighting* Christmas episode titled " 'Twas the Episode Before Christmas" coincidences accumulate to the point where David warns both Maddie and the audience, "Hang onto your suspension of disbelief!" In this episode a woman named Mary, who lives in the same apartment building as Blue Moon secretary Agnes Dipesto, leaves her baby in Ms. Dipesto's laundry basket for safety as she tries to escape from two mobsters. These mobsters threw her husband, Joseph Goodman, over the apartment balcony to his death after penetrating his witness protection cover. Subsequently, Joseph's "apparent suicide" is investigated by FBI investigators who "happen" to be three brothers whose surname is King. A day later, a bedraggled Mary arrives at the Blue Moon Detective Agency seeking Ms. Dipesto and the baby. Mary apologetically explains to David that she looks so rumpled because it is the day before Christmas and there is no room in any of the inns. At this point David verbally alerts both Maddie and the viewer to the connected thread of coincidence:

> David: [sotto voce to Maddie] You hear that? No room at the inns!
> Maddie: So?
> David: So! A woman named Mary, a baby, three kings. Confidentially, I'm worried.
> Maddie: About what?
> David: Maddie, I think we're trapped in an allegory.
> Maddie: A what?
> David: I'm telling you, we've got everything in this story except a camel.

> Mary: [From across the room] Would anyone care for a smoke?
> [She pulls out a pack of Camel cigarettes.]
> Maddie: Can I—
> David: See you outside? Sure, my manger's your manger.

The hyperbolic mixture of sacred and secular coincidences in this episode concludes with the protagonists and baby being rescued from the mobsters on Christmas Eve by the three FBI Kings, who arrive at Maddie's house dressed as Santa Claus, bearing sacks of gifts and carrying guns. As illustrated in this Christmas episode and in "The Lady in the Iron Mask" episode discussed earlier, the syntactic technique of hyperbolic coincidence is yet another comedic device through which the dramedy *Moonlighting* calls attention to textual artifice and generic conventions.

These dimensions of comedy syntax constitute central organizing principles of the dramedy *Moonlighting*. As a result, in both the dramedy *Moonlighting* and in television comedy a benevolent moral principle clearly governs the often confused, sometimes violent, usually ironic world of human affairs. That a comedic syntax organizes the serious detective plot premise of *Moonlighting* does not mean that dramatic subject matters such as intentional and unintentional mistakes and crimes perpetrated by confused, selfish, greedy people are magically erased. What does happen, however, is that the stories of crime and criminals are absorbed into a comedic frame in which good and evil, seriousness and silliness, drama and comedy fuse. And this essential and complementary duality is the essence of the generic hybrid, dramedy.

Concluding Observations

This analysis of the dramedy *Moonlighting* indicates that Altman's (1986) semantic/syntactic approach to Hollywood film genre studies can be applied to television genre studies in order to help explain how new genres emerge in television. The Directors Guild nominated *Moonlighting* for both best drama and best comedy awards because, as this analysis has demonstrated, *Moonlighting* is indeed both drama and comedy. *Moonlighting* is a dramedy, a generic hybrid in which the fusion of drama and comedy was accomplished through the reflexive technique of enacting in one genre the features of another genre.

Such self-reflexivity is a technique of defamiliarization which makes familiar genre conventions seem strange, and according to formalist critics such as Shklovsky (1965) its use in a text establishes that text as "artistic." According to Shklovsky (1965), an artistic text is one which is "obviously created to remove the automatism of perception" (p. 22). By this definition, as the analysis has demonstrated, the dramedy *Moonlighting* is clearly an artistic text.

The dramedy *Moonlighting* overtly calls attention to its inclusion of conventionally dramatic elements in a conventionally comedic syntax, thereby simultaneously fusing the two genres and questioning their generic features. Thus, the familiar generic features of both drama and comedy are made to seem strange and the viewer is forced into an awareness of how powerfully narcotizing generic conventions can become. This analysis of the generic hybrid *Moonlighting* suggests that one way artistic texts emerge is through self-reflexive generic fusion. This study, then, has enhanced our understanding of how artistic texts and new genres emerge.

"Artistic" texts such as *Moonlighting* are precisely the sorts of works many Hollywood writers and producers say they want to produce but cannot because of the nature of television as a commercial mass medium. This constraint, they say, means that they must create works that produce pleasure and do not disenchant the large, diverse audience which network television needs. As a result, Hollywood television writers assert that they generally have to create more conventional, formulaic, highly generic and less artistic series which innovate slightly on previous generic fare (Gitlin, 1983). However, the dramedy *Moonlighting* has been both popular and "artistic"; its self-reflexive techniques of intertextuality, witty dialogue, and generic fusion have garnered critical acclaim and popular approval (Horowitz, 1986; Sunila, 1987; Williams, 1988).

The popular and critical success of the dramedy *Moonlighting* invites two speculative conclusions. First, it suggests that since this emergent generic hybrid is able to meet simultaneously the needs of popular audiences and Hollywood artists, it may become a stable "successful" genre (Altman, 1986). If that is so, we should see increasing numbers of dramedies appearing and receiving both popular and critical appreciation in the coming television seasons.

Second, the dramedy *Moonlighting* achieved its level of popularity while violating—perhaps partly by violating—conventional genre expectations and at the same time requiring a substantial level of cultural (popular and classic) literacy from viewers for full appreciation of its allusions and nuances. This signifies a change in the relationships among television, audiences, and society. In the other arts (theatre, literature, painting, film), when an artistic form both indicates that it recognizes the traditions that have shaped it and self-consciously comments and departs from those traditions in the artistic works themselves, the critical/artistic community often concludes that the artistic medium has "come of age" and attained a respected place within the cultural community. The popular success and critical appreciation of the self-reflexive dramedy *Moonlighting* suggests that such a moment has arrived for television. Like Pirandello's *Six Characters in Search of an Author*, *Moonlighting* has invited viewers and critics to question and "see" anew the artistic possibilities (and limitations) of generic forms.

Works Cited

Abrams, M. H. (1979). *A glossary of literary terms*. (3rd ed.). New York: Holt, Rinehart & Winston.

Alley, R. S. (1985). Medical melodrama. In B. Rose (Ed.), *TV genres: A handbook and reference guide* (pp. 73–90). Westport, CT: Greenwood Press.

Alley, R. S. (1979). Television drama. In H. Newcomb (Ed.), *Television: The critical view*. (2nd ed.). (pp. 118–151). New York: Oxford.

Altman, R. (1986). A semantic/syntactic approach to film genre. In B. K. Grant (Ed.), *Film genre reader* (pp. 26–40). Austin: University of Texas Press.

Burke, K. (1957). *Counter-Statement*. Chicago: University of Chicago Press.

Burke, K. (1969). *A Rhetoric of Motives*. (3rd ed.), Los Angeles: University of California Press.

Campbell, K. K., & Jamieson, K. H. (1976). Form and genre: Shaping rhetorical action. Falls Church, VA: SCA.

Carter, B. (n.d.). A new " 'Moonlighting' "—at last. *The Baltimore Sun*, n.p.

Cawelti, J. G. (1976). *Adventure, mystery and romance: Formula stories as art and popular culture*. Chicago: University of Chicago Press.

Cawelti, J. G. (1986/1979). Chinatown and generic transformation in recent American films. In B. K. Grant (Ed.), *Film genre reader* (pp. 183–201). Austin: University of Texas Press.

Craft, R. (1979). Elegy for Mary Hartman. In H. Newcomb (Ed.), *Television: The critical view*. (2nd ed.). (pp. 97–106). New York: Oxford.

deLauretis, T. (1979). A semiotic approach to television as ideological apparatus. In H. Newcomb (Ed.), *Television: The critical view*. (2nd ed.). (pp. 107–118). New York: Oxford.

Deming, C. J. (1985). Hill Street Blues as narrative. *Critical Studies in Mass Communication, 2*, 1–22.

Eaton, M. (1981). Television situation comedy. In T. Bennett, S. Boyd-Bowman, C. Mercer, and J. Wollacott (Eds.), *Popular television and film* (pp. 26–52). London: British Film Institute.

Fiske, J. (1984). Popularity and ideology: A structuralist reading of Dr. Who. In W. D. Rowland, Jr., & B. Watlins (Eds.), *Interpreting television: Current research perspectives* (pp. 165–197). Beverly Hills: Sage.

Fiske, J. (1986). Television: Polysemy and popularity. *Critical Studies in Mass Communication, 3*, 391–408.

Fiske, J. (1987). *Television culture*. New York: Methuen.

Forster, E. M. (1927/1962). *Aspects of the novel*. Harmondsworth.

Geertz, C. (1980). Blurred genres: The refiguration of social thought. *American Scholar, 49*, 165–179.

Gitlin, T. (1983). *Inside prime time*. New York: Pantheon.

Gronbeck, B. E. (1984). *Writing television criticism*. Chicago: SRA.

Handelman, D. (1987, March 26). Dark side of the moon. *Rolling Stone*, pp. 52–54, 144.

Horowitz, J. (1986, March 30). Sweet lunacy: The madcap behind 'Moonlighting.' *New York Times Magazine*, p. 24. [Reprinted in *The Chicago Tribune*, April 20, 1986, Entertainment Section, p. 1, 5-C.]

Jamieson, K. H. (1973). Generic constraints and the rhetorical situation. *Philosophy and Rhetoric*, 6, 162–170.

Jamieson, K. H., & Campbell, K. K. (1982). Rhetorical hybrids: Fusions of generic elements. *Quarterly Journal of Speech*, 68, 146–157.

Mintz, L. E. (1985). Situation comedy. In B. Rose (Ed.), *TV genres: A handbook and reference guide* (pp. 107–130). Westport, CT: Greenwood Press.

Monaco, J. (1977). *How to read a film*. New York: Oxford.

Neale, S. (1981). Genre and cinema. In T. Bennett, S. Boyd-Bowman, C. Mercer, and J. Woollacott (Eds.), *Popular television and film* (pp. 6–25). London: The British Film Institute.

Newcomb, H. (1974). *TV: The most popular art*. Garden City, NY: Anchor/ Doubleday.

Newcomb, H. (1978). Toward television history: The growth of styles. *Journal of the University Film Association*, 30, 9–14.

Rose, B. G. (Ed.), (1985). *TV Genres: A handbook and reference guide*. Westport, CT: Greenwood Press.

Rosenthal, S. (1986, September 22). Thanks to *Cosby* and *Moonlighting*, the new season's quality is up. *US*, pp. 18–20, 22.

Schrader, P. (1986). Notes on film noir. In B. Grant (Ed.), *Film genre reader* (pp. 169–182). Austin: University of Texas Press.

Shklovsky, V. (1965). Art as technique and Sterne's Tristram Shandy: Stylistic Commentary. In L. T. Lemon & M. Reis, (Trans.), *Russian formalist criticism: Four essays* (pp. 3–60). Lincoln: University of Nebraska Press.

Sunila, J. (1987, March/April). Focus: More wordplay, I pray. *Emmy*, pp. 66–67.

Thorburn, D. (1987). Television melodrama. In H. Newcomb (Ed.), *Television: The critical view*. (4th ed.). (pp. 602–644). New York: Oxford.

Warshow, R. (1964). *The immediate experience*. Garden City: NY: Doubleday; Anchor Books.

Williams, J. P. (1988). When you care enough to watch the very best: The mystique of *Moonlighting*. *Journal of Popular Film and Television*, 16, 90–100.

Zoglin, R. (1985, March 25). Spring sparring partners: Mismatched couples provide spark for TV's "third season." *Time*, p. 74.

Television Credit

Moonlighting (ABC, a Picturemakers/ABC Circle Films Production; March 1985 to present). Creator and executive producer Glenn Gordon Caron. "The Lady in the Iron Mask" episode was written by Roger Director, directed by Christopher Leitch, produced by Jay Daniel and broadcast October 1, 1985. The " 'Twas the Episode Before Christmas" episode was written by

Glenn Gordon Caron, directed by Peter Werner, produced by Jay Daniel, and broadcast December 17, 1985. The episode "Knowing Her" was written by Jeff Reno and Ron Osborn, directed by Peter Werner, produced by Jay Daniel, and broadcast on November 12, 1985.

Notes

[1]Campbell and Jamieson's (1976) rhetorical definition of genre is quite similar to Altman's (1986) semantic/syntactic notion of genre. "A genre," they note, "is composed of a constellation of recognizable forms bound together by an internal dynamic" (p. 21).
[2]It should be pointed out, as Altman himself notes, that Altman's use of the term "semantic" differs from Fredric Jamieson's (1975) use of the term. Jamieson uses the term to signify the overall import of the text's semantic constituents while Altman's use of the term is more closely approximated by the notion of individual semantic elements or "lexical choices" (Altman, 1986, p. 40).

Family Photographs
A Generic Description

Sharon M. Varallo

In this essay, I will describe and analyze three photographs to determine if a genre of family photographs exists. I am interested in family communication and want to discover ways in which family members rhetorically construct themselves as a unit. Toward that end, I address the situational requirements necessary for a particular response, a description of the artifacts collected, an analysis of the substantive and stylistic features of the artifacts, and an overall pattern of organization for this genre.

Situational Requirements

The first step in generic description is the observation of similarities in rhetorical responses to particular situations. In other words, in order for an artifact to exist that might be called a *family photograph*, a number of elements must be present. The elements on which I briefly focus include the need for a family, a camera, a photographer, and an audience:

(1) The most obvious element required to be present is a family. The definition of *family* is much broader now than it has been in years past, as evidenced by new descriptors such as *blended families*, which did not exist a short time ago. The situational requirement, therefore, is a broadly defined one: whether the group members consider themselves to be traditional or nontraditional, the subjects being photographed must perceive themselves to be a family.

(2) The presence of a camera is necessary to the situation. Because many cameras are relatively inexpensive, they are accessible to the general population; people from almost every economic class, therefore, are able to present themselves as a family in front of a camera.

(3) A photographer must be present. Unless the photograph is taken with a camera with time-delay capability, family photos are taken with a non-family member as onlooker and producer.

(4) An audience is required. Why else would a family stop, pull together, smooth hair, and smile broadly at no one in particular? The family members know that the photograph will capture them in a

This essay was written while Sharon M. Varallo was a student in Sonja K. Foss' rhetorical criticism class at Ohio State University in 1994. Used by permission of the author.

particular moment, so they collect themselves enough to present themselves in ways that clearly show they are a family. The family itself could be the audience the photograph most persuades; in collecting family photos, we constantly reassure ourselves that we are members of the culturally valued group called a *family*.

Description of Artifacts

The artifacts I have chosen to analyze are three photographs of family groups. They include the Varallo family photograph, the Chryslee-Miller family photograph, and the Marty-Rhoades family photograph. All of the photographs are of immediate family members, and all of the families are white and middle class.

The Varallo family photograph was taken in December, 1973, during the Christmas holiday season. The photograph shows a mother, father, son, and daughter standing in front of a Christmas tree. The tree, decorated with plastic confections, is positioned in front of a window covered with white patterned curtains. The children are standing in front of their parents. The father's arm is encircling his wife, who, in turn, is touching her daughter. The son stands independently. The females are wearing primarily red, and the males are dressed primarily in white.

The Chryslee-Miller family photograph was taken in May of 1992 prior to a graduation ceremony for the older son. The photograph includes a mother and father and two sons, one of whom is dressed in a graduation cap and gown. The family members are standing in a line, all in close proximity to one another, obviously convening around the graduating son. The mother has her arms around both her sons, the father has his arm around his older son, and the younger son has his arm around his mother. The photograph was taken in front of a tree in the family's backyard.

The Marty-Rhoades photograph was taken during a vacation trip to visit family in August, 1992. The photograph includes two women who are partners and co-parents and their seven-year-old daughter. This family is shown huddled on a rock that is jutting out into the ocean, and the background is of the water and shoreline reefs. Both women are touching their daughter, and she appears to be leaning against them. They all are wearing casual clothing.

Substantive and Stylistic Elements

A substantive and stylistic analysis of the photographs uncovers the meanings present in the artifacts. In the case of non-discursive artifacts

Chryslee-Miller photograph

Varallo photograph

Marty-Rhoades photograph

such as photographs, substantive and stylistic elements cannot be separated; thus, both will be discussed together. This stage of generic description finds the similarities in the artifacts and considers what those similar elements might signify. As similarities in the photographs are uncovered, their importance or unimportance to a genre of family photographs also is addressed.

First, the children tend to be positioned in front of and physically lower than the adults. In the Varallo and Marty-Rhoades photographs, the children are positioned in front of and physically lower than the adults; this positioning is not surprising given that the children are, after all, shorter than the parents. However, in many family photographs where the children are taller than the parents, the children often are positioned so they are shorter than the parents. Julia Hirsch (1981) discusses a possible reason for this feature of family photography:

> The authority of these conventions, like the hold of traditional family roles which still makes us want strong fathers and nurturing mothers, loving children and sheltering homes, is difficult for any of us to resist. Professional as well as amateur photographers still place families in poses that express and cater to these longings. (p. 12)

Hirsch's revelation of the family as a metaphor for all of humankind gives any representation of the family a much greater significance. Families pose for formal photographs to show themselves as a family *should* be. The positioning of the subjects to ensure the distinction between the matriarch/patriarch and the children seems necessary to the genre.

A second similarity is that all the people are sitting or standing in close proximity to one another. Perhaps some of this closeness is required for everyone to fit into the picture, but the picture could be taken from a distance to produce a longer shot, so the physical closeness is not a necessity for the photograph itself. This closeness clearly suggests to an onlooker that the family is one unit. By standing near one another, the family members create a distinct and distinguishable group. To fit into the genre of the ideal family photograph, the members should be standing close to one another.

A third similarity related to the first two is that the mothers touch their children, while the fathers are less likely to do so. The Marty-Rhoades mothers are connecting the most obviously with their daughter; their warmth and intimacy are apparent from their comfortable connection with one another. The other mothers also touch their children in "natural" ways that the fathers do not. The Chryslee-Miller father has his hand on his son's shoulder but otherwise does not appear to be touching him and is standing directly forward in an independent stance. The Varallo father is touching only his wife. The connections of the mothers to the daughter show nurturing and protective women, and the separation of the fathers and the sons shows independence and distance: both are the kinds of behaviors that fit within the traditional family mold addressed by Hirsch and are an element necessary to the ideal genre.

Fourth, women seem to have paid more attention to their appearance than the men and, overall, seem to have been concerned more with presenting a pleasing image. The Varallo woman has on make-up and a wig and has thin, finely plucked eyebrows, as was the fashion at that time. The Chryslee-Miller woman has coordinated accessories—a red belt and red earrings—to add flair to her dress. Albeit more subtly, the Rhoades and Marty women also have on jewelry, and the daughter is wearing small post earrings. In all the photographs, the women's dress closely matches that of the other women in the photograph, as if they coordinated their efforts: the Varallo females are wearing red, and the Rhoades and Marty women are dressed similarly in style—they are wearing comfortable, kick-about clothing. Finally, all the women are smiling broadly. These elements combine to present an image of women as, perhaps, the filler of a more nurturing role. After all, the Chryslee-Miller and Varallo fathers—and the adult Chryslee-Miller sons—did not feel the need to smile: they present themselves as more independent and more of what traditionally might be called *strong*. The women perhaps are showing the traditional roles expected of them as part of a family. Their concern with a pleasing image is both individual and group oriented and influences the showing of the entire family.

Yet another characteristic that distinguishes the photographs is their optimism. The Marty-Rhoades family members have open-mouthed smiles as if laughing in response to a joke. The Varallo photograph is of people smiling for the camera, seemingly on command. The Varallo father is the only unsmiling person, and, as such, he stands out. The Chryslee-Miller photograph evidences optimism in yet another way: it celebrates a family milestone as the members have gathered for a son's graduation. These observations coincide with Hirsch's: "Family photographs, so generous with views of darling babies and loving couples, do not show grades failed, jobs lost, opportunities missed. . . . The family pictures we like best are poignant—and optimistic" (p. 118). We are motivated to fit the image. Optimism, not realism, is important to family photographs.

A sixth characteristic feature of the photographs is that the pictures are posed. These photographs, although seemingly natural, are not candid. Everyone except the Chryslee-Miller graduate is looking directly at the camera, and each person seems acutely aware of being photographed. In this way, photographs present a kind of normalcy that is not normal: my family never stood that way unless we were getting our picture taken, and chances are the Chryslee-Miller and Marty-Rhoades families usually did not stand in that fashion on a normal day. This awareness and posing seem important to the genre as well.

The backgrounds in the photographs clearly were important and consciously chosen, perhaps to help represent the image of the family; this is a seventh characteristic of the photographs. All the photographs were taken during a special event, an event that is clear from an analysis of the background details. The Varallo photograph was snapped at Christmas time, and the family members positioned themselves in front of the Christmas tree. The Chryslee-Miller family stood in front of a tree in their backyard, gathered around a graduate. The Marty-Rhoades family, standing with the ocean as a backdrop, were clearly out of the ordinary settings of their usual lives. Part of the catalyst for taking the photographs seems to have been the event itself. Special events, therefore, also may be integral to the ideal family photograph.

The backgrounds in these particular photographs may offer insights into a critique of the genre of family photographs. The decorations on the Varallo tree, for instance, are sugar-coated, plastic candy ornaments. The Christmas tree was a pretend tree, the decorations were pretend confections, and our presentation of ourselves as the ideal family was pretend. We also stood in front of a window, perhaps symbolizing our desire for public approval, and the window is covered with curtains, perhaps symbolizing our need to hide the "real" family. The star on the Christmas tree is directly above the patriarch's head, crown like, giving the male a kingly air. The Chryslee-Miller photograph was taken in front of a tree in the backyard, and part of the house is visible in the background, serving to reinforce the representation of the traditional family. The most open background of all the photographs is in the photograph of the Marty-Rhoades family. Interestingly, their environment is natural. While the Varallo family seems limited to one way of showing a family, the Marty-Rhoades family is the most open of all, not just in background but in the family structure itself. As lesbian partners and parents, they present a family that likely would garner objection in traditional circles. Their family photograph, however, shows a more open, natural setting and clearly shows the most sincere warmth. Their smiles are genuine, while the others, though not necessarily fake, are obviously primarily for the camera.

That these photographs rarely capture the subjects' feet is an eighth characteristic of the genre of family photographs. Only upper torsos are visible in the Varallo and Chryslee-Miller photographs, and we barely see the feet of the Marty and Rhoades women. Although this photographic choice may have some symbolic significance, it does not appear vital to the genre.

Finally, similarities exist in the physical presentations of the photographs. The Marty-Rhoades photograph is enlarged and framed and usually sat on a table in the family's living room. The framing and public showing of the picture added to the impression that the family is special. The photograph was set apart, given a place of honor on a table, put out to be admired and to remind those who saw it most often— the two women and their daughter—that they were, indeed, a family. Although the framing and presentation of the photograph reinforces the ideal family it presents, that the photograph be framed is not vital to the genre. The other two photographs, for instance, are normal-sized photographs and have been in both private and public places, ranging from the "photo drawer" to a bulletin board; they still seem to qualify as participants in this genre.

Organizing Principles of the Genre

In summary, the substantive and stylistic elements that seem vital to the genre include the presentation of:

(1) higher (status) positioning of the patriarch and/or matriarch

(2) close physical proximity of the family members

(3) mothers touching the children and touching more in general

(4) women more concerned with presenting a pleasing image

(5) optimism, usually evidenced in smiles

(6) a posed group

(7) backgrounds showing a special event

If all of these elements are present and the situational requirements are met, a photograph would seem to fit into a distinct category of family photography. From these observations, I conclude that there is, indeed, a genre of family photographs. The necessary elements noted in the previous section are substantial enough to warrant the inclusion of a new genre in the realm of generic criticism.

Conclusion

These photographs undoubtedly serve to convince and reinforce the "proper" family image to society at large and also to the families themselves. The photographs probably serve as a strong element of self-persuasion; in Hirsch's words, perhaps we are both seller and consumer of the idea of the ideal family. Formal family photography deals with character (Hirsch, p. 82), and few are willing to preserve for eternity a flawed image. None of the families evidenced in these photographs remains intact today—all three dissolved through divorce or separation of the parents. Nowhere, however, is family strife shown in any of these photographs. We all have our central identities at stake, and we therefore present ourselves as a unified family, the rules of which implicitly seem to be known.

Reference

Hirsch, J. (1981). *Family photographs*. New York: Oxford University Press.

"A Time of Shame and Sorrow"
Robert F. Kennedy and the American Jeremiad

John M. Murphy

On April 4, 1968, an assassin's bullet ended the life of Martin Luther King, Jr. In the next week, seventy-six American cities dealt with the consequences. Forty-six people died, all but five of them black, and 2,500 were injured. Nearly thirty thousand people were arrested and 70,000 Federal and National Guard troops tried to cope with the disorder by turning many American cities into armed camps (Newfield 269–70). The White House worried that it might actually run out of troops (Kaiser 148). Readers of the *New York Times* awoke the Saturday after King's death to a front-page picture of American troops setting up machine guns to protect the Senate of the United States.

Public figures responded to King's death and the subsequent violence with rhetoric familiar to the American people. Some deplored the kind of nation that would allow such an act to occur, such as James Farmer's reaction: "Evil societies always destroy their consciences" (Van Gelder 1). On the opposite end of the political spectrum, some implied that King had brought on his own fate. Governor Ronald Reagan of California, polishing his conservative credentials for a presidential campaign, noted that this was the kind of "great tragedy that began when we began compromising with law and order, and people started choosing which laws they'd break" (Chester, et al. 18). Governor John B. Connally replied in a similar vein, claiming that King had "contributed much to the chaos and the turbulence in this country but he did not deserve this fate" (Van Gelder 26). Three of the 1968 presidential candidates, with a more cautious approach, decided that the situation was too dangerous or difficult for extended public comment. Richard Nixon, Eugene McCarthy and George Wallace expressed their regret at the incident, although only Nixon and McCarthy chose to do so personally to Coretta King while attending the funeral (Van Gelder 26; Larner 66; Chester, et al. 19; Hofmann 25).

Other political leaders attempted to give meaning to King's death by proposing legislation as an appropriate tribute to the man and his work.

From *Quarterly Journal of Speech*, 76 (1990): 401–414. Used by permission of the Speech Communication Association and the author.

In other words, they chose to combine the epideictic aspects of a eulogy with deliberative strategies aimed at bringing about the passage of civil rights bills (Jamieson and Campbell). The President and the Vice-President issued statements using such strategies (Johnson 23; "Humphrey Appeals" 24), as did Governor Nelson Rockefeller in New York (Witkin 24). Such legislative reform, they hoped, would carry on King's work, ameliorate the injustices of racial prejudice, and end the turmoil. The *New York Times*, noting the power of such appeals, predicted that they would be successful (Hunter 25).

One powerful politician, however, specifically rejected a legislative response to King's death. Senator Robert F. Kennedy argued that the "question is not what programs we should seek to enact" ("Cleveland" 1). Perhaps recognizing the mood of a country that generally failed to see how previous legislation had helped matters, Kennedy found the cause of King's death in America's toleration of "a rising level of violence that ignores our common humanity and our claims to civilization alike" ("Cleveland" 1). In a striking move for a presidential candidate, Kennedy called not for new policy initiatives, but rather he demanded that each American take individual responsibility for the disorder and work to "remove this sickness from our soul" ("Cleveland" 1).

This essay argues that, in order to interpret the meaning of the chaos around him, Senator Kennedy adopted the traditional rhetorical form of the jeremiad. His speeches on this occasion offer the opportunity to examine the function of the modern jeremiad as a means to restore social harmony in a time of crisis. Kennedy made an outstanding strategic choice by attempting to fashion the response of the audience so that they would seek to bring "good out of evil" (Bormann 1977, 1985). This case illustrates, however, that while rhetors employing the jeremiad may call for political change to end discord, the jeremiad limits the scope of reform and the depth of social criticism. Analysis of Robert Kennedy's discourse reveals the strengths and the limitations of the jeremiad as a response to social crisis.

Kennedy used the jeremiad to shape the audience's response to the tragedy of King's death and the resulting disorders. The epideictic exigency to eulogize King dominated the situation. In this case, then, the jeremiad can be viewed within what Celeste Condit has called the "macro-genre" of epideictic speaking (284). Condit argues that the most complete type of epideictic speeches, what she terms "communal definition" (291), performs a series of functions for the audience and for the speaker. They define the problems the community faces and enable the community to understand itself and its values. At the same time, the audience can judge the speaker's potential for leadership through evaluation of his or her eloquence and "humane vision" (Condit 291). The epideictic speech builds and creates a community for both speaker and audience, particularly, as Condit emphasizes, in times of crisis that threaten the society. Senator Kennedy used the jeremiad to interpret the problems that faced American society, to provide the audience with an understanding of events, and to suggest the way toward a brighter future.

Robert Kennedy's vision of the future, however, evolved from the interpretation of the American past inherent within the jeremiad. Kennedy's rhetoric serves as an example of the ways in which the jeremiad acts as a rhetoric of social control. I argue that jeremiadic strategies function to transform dissent and doubt about American society into a rededication to the principles of American culture. Such discourse aids in the traditional task of epideictic speakers: overcoming crisis and restoring social harmony. However, it also precludes a searching examination of the "Establishment" or the system: what James Q. Wilson recently labeled the "American Way" of structuring the government and social relationships (p. 34). The jeremiad deflects attention away from possible institutional or systemic flaws and toward considerations of individual sin. Redemption is achieved through the efforts of the American people, not through a change in the system itself.

Study of Kennedy's discourse also provides important insight into his success as a presidential candidate and into the continuing influence of his words today. In the week before King's death, the Kennedy campaign was drifting, shaken by the withdrawal of Lyndon Johnson and his new peace policies regarding Vietnam (Newfield 268). The eulogy Kennedy gave in Indianapolis and the speech he delivered the following day in Cleveland are regarded as the best of his public career and are widely reprinted today (Cook 292-293; Newfield 272; Schlesinger 939-943; "TRB" 1). The themes Kennedy discovered in those speeches helped him to redefine his campaign. By using the jeremiad, Kennedy could explain the troubles of the time while speaking for fundamental national values. His eloquence in this trying situation revealed important leadership qualities, indicating that variations on the jeremiad function well as campaign rhetoric. The balance of this essay will review the important features of the jeremiadic tradition in American public address, examine Senator Kennedy's remarks after the assassination in light of that tradition, and conclude with a discussion of the strengths and limitations of the modern American jeremiad.

The American Jeremiad

Senator Kennedy's repeated emphasis on crisis and redemption as he spoke in Cleveland the day after the killing suggests that his rhetoric might profitably be examined within the American jeremiadic tradition. As a rhetorical type, the jeremiad began making its mark with the arrival of the Puritans in North America (Bercovitch 3–9). This "political sermon," which was delivered on ritualistic occasions, intertwined practical spiritual guidance with advice on public affairs. Identifying the Kingdom of God with the progress of the American settlements, these speeches assumed that the Puritans were God's chosen people with a special mission on earth to bring all people under His domain. With the passage of time and troubles, the vision expanded to include all American citizens by the time of the Revolution (Bercovitch 128–34).

The typical jeremiad in Puritan New England first explained the spiritual or Biblical precedent that served as the communal norm. The speech then would demonstrate in great detail the failure of the community to adhere to that norm and the catastrophes that have resulted. Finally, the minister would offer a prophetic vision of the utopia to come if only the people would repent and reform (Johannesen 158). Bercovitch emphasizes the importance of this vision of the future. Jeremiads went beyond cataloguing the evils of the audience. They combined lamentations with a firm optimism about the eventual fate of the community (Bercovitch 23). That vision of the "shining city on a hill" worked to unite the audience in pursuit of the goal and to reaffirm the values of the community.

Since fulfillment "was never quite there," Bercovitch argues that the function of the jeremiad "was to create a climate of anxiety that helped release the restless 'progressivist' energies required for the success of the venture" (23). Johannesen notes that the balance between lamentation and exultation was "in keeping with the historic Jeremiah's role of both castigating apostasy and of heralding a bright future" (159). After all, Jeremiah used discourse "to root out, to pull down, and to destroy, and to throw down, to build, and to plant" (Johannesen 159). Thus, the jeremiad emphasized the ways to "fetch good out of evil" and provided for renewal in a time of troubles (Bormann "Good Out of Evil" 132).

A number of critics have noted that the modern jeremiad still performs these functions for its audience. The civil religion of the American Dream now serves as the grounding for arguments (Johannesen 138; Ritter 158–59). Modern "Jeremiahs" assume that Americans are a chosen people with the special mission of establishing that "shining city on a hill." They point to the difficulties of the day as evidence that the people have failed to adhere to the values that made them special, to the great principles articulated by patriots such as Jefferson and Lincoln. The evils demonstrate the need to renew the American covenant and to restore the principles of the past so that the promised bright future can become a reality. From the speeches of presidential candidates to newspaper columns, the modern jeremiad has played a major role in recent American public address (Ritter; Johannesen).

But the restoration theme inherent in the jeremiad suggests that this rhetorical form has considerable limitations. While critics have documented its ability to unify and shape a community, traditional functions of epideictic speech, the jeremiad cannot serve as a vehicle for social criticism. This limitation is serious because jeremiads usually appear in a time of questioning and societal crisis that may well demand such examination. Instead of questioning American values, however, jeremiadic speakers urge a more stringent adherence to those values as a way to bring "good out of evil" and as a means to fulfill the prophecies of the past that assured the eventual success of America. Sacvan Bercovitch writes of the Puritan ministers: "Despite their insistent progressivism, the future they appealed to was necessarily limited, by the very prophecies they vaunted, to the ideals of the past" (179). The form of the jeremiad directs what might otherwise be a search for social and political alternatives into a celebration of the values of the culture and of change within the status quo. Bercovitch notes that a major rhetorical goal of colonial jeremiads was to "assert progress through continuity" (71). The difficulty of achieving social change by relying on the precepts of the past is particularly apparent when the issue is American racism.

1968

By early April of 1968, many Americans saw little hope of restoring the ideals of the American Dream. In fact, columnist Joseph Kraft wrote a column entitled "National Dissensus: Mental and Moral Decay is Eating Out The Vitals Of The Country" (B7). In the first few months of the year, Americans endured the capture of the *Pueblo*, the Tet offensive, a crisis with the dollar, the Kerner Commission report on racism in America, the defeat and abdication of President Johnson, and the assassination of King with the subsequent disorders.

The Kerner Commission report and the polling data done by the University of Michigan Institute for Social Research help explain the depth of the bitterness in America and the extent of the disorders following King's death. Those reports indicated that the perceptions of whites and blacks on the state of the nation were diverging sharply. Increasing numbers of whites felt that enormous efforts had been made, much money had been spent, and extensive legislation had been passed, to no avail. Racial tensions and violence continued to increase. Meanwhile, blacks, young men in particular, saw far less change in

America. True, "Jim Crow" laws had generally been eliminated. Most blacks, however, could not afford the restaurants to which they now had access. Conditions in the ghetto had not improved appreciably (Chester, et al. 35-40). Dangerous unravelings in the national fabric were becoming apparent and these racial tensions, combined with all of the other crises in 1968, led to serious doubts about the country itself. No less a figure than James Reston concluded: "The main crisis is not in Vietnam itself, or in the cities, but in the feeling that the political system for dealing with these things has broken down" (Quoted in White 109). Through it all, Senator Robert Kennedy sought to define his role in the fluctuating political situation.

After months of indecision that sapped his credibility with the American people, Robert Kennedy declared his candidacy for the Presidency on March 16, 1968. Kennedy ran because he strongly opposed the President on Vietnam and on urban policy and felt "that we can change these disastrous, divisive policies only by changing the men who make them" ("Announcement of Candidacy" 1). From the start his campaign was in trouble. Kennedy entered after Eugene McCarthy's New Hampshire primary showing demonstrated that a candidacy opposing the war in Vietnam could succeed. Senator Kennedy's late entry, combined with his previous reputation for "ruthlessness," damaged his position (Witcover 85-90; "Robert Kennedy—His Public Image" 14). President Johnson's withdrawal from the race and his peace initiatives on March 31 robbed RFK of his two main issues: the war and the President's record. Disconcerted by these events and worried about the strength of Vice-President Humphrey and Senator McCarthy as rivals for the Democratic nomination, the Kennedy campaign sought to start anew in the Indiana primary.

April 4 marked the first day of speaking in the Hoosier state. The advance teams booked Kennedy into places of strong support, college campuses and poor areas, to begin with momentum. At Notre Dame and Ball State Universities, "the crowds were good, if not ecstatic" (Witcover 139). At Ball State, a black student challenged Kennedy, asking if he truly believed that white America wanted to help minorities. Kennedy responded: "Most people in America want to do the decent thing" (Witcover 139). On the plane to his appearance in the ghetto of Indianapolis, Kennedy learned of King's killing. Keeping to the schedule, he eulogized King in Indianapolis that night and then canceled all appearances save one speech the next day before the Cleveland City Club.

The circumstances facing Senator Kennedy created significant rhetorical obstacles. The fact of King's death meant that Kennedy chose to use epideictic strategies to define the American community in light of the assassination. These strategies included providing the audience with an understanding of this terrible event, shaping a new sense of the community in response to the loss, and submitting his vision of the nation for the judgment of the audience (Condit 288). These demands were particularly strong because of the disorder that, by the Cleveland speech, was occurring in most American cities and because of the growing doubt about the viability of the American system. King's death crystallized all of the concern about the country; if Martin Luther King, Jr. was to be killed for his efforts on behalf of nonviolence, the nation was at risk.

In addition, Robert Kennedy had particular expectations attached to his words. The King assassination inevitably reminded the country of Dallas, and, as a Kennedy, the Senator was uniquely situated to shape the nation's response to this crisis. More than any other speaker, Kennedy represented a fondly remembered past and yet, given his opposition to the President, stood apart from the problems of the present. More pragmatically, the Senator was also a presidential candidate. His reaction to King's death could help or hinder his cause enormously. The state of the country, the Kennedy persona, and Robert Kennedy's own ambitions all helped to create his unique response to the death of Martin Luther King, Jr.

Senator Kennedy's eulogy for Dr. King the night of April 4 in Indianapolis has been highly praised (Newfield 270; "T.R.B." 1). Before a crowd that did not know of King's death, by urging adherence to King's method of nonviolence and by revealing his feelings about his brother's death, Kennedy channeled the natural anger and sadness of the audience in a positive direction (Cook 294–306; David and David 307–08). While this extemporaneous speech, written by Kennedy himself on the way to the rally, was not a jeremiad, it opened a key question and introduced important themes that Kennedy would address the next day in Cleveland.

After quieting the crowd, Senator Kennedy began the speech with a simple acknowledgement of King's death. He memorialized King in the next sentence, noting that he had "dedicated his life to love and justice for his fellow human beings, and he died because of that effort" ("Eulogy" 292). This line honored King's sacrifice, but it raised a disturbing question for Kennedy and the audience. Why should a man die because he pursued love and justice? The body of the speech, however, did not address that query. Instead, Kennedy chose to examine "what kind of a nation we are and what direction we want to move in" ("Eulogy" 292).

In the first section of the speech, he noted that people could react with hatred and violence and discussed the natural reasons for such a response ("Eulogy" 292). In the second section of this brief address, Kennedy turned to the superior alternative, asking the crowd to "make an effort, as Martin Luther King did, to understand and comprehend" and to replace violence with love ("Eulogy" 292). He argued that he knew, after his brother's death, the desire for revenge, but concluded that "we have to make an effort to understand, to go beyond these rather difficult times" ("Eulogy" 292). Kennedy tried to assure the audience that their current pain would result in knowledge and rebirth, just as his loss had led him to a new life.

Not surprisingly, the speech then wove together these personal concerns and the fate of the nation. Kennedy completed the body of the address with a series of parallel constructions that focused on America, dismissing hatred as an alternative and telling people that the country needed love, wisdom, compassion "and a feeling of justice toward those who still suffer within our country, whether they be white or whether they be black" ("Eulogy" 292).

Senator Kennedy's eulogy served what Condit calls the "definition/understanding" function of epideictic address by explaining a disturbing event within the frame of values and beliefs accepted by the audience (288). Kennedy focused on the need for reconciliation and compassion in that terrible time. His use of himself as an example created identification with the audience and provided proof positive that death could lead to rebirth. While he beautifully fulfilled the traditional requirements for a eulogy (Cook 303–305; Jamieson and Campbell 147), he did not explain why a man who gave so much for the country should be killed for that effort. In that sense, this epideictic address was incomplete because there was no clear reason why the audience should follow King's path, in light of his fate. Kennedy needed to provide a deeper understanding of the troubles, one that could explain the violence and offer a road to redemption that would enact King's values while offering hope for success. His speech in Cleveland the following day offered that opportunity.

"A Time of Shame and Sorrow"

Although Kennedy's first instinct had been to cancel all speaking engagements, he received calls from "concerned Negro leaders, some of whom wanted him to do something to help them discourage an outbreak of retaliatory violence" (Witcover 142). The Cleveland City Club speech on April 5 was a response to that plea, but the occasion also allowed Kennedy to provide a fuller analysis of the country's woes. Building on the themes suggested by the eulogy, Kennedy's speechwriters, primarily Adam Walinsky, Jeff Greenfield, and Ted

Sorensen, constructed what Jack Newfield has called "the best written text of the campaign, and perhaps of Kennedy's public career" (Newfield 272).[1]

The speech reflected the overwhelming epideictic exigence of King's death and the resulting disorders. To meet those demands, Kennedy chose to interpret the events of the day through the lens of the jeremiad. Focusing on the moral actions of individual Americans, Kennedy argued that those sins were responsible for the national malaise. Thus, Kennedy first detailed the violations of American ideals, then traced the causes of the disorders to the sins of the people, and finally, called for a greater adherence to the values of American traditions as the way toward redemption. This logic shaped a view of the troubles that directed the attention of the audience toward individual transgressions against American ideology. The American value system was not the problem; it was the solution. Consequently, Kennedy could explain the difficulties of the time while reaffirming the nobility and vitality of the nation. America could still fulfill its "sacred destiny" as a beacon of democracy for the rest of the world if the people would live up to the traditional values of the American covenant.

Kennedy began his address by defining the time as one of "shame and sorrow" ("Cleveland" 1). He depicted the growing menace of violence and put a human face on the victims of violence. All were "human beings whom other human beings loved and needed" ("Cleveland" 1). Seeking to find the reasons behind the epidemic, he noted that, pragmatically, violence accomplished nothing: "No martyr's cause has ever been stilled by an assassin's bullet" ("Cleveland" 1). He then turned to the morality of the people as a reason for the disorder.

Kennedy began that moral study by condemning the cowardice and madness of violence. Significantly, he created a close connection between the violence of individuals and the welfare of the state. Consistent with the age-old pattern of the jeremiad, Kennedy argued that each individual carried the responsibility for the success of the American experiment, claiming that "whenever we tear at the fabric of life another man has painfully and clumsily woven for himself and his children, the whole nation is degraded" ("Cleveland" 1). Kennedy intertwined an individual's choices and the country's future. The metaphor of a "national fabric" created an inescapable bond between Americans and their nation. Kennedy emphasized the futility of violence, and the ensuing violation of the American covenant, by resorting to the authority of Lincoln: "Among free men there can be no successful appeal from the ballot to the bullet; and those who take such appeal are sure to lose their cause and pay the cost" ("Cleveland" 1).

Bercovitch maintains that New England ministers, in an effort to redefine the American settlements as the New Jerusalem, created a "legend of New England's golden age" which elevated the original emigrants "into a mythical tribe of heroes—a race of giants in an age of miracles" (67–68). Similarly, Kennedy, drawing on the myth of Lincoln as the President who reunited the country and called for compassion at the end of the Civil War, urged Americans to act as their ancestors had done. The community could renew "its conception of itself and what is good" through reliance on the lessons of history (Condit 289).

Why did the nation need this instruction? Robert Kennedy discovered the reasons in the sins of individual people. Americans tolerated "a rising level of violence." Pinpointing commonplace actions, Kennedy claimed that we "calmly accept" stories of "civilian slaughter in far-off lands." Movies and television "glorify killing" and "call it entertainment." Americans "make it easy for men of all shades of sanity to acquire whatever weapons and ammunition they desire." People even "honor swagger and bluster and the wielders of force" ("Cleveland" 1). As the Senator enumerated such examples, the argument became clear. Killings such as King's and John Kennedy's were shocking, but they happened because of the consistent individual acceptance, even admiration, of violent acts every day in America. As a Puritan minister might have done, Kennedy catalogued, in some detail, the sins of the people. This list focused attention on individual acts by every American rather than on any flaws with the country itself. As Senator Kennedy defined problems of the community, he shaped a view of the disorder in the country as a natural consequence of individual, not systemic, sins. Kennedy concluded this section of the speech by making the reason for the carnage clear and calling for a spiritual solution: "Some look for scapegoats, others look to conspiracies but this much is clear: violence breeds violence, repression brings retaliation, and only a cleaning of our whole society can remove this sickness from our soul" ("Cleveland" 1).

Quickly, Senator Kennedy made the extent of the national cleansing explicit. He contrasted the "violence of institutions" with the caring of individual people. Civil disorders, he argued, were not the entire problem. Institutions in America sinned through "indifference, inaction, and slow decay" ("Cleveland" 1). While Kennedy began to deal with systemic problems in this short section of the speech, he did so by personifying American institutions. He did not present them as different from individual Americans nor did he acknowledge that the crisis might be caused by the structure of American society. Instead, he focused on their current behavior as he did with individual sinners. Kennedy wanted all to live out the values they professed to uphold.

Rather than seeing the death of King and the violence in the cities as a product of the system, Kennedy shaped a view of these events as the natural results of Americans' violation of the tenets of the American way. The actions necessary for renewal, logically, could be found in the American heritage. Condit argues that, as epideictic speakers shape a sense of community in the face of tragedy, they rely heavily on the group's shared history. Indeed, the "reference to heritage is usually very explicit" (Condit 289). The first two sections of the speech defined the nation's problems in terms of the people's failure to live up to their heritage. Naturally, Kennedy also found that the road to renewal led through American history.

In his conclusion, Kennedy urged Americans to admit their difficulties, to face them honestly, and, again, to emulate the actions of Abraham Lincoln. Significantly, Kennedy linked this process to the idea of leadership: "The question is whether we can find in our own midst and in our own hearts the leadership of human purpose that will recognize the terrible truths of our existence" ("Cleveland" 2). Implicitly, Kennedy argued that the function of a leader was to act as he was acting. In that sense, Kennedy was laying the groundwork for his later presidential campaign rhetoric and asking the audience to judge his vision of the country, a function, Condit argues, necessary to epideictic rhetoric (290–291). The speech then ended with the admission that the work would be hard, but, in another allusion to Lincoln, Kennedy assured people that the covenant could be restored: "Surely we can learn, at least, to look at those around us as fellow men and surely we can begin to work a little harder to bind up the wounds among us and to become in our hearts brothers and countrymen once again" ("Cleveland" 1).

This speech resembled a sermon more than a campaign address. Kennedy, detailing the horrors of the day, claimed that the nation was in terrible difficulty. The Lincoln quotation summarized the argument of the first half of the speech and served to remind the audience of the tragedy and waste of assassination. These words reinforced the notion that such violence had no place in the ideal of America. The principles of the society were not at fault. Why did violence occur then? Kennedy traced the cause to the sins of the people. They had departed from Lincoln's way and glorified killing in every way imaginable. From entertainment programming to Vietnam news reports, Americans welcomed violence into their homes every night. Kennedy made of all this death a seamless web. The only possible solution, in his view, was individual rebirth that could lead to a national revival. The nation could endure if the people would "bind up the wounds."

Robert Kennedy shaped perceptions of the King assassination and of violence in America in such a way as to absolve the system of blame. He explained the troubling events of the time as the natural consequence of individual failures to adhere to the values of the America covenant as articulated by men such as Abraham Lincoln. The jeremiad turns attention away from possible flaws in the covenant itself, such as institutionalized racism, and toward the failure of individuals to live out the appropriate values. The solution to the crisis lay in a greater dedication to the "ideals of the past."

Rhetorical Assessment and Implications

Jules Witcover has written that this "speech was, in a very real sense, a turning point in the presidential campaign of Robert Kennedy" (145). Witcover argues that Kennedy not only responded well to the death of King, but also discovered new themes for his struggling campaign. My analysis supports that conclusion. Robert Kennedy's use of the jeremiad held significant implications for his success as a speaker and candidate.

In the spring of 1968, the jeremiad, despite its problems, was a strategically apt choice for Kennedy because it allowed him to provide a coherent explanation for the rush of events. Ernest Bormann has written that the Puritan jeremiad "was a way of conceiving the inconceivable, of making intelligible order out of the transition from European to American experience" ("Good Out of Evil" 131). Kennedy sought to make intelligible the killing of King, the resultant disorders, and, in a broader sense, the long series of crises detailed earlier in this essay. The rhetorical form of the jeremiad allowed Kennedy to shape a plausible view of the situation for the American people, one that explained the crises, but assured the eventual triumph of the American system. The difficulties of the day could be understood and solved within the framework of American tradition. The balance between the terrible difficulty of the present and the promise of the future, as Bercovitch argues, released the energies necessary to make the changes to restore the covenant. The current crises became a test of the American character. The outcome was assured if the American people would respond with the spirit of their progenitors. The fact that Kennedy was a presidential candidate only made the possibility of reform that much more real and present. Kennedy offered himself to Americans who would "find in our own midst and in our own hearts the leadership of human purpose" that could lead the way to the promised land.

Moreover, unlike other leaders who responded to the assassination, Senator Kennedy had the personal authority to inveigh against violence. As he stated in Indianapolis, he spoke as a victim, as a man who had suffered and survived. He served as proof that death could lead to a new beginning. Further, in a peculiar way, Kennedy himself represented a way to restore the balance. In the minds of many Americans, the disorder had begun with the death of John Kennedy. From that time on, the tumult increased every year while nostalgia and guilt colored perceptions of 1961–63. In fact, *Time* magazine wrote about this feeling as early as 1966: "In part, the phenomenon grows out of what Indiana's Senator Vance Hartke calls 'a national guilt complex' over the assassination, a sort of politics of expiation whose chief beneficiary is Bobby" ("The Shadow and the Substance" 33). As a political Jeremiah, Kennedy could point to the troubles of the time, pinpoint the acceptance of violence as the reason, and, through his presidential campaign, offer a uniquely attractive means for restoring the covenant. While I hesitate to delve too deeply into the psyche of the American people, the appeal is clear. More than any other leader, Kennedy incarnated the past, the values of the American covenant, and a beloved martyred President. By electing Robert Kennedy, Americans could atone for that "original sin" and begin the process of working "a little harder to bind up the wounds among us."

Kennedy articulated these themes throughout the rest of the campaign, in a change from his earlier campaign rhetoric (Murphy). For instance, in his first campaign speech, at Kansas State University, Kennedy focused on the spiritual problems of the country but attributed their existence to the Vietnam War. American involvement in the war had brought about the crisis in the nation and the end of that war would resolve the problems ("Landon Lecture"). After the Cleveland speech, Kennedy spoke of Vietnam as a symptom of the underlying appetite for violence in America and called for a reaffirmation of American values as the solution. Later in the Indiana campaign, he contended that the campaign was a "voyage of discovery, a search into the heart of the American past for the enduring principles, to guide us toward the uncertain future" ("Indiana Televised Interview" 7). In California, the day after his defeat in Oregon, he quoted the Preamble to the Constitution and argued: "We can only restore these ancient values through imagination and ideas to suit the conditions of the future. This is what the founding fathers believed when they said our liberty needs to be freshly restored in every generation, and that is just what I'm trying to do" ("Airport Statement" 2). He argued for a restoration and the jeremiad was admirably suited for this task. His campaign possessed considerable rhetorical coherence and force.

This analysis suggests that variations on the jeremiadic form are excellent strategies for campaign speakers. Prior analyses of jeremiadic speaking have argued that such rhetoric creates the unity and drive necessary to meet and overcome crises. What earlier critiques have often neglected is the fact that the "jeremiahs" gain in prestige and stature because they are perceived as speaking for fundamental national values. Ritter (1980), for instance, notes the social cohesion created by nomination-acceptance addresses that use variations on the jeremiad but does not discuss in detail the power of these strategies to raise the *ethos* of the candidate. The case of Robert Kennedy argues strongly for the utility of such tactics. Speakers using the jeremiad seem to understand why the problems of the day exist and can offer solutions without threatening the basic structure of the country. In that sense, they offer the "humane vision" that audiences demand of epideictic speakers (Condit 290–291). As Condit notes, audiences rightfully take eloquence as a sign of leadership. The jeremiad provides a vision of America's future that is deeply rooted in its most fundamental values. Even in times of greatest tension, as after the death of King, the jeremiad affirms the nobility of the American experiment. By speaking so consistently for the "American way" and the American people, even as they criticize specific aspects of the culture, these "jeremiahs" go far toward establishing themselves as people worthy to lead the country.

The jeremiad also has limitations and these must be examined not only for future research on this rhetorical form but also to reach a full assessment of Kennedy's rhetorical choices. Robert Kennedy's speaking in this situation, however eloquent, ultimately served the purposes of the status quo. I do not mean to imply that Kennedy lacked concern for social progress. He justified that progress, however, through an appeal to the past and to the cause of "cultural revitalization" (Bercovitch 179). Kennedy's vision was confined "to the terms of the American myth" (Bercovitch 180). He sought to make the ideal America and the real America correspond but he could not propose policy alternatives or engage in social criticism outside of that ideal. His view of the ideal America restricted the changes he could propose for the real America.

In recent years, the study of the jeremiad has attracted the time and attention of a large number of critics. Their work details the ubiquity of the jeremiad, as this essay does, but the social and political consequences that undergird the jeremiad demand further examination. As the case of Kennedy demonstrates, the jeremiad calls for social change, but it also puts limits on reform. Bercovitch argues that one major contribution that the Whigs of post-Revolutionary America made to the rhetoric of the jeremiad was this insistence on control (134). When the founders contended that liberty needs to be "freshly restored" each generation, they meant that such "revolutions" would be within the confines of the American covenant. They saw the American Revolution itself as a continuation of the process begun by the Puritan emigration to a new land. Criticism and change served to restore and reaffirm basic American values not to overturn them. As Bercovitch notes:

> In the ritual of revolution [the Whigs] instituted, radicalism itself
> was socialized into an affirmation of order. If the condition of
> progress was continuing revolution, the condition of continuity (the

> Whig leaders insisted) was control of the revolutionary impulse. The
> social norms encouraged revolution, but the definition of revolution
> reinforced authority. (134)

The jeremiad, then, serves as a rhetoric of social control. In times of crisis, it functions to shape responses to the difficulties that reaffirm the viability and nobility of the American experiment. The jeremiad brings with it a definition of American history as a constant movement toward a special destiny, sanctioned by God, to establish that "shining city on a hill." By looking to the past through the jeremiad, Americans limit the kinds of choices they can make about the future. While reform within that tradition is possible, the jeremiad carries fundamental assumptions that make serious consideration of structural change difficult. Even though many Americans saw Robert Kennedy as a radical, he stood squarely within the American jeremiadic tradition. While he certainly spoke to and for radicals and outcasts in American society, he proposed that they enter American society on his terms. They would move up and out of poverty as Kennedy's family had done: by embracing the premises and values of the American Dream. The system itself did not need radical change.

During the Oregon primary, Eugene McCarthy used precisely these grounds to attack Kennedy on both urban policy and the philosophy of containment of Communism that led to the Vietnam War (Larner 94–110). On urban policy, for instance, McCarthy argued that Kennedy's proposals for ghetto revitalization could not possibly address the enormous economic and social problems faced by blacks and constituted a kind of "apartheid" (Larner 108). As indicated above, Kennedy felt that, with some governmental and private sector help, blacks could move up and out of the ghetto as the Irish before them had done. McCarthy responded that the basic racism of American society made such an analogy impossible and such a policy impracticable. If the country's problems inhered in its social structure, rather than in the sins of individuals, as McCarthy, James Farmer, and others argued in the wake of King's death, Kennedy could not step outside of the existing structure to propose appropriately radical solutions. The rhetorical form of the jeremiad clearly limits the range of political choices that are available even as it creates social cohesion. If the jeremiad is as pervasive as Bercovitch and others suggest, then rhetorical critics need to understand and explain both its strengths and its weaknesses.

These conclusions about the nature of the jeremiad also suggest that epideictic speaking itself may function in a similar manner to limit the political choices of the audience. Most research on epideictic speaking as a genre acknowledges its reliance on the values of the audience and on "*memoria*, or recollection of a shared past, . . . [as] an exceptionally important resource" (Condit; Campbell and Jamieson 204). Perelman and Olbrechts-Tyteca maintain that epideictic speeches, by emphasizing adherence to a particular system of values, may pave the way for policies that embody those values (49–52). While Condit does not accept that view as having explanatory power for all epideictic speaking, she acknowledges its relevance in some cases (286). If, in times of crisis, epideictic rhetoric is used to redefine the community in ways that reflect historically shared assumptions, then those values will restrict the range of political choices available to the audience. While this study can certainly come to no definitive conclusions on that matter, the deliberative ramifications of epideictic rhetoric need considerably more examination than they have yet received.

Senator Kennedy's assassination after the California primary has raised his presidential campaign to the status of myth and has often obscured a clear assessment of his rhetoric. In the wake of King's death, Robert Kennedy was one of the few national figures to attempt to bring "good out of evil." He deserves considerable praise for his persistent calls for compassion and for his strategically sound rhetorical choices. While Kennedy's rhetoric limited the means that he could offer the American people to reach those ends, it possessed the potential to unify the country behind a program of controlled progress, "the happy union of liberty and order" (Bercovitch 137). Whether such a policy could have met the needs of time is a question that remains unanswered.

Notes

[1]Accounts of the speechwriting process indicate a situation of considerable confusion. The three writers worked throughout the night, with Sorensen phoning in his suggestions from New York. Greenfield fell asleep at his typewriter trying to finish the text at 3:30 in the morning and was put to bed by Kennedy. While the speech reflects themes Kennedy had discussed before, the speech was clearly a collaborative effort, hastily composed, among all of the principals (Newfield 272; Schlesinger 942).

Works Cited

Aarons, Leroy. "Kennedy Launches Indiana Campaign." Washington Post 5 April 1968, final ed.: A2.

Aarons, Leroy. "RFK, His Voice Quavering, Tells Rally 'Very Sad News.'" Washington Post 6 April 1968, final ed.: A2.

"America Come Home." Editorial. New York Times 6 April 1968, late ed.: 38.

Bercovitch, Sacvan. The American Jeremiad. Madison: University of Wisconsin Press, 1978.

Bormann, Ernest. "Fetching Good Out Of Evil: A Rhetorical Use Of Calamity." Quarterly Journal of Speech 63 (1977): 130–39.

Bormann, Ernest. *The Force of Fantasy: Restoring the American Dream.* Carbondale: Southern Illinois University Press, 1985.

Condit, Celeste. "The Function of Epideictic: The Boston Massacre Orations as Exemplar," *Communication Quarterly* 33 (1985): 284–298.

Cook, Roger. "'To Tame the Savageness of Man': Robert Kennedy's Eulogy of Martin Luther King, Jr." In Lloyd E. Rohler and Roger Cook (Eds.) *Great Speeches for Criticism and Analysis.* Greenwood, IN: Alistair Press, 1988.

David, Lester and Irene David. *Bobby Kennedy: The Making Of A Folk Hero.* New York: Paperjacks, 1988.

Diffley, Kathleen. "'Erecting Anew the Standard of Freedom': Salmon P. Chase's 'Appeal of the Independent Democrats' and the Rise of the Republican Party." *Quarterly Journal of Speech* 74 (1988): 401–15.

Johannesen, Richard L. "The Jeremiad and Jenkin Lloyd Jones." *Communication Monographs* 52 (1985): 156–72.

Johannesen, Richard L. "Ronald Reagan's Economic Jeremiad." *Central States Speech Journal* 37 (1986): 79–89.

Johnson, Lyndon B. "Statement By The President." *New York Times* 6 April 1968, late ed.: 23.

Kaiser, Charles. *1968 In America.* New York: Weidenfeld and Nicolson, 1988.

Kennedy, Robert. "Announcement of Candidacy." 16 March 1968, *RFK Speeches and Press Releases Box #4* John F. Kennedy Presidential Library and Museum.

Kennedy, Robert. "Cleveland City Club Speech." 5 April 1968, *RFK Speeches and Press Releases Box #4* John F. Kennedy Presidential Library and Museum.

Kennedy, Robert. "Eulogy of Martin Luther King, Jr." In Lloyd E. Rohler and Roger Cook (Eds). *Great Speeches for Criticism and Analysis.* Greenwood, IN: Alistair Press, 1988.

Kennedy, Robert. "Interview with Senator Robert F. Kennedy." 17 April 1968, *RFK Speeches and Press Releases Box #4* John F. Kennedy Presidential Library and Museum.

Kennedy, Robert. "Statement of Senator Robert F. Kennedy: Press Conference, Los Angeles International Airport." 29 May 1968, *RFK Speeches and Press Releases Box #4* John F. Kennedy Presidential Library and Museum.

Kennedy, Robert F. *To Seek A Newer World.* New York: Bantam Books, 1968.

Kraft, Joseph. "National Dissensus: Mental and Moral Decay Is Eating Out The Vitals Of The Country." *Washington Post* 7 April 1968, final ed.

Larner, Jeremy. *Nobody Knows.* New York: The Macmillan Company, 1969.

Miller, Perry. *Errand Into The Wilderness.* Cambridge: Harvard University Press, 1964.

Miller, Perry. *The New England Mind: From Colony To Province.* Cambridge: Harvard University Press, 1953.

Murphy, John M. Renewing The National Covenant: The Presidential Campaign Rhetoric of Robert Kennedy. Diss. U. of Kansas, 1986.

Newfield, Jack. *Robert F. Kennedy: A Memoir.* New York: Berkley Publishing, 1978.

"RFK Denounces Slaying of Dr. King." *Washington Post* 6 April 1968, final ed.: A2.

Ritter, Kurt. "American Political Rhetoric and the Jeremiad Tradition: Presidential Nomination Acceptance Addresses, 1960–76." *Central States Speech Journal* 31 (1980): 153–71.

"Robert Kennedy—His Public Image." *Gallup Political Index Report No. 6* Nov. 1965: 14.

Schlesinger, Arthur M. *Robert Kennedy and His Times*. New York: Random House, 1978.

"The Shadow and the Substance." *Time* 16 September 1966:33.

Strout, Richard. "T.R.B. From Washington." *New Republic* 13 April 1968: 1.

Van Gelder, Lawrence. "Dismay in Nation." *New York Times* 5 April 1968, late city ed.: 1.

Vanden Heuvel, William and Milton Gwirtzman. *On His Own: Robert F. Kennedy 1964–1968*. Garden City: Doubleday and Co., 1970.

White, Theodore H. *The Making of the President 1968*. New York: Atheneum Publishers, 1968.

Wills, Garry. *The Kennedy Imprisonment*. New York: Pocket Books, 1981, 1982.

Wilson, James Q. "The Newer Deal." *New Republic* 2 July 1990: 33.

Witcover, Jules. *85 Days: The last Campaign of Robert Kennedy*. New York: G.P. Putnam, 1969.

Additional Samples
Generic Criticism

Aly, Bower. "The Gallows Speech: A Lost Genre." *Southern Speech Journal*, 34 (Spring 1969), 204-13.

Andrews, James R. "They Chose the Sword: Appeals to War in Nineteenth-Century American Public Address." *Today's Speech*, 17 (September 1969), 3-8.

Bass, Jeff D. "The Rhetorical Opposition to Controversial Wars: Rhetorical Timing as a Generic Consideration." *Western Journal of Speech Communication*, 43 (Summer 1979), 180-91.

Bennett, W. Lance. "Assessing Presidential Character: Degradation Rituals in Political Campaigns," *Quarterly Journal of Speech*, 67 (August 1981), 310-21.

Benoit, William L., and Susan L. Brinson. "AT&T": 'Apologies are not Enough.'" *Communication Quarterly*, 42 (Winter 1994), 75-88.

Benoit, William L., Paul Gulliform, and Daniel A. Panici. "President Reagan's Defensive Discourse on the Iran-Contra Affair." *Communication Studies*, 42 (Fall 1991), 272-94.

Benoit, William L., and Robert S. Hanczor. "The Tonya Harding Controversy: An Analysis of Image Restoration Strategies." *Communication Quarterly*, 42 (Fall 1994), 416-33.

Blair, Carole. "From 'All the President's Men' to Every Man for Himself: The Strategies of Post-Watergate Apologia." *Central States Speech Journal*, 35 (Winter 1984), 250-60.

Brown, Stephen H. "Generic Transformation and Political Action: A Textual Interpretation of Edmund Burke's *Letter to William Elliot, Esq.*" *Communication Quarterly*, 38 (Winter 1990), 54-63.

Brummett, Barry. "Premillennial Apocalyptic as a Rhetorical Genre." *Central States Speech Journal*, 35 (Summer 1984), 84-93.

Brummett, Barry. *Rhetorical Dimensions of Popular Culture*. Tuscaloosa: University of Alabama Press, 1991, pp. 125-46, 147-71.

Bryant, Donald C. "The Speech on the Address in the Late Eighteenth-Century House of Commons." *Southern Speech Communication Journal*, 51 (Summer 1986), 344-53.

Butler, Sherry Devereaux. "The Apologia, 1971 Genre." *Southern Speech Communication Journal*, 37 (Spring 1972), 281-89.

Campbell, Karlyn Kohrs. "The Rhetoric of Women's Liberation: An Oxymoron." *Quarterly Journal of Speech*, 59 (February 1973), 74-86.

Campbell, Karlyn Kohrs, and Kathleen Hall Jamieson, eds. *Form and Genre: Shaping Rhetorical Action*. Falls Church, Virginia: Speech Communication Association [1978], several essays, pp. 75-161.

Campbell, Karlyn Kohrs, and Kathleen Hall Jamieson. "Inaugurating the Presidency." In *Form, Genre and the Study of Political Discourse.* Ed. Herbert W. Simons and Aram A. Aghazarian. Columbia: University of South Carolina Press, 1986, pp. 203–25.

Carlson, A. Cheree. "John Quincy Adams' 'Amistad Address': Eloquence in a Generic Hybrid." *Western Journal of Speech Communication,* 49 (Winter 1985), 14–26.

Carlton, Charles. "The Rhetoric of Death: Scaffold Confessions in Early Modern England." *Southern Speech Communication Journal,* 49 (Fall 1983), 66–79.

Carpenter, Ronald H., and Robert V. Seltzer. "Situational Style and the Rotunda Eulogies." *Central States Speech Journal,* 22 (Spring 1971), 11–15.

Clark, Thomas D. "An Exploration of Generic Aspects of Contemporary American Campaign Orations." *Central States Speech Journal,* 30 (Summer 1979), 122–33.

Clark, Thomas D. "An Exploration of Generic Aspects of Contemporary American Christian Sermons." *Quarterly Journal of Speech,* 63 (December 1977), 384–94.

DeWitt, Jean Zaun. "The Rhetoric of Induction at the French Academy." *Quarterly Journal of Speech,* 69 (November 1983), 413–22.

Downey, Sharon D. "The Evolution of the Rhetorical Genre of Apologia." *Western Journal of Communication,* 57 (Winter 1993), 42–64.

Farrell, Thomas B. "Political Conventions as Legitimation Ritual." *Communication Monographs,* 45 (November 1978), 293–305.

Foss, Karen A. "Out from Underground: The Discourse of Emerging Fugitives." *Western Journal of Communication,* 56 (Spring 1992), 125–42.

Fulkerson, Richard. "*Newsweek* 'My Turn' Columns and the Concept of Rhetorical Genre: A Preliminary Study." In *Defining the New Rhetorics.* Ed. Theresa Enos and Stuart C. Brown. Newbury Park, CA: Sage, 1993, pp. 227–43.

Gold, Ellen Reid. "Political Apologia: The Ritual of Self-Defense." *Communication Monographs,* 45 (November 1978), 306–16.

Gronbeck, Bruce E. "The Rhetoric of Political Corruption: Sociolinguistic, Dialectical, and Ceremonial Processes." *Quarterly Journal of Speech,* 64 (April 1978), 155–72.

Hammerback, John C., and Richard J. Jensen. "Ethnic Heritage as Rhetorical Legacy: The Plan of Delano." *Quarterly Journal of Speech,* 80 (February 1994), 53–70.

Hoover, Judith D. "Big Boys Don't Cry: The Values Constraint in Apologia." *Southern Communication Journal,* 54 (Spring 1989), 235–52.

Ivie, Robert L. "Images of Savagery in American Justifications for War." *Communication Monographs,* 47 (November 1980), 279–94.

Jamieson, Kathleen Hall, and Karlyn Kohrs Campbell. "Rhetorical Hybrids: Fusions of Generic Elements." *Quarterly Journal of Speech,* 68 (May 1982), 146–57.

Johannesen, Richard L. "The Jeremiad and Jenkin Lloyd Jones." *Communication Monographs,* 52 (June 1985), 156–72.

Kahl, Mary. "*Blind Ambition* Culminates in *Lost Honor*: A Comparative Analysis of John Dean's Apologetic Strategies." *Central States Speech Journal,* 35 (Winter 1984), 239–50.

King, Janis L. "Justificatory Rhetoric for a Female Political Candidate: A Case Study of Wilma Mankiller." *Women's Studies in Communication*, 13 (Fall 1990), 21–38.

Kruse, Noreen Wales. "Apologia in Team Sport." *Quarterly Journal of Speech*, 67 (August 1981), 270–83.

Lucas, Stephen E. "Genre Criticism and Historical Context: The Case of George Washington's First Inaugural Address." *Southern Speech Communication Journal*, 51 (Summer 1986), 354–70.

Martin, Howard H. "A Generic Exploration: Staged Withdrawal, the Rhetoric of Resignation." *Central States Speech Journal*, 27 (Winter 1976), 247–57.

Miles, Edwin A. "The Keynote Speech at National Nominating Conventions." *Quarterly Journal of Speech*, 46 (February 1960), 26–31.

Nelson, Jeffrey. "The Defense of Billie Jean King." *Western Journal of Speech Communication*, 48 (Winter 1984), 92–102.

Olson, Kathryn M. "Completing the Picture: Replacing Generic Embodiments in the Historical Flow." *Communication Quarterly*, 41 (Summer 1993), 299–317.

Orr, C. Jack. "Reporters Confront the President: Sustaining a Counterpoised Situation." *Quarterly Journal of Speech*, 66 (February 1980), 17–32.

Quimby, Rollin W. "Recurrent Themes and Purposes in the Sermons of the Union Army Chaplains." *Speech Monographs*, 31 (November 1964), 425–36.

Ritter, Kurt W. "American Political Rhetoric and the Jeremiad Tradition: Presidential Nomination Acceptance Addresses, 1960–1976." *Central States Speech Journal*, 31 (Fall 1980), 153–71.

Rodgers, Raymond S. "Generic Tendencies in Majority and Non-Majority Supreme Court Opinions: The Case of Justice Douglas." *Communication Quarterly*, 30 (Summer 1982), 232–36.

Shaw, Punch. "Generic Refinement on the Fringe: The Game Show." *Southern Speech Communication Journal*, 52 (Summer 1987), 403–10.

Short, Brant. "Comic Book Apologia: The 'Paranoid' Rhetoric of Congressman George Hansen." *Western Journal of Speech Communication*, 51 (Spring 1987), 189–203.

Simons, Herbert W. "'Going Meta': Definition and Political Applications." *Quarterly Journal of Speech*, 80 (November 1994), 468–81.

Simons, Herbert W., and Aram A. Aghazarian, eds. *Form, Genre, and the Study of Political Discourse*. Columbia: University of South Carolina Press, 1986, numerous essays, pp. 203–77.

Valley, David B. "Significant Characteristics of Democratic Presidential Nomination Speeches." *Central States Speech Journal*, 25 (Spring 1974), 56–62.

Vartabedian, Robert A. "Nixon's Vietnam Rhetoric: A Case Study of Apologia as Generic Paradox." *Southern Speech Communication Journal*, 50 (Summer 1985), 366–81.

Ware, B. L., and Wil A. Linkugel. "They Spoke in Defense of Themselves: On the Generic Criticism of Apologia." *Quarterly Journal of Speech*, 59 (October 1973), 273–83.

Weaver, Ruth Ann. "Acknowledgment of Victory and Defeat: The Reciprocal Ritual." *Central States Speech Journal*, 33 (Fall 1982), 480–89.

White, Cindy L., and Catherine A. Dobris. "A Chorus of Discordant Voices: Radical Feminist Confrontations with Patriarchal Religion." *Southern Communication Journal*, 58 (Spring 1993), 239–46.

Wooten, Cecil W. "The Ambassador's Speech: A Particularly Hellenistic Genre of Oratory." *Quarterly Journal of Speech*, 59 (April 1973), 209–12.

For a more complete bibliography of genre studies, see: Fisher, Walter R. "Genre: Concepts and Applications in Rhetorical Criticism." *Western Journal of Speech Communication*, 44 (Fall 1980), 296–99; and Simons, Herbert W. and Aram A. Aghazarian, eds. *Form, Genre and the Study of Political Discourse.* Columbia: University of South Carolina Press, 1986, pp. 355–77.

8

Ideological Criticism

When rhetorical critics are interested in rhetoric primarily for what it suggests about beliefs and values, their focus is on the ideology manifest in an artifact. An *ideology* is a pattern or set of ideas, assumptions, beliefs, values, or interpretations of the world by which a culture or group operates. The ideology of a group typically includes "such things as the beliefs the members of the group hold, the concepts they use, the attitudes and psychological dispositions they exhibit, their motives, desires, values, predilections. . . ."[1] An ideology usually permeates everything produced in that culture or group, so its rhetorical artifacts— its works of art, religious practices, and institutions, for example— embody, enact, and express that ideology.[2]

Ideologies are obvious in the sets of beliefs that characterize, for example, the Republican or Democratic political parties, anti-Communism, Christianity, or supply-side economics. Moral and normative beliefs also constitute ideologies; the belief that women in our culture should be thin, young, and sexually attractive to men, for example, is an ideology that is manifest in a wide variety of cultural practices. But ideologies are not always explicit and fully articulated. They may be interpretations or beliefs about the world such as, "process is more important than product," "competition produces superior achievement and products," "all life forms are interconnected," "men are superior to women," and "the collective good is more important than the welfare of the individual."

A number of scholars have contributed to the development of ideological criticism in the communication field, including Philip C. Wander,[3] Michael Calvin McGee,[4] Raymie E. McKerrow,[5] Janice Hocker Rushing, Thomas S. Frentz,[6] Lawrence Grossberg,[7] and Celeste M. Condit.[8] These scholars have been influenced by a number of different perspectives and philosophies in their creation of an ideological approach to criticism.

One perspective that often informs ideological criticism is structuralism, a series of projects in which linguistics is used as a model for attempts to develop the "grammars" of systems such as myths, novels, or genres; these grammars are systematic inventories of elements and their relationships. Claude Lévi-Strauss' work is representative of a structuralist approach; he studied a wide range of myths in an effort to discover their structure or grammar.[9] By constructing such grammars, structuralists gain insights into the ideologies of artifacts because the grammars embody and provide clues to those ideologies.

A contributor to and form of structuralism that many ideological critics have found useful is semiotics or semiology, the science of signs. Developed by Ferdinand de Saussure[10] and Charles Sanders Peirce,[11] semiotics is a systematic attempt to understand what signs are and how they function. Signs are units that can be taken as substituting for something else and, consequently, they have meaning. All sorts of things can function as signs, suggesting particular meanings—words, font styles, camera angles, colors, clothing, and gestures, to name only a few. Semiotics provides a way to study components of an artifact as clues to its meaning and ideology. Among those who have contributed to the development of semiotics and its use in ideological criticism are Roland Barthes,[12] Arthur Asa Berger,[13] and Kaja Silverman.[14]

Marxism also informs the work of many ideological critics.[15] As an intellectual system, Marxism is a way of analyzing cultural products in terms of the social and economic practices and institutions that produce them. Although Marxist critics—such as Theodor Adorno,[16] Louis Althusser,[17] Walter Benjamin,[18] Bertolt Brecht,[19] Terry Eagleton,[20] Jürgen Habermas,[21] Georg Lukács,[22] and Herbert Marcuse,[23]—often differ in their interpretations and applications of Marxism, they are united by the belief that material conditions interact with and influence the symbols by which groups make sense of their world. Ideological forms are more than ideas, beliefs, and values; they have a material existence and are embodied in cultural institutions such as schools, churches, and political parties and in artifacts such as paintings, novels, and speeches.

Yet another influence on ideological criticism is deconstructionism, sometimes called *poststructuralism* because it developed after and in response to structuralism. The philosophy and critical method of deconstructionism is most closely associated with Jacques Derrida;[24] its foremost American exponent is Paul de Man.[25] The purpose of deconstructionism is to deconstruct the self-evidence of central concepts—to subject to critical analyses the basic structures and assumptions governing texts and how knowledge develops. Methodologically, deconstruction is directed to the questioning of texts—taking apart and exposing their underlying meanings, biases, and preconceptions—and then transforming or reconceptualizing the conceptual fields of those texts.

Postmodernism, a theory of cultural, intellectual, and societal discontinuity, also influences much ideological criticism. Postmodern theories are based on the notion that our culture has moved into a new phase—one that follows the period of Modernism, which championed reason as the source of progress in society and privileged the foundation of systematic knowledge. The new form of society has been transformed radically by the domination of the media and technology, which have introduced new forms of communication and representation into contemporary life. This postmodern society requires new concepts and theories to address the features that characterize the new era: fragmentation of individuals and communities, a consumer lifestyle, a sense of alienation, and destabilization of unifying discourses and principles. The postmodern project is useful to ideological critics in that it provides information about the context for many contemporary artifacts and suggests the exigence to which many of these artifacts and their ideologies are responding. Among the primary contributors to theories of postmodernism are Jean-François Lyotard,[26] Jean Baudrillard,[27] and Fredric Jameson.[28]

Yet another source from which ideological critics draw is cultural studies, an interdisciplinary project directed at uncovering oppressive relations and discovering available forces with the potential to lead to liberation or emancipation. As a loosely unified movement, cultural studies can be dated to the establishment of the Birmingham Centre for Contemporary Cultural Studies in Great Britain in 1964 by Richard Hoggart;[29] the Centre later was headed by Stuart Hall.[30] Although theorists associated with cultural studies adopt diverse approaches, including Marxist, poststructuralist, postmodern, feminist, and Jungian perspectives, they tend to be united by some basic assumptions about culture. Culture, they believe, consists of everyday discursive practices, with these discursive practices both embodying and constructing a culture's ideology. They see artifacts of popular culture as legitimate data for critical analysis because they are places where struggles take place over which meanings and ideologies will predominate.

The ideological criticism that has developed from perspectives such as structuralism, semiotics, and Marxism is rooted in some basic notions about ideologies and how they function. Primary is the notion that multiple ideologies—multiple patterns of belief—exist in any culture and have the potential to be manifest in rhetorical artifacts. Some ideologies, however, get privileged over others in a culture, and ideologies that present oppositional or alternative perspectives get repressed. The result is a dominant way of seeing the world or the development of a dominant ideology—in other words, one ideology comes to constitute a hegemony in the culture. *Hegemony* is the privileging of the ideology of one group over that of other groups; it thus constitutes a kind of social control, a means of symbolic coercion, or a form of domination of the more powerful groups over the ideologies of those with less power.[31]

When an ideology becomes hegemonic in a culture, certain interests or groups are served by it more than others—it represents the perspective of some groups more than others. The hegemonic ideology represents experience in ways that support the interests of those with more power. The dominance of one group's ideology over others can be seen in the contemporary discourse about new reproductive technologies such as in-vitro fertilization. Although many perspectives and ideologies are involved in the discourse about this issue—those of the Catholic church, feminists, lawyers, infertile couples, and doctors and medical researchers, for example—the dominant perspective that emerges and functions as hegemonic is that of the doctors and medical researchers. In part because they are the ones with the information about the technical procedures to supply to the journalists who cover the issue and because they have a commodity to offer to an audience of potential consumers, their perspective becomes privileged over that of other perspectives.[32]

The process by which an ideology becomes dominant or hegemonic typically is not one in which a powerful group coerces a less powerful group into accepting its ideology, nor is it usually deliberate and conscious. Instead, a particular ideology becomes hegemonic as a result of a process in which a variety of groups forge an accord with one another or tacitly give their consent that one perspective will be allowed to dominate.

A variety of factors give advantage to some groups over others in determining which ideologies come to dominate. Of primary importance in this process is the possession by a group of a broad-based and coherent ideology that is able to attract support from some groups and at least passive assent from others. Numerical superiority, access to resources or technologies not available to others, alliances with other groups that increase their legitimacy or authority, and the backing of other powerful groups all tend to advantage groups in the process of forging an accord that features an ideology as hegemonic.[33]

When an ideology becomes hegemonic through a process of accord and consent, it accumulates "the symbolic power to map or classify the world for others. . . ."[34] It invites "us to understand the world in certain ways, but not in others."[35] A dominant ideology controls what participants see as natural or obvious by establishing the norm; normal discourse, then, maintains the ideology, and challenges to it seem abnormal. A hegemonic ideology provides a sense that things are the way they have to be as it asserts that its meanings are the real, natural ones. In a culture where the ideology of racism is hegemonic, for example, the privilege accorded to whites seems normal, as does the lack of opportunity accorded to individuals of other races; if practices in the culture concerning people of color are questioned, the questions are seen as abnormal.

Resistance to the dominant ideology is muted or contained—its impact is limited—by a variety of sophisticated rhetorical strategies. Often, in fact, these rhetorical strategies incorporate the resistance into the dominant discourse in such a way that the challenge will not contradict and even may support the dominant ideology. In a culture in which an ideology of racism is dominant, for example, questions about why people of color are not given equal opportunities may be muted by depictions of these people as lacking in internal motivation; thus, the argument that they are not given equal opportunities is seen as irrelevant and thus is unable to have any impact on the dominant ideology.

To maintain a position of dominance, a hegemonic ideology must be constructed, renewed, reinforced, and defended continually through the use of rhetorical strategies and practices. One common mechanism for constructing and reinforcing ideologies is school, which shapes students in particular directions; we learn to obey orders, for example, through the educational process. This is just one of thousands of everyday activities and institutions that express, construct, and reinforce ideologies. Religion, families, the media, the legal system, and the rhetorical acts and artifacts of popular culture perpetuate the dominant ideology and convince participants in a culture to accept that ideology. Although, as individuals, we may adhere to ideologies different from the one that is hegemonic, we cannot help but participate in the hegemonic ideology as we participate in our culture through activities such as watching television, browsing through popular magazines, and attending school.

The primary goal of the ideological critic is to discover and make visible the dominant ideology or ideologies embedded in an artifact and the ideologies that are being muted in it. The critic who discovers that the dominant ideology revealed in an artifact suppresses the voices of important interests or groups seeks to explicate the role of communication in creating and sustaining the suppression and to give voice to those interests. The ultimate aim of the ideological critic, as a result, is the emancipation of human potential that is being thwarted by an existing ideology or ideologies.

Procedures

The critic whose focus is ideology analyzes an artifact in four steps: (1) formulating a research question and selecting an artifact; (2) selecting a unit of analysis; (3) analyzing the artifact; and (4) writing the critical essay.

Formulating a Research Question and Selecting an Artifact

The first step in the process of rhetorical criticism is to develop a research question to ask about rhetoric and to select a rhetorical artifact to analyze that provides an initial answer to the question. The ideological critic's primary interest in the ideology expressed in a rhetorical artifact leads to questions such as: What is the ideology embodied in this artifact? What are the implications of this ideology? How inclusive is the ideology expressed in the artifact? Does the dominant ideology expressed in the artifact represent the best possible concord that might be reached among the multiple groups and ideologies it reflects? What alternative interpretations of the world are possible to the one offered by the ideology manifest in the artifact? Are there aspects of the artifact that might support or facilitate emancipation? Can the artifact be used as the basis for proposing new ideologies that allow other ideologies and interests to be more visible?

Selecting a Unit of Analysis

The second step in the process of rhetorical criticism is to select a unit of analysis that can help the critic answer the research question. The unit of analysis is that aspect of the artifact to which the critic attends in the analysis. The units of analysis in ideological criticism are those mechanisms or aspects of the artifact that serve as traces of the ideology or ideologies embedded in it—those dimensions of the artifact that reveal its ideology. All artifacts are inscribed with ideology, and in ideological criticism, rhetorical artifacts are treated as symptoms or textual evidence of ideology.

Analyzing the Artifact

A critic who uses as the unit of analysis the traces of ideology manifest in a rhetorical artifact addresses three primary concerns in an analysis of the artifact:

Identification of Nature of Ideology.   The first step involves identification of the nature of the ideology that is dominant in the artifact. What is the preferred reading of the artifact? What does the artifact ask the audience to believe, understand, feel, or think about? What arguments are being made in the artifact and for what? What are the particular characteristics, roles, actions, or ways of seeing being commended in the artifact? What values or general conceptions of what is and is not good are suggested? What are the assumptions or premises of the artifact? What doesn't the artifact want the audience to think about? What ways of seeing does it ask the audience to avoid? What does the artifact suggest is unacceptable, negative, undesirable, marginal, and insignificant?

Identification of Interests Included.   The critic's second step is the identification of those whose interests are represented in the artifact. Who are the groups or voices whose interests are included in the dominant ideology? Whose interests are privileged or favored in the dominant ideology? Whose interests are negated, unexpressed, oppressed, or not represented in the dominant ideology?

Identification of Strategies in Support of the Ideology.   The critic then examines the artifact for the rhetorical features that promote one ideology over others. What rhetorical features of the artifact account for the rise to dominance of one ideology over others? What rhetorical strategies are used to create and support the dominant ideology? How does the rhetoric legitimate the ideology and the interests of some groups over others?

An infinite number of rhetorical strategies are available that promote one ideology over others. Do the rhetorical strategies employed by some groups or agents, for example, align with the interests of others to produce relative dominance of a particular ideology? Does the artifact universalize the ideology, portraying the interests of a particular group or groups as though they were general interests? Does the artifact homogenize, focusing on a single interest that unites diverse groups and playing down interests that might divide them? Is the artifact constructed to encourage identification with its form (as in a story with a happy ending), which then is transferred to identification with the content of a particular ideology? What rhetorical strategies are used to repress alternative ideologies? If alternative ideologies cannot be repressed, how are they pacified, appeased, or incorporated? What rhetorical strategies are used to defuse resentment that otherwise would be directed at dominant groups? What rhetorical strategies are used that discourage the audience from being reflective?[36]

Writing the Critical Essay

After completion of the analysis, the critic writes an essay that includes five major components: (1) an introduction, in which the research question, its contribution to rhetorical theory, and its significance are discussed; (2) description of the artifact and its context; (3) description of the unit of analysis, the evidence the critic finds in the artifact for a particular ideology; (4) report of the findings of the analysis, in which the critic describes the dominant ideology manifest in the artifact, the interests and groups it serves, and the rhetorical strategies that promote it over other ideologies; and (5) discussion of the contribution the analysis makes to answering the research question.

Sample Essays

In the essays that follow, ideological critics analyze a variety of artifacts to discover the ideologies they embody. Dana L. Cloud's analysis of television's coverage of the Persian Gulf War is guided by the research question, "What is the process by which television news represses and contains the opposition to its ideology?" In Karen E. Altman's analysis of the Better Homes in America Campaign, she seeks to answer the research question, "What are the discursive and media practices by which the formation of consumer culture is constructed and maintained?" Victoria A. Gillam analyzes *Late Show with David Letterman* to answer two research questions, "What is the dominant ideology expressed by *Late Show with David Letterman*?" and "How is that ideology constructed rhetorically?"

Notes

[1] Raymond Geuss, *The Idea of a Critical Theory: Habermas and the Frankfurt School* (New York: Cambridge University Press, 1981), p. 5.

[2] This definition comes largely from Stuart Hall, "Ideology," in *International Encyclopedia of Communications*, ed. Erik Barnouw (1981; New York: Oxford University Press, 1989), p. 307; and Antonio Gramsci, *Selections from the Prison Notebooks*, trans. and ed. Quintin Hoare and Geoffrey N. Smith (1971; rpt. New York: International, 1987).

³ Philip C. Wander, "Salvation Through Separation: The Image of the Negro in the American Colonization Society," *Quarterly Journal of Speech*, 57 (February 1971), 57–67; Philip C. Wander, "The John Birch and Martin Luther King Symbols in the Radical Right," *Western Speech*, 35 (Winter 1971), 4–14; Philip C. Wander, "The Savage Child: The Image of the Negro in the Pro-Slavery Movement," *Southern Speech Communication Journal*, 37 (Summer 1972), 335–60; Philip Wander and Steven Jenkins, "Rhetoric, Society, and the Critical Response," *Quarterly Journal of Speech*, 58 (December 1972), 441–50; Philip Wander, "'The Waltons': How Sweet It Was," *Journal of Communication*, 26 (Autumn 1976), 148–54; Philip Wander, "On the Meaning of 'Roots,'" *Journal of Communication*, 27 (Autumn 1977), 64–69; Philip Wander, "The Angst of the Upper Class," *Journal of Communication*, 29 (Autumn 1979), 85–88; Philip Wander, "Cultural Criticism," in *Handbook of Political Communication*, ed. Dan D. Nimmo and Keith R. Sanders (Beverly Hills: Sage, 1981), 497–528; Philip Wander, "The Ideological Turn in Modern Criticism," *Central States Speech Journal*, 34 (Spring 1983), 1–18; Philip Wander, "The Aesthetics of Fascism," *Journal of Communication*, 33 (Spring 1983), 70–78; Philip Wander, "The Rhetoric of American Foreign Policy," *Quarterly Journal of Speech*, 70 (November 1984), 339–61; Philip Wander, "The Third Persona: An Ideological Turn in Rhetorical Theory," *Central States Speech Journal*, 35 (Winter 1984), 197–216; Richard Morris and Philip Wander, "Native American Rhetoric: Dancing in the Shadows of the Ghost Dance," *Quarterly Journal of Speech*, 76 (May 1990), 164–91; and Philip C. Wander, "Introduction: Special Issue on Ideology," *Western Journal of Communication*, 57 (Spring 1993), 105–10.

⁴ Michael C. McGee, "In Search of 'The People': A Rhetorical Alternative," *Quarterly Journal of Speech*, 61 (October 1975), 235–49; Michael C. McGee, "'Not Men, but Measures': The Origins and Import of an Ideological Principle," *Quarterly Journal of Speech*, 64 (April 1978), 141–54; Michael Calvin McGee, "The 'Ideograph': A Link Between Rhetoric and Ideology," *Quarterly Journal of Speech*, 66 (February 1980), 1–16; Michael Calvin McGee, "The Origins of 'Liberty'": A Feminization of Power," *Communication Monographs*, 47 (March 1980), 23–45; Michael Calvin McGee and Martha Anne Martin, "Public Knowledge and Ideological Argumentation," *Communication Monographs*, 50 (March 1983), 47–65; Michael Calvin McGee, "Secular Humanism: A Radical Reading of 'Culture Industry' Productions," *Critical Studies in Mass Communication*, 1 (March 1984), 1–33; Michael Calvin McGee, "Another Philippic: Notes on the Ideological Turn in Criticism," *Central States Speech Journal*, 35 (Spring 1984), 43–50; Allen Scult, Michael Calvin McGee, and J. Kenneth Buntz, "Genesis and Power: An Analysis of the Biblical Story of Creation," *Quarterly Journal of Speech*, 72 (May 1986), 113–31; Michael Calvin McGee, "Power to the {People}," *Critical Studies in Mass Communication*, 4 (December 1987), 432–37; and Michael Calvin McGee, "Text, Context, and the Fragmentation of Contemporary Culture," *Western Journal of Speech Communication*, 54 (Summer 1990), 274–89.

⁵ Raymie E. McKerrow, "Critical Rhetoric: Theory and Praxis," *Communication Monographs*, 56 (June 1989), 91–111; and Raymie E. McKerrow, "Critical Rhetoric in a Postmodern World," *Quarterly Journal of Speech*, 77 (February 1991), 75–78.

⁶ Janice Hocker Rushing, "The Rhetoric of the American Western Myth," *Communication Monographs*, 50 (March 1983), 14–32; Janice Hocker Rushing, "E.T. as Rhetorical Transcendence," *Quarterly Journal of Speech*, 71 (May 1985), 188–203; Janice Hocker Rushing, "Mythic Evolution of 'The New Frontier' in Mass Mediated Rhetoric," *Critical Studies in Mass Communication*, 3 (September 1986), 265–96; Janice Hocker Rushing, "Ronald Reagan's 'Star Wars' Address: Mythic Containment of Technical Reasoning," *Quarterly Journal of Speech*, 72 (November 1986), 415–33; Janice Hocker Rushing, "Evolution of 'The New Frontier' in *Alien* and *Aliens*: Patriarchal Co-optation of the Feminine Archetype," *Quarterly Journal of Speech*, 75 (February 1989), 1–24; Janice

Hocker Rushing, "Power, Other, and Spirit in Cultural Texts," *Western Journal of Communication*, 57 (Spring 1993), 159–68; Thomas S. Frentz and Thomas B. Farrell, "Conversion of America's Consciousness: The Rhetoric of *The Exorcist*," *Quarterly Journal of Speech*, 61 (February 1975), 40–47; Janice Hocker Rushing and Thomas S. Frentz, "The Frankenstein Myth in Contemporary Cinema," *Critical Studies in Mass Communication*, 6 (March 1989), 61–80; Janice Hocker Rushing and Thomas S. Frentz, "Integrating Ideology and Archetype in Rhetorical Criticism," *Quarterly Journal of Speech*, 77 (November 1991), 385–406; and Thomas S. Frentz and Janice Hocker Rushing, "Integrating Ideology and Archetype in Rhetorical Criticism, Part II: A Case Study of *Jaws*," *Quarterly Journal of Speech*, 79 (February 1993), 61–81.

[7] Lawrence Grossberg, "Marxist Dialectics and Rhetorical Criticism," *Quarterly Journal of Speech*, 65 (October 1979), 235–49; Lawrence Grossberg, "Is There Rock after Punk?" *Critical Studies in Mass Communication*, 3 (March 1986), 50–73; and Lawrence Grossberg, "Cultural Studies and/in New Worlds," *Critical Studies in Mass Communication*, 10 (March 1993), 1–22.

[8] Celeste Michelle Condit, "Hegemony in a Mass-Mediated Society: Concordance about Reproductive Technologies," *Critical Studies in Mass Communication*, 11 (September 1994), 205–30; and Celeste Michelle Condit, "The Rhetorical Limits of Polysemy," *Critical Studies in Mass Communication*, 6 (June 1989), 103–22.

[9] See, for example, Claude Lévi-Strauss, *The Savage Mind* (Chicago: Chicago University Press, 1966); and Claude Lévi-Strauss, *Totemism*, trans. Rodney Needham (Boston: Beacon, 1963).

[10] See, for example, Ferdinand de Saussure, *Course in General Linguistics*, ed. Charles Bally, Albert Sechehaye, and Albert Reidlinger, trans. Roy Harris (London: Duckworth, 1983).

[11] See, for example, Charles Sanders Peirce, *Peirce on Signs: Writings on Semiotic*, ed. James Hoopes (Chapel Hill: University of North Carolina Press, 1991).

[12] See, for example, Roland Barthes, *Elements of Semiology*, trans. Annette Lavers and Colin Smith (1964; New York: Noonday, 1967); and Roland Barthes, *Mythologies*, trans. Annette Lavers (1957; New York: Noonday, 1972).

[13] See, for example, Arthur Asa Berger, *Signs in Contemporary Culture: An Introduction to Semiotics* (New York: Longman, 1984); and Arthur Asa Berger, *Media Analysis Techniques* (Newbury Park, CA: Sage, 1991).

[14] Kaja Silverman, *The Subject of Semiotics* (New York: Oxford University Press, 1983).

[15] See, for example, Karl Marx and Frederick Engels, *The German Ideology: Parts I and III*, ed. Roy Pascal (New York: International, 1947); and Karl Marx, *The Grundrisse*, ed. and trans. David McLellan (New York: Harper and Row, 1971).

[16] See, for example, Theodor Adorno, *Aesthetic Theory*, ed. Gretal Adorno and Rolf Tiedmann, trans. C. Lenhardt (London: Routledge and Kegan Paul, 1984); and Theodor Adorno, *The Jargon of Authenticity*, trans. Knut Tarnowski and Frederic Will (Evanston, IL: Northwestern University Press, 1973).

[17] See, for example, Louis Althusser, *For Marx*, trans. Ben Brewster (1965; rpt. London: Allen Lane, 1969); and *Lenin and Philosophy and Other Essays*, trans. Ben Brewster (New York: Monthly Review, 1971).

[18] See, for example, Walter Benjamin, *Illuminations*, ed. Hannah Arendt, trans. Harry Zohn (New York: Schocken, 1968); and Walter Benjamin, *Understanding Brecht*, trans. Anna Bostock (London: NLB, 1977).

[19] See, for example, Bertolt Brecht, *Brecht on Theatre*, ed. and trans. John Willett (New York: Hill and Wang, 1964).

[20] See, for example, Terry Eagleton, *Marxism and Literary Criticism* (Berkeley: University of California Press, 1976); and Terry Eagleton, *The Function of Criticism: From the Spectator to Post-Structuralism* (London: Verso, 1984).

21 See, for example, Jürgen Habermas, *Communication and the Evolution of Society*, trans. Thomas McCarthy (Boston: Beacon, 1979); Jürgen Habermas, *The Theory of Communicative Action, Volume I: Reason and the Rationalization of Society*, trans. Thomas McCarthy (Boston: Beacon, 1984); and Jürgen Habermas, *The Theory of Communicative Action, Volume II: Lifeworld and System: A Critique of Functionalist Reason*, trans. Thomas McCarthy (Boston: Beacon, 1987).

22 See, for example, Georg Lukács, *History and Class Consciousness*, trans. Rodney Livingston (London: Merlin, 1971); and Georg Lukács, *The Historical Novel*, trans. Hannah Mitchell and Stanley Mitchell (London: Merlin, 1962).

23 See, for example, Herbert Marcuse, *An Essay on Liberation* (Boston: Beacon, 1969); and Herbert Marcuse, *Counterrevolution and Revolt* (Boston: Beacon, 1972).

24 See, for example, Jacques Derrida, *Writing and Difference*, trans. Alan Bass (Chicago: University of Chicago Press, 1978); Jacques Derrida, *Margins of Philosophy*, trans. Alan Bass (Chicago: University of Chicago Press, 1982); and Jacques Derrida, "Structure, Sign, and Play," in *The Structuralist Controversy*, ed. Richard Macksey and Eugenio Donato (Baltimore: John Hopkins Press, 1972), pp. 247–72.

25 See, for example, Paul de Man, *Blindness and Insight: Essays in the Rhetoric of Contemporary Criticism* (New York: Oxford University Press, 1971); and Paul de Man, *Allegories of Reading: Figural Language in Rousseau, Nietzsche, Rilke, and Proust* (New Haven: Yale University Press, 1979).

26 See, for example, Jean-François Lyotard, *The Postmodern Condition: A Report on Knowledge*, trans. Geoff Bennington and Brian Massumi (1979; Minneapolis: University of Minnesota Press, 1984).

27 See, for example, Jean Baudrillard, *Simulations* (1981; rpt. New York: Semiotext(e), 1983); and Jean Baudrillard, *The Mirror of Production*, trans. Mark Poster (St. Louis, MO: Telos, 1975).

28 See, for example, Fredric Jameson, *Postmodernism, or the Cultural Logic of Late Capitalism* (Durham, North Carolina: Duke University Press, 1991); and Fredric Jameson, *The Geopolitical Aesthetic: Cinema and Space in the World System* (Bloomington: Indiana University Press, 1992).

29 See, for example, Richard Hoggart, *The Uses of Literacy: Aspects of Working-Class Life, with Special Reference to Publications and Entertainments* (New York: Oxford University Press, 1970); and Richard Hoggart, *On Culture and Communication* (1971; rpt. New York: Oxford University Press, 1972).

30 See, for example, Stuart Hall, "The Rediscovery of 'Ideology': Return of the Repressed in Media Studies," in *Culture, Society and the Media*, ed. Michael Gurevitch, Tony Bennett, James Curran, and Janet Woolacott (London: Methuen, 1982), pp. 56–90; Stuart Hall, "Encoding/Decoding," in *Culture, Media, Language*, ed. Stuart Hall, Dorothy Hobson, Andrew Lowe, and Paul Willis (London: Hutchinson, 1980), pp. 128–38; and Stuart Hall and Tony Jefferson, eds., *Resistance Through Rituals: Youth Subcultures in Post-War Britain* (London: Hutchinson, 1976).

31 Antonio Gramsci is credited with the initial conceptualization of this notion of hegemony. See Gramsci.

32 Condit, "Hegemony in a Mass-Mediated Society."

33 For a full description and illustration of this process, see Condit, "Hegemony in a Mass-Mediated Society."

34 Stuart Hall, "The Toad in the Garden: Thatcherism Among the Theorists," in *Marxism and the Interpretation of Culture*, ed. Cary Nelson and Lawrence Grossberg (Urbana: University of Illinois Press, 1988), p. 44.

35 Alan O'Connor, "Culture and Communication," in *Questioning the Media: A Critical Introduction*, ed. John Downing, Ali Mohammadi, and Annabelle Sreberny-Mohammadi (Newbury Park, CA: Sage, 1990), p. 36.

[36] These questions were suggested by: A. Susan Owen, syllabi and assignments, University of Puget Sound; Condit, "Hegemony in a Mass-Mediated Society"; Wander, "The Third Persona"; Wander, "Cultural Criticism"; McKerrow, "Critical Rhetoric: Theory and Practice"; David J. Sholle, "Critical Studies: From the Theory of Ideology to Power/Knowledge," *Critical Studies in Mass Communication*, 5 (March 1988), 16–41; and Hall, "Ideology."

Operation Desert Comfort

Dana L. Cloud

During the Persian Gulf War, U.S. television news played a key role in domesticating dissent by rearticulating political outrage as personal anxiety and reconfiguring the will to resist as the need to support our troops. The mobilization of the themes and language of psychological crisis and emotional support domesticated the homefront, as images of military families quietly coping with the threat of war served as the key icon for the manufacturers of appropriate public response.

News stories from national magazines to CNN defined questioning and/or protest of the war as harmful to the U.S. social body. Protest was labeled a social disease, a resurgent epidemic of the "Vietnam syndrome." Over and over again, news stories in print and on television suggested the mystical argument that troops were killed in the Vietnam War because of a lack of unified support on the homefront. Any voice of protest—and any news story covering that protest—was accused of being somehow complicit in the possible death of the troops in Desert Storm. The rhetorical cure these texts offered for the Vietnam Syndrome was silent coping and emotional unity along with support not only for the troops but for the war effort itself. The framing of responses to the war in terms of emotional support represented a therapeutic displacement of political energy, effectively cordoning off and muting the voices of opposition to the war, thereby protecting the fragile social space from the anger of protesters.

This strategy depended on a particularly gendered mapping of the homefront. During this and other U.S. wars, the discourse of family support for the troops feminizes and personalizes the "home" front. Gender divisions in society and their reinforcements in ideological texts are deployed during wartime to mobilize uncritical support for the war effort. The maintenance of pro-war interests thus depends on a particular definition of feminine support and domestic space. As women and families are constructed within support roles, a potentially divided and conflicted country is also "domesticated."

This essay shows how a pattern of initial anxiety and critique of the Persian Gulf War in news texts was answered by themes of comfort and consolation. Most widely watched news texts moved from reporting

An earlier version of this essay was published in Lauren Rabinovitz and Susan Jeffords, eds., *Seeing Through the Media: The Persian Gulf War* (New Brunswick, New Jersey: Rutgers University Press, 1994), pp. 155–70. Used by permission of Rutgers University Press and the author.

moments of incipient political critique to encouraging personal, emotional avenues for the expression of anxiety. This rhetorical move constituted the nation as a unified family supportive of the war. During the war, "coping," "waiting," and "healing" were the watchwords of families with members stationed in the Persian Gulf. Stories depicting families—especially military wives and children—were ubiquitous before and during the war, occurring for the most part at the end of television news broadcasts, seemingly in direct answer to anxiety-producing coverage of war technologies, tactics, casualties, and protests. Almost without exception, coverage of troops' families began with statements of ambivalence, anger, and opposition to the war on the part of the interviewed family members. By the end of each segment, however, the interviewees had resigned themselves to coping with their fears and helping others to do the same.

More than consoling the interviewees, support-group news during the Persian Gulf War consoled the nation as a whole. These stories, I will argue, effectively personalized the political in a therapeutic discourse that contained widespread unrest and resentment toward the deployment of U.S. troops. The themes of therapy—consolation, coping, support and adaptation—generally translate political problems into personal and emotional terms. During the war, this discourse worked to moderate the anti-war edge of "harder" coverage (of danger, prisoners, protests and the like). "Support-group" stories controlled news about anti-war protest through their placement in the broadcasts and their invocation and reinflection of the history of the U.S. "defeat" in the Vietnam War. Because therapeutic themes and motifs acknowledge unhappiness and anger while encouraging personal solutions to problems, they are ideal for the expression and containment of dis-ease in popular culture.[1]

Hegemony Theory: Domesticating Dissent

Hegemony theory enables critics to explain how popular and political texts can give voice to opposition and simultaneously mute critical voices.[2] In elaborating a theory of how culture, broadly conceived, works to ensure economic domination, Antonio Gramsci argued that culture plays an integral role in maintaining order and defusing resistance to the established social system by manufacturing the consent of its subjects through persuasion rather than coercion.

The process of hegemony acknowledges discontent but makes it difficult to translate oppositional outlooks into active or collective resistance. Hegemony is flexible, allowing the articulation of opposition interests—but it also defines the limits within which those articulations must be framed. The dominant culture provides a finite set of acceptable, legitimate rhetorical tools that can be appropriated in antagonistic ways. These tools simultaneously enable the expression of antagonism and limit the extent to which such movements can actually challenge political, economic, and social arrangements.

During the Persian Gulf War, the therapeutic discourse of coping, unity, and healing took what might have been resistance to the familial (and broader social) disintegration caused by the war and reinflected it as unconditional support for the war. In this way therapeutic discourse channeled collective anger and action into personalized, individualistic strategies of coping with the *status quo*.

Hegemony and the News

The news participates in maintaining the hegemony of established economic and political interests. Herbert Gans' landmark study of newsmaking routines and texts argues that journalistic habits and the ideological commitment to liberalism have made television news a short-sighted undemocratic enterprise that depoliticizes the public realm.[3] By *liberalism*, I mean not the commonsense "opposite of conservatism" but rather the political philosophy and set of core ideological assumptions of Western, capitalist nations. Liberalism's core values include individual autonomy and responsibility over and above collective identification and action.[4] Thus, liberal discourses typically frame social movements and other forms of collective protest as aberrations from an individualist norm.

Gans notes that newsmakers working within the assumptions of liberalism thereby promote an ideology, although that reality is obscured by journalistic constructs of "objectivity" and the liberal assumption that liberalism itself is not an ideology, whereas anyone with a distinct ideological position is a special interest with an axe to grind.[5] Furthermore, the structuring of news stories (especially on commercial television) follows a narrative format of introduction, rising action, crisis, falling action, and conclusion.[6] This structure, like narratives in general, poses news events in terms of authority, social cohesion, and order; disruptive challenges to that order; and the restoration of order and unity.

Most studies of news content and form suggest that mainstream news is conservative of the social order, reinforcing the everyday liberal common sense of its viewers and defining any event or statement that challenges that common sense as a disruptive force.[7] Especially during a social crisis (such as a war), news reinforces the values of national unity, individualist solutions to problems, consumerism, and a sense of self that is fundamentally isolated and passive. Because journalists operate within the "routine structures of everyday thought"[8] and perceive perspectives outside of those structures as belonging to "biased" "special interests," news narratives tend to frame social conflict in terms of the dominant value system. Gans writes, "To the extent that journalists help maintain order, warn against disorder, and act as moral guardians, they function as agents of social control."[9] From this perspective, the most important question is how news deals with political opposition to established ideological common sense during times of political crisis, such as the Persian Gulf War.[10]

The news works rhetorically to neutralize events categorized as social disorder news, and so each broadcast, or even segment, ends with the restoration of order. During the Vietnam War (and the ongoing civil rights struggle), marches, protests, sit-ins, and other political challenges were covered as "social disorder news." Gitlin's study of media coverage of the New Left during the Vietnam conflict provides additional evidence for the claim that media frames[11] incorporated New Left events and claims but undercut them with implicit assumptions reinforcing the liberal ideology. The result for the New Left was marginalization, distortion of central contentions, and most importantly, the false opposition between activism on the one hand and rational, moderate debate on the other (as if activists never made rational sense). The result of this process of marginalization is that "discrepant statements of reality are acknowledged—but muffled, softened, blurred, fragmented, domesticated at the same time."[12]

Thus, the news frames demonstrations and conflict not as legitimate alternative suggestions but rather as disruptions of an order presumed to be the only legitimate option. Reporters attend to radical activists not to give their views supportive airplay, but to call attention to the threat activists pose to the security of the social system. One key way in which the news attempts to undermine the persuasiveness of activists is through personalized news that reduces viewers' involvement in the world to the affairs of their personal lives.

Personalized news refers to the attempts of news producers and writers to link national and international events to the "real" lives of individuals in their home towns. Normally this kind of news serves to "wrap up" the day's events in cheerful stories at the end of the broadcast, to leave the listener or viewer with a pleasant sense of security.[13] Personalized news is one way in which news producers structure information about opposing interests and events into narrative forms that make illegitimate any opposition to the basic assumptions of liberal capitalism.

Since its emergence in the middle of the 19th century, this form of news has been symbolic rather than informative, designed to achieve audience identification with certain national values in dramatic form.[14] The human interest story is a key component of "wrapping up" a news segment or broadcast featuring social discord. It can serve to restore a sense of unity and coherence, providing a "solution" to the problems posed in the text's earlier moments. The problem with this kind of news is that it suggests that the resolution of social problems lies in individuals rather than in the structural or political causes of problems. This individualistic and personal focus can work to persuade people that they do not need to work politically for social change as the solution to social problems.[15]

Personalized news was a pervasive component of Persian Gulf War coverage, portraying ordinary families coping with the stress of war and taking personal responsibility for getting through the crisis. Family support stories at the end of national news broadcasts served to "wrap up" earlier news about the war (and opposition to it) in a neat, clean package with a yellow ribbon, putting a tidy end to dissent and disunity.

Yellow (Ribbon) Journalism

Reassuring family support stories seemed like a direct response to war-induced anxiety. One headline proclaimed, "24-hour war coverage makes viewers anxious."[16] The news described how military families sometimes avoided footage of combat and favored the suggestion that the news be totally blacked out due to fear of trauma.[17] The day after the war began, the *New York Times* interviewed wives of Marines stationed in the Gulf. One said, "I try not to watch the news. It disturbs me too much." Another agreed: "I don't watch the news . . . I do not pretend to understand what makes the world tick. I know only how it affects me."[18]

Around the country, support groups (numbering in the dozens in each major metropolitan or military community) sprang up to help people deal with the emotional stresses of war. While the groups themselves consoled the individuals and the families wracked with worry, news coverage of support groups and family crisis—or yellow ribbon journalism—served to console the nation as a whole. Two important patterns emerged in this coverage. First, although some men were left at home to care for children and wait for the return of the troops, the stories (except a few investigating single fatherhood as an anomaly) focused on anxious women (military wives) and children. Second, in the accounts of these families, a dialectic of anxiety about the war and therapeutic solutions to that anxiety was played out. Operation Desert Storm was answered on the homefront by "Operation Desert Comfort."[19]

Many military families were critical of the war.[20] A national organization called the Military Family Support Network (MFSN), an anti-war group of military families, had 136 chapters and 6500 supporters at the height of the war.[21] While many military support networks refused disturbing political debate in favor of comfort strategies, the MFSN located blame for stress with public, political factors rather than interpersonal ones.

But the MFSN and the coverage of its particular version of "support the troops" (by bringing them home) rhetoric were not featured in the popular media. Most stories were structured around the principle of ameliorating anxiety and finding ways to cope. Personal conflict over the war was the dramatic crux of military family news coverage; personal solutions made for a comforting (and rhetorically effective) denouement to the drama. For example, an account in the *Baltimore Sun* of a military support group reported initial anger toward the war but went on to say that the group was comprised of both war supporters and war opponents.[22] "But whatever their differences," the article continued, "these groups share a common goal: helping people cope with the loneliness, fear, and frustration that comes from separation from loved ones."[23] This passage marked the transition to suggested strategies for coping with the stress of war: swapping information, "getting things done for others," avoiding television, and talking about their fears. The article concluded with a list of support groups in the Baltimore area. A list of political anti-war organizations was, predictably, absent.

This article was typical of most coverage of support groups in its movement from anger to coping, its emphasis on women, its plea for therapeutic unity between anti- and pro-war citizens, and its assumption that women work through anxiety by helping other people rather than acting on their own behalf. In many of these articles, protesting the war was upheld but trivialized, on the one hand, as just another coping strategy (a way to "pretend" that one had some control over events). On the other hand, protest was articulated within the context of family support news as just another source of stress.

The inclusion of war supporters and protesters under the umbrella of "support" was a common framing device during the war. Support for the troops was an ambiguous construction, often becoming equated with support for the war. The rhetorical upshot of the imperative to community support was that we needed to be so careful of one another's feelings that politics was out of bounds. In other words, when political issues were framed in emotional terms, outright criticism and dissent were excluded in favor of nurturing and protecting others from potential critique. "Support"—translated to mean uncritical acceptance of existing conditions and one's ultimate powerlessness to do anything to change them—was the order of the day. The therapeutic function was to nullify anger and to silence debate in the context of an emotional mutuality that precluded political discussion.

The focus on women and especially children played a large part in this work. Articles on how to talk to children about war and death, respond to their questions, and deal with the absence of one or more parents proliferated in the press. In response to what was called a "national collective anxiety attack,"[24] the press advised adults and children alike to do two things: unite and adapt to the situation. One psychiatrist advocated yellow-ribbon wearing as a signifier of group identity.[25] The psychiatric discourse invoked in the popular news deployed therapeutic motifs of consolation and identification in order to encourage adaptation to the crisis rather than protest against it. In addition, readers were encouraged to find comfort in the private sphere rather than take public action. The obsession with children's needs during the war thus might be regarded as an attempt to render the entire homefront docile and childlike, seeking comfort and refuge from the war. Like the press, television overall took the therapeutic advice of one reporter to "temper reality with reassurance."[26]

Television's Cure for the Vietnam Syndrome

The therapeutic went national as television news and national news magazines picked up and ran with coverage of families coping with war stress. *Newsweek* divided its war news into "Desert Storm" and "The Home Front," the latter devoted to news about protests, media coverage analysis, opinion polls, and—last but not least—coverage of military families coping with the war. *Time* employed a similar format, as in a story about a peace activist who had changed her mind and joined in her community's "support the troops" campaign.[27]

Photographs or televised images of tearful goodbyes and anxious families huddled around the television further personalized the experience of war. Coverage of families supporting the war followed and reframed coverage of protests, emphasizing the need for emotional unity so as to avoid another Vietnam War. As Steven Roberts put it in *U.S. News and World Report*, "Vietnam etched an indelible pattern on our identity, fragmenting our families and poisoning our patriotism."[28] His article featured young pro-war activists who ostensibly had gotten over the cynicism and shame of the Vietnam War era and could rally around the flag in good conscience. National pride and emotional support for the troops functioned in this kind of coverage as therapy against the Vietnam Syndrome.

In February, *Time* covered the construction of an enormous human flag in San Diego, under the headline, "Land That They Love: Patriotism and its symbols dominate the debate over the Gulf war as both sides emphasize concern for the soldiers and for the fate of the nation."[29] The reporter wrote, "There is a measure of atonement in this by a country that treated Vietnam veterans with unjustified contempt."[30] This passage identified what was so compelling about "support the troops" rhetoric: It served the therapeutic function of assuaging national guilt in the wake of the Vietnam War.

Television newscasts were blamed for reinvoking Vietnam War related anxiety. "Just watching the war is stressful," and "War takes toll on TV viewers," rang the headlines.[31] Meanwhile, President George Bush and Vice President Dan Quayle kept insisting that Desert Storm would not become another Vietnam War.[32] Persian Gulf War presidential and news versions of the Vietnam War continually suggested that lack of support was a major cause of the "failure" of the U.S. troops in the Vietnam War. In this revised historical account, the media were partly to blame for bringing vivid scenes of the horror of war before the U.S. public. If reporters of the Persian Gulf War were to escape blame this time around, they needed to "temper reality with reassurance."

During the first week of the war, one *Newsweek* article noted the eruption of a dedicated anti-war groundswell once fighting began.[33] The article went on to say how peaceful and mainstream most anti-war protesters were, labeling the ones who did not approve even of sanctions as "conspicuously more radical."[34] This strategy attempted to define the outer margins of acceptable dissent and, as in other similar stories, warmly accepted anti-war activists who still waved the American flag and paid emotional lip service to the "support the troops" mantra.

The article reported that 57 percent of Americans wished that all protests would stop. To drive that suggestion home, an additional short article ran within a box inside of the protest coverage with the headline, "'One Big Family' in Crystal Springs."[35] Its subject was a city with 160 of its residents stationed in the Persian Gulf. The article emphasized the community's support of the troops, the administration, and the war itself. Despite the anxiety over the possibility of the soldiers' deaths, people in Crystal Springs bonded together for "strength and solace" and "words of consolation."[36] Crystal Springs was a town "poised to pay the price for the war in the Gulf."[37]

The juxtaposition of a unified "family" alongside the condemnation of protesters made an implicit argument. In contrast to the "family" of Crystal Springs, anti-war demonstrators, by implication, lacked "strength and solace." They were constructed as outsiders to the national community enacted in the media and were rhetorically scapegoated for the anxieties and risks attendant to the war. Such stories constituted ritual expulsion of dissent and difference. The war and discussion about its merits were subjects reserved for the domestic space of the community-family, a space in which consolation was more appropriate than dissent as a response to the crisis.

Like newspapers and magazines, television constructed an emotionally harmonious space for supporting the troops. According to a *Tyndall Report* study, the television networks (including CNN) spent more time (measured in minutes) on "yellow ribbon" stories (focusing on domestic support for the troops) than any other war-related news stories in a ratio of almost two to one.[38] The Gannett Foundation explains this imbalance as a consequence of a similar rhetorical ploy in presidential discourse: "The President united the country under the umbrella of support for the troops [in his State of the Union speech] rather than seeking to win over skeptics to his approach."[39] Todd Gitlin and Daniel Hallin have argued that local nightly news emphasized support groups and rallying around the flag in an effort to build community morale and support for the war.[40] Between November 1, 1990 and March 17, 1991, the three primary networks (CBS, ABC, and NBC) ran a total of 115 stories about the families of troops and domestic support for the war during the evening news (ABC, 36; CBS, 34; NBC, 45).[41]

These stories always ran after "harder" news about troop deployments, battle developments, casualties and prisoners, and—most importantly—after news about anti-war demonstrations or criticisms of the war. For example, an NBC reporter interviewed a black soldier eating his Thanksgiving rations. The soldier criticized the racism of the military, noting that the nation's wealthy would not be fighting this war and that military service is often the only option for blacks seeking their way out of impoverished ghettoes. This critical story (occurring 20 minutes into the newscast) was followed immediately by a family support story, in which a (white) military wife expressed her support for her husband via satellite video.[42] Similarly, stories about support groups, goodbye parties, and family reunions also framed stories about medical readiness for war, American hostages—and Vietnam War flashbacks.

Like the other networks, CNN juxtaposed yellow-ribbon therapeutic news with hard news—only it did it around the clock in continuous newscasts that recycled story after story about support for the troops on the homefront.[43] The sheer number of such CNN stories is impossible to know. According to CNN archivist John Robinson, stories with themes of family support groups and the psychological effects of the war were so numerous as to render a thorough database search unwieldy.[44]

In Every Hamlet, It's a War of Emotions

A close examination of two representative CNN clips from January 26 and 28, 1991, reveals that the pattern of critique and consolation occurred within news segments as well as across them. On January 26, 1991, CNN *Headline News* introduced into its rotation a segment about a black family in Houston with 30 of its members stationed in the Persian Gulf. Pearlie Cooper, the mother of several of these soldiers, first was shown in a close-up, saying, "I really feel sad. It's just too high a price to pay." Throughout the story, family members expressed critical attitudes toward the war. Bettie Cooper, a young woman (presumably a sister or cousin) made a case against the war from an anti-racist perspective:

> *Bettie:* Now they're over there in a bad fix. They're scared, wondering whether or not they might not be coming back home.
>
> *Andrea* (brief close-up): I wish they hadn't joined the army.
>
> *Bettie:* And they say they don't want to go over there and die over nothing they don't have anything to do with or know anything about. . . . We're over there fighting a war and when we come back here we're fighting civil rights! It's like we're on the front lines out there, and that's not fair.

Bettie's opposition was reinforced by the CNN correspondent who provided background in a voice-over, "Like the rest of his enlisted relatives, Ronnie Johnson and his brother Russell joined the army. They wanted a job, the money, and a free education. Their sisters . . . now regret it." During this summary, the camera panned a photograph of all the members of the Johnson clan currently serving Uncle Sam. The image of rows and rows of solemn black faces strengthened the emerging critique. (At least one woman was visible; none of the men or women were decorated as officers.)

However, three elements of the text resisted its critical edge. First, there was a reference to the Vietnam War, which occurred right after Bettie's statement. Pearlie said, "I had several family members in the Vietnam War, and when they came back they got no recognition whatsoever." The correspondent said, "This war could wipe out an entire generation of men in this family. [She ignored the women in the photograph; the presumption was that troops are male, supporters are female.] It's one more reason the Johnsons are ready for the fighting to end." Next, the text appealed to unity and religion. Sherry Hawkins (another relative) stated, "We're such a close-knit, tight family. All we can do now is pray and put it in God's hands, 'cause he can take care of, he will take care of us." This verbal expression of the theme of family unity was echoed in the visuals of the segment. There were four long shots of the entire family clustered unnaturally close together, watching CNN on television. As Sherry concluded her remarks, the camera pulled out into an extreme long shot, foregrounding a dome clock, possibly to symbolize the need to wait patiently—or to suggest that for the Johnsons, time was running out.

The brief attempts at the end of the story to contain Bettie's clearly stated critique seemed desperate. The black, working-class women refused, for the most part, to take up the faithful supportive roles required of white, middle-class women during the war. The critique of racism offered by Bettie politicized the personal in this story in a way that significantly injured the fragile rhetoric of support for the troops. In this way, the segment offered viewers a critical stance toward the war.

"Doing Something for the Emotional End of It"

More often than not, however, family support news on television resembled not the Johnson story but a segment aired by CNN on January 28, 1990. Anchor Lynn Russell introduced a story about a support group in Concord, New Hampshire. Over her left shoulder (our right), a map of New Hampshire was framed in a box. Below it, in blocked capitals, appeared the word "SUPPORT," itself both a label and an implicit command. The segment cut to a scene of the town, where, as Russell said, people were "coping with the war." The story moved from street scenes to interviews with women in a mall, back to houses bedecked with yellow ribbons and American flags against a background of sparkling snow and crystal-blue sky, back to more interviews at the mall followed by a cutaway to a rural woman alone at home and then with a group of supporters, then finally to Norma Quarrels, the correspondent, who wrapped the whole thing up: "On the homefront, the Persian Gulf conflict is a war of emotions—as evidenced in small towns like Concord, New Hampshire."

Unlike the January 26 segment, however, this war of emotions was one-sided. Concord, as the town's name suggests, was a place of unity and mutual support, not division, critique, or conflict. All of the people in the story were white and clearly middle or upper class, dressed in furs or fashionable sweaters, their hair carefully coiffed. They inhabited malls and shining white suburban homes. Dissent spoke here in a lonely voice. Coral Nieder, a rural woman with two sons in the Persian Gulf, described her initial reaction to news of their deployment: "Oh God, I wish we weren't there. I wish my sons weren't there." Earlier in the story, a token protester (a well-dressed, young white woman), walking alone in a shopping mall, provided the illusion of journalistic balance: "I think we should get the hell out of there." But these statements were subject to several strategies of recuperation. Foremost among these was the appeal in both language and imagery to rural, traditional family and community values.

Introducing the story, correspondent Norma Quarrels stated, "The war in the Persian Gulf is reaching into towns, villages, and hamlets across the United States, touching many lives." The choice of nouns, "towns, villages, and hamlets," evoked a rural, small-town age of people who pull together for the common good and whose sense of community has not become a casualty of modern urban life. The text constructed such a space in its choices of images of Concord and Bow, both towns in New Hampshire. Nostalgia for community saturated the text, rhetorically exhorting viewers to emulate the supportive solidarity exemplified by these small-town residents.

In one passage, the reporter made the following statement in voice-over:

> People in Concord, New Hampshire, are doing whatever they can to show their support for the troops serving in the Gulf. In addition to the flags and the yellow ribbons, there are letter-writing campaigns, and this month, pictures are being taken and sent to the Gulf in time for Valentine's Day.

The visuals accompanying these words were a white, spacious, two-story house, crusty with glistening snow. A man shoveled the sidewalk, but the camera focused on the yellow ribbons adorning the house and on the flag waving in the breeze. The segment cuts to a closer view of the ribbons, yellow on white, then to a bumper sticker on a pickup truck: "I SUPPORT OUR TROOPS IN OPERATION DESERT SHIELD." The segment concluded with an aestheticized low-angle shot of the flag with yellow ribbons in foreground. The camera, using a starburst filter, zoomed in on the flag and captured the sun glistening on the waving fabric. Later in the story, similar shots constructed a pastoral, patriotic vision of the rural community of Bow, New Hampshire.

When the segment moved from the quiet outdoor scene to the bustling shopping mall, where families gathered for a photo session and letter-writing stint, we were asked to connect the positive images of patriotic domesticity with the support-group effort. The woman who spoke out against the war was shown alone, in contrast to framing scenes that showed large numbers of community members engaged in a letter-writing campaign to the troops for Valentine's Day. The lone woman was young and angry, whereas the support-group members were more mature, community identified, family oriented, and respectful. The report did not tell us her name or provide any information about her identity in or attachments to this community. In this mythic opposition of characters, protest was defined as the willful abnegation of community spirit and belonging.

The iconography of the photograph contributed to this process. A common emotional ploy of support-group segments was to zoom in on or to pan across photographs (usually adorned with yellow ribbons) of relatives stationed in the Persian Gulf, evoking a kind of emotional connection with the soldiers and an anxiety over their absence made present by the photos. In this story, one woman at the mall wore a photograph of her son pinned to her chest; later in the segment, the camera panned across the images of Coral Nieder's four sons on a wall. Images of those whose lives were at stake could be read oppositionally (as I think the Johnson photograph discussed above encouraged us to do). The fetishization of the absent soldier indicated a measure of anxiety over the lives of the troops and a desperate desire to have some control over the fate of those lives. In this way, photography and death were bound up with one another.

One way in which the anxiety evoked by the photographs was channelled into support for the war was through Vietnam War references. The woman who wore the lapel photo in this segment said, "They really do need our support. I don't want them to be unsupported like the men in Vietnam felt that they were unsupported." This statement preceded the brief cutaway to the unidentified woman who spoke out against the war, as if to chastise her for potentially creating another Vietnam War with her words.

Despite her initial anger at her sons' fate, Coral Nieder was lauded for channelling her energy into community-support work, collecting more than 400 names of New Hampshire families with members in the Persian Gulf and organizing letter-writing campaigns. She recalled her initial reactions: "It hit me . . . during the church service that they could die. My sons could die over there. But they chose to be there and I'll back them one hundred percent." The reference to the church service reinforced the theme of small-town values. The emphasis on the voluntary nature of military service can be read as an implicit response to the critique illustrated by Bettie Johnson, that African Americans joined the army out of economic necessity, not out of choice. But like the Johnsons, Coral Nieder resolved simply "to do something for the emotional end of it," as she stated toward the segment's end.

The Support-Group Nation

Support-group news during the Persian Gulf War constituted a hegemonic dislocation of social anger and discontent. The "Operation Desert Comfort" theme reinforced traditional and oppressive constructions of womanhood and family to enforce a sense of national *emotional* unity as a diversion from political fragmentation, conflict, and criticism of a brutal war that decimated a country and slaughtered 20,000 people, all essentially over the control of oil.[45] But emotional unity, created in the language of therapy, precluded the possibility of political awareness and action.

This study of therapeutic discourse during the Persian Gulf conflict reveals that the popular news media actively constructed a dysfunctional democracy based on the metaphor of family support. They persuaded us to find comfort in the flight from "independent thought and action." They told us it was all right to be clients instead of citizens. "We're a support-group nation," said University of Iowa professor Kathleen Farrell. "We don't talk about whether something is right or wrong, we just talk about making it through it."[46]

The imagined interpersonal harmony and emotional unity of the family are a metaphor for an ideal national consensus. But when private-sphere virtues and spaces are constructed as models for public discussion, therapy also works to close down on the perceived desirability of public debate, conflict, and change. In a privatized sphere of response to politics and war, the scope of one's power as a social agent is limited to interpersonal negotiation and, ultimately, passivity in the face of structured events in the public sphere that affect our lives.

Notes

[1] In this essay, I develop a broad critical sketch of the family-support coverage in network news, the popular press, and CNN Persian Gulf War coverage. My method is based on wide critical reading of primary news sources (including the New York Times, the Los Angeles Times, various other city daily newspapers, popular national news magazines, and alternative news periodicals such as The Nation), in addition to nearly constant viewing of mainstream news coverage (particularly CNN's Headline News) of the war. I also consulted with CNN archivists and scanned the Vanderbilt Archives television index and abstracts to the network nightly news over the course of the war, counting the numbers of stories related to family-support groups.

[2] Excellent syntheses, explanations, applications, and critiques of Gramsci's theory of hegemony abound. See Antonio Gramsci (ed., and trans. Quentin Hoare and Geoffrey Nowell Smith), Selections from the Prison Notebooks (New York: International, 1971); also Perry Anderson, "The Antimonies of Antonio Gramsci," New Left Review 100 (1976–77): 5–75; Stuart Hall, "Gramsci's Relevance for the Study of Race and Ethnicity," Journal of Communication Inquiry 10, no. 2 (1986): 5–27; T. J. Jackson Lears, "The Concept of Cultural Hegemony: Problems and Possibilities," American Historical Review 90, no. 3 (1985): 567–593; John Murphy, "Domesticating Dissent: The Kennedys and the Freedom Rides," Communication Monographs 59 (1992): 61–78; and Raymond Williams, "Base and Superstructure in Marxist Cultural Theory," New Left Review 82 (1973): 3–16.

[3] Herbert Gans, Deciding What's News (New York: Pantheon, 1979).

[4] See Stuart Hall, "Variants of Liberalism," in J. Donald and Stuart Hall, eds., Politics and Ideology (Philadelphia: Open University, 1986), pp. 34–69; also Louis Hartz, The Liberal Tradition in America (New York: Harcourt Brace Jovanovich, 1955).

[5] Gans, Deciding What's News, 190–191.

6 See Catherine A. Collins and Jeanne E. Clark, "A Structural Narrative Analysis of *Nightline*'s 'This Week in Holy Land,'" *Critical Studies in Mass Communication* 9 (1992): 25–43; and Todd Gitlin, "News as Ideology and Contested Arena: Toward a Theory of Hegemony, Crisis, and Opposition," *Socialist Review* 9, no. 6 (1979): 11–54; Todd Gitlin, "Prime-Time Ideology: The Hegemonic Process in Television Entertainment," *Social Problems* 26, no. 3 (1979): 251–266.

7 There is some debate over whether journalism routines (N. Eliasoph, "Routines and the Making of Oppositional News," *Critical Studies in Mass Communication* 5 [1988]: 313–334; E. Herman and Noam Chomsky, *Manufacturing Consent* [New York: Pantheon, 1988]; Gaye Tuchman, *Making News* [New York: Free Press, 1978]); structures of ownership (Douglas Kellner, *Television and the Crisis of Democracy* [Boulder, CO: Westview, 1990]); advertising and control (Ben Bagdikian, *The Media Monopoly* [Boston: Beacon, 1990]); narrative generic constraints (E. J. Epstein, *News From Nowhere* [New York: Random House, 1973]; pp. 164–65 describes the limited repertoire of news "plots"); conscious "bias"; internalized liberal and anticommunist ideologies (Herman and Chomsky, *Manufacturing Consent*); or some combination of these elements produces the uniformity that characterizes commercial broadcast news in the United States.

8 Gitlin, "Prime-Time," 251.

9 Gans, *Deciding What's News*, 295.

10 See Gitlin, "News and Ideology"; Gitlin, *Whole World*; Daniel Hallin, *The Uncensored War: The Media and Vietnam* (New York and Oxford: Oxford University Press, 1986); Daniel Hallin, "TV's Clean Little War," *Bulletin of Atomic Scientists* 47 (1991): 17–24; Douglas Kellner, *The Persian Gulf TV War* (Boulder: Westview, 1992). I am particularly indebted to Kellner's comprehensive analysis.

11 "Frames are principles of selection, emphasis, and presentation composed of little tacit theories about what exists, what happens, and what matters. . . . We frame reality in order to negotiate it, manage it, comprehend it, and choose appropriate repertoires of cognition and action. Media frames, largely unspoken and unacknowledged, organize the world both for journalists who report it and . . . for us who rely on their reports. *Media frames are persistent patterns of cognition, interpretation, and presentation, of selection, emphasis, and exclusion, by which symbol-handlers routinely organize discourse*" (Gitlin, *Whole World*, 6–7, emphasis in original).

12 Gitlin, *Whole World*, p. 271, italics in original.

13 For a review of this issue and bibliography, see Dianne Rucinski, "Personalized Bias in the News: The Potency of the Particular?" *Communication Research* 19, no. 1 (1992), 91–108.

14 Harriet M. Hughes, *News and the Human Interest Story* (New York: Greenwood, 1940).

15 Rucinski, "Personalized Bias," 92.

16 Holly Selby, "24-Hour War Coverage Makes Viewers Anxious," *Baltimore Sun*, 23 January 1991.

17 Steve Scott, "Families Favor Blackout," *Dallas Morning-News*, 25 February 1991.

18 Robert Reinhold, "Tensions Crackle as Reality Invades," *New York Times*, 17 January 1991, section A.

19 A phrase coined by Noam Neusner, "Operation Desert Comfort," *Baltimore Sun*, 6 Feb. 1991.

20 For example, see Alex Molnar, "If My Marine Son Is Killed," in Micha Sifry and Christopher Cerf, eds., *The Gulf War Reader* (New York: Times Books/Random House, 1991). Molnar first published this piece critical of the war in newspapers across the country.

21 Jane Creighton, "War at Home," *Mother Jones*, May/June 1991, 22–23.

[22] Neusner, "Desert Comfort."

[23] Neusner, "Desert Comfort."

[24] Gerri Kobren, "War on our Peace of Mind," *Baltimore Sun*, 5 Feb. 1991.

[25] Quoted in Steve Moore, "Psychologist Offers Advice on War Stress," Pitsfield (Mass.) *Berkshire Eagle*, 3 Feb. 1991. In the *New York Times*, Russell Banks ("Red, White, Blue, Yellow," 26 February 1991) reads the yellow ribbon phenomenon differently. He suggests that the ribbons signify "our desire to bring home Americans who were being held against their wills in foreign lands (which, since Vietnam, is how I have regarded enlisted men and women anyhow)." Banks argues that it is only when the yellow ribbon gets inextricably linked to the American flag and patriotism (which he argues contradicts the motive of getting the troops home) that it becomes an unequivocal nationalist symbol.

[26] Suzanne Sataline, "Kids and War: Tempering Reality with Reassurance," Hartford (Conn.) *Courant*, 3 Feb. 1991.

[27] Nancy Gibbs, "The Homefront: A First Thick Shock of War," *Time*, 28 January 1991, 34.

[28] Steven Roberts, "New Generation, Old Lessons," *U.S. News and World Report*, 4 March 1991, 11.

[29] Nancy Gibbs, "The Home Front: Land That They Love," *Time*, 4 Feb. 1991, 52.

[30] Gibbs, "Home Front," my emphasis.

[31] Jim Calhoun and Kevin O'Hanlon, "Just Watching War Is Stressful," Cincinnati *Enquirer*, 20 Jan. 1991; John O'Connor, "War Takes Toll on TV Viewers," San Francisco *Examiner*, 25 Jan. 1991.

[32] "Transcript of the Comments by Bush on the Air Strikes Against the Iraqis," *New York Times*, 17 Jan. 1991, section A; Dan Quayle, "American Support for Desert Shield: Address Before the U.S. Gulf Forces, Saudi Arabia, 1 Jan. 1991," *U.S. Dept. of State Dispatch*, 7 Jan. 1991, 4.

[33] Jerry Adler, "Prayers and Protest," *Newsweek*, 28 Jan. 1991, 36–39.

[34] Adler, "Prayers and Protest," 37.

[35] Vern Smith and Annetta Miller, "'One Big Family' in Crystal Springs," *Newsweek*, 28 Jan. 1991, 39–40.

[36] Smith and Miller, "One Big Family," 38.

[37] Smith and Miller, "One Big Family," 38.

[38] This research was cited in Gannett Foundation, *The Media at War* (New York: Gannett Foundation Media Center, 1991), 48–49.

[39] Gannett, *Media at War*, 48.

[40] Todd Gitlin and Daniel Hallin, "Prowess and Community: The Gulf War as Popular Culture and as Television Drama" (Paper delivered at the 42nd Annual Conference of the International Communication Association, Miami, FL, 1992), 15–21.

[41] *Vanderbilt Television News Archive Index and Abstracts*, Nov. 1990—March 1991. The ratio is about five stories every six days for all networks in 137 days of coverage. This count includes only those stories containing the words "family" and "support" in the same context. The occurrence of support-group stories peaked at times of crisis and stress: Thanksgiving and Christmas, 1990, as the troops celebrated holidays away from home; around news of American hostages in Iraq; around news about the failure of diplomacy; the beginning of the air war; the beginning of the ground war; and, most notably, immediately framing news about anti-war demonstrations.

[42] *Vanderbilt Index*, November 1991, pp. 1976–77.

[43] At the war's beginning, a record 10.7 million people tuned in to CNN while other stations tallied losses. Nielsen ratings showed CNN with a 19.1, ABC 14.4, NBC 13.8, and CBS 10.9 the day after the war; see *Broadcasting*, January 1991, 23. A Times-Mirror poll late in the war found that 61 percent of those questioned thought CNN had the best war coverage, compared to 12 percent, 7 percent, and 7 percent respectively for ABC, NBC, and CBS (B. Thomas, "The Bad News Bearers at CNN," *Los Angeles Times*, 3 March 1991).

44 Robinson made these remarks during a telephone interview with me on July 21, 1992. Because CNN does not index its programs (and thus information is only available by commissioning a search by the professional archivists there), numerical data on CNN family-support coverage is inaccessible.

45 See Kellner, *Persian Gulf TV War*, for detailed accounts of the economic and political motives for the war.

46 Quoted in Les May, "UI Professor Claims TV Dictates Opinions," *The Daily Iowan* (Iowa City), 7 Feb. 1991, 1Aff. Farrell's comment inspired this essay.

Consuming Ideology
The Better Homes in America Campaign

Karen E. Altman

Historical and cultural scholarship characterizes the turn of the twentieth century as that period when consumption of industrially produced commodities became a defining characteristic of the American economy and way of life: that is, when a commercial consumer culture arose.[1] Histories of housework describe the consuming function that women began to perform as part of their home labor and with the proliferation of household technologies; Cowan (1976) calls the period "the industrial revolution in the home."[2] Women's labor changed dramatically as industry took over the productive aspect of the home. Housework became service-oriented rather than productive and included the consumption of those commodities that once had been homemade goods.

By the end of the 1920s, a distinct image of the consumer as a white, middle-class housewife had been constructed in the public imagination. Many public discourses, popular artifacts, and professional publications, especially Christine Frederick's 1929 Selling Mrs. Consumer, suggest that a particular ideology of gender and consumption in the home developed with the expansion of corporate industrial capital. One home reform campaign contributed to the formation of consumer culture and to changed meanings of the American home and housework. That campaign was Better Homes in America.

Better Homes in America (BHA) began in 1921 under the leadership of Marie Meloney, the editor of a then popular women's magazine, The Delineator. Meloney worked with Secretary of Commerce Herbert Hoover, other federal officials, leaders of the General Federation of Women's Clubs, and experts in the new discipline of home economics to orchestrate the building and display of model homes in communities around the country. Although Better Homes activities occurred throughout the year, its major work was a week-long event of exhibitions, displays, and lectures in "demonstration homes." The institutions that coalesced in this campaign—The Delineator magazine, the U.S. Department of Commerce, and the discipline of home economics—all used the Better Homes in America campaign as a "non-commercial, educational" vehicle for home ownership and better quality homes, but

From Critical Studies in Mass Communication 7 (September 1990), 286–307. Used by permission of the Speech Communication Association and the author.

each did so for different purposes. The federal agencies promoted social order and stability through BHA; the publishing company used BHA to sell magazines and to attract advertisers; and the new field of home economics supported BHA to create opportunities for the application of their "expertise." Within two years, the campaign grew so large and unwieldy that its leaders decided to incorporate it as a nonprofit organization attached to the U.S. Department of Commerce, where it operated as a "propaganda apparatus" until 1935. Their demonstration work increased steadily throughout the 1920s, with 502 communities participating in the first annual demonstration week in 1922 and over 7,200 communities participating in 1930.[3]

The significance of the Better Homes in America campaign lies in its claim of "non-commercial, educational" interests in an economy of expanding capital and in a body politic where women were newly enfranchised citizens. Its "non-commercial, educational" discourse constituted a particular ideology of home ownership, housework, and consumption built on specific social differences of gender, class, and race.

This study analyzes the discursive and media practices by which BHA defined the modern home and addressed an American public as consumers. Informed by critical and feminist theories that see even the seemingly most personal and private dimensions of human worlds as constituted in political and ideological relations, the examination of BHA provides empirical, historical evidence that "the most effective ground of ideology is not the domain officially defined as 'politics,' but rather the domain of everyday life—the home, the workplace, the school, the media" (Thompson, 1984, p. 83).

This essay is organized into four sections that correspond to my major claims. I argue that BHA's discursive and media practices (a) reified political, economic, and social realities of the 1920s as natural or universal, (b) linked the values of patriotism and science to define the modern home, its work, and consumption, (c) utilized multiple rhetorical strategies and forms of representation to reproduce its values and ideals, and (d) articulated a modern social order built on gender, class, and racial differences in the home. I then conclude by discussing the mobilization of better homes discourse beyond the BHA campaign and by drawing implications about the discursive constitution of ideology and the social construction of gender.

Reifying Discourse

The discourse of the Better Homes in America campaign reified conditions of the 1920s by naming specific economic necessities, political realities, and cultural values "natural" or "universal." The articulation of culturally and historically specific conditions as natural or universal is the work of ideology (Grossberg, 1986; Hall, 1985; Jessop, 1982, pp. 191–209; Mouffe, 1979).

Naturalization occurs in discourse that claims historical conditions are natural, instinctual, innate, or inborn (Barthes, 1972; Giddens, 1979; Thompson, 1984; Volosinov, 1973; R. Williams, 1977). "There is a primal instinct in us all for home ownership," Secretary of Commerce Hoover wrote in a widely published article, "The Home as an Investment" (1922b), which celebrated the opening of the first BHA demonstration week in 1922.[4] There is a "universal yearning for better homes and the larger security, independence, and freedom that they imply," Hoover continued. Both home ownership and improving home quality were considered natural or universal.

Home instincts, however, were not the same for all American people. There were so-called natural sex differences in who was to own homes and who was to labor in homes for their betterment. Men yearned to own homes and would fight for such ownership. "No man ever worked or fought for a boarding house," Hoover proclaimed (1922b). Women, on the other hand, had the "feminine instinct" or "intuition" of adorning the home (Coolidge, 1922, p. 16; "Original of 'Home,' " 1923). In Meloney's words, "women are born to serve" (1924b). The socially structured character of gender and relations between the sexes disappeared when attributes were said to be inborn.

Ideological processes also work through discourse that claims historical realities are universal, transcendent, or timeless. Claims of a "universal yearning" for home ownership displaced the conditions of corporate, industrial capital in postwar America. The values and practices of individual home ownership, however, made sense within the 1920s configuration of liberalism and industrial capitalism, where the individual was privileged and where ownership was an economic possibility and valued social practice.

In the beginning years, campaign officials declared repeatedly that the country was short a million homes but that housing construction was not their principal effort ("Better Homes in America," 1922). America needed better quality homes, not simply housing, to meet the goals of BHA:

> Better Homes mean better communities—a finer nation.
> Better Homes mean better babies.
> Better Homes mean boys and girls staying at home.
> Better Homes mean healthier families.
> Better Homes mean happier people.
> Better Homes mean better times. (Meloney, 1923b)

Far from BHA's claims of natural instincts or universal desires, campaign discourse presented conditions and relations peculiar to 1920s America.

In the next section an examination of BHA's primary value appeals will provide details on the historical specificity of the modern home order.

Patriotism Meets Science in the Home

BHA's primary appeals drew upon old values of the American republic and combined them with new values to construct a modern American ideology of the home. Old values of patriotism, citizenship, and property were configured in BHA discourse with new values of science, standardization, and expertise.

The theme of patriotism and citizenship pervaded BHA's discourse during 1922, the first full year of campaign organizing. In a time of labor and socialist activism, BHA called for traditional patriotic values in the home. Federal officials were foremost in advocating the relationship between patriotism and the BHA campaign. Vice-president Calvin Coolidge wrote of such values in his endorsement of the first demonstration week activities:

> We believe in American institutions. . . . We believe in the right of self government. We believe in the protection of those personal rights of life and liberty and the enjoyment of the rewards of industry. We believe in the right to acquire, hold, and transmit property. (1922, p. 17)

Theodore Roosevelt, Jr., announced that BHA

> strikes pretty close to . . . the underlying tenets of our American theory of a republic. The best types of citizens are men and women who have homes and children, because they are the ones that have a real interest in the country. . . . They will work or pay the final sacrifice for the good of the nation. (Meloney, 1923a)

And Secretary of Commerce Hoover, confident of the citizenship entailed with ownership, stated, "One can always safely judge the character of a nation by its homes" (1922b).

The "good soldiers" called forth to organize and support the BHA campaign in "the defense of the nation" were American women. To recruit organizers and volunteers, campaign headquarters made a patriotic appeal: "American women are again summoned to the Colors, this time to stop the post-war inroads upon the home life of the American people by getting Good Americans back into good homes" (*Advance General Information*, 1922). Further patriotic appeals were published in different departments of *The Delineator* between 1922 and 1926 (when editor Meloney resigned from the magazine).[5] Regularly featured articles on better homes' architecture often included inspirational illustrations of home life from the past. Occasional or solicited articles from federal officials, such as Coolidge's "Books for Better Homes" (1923), made persuasive arguments for the sense of American spirit cultivated in the home. The homemakers' department discussed housework in terms of American ideals, and Meloney's editorials imparted a patriotic tone whenever possible.

BHA officials built arguments against the seemingly unpatriotic appeals for kitchenless homes and communal domestic services advocated by utopianists, housing experimentalists, and socialist activists of the previous decades (Allen, 1988; Hayden, 1981). Charlotte Perkins Gilman, for instance, had advocated centralized kitchens and commercialized domestic services in her evolutionary vision of social life. Herbert Hoover, in contrast, argued that "with all of our American ingenuity and resourcefulness [in designing plants and factories], we have overlooked·the laundry and the kitchen" (1922b).

Creating better homes also meant standardizing housework through science. The labor involved in turning a house into a home was standardized by "scientific minds" whose "fundamentals of construction, arrangement, and equipment . . . are so simple that we wondered why we had never thought about them before" ("Better Homes in America," 1924). Those responsible for developing scientific, standardized procedures for housework were the new experts in the field of home economics.[6] One prominent home economist, Martha Van Rensselaer, became involved in BHA through her editorial position in the "Homemaker's Department" at *The Delineator*. Because the "house and housekeeping are only half-standardized . . . [and] the machinery of the household is not quite good[,] the individual earner and the state are paying a high price," Van Rensselaer stated (1922). The Better Homes campaign aimed to educate housekeepers in the skills of scientific home management.[7] "A convenient workshop with labor-saving equipment and a floor plan requiring the fewest steps" (Van Rensselaer, 1922) were among the basic aims of standardized homemaking, "but it is just such little things that make all the difference between happy labor in your home and drudgery" (Meloney, 1922a). Home economics principles claimed to turn drudgery into "homemaking."

BHA legitimized consumerism by associating it with both the old American values of property and ownership and with the new, modern values of standardization and expertise. Hoover declared that owning a home was a primal instinct and Coolidge upheld the right to acquire and transmit property, but Meloney's words crystallized the ideology of consumption:

> It is [our] ambition . . . to make every new house built . . . all that a house must be if it is worthy of the name home. It is our ambition,

also, to help America become a nation of home *owners*—not of
renters. . . . Less than fifty percent of the American people own their
homes. Housing experts claim that only about twenty-five percent
of these dwellings come up to recognized standards for a *good* home.
(Meloney, 1922a)

Americans not only needed to own more homes, they also needed to
furnish and equip their houses according to experts' standards. This
meant purchasing newly standardized products—from sinks to vacuum
cleaners to lighting equipment—all for the good of the nation:

To raise the standard of the American home is to raise the standard
of the American people. The home is the foundation of society.
. . . It is the conclusive reply to every threat against the fundamental
principles upon which our government is based. ("Better Homes in
America," 1924)

The "educational propaganda" of BHA, therefore, corresponded with
the economics of expanding corporate capital in the 1920s: Buy more
commodities.

The national organization of the first Better Homes Week established
standards for local communities' use in setting up their demonstration
houses and displays. BHA headquarters at *The Delineator* provided local
leaders with a *Plan Book for Demonstration Week* (1922). All demonstrations were to be conducted "cooperatively" by chambers of
commerce, local retailers, and businesses, school boards, and prominent
citizens. The demonstrations were not "to help special interests,
particular firms, or individuals . . . [but] to benefit every line of business"
in the community (*Plan Book*, 1922, p. 11). BHA was noncommercial,
then, in that it did not sponsor any one business or individual. It avoided
commercialism, but promoted commodification per se and educated "the
people" about commodities and their use in the home (McGee, 1975).
Hoover stated:

I realize that if people are to have better homes and the percentage
of home ownership is to increase, that there must be greater
purchases of articles for the home and of homes themselves. But,
except where unusual precautions are taken, the people frequently
judge such efforts to be purely commercial. (Hoover, 1922a)

The June 1923 demonstration week received much more publicity and
participation at both the local and national levels than the 1922 demonstration week, and it centered on a specific theme—"Home, Sweet
Home." The national demonstration house built in Washington, D.C.,
was modeled after the boyhood home of John Howard Payne, composer
of the song "Home, Sweet Home."[8] News releases, *Delineator* articles
and editorials, and speeches proclaimed the model as the "ideal" for

all homes ("Original of 'Home,'" 1923). A *Delineator* architectural writer
described the seven-room house down to the details of its walnut stair
treads and flat-gloss bathroom enamel (Barber, 1923c). This "first
national better home" was equipped with modern, labor-saving devices
and designed for efficiency in housekeeping. But the theme of "Home,
Sweet Home" articulated larger national purposes during the years of
red scare antiunionism, antisocialism, and antifeminism (Hawley, 1979,
pp. 49–53; Leuchtenburg, 1958, pp. 66–83). As stated in the 1923 *Plan
Book for Demonstration Week*, its aims were "to emphasize the importance of the home in our national and community life, to encourage thrift
for home ownership, to give helpful suggestions regarding the selection
and building of the home, its equipment and management" (p. 8).
Theodore Roosevelt, Jr., supported the 1923 campaign by saying:

> It makes but little difference what we . . . may do in the arrangement
> of governmental machinery or in the adjustment of our relationship
> with other nations if we do not also see that the children are brought
> up to . . . carry on the ideals of our country. (Roosevelt, 1923)

A state rent commissioner was more direct in her endorsement: "without
a real home we will stop rearing children and without them our real
Americans will be gone" ("Original of 'Home,'" 1923).[9] Buying a home,
furnishing it with standardized commodities, and doing its labor by
following expert advice were patriotic acts that supported a historically
formed political, economic, and social order in the postwar expansion
of capital.

Strategies and Forms of Representation

The BHA campaign utilized multiple rhetorical strategies and forms
to promote its ideals for home ownership, housework, and consumption.
Dedication speeches exhorted patriotism, homemaking articles demonstrated scientific principles, fiction narrated the romance, and nonfiction argued for transitional family values—all in the name of better
homes.

Better Homes in America awarded annual prizes to the local communities judged as demonstrating top model homes or exhibits. In
awarding a $500 prize to New Haven for its outstanding demonstration,
Herbert Hoover (who delivered many of the congratulatory statements)
praised the city for acquiring "the cooperation of 26 organizations
representing the patriotic, religious, social, and commercial interests
of New Haven" ("Better Homes in America," 1923, p. 1). Epideictic
oratory and writings celebrated cooperation and patriotism.

As the primary communication medium of the campaign before BHA
became incorporated, *The Delineator* used many of its departments to

present better homes ideals. The homemakers' department, for example, valorized scientific management in the modern home. "Once a woman becomes interested in the fundamental principles of homemaking, to that woman homemaking will always be interesting," editor Martha Van Rensselaer claimed (1923b). It required the application of scientific principles and standard equipment: "one may preach about a good home, but if someone is working . . . with poor equipment," the science and sentiment of homemaking cannot be sustained. Furthermore, child care could be improved by the new science of psychology, which promised to control children in a way that was "safe and sure . . . to bring future happiness to the individual and to cut down on the expense to the State of misdirected human beings" (Van Rensselaer, 1923a).

The importance of child health as a homemaker's responsibility received much attention in another campaign that The Delineator ran simultaneously with BHA: the Save the Race campaign. Beginning in June 1922, The Delineator persuaded "eminent scientists" and medical "specialists" to write on child betterment for the "average mother" (Meloney, 1922c). Mothers had not kept pace with the "progress of science" and needed the advice of experts. For the next sixteen months, articles on the happy child and scientific baby care were featured. Appeals to science and experts in these articles complemented the claims that science and expert applications were fundamentals for making better homes.

A series of practical advice articles for Mr. Home Builder and Mrs. Homemaker focused on better homes' activities and values. Donn Barber, an American Institute architect, published many pieces on BHA plans for the better home (see, e.g., 1923a, 1923b). Other columns such as "Her Electric Home" and "The Well-Equipped Bathroom" introduced new commodities and instructed women in how to use these "electric servants" or other fixtures. Although BHA was not often mentioned in these articles, the values of science, standardization, and expert advice reproduced similar themes.

The Delineator's fiction supported BHA by glorifying homemaking. A series called "Romances of the American Home" began in 1922 and included "Where Poe Once Lived and Loved" (Towne, 1922). Other nonfiction articles, such as "When Marriage Goes on the Rocks" (1922) and "Why Boys Leave Home" (Adams, 1921), strongly argued for the traditional family values in a better home life.

When BHA was incorporated as a nonprofit educational organization and attached to the Department of Commerce, its use of print media expanded beyond The Delineator to circulars, pamphlets, brochures, and guide books. The 32-page booklet titled "How to Own Your Home" (Gries & Taylor, 1925) illustrated the joint ventures of BHA, Inc., and the U.S. Department of Commerce, and BHA activities began to be reported in government publications such as *The Twelfth Annual Report of the Secretary of Commerce* (1925). The University of Chicago Press published the massive *Better Homes Manual* (Halbert, 1931). And without *The Delineator*'s control, BHA, Inc., sought publishing opportunities with such magazines as *McCall's, Woman's Home Companion, Household, Child Welfare,* and *Pictorial Review*.[10]

BHA, Inc., also utilized the new medium of radio to reach wider audiences in both rural and urban areas. Talks by various BHA supporters were broadcast early in radio history, such as the one by Children's Bureau Chief Grace Abbott in May 1924. At least one film project, the fifteen-minute "Own Your Home," was proposed in conjunction with the National Motion Picture Bureau.[11]

Order Built on Difference: Gender, Class, Race

The Better Homes in America campaign built a modern sense of order on gender, class, and racial differences in the home. These differences were explicitly stated, often celebrated, occasionally denied, and typically forged into interlocking relations. Most obviously, the economic difference of home ownership and unpaid housework was linked with the gender difference of man and woman, respectively.

BHA discourse on cooking, cleaning, decorating, child care, and consumption was addressed to women as housewives, homemakers, or mothers. For example, John Gries, Chief of the U.S. Department of Commerce's Division of Building and Housing and advisory member to BHA, wrote that "work has been started on a publication to aid the housewife in the selection and purchase of commodities for the home." The specifications of these commodities had been "prepared by and for the use of 'experts,'" but the goal was that "the housewife can make use of [them] when making her purchases" (1926a, p. 136). Although campaign discourse asserted woman's natural instinct for housework, it simultaneously constructed a specific gendered image: the white woman as housewife, mother, and consumer, guided by science or expert advice.

By contrast, appeals to the value of property constituted the ideology of acquisition and accumulation for the individual man. Such appeals united the practices of individual men with the practices of capital. Men were featured in home planning, building, and ownership publications, and in celebratory speeches about the home's purpose in American life. For instance, Herbert Hoover claimed, "the home is fundamental to our national life. . . . While good housekeeping does not necessarily make a home, it is essential to happy family life. . . . It is indeed a task that few men essay to perform" (1923a). In BHA discourse and images, Mr. Homeowner married Mrs. Consumer (Hayden, 1981, p. 284).

BHA's homemaker ideal featured the feminine, self-sacrificing, married woman and mother. However, by the early 1920s, there were many "new women": feminists, reformers, athletes, scientists, aviators, and businesswomen, especially those in the Federation of Business and Professional Women (Brown, 1987, pp. 29–47). The "new woman" also wanted better homes, Meloney reasoned, because when her day's work was done, she wanted to stay home (1922b). BHA did not exclude the "new woman" from their address, but she did not fit the ideal.

The campaign's conflictual stance toward the career woman became part of a much larger complex of social problems that BHA envisioned. It was widely stated that women who placed more importance on their career than on labor in the home often sacrificed their home and marriage, as the article "Despoiled: The Confession of a Wife Who Failed" warned *The Delineator*'s readers (1923). In 1926, BHA, Inc., argued for extended funding from the Laura Spelman Rockefeller foundation to deal with "a big national problem" in raising the standards of home life in light of women's political and economic changes (Hoover, 1926). Girls and young women "who know nothing of homemaking and have no interest except economic independence and the easy solution of married life without home responsibilities" were said to be turning away from the home. It was "vitally necessary," Hoover argued, to "cure" this "evil" by thoroughly instructing girls and young women in home life, and BHA, Inc., could provide such instruction. BHA, as well as many other conservative organizations during the 1920s, worked against women's political gains and economic advances. The powerful American Medical Association, for example, defeated the national Sheppard-Towner plan, a piece of maternity and infant protection legislation that had been mobilized largely by women (Lemons, 1973, pp. 153–180).

The conflation of gender and class differences is most readily observed in the campaign's positioning of men as home owners and women as home laborers. These intertwined gender and class differences organized property, work, and familial relations around the home for national order. The more complicated ways in which BHA built order out of difference, however, can be grasped when the multiplicity and contradictions of difference are seen *among* women rather than *between* white women and men of the generalized middle classes.[12]

The first BHA campaign attempted to unite those women who were involved as sponsors and those women toward whom the campaign was directed—twenty million American housekeepers. Organized women's groups, such as the General Federation of Women's Clubs and home economists, spoke to American housekeepers. In the following year, the demonstration week was called "essentially a women's campaign," and BHA public discourse began to change ("Broad Campaign," 1923). What had started in 1922 to educate twenty million housekeepers became a movement representing "organized women of America, those who are always at last responsible for making the home," according to President Warren Harding in his 1923 demonstration week dedication address ("Harding Calls Home," 1923). American housekeepers were not organized nor had they requested a Better Homes campaign. Although organized women's groups had joined journalists and federal officials to promote BHA, they were not representative of the housekeepers. Matters of audience and representativeness among women became confused in campaign statements.

One conflict between Better Homes in America and the national women's clubs concerned whether the campaign was a "[club] woman's movement." President Harding's dedication speech and other public statements claimed that BHA was a woman's movement; other statements suggested otherwise. Three women's clubs, the General Federation of Women's Clubs and the Federation of Business and General Federation of Women's Clubs and the Federation of Business and Professional Women, were on the Better Homes advisory council, and the GFWC, in particular, was active in the annual demonstration weeks. The chair of the federation made public statements supporting BHA and attended the 1923 "Home, Sweet Home" dedication ceremony ("Harding Calls Home," 1923; "Hoover Lauds Better Homes," 1923). Meloney worried that the GFWC would take charge and get credit for the organization instead of Hoover and the Department of Commerce. She claimed, without citing evidence, "it will destroy the [BHA] movement to put it in the hand of the General Federation," and she insisted that the campaign be incorporated to "definitely fix the credit for the organization" (Meloney, 1923c; Rickard, 1923). Even with the BHA's incorporation, however, some tension continued over the GFWC's involvement. In 1927, the president of the GFWC resigned from her position on the BHA board of directors because her board membership resulted "in much misunderstanding and confusion among the club and Federation women" (Sherman, 1927; see also Meloney, 1928).

BHA's "instruction" focused on the two aspects of women's household duties: housekeeping and consuming. "Housewives, both as *consumers* of household equipment, and as *makers* of homes, have a chance to meet in a demonstration house and discuss their problems together," Hoover claimed (1923a). The needs, wants, and desires of such audience members were hardly the same, yet BHA discourse diminished class differences among women through various modes of address. One mode of address referred to all women in the same manner— housewife, homemaker, housekeeper—with no acknowledgment that some women worked outside the home for wages as well as did their own housework. Similarly, BHA did not recognize those women whose paid employment outside the home came from doing other people's housework. By not speaking of these differences, the campaign appeared to be indifferent to class or economic relations. To speak of the "great middle class," as one commissioner did, implied that all people were of this class or that America was principally a one-class society ("Original of 'Home,'" 1923).

When BHA officials spoke of economic or class differences, they often did so through euphemisms. Terms such as "modest income" or "limited income" blurred economic differences among the middle, lower-middle, and working classes while dividing these classes from the elite or dominant classes, which in turn were euphemistically termed "well-to-do" or "prominent." The "well-to-do" organizers and community leaders, for instance, sponsored the demonstrations for those with "modest" or small incomes, and "specialists aimed to help men and women of modest means rather than owners of costly homes" ("Better Homes in America," 1923, p. 12).

The term "better homes" itself had multiple and contradictory meanings within BHA's own practices. The actual building and display of model homes were organized around economics. In praising the community that had built the winning demonstration home, Hoover stated, "it is important that you not only developed a model house for the family in moderate means, but that you recognized the needs of the less fortunate citizens and exhibited a model tenement" ("Better Homes in America," 1923, p. 12). This clear acknowledgment of differences, however, seemed to contradict other BHA discourse. When a funding agency director (Perry, 1924) specifically asked BHA, "What classes of people do you want to witness the demonstration?" BHA director James Ford answered, "We naturally wish to interest everybody" (Ford, 1924). Such a response denied, or perhaps displaced, difference for a number of possible interests or reasons. Phrases such as "Better Homes for Better Business and Better Citizens" removed economic difference from the center of public attention.

Race and ethnicity also were categories used for building order out of difference. One profound articulation of ethnic difference concerned access to home demonstration training:

> The most significant fact in all this movement is the building in a number of cities of model homes which belong to high schools and where the science of home-making will be taught to girls in the morning, married women in the afternoon, and the foreign-born at night. ("Better Homes in America," 1924)

BHA discourse assumed that girls and married women were white or Anglo-American, but the dominant racial group, in Barthes's terms, "obliterated its name in passing from reality to representation" (1972, p. 138). This assumption, or exnomination, contrasts with the use of terms to identify other groups. Black girls and women were identified by the marker "Negro." The term "foreign-born" named women in relation to those who were American-born, not by their own ethnicity or heritage. Furthermore, no distinction was drawn between the foreign-born who had become American citizens and those who had not. "Foreign-born" women went to demonstrations at night because they were most likely to be employed during the daytime—another unspoken class difference.

Americanizing immigrants was part of BHA's overall project. Blanche Halbert, a BHA research director, wrote magazine articles such as "Making Americans Through Flower Gardening" (see Halbert, 1926). Halbert also coordinated demonstrations for Americanizing immigrants. For instance, she claimed that "the Better Homes demonstration at Fullerton [California] illustrates so well the Americanization work that is being carried out in a colony of Mexican fruit workers." ·

BHA also addressed black Americans separately. The annual awards for the 1923 demonstration week, for example, included a first-place prize to Port Huron, Michigan, for a demonstration home that cost $5,500. The second-place prize went to St. Helena's Island, South Carolina, for "a perfect demonstration to Negroes." On an island of 6,000 blacks and 50 whites, the demonstration "house itself was a small Negro cottage built at the cost of $643.90," about one-tenth the cost of the model in a white, middle-class, suburban neighborhood (*Better Homes in America*, no date). The campaign distinguished among racial and ethnic groups even while claims that Better Homes in America was for all the people masked or naturalized difference.

BHA principally addressed adult women and men over its fifteen-year campaign. In 1924, however, it involved American girls, when the 1923 "Home, Sweet Home" demonstration model in Washington, D.C., was given to the Girl Scouts of America. In this national model home, the Girls Scouts established a permanent demonstration center called the "Little House." It was dedicated in May 1924 by Mrs. Calvin Coolidge, but the organizational work had been carried out by Mrs. Herbert Hoover, president of the Girl Scouts.[13]

By the 1920s, the service ideals of the Girl Scouts corresponded to BHA's ideology of the homemaker:

> Since the organization of the Girl Scouts in 1912, a half million girls have received scouting training. They have been taught to cook, sew,

and care for children. Ideals of service . . . have been instilled in
the minds of hundreds of thousands of girls. ("Big Gifts," 1924)

Having begun in the 1910s as an outdoors scouting organization, the
Girl Scouts now became the training ground for the youngest modern
homemakers.

According to Lou Henry Hoover, the "Little House" was to be the
national center of Girl Scout activities in homemaking. She saw it as
a "half way house between the playhouse of childhood and the home
every girl hopes to achieve some day" (quoted in Entz, 1930). Dusting,
cooking, laundry, and other tasks occupied the girls at "Little House."
The seven-room house was so useful for training that by 1930 it became
the model for 69 Girl Scout houses around the country (Entz, 1930).

Girl Scout pamphlets, reports, and *American Girl* magazine presented
a modern ideology of housework. "Homemaking" was "a delightful
game" with much "zest in cooking, dusting . . . and other homey tasks"
(*Annual Report*, no date). Girl Scouts train to create a home that is "a
refuge from the world's frets" and "something more than a house filled
with furniture" (*Broadcast from Station "Girl Scout,"* 1928). At the
"Little House," Girl Scouts "demonstrate their abilities as real
homemakers. Girl Scouts today mean *better homes* [italics added]
tomorrow" (*Annual Report*, no date). Homemaking became such a
featured part of Girl Scouting during the 1920s that merit badge
proficiencies changed over the decade. In 1923, Health merit badges
were the ones most earned; in 1928, twice as many Homemaking merit
badges as Health badges were earned (*Broadcast from Station "Girl
Scout,"* 1928).

The "Little House" frequently put on demonstration luncheons based
on two types of American budgets, "average" and the "low." Federal
officials, home economists, and other dignitaries were invited to these
luncheons, which often initiated the opening of the annual Better Homes
Week.

Even with all of this training and demonstration work to prepare girls,
Lou Henry Hoover and other Girl Scout leaders continued to argue that
homemaking was "natural" for girls. Hoover believed there was a
"feminine urge" for housekeeping and "domesticity." The "Little
House" "provides an outlet for this instinct."

Girl Scouts of America was the major national organization to address
young people, but local school boards also became involved. School
systems took one of two approaches toward better homes: civics lessons
or vocational education. For civics lessons, schools held contests for the
best essays, posters, and speeches, and provided volunteer help at the
community demonstration. Girls and boys participated in the week's

activities through projects designed in such courses as history, chemistry, and elocution (Carlisle, 1924; Ford, 1925).

Vocational or practical education about better homes was divided by gender. Literature distributed to school systems from BHA, Inc., made this division very clear: "Most American boys will be householders and most American girls will be homemakers in their adult years" (Ford & Halbert, 1925). School practice houses were where theory and experimentation were "converted into real homemaking knowledge."

School practice houses taught girls how to "eliminate drudgery and unnecessary waste of time and energy in doing necessary housework." Using labor-saving devices and arranging equipment conveniently would make available more time for civic affairs and for self-improvement. "The standards of homemaking, as outlined by specialists, have developed with the changing needs of our civilization," the executive director of BHA, Inc., stated (Ford & Halbert, 1925). Training intelligent homemakers aimed to make better citizens.

Boys, on the other hand, built school practice houses or the community's model home. BHA, Inc., research director Halbert claimed, "Boys work best at creative tasks. They like to do serious work and to see results" (Halbert, 1927, p. 1). Such student "labor," to BHA, was a practical educational device that had civic value in raising the standards of the home in the community.

The meaning of work for boys and girls, men and women was constituted in such discourse. The work boys did was called "labor"; the work girls did was called "homemaking." Labor was productive and worthy of pay; homemaking was service or servitude and performed out of love, instinct, or feminine urges.

In its efforts to make better homes and to raise standards of living, BHA encouraged consumer desire even among youth. In one city, for instance, high-school students voted on "The Things I Want in My Own Home," for part of the community's demonstration week activities. Their list of commodities totaled over $30,000 ("The Story of the 1923 Campaign," 1924).

Conclusion: Mobilization of Better Homes Discourse

Despite its claims to be strictly noncommercial, BHA nonetheless contributed to the formation of consumer culture in the 1920s. While the campaign was adamant about not promoting any one specific product, business, or industry, it did promote individual property ownership, the purchase of standardized commodities, and the use of household technologies. But "better homes" discourse spread beyond the organization called Better Homes in America and the institutions that had originally coalesced in the campaign. "Better homes" began to be used by institutions with specific commercial interests, and conflict among powerful organizations ensued. Some of these conflicts over the use of discourse pushed the move toward BHA's incorporation.

When commercial organizations advertised for better housing and homes, it became difficult to distinguish which groups were "cooperating" with BHA and which were coopting it. One lumber company, for example, ran an advertisement during the week of the second national demonstration using Department of Commerce housing policies to promote its commercial services. "HERBERT HOOVER SAYS," the ad stated, that if the family is the unit of civilization, the home should have as much attention as the factory. Western Lumber Company (1923) was ready to offer its "experts in all lines [to] assist in planning those home conveniences." Conflict also occurred between BHA and certain trade associations. A group of "furniture people" campaigned for better housing under the name of the American Home Bureau and used Coolidge's endorsement of Better Homes in America for itself. Meloney declared, "We must distinguish Better Homes . . . [from this] rival, commercial, non-educational movement" (Meloney, 1924a; see also Gries, 1924). As Meloney said in "The 1922 National Campaign Report": "*The Delineator* did not in any way put a commercial stamp on this campaign. . . . Two commercial groups, [however,] attempted to make the campaign merely a selling week because they appropriated much of [our] material."

Conflicts between commercial and noncommercial ventures began to plague BHA. As of June 1923, Hoover noticed that commercial agencies not involved with BHA "were claiming credit and that the future will resolve itself into contests between houses and commercial organizations . . . for the exploitation of [BHA]" (1923b). When George Wilder, publisher of *The Delineator*, heard of the push for BHA incorporation, he was relieved for none other than commercial reasons: BHA was draining the resources of *The Delineator* with little payoff. *The Delineator* supported the campaign financially, but, he claimed, received no business advantage from it. "We have refrained from approaching possible advertisers on account of it and kept it free altogether from commercialism," Wilder argued. He pledged to continue support for BHA through Meloney's editor's page, but he warned that another form of commercialism would exploit BHA. "When we give up special claim to it, all magazines of [our] type . . . will then promote and use the movement as long as it is to their advantage" (Wilder, 1923). Once *The Delineator* relinquished its official claims to BHA, Meredith Publications capitalized on it, almost as Wilder had predicted.

In August 1924, four months after *The Delineator* withdrew its official sponsorship, Meredith changed the name of its failing magazine, *Fruit, Garden, and Home*, to *Better Homes and Gardens* (Meredith, 1924; Reuss, 1971, pp. 38–41). *Fruit, Garden, and Home* was a low circulation magazine and (due to its name, it was speculated) had difficulty raising advertising revenue. But this did not alter the aspirations of editor Chelsa Sherlock, who wrote to publisher E. T. Meredith in December 1923, "our first goals must be to DOMINATE this field before anyone else has time and chance to beat us to it" (quoted in Reuss, 1971, p. 38). A name change had been discussed for months and, finally, in the summer of 1924, *Better Homes and Gardens* was selected. At that time, the price of the magazine tripled; by 1928, its circulation exceeded one million (Mott, 1968, p. 37; Reuss, 1971, pp. 40–41).

Advertisers also used "better homes" discourse. Ads filled with better furniture, better children, and better food reproduced the notions of women working in the home, shopping for commodities, and improving home life through consumption. One Campbell's soup ad (1924) began with the same words that Meloney used in starting BHA: "To the Eighteen Million American Women Who Do Their Own Work." Campbell's claimed to offer "real emancipation" for women. By using suffrage discourse in combination with better homes discourse, Campbell's sought to associate emancipation with new standards of work in the modern home: "Campbell's soups are helping to bring this emancipation to the women of America—better food with less work."

This examination of the BHA campaign and of better homes discourse reveals several dimensions of the discursive constitution of ideology and the social construction of gender. Most fundamentally, the analysis shows that the domain of everyday life is an effective ideological ground. In public discourse and images, the home is a place where culture and history are erased and where partial ideals are represented as reality. In addition to arguing *that* the domain of everyday life is an ideological site, the analysis also shows *how* the ideological was constituted in discursive and media practices. Across speeches, demonstration talks, editorials, news coverage, magazine articles, and other forms of media, BHA discourse constructed and reproduced relationships among home ownership, housework, and consumption. Various rhetorical strategies, such as editorial arguments, official endorsements, romantic narratives, and demonstrative "how-tos," linked patriotic, scientific, and gendered ideals, but left no or little trace of the specific historical conditions that enabled these values and ideals to be combined meaningfully. "Cultures try to pass off as natural features of the human condition arrangements and practices that are in fact historical" (Culler, 1983, p. 24); my attempt has been to show one significant way such "passing off" occurs—in discursive practices reproduced across media.

Several institutions had important stakes in redefining the American home and in addressing newly enfranchised women as consumers in the 1920s. Discourse about the home became a site of power relations among these institutions, for it was in discourse that some institutions aligned into a campaign and that other institutions operated in conflict. Federal officials, journalists, and home economists used better homes discourse for a related set of political and educational interests, while publishers, advertisers, and trade organizations did so for another set of business interests. "Structures of signification are mobilized to legitimate the sectional interests of hegemonic groups" (Giddens, 1979, p. 188), and this mobilization among hegemonic leadership is conflictual and negotiated rather than harmonic and monolithic.

Hegemonic groups do not impose ideology in manipulative, coercive, or dominating discourse. Instead, an ideological "effect" or outcome of their public, mass-mediated discourse is "the tendency . . . to make some forms of experience readily available to consciousness while ignoring or suppressing others" (Lears, 1985, p. 577). Public discourse calls attention to particular realities, legitimates specific values, and cultivates wide audience identification. Although institutions and campaigns have no guarantees that they will secure acceptance, participation, or even a hearing from actual audience members, they unify an audience discursively. Through modes of address that generalize across differences, public discourse creates one "people" rather than multiple groups.

As feminist theories emphasize, however, no universal audience, generalized person, or gender-neutral individual exists, regardless that such representations fill many canonical texts of Western civilization. The analysis of BHA reveals most clearly the social construction of gender formed into complex relations with class and race.[14] The campaign produced images of genders, classes, and races and arranged relations among them based on difference. As a social construct, gender is not a wholly discrete category, display, or performance, but is heavily intertwined with race, ethnicity, class, age, and other social differences. Relations between men and women and among women become organized or patterned in the interconnections with these other constructs of social difference. As a way of thinking and speaking, difference forms the links that organize relations, and in the case of BHA, the organizational pattern was hierarchical. Hierarchy is configured among multiple gender, racial, and class differences (Kramarae, 1989): (white) man as owner versus (white) woman as laborer; woman as prominent campaign organizer (who has leisure time created by another's domestic labor) versus woman as housewife (who does her own housework); and whites or Anglo-Americans as well-to-do, costly home dwellers versus Negroes and foreign-born as tenement or modest cottage dwellers. Difference in discourse may form many patterns of social relations, and one important feminist challenge remains the formation of differences into patterns alternative to hierarchy.

During the 1920s, ownership, work, and consumption congealed in the name of better homes. Today's "Born to Shop" bumper stickers and tee shirts are only the latest examples of discourse that reifies peculiar historical conditions of consumption.

Notes

1 The literature on consumer culture has expanded greatly since the 1976 publication of Ewen's *Captains of Consciousness*. See Benson (1986), Bowlby (1985), Erenberg (1981), Ewen and Ewen (1982), Fox and Lears (1983), Harris (1981), Kasson (1978), Leach (1984), Lears (1982), Marchand (1985), May (1980), Rydell (1984), Schudson (1984), and R. H. Williams (1982). For articles, a bibliography, and review essays on consumer culture in the 1940s and 1950s, see Gaines and Renov (1989).

2 For histories of housework, see Cowan (1976, 1983), Ehrenreich and English (1978), Hayden (1981), Kessler-Harris (1981), and Strasser (1982). For a social history of American housing, see Wright (1981). For a history of ideas about the home, see Rybczynski (1986).

3 My research on Better Homes in America was conducted at the Herbert Hoover Presidential Library in West Branch, Iowa, and the Hoover Institution on War, Revolution, and Peace at Stanford University in Palo Alto, California. The data on demonstration week organization and participation are from "Better Homes Week" (1922) and Ford (1928, 1931). Words in quotation without citation were pervasive campaign terms.

4 The article was printed in the BHA *Plan Book for Demonstration Week, 1922* and in many U.S. newspapers.

5 As a principal founder of BHA, Meloney used *The Delineator* in many ways to promote the campaign. Part of the events precipitating her resignation concerned publisher George Wilder's refusal to continue BHA support (Gries, 1926b; Meloney, 1926).

6 Historians present different views on the beginnings of home economics, which had been known earlier as domestic science, home science, household administration, and domestic economy. The professionalization of home economics accelerated during the first two decades of the twentieth century and included the establishment of the American Home Economics Association in 1909, the publication of its *Journal of Home Economics*, and the institutionalization of home economics as an agency of the federal government when the Office of Home Economics was first created under the U.S. Department of Agriculture in 1915 and became the Bureau of Home Economics in 1923 (Betters, 1930; Fritschner, 1977; Weigley, 1974).

7 For examples of texts or manuals using scientific home management and efficiency principles, see Frederick (1912, 1920) and Gilbreth (1927). For critiques of scientific home management, see Berch (1980) and Ehrenreich and English (1978). For a look at how scientific home management was used in public discourses about home technologies, see Altman (1990).

8 There is some controversy about the rights to this 1823 song. BHA and news articles identified Payne as its composer. Lax and Smith (1984, p. 231) state that the words were by Payne and the arrangement by Henry Bishop but that Payne was denied authorship to the song.

⁹ The phrase "real Americans" was frequently used by fervent patriots of the decade. See, for example, Hawley (1979, p. 50).

¹⁰ For matters related to magazine and journal outlets for BHA, see Better Homes in America, Inc., Papers, Boxes 26-30, at the Hoover Institution on War, Revolution, and Peace.

¹¹ On BHA radio broadcasts, see the files on radio stations WEAF, WRC, WBAL, WJZ, and WMAL, and the file titled "Abstracts of Radio Talks" in the Better Homes of America, Inc., Papers, Box 30, at the Hoover Institution on War, Revolution, and Peace. Also see the file titled "National Motion Picture Bureau, Motion Pictures" in the Better Homes in America, Inc., Papers, Box 23.

¹² Feminist theories have moved from an initial focus on gender to an interest in the multiple ways in which gender intersects with other social differences. A key topos in feminism since 1980 is "difference." For examples in the humanities and social sciences, see Barrett (1987), de Lauretis (1986), Doane and Hedges (1987), Eisenstein and Jardine (1980), Hare-Mustin and Maracek (1988), Joseph and Lewis (1981), Scott (1986), and Spivak (1987). For a critique of feminist uses of difference, see Altman (1989).

¹³ Important records on the Girl Scouts of America are housed in the Lou Henry Hoover Papers and the Gertrude S. Bowman Papers at the Herbert Hoover Presidential Library. For information on the founding and dedication of the "Little House," see "Girl Scouts Move" (1923), "Home, Sweet Home" (1923), and "House Built for Better Homes" (1924).

¹⁴ For debates on constructionism and essentialism in feminist theory, see Alcoff (1988), "The Essential Difference" (1989), Fuss (1989), and Spelman (1988).

References

Adams, Samuel Hopkins. (1921, March). Why boys leave home. *The Delineator*, pp. 4-5, 69-71.

Advance general information (Bulletin No. 1.) (1922, July 31). Personal Correspondence, Meloney, Marie M., Lou Henry Hoover Papers, Herbert Hoover Presidential Library, West Branch, IA.

Alcoff, L. (1988). Cultural feminism vs. post-structuralism: The identity crisis in feminist theory. *Signs, 13*, 405-427.

Allen, P. W. (1988). *Building domestic liberty*. Amherst: University of Massachusetts Press.

Altman, K. E. (1989). Rhetorics of difference in feminist argument. In B. E. Gronbeck (Ed.), *Spheres of argument: Proceedings of the sixth SCA/AFA conference on argumentation* (pp. 346-353). Annandale, VA: Speech Communication Association.

Altman, K. E. (1990). Modern discourse on American home technologies. In M. J. Medhurst, A. Gonzalez, and T. R. Peterson, (Eds.), *Communication and the culture of technology* (pp. 95-111). Pullman: Washington State University Press.

Annual Report of the Girl Scouts for 1923. (no date). Girl Scouts Pamphlets, Herbert Hoover Commerce Papers, Herbert Hoover Presidential Library, West Branch, IA.

Barber, D. (1923a, March). Pitfalls for the home builder. *The Delineator*, p. 14.

Barber, D. (1923b, April). New plans for better homes. *The Delineator*, p. 16.

Barber, D. (1923c, September). Our first national better home. *The Delineator*, pp. 2, 78.

Barrett, M. (1987, June). The concept of "difference." *Feminist Review, 26,* 29–41.

Barthes, R. (1972). *Mythologies.* (A. Lavers, Trans.). New York: Hill & Wang.

Benson, S. P. (1986). *Counter cultures: Sales women, managers, and customers in American department stores, 1890–1940.* Urbana: University of Illinois Press.

Berch, B. (1980). Scientific management in the home: The empress's new clothes. *Journal of American Culture, 3,* 440–445.

Better Homes in America (Bulletin No. 8). (no date). Building and Housing, 23, Herbert Hoover Commerce Papers, Herbert Hoover Presidential Library, West Branch, IA.

Better Homes in America. (1922, October). *The Delineator,* p. 16.

Better Homes in America. (1923, May). *The Delineator,* pp. 1, 12–13.

Better Homes in America. (1924, February). *The Delineator,* p. 1.

Better Homes Week is here. (1922, October 9). *New York Evening Post* (no page). Housing Clippings File, 1921–1928, Herbert Hoover Commerce Papers, Herbert Hoover Presidential Library, West Branch, IA.

Betters, P. V. (1930). *The Bureau of Home Economics: Its history, activities and organization* (Service Monograph of the United States Government, No. 62). Washington, DC: Brookings Institution.

Big gifts help Girl Scouts in national drive. (1924, November 21). *Aberdeen World* (no page). Clippings, 1924, Girl Scouts, Lou Henry Hoover Papers, Herbert Hoover Presidential Library, West Branch, IA.

Bowlby, R. (1985). *Just looking: Consumer culture in Dreiser, Gissing, and Zola.* New York: Methuen.

Broad campaign for Better Homes. (1923, June 4). *The New York Times* (no page). Housing Clippings File, 1921–1928, Herbert Hoover Commerce Papers, Herbert Hoover Presidential Library, West Branch, IA.

Broadcast from Station "Girl Scout." (1928). Girl Scouts Pamphlets, Herbert Hoover Commerce Papers, Herbert Hoover Presidential Library, West Branch, IA.

Brown, D. M. (1987). *American women in the 1920s: Setting a course.* Boston: Twayne.

Campbell's Soup. (1924, February). Advertisement. *The Delineator,* p. 37.

Carlisle, E. (1924, March). *Why and how to teach civic effectiveness* (Publication No. 2). Building and Housing, Better Homes in America, Printed Matter, Herbert Hoover Commerce Papers, Herbert Hoover Presidential Library, West Branch, IA.

Coolidge, C. (1922, October). A nation of home owners. *The Delineator,* pp. 16–17.

Coolidge, C. (1923, August). Books for better homes. *The Delineator,* pp. 2, 70.

Cowan, R. S. (1983). *More work for mother.* New York: Basic.

Cowan, R. S. (1976). The "industrial revolution" in the home: Household technology and social change in the 20th century. *Technology and Culture, 17,* 1–23.

Culler, J. (1983). *Roland Barthes.* New York: Oxford University Press.

de Lauretis, T. (Ed.). (1986). *Feminist studies, critical studies.* Bloomington: Indiana University Press.

Despoiled: The confession of a wife who failed. (1923, March). *The Delineator,* pp. 17–18, 73.

Doane, J., & Hedges, D. (1987). *Nostalgia and sexual difference*. New York: Methuen.

Ehrenreich, B., & English, D. (1978). *For her own good: 150 years of the experts' advice to women*. Garden City, NY: Anchor.

Eisenstein, H., & Jardine, A. (Eds.). (1980). *The future of difference*. New Brunswick, NJ: Rutgers University Press.

Entz, A. (1930). Girl Scout homemaking activities stimulated by aid of Mrs. Hoover (no page). Clippings and Printed Matter, Girl Scouts and Other Organizations, Lou Henry Hoover Papers, Herbert Hoover Presidential Library, West Branch, IA.

Erenberg, L. A. (1981). *Steppin' out: New York nightlife and the transformation of American culture, 1890-1930*. Chicago: University of Chicago Press.

The essential difference. (1989, Summer). *Differences: A Journal of Feminist Cultural Studies* (1).

Ewen, S., & Ewen, E. (1982). *Channels of desire*. New York: McGraw-Hill.

Ford, J. (1924, February 13). Letter to Clarence A. Perry. Laura Spelman Rockefeller to "T" file, Russell Sage Foundation, Better Homes in America, Inc., Hoover Institute on War, Revolution, and Peace, Stanford University, Palo Alto, CA.

Ford, J. (1925). How home economics departments work with Better Homes in America. *Journal of Home Economics, 17*, 136-139.

Ford, J. (1928, July 25). Letter to Herbert Hoover. Building and Housing, Better Homes in America Inc., Herbert Hoover Commerce Papers, Herbert Hoover Presidential Library, West Branch, IA.

Ford, J. (1931). Better Homes in America. In B. Halbert (Ed.), *Better Homes manual*. Chicago: University of Chicago Press.

Ford, J., & Halbert, B. (1925, October). *School cottages for training in homemaking* (Publication No. 8). Building and Housing, Better Homes in America, Printed Matter, Herbert Hoover Commerce Papers, Herbert Hoover Presidential Library, West Branch, IA.

Fox, R. W., & Lears, T. J. (Eds.). (1983). *The culture of consumption*. New York: Pantheon.

Frederick, C. (1912). *New housekeeping*. Garden City, NY: Doubleday, Page.

Frederick, C. (1920). *Household engineering: Scientific management in the home*. Chicago: American School of Home Economics.

Frederick, C. (1929). *Selling Mrs. Consumer*. New York: Business Bourse.

Fritschner, L. M. (1977). Women's work and women's education: The case of home economics, 1870-1920. *Sociology of Work and Occupations, 4*, 209-234.

Fuss, D. (1989). *Essentially speaking: Feminism, nature, & difference*. New York: Routledge.

Gaines, J., & Renov, M. (Eds.). (1989). Female representative and consumer culture [Special issue]. *Quarterly Review of Film and Video* (11).

Giddens, A. (1979). *Central problems in social theory*. Berkeley: University of California Press.

Gilbreth, L. (1927). *The homemaker and her job*. New York: Appleton.

Girl Scouts move to model house. (1923, December 12). *The Washington Times* (no page). Clippings, 1923, Girl Scouts, Lou Henry Hoover Papers, Herbert Hoover Presidential Library, West Branch, IA.

Gries, J. M. (1924, January 24). Letter to Herbert Hoover. Building and Housing, Better Homes in America, Inc., Herbert Hoover Commerce Papers, Herbert Hoover Presidential Library, West Branch, IA.

Gries, J. M. (1926a). Bureau of Standards report. In *The thirteenth annual report of the Secretary of Commerce, 1925.* Washington, DC: U.S. Government Printing Office.

Gries, J. M. (1926b, July 19). Letter to H. P. Stokes. General Accession, Mears to Merchant, Herbert Hoover Commerce Papers, Herbert Hoover Presidential Library, West Branch, IA.

Gries, J. M., & Taylor, J. S. (1925). *How to own your home.* Washington, DC: U.S. Government Printing Office. Building and Housing, Better Homes in America, Printed Matter, Herbert Hoover Commerce Papers, Herbert Hoover Presidential Library, West Branch, IA.

Grossberg, L. (Ed.). (1986). On postmodernism and articulation: An interview with Stuart Hall. *Journal of Communication Inquiry, 10,* 45–60.

Halbert, B. (1926, December 27). Letter to Paul V. Kellogg. Publicity to Publications, Publicity "S" file, Better Homes in America, Inc., Hoover Institution on War, Revolution, and Peace, Stanford University, Palo Alto, CA.

Halbert, B. (1927, June). *Boy built houses* (Publication No. 13). Building and Housing, Better Homes in America, Printed Matter, Herbert Hoover Commerce Papers, Herbert Hoover Presidential Library, West Branch, IA.

Halbert, B. (1931). *Better Homes manual.* Chicago: University of Chicago Press.

Hall, S. (1985). Signification, representation, ideology: Althusser and the post-structuralist debates. *Critical Studies in Mass Communication, 5,* 91–114.

Harding calls home nation's best industry. (1923, June 5). *The New York Times* (no page). Housing Clippings File, 1921–1928, Herbert Hoover Commerce Papers, Herbert Hoover Presidential Library, West Branch, IA.

Hare-Mustin, R. T., & Maracek, J. (1988). The meaning of difference: Gender theory, postmodernism, and psychology. *American Psychologist, 45,* 455–464.

Harris, N. (1981). The drama of consumer desire. In O. Mayr & R. C. Post (Eds.), *Yankee enterprise* (pp. 189–216). Washington, DC: Smithsonian Institution Press.

Hawley, E. W. (1979). *The Great War and the search for a modern order.* New York: St. Martin's.

Hayden, D. (1981). *The grand domestic revolution.* Cambridge, MA: MIT Press.

Home, Sweet Home to be moved soon. (1923, December 12). *Washington Star* (no page). Clippings, 1923, Girl Scouts, Lou Henry Hoover Papers, Herbert Hoover Presidential Library, West Branch, IA.

Hoover, H. (1922a, September 13). Letter to Irving B. Hiett. Building and Housing, Better Homes in America, Herbert Hoover Commerce Papers, Herbert Hoover Presidential Library, West Branch, IA.

Hoover, H. (1922b, October). The home as an investment. *The Delineator,* p. 17.

Hoover, H. (1923a, June 4). Address at dedication of "Home, Sweet Home" house. Building and Housing, Better Homes in America, 1923, Herbert Hoover Commerce Papers, Herbert Hoover Presidential Library, West Branch, IA.

Hoover, H. (1923b, June 14). Letter to George Wilder. Building and Housing, Better Homes in America, 1921-1923, Herbert Hoover Commerce Papers, Herbert Hoover Presidential Library, West Branch, IA.

Hoover, H. (1926, January 26). Letter to Mrs. William Brown [Marie M.] Meloney. Building and Housing, Better Homes in America, Inc., Herbert Hoover Commerce Papers, Herbert Hoover Presidential Library, West Branch, IA.

Hoover lauds Better Homes campaign. (1923, April 23). The Washington Times (no page). Housing Clippings File, 1921-1928, Herbert Hoover Commerce Papers, Herbert Hoover Presidential Library, West Branch, IA.

House built for Better Homes in America given to Girl Scouts. (1924, May 11). Tribune (no page). Clippings, 1923, Girl Scouts, Lou Henry Hoover Papers, Herbert Hoover Presidential Library, West Branch, IA.

Jessop, B. (1982). The capitalist state. New York: New York University Press.

Joseph, G., & Lewis, J. (1981). Common differences. Boston: South End Press.

Kasson, J. F. (1978). Amusing the million. New York: Hill & Wang.

Kessler-Harris, A. (1981). Women have always worked. Old Westbury, NY: Feminist Press.

Kramarae, C. (1989). Redefining gender, class, and race. In C. M. Lont & S. A. Friedley (Eds.), Beyond boundaries: Sex and gender diversity in communication (pp. 317-329). Fairfax, VA: George Mason University Press.

Lax, R., & Smith, F. (1984). The great song thesaurus. New York: Oxford University Press.

Leach, W. R. (1984). Transformations in a culture of consumption: Women and the department stores, 1890-1925. Journal of American History, 71, 319-342.

Lears, T. J. (1982). Some versions of fantasy: Toward a cultural history of advertising. In J. Solzman (Ed.), Prospects (Vol. 9, pp. 349-405). New York: Bert Franklin.

Lears, T. J. (1985). The concept of cultural hegemony: Problems and possibilities. American Historical Review, 90, 567-593.

Lemons, J. S. (1973). The woman citizen: Social feminism in the 1920's. Urbana: University of Illinois Press.

Leuchtenburg, W. E. (1958). The perils of prosperity, 1914-32. Chicago: University of Chicago Press.

Marchand, R. (1985). Advertising the American dreams: Making way for modernity, 1920-1940. Berkeley: University of California Press.

May, L. (1980). Screening out the past: The birth of mass culture and the motion picture industry. New York: Oxford University Press.

McGee, M. C. (1975). In search of "the people": A rhetorical alternative. Quarterly Journal of Speech, 61, 235-249.

Meloney, M. M. (1922a, November). Better Homes in America. The Delineator, p. 18.

Meloney, M. M. (1922b, November). The new woman. The Delineator, p. 1.

Meloney, M. M. (1922c, June). From the editor's point of view. The Delineator, p. 1.

Meloney, M. M. (1923a, January). From the editor's point of view. *The Delineator*, p. 1.

Meloney, M. M. (1923b, April). From the editor's point of view. *The Delineator*, p. 1.

Meloney, M. M. (1923c, November 19). Letter to Herbert Hoover. Building and Housing, Better Homes in America, 1921–1923, Herbert Hoover Commerce Papers, Herbert Hoover Presidential Library, West Branch, IA.

Meloney, M. M. (1924a, January 17). Letter to Herbert Hoover. Building and Housing, Better Homes in America, Inc., Herbert Hoover Commerce Papers, Herbert Hoover Presidential Library, West Branch, IA.

Meloney, M. M. (1924b, April). From the editor's point of view. *The Delineator*, p. 1.

Meloney, M. M. (1928, February 10). Letter to Herbert Hoover. Meloney, Marie M., Herbert Hoover Commerce Papers, Herbert Hoover Presidential Library, West Branch, IA.

Meloney, Mrs. W. B. [M. M.]. (1926, July 17). Letter to Herbert Hoover. General Accession, Mears to Merchant, Herbert Hoover Commerce Papers, Herbert Hoover Presidential Library, West Branch, IA.

Meredith, E. T. (1924, August). Better homes and gardens. *Better Homes and Gardens*, p. 1.

Mott, F. L. (1968). *A history of American magazines, Vol. 5: Sketches of 21 magazines, 1905–1930*. Cambridge: Belknap Press of Harvard University Press.

Mouffe, C. (1979). Ideology and hegemony in Gramsci. In C. Mouffe (Ed.), *Gramsci and Marxist theory* (pp. 168–204). Boston: Routledge & Kegan Paul.

The 1922 national campaign report. (no date). Building and Housing, Better Homes in America, 1921–1923, Herbert Hoover Commerce Papers, Herbert Hoover Presidential Library, West Branch, IA.

Original of "Home, Sweet Home" selected as ideal of all homes. (1923, June 3). *The New York Times* (no page). Housing Clippings File, 1921–1928, Herbert Hoover Commerce Papers, Herbert Hoover Presidential Library, West Branch, IA.

Perry, C. A. (1924, February 11). Letter to James Ford. Laura Spelman Rockefeller to "T" file, Russell Sage Foundation, Better Homes in America, Inc., Hoover Institution on War, Revolution, and Peace, Stanford University, Palo Alto, CA.

Plan book for demonstration week, October 9 to 14, 1922. (1922). New York: The Delineator. Building and Housing, Better Homes in America, Printed Matter, 1923–1927, Herbert Hoover Commerce Papers, Herbert Hoover Presidential Library, West Branch, IA.

Plan book for demonstration week, June 4–10, 1923. (1923). New York: The Delineator. Building and Housing, Better Homes in America, Printed Matter, 1923–1927, Herbert Hoover Commerce Papers, Herbert Hoover Presidential Library, West Branch, IA.

Reuss, C. (1971). *"Better Homes and Gardens" and its editors*. Unpublished doctoral dissertation, University of Iowa, Iowa City.

Rickard, E. (1923, May 16). Letter to Herbert Hoover. Better Homes in America, General File, Belgium-American Education Foundation, Incorporated Papers, Herbert Hoover Presidential Library, West Branch, IA.

Roosevelt, T. (1923, June). Better Homes in America. *The Delineator*, p. 1.

Rybczynski, W. (1986). *Home: A short history of an idea*. New York: Penguin.

Rydell, R. (1984). *All the world's a fair*. Chicago: University of Chicago Press.

Schudson, M. (1984). *Advertising, the uneasy persuasion*. New York: Basic.

Scott, J. W. (1986). Gender: A useful category of historical analysis. *American Historical Review, 91,* 1053-1075.

Sherman, Mrs. J. D. (1927, November 21). Letter to Herbert Hoover. Building and Housing, Better Homes in America, Inc., Herbert Hoover Commerce Papers, Herbert Hoover Presidential Library, West Branch, IA.

Spelman, E. V. (1988). *Inessential woman*. Boston: Beacon.

Spivak, G. C. (1987). *In other words: Essays in cultural politics*. New York: Methuen.

The story of the 1923 campaign. (1924, January). *The Delineator*, p. 1.

Strasser, S. (1982). *Never done: A history of American housework*. New York: Pantheon.

Thompson, J. B. (1984). *Studies in the theory of ideology*. Berkeley: University of California Press.

Towne, C. H. (1922, May). Where Poe once lived and loved. *The Delineator*, p. 18.

The twelfth annual report of the Secretary of Commerce, 1924. (1925). Washington, DC: U.S. Government Printing Office.

Van Rensselaer, M. (1922, October). The homemaker's department. *The Delineator*, p. 43.

Van Rensselaer, M. (1923a, February). The homemaker's department. *The Delineator*, p. 43.

Van Rensselaer, M. (1923b, November). The homemaker's department. *The Delineator*, p. 19.

Vološinov, V. N. (1973). *Marxism and the philosophy of language*. (L. Matejka & I. R. Titunik, Trans.). Cambridge: Harvard University Press.

Weigley, E. S. (1974). It might have been euthenics: The Lake Placid conferences and the home economics movement. *American Quarterly, 26,* 79-96.

Western Lumber Company. (1923, June 6). Advertisement. Housing Clippings File, 1921-1928, Herbert Hoover Commerce Papers, Herbert Hoover Presidential Library, West Branch, IA.

When marriage goes on the rocks. (1922, November). *The Delineator*, p. 3.

Wilder, G. (1923, July 20). Letter to Herbert Hoover. Building and Housing, Better Homes in America, 1921-1923, Herbert Hoover Commerce Papers, Herbert Hoover Presidential Library, West Branch, IA.

Williams, R. (1977). *Marxism and literature*. New York: Oxford University Press.

Williams, R. H. (1982). *Dream worlds*. Princeton: Princeton University Press.

Wright, G. (1981). *Building the dream: A social history of housing in America*. Cambridge, MA: MIT Press.

Late Show with David Letterman
An Ideological Critique

Victoria A. Gillam

Television junkies and critics alike have raved about David Letterman since the creation of his *Late Night with David Letterman* for NBC in 1982. When the show moved to CBS in August, 1993, and was renamed *Late Show with David Letterman*, the positive responses continued. From exposing the modes of production to lampooning structured formats to sticking his nose right up to the lens of the camera, Letterman has learned to mock and manipulate the medium through which he courts consumers into a love affair with show business.

Letterman is on his way to becoming an American icon. As the host of the most successful talk show on television, Letterman enjoys, among other perks, thronging lines for his studio audience, steady Nielsen ratings, $14 million a year, a clothing and souvenir line promoting the *Late Show*, his name as a household word, and *warnings* for 140-miles-per-hour speeding violations (*Late Show*, 1994, Dec. 8). Letterman's wild popularity is directly responsible for the success of the new show. According to Rose (1985), "the success of a talk show rests on the ability of its star to unify a variety of mostly unscripted segments by the sheer force of his or her 'real life' character" (p. 341). To understand why millions of Americans ritually tune in nightly to see the "real-life" Letterman in action, one first must understand the design of the program, which follows the format of late-night talk shows.

General Characteristics of the Late-Night Talk Show

The talk show, according to Rose (1985), "combines some of the principal qualities of other successful dramatic forms—the emotional intimacy of melodrama, the sprightliness of comedy, for instance—while offering a compelling immediacy no work of TV fiction can provide" (p. 329). Unlike the syntagmatic narrative flow of a serial, the talk show is, instead, a series of presentational formats. Although framed as casual and spontaneous, careful planning is required to ensure a predictable organization for the talk show (Rose, 1985, p. 329). In the talk show's 30-year history, it "has usually been dedicated to either light entertainment, complete with comedy, skits, music, and show business

This essay was written while Victoria A. Gillam was a student in a A. Susan Owen's television criticism class at the University of Puget Sound in 1994. Used by permission of the author.

guests, or to more serious discussion, in a simple studio, with just an interviewer and an interviewee" (Rose, 1985, p. 330). The Late Show follows the former approach.

Premiering on NBC with host Steve Allen on September 27, 1954, Tonight! established the format with which today's audiences are familiar. The following features have been assimilated into modern late-night talk shows (including the Late Show): "an opening segment featuring the host in a solo turn at center stage, occasional forays into the audience or streets, a shift to a different platform where the host sits behind a desk flanked by chairs, chats with the orchestra leader and announcer, and, finally, a procession of appearances and discussions with visiting stars and momentary celebrities" (Rose, 1985, p. 332). The program lasted 3 1/2 years and, after being cancelled, was brought back as The Tonight Show with a new host, Jack Paar. Unlike Allen, Paar used the opening segment for a comedy monologue, but otherwise, Paar was committed to the same structure that had been used on Tonight!. Engaging and personable, Paar led the show to heightened popularity through his skillful interviewing, charming honesty, and lack of fear of intellectuals and political topics. In these ways, he stretched the previous notions of talk television. Paar lasted almost five years and was replaced by Johnny Carson, whose amazing 30-year reign as host cemented these features of the late-night talk show.

Surprisingly, Letterman's act started out in the 10:00–11:00 A.M. slot on NBC with a primary audience of homemakers; it debuted on June 23, 1980, as The David Letterman Show. Satiric and sly, Letterman's antics and style were well received by critics but ill suited to his audience. The show was cancelled after four months, renamed Late Night with David Letterman, and moved to the slot directly after The Tonight Show, where producers figured his act would fit the late-night audience more appropriately. Rose (1985) suggests that the program followed the format established by previous late-night talk shows:

> "Late Night" still honored the formula's primary conventions. David Letterman opened each show with a comic monologue; he took part in skits, he talked to his band leader, and he interviewed his guests from behind a desk. For all its mocking tone and campy irony, "Late Night with David Letterman" was essentially an affectionate salute to the talk show, designed for a generation that had grown up with the genre. (p. 340)

Organizational and Structural Elements of the Talk Show

The Late Show honors the historical form of the organization and structure of late-night talk shows, as illustrated in the November 2, 1994, program I chose to analyze. Opening with a graphic montage, a voice announces the night's celebrity guests. Following this segment, the camera moves into the Ed Sullivan Theater, where, after the traditional establishing shots of the audience, band, and stage, Letterman begins his comedy monologue. Next, he moves to the raised platform that represents his "office" and takes his place behind his desk. Interrupting the comic discourse is a short "court-scene" skit with *Late Show* regulars Mujibar and Sirijul. Letterman moves the action along with the "warning-labels" segment for which the CBS orchestra plays a theme song and the production staff has created graphic visuals. Letterman then converses and jokes with the audience, interrupted by a flashback to the "court scene." The "top-ten list," introduced by music and a graphic montage, is next. Radio personality David Brenner and child actor Elijah Wood are the celebrities for the evening and are interviewed by Letterman, with Brenner's interview punctuated by a short skit of Letterman blowing up pumpkins on Halloween. Blues Traveler performs last—as is typical for musical guests—and Letterman joins the group on stage. Finally, Letterman signs off with a "Thanks for watching! Good night, everybody!" Just when the credits are about to play, the final "court-scene" skit is flashed on screen.

As is evidenced in the formal structure of this program, the *Late Show* follows the traditional talk-show organization and varies only to the degree that Letterman is able to personalize and render the show unique. Maintenance of this structure across historical time but also across each *Late Show* program is important, as Rose (1985) suggests:

> In the absence of the dynamic story elements of fictional formats, the talk show stresses the familiarity . . . of its structure. The genre's rigidity, in fact, helps contribute to its appeal. . . . [It] offers viewers a satisfying demonstration that form is just as important as content. The endlessly repeatable structure provides orientation as well as a sense of expectation. . . . This predictable progression gives the illusion of dramatic action and movement to a format that is essentially static. (p. 342)

Without the assuring plot or action dependence of a series, the talk show compensates by establishing, developing, and perpetuating a format familiar to viewers. Not only does this organization assure the interpretability of the text (Feuer, 1992, p. 144), but it lends a common ground on which viewers can depend every week night. Thus, the talk show becomes a point of reference for viewers through its organizational structure.

In addition to its organization, there are several other important features in the talk show's structure. First, the talk show is fast paced. Angelo (1977) claims, "the cardinal rule is simply, 'Keep it moving!'

If you can't get any voltage out of the interview, the least you can do is don't stop. So there's rarely even a *hmmm* in the conversation. There's no time for one'' (p. 228). In the episode of the *Late Show* I analyzed, the program is, as usual, packed with action. The CBS orchestra offers musical numbers between and during segments, notably the "warning-labels" segment, to spice up the presentational formats and create the illusion of breathlessness. Letterman also adds to this sense of being rushed with his guests. He cuts off David Brenner when he talks too long, and he consistently interrupts Elijah Wood in an effort to move forward in the interview.

Another feature of a talk show is its apparent spontaneity, a spontaneity that sometimes is scripted and sometimes is genuine. One of the most distinctive features of the *Late Show* is the host's and the production team's ability to create "spontaneity" skillfully and to handle the unexpected. In the episode I analyzed, Letterman wrests a canned ham from a man in the audience, only to give it to someone else. When the audience boos him, he shouts to his crew, "Can I have another ham? Get me another damn ham!" Almost instantly, another ham is produced. Letterman's reaction to the audience's boos seemed to prompt him to revise his behavior, but in reality, the whole interaction was carefully predicted, scripted, and acted to appear to be a spontaneous reaction. On the other hand, Letterman has a knack for rescuing himself from the truly unexpected. While he is showing different products with warning labels at his desk, the box of fish sticks falls off his desk. Letterman is obviously surprised and gets up to walk around the desk to retrieve the box. He mutters, "Warning, carton is improperly balanced," and as he walks to the other side of the desk, the band plays a tune to which Letterman improvises a little dance.

One final element that characterizes the show is the structured relationships that exist between the host and the supporting cast. Rose (1985) claims that the supporting cast acts as a mini-family for the host (p. 341). The members of the production team for the *Late Show* were carried over from NBC's *Late Night* and therefore know Letterman well. Letterman often talks to his producer and director, Hal Gurnee, during the show. In the episode I analyzed, he calls out, "Hal, do me a favor. Punch up that court-room scene." He also talks to the camera person, Bob, in this episode, displaying his intimacy with his camera team and illuminating Letterman's ultimate control over the modes of production. At the same time, of course, he exposes those modes, thus breaking the invisible-camera convention observed by much of the television industry. The most important member of the supporting cast, however, is the sidekick. Rose (1985) asserts that the sidekick stabilizes the group as a reference point throughout the presentational formats (p. 342). He is a reminder of an assuring, non-changing relationship in the midst of chaos. Band director Paul Shaffer is Letterman's faithful sidekick. In the November 2, 1994, episode, Letterman uses Shaffer to affirm his memory of blowing up pumpkins in the Halloween dream skit. Shaffer is often used in similar ways to advance drama, to confirm the opinions and actions of Letterman, and to act as a dependable force.

During the November 2, 1994, episode of the *Late Show*, both the host and the guests met the expectations placed on them by the talk-show genre. Letterman honors the traditional structural qualities of the talk-show genre set forth by Steve Allen in *Tonight!*, perpetuated by Jack Paar on *The Tonight Show*, and made famous by Johnny Carson. Letterman's sly wit, coupled with his constant flirtation with chaos, however, distinguish him from his predecessors. The computer-generated graphic montages introducing his discourse, the occasional videotaped forays into suburban neighborhoods, and the frequent reappearances of novelty characters (made famous by Letterman) also propel the *Late Show* into uncharted territory. Letterman is a risk taker and innovator and the driving force behind his production crew, content, and form. "TV's funniest lame duck," as Letterman was called by *Entertainment Weekly* (Tucker, 1993), has set the standard for the modern talk show of the 1990s.

Understanding the development and nature of the traditional talk-show genre is critical to grasping the difference between a talk show's overt purposes and its underlying aims. The purpose of the talk show, as I have established, ostensibly is to showcase entertainment stars and their work. However, while this forum with celebrities appears to be "entertainment" and "conversation," it actually is driven by a profit motive in an environment of promotional appeals. Although the talk show *seems* to prize nostalgic structure, fast-paced banter, spontaneity, cast relationships, and host-guest interactions, the real premium is being placed on advancing the interests of the entertainment industry. In order to gain a deeper critical perspective of this talk show, I will analyze the November, 2, 1994, *Late Show* to discover the ideology that permeates the genre of the late-night talk show and the *Late Show* in particular.

Ideology of the *Late Show*

Ideological analysis is concerned with understanding "culture as a form of social expression . . . how a cultural text specifically embodies and enacts particular ranges of values, beliefs, and ideas" (White, 1992, p. 163). Because the *Late Show* is an artifact bound in time and culture to the social formation in which it is created, it constitutes a cultural text. Examination of its meaning and how it is produced and manifest illuminates the social formation in which it exists. Ideological analysis is "concerned with the ways in which cultural practices and artifacts . . . produce particular knowledges and positions for their users . . ." (White, 1992, p. 163). The *Late Show*, I will argue, is an artifact that produces knowledge about the show-business industry for its viewers, advocating certain life and consumption styles, and thus advances the economic interests of the industry. Ideological critics suggest that the commercial message is "the linchpin between television as information-entertainment and television as an industry, with the viewer as the place where these meanings or forces converge" (White, 1992, p. 172). Perhaps nowhere in television is the economic motive as clear as in the traditionally formatted late-night talk show.

In the case of the *Late Show*, the viewer is both a consumer and a commodity. Advertisers pay tens—even hundreds—of thousands of dollars to buy commercial air time to promote their products: "Because commercial television is first and foremost a mass-advertising medium, viewers are positioned as potential consumers. . . . [T]hey are regularly subject to a range of appeals for a variety of products" (White, 1992, p. 171). *Late Show* viewers tune in to "consume" their favorite stars— Letterman is one of them. Guests are chosen because they are working on projects of interest. Letterman's guests are "desirable," or they would not have been invited on the show. If Letterman likes them, so do the viewers. He creates a desire for the guests in the viewers through facial expressions, warm greetings, and bantering with guests about their recent successes. He is being paid $14 million a year to make his guests look good and to share in those guests' profit when he does. The show presents positive images of celebrity guests, acting as an advocate of each star, thereby establishing positive attitudes of reception among viewers toward the stars and their work.

But the *Late Show* is more blatant about its function as a platform for promotional advertising. Letterman does not simply make his guests desirable so that viewers will want to consume them, but he engages in explicit promotion of the activities and projects of those guests. In the episode of the *Late Show* I analyzed, David Brenner discussed how he recently took over Larry King's radio show and is moving the show to a live format, which will be broadcast five days a week from New York's Planet Hollywood. He also tells the audience that he will do a "radiomentary" on the *Late Show* on his radio program—he will promote Letterman's program on radio, just as his radio program is being promoted on Letterman's television program. Letterman ends his interview with an explicit persuasive appeal for Brenner by looking into the camera and reminding the audience, "Let me mention here. David Brenner will be at the Clairidge Hotel Casino November 18th, 19th, and 20th, so go down there and see David Brenner in Atlantic City at the

Clairidge Hotel!'' Elijah Wood comes on to advertise his new film, *The War*, with Kevin Costner. He also ends up sharing how he became a child movie star, with a reference from Letterman about Wood's work in the movie, *The Good Son*. Viewers of the *Late Show*, then, are subjected to promotions and appeals designed to induce viewers to consume products and projects from which the guests on the show will profit.

People are not the only commodities on the *Late Show*. Viewers also are asked to buy products. In the ''warning-labels'' comedy segment in the program I analyzed, viewers were subjected to many rapid appeals as these products were showcased: Light & Lively cottage cheese, Arm & Hammer baking soda, Nabisco shredded wheat, Gorton's fish sticks, and Zima alcohol. All promoted the packaged food industry and suggested the desirability of a consumptive life style. Also sold to viewers were R.E.M.'s album, *Monster* (promoting another branch of the entertainment industry); a *Late Show* ticket (promoting the show itself); *T.V. Guide* (promoting the television industry); and Baci chocolates, about which Letterman says, ''it's a Gumpism!,'' promoting the movie, *Forrest Gump*, and thus the film industry). These products, all linked to the entertainment industry and designed to enhance its profits, were sold to viewers as they watched the *Late Show*.

But the audience for the show not only functions as a consumer but as a commodity. As White (1992) explains, ''Because they are 'sold' to advertisers, viewers themselves become commodities in the act of watching television'' (p. 171). The viewer as consumer is sold to advertisers when the show gets Nielsen rating points based on viewership. The viewer thus becomes currency—a form of exchange among players in the entertainment industry. Viewers of the program also were sold as potential audiences to the Clairidge Hotel Casino while watching Letterman promote Brenner and to the movie, *The War*, as a potential audience under the guise of an interview with one of its stars, Elijah Wood.

The *Late Show*, then, seems to operate on the you-scratch-my-back-I'll-scratch-yours principle. On the program, Letterman or the producers invite guests to appear on the show. People tune in to watch these guests, and CBS makes a profit. As guests amuse, entertain, and promote, interest in and support for these guests is developed, and the potential for further consumption of these guests is created. CBS makes a profit, and guests make profits off of the *Late Show*.

Viewers, of course, are willing participants in this economic exchange. They take part in their subjection to promotional appeals and in their own commodification. Every time they ''shop'' the networks and tune back in to the *Late Show*, they willingly have made another purchase and become another potential commodity for another business venture. They like Letterman; they get pleasure from the *Late Show*. Their liking perpetuates their loyalty, which translates into rating points, which translate into dollars for advertisers. Their consumption pattern meets a need for them—perhaps one of entertainment, escape, or engagement—but it appears to be a need created by economic interests and sold to American audiences as a natural and appropriate desire. Everyone is making a profit off of this constructed desire except the viewers; as both consumers and commodities, they continually feed the entertainment industry, all the while believing they are being entertained.

References

Angelo, L. (1977). Confessions of a talk show host. In J. Fireman (Ed.), *TV book: The ultimate television book* (pp. 226–228). New York: Workman.

Feuer, J. (1992). Genre study and television. In R. C. Allen (Ed.), *Channels of discourse, reassembled* (pp. 138–59). Chapel Hill: University of North Carolina Press.

Rose, B. (1985). The talk show. In B. Rose (Ed.), *TV genres: A handbook and reference guide* (pp. 329–352). Westport, CT: Greenwood.

Tucker, K. (1993, June 25–July 8). David Letterman: With million dollar clout and a new home at CBS, TV's funniest lame duck has nothing to scowl about. *Entertainment Weekly*, pp. 24–26.

White, M. (1992). Ideological analysis and television. In R. C. Allen (Ed.), *Channels of discourse, reassembled* (pp. 161–202). Chapel Hill: University of North Carolina Press.

Additional Samples
Ideological Criticism

Berger, Arthur Asa. *Media Analysis Techniques*. Newbury Park, CA: Sage, 1991, numerous essays.

Bodroghkozy, Aniko. "'We're the Young Generation and We've Got Something to Say': A Gramscian Analysis of Entertainment Television and the Youth Rebellion of the 1960s." *Critical Studies in Mass Communication*, 8 (June 1991), 217–30.

Condit, Celeste Michelle. "Hegemony in a Mass-Mediated Society: Concordance about Reproductive Technologies." *Critical Studies in Mass Communication*, 11 (September 1994), 205–30.

Cooks, Leda M., Mark P. Orbe, and Carol S. Bruess. "The Fairy Tale Theme in Popular Culture: A Semiotic Analysis of *Pretty Woman*. *Women's Studies in Communication*, 16 (Fall 1993), 86–104.

Fang, Yew-Jin. "'Riots' and Demonstrations in the Chinese Press: A Case Study of Language and Ideology." *Discourse and Society*, 54 (October 1994), 463–81.

Franklin, Sarah. "Deconstructing 'Desperateness': The Social Construction of Infertility in Popular Representations of New Reproductive Technologies." In *The New Reproductive Technologies*. Ed. Maureen McNeil, Ian Varcoe, and Steven Yearley. London: MacMillan, 1990, pp. 200–29.

Frentz, Thomas S., and Thomas B. Farrell. "Conversion of America's Consciousness: The Rhetoric of *The Exorcist*." *Quarterly Journal of Speech*, 61 (February 1975), 40–47.

Frentz, Thomas S., and Janice Hocker Rushing. "Integrating Ideology and Archetype in Rhetorical Criticism, Part II: A Case Study of *Jaws*." *Quarterly Journal of Speech*, 79 (February 1993), 61–81.

German, Kathleen M. "Frank Capra's *Why We Fight* Series and the American Audience." *Western Journal of Speech Communication*, 54 (Spring 1990), 237–48.

Hackett, Robert A., and Zuezhi Zhao. "Challenging a Master Narrative: Peace Protest and Opinion/Editorial Discourse in the US Press During the Gulf War." *Discourse and Society*, 5 (October 1994), 509–41.

Haines, Harry W. "'What Kind of War?': An Analysis of the Vietnam Veterans Memorial." *Critical Studies in Mass Communication*, 3 (March 1986), 1–20.

LaFountain, Marc J. "Foucault and Dr. Ruth." *Critical Studies in Mass Communication*, 6 (June 1989), 123–37.

Lessl, Thomas M. "Science and the Sacred Cosmos: The Ideological Rhetoric of Carl Sagan." *Quarterly Journal of Speech*, 71 (May 1985), 175–87.

Marvin, Carolyn. "Theorizing the Flagbody: Symbolic Dimensions of the Flag Desecration Debate, or, Why the Bill of Rights Does Not Fly in the Ballpark." *Critical Studies in Mass Communication*, 8 (June 1991), 119–38.

McGee, Michael Calvin. "The Origins of 'Liberty': A Feminization of Power." *Communication Monographs*, 47 (March 1980), 23–45.

Morris, Richard, and Philip Wander. "Native American Rhetoric: Dancing in the Shadows of the Ghost Dance." *Quarterly Journal of Speech*, 76 (May 1990), 164–91.

Murphy, John M. "Domesticating Dissent: The Kennedys and the Freedom Rides." *Communication Monographs*, 59 (March 1992), 61–78.

Nakayama, Thomas K. "Show/Down Time: 'Race,' Gender, Sexuality, and Popular Culture." *Critical Studies in Mass Communication*, 11 (June 1994), 162–79.

Parry-Giles, Trevor. "Ideological Anxiety and the Censored Text: *Real Lives— At the Edge of the Union.*" *Critical Studies in Mass Communication*, 11 (March 1994), 54–72.

Rojo, Luisa Martín. "Division and Rejection: From the Personification of the Gulf Conflict to the Demonization of Saddam Hussein." *Discourse and Society*, 6 (January 1995), 49–80.

Rushing, Janice Hocker. "E.T. as Rhetorical Transcendence." *Quarterly Journal of Speech*, 71 (May 1985), 188–203.

Rushing, Janice Hocker. "Evolution of 'The New Frontier' in *Alien* and *Aliens*: Patriarchal Co-optation of the Feminine Archetype." *Quarterly Journal of Speech*, 75 (February 1989), 1–24.

Rushing, Janice Hocker. "Mythic Evolution of 'The New Frontier' in Mass Mediated Rhetoric." *Critical Studies in Mass Communication*, 3 (September 1986), 265–96.

Rushing, Janice Hocker. "The Rhetoric of the American Western Myth." *Communication Monographs*, 50 (March 1983), 14–32.

Rushing, Janice Hocker. "Ronald Reagan's 'Star Wars' Address: Mythic Containment of Technical Reasoning." *Quarterly Journal of Speech*, 72 (November 1986), 415–33.

Rushing, Janice Hocker, and Thomas S. Frentz. "The Frankenstein Myth in Contemporary Cinema." *Critical Studies in Mass Communication*, 6 (March 1989), 61–80.

Salvador, Michael. "The Rhetorical Subversion of Cultural Boundaries: The National Consumers' League." *Southern Communication Journal*, 59 (Summer 1994), 318–32.

Scult, Allen, Michael Calvin McGee, and J. Kenneth Kuntz. "Genesis and Power: An Analysis of the Biblical Story of Creation." *Quarterly Journal of Speech*, 72 (May 1986), 113–31.

Shah, Hemant, and Michael C. Thornton. "Racial Ideology in U.S. Mainstream News Magazine Coverage of Black-Latino Interaction, 1980–1992." *Critical Studies in Mass Communication*, 11 (June 1994), 141–61.

Short, Brant. "'Reconstructed, But Unregenerate': *I'll Take My Stand's* Rhetorical Vision of Progress." *Southern Communication Journal*, 59 (Winter 1994), 112–24.

Sloop, John M. "'Apology Made to Whoever Pleases': Cultural Discipline and the Grounds of Interpretation." *Communication Quarterly*, 42 (Fall 1994), 345–62.

Solomon, Martha. "'With Firmness in the Right': The Creation of Moral Hegemony in Lincoln's Second Inaugural." *Communication Reports*, 1 (Winter 1988), 32–37.

Taylor, Bryan C. "*Fat Man and Little Boy*: The Cinematic Representation of Interests in the Nuclear Weapons Organization." *Critical Studies in Mass Communication*, 10 (December 1993), 367–94.

Trujillo, Nick. "Interpreting (the Work and the Talk of) Baseball: Perspectives on Ballpark Culture." *Western Journal of Communication*, 56 (Fall 1992), 350–71.

Trujillo, Nick, and Leah R. Ekdom. "Sportswriting and American Cultural Values: The 1984 Chicago Cubs." *Critical Studies in Mass Communication*, 2 (September 1985), 262–81.

Wander, Philip. "The Aesthetics of Fascism." *Journal of Communication*, 33 (Spring 1983), 70–78.

Wander, Philip. "The Angst of the Upper Class." *Journal of Communication*, 29 (Autumn 1979), 85–88.

Wander, Philip C. "The John Birch and Martin Luther King Symbols in the Radical Right." *Western Speech*, 35 (Winter 1971), 4–14.

Wander, Philip. "On the Meaning of 'Roots.'" *Journal of Communication*, 27 (Autumn 1977), 64–69.

Wander, Philip. "The Rhetoric of American Foreign Policy." *Quarterly Journal of Speech*, 70 (November 1984), 339–61.

Wander, Philip C. "Salvation Through Separation: The Image of the Negro in the American Colonization Society." *Quarterly Journal of Speech*, 57 (February 1971), 57–67.

Wander, Philip C. "The Savage Child: The Image of the Negro in the Pro-Slavery Movement." *Southern Speech Communication Journal*, 37 (Summer 1972), 335–60.

Wander, Philip. "'The Waltons': How Sweet It Was." *Journal of Communication*, 26 (Autumn 1976), 148–54.

Zagacki, Kenneth S. "The Rhetoric of American Decline: Paul Kennedy, Conservatives, and the Solvency Debate." *Western Journal of Communication*, 56 (Fall 1992), 372–93.

9

Metaphoric Criticism

The first extended treatment of metaphor was provided by Aristotle in the *Rhetoric* and *Poetics*. "Metaphor," he asserted, "is the transference of a name from the object to which it has a natural application; . . ."[1] Aristotle's definition and the treatment of metaphor by those who continued to build on it set the direction for the study of metaphor for the next several centuries.

A major dimension of the early and narrow view of metaphor was that metaphor is decoration or ornamentation. It was seen as a figure of speech or linguistic embroidery that the rhetor uses only occasionally to give extra force to language. Metaphor, explained Aristotle, "gives clearness, charm, and distinction to the style; . . ."[2] Cicero also held this view, believing that "there is no mode of embellishment . . . that throws a greater lustre upon language; . . ."[3] To summarize this dimension of metaphor, metaphors "are not necessary, they are just nice."[4]

When metaphor is seen as decoration, it also is regarded as a matter of extraordinary rather than ordinary language; it is a deviant form of language. As Aristotle wrote in the *Poetics*, metaphors "create an unusual element in the diction by their not being in ordinary speech."[5] The view that metaphor deviates from normal language use continued to be held long past the Classical Age. Thomas Hobbes, in the sixteenth and seventeenth centuries, held that metaphor frustrates the process of communicating thoughts and thus knowledge. He considered metaphor to be one of four abuses of speech because we "deceive others" when we use metaphor.[6] Rhetorical theorists into the nineteenth century expressed a similar view of metaphor. Richard Whately, for example, suggested that the use of metaphor departs "from the plain and strictly appropriate Style. . . ."[7]

Because metaphor was seen as linguistic embellishment that made it different from the usual use of language, theorists saw the formulation of rules for its use as quite appropriate. Throughout the history of the treatment of metaphor, strong warnings have been given against the improper use of metaphor. Although Aristotle stated in the *Poetics* that metaphor is not something that can be taught,[8] he provided guidelines for its proper use; a metaphor should not be "ridiculous," "too grand," "too much in the vein of tragedy," or "far-fetched."[9] Cicero's writings on metaphor provide another illustration of the kinds of rules offered for its proper use. A metaphor must bear some resemblance to what it pictures, and it should give clarity to a point rather than confuse it.[10]

An expanded view of metaphor goes beyond the notion that it is a decorative use of language and is the perspective assumed by the metaphoric critic, a perspective developed in the communication field by theorists such as Michael Osborn[11] and Robert L. Ivie.[12] The starting point for this new perspective that has developed on metaphor is how language relates to reality. Underlying this view is the assumption that we cannot know reality in any objective way.[13] We do not stand apart from the world and perceive reality and then interpret or give it meaning. Rather, we have or know a reality only through the language by which we describe it. We constitute reality through our use of symbols.

Metaphor is a basic way by which the process of using symbols to know reality occurs. Whatever language we select as the means through which to view reality, it treats that portion of reality *as* something, thus creating it and making it an object of experience for us. Reality, then, is simply the world as seen from a particular description or language; it is whatever we describe it *as*. Whatever vocabulary or language we use to describe reality is a metaphor because it enables us to see reality *as* something. Phenomena in the world become objects of reality or knowledge only because of the symbols/metaphors that make them accessible to us.

A number of theorists in various fields have helped to transform the narrow view of metaphor into one in which it is seen as central to thought and to our knowledge and experience of reality.[14] Although his equation of metaphor with thought was largely ignored, in the late nineteenth century, Friedrich Nietsche argued that metaphor is a process by which we encounter our world: "A nerve-stimulus, first transformed into a percept! First metaphor! The percept again copied into a sound! Second metaphor! And each time he leaps completely out of one sphere right into the midst of an entirely different one.''[15] I. A. Richards, whose contributions to the development of an expanded view of metaphor were particularly significant, saw metaphor as ''a borrowing between and intercourse of *thoughts*, a transaction between contexts.'' Thus, metaphor is an omnipresent principle of thought and language: ''Thought is metaphoric, and proceeds by comparison, and the metaphors of language derive therefrom.''[16] All thought is metaphoric, Richards argued, because when we attribute meaning, we are simply seeing in one context an aspect similar to one we encountered in an earlier context.

Kenneth Burke, too, suggested that metaphor plays a critical role ''in the discovery and description of 'the truth.' ''[17] ''If we employ the word 'character' as a general term for whatever can be thought of as distinct (any thing, pattern, situation, structure, nature, person, object, act, rôle, process, event, etc.,),'' he explained, ''then we could say that metaphor tells us something about one character as considered from the point of view of another character. And to consider A from the point of view of B is, of course, to use B as a *perspective* upon A.''[18] In the view of metaphor expressed by Burke and others, then, metaphor occurs prior to and generates the discovery of ideas.

The metaphoric process that allows us to know and experience reality constructs a particular reality for us according to the terminology we choose for the description of reality. It serves as a structuring principle, focusing on particular aspects of a phenomenon and hiding others; thus, each metaphor produces a different description of the ''same'' reality. In Max Black's words: ''Suppose I look at the night sky through a piece of heavily smoked glass on which certain lines have been left clear. Then I shall see only the stars that can be made to lie on the lines previously prepared upon the screen, and the stars I do see will be seen as organized by the screen's structure. We can think of a metaphor as such a screen. . . .''[19]

The metaphor that ''time is money'' demonstrates in more concrete terms how the use of a particular metaphor can affect our thought and experience of reality. This metaphor, reflected in common expressions in our culture such as, ''This gadget will *save* you hours,'' ''I've *invested* a lot of time in her,'' and ''You need to *budget* your time,'' has led us to experience the reality of time in a particular way. Because we conceive of time as money, we understand and experience it as something that can be spent, budgeted, wasted, and saved. Telephone-message units, hotel-room rates, yearly budgets, and interest on loans are examples of how time is money.

Yet another case of how our selection of a particular metaphor affects our perception and experience of reality is the metaphor that "argument is war." That we tend to see an argument through the metaphor of war is evidenced in such expressions as, "He *attacked* my argument," "I *demolished* her argument," "I *won* the argument," and "He *shot down* all of my arguments." As a consequence of the war metaphor, we experience an argument as something we actually can win or lose. We view the person with whom we engage in the argument as an opponent. We may find a position indefensible and thus abandon it and adopt a new line of attack. In contrast, if we used a different metaphor on argument, "argument is a dance," participants would be seen as performers; their goal would be performing in a balanced, harmonious, and aesthetically pleasing way. With the selection of a different metaphor, we would view and experience arguments differently.[20]

By organizing reality in particular ways, our selected metaphors also prescribe how we are to act. Metaphors contain implicit assumptions, points of view, and evaluations. They organize attitudes toward whatever they describe and provide motives for acting in certain ways. Because of the metaphor that time is money, for example, we expect particular actions from others. We expect to be paid according to amount of time worked, and we decide whether to engage in certain activities according to whether the time spent will be worthwhile or sufficiently valuable. Similarly, once a metaphor of "blighted area" is used to describe a neighborhood—a metaphor of disease—we are motivated to remove the blight and thus cure the disease. Were the same neighborhood to be labeled a "folk community," our evaluation of it would be positive and would focus on the neighborhood's homeyness, stability, and informal networks of support. We then would be motivated to preserve the community as it is.[21] Whatever metaphor is used to label and experience a phenomenon, then, suggests evaluations of it and appropriate behavior in response.

With a view of metaphor as a way of knowing also came new perspectives on how metaphor functions. One influential theory of this process, interaction theory, was suggested by Black. An interaction view of metaphor begins with the notion that metaphor consists of a juxtaposition of two terms normally regarded as belonging to different classes of experience. One term is called the *tenor, principal subject,* or *focus;* the other is the *vehicle, secondary subject,* or *frame.*[22] In the metaphor, "My roommate is a pig," for example, the roommate is the tenor, principal subject, or focus, and pig is the vehicle, secondary subject, or frame.

The interaction theory's unique contribution lies in its explanation of how the tenor and vehicle are related. The two are seen as related by a "system of associated commonplaces," entailments, or characteristics that we habitually associate with objects and events.[23] Each tenor and vehicle entails certain characteristics, and in their interaction to create a metaphor, those associated with the vehicle are used to organize conceptions of the tenor. When the tenor and vehicle share some associated commonplaces, they join in a metaphor.[24] In the metaphor, "My roommate is a pig," we use one system of commonplaces (those dealing with pigs) to filter or organize our conception of another system (that of the roommate). As the associated characteristics of the tenor and vehicle interact, some are emphasized and others are suppressed. In addition, we recognize that there are both similarities and differences between the two systems of characteristics.[25]

When metaphor is seen as a way of knowing the world that emerges from the interaction of the associated characteristics of the tenor and vehicle, metaphor comes to have a particular relationship to argument. When metaphor was seen as decoration and as a deviant form of language, metaphor was thought to play no role in argument; it was a matter of style without argumentative function. In the new under-standing of metaphor, in contrast, metaphor serves an argumentative function in a very basic way: metaphor constitutes argument. Metaphor does not simply provide support to an argument; the structure of the metaphor itself argues. It explicates the appropriateness of the associated characteristics of the vehicle to those of the tenor and thus invites auditors to adopt the resulting perspective. If the audience finds the associated characteristics acceptable and sees the appropriateness of linking the two systems of characteristics, the audience accepts the argument.[26]

Steven Perry explains how metaphor constitutes (rather than merely illustrates) argument in his study of the infestation metaphor in Hitler's rhetoric: "Hitler's critique of the Jew's status as a cultural being . . . is not illustrated by the metaphor of parasitism; it is *constituted* by this metaphor. . . ."[27] The figurative language is not supplementary or subordinate to the argument; it is itself Hitler's argument. The listener or reader who does not reject the interaction of the characteristics of *infestation* and *Jews* has accepted a claim about what the facts are and the evaluation expressed in the metaphor. A disease metaphor argues with particular force as a result of this same process. The horror, mystery, and repugnance associated with diseases such as AIDS and cancer are suggested to inhere in the metaphor's tenor as well.[28] A metaphor, then, argues just as typical argumentative structures do, but it usually does so more efficiently and comprehensively.[29]

Procedures

Using metaphors as units of analysis, the critic analyzes an artifact in a process of four basic steps: (1) formulating a research question and selecting an artifact; (2) selecting a unit of analysis; (3) analyzing the artifact; and (4) writing the critical essay.

Formulating a Research Question and Selecting an Artifact

The first step in the process of rhetorical criticism is to develop a research question to ask about rhetoric and to select a rhetorical artifact to analyze that will provide an initial answer to the question.

Selecting a Unit of Analysis

The critic's next step is to select a unit of analysis that can help the critic answer the research question. The unit of analysis is that aspect of the artifact to which the critic attends in the analysis. The unit of analysis provided by metaphoric criticism is the metaphor.

Analyzing the Artifact

In criticism in which metaphors are used as units of analysis, the critic analyzes an artifact in four steps: (1) examination of the artifact for a general sense of its dimensions and context; (2) isolation of the metaphors in the artifact; (3) sorting of the metaphors into groups according to vehicle if the metaphors deal with the same tenor or subject or according to topic if the metaphors deal with various subjects; and (4) analysis of the metaphors to discover how they function for the rhetor and audience.[30]

Examination of Artifact as a Whole. The first step for the critic is to become familiar with the text or elements of the artifact and its context to gain a sense of the complete experience of the artifact. Attention to the context is particularly important because although some metaphors generally are understood in particular ways without attention to the context in which they are used, the meaning of most metaphors must be reconstructed from clues in the setting, occasion, audience, and rhetor. The meaning of calling a person a pig, for example, would be different when applied to a police officer in the context of the late Sixties than if applied to a teenager in her messy room. Information about the context of the artifact can be gathered in a variety of ways, including a review of rhetoric contemporaneous with the artifact, the audience's reactions to the artifact, historical treatments of the context, and previous essays of criticism on the artifact.

Isolation of Metaphors. The second step in metaphoric analysis is to isolate the metaphors employed by the rhetor, focusing on particular vehicles or tenors according to the critic's research question. A brief selection from Martin Luther King, Jr.'s speech, "I Have a Dream," illustrates this procedure. In the introduction of his speech, King said: "Five score years ago, a great American, in whose symbolic shadow we stand today, signed the Emancipation Proclamation. This momentous decree came as a great beacon light of hope to millions of Negro slaves, who had been seared in the flames of withering injustice. It came as a joyous daybreak to end the long night of their captivity."

The critic who seeks to understand King's worldview could identify these metaphors: *in whose symbolic shadow we stand, great beacon light of hope, seared in the flames of withering injustice, daybreak,* and *long night of their captivity.* In many instances, only the vehicle is actually present in the artifact, and the tenor is implied. In this passage, King includes both tenor and vehicle in most of his metaphors: hope is a beacon light, injustice is flame, the Emancipation Proclamation is daybreak, captivity is the long night. His metaphor of standing in the symbolic shadow of Lincoln, however, does not explicitly include a tenor. Implied is a tenor of history and past struggles that cast their shadow and lend their spirit to the current situation. The critic, then, needs to look for metaphors where both tenor and vehicle are present and where only the vehicle is stated.

Many metaphors are so basic to our way of conceptualizing experience that their analysis does not yield particularly productive insights. The critic probably does not want to include such metaphors in the list of metaphors developed at this step. The metaphors of being *in* love or of *falling* into a depression, for example, may not be important enough to identify as metaphors in the artifact being analyzed. Typically, though, each examination of the artifact produces previously overlooked metaphors as the critic becomes more sensitized to metaphors that are disguised initially by their apparently literal usage. At the end of this part of the process, the critic has reduced the text of the artifact to an abridged version of metaphors and brief descriptions of their context.

Sorting of Metaphors.   In the next step of the procedure, the critic sorts the identified metaphors into groups, looking for patterns in metaphor use. The metaphors are sorted or grouped either according to vehicle or tenor, depending on the research question. In Martin Luther King, Jr.'s speech, for example, the critic may group metaphors used by King into tenors—those that deal with Blacks, the Constitution, and America. If the critic is studying the rhetor's use of metaphor around one topic, then the metaphors may be grouped around similar vehicles. In a study, for example, of how the arts are presented in the publicity surrounding blockbuster art shows—such as the King Tut, Picasso, or impressionist exhibitions—a critic may discover that the metaphors used for the arts may be grouped into a number of vehicles. Vehicles to

describe art such as *parade, hoopla, extravaganza, show-stopper, makes
a debut, trails heavy clouds of hype,* and *thrills* could be grouped into
a category of art as entertainment because the vehicles all have to do
with notions we associate with viewing performances and shows. Other
vehicles used to describe art in the discourse surrounding the exhibition,
such as *treasure, jackpot, riches, the shine of gold, priceless, golden
gleam, resplendent,* and *economic impact* would be placed in a different
category—perhaps art as wealth.[31]

Analysis of Metaphors.   In this step, the groups of metaphors—either
metaphors around various tenors or various vehicles around the same
tenor—are analyzed to reveal the system of metaphorical concepts in
the artifact. Here, the critic suggests what effects the use of the various
metaphors may have on the audience and how the metaphors function
to argue for a particular attitude toward the ideas presented. In the effort
to analyze the metaphors used and how they limit and facilitate the
audience's likelihood of adopting particular perspectives, the critic may
find the following questions useful. These are not, of course, the only
questions the critic can ask to help in the analysis of the metaphors
identified. Depending on the critic's interest, only one or two of these
may be asked, or other questions may be developed to get at the critic's
particular concerns.[32]

1. What ideas are highlighted and what ideas are masked as a result
   of the metaphors used?
2. What image do the metaphors convey of the tenor or tenors of the
   artifact?
3. What do the metaphors suggest about the worldview of the rhetor?
4. Do the metaphors used by the rhetor facilitate or hinder the
   accomplishment of the rhetor's goals?
5. What attitudes and values undergird the metaphors, and how do
   these attitudes and values direct audiences' attitudes and motivations to act?
6. Are the metaphors internally consistent? If not, what is the effect
   of the inconsistency?
7. How are the metaphors organized in the artifact? Do they occur
   primarily in the introduction or the conclusion? Do they recur
   throughout the rhetoric? Does one metaphor dominate the others
   because of its placement in the structure?
8. Do the metaphors that characterize a body of rhetoric change over
   time? If so, how and by what apparent pressures?
9. Do the metaphors corroborate otherwise inconclusive rhetorical
   cues? Do the rhetor's metaphors, when compared with other
   habitual rhetorical behaviors of the rhetor, reinforce tentative
   conclusion the critic is drawing from the artifact?

Writing the Critical Essay

After completion of the analysis, the critic writes an essay that includes five major components: (1) an introduction, in which the research question, its contribution to rhetorical theory, and its significance are discussed; (2) description of the artifact and its context; (3) description of the unit of analysis, the metaphor; (4) report of the findings of the analysis, in which the critic reveals the metaphors, their patterns, and their function in the text; and (5) discussion of the contribution the analysis makes to answering the research question.

Sample Essays

The following essays provide samples of criticism in which metaphors are used as units of analysis to answer various research questions. In Michael P. Graves' essay on metaphors in Quaker sermons, he is guided by the research question, "What conceptual functions do metaphors serve?" In his analysis of an advertisement for Honda, Robert Huesca asks the research question, "How can metaphors be used to target particular audiences without alienating those who do not fit precisely the characteristics of those audiences?" Marla Kanengieter-Wildeson's essay analyzing a building by architect Michael Graves focuses on visual metaphors, and her analysis is directed toward answering the research question, "How are ideologies subverted through the use of visual metaphors?"

Notes

[1] Aristotle, *Poetics*, 21.

[2] Aristotle, *Rhetoric*, 3.2.

[3] Cicero, *On Oratory and Orators*, 3.41.

[4] Andrew Ortony, "Metaphor: A Multidimensional Problem," in *Metaphor and Thought*, ed. Andrew Ortony (Cambridge: Cambridge University Press, 1979), p. 3.

[5] Aristotle, *Poetics*, 22.

[6] Thomas Hobbes, *Leviathan*, ed. C. B. MacPherson (1651; rpt. New York: Penguin, 1951), pt. I, chpt. 4, p. 102.

[7] Richard Whately, *Elements of Rhetoric* (New York: Harper, 1864), pt. 3, chpt. 2.3.

[8] Aristotle, *Poetics*, 22.

[9] Aristotle, *Rhetoric*, 3.34.

[10] Cicero, 3.39.

[11] Michael M. Osborn and Douglas Ehninger, "The Metaphor in Public Address," *Communication Monographs*, 29 (August 1962), 223–34; John Waite Bowers and Michael M. Osborn, "Attitudinal Effects of Selected Types of Concluding Metaphors in Persuasive Speeches," *Communication Monographs*, 33 (June 1966), 147–55; Michael Osborn,

"Archetypal Metaphor in Rhetoric: The Light-Dark Family," *Quarterly Journal of Speech*, 53 (April 1967), 115–26; Michael M. Osborn, "The Evolution of the Theory of Metaphor in Rhetoric," *Western Speech*, 31 (Spring 1967), 121–31; and Michael Osborn, "The Evolution of the Archetypal Sea in Rhetoric and Poetic," *Quarterly Journal of Speech*, 63 (December 1977), 347–63.

12 Robert L. Ivie, "The Metaphor of Force in Prowar Discourse: The Case of 1812," *Quarterly Journal of Speech*, 68 (August 1982), 240–53; Robert L. Ivie, "Speaking 'Common Sense' About the Soviet Threat: Reagan's Rhetorical Stance," *Western Journal of Communication*, 48 (Winter 1984), 39–50; Robert L. Ivie, "Literalizing the Metaphor of Soviet Savagery: President Truman's Plain Style," *Southern Communication Journal*, 51 (Winter 1986), 91–105; and Robert L. Ivie, "Metaphor and the Rhetorical Invention of Cold War 'Idealists,'" *Communication Monographs*, 54 (June 1987), 165–82.

13 See, for example, Richard Rorty, *Philosophy and the Mirror of Nature* (Princeton: Princeton University Press, 1979), pp. 163, 170.

14 For summaries of the history of the treatment of metaphor, see: Osborn, "The Evolution of the Theory of Metaphor in Rhetoric"; and Mark Johnson, "Introduction: Metaphor in the Philosophical Tradition," in *Philosophical Perspectives on Metaphor*, ed. Mark Johnson (Minneapolis: University of Minnesota Press, 1981), pp. 3–47.

15 Friedrich Nietzsche, "On Truth and Falsity in their Ultramoral Sense," in *The Complete Works of Friedrich Nietzsche*, ed. Oscar Levy, trans. Maximilian A. Mügge, II (New York: Macmillan, 1911), p. 178.

16 I. A. Richards, *The Philosophy of Rhetoric* (London: Oxford University Press, 1936), p. 94.

17 Kenneth Burke, *A Grammar of Motives* (1945; rpt. Berkeley: University of California Press, 1969), p. 503.

18 Burke, pp. 503–04.

19 Max Black, *Models and Metaphors: Studies in Language and Philosophy* (Ithaca, New York: Cornell University Press, 1962), p. 41.

20 These examples were suggested in George Lakoff and Mark Johnson, *Metaphors We Live By* (Chicago: University of Chicago Press, 1980), pp. 4, 7–9.

21 This example was suggested in Donald A. Schön, "Generative Metaphor: A Perspective on Problem-Setting in Social Policy," in *Metaphor and Thought*, ed. Andrew Ortony (Cambridge: Cambridge University Press, 1979), pp. 265–68.

22 The terms, *tenor* and *vehicle*, were suggested by Richards, p. 96; *principal subject* and *secondary subject* by Max Black, "More About Metaphor," in *Metaphor and Thought*, ed. Andrew Ortony (Cambridge: Cambridge University Press, 1979), p. 28; and *focus* and *frame* by Black, *Models and Metaphors*, p. 28.

23 The term, *associated commonplaces*, was suggested by Black, *Models and Metaphors*, p. 40; *entailments* was suggested by Lakoff and Johnson, p. 9.

24 For a summary of the interaction theory of metaphor and of the contributions of various theorists to it, see Johnson, pp. 27–35.

25 For more on the notion of differences in the operation of metaphor, see Richards, p. 127.

26 Steven Perry, "Rhetorical Functions of the Infestation Metaphor in Hitler's Rhetoric," *Central States Speech Journal*, 34 (Winter 1983), p. 230; and Carroll C. Arnold, *Criticism of Oral Rhetoric* (Columbus, Ohio: Charles E. Merrill, 1974), p. 203.

27 Perry, p. 230.

28 Perry, p. 231; and Susan Sontag, *Illness as Metaphor* (New York: Farrar, Straus and Giroux, 1978), pp. 82–88.

29 Michael Leff, "I. Topical Invention and Metaphoric Interaction," *Southern Speech Communication Journal*, 48 (Spring 1983), 226.

[30] These steps in the process of metaphoric criticism came largely from Robert L. Ivie, "Metaphor and the Rhetorical Invention of Cold War 'Idealists,'" *Communication Monographs*, 54 (June 1987), 167–68.

[31] Sonja K. Foss and Anthony J. Radich, "Metaphors in 'Treasures of Tutankhamen': Implications for Aesthetic Education," *Art Education*, 37 (January 1984), 8.

[32] These questions were suggested by: Kathleen Hall Jamieson, "The Metaphoric Cluster in the Rhetoric of Pope Paul VI and Edmund G. Brown, Jr.," *Quarterly Journal of Speech*, 66 (February 1980), 51, 53, 63, 64, 71, 72; Michael M. Osborn, "Archetypal Metaphor in Rhetoric: The Light-Dark Family," *Quarterly Journal of Speech*, 53 (April 1967), 115–26; Robert L. Ivie, "Literalizing the Metaphor of Soviet Savagery: President Truman's Plain Style," *Southern Speech Communication Journal*, 51 (Winter 1986), 96–100, 105; Roderick P. Hart, *Modern Rhetorical Criticism* (Glenview, Illinois: Scott, Foresman, 1990), pp. 219–28; Perry, p. 235; and Sontag, pp. 82–88.

Functions of Key Metaphors in Early Quaker Sermons, 1671–1700

Michael P. Graves

Scholarly interest in metaphor in rhetorical discourse has been prominent in speech communication journals.[1] Scholars have sought to explain
how metaphors function in several kinds of rhetorical situations. There
has been a similar burgeoning of inquiry into metaphor by anthro-
pologists and sociolinguists.[2] This essay seeks to contribute to our
understanding of metaphor by analyzing key metaphors[3] in surviving
Quaker sermons from the years 1671–1700.[4]

These sermons provide a rich body of discourse for the study of
metaphor. The early Quaker notion of homiletics placed supreme
importance on the immediate revelation of truth from God. The preacher
acted as "midwife" or "medium" in the communication of truth to an
audience.[5] In such a context, advanced preparation was shunned,
including the use of notes or manuscripts. One of the keenest statements
revealing early Quaker attitudes toward preaching was made by William
Penn: "Christian ministers are to minister *what they receive* . . . so that
we are not only not to *steal* from our neighbors, but we are not to *study*
nor to speak our *own words*. . . . We are to minister, *as the oracles of
God*; if so, then we must receive *from Christ*, God's great oracle, what
we are to minister."[6] Because they spoke impromptu, Quaker preachers
tended to reject detailed theological arguments and extended scriptural
exposition, both of which would pose considerable challenges to a
speaker in an impromptu setting. They also rejected the "doctrine-use"
pattern of sermon organization which was widely accepted in the century
by Puritans.[7] Instead, Quaker preachers relied on metaphor to tie their
sermons together conceptually. In a seminal essay on early Quaker style,
Jackson Cope identified "the essential quality of seventeenth-century
Quaker expression" as "a tendency to break down the boundary between
literalness and metaphor, between conceptions and things."[8] For early
Quakers, metaphor not only transcended its traditional function as
ornament in Renaissance rhetoric, but became the conceptual
underpinning of discourse.[9]

From *Quarterly Journal of Speech*, 69 (November 1983), 364–378. Used by permission
of the Speech Communication Association and the author.

Let us look at the major kinds of metaphors used by Quaker preachers in the seventeenth century. Then we shall look at how they functioned in the discourse.

I

The surviving sermons contain five recurrent clusters[10] of metaphors that are employed throughout the period 1671–1700 and across the twenty-one preachers included.[11] The five clusters which will be examined include: (1) the *Light/Dark* cluster, (2) the *Voice* cluster, (3) the *Seed* cluster, (4) the *Hunger/Thirst* cluster, and (5) the *Pilgrimage* cluster.[12]

Light/Dark

Early Quakers assimilated light/dark imagery from the Bible and built a belief system around the concept of the "Inward Light" (never "Inner Light") of Christ, taking literally the first chapter of John's Gospel which announces that Christ is the light that enlightens every person. In contrast to Calvinists, Quakers taught that everyone could be saved because the Light could open anyone's eyes to spiritual reality. They maintained that people, even religious people, dwelt in the realm of shadow but that the Light dispelled the shadow and the clouds of spiritual ignorance.

In the sermons, light/dark imagery is so pervasive that it is impossible to understand other clusters of metaphor without understanding the early Quaker vision of light and dark. Light imagery appears in sixty-five of seventy-four sermons; darkness or night imagery appears in fifty-five. Only five sermons do not express a variant of either light or dark imagery.[13]

Natural phenomena such as the sun, moon, stars, clouds, and fog become the most common vehicles for light/dark metaphors in the sermons. The "sun" or the "day" appeared in thirty-four of the sermons. The typical pattern was a variation of that presented by George Fox, the acknowledged founder of Quakerism, in a 1674 sermon:

> They come to se[e] him when ye Day is Come[,] ye Day Spring from on high. There is a naturall Day Springs upp—Rise to work[;] lye not in bed, till the Sun Rises, as outwardly: so Inwardly, The Day Spring from on high:—People have been in Darkness Long enough, when Immortality is brought to Light[,] then thei[r] Day Springs from on high that know, & ye Shadowes & Clouds to fly away, when ye morning breaks, the Sunn of Righteousness Arises with his heavenly praises, so now this day is Sprung from on high[. T]his is witnessed

> when he Comes to Rule in ye Day,—Soe now[,] as every man Comes
> under God[']s Teaching . . . the[y] Come to know ye Day of God .
> . . So here is god[']s Day[,] his everlasting day[,] his heavenly Day;
> his spirituall Day.[14]

The passage is a verbal mosaic of light and dark which focuses on the
dawning of day. It illustrates well Cope's description of the "incantatory
style": "an incredible repetition, a combining and recombining of a
cluster of words and phrases drawn from Scripture."[15] The appeal of
the passage lies in the identification of "God[']s Teaching," presumably
that reflected in the beliefs of Quakers, with the "Day spring on high."
"Shadows and clouds," along with "darkness," are identified with
unrighteousness and, by implication, false teaching.[16]

Quakers sometimes coupled false teaching with the ill effects of the
sun's heat. In a 1675 sermon, Fox contrasted the good effects of the
"righteous" sun with the evil effects of the "Papists['] Sun," which
"scorched ye Blade," and the sun of Anglicans, which "Scorched & went
down."[17] Those who beheld the "Sun of Righteousness," Fox told his
hearers, "never fear ye Persecutor[']s Sun."[18]

Early Quaker faith in the power of the Light is nowhere seen to better
advantage than in the following from Stephen Crisp, one of the best
itinerant preachers:

> What if a Company of People should combine together, and say, We
> will not have the Sun to shine upon the City of London; what course
> must we take? When the Sun is down, we will build a Bank or high
> Wall to intercept its Light; but notwithstanding all their Endeavours,
> when the Sun riseth, it will get over their high Banks and Wall; so
> all their Designs, and all the Contrivances against the Light of the
> Gospel, and against Christ the Sun of Righteousness, and against
> the Spirit of Christ, the Light will ascend and get over them, and
> break through all opposition.[19]

Here, the sun is the vehicle for the "Light of the Gospel," or the
"Spirit of Christ." The inevitability of the sun's rising in human
experience is called upon as witness to the inevitable rising of the "Sun
of Righteousness."

Sunlight, of course, provides vision, illuminating objects and path-
ways, and this natural characteristic also found metaphorical expression.
Samuel Waldenfield, in a classic statement of the core of early Quaker
belief, employed this motif for his appeal: "as the Light of the Sun
outwardly makes a discovery of Visible Things, so the inward Light of
the Son of God makes a Discovery of the invisible Things."[20] Many
similar examples could be cited. The use of light and vision is especially
important because of the blending of metaphor implied in the passage.
I will discuss this phenomenon later. Here I want only to note that there

is a natural blending of *Light/Dark* and *Pilgrimage* clusters since travel demands the light of day (or artificial light) to avoid dangers and reckon accurate directions.

Whereas the Quakers identified light with good (with the exception of its use to indicate persecution), they identified all that was dark with evil. The preachers referred to the state of the contemporary non-Quaker church as a "long Night of Darkness."[21] Crisp's estimate of the days prior to the advent of Quakerism is captured in this brief quotation: "There hath been a very Dark and Cloudy Day upon our Fore-Fathers, and also upon us, in the Days of our Ignorance."[22] Benjamin Coole used "clouds" to illustrate why people rejected God's grace: "Man by Sin hath darkened his own Mind, and clouded his Understanding, that he cannot see the Glory of God."[23] According to Richard Ashby, people in their natural state "are in the Dark, they are groping for the Wall, they are at an uncertainty."[24] Crisp spoke of a "Veil of Ignorance" that had fallen over people and asked, "what can Darkness see? What can Darkness discover?"[25] For anyone in the meeting who understood but rejected the message of Light, a "Curtain of Darkness"[26] would be drawn between God and his/her soul, and as Penn said, "There is nothing will remain, then, but Chains of Darkness, they that Loved Darkness here, shall be cast into utter Darkness, hereafter, even the Blackness of Darkness for ever."[27]

Light/Dark imagery was amplified in psychological force when contrasted in the same context. The quotations cited exhibit the strength of implied or explicit light-dark antithesis. On many occasions, notably during closing prayers, the preachers relied upon the tension. In 1687 Crisp prayed that God would "dispel the Clouds of Darkness that hath been upon the Sons and Daughters of Men." He also prayed for those "that have been driven away in a cloudy and dark Night," that they be "brought to a glorious and blessed Day, wherein they may enjoy the Gospel that brings Light to dark Souls."[28]

Many similar passages could be cited, but these are enough to show that the opposition of light to dark was the primary metaphor cluster of the sermons.

Voice

Second in importance to the *Light/Dark* cluster, and often used in conjunction with or juxtaposed to it, were images drawn from the early Quaker propensity to perceive the world in terms of silence and sound.[29] Quaker lifestyle placed high importance on silence and upon weighing one's words. Silent waiting was prerequisite to worship. The sermons, arising as impromptu expressions out of the silence, drew on the power of silence practiced as a discipline. Silence, as such, was mentioned in only five of the extant sermons. However, this fact should not be interpreted to mean that silence was viewed as unimportant by the preachers. Silence was a significant topic in Quaker journals, tracts, and theological writings.[30] Furthermore, the context of silent waiting which surrounded the sermons acted as nonverbal reaffirmation of its importance. The *Voice* metaphor, the other polarity from silence, was chosen almost as often as light imagery in the sermons. "Hearing the Voice" of God (or Christ, the Spirit, or even the Light) was used in thirty-nine sermons; similarly, Christ or God referred to as the "speaker" or "teacher," implying the Voice to be heeded, was used in seventeen sermons.

Fox's sermons are a repository of statements which reiterate the belief that people, if they wait patiently in silence, will hear the silence broken by the Voice of Christ. One of his appeals began with a recapitulation of the Adam and Eve story in which God was viewed as the "first speaker" who communicated with man and woman; Satan was the "second speaker," who beguiled the two with false words. Christ was seen as the "third speaker" who "bruises ye head of all false Teachers."[31] The following quotation typifies Fox's use of oral-aural imagery: "God is become ye Speaker againe, that was ye first Speaker in Paradise, God hath spoken to us by his Son. Here doe people come to hear his voice from Heaven."[32] It was, after all, the *Voice* of Christ, not the *Light*, that Fox used to describe his own spiritual experience after long search, and perhaps therein his emphasis on hearing the "voice of the teacher" finds psychological antecedent.[33] According to Fox, if people could shut out the opposing voices, especially that of the "second speaker," they would hear the Voice of the "first speaker" once again. Crisp, in 1688, also expressed concern about shutting out the false voices when he observed that those who are under the government of Christ "have been able . . . to make such a Distinction of Voices, and of Sounds, that they have been preserv'd from the Delusions of the Age."[34]

When Quaker preachers used "Word of God" (or "Word of the Lord"), they did not use the phrase to indicate the Bible. In the forty-four sermons that refer to the "Word" of God, the use clearly means "Christ the Word" or the "Word as spoken by God." Crisp is typical: "This great Change hath been wrought in many a Soul, by the Operation of the Word of God, of the inward Word, that inward Voice, when the Lord hath taken Men in hand himself."[35] This usage was consistent with early Quaker epistemology, which placed secondary emphasis on the Bible and primary importance on direct revelation.[36]

Crisp often used the imagery of the *Voice*. Sixteen of the thirty-two sermons of his which survive employ the metaphor. On one occasion he revealed: "It is Christ that they must hear; he is come so near to Men that they hear his Voice, and hear him tell us our very Thoughts."[37] Other preachers rehearsed essentially the same imagery. William Dewsbury expressed confidence that salvation "is entailled upon such Souls as hear the Voice of Christ."[38] Similarly, Waldenfield hoped "that People might be mindful of the Inward Voice of Christ to their Souls, that when he Speaks, they might hear."[39] In the passages cited thus far, especially those by Fox and Crisp, the blending of literalness and metaphor is striking. In fact, in most of these quotations, the reader cannot be certain if a literal voice or a metaphorical one is implied.

Given the Quaker view of man as the creature who lives in darkness, it is almost predictable that their imagery would at some point emphasize not only the importance of light, but also the presence of a voice that would guide a person along a dark path. The *Light/Dark* and *Voice* clusters were easily mixed, as in this quotation from Crisp:

> Blessed be God this Darkness is removed, this Vail [sic] is gone over and taken away; the Brightness of the Glory of the Gospel hath expell'd this Darkness, and thousands now a-days not only hear the Minister reprove them, but they hear a Voice within that doth reprove them for Iniquity. . . . God hath an immediate way of counselling and instructing.[40]

In another sermon, the blending of the *Voice* cluster with what I shall presently describe as the *Pilgrimage* cluster occurs: "There is a Voice that calls to People in our Days, to look behind them, for they are out of the way."[41] Thus, the images of *Light/Dark* and *Voice* are sometimes interchangeable and easily blended, and either suggests the idea of guidance while traveling on a journey or pilgrimage. The fascinating interaction of *Light* and *Voice* is set forth in a quotation from Crisp summarizing the goal of Quaker preaching: "To persuade all Men every where, that they believe in the Light, and hearken to the Voice of the Light in their own Consciences."[42] In the arresting juxtaposition, "Voice of the Light," Crisp seemed to be essaying the limits of early Quaker concepts through metaphor.

Seed

The third most common key metaphor was the *Seed*. The cluster partook of sets of interrelated animal and vegetable associations. On the one hand, it referred to the progeny of humans—we are all the "seed" of our ancestors. At the same time, it alluded to the phenomenon of botanical germination and growth. The principle of growth according to inherited traits is the same in either case. In the sermons, especially when the word "seed" was used apart from contextual modifiers, a rich integration of associations from both animal and vegetable realms was evoked. A variation of the *Seed* metaphor appears in twenty-six early Quaker sermons. It is used in three ways: (1) the Seed as the symbol of good or evil, Christ or Satan; (2) the Seed as the image of the indwelling of good or evil in a person's life; and (3) the Seed as the faithful believers, the progeny of Christ, the good seed.

Fox's use of "seed" referred back to the Old Testament promise that God "will put enmity between thee [the serpent] and the woman [Eve], and between thy seed and her seed; it shall bruise thy head, and thou shalt bruise his heel."[43] He identified the Seed with Christ: "All nations shall come to the blessing of this seed. *This seed is Christ*, that was promised to break the Serpent's power."[44] According to Fox, one could reject the good seed in favor of the serpent's seed: "They yt Crucifie ye Seed to ym selves a fresh, & quench ye Spirit of God in ym selves . . . entertain ye Evil Seed, and ye Evil Spirit yt brings ye Curse upon ym."[45]

Other preachers also talked to two seeds—one standing for the evil potential in humans, the other standing for human potential for good through Christ. Crisp said that "there is in every Man by nature the Seed and Root of all Sin and Rebellion against God."[46] On the other hand, there was offered hope "in him that was the promised Seed, whom God promised should break the Serpent[']s head."[47] Crisp talked about the "Persecution, Hatred and Enmity, between the Woman[']s Seed, and the Serpentine Seed. . . . So that it is not to be expected that the Seed of the Serpent . . . can love those that are born of the Woman's Seed.[48]

Eventually, the progeny of the union between Christ and man—the "planting of the Seed"—would come to resemble the parentage. Ultimately, the product itself would be called the "Seed." Crisp reminded listeners that the blessing of Abraham was promised "to the Seed, that is, to those that are in Christ."[49] He went on to refer to the Seed as Christ: "The Faithful are those that are obedient to Christ, who is the Seed of the Promise. . . . They must come to Christ the Seed."[50]

Quotations using the "Seed" thus far reveal a closer affinity to human heredity than to botany. However, many of the sermons employ the Seed image in a context explicitly tied to the process of germination and growth in plants.[51] Robert Barclay, the movement's most able apologist, likened Christ to a seed in the same way that Christ explained his impending death and resurrection to his disciples: "Every Plant, Seed or Grain that is placed in the Earth, it dies before it grows up. . . . It was necessary that the Son of God (the Prince of Life) should die . . . else he could not finish . . . the Sowing of that Seed . . . whereby we might come to have a share with him."[52] Thus Barclay identified Christ not only as fulfillment of the "seed" prophecy in the story of the Fall, but also as archetypal reenactment of the life-death cycle in nature.[53]

Quaker preachers also saw the Seed in terms dictated by Jesus in the Parable of the Sower.[54] Penn, for example, reminded his hearers to keep watch that Satan not "hinder the good Seed (the Word) from taking Root; and bringing forth Fruit."[55] Here we see the blending of the *Seed* and *Voice* clusters through the identification of "seed" and "word."

Although not employed to the extent of the *Light/Dark* or *Voice* metaphors, the image of the *Seed*, whether in the context of human progeny or that of agriculture, was an important metaphor in the sermons. It became a significant way to conceptualize the potential for growth, fruitfulness, life itself, and the life-death-rebirth cycle of Christian teaching. It also allowed the preachers to extend the polarizations of light-dark and voice-false voice to the good seed-evil seed, all of which conceptualized the world as enmity between two forces. The growth potential inherent in the Seed, however, introduced the ominous possibility that, given the proper encouragement, *either* seed could grow to maturity and bear fruit in any person.

Hunger/Thirst

The need for nourishment is universal. Only when hunger and thirst are satisfied can we turn to other human concerns such as shelter, clothing, protection from danger, development of relationships, etc. Early Quakers drew on the primal power of metaphors clustered around the needs for food and drink. They assimilated the patterns from the Bible and repeated, developed, and extended them in their sermons. They believed that people should hunger and thirst for God, just as they experience hunger and thirst for physical nourishment. Furthermore, they maintained that if people did not hunger and thirst after God, they would not find him: "These Persons are not hungry, and so they are not fed; they are not thirsty, and so they never obtain that which can satisfy the Soul."[56]

Quakers used several vehicles in the *Hunger/Thirst* cluster, but the two most prominent were "bread" and "water" (also including specific terms relating to water such as "fountain" and "well").[57] The former appears in twenty-three sermons, and the latter in seventeen. Either or both appear in thirty-three sermons.[58]

Passages of simple beauty are produced in the sermons when both bread and water images are combined. Fox announced that when people possess the Seed, they "all come to Eat of ye Living Bread yt comes down from Heaven & drink of ye Living Waters. . . . Here is ye pure standing Fellowship; Meet here, Feed here, Drink here."[59] Relying on concrete and universal experiences such as hunger and thirst, Fox was able to amplify abstractions such as "peace" and "reconciliation" which appeared prior to the passage just quoted. John Butcher later repeated the same image when he pointed out that in Quaker meetings, "many a time the Hungry have been satisfied with Bread, And the Fountain of Living Water hath been opened, and the Thirsty have been Drinking of it."[60]

In the sermons, God's "bread," used apart from "water," always implies the nourishment and comfort of a satisfied desire for food. James Park, for example, explained the result of drawing close to God in terms of the simple comfort of bread: "Then will your Bread (your Heavenly, Living Bread) be sure, and you will know the Breaking of it, and the Eating of it; that Bread which Christ gives, is that whereby we are Comforted and Refreshed."[61]

"Water," employed alone in a passage, was used in a manner paralleling "bread" that stressed its thirst-quenching rather than cleansing function. An anonymous preacher used water imagery to dissuade his hearers from following the preacher instead of discovering the true source of spiritual water: "O come and tast[e] and see, for your selves, don't come to us, to take Water at second-hand, but come to the Springs, where Water runs swiftly and sweetly. Come Friends, Drink of the Stream."[62]

The Hunger/Thirst cluster was blended with other key clusters. Crisp, for example, associated "bread" with "word": "For this is the Nourishment and the Heavenly Bread. . . . The Begotten of God are come to know the Vertue [sic] of the Divine Life, Christ Jesus, their Feeding and their Nourishment is by every Word that proceedeth out of the Mouth of God."[63] Similarly, Fox associated "hearing" with "feeding": "So now feed not on ye Serpent[']s food but feed on God[']s bread, & hear him from heaven:—see what all mankinde, hath gott, by feeding, & hearing of ye serpent."[64]

An incredible blending of Light/Dark, Seed, and Hunger/Thirst clusters is discovered in the following passage from Fox, illustrating the ease with which the metaphors were articulated together:

> In ye Old Covenant they had ye Outward Booths, & Feasts of Tabernacles; Now in ye New Covenant they come to be grafted into Christ Jesus, & in him everie Plant grows green allwaies in ye Second Adam. . . . As Christ said her [sic] yt believes in me Out of [his] belly shall flow Rivers of Living Water: Now is this True? Can Rivers Spring out of his Belly? This spake he of ye Spirit: You being Grafted into Christ ye Fountain by believing in ye Light. . . . From him ye Living Fountain do these Springs of Living Waters come; this spoke he of ye Spirit, this Spirituall River, & Fountain.[65]

Early Quaker preachers placed considerable reliance upon refer-ence to the primal drives for satisfaction of hunger and thirst. They conceptualized through metaphor the satisfaction and comfort they believed were afforded people who chose their manner of belief. The preference for simple food and drink, such as bread, water, milk, or fruit, reflected Biblical usage, but also implicitly reinforced the Quaker emphasis upon simplicity of lifestyle.

Pilgrimage

The fifth key metaphor cluster found in early Quaker sermons identified Quaker beliefs with the vision of life as a pilgrimage or journey. The pattern is a reflection of the metaphor of the journey found widely in the literature of many disparate cultures.[66] Pilgrimage as an act and metaphor permeates Biblical literature and historical Christianity, and was especially significant in seventeenth-century Christian writings.[67] There were several variations of the metaphor in the sermons, all involving the conception of life as a journey from an evil to a good place, from Egypt to Canaan, from "Death to Life, and from Darkness to Light."[68] Pilgrimage was either developed or implied in twenty-seven of the extant sermons.[69]

A typical example of the Pilgrimage cluster, complete with the identification of the believer's life with the Hebrews in the wilderness, is seen in this passage from Fox: "These that are Come to be Convinced now . . . & that have stood still, & seen salvation, & have been preserved through ye Redd Sea, & have come into ye Wilderness, & out of Egypt, & bondage . . . they finde abundance of trouble, before they Come to Canaan."[70] Just as the journey to the Promised Land was difficult for the Hebrews, so it was for the pilgrim. Crisp spoke of the people who had come away from the evil cities only to be ensnared by the troubles of the wilderness: "We have before our Eyes from day to day, those that have . . . been in great measure brought out of Sodom, and out the way of Egypt. . . . But at last they have taken and arrogated those Gifts to themselves."[71] Approximately one month after Crisp had spoken, Penn preached a funeral sermon in which he contrasted the Land of Promise with the trouble of the present "wandering" life:

> We are Travellers here in this Vale of Tears, in this Earthly Pilgrimage, into the Land of Rest the Heavenly Canaan; Let us follow our blessed Joshua, that is leading us into that Land of Promise, and he will give to every one his Lot. . . . O Blessed are they that are waiting for their Lot and Portion in that Heavenly Country to which Abraham had his Eye, the City, the New Jerusalem.[72]

The Pilgrimage cluster expressed an otherworldliness on the part of the preachers, especially with regard to life's pleasures. Fox explained: "Our Religion is Practicall, it brings & bowers [sic] down every mind to seek after things above, as Heirs of another Kingdom, & not these Outward Transitory things here below; Pilgrims & Strangers yt are hastning [sic] to another Countrey or Kingdom; are not much affected & taken wth any thing they meet wth as they travell along."[73] The journey was so dangerous that, as Crisp maintained, "The Children of *Israel* might as well have gone through the Red Sea, without the help of God, as the Christian Traveller can go through the many difficulties . . . he is to meet with in his Way, without the assistance of God's Holy Spirit."[74]

The image of the traveller, whether used by Fox, Crisp, Penn, or another preacher, was at once familiar and strong because it was built on a lengthy history of associations from Biblical times through Puritan. It was also an expression of the "quest" story which is discovered over a wide cultural base in both sacred and secular writings as well as oral literature. Hermann G. Stelzner has isolated five elements of the "quest" metaphor, all of which are found in the *Pilgrimage* cluster used by early Quaker preachers. Reinterpreted to fit the requirements of the Quaker metaphor, the five elements become (1) "a precious object and/or Person to be found and Possessed or married"—Jerusalem, Canaan, the Land of Promise (or Christ, God), etc.; (2) "a long journey to find the Object"—the Pilgrimage; (3) "a Hero"—the Pilgrim-Traveller; (4) "the Guardians of the Object who must be overcome before it can be won"—the voice of the "second speaker," the lusts of the "world," stumbling in the dark, etc.; and (5) "the Helpers who . . . assist the Hero"—the Light, Voice, etc.[75] By employing this metaphor, the preachers offered their hearers a conceptualizing image that informed human experience to such an extent that, in Stelzner's words, "Occasionally universal human reactions are elicited."[76]

II

The five key metaphor clusters served three functions, all of which are implicit in the analysis presented above; (1) they provided a means of summarizing and conceptualizing a "world" that made psychological and theological sense to the speakers and listeners; (2) they stood as a means of elaborating the implications of the beliefs in individual Quakers' lives; (3) they constituted an important inventional tool used by speakers enjoined to preach without preparation.[77]

The Summarizing Function

Quaker preachers spoke against a backdrop of rapid change in England. English society had undergone unprecedented revolutions in politics, religion, and science.[78] Quakers participated to greater or lesser degrees in the liminality of their cultural surroundings, and early Quaker journals attest to the personal confusion, search, and general sense of personal alienation prior to "convincement" (the Quaker term for religious conversion).[79] For these people, then, the telling of religious truth in familiar metaphors which they could identify in terms of personal response shared by others became a way to offset the ubiquity of change and flux that surrounded them. The five clusters "summarized" the Quaker's world. They compounded and synthesized a complex system of ideas.[80] The preachers could thus avoid having to develop long theological arguments or extensive scriptural expositions in favor of rehearsing and combining easily understood metaphors.

The metaphors possessed an additional advantage inasmuch as they not only summarized positive theological (and, by implication, behavioral) information, but they also summarized negative theological (and behavioral) information through the process of polarization: Light assumed *dark* (as well as spurious light); the *Voice* stood opposite the *false voices* or the *second speaker*; the *Seed* opposed the *evil seed* or the *serpent's seed*; the *Hunger/Thirst* cluster assumed either the possession of hunger and thirst for God (and finding satisfaction) or possessing false satisfaction which would obviate the drives; the *Pilgrimage* from Babylon to Canaan implied movement from an evil to a holy place and assumed that one could choose *not* to be a pilgrim. Thus, a set of either-or rhetorical options tended to provide structure for the early Quaker's world. They helped produce unity through binary opposition.

When the metaphors were used in combination, two forces helped bring about a unification of the Quaker's world. First, the metaphors were identified together in the preacher's and hearer's minds through repetition and frequent blending. Second, because the metaphors each implicated one or more of the senses, when the images were combined, an overlapping of the senses—a synesthesia—was suggested metaphorically.[81] In Crisp's phrase "hearken to the Voice of the Light," both sound and sight were provoked in such a way that listeners must have been aware, if only subconsciously, that God was not bound to one channel of sensory input. If light possessed a voice, and if one could feed on the light, then the metaphors indicated that the entire sensorium was vulnerable in a metaphorically unified way to the claims of God mediated through the preachers. The metaphors also implied that religion was not simply a pursuit of the mind detached from the body, and that Quakerism, at least, was a commitment that demanded participation in a world in which the senses played a vital role.[82]

The Elaborating Function

The five key metaphor clusters not only provided a unifying picture of the world for early Quakers, they also became a means of extending their thought and, in Burkean terms, "revealing hitherto unsuspected connectives . . . by exemplifying relationships between objects which our customary rational vocabulary has ignored."[83] Ortner calls this process "elaboration" and contends that the end product of the process does not stop short at the level of understanding but ultimately makes the symbol "translatable into orderly action."[84]

Both Burke's and Ortner's comments are germane to the elaborating function of metaphors because (1) the naming property of metaphors, by its "connective" nature, reveals new and "extended" relationships in the user's and hearer's mind; (2) the implications of the metaphor, what may be described as the reinterpretation of it in personal terms, of necessity assume a personal sorting process that can lead to personal commitment and action. For example, to name life a *Pilgrimage* overlays a gloss of geographic factors which may never have occurred to the person who hears the metaphor applied to life for the first time. At the very least, the idea of pilgrimage may call forth associations which have lain dormant. Upon assimilating the metaphor, however, the hearer may begin to translate the events in his or her world into terms of the metaphor (e.g., living in an evil place; finding a straight path; traveling light [and in the light], etc.), make changes in his or her personal lifestyle, or be reaffirmed in changes already made.[85]

It is significant that none of the metaphors differentiate between the sexes as many Biblical (and non-Biblical) metaphors do. It was axiomatic among early Quakers that women and men are equal in all respects,[86] and women were capable and well-respected preachers in early Quaker circles.[87] Thus, all auditors, women and men alike, could easily elaborate and personalize these metaphor clusters into their own spheres of life without having to undergo metaphoric sex change as one must do in order, for example, to be both "sons of God" and "Brides of Christ" at the same time.

The Inventional Function

Unlike their Puritan and Anglican counterparts, Quaker preachers spoke without assistance of notes, manuscripts, or memorization. Yet they managed to compose sermons which approximate the length of other seventeenth-century sermons. The investigator is naturally led to question how they managed it and to search for mnemonic aids, such as formulaic structures, in the sermons.[88] The key metaphors, although not formulaic structures in the sense of being predictable in a certain form in a particular place in a given sermon, did function as a basic inventional tool—a set of topoi. They allowed the preacher several options of acceptable, dense metaphor clusters which he or she could build upon, combine, unravel, and particularize according to the demands of audience or "inspiration." The five key clusters are recognized by anyone familiar with the King James Bible as having their roots in its content and language. The combining of these Biblical terms, their elaboration and particularization, and, most important, the preachers' preference for these metaphors out of a host of other Biblical metaphors, signal the inventiveness of the speakers. The Biblical source also allowed the preachers to string together appropriate Scripture passages from memory as they were suggested by a particular word in a metaphor cluster. In this manner they were able to "gain time" while quoting a passage from the Bible in order to think ahead to their next point. There is no evidence that the speakers consciously chose the metaphors because of their advantages in the process of invention. It is difficult to imagine one of the preachers admitting to the use of Biblical quotation to fill time while thinking of the next point. After all, they saw themselves as God's oracles and were enjoined not to speak unless they were certain of their role. On the other hand, the argument that the preachers were not aware of the invention advantages of the metaphors, or at least did not choose them for their inventional advantages, is a moot point. Regardless of their motivation, they chose an adaptable rhetorical tool that, in addition to its summarizing and elaborating potential, could also function as a form of topoi and, if need arose, as a stalling device.[89]

Conclusion

Early Quaker preaching offers a provocative example of the use of metaphor. Furthermore, Quaker sermons provide examples of metaphors responding to knotty theological and rhetorical problems. Early Quakers faced a paradox: how to encourage a sense of group unity and identity and maintain a theological stance that stressed the belief that direct revelation from God to man had not ceased with the canonization of Scripture? Too much emphasis on the individual's revelation could split the group. The individual was always potentially at odds with group unity.[90] Early Quakers met the demands of the paradox on two levels. The first encouraged the impromptu sermon, which allowed the individual to become God's spokesperson, God's oracle. The impromptu format, however, presented its own rhetorical problem: invention. One answer to the demands of the impromptu format was the use of metaphors functioning as inventional topoi. The second-level response to the group-individual paradox also lay in the use of metaphors. The key metaphors allowed preachers to stay within the conceptual boundaries of group belief, yet present a message which could stretch the boundaries through elaboration and personalization, and have the earmarks of the word of truth from God.

By combining and recombining the five clusters of metaphors, the preachers were able to (1) establish familiar ground by using images acceptable to their audiences' sense of reality, (2) extend their own and their audiences' conceptual worlds through elaboration of the images, and (3) discover an inventional tool that solved rhetorical problems inherent in the impromptu sermon.

Notes

[1] A partial listing would include the following: Michael M. Osborn and Douglas Ehninger, "The Metaphor in Public Address," *Speech Monographs*, 29 (August 1962), 223–234; Michael Osborn, "Archetypal Metaphor in Rhetoric: The Light-Dark Family," *Quarterly Journal of Speech*, 52 (April 1967), 115–126; William Gribbin, "The Juggernaut Metaphor in American Rhetoric," *Quarterly Journal of Speech*, 59 (October 1973), 297–303; Paul Newell Campbell, "Metaphor and Linguistic Theory," *Quarterly Journal of Speech*, 61 (February 1975), 1–12; J. Vernon Jensen, "British Voices on the Eve of the American Revolution: Trapped by the Family Metaphor," *Quarterly Journal of Speech*, 63 (February 1977), 43–50; Michael Osborn, "The Evolution of the Archetypal Sea In Rhetoric and Poetic," *Quarterly Journal of Speech* (December 1977), 347–363; Kathleen Hall Jamieson, "The Metaphor Cluster in the Rhetoric of Pope Paul VI and Edmund G. Brown, Jr., *Quarterly Journal of Speech*, 66 (February 1980), 51–72; and Robert L. Ivie, "The Metaphor of Force in Prowar Discourse: The Case of 1812," *Quarterly Journal of Speech*, 68 (August 1982); 240–253.

[2] See, for example, James W. Fernandez, "Persuasions and Performance: Of the Beast in Every Body . . . And the Metaphors of Everyman," *Daedalus*, 101 (Winter 1972), 39–60, and "The Mission of Metaphor in Expressive Culture," *Current Anthropology*, 15 (June 1974), 119–133; Sherry B. Ortner, "On Key Symbols," *American Anthropologist*, 75 (October 1973), 1338–1346; Brenda E. F. Beck, "The Metaphor as a Mediator Between Semantic and Analogic Modes of Thought," *Current Anthropology*, 19 (March 1978), 83–88; and *The Social Use of Metaphor*, ed. J. David Sapir and J. Christopher Crocker (Philadelphia: University of Pennsylvania Press, 1977). For examples of specific applications of metaphorical analysis to specific cultures, see Michele Zimbalist Rosaldo, "Metaphors and Folk Classification," *Southwestern Journal of Anthropology*, 28 (1972), 83–99, and "It's All Uphill: The Creative Metaphors of Ilongot Magical Spells," in *Sociocultural Dimensions of Language Use*, ed. Mary Sanches and Ben Blount (New York: Academic Press, 1975), 177–203; Gustav Thaiss, "The Conceptualization of Social Change Through Metaphor," *Journal of Asian and African Studies*, 13 (January and April 1978), 1–13; and Nels Johnson, "Palestinian Refugee Ideology: An Enquiry into Key Metaphors," *Journal of Anthropological Research*, 34 (Winter 1978), 524–539.

[3] I follow Nels Johnson's use of the term "key metaphor," which is an adaptation of the concept "key symbol" used by Sherry Ortner [Johnson, "Palestinian Refugee Ideology"; Ortner, "On Key Symbols"]. A key symbol, according to Ortner, is recognized because: (1) people in the culture tell you that it is important; (2) people in the culture are positively or negatively aroused by it, rather than indifferent; (3) the symbol comes up in many different contexts; (4) there is greater cultural elaboration surrounding it; and (5) greater cultural restrictions surround it (p. 1329). The metaphors discussed in this essay are thought to be "key" in seventeenth-century Quaker culture because: (1) the metaphors are prominent both in terms of quantity and placement in significant passages in the sermons, and (2) because evidence extrinsic to the sermons (from tracts, journals, epistles, etc.) corroborates that the metaphors are among key cultural indicators for early Quakers [See, for example, *The Journal of George Fox*, ed., John L. Nickalls, rev. ed. (Cambridge, Eng.: Univ. Press, 1952), and *Early Quaker Writings*, ed. Hugh Barbour and Arthur O. Roberts (Grand Rapids: William B. Eerdmans Publishing Company, 1973)].

[4] Although there is only one extant sermon fragment of the thousands of sermons spoken in Quaker meetinghouses during the first twenty years of the sect (1650–1670), seventy-four sermons from the period 1671–1700 exist in manuscript form or in published versions. References to sermon sources in subsequent notes will be by letter as follows:

A. *A Collection of Several Sermons and Testimonies. . . .*, London: B. Beardwell, 1701.

B. *A Sermon . . . by Thomas Story . . . with an Appendix Containing an Original Sermon of George Fox* (Philadelphia: S. Potter Co., 1825).

C. Thomas Chalkley, *Mr. T. Chalkley's Sermon & Prayer . . .*, MS at Friends Historical Library, Swarthmore College.

D. Stephen Crisp, *Scripture-Truths Demonstrated. . .*, London: J. Sowle, 1707.

E. George Fox [Sermon] in *Severall Letters to the Saints of the Most High*. No place, no publisher, 1654.

F. Headley MSS. Friends House Library, London.

G. Richardson MSS. The Quaker Collection, Haverford College Library. For a description of the MSS and an account of their content, see Henry Cadbury, "Richardson MSS," *Journal of the Friends Historical Society*, 32 (1935), 34–37.

H. *The Concurrence and Unanimity; Of the People Called Quakers . . .*, London: J. Sowle, 1711.

I. *The Harmony of Divine and Heavenly Doctrines . . .*, London: J. Sowle, 1696.

The sermons contained in sources D, H, and I, representing fifty-eight of the seventy-four sermons, were pirated by non-Quaker publishers and later published by the Quakers themselves [For details of this episode, see Luella M. Wright, *The Literary Life of the Early Friends, 1650–1725* (New York: Columbia University Press, 1932), pp. 145–146]. The piracy was possible because the sermons in this study represent the work of note-takers rather than the notes of the preachers themselves, thus they are a close record of what Quaker preachers actually said, i.e., they are probably closer to verbatim accounts than is discovered in other seventeenth-century sermons representing manuscripts written by the preachers themselves, knowing that the preachers could (1) deviate from the manuscripts in actual performance, and (2) alter the manuscripts after the performance for the demands of print.

[5] Both metaphors are possible. The preachers were "midwives" because they sought to bring to life the Light that they believed shines in all persons, what they called "that of God in every man." The term "medium" in this context is Richard Bauman's (personal conversation, University of Texas, Austin, summer 1982). Bauman argues that Quaker preachers saw themselves as mouthpieces through which the inspiration of God (the Word) flowed. On the other hand, Hugh Barbour prefers the term "matchmaker," noting

that "Human actions of either the preacher or the repentant hearer were intended only to prepare the way for what God would do" [*The Quakers in Puritan England* (New Haven: Yale University Press, 1964), p. 130].

[6] *Primitive Christianity Revived . . .* , (Philadelphia: Henry Longstreth, 1877), pp. 71–72, first published in 1696.

[7] Puritan divines began with a definite Biblical text, clarified it, "raised the doctrine" from it, gave reasons for the doctrine, and applied the doctrine for the use of the hearers [see Babette May Levy, *Preaching in the First Half Century of New England History*, Studies in Church History, Vol. 6 (New York: Russell & Russell, 1967), pp. 88–95.]. The process depended upon the preacher's ability to develop arguments, marshall evidence and make both appear relevant to the listeners. Early Quakers were not deficient in these skills, as their numerous tracts and epistles indicate. When it came to preaching, however, exegesis and lengthy arguments played a secondary role.

[8] "Seventeenth Century Quaker Style," *PMLA*, 71 (September 1956), 79. Cope's work does not cite any of the sermons of this essay and tends to concentrate on an earlier period relying largely upon journals and tracts for his evidence. The sermons reveal that what he concluded about the use of metaphor by Quakers during the 1650s and 1660s is accurate for the only surviving record of *spoken* language (rather than what was composed for print) in the last three decades of the seventeenth century.

[9] Renaissance rhetoric was bent on viewing the speaker's craft as "an aesthetically oriented art of ingratiation—a form of conscious flattery or supplication" [Douglas Ehninger, "On Rhetorics and Rhetoric," *Western Speech*, 31 (Fall 1967), 244]. Quakers consciously avoided verbal ingratiation, preferring the "plain speech" of Puritans and going beyond them in group strictures on language use. For an excellent consideration of Quaker language against the background of other-widespread language experimentation, see Hugh Ormsby-Lennon, "'The Dialect of Those *Fanatic Times*'; Language Communities and English Poetry from 1580 to 1660," Diss. University of Pennsylvania 1977, pp. 379–388. The subject of literalness and metaphor has attracted the attention of philosophers of late. See, for example, Michael McCanles, "The Literal and the Metaphorical: Dialectic or Interchange," *PMLA*, 90 (March 1976), pp. 279–290.

[10] I follow Jamieson in the use of the term "clusters," meaning related metaphors obviously belonging to the same imagery pattern or conceptual structure ("The Metaphoric Cluster in the Rhetoric of Pope Paul VI and Edmund G. Brown, Jr.," pp. 51–52).

[11] One of the sermons included in the study is anonymous, but may have been preached by one of the other named preachers in the study.

[12] The five key metaphors discovered in the sermons exhibit the characteristics of archetypal metaphors posited by Osborn: (1) they are relatively immune to changes in time and culture; (2) they are based on some inexorable part of human experience; and (3) they possess an appeal based upon identification with primal human motivations ["Archetypal Metaphor in Rhetoric," pp. 115–126]. Their identity as archetypal, however, is irrelevant to the argument of this essay since key metaphors may be discovered in a culture's rhetoric irrespective of their classification as archetypal. We should expect many cultures to develop key metaphors which are bound temporally and culturally.

[13] Two of the five are by Stephen Crisp and George Fox who employ the imagery in their other sermons. The remaining three sermons that do not express Light/Dark patterns do not employ any of the five clusters (one sermon by Leonard Fell, n.d., source A; two sermons by Philip Hermon, 1700, source A. These are the only sermons that survive Fell and Hermon.

[14] A sermon preached at Yearly Meeting, London, May 9, 1674, source F, 253–254. As was common in writings of the century, some of Fox's sermons employ the "y" for the voiced "the." Except where necessary for purposes of avoiding ambiguity, I have

not changed spelling or altered grammar, punctuation, or capitalization in the sermon quotations. All sermons were delivered in the vicinity of London, except where indicated.

[15] Cope, p. 733.

[16] The quotation also illustrates the early Quaker propensity to express concepts in spatial terminology. See Maurice A. Creasey, "'Inward' and 'Outward': A Study in Early Quaker Language," *Supplement No. 30, Journal of the Friends Historical Society*, 1-24.

[17] A sermon preached at Yearly Meeting, May 25 or 26, 1675, source G, typed copy, 439-440.

[18] *Ibid.*

[19] "Bearing the Cross of Christ, the true Mark of a Christian," a sermon preached at Devonshire House, October 12, 1690, source D, 33.

[20] "Christ Altogether Lovely," a sermon preached at Grace Church Street, March 11, 1693, source I, 206.

[21] Crisp, "Bearing the Cross of Christ," source D, 14.

[22] "The Dawning of the Day of Grace and Salvation," a sermon preached at Grace Church Street, August 2, 1691, source D, 110.

[23] "Christ the Mighty Helper of *Poor Helpless Man*," a sermon preached at Grace Church Street, May 12, 1694, source I, 184-185.

[24] A sermon preached at St. Martins le Grande, February 16, 1693, source H, 102.

[25] "The Standard of Truth," a sermon preached at Grace Church Street, May 29, 1692, source D, 70.

[26] Coole, source I, 186.

[27] "Two Made One; Or, The happiness of Marrying in the Lord," a sermon preached at Devonshire House, October 3, 1694, source I, 146.

[28] "The Mighty Work of Man's Redemption," a sermon preached at Grace Church Street, February 8, 1687, source D, 26.

[29] For excellent discussions of the tension between silence and speech see Richard Bauman, "Aspects of Seventeenth Century Rhetoric," *Quarterly Journal of Speech*, 56 (February 1970), 67-74; and "Speaking in the Light: The Role of the Quaker Minister," in *Explorations in the Ethnography of Speaking*, ed. Richard Bauman and Joel Sherzer (New York: Cambridge University Press, 1974), pp. 144-160.

[30] See, for example, Robert Barclay's *Apology for the True Christian Divinity*, proposition VII (Manchester: William Irwin, 1869). First ed. 1678.

[31] A sermon preached at Yearly Meeting, June 9, 1674, source F, 248.

[32] A sermon preached at Yearly Meeting, June 11, 1674, source F. 282.

[33] Fox recorded that when his hopes in men were exhausted, "then, Oh then, I heard a voice which said, 'There is one, even Christ Jesus, that can speak to thy condition,' and when I heard it my heart did leap for joy . . ." [*The Journal of George Fox*, ed. John L. Nickalls, rev. ed. (Cambridge, Eng.: University Press, 1952), p. 11]. In the journal, Fox appears to speak of a literal voice. The sermons are highly ambiguous as to whether the voice is literal or figurative.

[34] "The Sheep of Christ hear his Voice," a sermon preached at Devonshire House, May 10, 1688, source D, 14.

[35] "The Word of God a Christian's Life," a sermon preached at Grace Church Street, March 14, 1687, source D, 28.

[36] Arthur O. Roberts, in his *Through Flaming Sword: A Spiritual Biography of George Fox* (Newberg, Oregon: The Barclay Press, 1959), has stated the early Quaker position of the "Word" in this way: "He who knows Jesus Christ experimentally knows the revelation of God about which the Scriptures speak authentically. Scriptures are the *words of God*, Jesus Christ is the *Word of God*" (p. 92).

[37] "The Excellency of Peace with God," a sermon preached at Devonshire House, August 5, 1691, source D, 128.

[38] *Ibid.*, p. 139.

[39] A sermon preached at Grace Church Street, May 6, 1688, source H, 17.

[40] "The Word of God a Christian's Life," source D, 35.

[41] Crisp, "The Great Duty of Remembering our Creator," a sermon preached at Devonshire House, April 6, 1692, source D, 102.

[42] "Christ the Way to Eternal Life," a sermon preached at Grace Church Street, May 6, 1693, source D. 4.

[43] Genesis 3:15, King James Version.

[44] A sermon preached at Wheeler Street, June 1, 1680, source B, 65.

[45] A sermon preached at a men's meeting, Barbados, October, 1671, source G, 200-201.

[46] "The Wonderful Love of God to Mankind," a sermon preached at St. Martins le Grand, November 9, 1690, source D, 177.

[47] John Bowater, a sermon preached at St. John's Street, March 18, 1693, source H, 47.

[48] "Bearing the Cross of Christ," source D, 30-31.

[49] "The Excellency of Peace with God," source D, 140.

[50] *Ibid.*

[51] Many of the variations of the *Seed* cluster are related to plants and trees and other agricultural images. "Plants" and "trees" appear in twenty-six sermons; the "vineyard" or the "vine" appear in ten sermons; and "grafting," essential to St. Paul's letter to the Romans (11:17-24), in eleven sermons.

[52] A sermon preached at Grace Church Street, May 16, 1688, source H, 2. See also John 12:24.

[53] Maud Bodkin notes that the symbol of the seed of wheat transports us "to a world whose less discriminating mode of thought has upon us the power of an inchoate or unconscious poetry. Within that world, the sequence of rain, flood, and springing corn constitutes a holy rebirth wherein man participates and finds an expression of his own nature" [*Archetypal Patterns in Poetry* (London: Oxford University Press, 1934), p. 274].

[54] Matthew 13:3-23; Mark 4:3-20; Luke 8:5-15.

[55] "The Heavenly Race," a sermon preached at Grace Church Street, January 16, 1694, source I, 97.

[56] Crisp, "The Acceptable Sacrifice," a sermon preached at Grace Church Street, source D, 207.

[57] Terms for water are not used in the sermons to refer to Baptism or cleansing.

[58] Other terms drawing on the *Hunger/Thirst* pattern not discussed here include: "fruit," "milk," "nursing," and "wine."

[59] Yearly Meeting, May 25, 1681, source G, 538-539.

[60] A sermon preached at Grace Church Street, March 11, 1694, source H. 163.

[61] A sermon preached at Ratcliff, April 19, 1694, source H, 183.

[62] A sermon preached at Savoy Meetinghouse, n.d., source A, 11.

[63] "The Divine Life of Christ Jesus," a sermon preached at Grace Church Street, March 16, 1691, source D, 69.

[64] Yearly Meeting, May 9, 1674, source F, 249.

[65] Yearly Meeting, May, 1678, source G, 479.

[66] The journey metaphor is carefully discussed by Georg Roppen and Richard Sommer, in *Strangers and Pilgrims: An Essay on the Metaphor of Journey* (New York: Humanities Press, 1964). Roppen and Sommer call the journey the "metaphor of narration, of duration, extension, and purpose. Space and time operate in the metaphor under the control of a single element, a purpose or teleological force" (preface, n.p.).

[67] The journey of the Jewish nation from Egypt to the Land of Promise is perhaps the best Biblical example of the metaphor. In seventeenth-century England, the image of the Pilgrim was immortalized by John Bunyan's *Pilgrim's Progress* (1678). In 1691, Crisp

wrote his *Short History of a Long Travel from Babylon to Bethel* (published in 1711), which paralleled Bunyan's work at several points.

[68] Crisp, "The Spirit of Christ the only true Guide," a sermon preached at Grace Church Street, October 10, 1690, source D, 51.

[69] Several of the sermons use the phrases "spiritual journey," "heavenly journey," and "spiritual travel."

[70] Yearly Meeting, June 11, 1674, source F, 269.

[71] "The Sheep of Christ hear his Voice," source D, 147.

[72] A sermon preached Upon occasion of the Death of Mrs. *Rebecca Travers*, June 19, 1688, source H, 6.

[73] Women's meeting, Barbados, October, 1671, source G, 273.

[74] "The Undefiled Way to Eternal Rest," a sermon preached at Devonshire House, July 29, 1691, source D, 97.

[75] "The Quest Story and Nixon's November 3, 1969 Address," *Quarterly Journal of Speech*, 57 (April 1971), 164.

[76] *Ibid.*, p. 163.

[77] The terms "summarizing" and "elaborating" are borrowed from Ortner. Summarizing symbols "operate to compound and synthesize a complex system of ideas" ("On Key Symbols," p. 1340). On the other hand, elaborating symbols work by "sorting out complex and undifferentiated feelings and ideas, making them comprehensible to oneself, communicable to others, and translatable into orderly action." She also asserts that she is "distinguishing not only types of symbols, but types of symbolic functions" (p. 1344).

[78] See, for example, Christopher Hill, *The Century of Revolution 1603-1714*, Vol. V. of *A History of England*, ed. Christopher Brooke and Denis Mack Smith (8 vols; London: Thomas Nelson and Sons, Ltd., 1961), pp. 4-5.

[79] Fox's *Journal*, p. 11, supra. Cf. *The History of the Life of Thomas Ellwood* [1639-1713] (Philadelphia: Friends' Book Store, n.d.), pp. 24-36.

[80] Ortner, p. 1340.

[81] See Fernandez, "The Mission of Metaphor," p. 124.

[82] Fox's *Journal* is particularly full of references to the senses. During one of Fox's religious experiences, he recorded: ". . . I was come up in Spirit through the flaming sword into the paradise of God. All things were new, and all the creation gave another smell unto me than before, beyond what words can utter" (p. 27).

[83] Kenneth Burke, *Permanence and Change* (Indianapolis: The Bobbs-Merrill Company, 1965), p. 104.

[84] Ortner, p. 1340.

[85] George Lakoff and Mark Johnson map major metaphors in Western thought and illustrate their profound effects on our lives in their provocative volume, *Metaphors We Live By* (Chicago: The University of Chicago Press, 1980).

[86] Thaiss notes that the metaphors of Iranian rhetoric build upon cultural assumptions regarding distinctions in status and function among the sexes ("The Conceptualization of Social Change Through Metaphor," pp. 5-10).

[87] Regrettably, no sermons delivered by women have survived, which probably reflects a bias of the note-takers who transcribed the sermons, most of whom were not Quakers.

[88] See Bruce Rosenberg, "The Formulaic Quality of Spontaneous Sermons," *Journal of American Folklore*, 83 (1970), 3-20.

[89] *Ibid.*, p. 9. The "stall formula" as used by American folk preachers consists of words or phrases repeated, usually in an exaggerated emotional pattern, in order to gain time. Quaker metaphors leading to the recitation of memorized scripture passages are hardly the same thing, yet they may have served a similar purpose on occasion.

[90] The infamous case of James Nayler is dealt with by William C. Braithwaite in *The Beginnings of Quakerism*, 2nd ed. (Cambridge: University Press, 1955), 241-278.

Honda
The Ultimate Trip

Robert Huesca

With the growth of the Latino population in the United States has come a plethora of advertisements aimed at this market. A 1991 ad by Honda demonstrates that demographic characteristics particular to Latinos are being incorporated into verbal and visual metaphors. Although the metaphors are grounded in culturally specific characteristics, the imagery is sufficiently vague to attract even those who do not fit precisely those specific characteristics. The source of power in the advertisement I have chosen to analyze, then, lies in the nature of the metaphors it features—they are specific enough to target a particular audience but ambiguous enough not to exclude individuals within that audience who may differ in significant ways from qualities associated with the audience.

Honda Advertisement

The artifact I have selected is an advertisement for Honda taken from *Más* magazine, a publication aimed at a general audience interested in Hispanic issues. The advertisement consists of three basic images—a car, a family, and sky—and it works with three muted colors—white, blue, and black.

Across the top of the page, in 72-point type, is the Spanish word, "familiarízate," which means "familiarize yourself" or "get to know it." This single word dominates the ad and is balanced by a picture of a blue Honda Civic, shown from the side at the bottom of the page. The car appears to be parked on a level piece of pavement, which occupies the base of the ad. Inside the car are four people, although they are not instantly noticeable due to the semi-opaque glare on the windows. On closer inspection, the people in the car appear to be a family with a mother and father in the front seat and either two children or a child and a grandparent in the back seat.

The car and the word "familiarízate" are displayed against a blue and white field of cotton-like clouds and sky. The clouds occupy the lower portion of the page, giving way to a clear blue sky that takes up the top half of the page. Five paragraphs in black type are written in Spanish

This essay was written while Robert Huesca was a student in Sonja K. Foss' rhetorical criticism class at Ohio State University in 1991. Used by permission of the author.

across the cloudless portion of the sky. The paragraphs discuss the size of the car in relation to the needs of a family: "father, mother, grandma, the children." The copy mentions the practical and reliable characteristics of the car in non-technical language before suggesting a trip to the dealer to "familiarize yourself." The final words of the page are "Honda," written in the company's trademark font, and the slogan, " Algo grande está pasando!" or "Something big is happening!"

The Metaphors

The tenor in this advertisement is the Honda, which appears both verbally and visually. The numerous vehicles (ha ha) are clustered around two themes, family and spiritual realization, and are expressed both visually and verbally. Both notions, family and spirituality, are specific characteristics of the Latino population. Without going into census data, I safely can say that Latinos generally have larger families than the general U.S. population, and they claim religious affiliations in greater proportions than the overall population. Furthermore, family and religion are important components of the Latino culture.

The family metaphor is suggested by the dominant word in the ad, "familiarízate," which contains the root *familia*, or family. Although this word suggests the importance of the family, it cannot be taken on its face to reference or mean family. The remainder of the ad, however, encourages the reader to extract *family* from the word. The first paragraph in the sales text begins: "Papá, mamá, abuelita, los niños." This works immediately to reinforce the family referent for "familiarízate." Note that the copy writer included "abuelita" or "grandmother," which speaks to a culturally specific notion of the Latino family. Rather than introducing the modern U. S. concept of the nuclear family—mother, father, and 1.5 children—the ad extends the concept of family to include the eldest generation, a common component of Latino families. Also, the copy is written in the diminutive form by ending the word for grandmother in *ita*. This conveys a notion of closeness and value. It also harkens to the way in which the word tends to be used in Latino families. The word *abuela* is used to describe a relative other than one's own; *abuelita*, on the other hand, only is used by a blood relative of the grandmother.

The notion of family is reinforced by picturing a family inside the car. But the nature of this family is not clear because the windows are obscured by the light reflecting off the windows. Exactly who is in the car cannot be discerned. What the lack of clarity in presenting the family suggests is an ambiguity about the nature of the family to which an individual might belong. Although many Latinos still may belong to conventional kinds of families of the types associated with the Latino culture, the changing nature of the American culture is affecting Latinos as well as other Americans. Many Latinos may not belong to families that include two parents, many children, and other relatives. With the ambiguity of the metaphor, such individuals are allowed to identify with the cultural sense of a Latino family even though their own experience does not fit the traditional conception.

Vehicles clustered around the concept of spiritual realization operate in a way similar to the family metaphor. The image of billowing white clouds rising to an open blue sky introduces the concept of spiritual transcendence. ''Something big is happening!'' reinforces this concept, suggesting that the clouds and sky are not included as mere decoration. A closer look at the entire ad reveals that, indeed, something big is happening. The clouds appear to be spreading apart, allowing passage to some higher reality. The family members also appear to be moving into a new realm of consciousness, conveyed in their transfixed, placid, serene expressions and in the glare on the window. Because the family is not clearly visible, it appears to be vanishing to another world. Finally, the use of reflection on the car creates the illusion of movement upward. The bright, horizontal reflection on the upper half of the car makes the car seem as though it is disappearing from the picture.

Although the image of the sky has a spiritual, archetypal quality, it does not reference any particular kind of spirituality. The spiritual images in this ad work in an almost magical way. The transcendence to spiritual realization is accomplished through archetypes and technology rather than a reliance on religious icons typical of Latino culture. The advertisers could have shown the family in front of church at a wedding or baptism. They could have used images such as crosses, saints, and virgins commonly found in the cars driven by Latinos. But such an approach would have required a religious-specific approach. Whereas most religious Latinos are affiliated with the Catholic church, many are branching off into other sects, and others are eschewing institutional religion. To link advertising to specific religious symbols would have run the risk of alienating Latinos affiliated with other churches or religious philosophies. Honda took the safe road by maintaining neutrality when offering spiritual realization. The company also succeeded in subliminally proselytizing consumerism as the redemptive religion, a religion that has appeal whatever the nature of the targeted audience member's spiritual religion.

Conclusion

Clearly, the importance of family and religion in Latino culture was recognized and manipulated in this ad. The focus on the family reflected the importance of family in the culture but did not define in specific terms the nature or size of that family. Similarly, the attention to religion through non-specific metaphors suggests that religion is an important element in the Latino identity but allows space for those within the ethnic group who are moving outside the traditional boundaries of the Catholic church to be included in the audience for the ad.

The success of this ad in tapping traditional cultural values rests in large part on the subtlety and ambiguity of the metaphors. Sensitive political topics, such as religion, are avoided yet not ignored by these metaphors. Through the metaphors used in this ad, an audience is targeted, but variations and differences within that audience are not discounted or devalued.

Architectural Metaphor as Subversion
The Portland Building

Marla Kanengieter-Wildeson

Susanne Langer described the role and function of architecture as shaping a culture's image by creating a human environment that expresses "characteristic rhythmic patterns within that culture."[1] She explains:

> Such patterns are the alternations of sleep and waking, venture and safety, emotion and calm, austerity and abandon, the tempo and the smoothness or abruptness of life; the simple forms of childhood and the complexities of full moral stature, the sacramental and the capricious moods that mark a social order.[2]

As these rhythmic patterns transform and shift within a specific culture, so do the symbols, icons, and monuments built by its members. Whether its language is the ideal symmetry of Greek *arete* expressed by the builders of the Parthenon or the sterility of Orwell's *1984* raised by the technocrats of steel and glass boxes, architecture relies on a poetic process—a process characterized by the use of metaphor.

In this essay, I will argue that, through the use of metaphor, architectural forms can subvert or reaffirm existing ideologies, and I will demonstrate this process in architect Michael Graves' Portland Building. In 1980, the city of Portland, Oregon, chose Michael Graves' design for its new public service building. Completed in 1982, the building sits on a 200-foot-square block between the City Hall on the east, the County Courthouse on the west, a public transit mall on the north, and a park on the west. Since its construction, the Portland Building remains an enigma in American architecture. Some have called the building's design "offensive rather than open and inviting,"[3] "a joke,"[4] and "dangerous,"[5] while others have proclaimed that it "would be a landmark from inception"[6] and "brings some not-so-old but almost forgotten American traditions to life."[7] That the Portland Building has influenced the landscape of architectural design and caused people to think and talk about their environment is clear.

I suggest that Graves, through his use of metaphor, has molded a carefully articulated statement that reshapes traditional notions about

This essay was written while Marla Kanengieter-Wildeson was a student in Sonja K. Foss' rhetorical criticism class at the University of Oregon in 1989. Used by permission of the author.

government institutions. His non-discursive message reaffirms the belief that humans play an intrinsic role in civic affairs and concurrently subverts the conventional assumption that efficient governmental bureaucracies are imperious, inelegant, and immutable rather than hospitable and humane.

The first metaphor Graves incorporates in the Portland Building is the metaphor of the building as toy. He associates various dimensions of the building with children's toys and activities, thus extending toy-like images to a building that is supposed to be the epitome of efficiency. For example, many geometric shapes—trapezoidal figures, squares, and rectangles—flippantly decorate the facade, with the shapes fitting together much like a three-dimensional puzzle. The toy metaphor also is characterized by the shape of the building—a truncated jack-in-the-box—flanked on four sides by small, square, blackened windows, evoking images of small building blocks used by children in their play. Approaching the Fourth Avenue entrance, the building reveals the features of a robotic face, complete with two eyes (two inverted, three-dimensional triangles) staring out in wide-eyed wonder. Across the top of the columns on one side of the building are bas-relief "ribbons," reminiscent of colorful streamers on May poles. The two-dimensional quality of these ribbons is cartoonish, and, as one reviewer notes, the building "looks as though it just won first prize at the county fair."[8] Thus, these playful accoutrements serve as facetious caricatures of the red tape usually associated with government.

The building's anthropomorphic quality is the second metaphor Graves uses to engage viewers. Richard Sennett underscores the prevalence of the human form in the history of architecture when he argues that in "the course of urban development master images of 'the body' have frequently been used, in transfigured form, to define what a building or an entire city should look like."[9] The building as human is seen in the Portland Building's three-part structure—a structure like that of a human body—legs (the base of the building is weighted in green), torso (the middle section is painted a parchment color), and head (coiffed in a receding tier). The context in which these images occur invites the metaphor of the body politic. By endowing the building with human form, Graves takes the bite out of Portland's political machine. Instead of an austere, looming edifice housing cynical politicians, nameless workers, or, in the words of T. S. Eliot, "hollow men," the Portland Building is shaped into a humane structure—one that reflects the kind of citizens visitors hope work inside. The building's human-like characteristics celebrate the role of humans, not machines, in civic affairs.

The third metaphor Graves employs is a metaphor of building as romance. The Portland Building embraces a feeling of sensuality rather than utility. Citizens generally assume that a public service building first and foremost is functional. They have been conditioned to think that, in such buildings, walls are gray, furniture is brown, and lighting is fluorescent. Instead of the colorless neutrality of black, gray, and shiny steel dominant in virtually every streamlined slab of the modernist style, however, the Portland Building is dipped in a soft color scheme of pastels—maroon, blue, and green. The colors and the way in which they interact with light suggest the ambience of a Maxwell Parrish painting. By integrating color, form, light, and shadow, Graves erases the mundane and replaces it with a careful mixture of the sublime and the sensuous—with romance.

Although viewers and users of the Portland Building may appreciate it from an aesthetic perspective, my concern as a rhetorical critic is to understand how Graves' metaphors work in generating particular rhetorical responses to the building. The metaphors Graves selected work to encourage a transformation of viewers' usual attitudes toward government because they are rooted in and strongly linked to various positive patterns of experience. Graves references and articulates specific images and experiences that tend to generate positive emotions and to be associated with desirable and valued dimensions of human life (childhood memories, the joy of human contact, and romance). By juxtaposing these with equally strong but negative referents connected with government (bureaucracy, political machinery, sterility, and red tape), Graves gives visitors an opportunity to reconstruct their frame of reference for the offices and processes the building houses. The Portland Building's metaphors create a dialogue with visitors, encouraging them to readjust their perceived order—giving them an opportunity to reconstruct that order in a more positive way. The Portland Building, then, subverts the existing ideology of bureaucracy and invites citizens to revise their perspectives when approaching their city governmental structures— adopting a perspective of optimism, humor, and perhaps even delight.

I suggest that non-discursive metaphors often play a major role in the environment created by architecture; thus, such metaphors deserve the attention of rhetorical critics. Such non-discursive metaphors suggest that buildings are more than aesthetic sites upon which verbal discourse takes place; rather, through the metaphors they suggest, they can become, literally, a ground of ideology and argument, reaffirming conventional perspectives or, as in the case of the Portland Building, inviting viewers to apprehend, experience, and interpret their worlds in new ways.

Notes

¹ Susanne Langer, *Feeling and Form* (New York: Charles Scribners, 1953) 96. *0*

² Langer 96.

³ Gary Clark, letter, *Oregonian* 4 Mar. 1980: B6.

⁴ Robert K. Schroeder, letter, *Oregonian* 16 Mar. 1980: D2.

⁵ Wolf von Eckhardt, "A Pied Piper of Hobbit Land," *Time* 23 Aug. 1983: 62.

⁵ Steve Jenning, "Architects Favor Temple Design for City Office Building," *Oregonian* 18 Feb. 1980: B1.

⁷ Vincent Scully, "Michael Graves' Allusive Architecture," *Michael Graves Building and Projects 1966–1981*, ed. Karen Vogel Wheeler, Peter Arnell, and Ted Bickford (New York: Rizzoli, 1982) 297.

⁸ John Pastier, "First Monument of a Loosely Defined Style," *AIA Journal*, 72 (May 1983): 236.

⁹ Richard Sennett, *Flesh and Stone, the Body and the City in Western Civilization* (New York: W. W. Norton, 1994) 24.

Additional Samples
Metaphoric Criticism

Adams, John Charles. "Linguistic Values and Religious Experience: An Analysis of the Clothing Metaphors in Alexander Richardson's Ramist-Puritan Lectures on Speech." *Quarterly Journal of Speech*, 9 (February 1990), 58-68.

Aden, Roger C. "Back to the Garden: Therapeutic Place Metaphor in *Field of Dreams*." *Southern Communication Journal*, 59 (Summer 1994), 307-17.

Aden, Roger C. "Entrapment and Escape: Inventional Metaphors in Ronald Reagan's Economic Rhetoric." *Southern Communication Journal*, 54 (Summer 1989), 384-400.

Aden, Roger C., and Christina L. Reynolds. "Lost and Found in America: The Function of Place Metaphor in *Sports Illustrated*." *Southern Communication Journal*, 59 (Fall 1993), 1-14.

Akioye, Akin A. "The Rhetorical Construction of Radical Africanism at the United Nations: Metaphoric Cluster as Strategy." *Discourse and Society*, 5 (January 1995), 7-31.

Blankenship, Jane. "The Search for the 1972 Democratic Nomination: A Metaphorical Perspective." In *Methods of Rhetorical Criticism: A Twentieth-Century Perspective*, ed. Bernard L. Brock and Robert L. Scott (Detroit: Wayne State University Press, 1980), pp. 321-45.

Brown, Richard Harvey. "Rhetoric and the Science of History: The Debate Between Evolutionism and Empiricism as a Conflict in Metaphors." *Quarterly Journal of Speech*, 72 (May 1986), 148-61.

Brummett, Barry. "The Representative Anecdote as a Burkean Method, Applied to Evangelical Rhetoric." *Southern Speech Communication Journal*, 50 (Fall 1984), 1-23.

Carpenter, Ronald H. "America's Tragic Metaphor: Our Twentieth-Century Combatants as Frontiersmen." *Quarterly Journal of Speech*, 76 (February 1990), 1-22.

Daughton, Suzanne M. "Metaphorical Transcendence: Images of the Holy War in Franklin Roosevelt's First Inaugural." *Quarterly Journal of Speech*, 79 (November 1993), 427-46.

Farrell, Thomas B., and G. Thomas Goodnight. "Accidental Rhetoric: The Root Metaphors of Three Mile Island." *Communication Monographs*, 48 (December 1981), 271-300.

Foss, Sonja K., and Anthony J. Radich. "Metaphors in 'Treasures of Tutankhamen': Implications for Aesthetic Education." *Art Education*, 37 (January 1984), 6-11.

Gribbin, William. "The Juggernaut Metaphor in American Rhetoric." *Quarterly Journal of Speech*, 59 (October 1973), 297-303.

Ivie, Robert L. "Literalizing the Metaphor of Soviet Savagery: President Truman's Plain Style." *Southern Speech Communication Journal*, 51 (Winter 1986), 91-105.

Ivie, Robert L. "Metaphor and the Rhetorical Invention of Cold War 'Idealists.'" *Communication Monographs*, 54 (June 1987), 165–82.

Ivie, Robert L. "The Metaphor of Force in Prowar Discourse: The Case of 1912." *Quarterly Journal of Speech*, 68 (August 1982), 240–53.

Jamieson, Kathleen Hall. "The Metaphoric Cluster in the Rhetoric of Pope Paul VI and Edmund G. Brown, Jr." *Quarterly Journal of Speech*, 66 (February 1980), 51–72.

Jensen, J. Vernon. "British Voices on the Eve of the American Revolution: Trapped by the Family Metaphor." *Quarterly Journal of Speech*, 63 (February 1977), 43–50.

Kaplan, Stuart Jay. "Visual Metaphors in the Representation of Communication Technology." *Critical Studies in Mass Communication*, 7 (March 1990), 37–47.

Koch, Susan, and Stanley Deetz. "Metaphor Analysis of Social Reality in Organizations." *Journal of Applied Communication Research*, 9 (Spring 1981), 1–15.

Mechling, Elizabeth Walker, and Jay Mechling. "The Jung and the Restless: The Mythopoetic Men's Movement." *Southern Communication Journal*, 59 (Winter 1994), 97–111.

Osborn, Michael. "Archetypal Metaphor in Rhetoric: The Light-Dark Family." *Quarterly Journal of Speech*, 53 (April 1967), 115–26.

Owen, William Foster. "Thematic Metaphors in Relational Communication: A Conceptual Framework." *Western Journal of Speech Communication*, 49 (Winter 1985), 1–13.

Perry, Stephen. "Rhetorical Functions of the Infestation Metaphor in Hitler's Rhetoric." *Central States Speech Journal*, 34 (Winter 1983), 229–35.

Smith, Ruth C., and Eric M. Eisenberg. "Conflict at Disneyland: A Root-Metaphor Analysis." *Communication Monographs*, 54 (December 1987), 367–80.

Solomon, Martha. "Covenanted Rights: The Metaphoric Matrix of 'I Have a Dream.'" In *Martin Luther King., Jr., and the Sermonic Power of Public Discourse*, Ed. Carolyn Calloway-Thomas and John Louis Lucaites. Tuscaloosa: University of Alabama Press, 1993, pp. 66–84.

Stelzner, Hermann G. "Analysis by Metaphor." *Quarterly Journal of Speech*, 51 (February 1965), 52–61.

Stelzner, Hermann G. "Ford's War on Inflation: A Metaphor that Did Not Cross." *Communication Monographs*, 44 (November 1977), 284–97.

van Teefelen, Toine. "Racism and Metaphor: The Palestinian-Israeli Conflict in Popular Literature." *Discourse and Society*, 5 (July 1994), 381–405.

10

Narrative Criticism

Alasdair MacIntyre has described the human being as "essentially a story-telling animal."[1] Narratives help us impose order on the flow of experience so that we can make sense of events and actions in our lives. They allow us to interpret reality because they help us decide what a particular experience "is about" and how the various elements of our experience are connected.[2]

Recognition of the capacity of stories to reveal how we organize experience has led to the study of narrative by scholars in a wide range of disciplines. Contributions to the study of narrative can be traced to classical Greece and Rome; Aristotle and Quintilian, for example, both wrote about narration.[3] Contemporary contributions to our understanding of various aspects of narrative include Walter R. Fisher's work on the narrative paradigm;[4] Ernest G. Bormann's theory of symbolic convergence and fantasy-theme analysis;[5] the cultural perspective on communication, represented by, among others, Nick [O'Donnell] Trujillo, Michael E. Pacanowsky, Linda L. Putnam, and Stanley A. Deetz;[6] and Kenneth Burke's notions of dramatism and the pentad.[7] The performance perspective on communication, in which human beings and cultures are seen as constituting themselves through performances of various kinds, including stories, is another component of the study of narrative; this approach is represented by the work of Victor Turner,[8] Clifford Geertz,[9] Richard Bauman,[10] and Dwight Conquergood.[11]

Because of the conceptual diversity that characterizes narrative theory, *narrative* has been defined in a number of ways. A narrative generally is recognized to be a way of ordering and presenting a view of the world through a description of a situation involving characters, actions, and settings. Most definitions also include the idea that a narrative involves a sequence of some kind so that at least two events or states are organized sequentially.[12] In many narratives, the sequences are temporally organized, with the order of events moving chronologically through time. In other narratives, the sequences are constructed through means other than time—by a theme, a character, or a quality, perhaps. Narratives are found in all types of symbol use. They constitute the basic form of short stories, novels, comic strips, films, and many songs and also occur as part of larger discursive forms such as conversations with friends, interviews, and speeches.[13]

The critic who uses narrative or features of narrative as the unit of analysis in rhetorical criticism focuses on the story form itself. The critic may be interested in discovering how the construction of a particular narrative directs the interpretation of a situation. A narrative, as a frame upon experience, functions as an argument to view and understand the world in a particular way, and by analyzing that narrative, the critic can understand the argument being made and the likelihood that it will be successful in gaining adherence for the perspective it presents.

A critic whose interest is in how narratives construct particular interpretations also may choose to investigate how different types of narratives, with their distinctive structures and styles, persuade differently. Habitual narratives, for example, in which events happen over and over with no peak in the action, are structured differently from hypothetical narratives, which depict events that did not happen. Various types of narratives may create particular kinds of arguments, and these differences may constitute the rhetorical phenomena in which the critic is interested.

Critics also may choose to use narratives or aspects of narratives as units of analysis because they want to discover the effects or likely effects of particular narratives on audiences. If narratives are being used in a political campaign, for example, the critic might be interested in finding out the impact those narratives have on voters' perceptions of a candidate. Narratives might be examined, as well, to discover how they discourage or facilitate particular outcomes—possibilities for dispute resolution or peace negotiations, for example; the perceptions they create of a particular cause, issue, or group; or the impression they convey of a rhetor. A critic also may be interested in the effects of narratives on the storytellers themselves—how they function as tools for empowerment or to build community within a group, for example.

Narratives can be examined, as well, for what they reveal about an individual's or a culture's identity. Because stories "have to do with how protagonists interpret things, what things mean to them,"[14] they provide clues to the subjectivity of individuals and to the values and meanings that characterize a culture. The stories told by a rhetor or group of rhetors, then, provide clues to their worldviews and thus to their motivations for action. Similarly, the stories commonly told in a culture provide glimpses into that culture—the meanings attributed to particular events, those aspects of the culture that are privileged and repressed, its values, and its ethical system, for example.

All of the symbolic forms that can be studied from a narrative perspective also can be analyzed from pentadic or fantasy-theme perspectives; all three include as units of analysis characters, actions, and settings and thus enable similar insights to be developed about an artifact in these areas. What narrative criticism offers that these other perspectives do not, however, is the opportunity to investigate a greater number of dimensions of the narrative itself—dimensions beyond characters, settings, and actions—and the opportunity to analyze not simply the content of a worldview but the form and structure of that worldview.

Procedures

Using dimensions of narratives as units of analysis, the critic proceeds through four steps: (1) formulating a research question and selecting an artifact; (2) selecting a unit of analysis; (3) analyzing the artifact; and (4) writing the critical essay.

Formulating a Research Question and Selecting an Artifact

The first step in the process of rhetorical criticism is to develop a research question to ask about rhetoric and to select a rhetorical artifact to analyze that will provide an initial answer to the question.

Selecting a Unit of Analysis

The critic's next step is to select a unit of analysis that can help the critic answer the research question. The unit of analysis is that aspect of the artifact to which the critic attends in the analysis. The units of analysis provided by narrative criticism are the various dimensions of narratives.

Analyzing the Artifact

The basic procedure for conducting narrative criticism involves two steps: (1) a comprehensive examination of the narrative; and (2) selection of elements on which to focus. The first step involves examining the narrative in detail to gain a comprehensive understanding of it as a whole. The second involves focusing on those aspects of the narrative that allow the critic to answer the research question that guides the analysis.

Comprehensive Examination of the Narrative. In order to understand the narrative as a whole, the critic explores the various dimensions of the narrative. The following questions are offered as starting places for identifying features of the narrative:

1. *Setting:* What is the setting or scene in the narrative? Is there a change in setting over the course of the narrative? How does the setting relate to the plot and characters? How is the particular setting created? Is the setting textually prominent—highly developed and detailed—or negligible?[15]

2. *Characters:* Who are the main characters in the narrative? Are some of the characters non-human or inanimate phenomena, described as thinking and speaking beings? What are the physical and mental traits of the characters? In what actions do the characters engage? Do the traits or actions of the characters change over the course of the narrative?

How are the characters presented? Are they flat or round? A flat character has one or just a few dominating traits, making the behavior of the character highly predictable. Round characters, on the contrary, possess a variety of traits, some of them conflicting or even contradictory. Their behavior is less predictable than that of flat characters because they are likely to change and to continue to reveal previously unknown traits.[16]

3. *Narrator:* Is the narrative presented directly to the audience, or is it mediated by a narrator? In direct presentation of the narrative, the audience directly witnesses the action, and the voice speaking of events, characters, and setting is hidden from the audience. In a narrative mediated by a narrator, the audience is told about events and characters by a narrator whose presence is more or less audible. If a narrator is audible, what features mark the presence of the narrator? What in the narrative creates a sense of the narrator's presence? What makes the narrator intrusive or not?

What kind of person is the narrator? A narrator who apologizes, defends, and pleads, for example, is different from one who evaluates, criticizes, and preaches. What kind of vocabulary does the narrator use? Does the narrator favor certain types of words, sentence structures, metaphors, or types of arguments? Is the narrative vividly told and detailed? Is the narrator wordy and verbose or straightforward and direct? How coherent is the narrative? Does the narrator adequately connect the various elements of the narrative to one another to create a cogent and meaningful narrative? What is the narrator's attitude toward the story being told, the subject matter of the story, the audience, and him or herself?

If the narrative is being presented orally, what characterizes the narrator's pitch, pauses, tone of voice, gestures, emphasis, pronunciation, and other features of speech? Style also may be visual in narratives that are predominantly or exclusively visual, accomplished through such elements as types of shots in video or film, motions in dance, or styles of painting.

What kinds of powers are available to the narrator? What kind of authority does the narrator claim?[17] What is the point of view adopted by the narrator? Point of view is the perceptual and psychological point of view in the presentation of the narrative. Is the narrator omniscient, knowing the outcome of every event and the nature of every character and setting, thus telling the story from a god-like vantage point? Is the narrator omnipresent—able to skip from one locale to the other in the narrative? Is the narrator allowed to range into the past or future or restricted to the contemporary story moment? Does the narrator engage in time and space summarizing, a process in which vast panoramas and large groups of people are characterized in certain ways as seen from the narrator's exalted position? Does the narrator go beyond describing to engage in commentary such as interpretation and evaluation? Does the narrator engage in metanarrative discourse, or discourse in which the narrative itself is discussed and elements in the narrative are commented on explicitly—such as definitions of terms or translations of foreign words? How does the narrator report characters' discourse? Does the narrator use direct forms of representation, in which the exact words of the characters are reported? Does the narrator use indirect forms, in which the characters' speech and thought are paraphrased, suggesting more intervention by the narrator?

How reliable is the narrator? In unreliable narration, the narrator's account is at odds with the audience's inferences and judgments about the story. The audience concludes that the events and characters depicted by the narrator could not have been as the narrator describes them. What seems to be the cause of the narrator's unreliability—gullibility, innocence, or a desire to mislead?[18]

4. *Events:* What are the major and minor events—plot lines, hap-
penings, or changes of state—in the narrative? Major events are called
kernels; these are events that suggest critical points in the narrative and
that force movement in particular directions. They cannot be left out
of a narrative without destroying its coherence and meaning. Minor plot
events, called *satellites,* are the development or working out of the
choices made at the kernels. Their function is to fill out, elaborate, and
complete the kernels. Satellites are not crucial to the narrative and can
be deleted without disturbing the basic story line of the narrative. Their
omission, of course, would affect the form of the narrative and the form's
rhetorical effects.[19]

How are the events presented? Are they characterized by particular
qualities? How fully are the kernels developed by satellites? How do
the satellites affect the nature of the kernels? Are the events active
(expressing action) or stative (expressing a state or condition)?[20]

5. *Temporal Relations:* What are the temporal relationships among
the events recounted in the narrative? Do events occur in a brief period
of time or over many years? What is the relationship between the natural
order of the events as they occurred and the order of their presentation
in the telling of the narrative? Does the narrator use flashbacks and
flashforwards, common devices to reorder events as they are narrated?[21]
How is the story that is told located in time with respect to the act of
narrating it? Is the telling of the story subsequent to what it tells—a
predictive or prophetic form? Is the telling in present tense, simultaneous
or interspersed with the action depicted? Is the narration in the past
tense, coming after the events recounted?[22]

What is the speed of the narrative? Speed is the relationship between
the length of time the events in the narrative go on and the length of
the narrative. Are particular events and characters narrated with higher
speed than others? Does use of speed emphasize some events and
characters over others?[23]

6. *Causal Relations:* What cause-and-effect relationships are established in the narrative? How are connections made between causes and
effects? Is cause presented prior to effect or after it? How clearly and
strongly are the connections between cause and effect made? Which
receives the most emphasis—the cause or the effect? What kinds of
causes are dominant in the narration? Are events caused largely by
human action, accident, or forces of nature? In how much detail are the
causes and effects described?

7. *Audience:* Who is the audience or the person or people to whom
the narrative is addressed? Is it addressed to an individual, a group, or
the narrator him or herself? Is the audience a participant in the events
recounted? What are the signs of the audience in the narrative? What

can be inferred about the audience's attitudes, knowledge, or situation from the narrative? Is the audience represented in a detailed or sketchy manner? What seems to be the narrator's evaluation of the audience's knowledge, personality, and abilities?[24]

8. *Theme:* What is the major theme of the narrative? A theme is a general idea illustrated by the narrative; it is what a narrative means or is about and points to the significance and meaning of the action. A narrative's theme might be that good triumphs over evil, oppression is unjust, everyone can succeed with hard work, and violence is sometimes justified. How is the theme articulated in the narrative— through the depiction of setting, characters, or events or through the narrator's commentary? How obvious and clear is the theme?[25]

As a result of an examination of the elements of the narrative suggested by these questions and other elements the critic notices while investigating the narrative, the critic develops a comprehensive picture of the narrative. All of this information, however, is not included in the critic's essay. What the critic includes is developed in the second step of the process of narrative criticism: identification of the feature or features of the narrative that are significant for and most relevant to the research question that is guiding the critic's analysis.

Selection of Significant Elements. At the end of the process of identifying the basic features of the narrative, the critic has examined in a detailed fashion the content and means of expression of the narrative. The critic's task now is to identify which of those features are of most significance and relevance to the research question the critic is asking. These features are those that provide the clearest, most coherent, and most insightful answer to the research question. If the critic is using narrative to understand the persuasive appeal of a particular discourse, for example, the critic would discuss how the significant elements of the narrative identified help to explain the persuasive appeal. Perhaps the nature of the characters and how they are presented provide the most useful clues to the source of a narrative's persuasive appeal. If the critic's interest is in the impact a narrative is likely to have on efforts to negotiate a peace treaty between two countries, the critic would use the significant features identified—perhaps the temporal and causal relations of the narrative—to suggest what that impact is likely to be.

In selecting the elements of the narrative on which to focus, the critic may find that elements of the story itself (the substance or content of the narrative or the story line), are the most important. In other instances, elements of the expression of the story (the means by which the content is communicated or the form of the narrative) may appear to be most significant.[26] Because the interconnection of form and content makes separating the *what* of the narrative from its *how* difficult, however, most critics choose to use as units of analysis aspects of both the substance and form of the narrative. A critic who is interested in discovering what a political leader's narratives about his experiences during World War II suggest about his view of war, for example, might discover that the nature of the characters and the way they are depicted are the most important features of the narratives in terms of explaining his attitude toward war—an interest in both content and form. A critic who is interested in the values that are suggested in the stories told in therapeutic groups, on the other hand, may discover that the content of the stories—the nature of the characters, settings, and events—are of far greater importance than the forms of expression through which these are conveyed.

Writing the Critical Essay

After completion of the analysis, the critic writes an essay that includes five major components: (1) an introduction, in which the research question, its contribution to rhetorical theory, and its significance are discussed; (2) description of the artifact and its context; (3) description of the unit of analysis, the dimensions of narrative; (4) report of the findings of the analysis, in which the critic suggests the dimensions of the narrative that are most significant for answering the research question; and (5) discussion of the contribution the analysis makes to answering the research question.

Sample Essays

In the following samples of narrative criticism, narratives are used as units of analysis to answer a variety of research questions. Catherine A. Collins and Jeanne E. Clark's essay on *Nightline's* series on the conflict between Israelis and Palestinians contributes to an understanding of how the construction of a narrative directs the interpretation of a situation. They are guided by the research question, "How do structural choices in narrative encourage particular readings of the events depicted?," and answer it by focusing on the dimensions of narrator, narrative order, characters, and narrative segmentation. In the essay by Thomas A. Hollihan and Patricia Riley, the focus is on the substantive themes of the narratives; they are interested in discovering an answer to the research questions, "What is the nature of therapeutic narratives told in support groups?," "What in these narratives accounts for their appeal?," and "What are the effects of these narratives on their audiences?" Linda Cooper Berdayes' analysis of a narrative about the information highway is designed to answer the research question, "What role for women is suggested in the assumptions and values that underlie the narrative told about the information highway?" She selected setting, characters, narrator, and major event as features of the narrative that provide the most relevant information for answering the question.

Notes

[1] Alasdair MacIntyre, *After Virtue: A Study in Moral Theory* (1981; rpt. Notre Dame, Indiana: Notre Dame University Press, 1984), p. 216.

[2] W. Lance Bennett, "Storytelling in Criminal Trials: A Model of Social Judgment," *Quarterly Journal of Speech,* 64 (February 1978), 1–22; and Catherine Kohler Riessman, *Narrative Analysis* (Newbury Park, California: Sage, 1993), pp. 1–4.

[3] For a good summary of Aristotle's and Quintilian's discussions of narrative, see John Louis Lucaites and Celeste Michelle Condit, "Re-constructing Narrative Theory: A Functional Perspective," *Journal of Communication,* 35 (Autumn 1985), 90–108.

[4] Walter R. Fisher, *Human Communication as Narration: Toward a Philosophy of Reason, Value, and Action* (Columbia: University of South Carolina Press, 1987). For responses to Fisher, see: Barbara Warnick, "The Narrative Paradigm: Another Story," *Quarterly Journal of Speech,* 73 (May 1987), 172–82; Robert C. Rowland, "Narrative: Mode of Discourse or Paradigm?" *Communication Monographs,* 54 (September 1987), 264–75; and Michael Calvin McGee and John S. Nelson, "Narrative Reason in Public Argument," *Journal of Communication,* 35 (Autumn 1985), 139–55.

[5] See, for example, Ernest G. Bormann, "Fantasy and Rhetorical Vision: The Rhetorical Criticism of Social Reality," *Quarterly Journal of Speech,* 58 (December 1972), 396–407. Other sources on symbolic convergence theory and fantasy-theme analysis can be found in chapter 5 of this book.

[6] Two sources contain a number of essays articulating the notion of organization as culture, including ones by Trujillo, Pacanowsky, Putnam, and Deetz: *Western Journal of Speech Communication,* 46 (Spring 1982); and Linda L. Putnam and Michael E. Pacanowsky, eds., *Communication and Organizations: An Interpretive Approach* (Beverly Hills: Sage, 1983).

[7] See, for example, Kenneth Burke, "Dramatism," *International Encyclopedia of the Social Sciences,* ed. David L. Sills ([New York]: Macmillan/Free, 1968), VII, 445–52; and Kenneth Burke, *A Grammar of Motives* (Berkeley: University of California Press, 1969), pp. xv, xvi, xxx.

[8] See, for example, Victor W. Turner and Edward M. Bruner, eds., *The Anthropology of Performance* (Urbana: University of Illinois Press, 1986).

[9] See, for example, Clifford Geertz, *The Interpretation of Cultures* (New York: Basic, 1973).

[10] See, for example, Richard Bauman, *Verbal Art as Performance* (Prospect Heights, Illinois: Waveland Press, 1977).

[11] See, for example, Dwight Conquergood, "Between Experience and Meaning: Performance as a Paradigm for Meaningful Action," in *Renewal and Revision: The Future of Interpretation,* ed. Ted Colson (Denton, Texas: Omega, 1986), pp. 26–59.

[12] Gerald Prince, *Narratology: The Form and Functioning of Narrative* (New York: Mouton, 1982), pp. 4, 145.

[13] Some theorists distinguish among various kinds of communication and see narrative as functioning differently in each, but I am not making such distinctions. See, for example, Lucaites and Condit; and Thomas B. Farrell, "Narrative in Natural Discourse: On Conversation and Rhetoric," *Journal of Communication,* 35 (Autumn 1985), 109–27.

[14] Jerome Bruner, *Acts of Meaning* (Cambridge, Massachusetts: Harvard University Press, 1990), p. 51.

[15] For more on setting, see Seymour Chatman, *Story and Discourse: Narrative Structure in Fiction and Film* (Ithaca, New York: Cornell University Press, 1978), pp. 101–07, 138–45; Robert Liddell, *A Treatise on the Novel* (London: Jonathan Cape, 1947), pp. 110–28; and Prince, pp. 73–74.

[16] For more on characters, see Chatman, *Story and Discourse*, pp. 119–38, 198–209; Prince, pp. 13–16, 47–48, 71–73; and Gérard Genette, *Narrative Discourse: An Essay in Method*, trans. Jane E. Lewin (Ithaca, New York: Cornell University Press, 1980), pp. 169–85.

[17] Lanser suggests that a narrator's authority arises from three features: status, a function of the narrator's credibility, sincerity, and storytelling skill; contact, the pattern of the narrator's relationship with the audience; and stance, the narrator's relationship to the story being told. Susan Sniader Lanser, *The Narrative Act: Point of View in Prose Fiction* (Princeton, New Jersey: Princeton University Press, 1981), pp. 85–94.

[18] For more on the narrator, see Chatman, *Story and Discourse*, pp. 146–262; Prince, 7–16, 33–47, 50–54, 115–28; Genette, pp. 185–211; and Bauman, pp. 61–79.

[19] For more on kernel and satellite events, see Chatman, *Story and Discourse*, pp. 53, 54; and Prince, pp. 83–92.

[20] Active and stative events are discussed by Prince, pp. 62–63.

[21] For more on temporal relations, see Prince, pp. 48–50, 64–65; and Seymour Chatman, "What Novels Can Do That Films Can't (and Vice Versa)," in *On Narrative*, ed. W. J. T. Mitchell (Chicago: University of Chicago Press, 1980), p. 118.

[22] For more on the relationship between story time and narrating time, see Paul Ricoeur, "Narrative Time," in *On Narrative*, ed. W. J. T. Mitchell (Chicago: University of Chicago Press, 1980), pp. 165–86; Chatman, *Story and Discourse*, pp. 63–84; and Genette, pp. 33–160, 215–27. Genette distinguishes among three categories of relations: order (the order in which the events of the story are presented), duration (the relation of the time it takes to read out the narrative to the time the story-events themselves lasted), and frequency (number of representations of story moments).

[23] For more on speed of the narrative, see Prince, pp. 54–59.

[24] For more on the audience, see Prince, pp. 16–26; and Genette, pp. 259–60.

[25] For more on theme, see Prince, p. 74.

[26] Seymour Chatman, *Story and Discourse*, p. 19; and Prince, p. 7. Some narrative theorists suggest that a narrative contains three parts rather than two: story, narrative, and narrating. The *story* is the sequence of events related or the content of the story; the *narrative* is the narrative text in which the story is manifest or the statement of the story in a particular medium such as a novel, myth, or film; and the *narrating* is the telling of the story or the act of narrating. See, for example, Genette, p. 27; and Edward M. Bruner, p. 145.

A Structural Narrative Analysis of *Nightline's* "This Week in the Holy Land"

Catherine A. Collins and Jeanne E. Clark

For 4 years, Palestinians and Israelis have been caught up in a cycle of violence they call the *intifadeh*, the uprising. During these years count-less news stories have reported the violence and attempted to explain why it continues. One of the most comprehensive attempts early in the *intifadeh* to provide a coherent story came with *Nightline's* five-part series titled "This Week in the Holy Land." The series intended to "provide some context—historical, political, military and religious—for the news stories that so dominate our headlines" (*Nightline*, I, p. 2).[1] As narrator, Ted Koppel tells us that to understand the *intifadeh* requires an understanding of the new and ancient stories told by the Israelis and Palestinians. Koppel arranges to let the participants tell their own story in a Town Meeting, bringing them together to talk with one another. ABC assigns reporters to interview participants on both sides of the conflict and encourage them to explain the conflict.

Nightline adopts an overtly neutral stance in chronicling the events of the *intifadeh*. White (1987) would describe this as discourse that narrativizes. Rather than openly adopting a perspective and viewing the events of the uprising from that stance, the series "feigns to make the world speak itself and speak itself as a story" (White, 1987, p. 2). It is apparent in watching the series that both its structure and its subject matter are closely tied to stories told and retold by the parties to the conflict, journalists, historians, international leaders, and others seeking to explain and end the cycle of violence. What is also apparent with a close textual analysis is that choices in the way *Nightline* constructs the series contradict the overt effort to let the participants tell their own story. *Nightline* privileges a particular reading of the conflict. This paper seeks to deconstruct the way narrative choices in the series construct a reality for the audience. *Nightline's* "This Week in the Holy Land" serves as a case study in how structural choices—some intentional, others

From *Critical Studies in Mass Communication*, 9 (March 1992), 25–43. Used by permission of the Speech Communication Association and the authors.

culturally proscribed—argue for particular readings of events, particular characterizations and attributions of motives.

Through varied foci, media studies have turned our attention to how news participates in the social construction of reality: news production (Gans, 1979; Tuchman, 1978); the ideological function of the news (Glasgow University Media Group, 1976, 1980, 1982); news language (Edelman, 1987; Sigman & Fry, 1985; Trew, 1979), discourse analysis (van Dijk, 1988); and the normalization of news (Bennett, Gressett, & Haltom, 1985; Eliasoph, 1988). Taken together, these studies build a rich sense of how the news, as a communicative act, comes to have meaning for an audience. The news tells a story. A story involves relationships between the text—the story being told, the teller—the narrator, and the audience whose recreation of the story gives it meaning. No single approach explains how audiences construct meaning from media messages. Each, however, adds to our appreciation of how news choices influence the social construction of meaning.

A structuralist approach to narrative theory (Barkin & Gurevitch, 1987; Chatman, 1978; Genette, 1983; Rimmon-Kenan, 1983) provides a lens for discovering how textual structures in news discourse belie the overtly narrativizing posture. This approach assumes that whether the text is literature, television, film, or a news report, it reveals structural choices of inclusion, order, duration, voice, and mood that narrow the scope of potential readings (Genette, 1983). In the case of news documentary, conventional form dictates a posture of detachment, of objectivity, but attention to textual structures reveals the countering control wielded through choices of structural elements. The news documentary is supposed to balance pro and con, liberal and conservative, or in this case Palestinian and Israeli voices. But this series' linguistic choices and reliance on particular narrative selections from among potential details, spokespersons, and relationships deflect us from an alternative reading into a privileged reading.

Bennett and Edelman (1985) remind us that the power of narrative in news discourse comes from the "sequence of evocations that are accepted unself-consciously" (p. 165) in news texts as in any other narrative text. Not all readers will understand the text in the same way, but their individual readings are "not likely to be idiosyncratic either. The cues in a text set off similar resonances in people who share a common characteristic like class, gender, ideology, ethnicity, or color" (p. 165). Meaning ultimately rests with the audience's reconstruction of the text, but structural variables narrow the range of reconstructions. "The selection of documentary detail becomes all the more convincing (i.e., the selected details become 'facts') when the audience can fill in a time-honored favorite narrative plot that makes sense of emerging facts" (p. 164). Attention to structural narrative decisions informs our understanding of the relationship between media representations and audience perceptions.

Understanding the way narratives frame audience perceptions requires a close textual analysis. How does the authoritative stance of the narrator focus an audience's reading of the text? What anthology of stories does the news documentary evoke? How do choices of narrative order, movement, and segmentation privilege a particular perspective? How do choices in plot and character development make a reconstruction coherent? The *Nightline* series illustrates how structural elements forefront a particular reconstruction for the audience.

The complexity of the conflicting stories generated by Israelis and Palestinians during the early months of the *intifadeh* justify the overt attempts of Koppel, as the visible narrator for the ABC *Nightline* effort, to deconstruct the stories from the Holy Land, to privilege one particular reconstruction of the *intifadeh* story. On the surface, the five-part series gives the participants an incredible opportunity to tell their own story; but careful attention to the structure of the series reveals a compelling funneling of the audience into one reading of the discourse. This is nowhere more obvious than in Part III. In the introduction, Koppel proclaims:

> For several months now, our correspondents and producers have been compiling versions of history, stories and legends, some of them carved out of our lifetimes and those of our parents and grandparents. . . . But the same events are remembered in different ways. . . . Get ready to be outraged by history. By the time this program is over, you will have learned what professional historians already know: history is not objective recitation of truth, it is a story shaded and sculpted by those temporarily in control. . . . George Santayana's famous aphorism that those who forget the lessons of history are condemned to relive them is incomplete. In the Holy land, it is precisely the ancient and not-so-ancient stories, told and retold, that are used to justify this repetition. (p. 2)

We will do two things to develop the *Nightline* case study: describe local stories the *Nightline* team encounters during research and live interviews—e.g, how the participants in the conflict explain their actions—and then offer a narrative structural analysis of the story, with its authoritative voice, created by editing and Koppel's interventions. The *Nightline* series gives us a rich understanding of how stories shape a culture and its people. Koppel's deconstruction of the overall story reveals an American, or at least American journalistic, narrative form into which the events of history are forced to fit. Koppel acknowledges this by the end of the series, stating:

> An American perspective on history is a handicap in this part of the
> world. . . . When we wonder at the capacity of Palestinians and Jews
> to inflict and absorb punishment on and from one another, we merely
> reflect our own impatience, and the brevity of our attention span.
> (Nightline, V, p. 9)

While admitting that television distorts the message, Koppel assures us
this is not a case of agenda-setting. The agenda has already been set by
the participants: "They had it before we came, and they'll have it after
we leave. A few thousand hours of television coverage, in that context,
doesn't even amount to a heartbeat" (Nightline, V, p. 9).

Nightline: The Israeli-Palestinian Conflict Story

The series ran for 5 nights. Part I introduces the conflict between
Palestinians and Israelis. Koppel interviews a special advisor to Yasir
Arafat and the Israeli Defense Minister, employing the Nightline
pattern—an interview with taped inserts to which guests respond. Part
II, a 3 hour and 10 minute Town Meeting, brings together a panel of
Palestinians and Israelis (President, Gaza Red Crescent; Palestinian
professors; Knesset members from Likud, Labor, and Citizens Rights).
This group speaks and answers questions before an audience representing the spectrum of Israeli and Palestinian views on the intifadeh.
Participants are asked to tell their story of what is happening, why, and
what needs to be done to resolve the conflict. Part III is Koppel's attempt
to explain the history of tensions between the parties. He interviews
historians Walid Khalidi and Yehuda Bauer and inserts brief clips from
the Town Meeting taped the previous night. Part IV focuses on the cycle
of violence Koppel sees in the Holy Land. Interviews with a West Bank
commander, a Palestinian attorney, and a former Israeli Foreign Minister
are contextualized for the television audience by a reading of Israeli and
Palestinian poetry that eloquently evokes the violence, the intransigence,
and the inevitability of conflict between these two groups. In Part V
Koppel confronts Shimon Peres and Yitzhak Shamir with the inevitability of generations caught in the hatred—a "dialogue of the deaf" (p 2).

Over the course of the week's interviews, discussion, and news
reports, people tell seemingly hundreds of mini-narratives, recounting
their roles in and memories of the past and present crisis. Such narratives
consist of story—a chronological series of events—and plot—the configuration of story elements in an interpretive frame to maximize
"emotional effect and thematic interest" (Scholes, 1976, p. 80). Several
shared plotlines emerge from the narrative multiplicity of the week.

These plotlines are drawn from statements made by the conflict participants and occasional representative summaries by reporters assigned to
a given perspective. Together these plots establish a monolithic "we-
they" division of noble victim and evil villain as each is presented with
Israeli and Palestinian versions, and often mutual refutations. Within
the contradictory and divisive plots, shared stories indicate shared
values, but counterpointing structure obscures commonality. The
narrative choices made by the stories' tellers and reinforced by the
program editors in their selection of stories to air serve to emphasize
the division rather than the identification.

Three broad anthologies of related plotlines form the corpus of rhetoric
from the Holy Land as seen in *Nightline*. These anthologies are not
mutually exclusive, nor do they cover the range of stories available from
excluded perspectives. We hear little of the stories of multiple factions
on both sides. While there is talk of Israeli debate, the mutually contradictory narratives of the anthologies reinforce a simpler sense of Arab-
Israeli polarity. Neither, however, are the stories manufactured by
Nightline. The anthologies resemble plotlines found in the *Jerusalem
Post International Edition* and *Al-Fajr Jerusalem* during the early months
of the *intifadeh*. Older stories compare with the "myths" Flapan (1987)
analyzes in his discussion of the birth of Israel. The narrative decision
to isolate one story line and bring it to the forefront or to interweave
the anthologies privileges a particular interpretation of individuals or
events within the conflict.

The *victimage* anthology contains three related plotlines: the story of
the Holocaust; the story of the Diaspora; and the terrorism story. The
anthology of *self and other* explains the way both sides develop heroes,
villains, and victims in their stories. Plotlines in the anthology of *land
claims* explain the motivation for the current conflict by justifying the
speakers' claims and denigrating the claims made by the other party.

An Anthology of Victimage

American media have traditionally told victimage stories from the
Israeli perspective; the Arabs are terrorists against the Jews whose
historically most dramatic suffering during the Holocaust inevitably led
to their desire to return to the Holy Land from which they had been
exiled. But each of these victimage stories is also a Palestinian story;
they are the homeless, forced out of their land, who currently suffer their
own holocaust at the hands of the Israeli occupiers. Tied to divergent
understandings of national beginnings and self-defense, the terrorist and
victim labels, once set, provide a public justification for actions during
and preceding the *intifadeh*. In each of the related plotlines both sides
claim the role of victim.

The holocaust story is the most familiar victimage plot. Two Israelis employ it during the Town Meeting (*Nightline*, II)—once justifying an Israeli action (p. 29) and once refuting a Palestinian's use of the story (p. 23). An Israeli historian dubs it a "major point" (*Nightline*, III, p. 13) in the history of the region. The Palestinian version of the holocaust story results from the Jewish demand for statehood: "What is the war of independence to Israel is the war of the catastrophe to the Arabs" (*Nightline*, III, p. 9). The Jews implemented "a carefully thought-out scheme": "Occupy land, remove Arabs and remove any signs of their existence, and bring Jewish people and replace them" (*Nightline*, III, p. 10). Victims become victimizers, and the two stories are merged.

Nightline introduces the story of the Diaspora from an unexpected perspective with a news clip of Palestinian refugees in 1948; the narrator remarks, "How many were evicted, how many just fled, will never be known," but "a million [homeless Arabs] . . . in refugee camps in Jordan, Gaza, Syria and Lebanon . . . created a Palestinian diaspora" (*Nightline*, I, p. 4). On the next night, conflict participants use the story repeatedly (e.g., p. 10 & p. 12). A Likud representative denies the Palestinian diaspora story. "Six hundred thousand Arabs fled Palestine in 1948 upon Arab leadership's invitation and appeal and call. . . . Arabs need martyrdom, I'm sorry to say it. And this is why they've kept refugees in refugee camps." The Jewish diaspora story is accepted and assumed, but that story is at an end, ". . . there are no Jewish refugees today." Victimage had ended for one group as it was beginning for the other.

From the holocaust and diaspora stories a third plotline emerges in which both sides use their own earlier victimage to justify efforts to establish and maintain a nation; violent acts are necessary. Similar actions by the other side are labeled terrorism. Both sides offer a central action of terror from earlier history "to bring the world's attention to the cause of this disgruntlement" (*Nightline*, II, p. 19). For the Palestinians it is the story of the Deir-Yassin massacre:

> As many as 250 Palestinian men, women and children were slaughtered. Some women were raped, then shot dead. Bodies were mutilated and stuffed down wells. Anwar Kateeb helped gather together 25 children who had been orphaned by the massacre, which he said was part of a deliberate campaign to terrify Palestinians. (*Nightline*, III, p. 9)

A reporter thus explains the story with interjections from eyewitnesses. This Palestinian shibboleth had already been used in the Town Meeting (*Nightline*, II, p. 13). Israelis throughout the week recall a litany of terrorism with references to the PLO: "a murderous organization . . . a terrorist organization" (*Nightline*, II, p. 27). A reporter carefully summarizes that litany of over 1,000 attacks. The Israelis need not give additional detail; the name of the organization evokes the Israeli plotline. Shamir, already labeled as a terrorist himself (*Nightline*, II, p. 13), dubs the *intifadeh* a new form of terrorist warfare (*Nightline*, V, p. 6). By contrast, the President of the Gaza Red Crescent dubs it "the legacy of Jewish terrorism" as he remembers Jewish bombing of Arab sites (*Nightline*, II, p. 24). This persistent story becomes a corrosive agent as participants use it repeatedly to place blame and evade responsibility. The story, central to both sides and fostered in its continual reappearance by Koppel, embodies the cycle of violence in escalating victimage.

An Anthology of Self and Other

Three sets of plotlines emphasize characterization of the participants: the David and Goliath story; the story of the intransigent other; and the story of the political reality. Each of these stories can be told from the perspective of the Israelis or the Palestinians, but an American audience is most familiar with the Israeli perspective.

One of the most often told stories in the conflict is the Bible story of the little shepherd David, armed only with a sling, taking on the mighty armor-clad giant Goliath. Ambassador Ben-Elissar gives the Israeli version of the story quickly and simply: "The Arab side has all the territories in the world. All the riches in the world. Everything. We have got only this small, tiny territory" (*Nightline*, II, p. 16). The resulting national security emphasis is sometimes called the Masada complex, recalling Zealots of tiny ancient Israel who chose mass suicide rather than surrender to Roman might.

Ironically, this security obsession fuels the Palestinian claims that the roles are reversed and that Israel is the Goliath to a helpless Palestinian population. "We are a civilian population, totally unarmed and defenseless and we are at the mercy of the greatest war machine that you have seen right here on TV" (*Nightline* II, p. 13).

The second plotline shifts from military menace to reluctant negotiators. Each side presents the other as a self-destructive obstinate opposite who threatens to destroy everyone. A representative of the American-Arab Anti-Discrimination Committee firmly casts the Israelis in this role: "My view is the greatest threat to Israel is itself. It has armed itself to the teeth. It's refused to make peace with its neighbors. It tries to bully and intimidate its neighbors" (*Nightline*, I, p. 8). No less inflammatory is Shamir's characterization of the Palestinians: "Their philosophy is a philosophy of hatred, of extermination. It's very danger-ous. But I'm sure that we will win, because we are motivated. We are reasonable. They are not reasonable. They are very extreme" (*Nightline*, V, p. 7). Both stories offer an extreme, almost racist, characterization of the other, precluding the possibility of negotiation. Even as neither sees its own role as Goliath, neither recognizes its own intransigence.

The story of political reality examines the nature of the uprising and the occupation and questions who can claim the prized label, "democratic." Israelis traditionally characterize their state as the sole democracy in the Middle East (e.g., *Nightline*, II, p. 14). This characterization erodes under Palestinian descriptions of the Israeli occupation as "slavery" (*Nightline*, I, p. 7) and the Palestinian uprising as a grass-roots, hence democratic, movement based on committees of "all sorts of people" (*Nightline*, IV, p. 2). For the Israelis the reality is reversed: the uprising is not democracy in action, but "anarchy" (*Nightline*, IV, p. 3), while the occupation offers "security, services, and . . . a normal life" (*Nightline*, IV, p. 3) rather than slavery.

An Anthology of Land Claims

"If you have no land you have no honor" (*Nightline*, III, p. 4). This Palestinian proverb is an apt introduction for both sides' plotlines concerning land ownership—plots centering on historical claims. The mutually contradictory plots leave the tellers at a narrative impasse like that described in 1940 by a Zionist land acquisition program spokesman: "There is no room for both peoples" (*Nightline*, III, p. 6).

Two primary stories justify national ownership of the land. The Israeli story returns to God's covenant with Abraham. Two Israeli children are quite explicit: "God gave it to us. He promised Abraham that we'll get this land." "I believe that we are the chosen people . . . chosen to live in this country. And they weren't. And that's all" (*Nightline*, V, p. 8). The Israeli story claim is undercut by a Palestinian counterclaim: "It's very difficult for the Jewish nice, unique history to know that I'm Semite. We're cousins. . . . We're the son of Abraham" (*Nightline*, II, p. 22).

Prior contemporary ownership is the other narrative basis for the Palestinian claim: "My family has been in Jerusalem continuously for the last 1,000 years, which is a little bit longer than the Mayflower, and is virtually 1,066 more like the Norman invasion of England" (*Nightline*, III, p. 5). An Israeli historian offers a Jewish counterstory: "although they [the Jews] were a minority in this country, there was never a time when there was no Jewish occupation of part of this land" (*Nightline*, III, p. 12).

Both sides present themselves as caregivers tormented by their dreams for the land, fulfilled in fructifying the land, and unable to leave it lest they be lost in rootless diaspora.

Their Story: Implications

The three anthologies of victimage, land claims, and self and other are not mutually exclusive; nevertheless, together they provide the basic stories used by the participants to justify action and perception in the conflict as it is portrayed by *Nightline*. The multiple plotlines in the "live" stories of Part II clarify participant ownership of the stories we hear throughout the week. These capsule narratives are not *Nightline* fabrications, but equally clearly they are not unaffected by their *Nightline* inclusion: "live" stories are reinforced, emphasized, by correspondent reports and selected taped interview segments.

All of the highlighted stories are set in the dichotomous frame of the anthologies. That the plotlines are shared suggests that the tellers hold similar values—that grounds exist for mutual recognition and peaceful coexistence. The story pairings in the anthologies, however, build a sharp "we-they" distinction; we are encouraged to see difference rather than similarity. The anthologies present an apparently insoluble conflict between justly aggrieved parties, victimized by each other and the world. Polarized accounts of the political reality in stories center on traditional Western values like democracy, cooperation/compromise, and the underdog hero. As we repeatedly hear story broken by counterstory, we begin to perceive the larger story *Nightline* constructs of two sides locked in combat, unable to recognize the humanity and similarity of the other. The second section of this paper extends our understanding of the distinctive *Nightline* story as it is narrated by Koppel.

Structural Choices in *Nightline*: Koppel's Palestinian-Israeli Story

We can better understand the story Koppel privileges by examining *Nightline*'s choices in plot, character development, and structural positioning. These choices transform our understanding of the chronological events of story—the conflict in the Holy Land. White (1987) argues, "the narrative figurates the body of events that serves as its primary referent and transforms these events into intimations of patterns of meaning that any literal representation of them as facts could never produce" (p. 45). Each choice of order, plot, or character development leads the reader to a particular pattern of meaning. We have been shown a cultural and narrative blindness in the Israeli and Palestinian storytellers. We may read *Nightline* as contemporary history or as a fiction created by ABC's journalists. Regardless, our understanding is changed by the progression of the story and the tone of acceptance or disbelief afforded individual characters' interpretation by the narrator.

Koppel as Narrator

Preparing for negotiations between the warring parties, the *Nightline*
series attempts to deconstruct the enumerated stories assumed to perpetuate the cycle of violence. The central character and narrator for this
overarching story is Ted Koppel, who switches between several roles—
peacebroker, objective news reporter, historian. This confusion of roles
leads to problems in *Nightline*'s deconstruction of the *intifadeh*.

As news reporter, Koppel's is the authoritative voice for unraveling
the tensions and seemingly insurmountable obstacles presented by the
Israeli-Palestinian conflict. The narrator as reporter shows us the
complexity of the events in a story form familiar and acceptable to
American culture: a conflict that is unresolvable given the attitudes of
the participants (e.g., Northern Ireland, South Africa). This reporter-
with-a-familiar-story is the narrative stance an American audience
expects of Koppel, but his dual controlling function as interviewer and
story unraveler leads easily into other narrative stances.

Although the series overtly tells us the purpose is not to instigate an
on-the-spot negotiation—"No one is here tonight to negotiate" (*Nightline*, II, p. 1); "we're not going to negotiate any settlements here tonight"
(*Nightline*, II, p. 10)—the context tells a different story. It moves us from
viewing Koppel as news reporter/moderator to viewing him as would-
be peacebroker.

Immediately preceding the denial of negotiation as a goal, an Israeli
spokesperson says, "I think that their leadership is our problem just like
our leadership is their problem. There is hope while we have this show
with Ted Koppel" (*Nightline*, II, p. 10). The previous night Koppel had
asked a PLO spokesman whether a joint announcement of Israeli willingness to negotiate with the PLO and PLO recognition of Israel's right
to exist "within secure boundaries" might be possible with the intervention of "someone independently, let's say some broker" (*Nightline*,
I, p. 6).

When Rabin, the Israeli Defense Minister, firmly rejects negotiation
with the PLO, Koppel pulls back: "I understand, we're not going to do
it here, but why is it not possible that there can be private meetings?"
(*Nightline*, I, p. 9). The similar modest denial on the second night,
Koppel's constant probes to see if panelists at the Town Meeting are
willing to negotiate, and his challenges to the official stories all mitigate
the denial.

Instead we are subtly given the image of Koppel as peacebroker and
of *Nightline* as the Camp David of the late '80s. The preparation for the
Town Meeting itself, Koppel says, involved "negotiations" of some
"delicacy," including the placement of a fence between the Israeli and
Palestinian panelists. Koppel, the interviewer/mediator, carefully says
of the fence: "I must tell you that it has been so difficult to arrange

this broadcast that that was one small price that we were prepared to pay, so here it is, I will try and spend as much time on one side as on the other" (*Nightline*, II, p. 3).

Koppel controls the *Nightline* story: as journalist he calls forth the story form of unending conflict; as potential peacebroker he offers the possibility of order in a chaotic land. To unlock this dilemma Koppel explores the contradictory plotlines of the participant anthologies. Using these lesser accounts to tell the central *Nightline* story, he assumes the role of narrator as historian, and, on the offense, he rejects the validity of the participants' understanding of the conflict.

During the third evening, Koppel undermines the basis for all of the stories we discussed in the first section by challenging the worth of history as justification, at least the history told by Palestinians and Israelis. Koppel tells us that "history is not the objective recitation of truth, it is a story shaded and sculpted by those temporarily in control" (p. 2). We are offered a series of history stories, but when the guest historians begin to critique or justify their varying histories, Koppel concludes that such contradictory history is irrelevant to the solution of the conflict.

The Israeli historian contends, "Like every civilization, like every culture, they [the Jews] base their claims, their hopes, their future, on literature, on scripts, on religion, on understanding of their own past" (pp. 7–8). Koppel intervenes, "while everyone quotes history when it is convenient to his particular cause, it almost seems to me as though what you gentlemen are underscoring is the absolute irrelevance of history" (p. 8). The Palestinian historian rejects this claim of historical irrelevance and begins an evaluation of the Israeli argumentative claims to the land. Koppel shuts that down with a rejection of such theory and a focus on action: not who has the right, or the right story, but who has the power. In effect, while telling us that history is not undebatable truth but stories with set perspectives, Koppel rejects the worth of those stories. Conflicting stories cannot lead to a solution; conflicting truths will not tell us who is right. Koppel devalues the historians' recognition of the importance of the stories—true or not—to the reasoning of the populace. Koppel replaces these conflicting cultural truths with his own narrative truth. He rewrites the history of the conflict.

In all three narrative roles, balancing his physical presence and allocation of time between the two parties, Koppel manipulates structural elements to tell "his" (ABC/*Nightline*'s) story of the conflict. One such manipulation is temporality. The events of a story are always chronological; but narrative time is not bound by historical chronologies. Genette (1983) distinguishes the temporal order from the pseudo-temporal order of events as they are arranged in the narrative. When the narrative moves backward in time from the present or projects into the future, our understanding of events changes. Narrative order can change how we punctuate causality, which characters' point of view we accept as most reasonable, and whether the tale has fidelity to competing stories about these historical events.

Narrative Order

Koppel begins the series with the Israeli story of Masada. He could legitimately have begun with the Palestinian story of their Canaanite forebears, with the story of the uprising, with the United Nations mandate to form the independent state of Israel, etc. How do we, with Koppel, begin to unravel the complexities of the current uprising? With a Jewish story of strength, persistence, and determination that Masada "shall not fall again."

Shots of contemporary Jews at the Western Wall reinforce the first legitimized story (Israeli) while Koppel explains the purpose of the week-long series. Until the 1967 war, this Western Wall was held by Arabs. The next segment reinforces the claim that further action is necessary.

Following Koppel's brief historical explanation, the "obsession" of the Masada story is played out in the Israeli story about national security as illustrated by an Israeli government film. *The Strategic Equation.* We are given the David and Goliath narrative of the underdog engaged in self-defense.

We abruptly begin Koppel's deconstruction of this story: Israeli strength and excessive firepower versus women and children with rocks and rhetoric. The reversed David and Goliath story becomes a major plotline during the 5 days, molding how we interpret events and understand participant stories. Both verbal and visual scripts reinforce this primary story. One of the most frequent visuals shows Arab children, accompanied by women, throwing rocks at armed Israeli soldiers. This scene appears first in the Israeli security story, foreshadowing its fuller exposition as plotline. It becomes a major story in Part II, "Town Meeting," and in Part III, where Koppel tells us that the "history" we are about to hear is written by the warring parties and reflects their story. The Arab story consistently focuses on Israeli might versus their symbolic might in rock throwing. Dr. Mikhail-Ashrawi expressed the story most clearly in response to Koppel's assertion that Palestinian-Israeli relations were characterized by violence rather than dialogue: "Violence I'd say on the part of the Israelis. Symbolic violence on the part of the Palestinians. You cannot equate stone-throwing, which is essentially a symbolic act, with the military machine, with the might of rubber bullets . . . do you call that a parity situation?" (*Nightline*, II, p. 4).

The juxtaposition of conflicting versions of the David and Goliath story reinforces the message Koppel introduces in Part I: The land and violence are linked. When both sides employ the same story forms to justify their violence, and when the stories are ordered so that the Palestinian story sets the context for the Jewish story and vice versa, the audience can read the text of the Koppel story clearly; the conflict will continue.

Narrative movement in *Nightline* is continually from the past to the present, with the past violence and subjugation of the land as a guide to interpreting the current uprising and the unlikelihood that the two parties, alone, will resolve their differences. The past provides context for the present, justifying Koppel's central story—the cycle of violence.

Early on the first night Koppel foreshadows the conclusion of the series. He interviews "the soldier in the street" who sees "no winners in this war." The soldier sees the children not "as an enemy" but "cute." Koppel undercuts this humanizing tone with a "Cute, but also suspect" voiceover. Returning to the interview, Koppel comments, "The problem is you may so radicalize them that you end up with more enemies than before." An Israeli spokesman concludes that "military might" is not a guaranteed solution: "sometimes, power becomes powerless" (*Nightline*, I, p. 3). While clarifying the need for some nonmilitary response, Koppel has already established the cycle of violence and prepared us to regretfully accept the radicalized children who will project the inevitability of the cycle as they speak to us on the fifth night. Koppel concludes the second night by saying that dialogue "is not an easy thing to achieve here in Israel" (p. 32).

Part III begins with Koppel's recapitulation of the historical violence: "To this day, what is known as the Turkish Wall encircles the Old City of Jerusalem and the history of 15 different cultures and empires that have ruled this city over the past 4,000 years" (p. 2). What follows is another blatant coercion of the overall narrative in the direction of the cycle of violence. As the Palestinian historian, Walid Khalidi, is attempting to offer a critique of the "four bases" of the "Zionist claim to Palestine," Koppel interrupts and refocuses the question in a return to the cycle: "Among the four points that you have raised, the one point that you have not raised—which is really the cornerstone of all historical conquest—is that might makes right. Ultimately, what really counts is not the history, but who has the power, isn't it?" (p. 8). Koppel has revalued the cycle of violence. Might is the real, the practical winning tool. Having taken us through competing stories of violence, the evening ends with Khalidi saying: "All one has to do is look at the archaeological debris of empires of ancient times that sprinkle the entire region to reach the conclusion that power is an ephemeral phenomenon. . . . And I think that is something that everybody should contemplate, not least of all the Israelis" (p. 14). Thus we return to the powerless power of Part I.

Part IV again begins with the cycle of violence story, this time recounting 190 years of "Christian crusades variously led by French, Italian, German and English knights [who] conquered, lost and regained regions of the Holy Land" (p. 2). Koppel, as peacebroker, argues that mutual recognition, discovered in shared values, a shared appreciation of the land, can break this cycle of violence. An interviewee explains what is required for negotiation. "If you can begin to see that they are children, and women, and men . . . who care about their homes and their olive trees and places they've lived . . . then maybe you can begin to think about ways of negotiating. You can't negotiate with people unless you accept them as human" (p. 3).

Part V begins with highlights of the Town Meeting, during which Koppel says, "Israelis and Palestinians demonstrated the extraordinary difficulty of achieving peace here by engaging in what one reporter later described as a dialogue of the deaf." Koppel chooses excerpts that, with one exception, illustrate the intransigence of the Israelis.

An even more powerful rendition of the cycle of violence story concludes Part V. Koppel ends the series with a taped interview with Prime Minister Shamir, an opponent of territorial compromise, "a right-wing hardliner since he led underground fighters before the state was born" (*Nightline*, I, p. 8). The interview is intercut with a taped story of Israeli and Palestinian children. The children's stories reflect ingrained prejudices, fear and intolerance of the other, and commitment to the non-productive solutions advocated by their elders. The final clip is of a Palestinian girl who, with upraised fist of defiant power, proclaims, "I am the child of Palestine. I will never forget. I will never forget. I will never forget. I will never forget" (p. 9). Shamir's response, "You know, you can hear from some, some voices, of brainwashing, of indoctrination" (p. 9), reiterates the cycle of violence story. It is the last story after 5 days of stories, and the story that has, as Koppel deconstructs the Israeli-Palestinian conflict, finally linked the multiple myths, legends, and stories we are told.

Development of Characters

The deconstruction of the cycle of violence story continues the characterization of participants as villains or victims. Koppel introduces the story of the children as victim/participants early in the first segment during his interview about the "cute" but "suspect" Palestinian children. He continues, "we must not forget that an estimated 170 Palestinians, children among them, have died" (p. 3). An introductory tag quotation later in the week offers a PLO spokesperson seeing all the youths as victims:

> I felt miserable that this young boy, instead of playing basketball,
> is throwing stones at the occupation army. . . . there are two parties,
> almost of the same age. One is responding to 20 years of oppression,
> and his eagerness to be free. And the other one is carrying out orders,
> and in most cases does not believe in those orders. (Nightline, IV,
> p. 4)

A further reminder of the fate of the children comes with the frequent repetition of a scene with a small boy riding a donkey accompanied by a village woman and another child. This scene of peaceful peasant life, a depiction of potential innocent sufferers, punctuates segments before and after commercial breaks and stimulus remarks by world leaders. Each time it appears we are brought back to the issue of victims and the reasons for victimage.

The stories told by each side contribute to the victimage; but we are shown that part of the blame rests with the character of the leadership for each side. Koppel-ABC/Nightline constructs the intransigent, objectionable character of the Israeli and Palestinian leadership. Although Koppel does not overtly take one side, the editing of Nightline defines the character of the PLO. In the first night, the segment introducing the PLO tells us, "Palestinians see violence against Israel not as terror but as heroic action" (p. 5) but concludes with a litany of deeds the world has viewed as terrorism. The label adheres to the organization.

In this constructed context, a PLO spokesman is introduced. Responding to the assassination of Abu Jihad, Bassam Abu Sharif terms the Israelis the seekers of "bloodshed in the Middle East. We are not for bloodshed" (p. 5). The shifting of the terrorist label to the Israeli leadership is carefully intensified through editing. As Abu Sharif makes his arguments, Nightline superimposes his credentials: "Wounded in 1972 by a letter bomb." The sender of the letter is not labeled, but the implied link to the presumably Israeli assassination of Abu Jihad is clear. Editing negatively defines the character of both Palestinian and Israeli leadership. The importance of this leadership degradation lies with Koppel's belief that neither side really wants to negotiate and that both sides act to perpetuate a cycle of violence.

In the last program Koppel shows Shamir a taped segment of the Town Meeting where he is accused of having been a terrorist. Koppel says:

> Now, here I sit, with the man who was just described as the terrorist
> Shamir who blew up the King David hotel. And the question I have
> has to do with the violence of rhetoric. As long as you keep describing
> them as terrorists, and they keep describing you as terrorists . . .
> doesn't it make the possibility of negotiating totally remote? (p. 7)

Such polarization of character shows the viewer that the leadership on both sides is guilty of perpetuating the cycle of violence in the Holy Land.

Choices of order in structuring the telecast shape the central plotline, the cycle of violence story, and major characters—narrator, villainous leadership, and suffering victims. They privilege a particular reading of the situation, a reading that denies the narrativizing posture Koppel seemingly adopted at the outset. Further shaping is apparent when we consider the narrative segmentation in the five-part series.

Narrative Segmentation

Koppel's story of continuing violence in the Holy Land is shaped as he edits together taped stimulus segments, live interviews, and film footage from the Town Meeting; as he probes the statements made by panelists and guests; and as he visually reinforces the character of victims and villains with film footage. Choices in segmentation manipulate the images we see of the *intifadeh* and thereby condition the way we read the messages that precede and follow these images.

The events of a story exist as a continuum that narrative discourse segments—foreshortening, stretching, and reordering events to create a narrative truth. The segmentation process, natural to narrative, stretches and bends reality further when television intermixes live and taped discourse. Part II of *Nightline*, the Town Meeting, is a live confrontation/dialogue between panelists and audience, Israeli and Palestinian. But the course of the discussion, segmented by Koppel as moderator, is manipulated by taped segments designed to stimulate discussion. As they are inserted, the segments shape our interpretation of the comments we have just heard live.

Several examples illustrate the editing. Before a commercial break, the Palestinian political scientist argues that the question to be addressed is how to bring the two sides to the negotiating table. He sees the refusal by Israelis and Americans to let the Palestinians choose who will speak for them as the central issue blocking negotiations: "All Israeli political establishment want to choose my representatives for me, and it's never happened in the history of mankind, that two enemies who are about to make peace, that one party is to choose both people's representatives" (p. 15). Koppel promises Erakat he can finish his response after the commercial break. But the dialogue does not resume immediately. Instead, ABC inserts a taped statement by Michael Dukakis saying that, before progress can be made in the negotiations, Arab leaders must make the concession that Sadat did—recognize Israeli borders and allow them to live securely within them. Koppel opens the discussion turning to Erakat as promised, but changes the issue from the right to choose one's own negotiator/leader to recognition of Israel. Koppel thus shifts the focus, bringing the cycle of violence story into the foreground. When a Peace Now questioner then challenges the Likud panelists to end the cycle of violence, Koppel offers the question to the more radical Likud representative, ensuring a rejection of negotiation.

In a second example, the taped stimulus refocuses the discussion to tell the story Koppel sees as important. Ms. Mikhail-Ashrawi introduces a discussion about an International Conference for negotiating a peace with the sentence: "I find it extremely ironic that the state that has won every single military confrontation is asking for assurances from its victims" (p. 17). For almost 10 minutes the discussion centers on preconditions for negotiations.

The taped stimulus picks up on her earlier sentence rather than the subject of the ensuing discussion. Koppel says, "Let me interrupt for one moment. And Hanan, I want to come back to something, to a question you raised before" (p. 18). He shows a story about the number of PLO attacks, inside and outside of Israel; he offers a litany of victims. By thus inserting the taped story, Koppel takes the discussion away from the preconditions for negotiation and back to the inevitability of the cycle of violence. Koppel says, "Perhaps, rhetorically at least, your question has been answered. Why there is such mistrust on the part of Israelis to what Palestinians—but now let me give you a chance to move on" (p. 19). From a journalistic perspective, Koppel's insertion of the tape at that point strains ethical standards for reporting. Rather than encouraging further discussion or exploring an alternative side of the story, Koppel's timing editorially redefines the discussion to highlight one particular interpretation of the events—the preeminence of an inevitable cycle of violence in this land. It is an act curiously in conflict with his role as peacebroker, moving the discussion away from conditions for negotiation and back to violent acts neither side wants to forget.

Mikhail-Ashrawi tries to break the cycle story by suggesting that violence is a symptom and that dialogue needs to get to the root cause. She lays out an argument about self-determinism that Koppel interrupts, questioning her assumptions and shifting the floor to Erakat. As the program evolves, Koppel appears to have a story into which comments will be made to fit—the inevitability of the cycle of violence.

Yet again, when a Palestinian panelist speaks of "acknowledging the principle of equal rights as a basis for meaningful negotiations" (p. 26), Koppel cuts away to a taped interview containing a call for mutual recognition as the road to negotiation. When Koppel returns to an Israeli panelist he frames the question purportedly asked by the Palestinian as "Why can't there be mutual recognition?" (p. 26). The Israeli objects, recalling the equality of rights focus, but ultimately bows to Koppel's overriding interpretation. Hence, Koppel again shifts the argument from a shared value concern to a point of negotiator intransigence.

Isolating the taped stimulus segments suggests that Koppel and the *Nightline* writers had a story in mind when they began—a story that does not promote the constructive management of conflict. Koppel explains the taped segments, "What we're going to be doing during the course of this broadcast in addition to the discussion that we'll be having, is a series of events that have been recorded on tape" (II, p. 2). These taped news stories and brief interviews, overtly "intended to stimulate discussion" (II, p. 3), powerfully structure the story ABC tells. An overview of Parts II and IV illustrates narrative manipulation.

Part II, the Town Meeting where participants have a chance to tell their own story, begins with Koppel's perspective: each side sees the other as terrorist, hence untrustworthy. One news story opening with an Arab hospital scene concludes with the antagonizing Israeli practice of collective punishment. It is "balanced" by a story opening on Israeli soldiers fearful of attack in Nablus. One soldier confesses, "I think about the two-by-four that's going to land on my head, that's what I think about so I'm looking, you know they throw these huge cement blocks and boulders, you know they're not throwing little rocks" (p. 6). A reserve soldier remarks, "I know they hate us; maybe they have a reason, maybe they don't. I don't know. But the fact is they hate us" (p. 6). The correspondent notes the world's disapproval of the seemingly excessive response, "Live ammunition, then tear gas or rubber bullets. Mace against women" (p. 6). Even though the story contains statements about the Israeli goal to keep the peace, thus fostering a political rather than violent solution, the salient image is of continuing and directionless violence. Narrative segmentation promotes one reading.

Four interview excerpts are used. Bush asserts that negotiations will be between Israel and Hussein, an assumption the Palestinians violently reject. Dukakis says that it is the Palestinians who must compromise by recognizing Israel, a precondition the Palestinians again reject. A representative of the American Jewish Organizations proclaims that the only obstacle to peace is "the Arab states, six united in a continuing war against Israel" (p. 26), which the Palestinians obviously reject. Finally, Jesse Jackson calls for "land for peace" (p. 29), a major sore point that the conservative Israeli Likud Party rejects. The dialogue during Parts I and II makes it difficult to read the blithe American "solutions" as likely.

Taped stories about homeland demands, collective punishment, and PLO negotiating legitimacy reveal Palestinian roadblocks to a solution. Israeli roadblocks are apparent in stories and interviews about PLO violence. A West Bank settler, fearing for his life, declares a commitment to violence: "I'll do whatever I have to do to protect myself. If someone tries to kill me, I'll try to kill him first" (*Nightline*, II, p. 25). One Israeli settler asserts that a 15-year-old Israeli girl had been killed earlier in the month by an Arab. In fact, we are told by the commentator, the girl was accidentally killed by another settler. The quick attribution of blame to the other makes continuing violence seem likely. Inclusion of particular details makes it easy for the viewer to fit the events and characters into a now-familiar cycle of violence story.

Part IV contains three taped interview excerpts. The first two reinforce the Koppel story: a *New York Times* columnist argues that the mutual assumption of the other's inhumanity prevents serious negotiations; a PLO observer to the United Nations sees the inevitability of rebellion in Israeli repression. In a more neutral interview, a member of the American Jewish Congress sees the explosive Arab growth rate inside Israel as necessitating serious consideration of the land for peace proposal. Given the Likud's vehement rejection of this course, this stimulus similarly leaves us in the cycle of violence.

The strongest taped news story in Part IV for deconstructing the crisis as a cycle of violence story discusses Palestinians establishing committees to care for the refugees. The report ends with a Palestinian remarking, "We have now fought five months in the uprising, and we are not tired" (p. 2). This counters the Israeli assertion that the *intifadeh* will burn itself out.

The final taped story in Part IV is Bill Blakemore reading Jewish and Palestinian poetry. The poetry and visual images recall the stories of Part III, the dreams and justifications that divide rather than seek commonality between the two groups.

Throughout the week, the taped interviews and stories, overtly designed to stimulate discussion, construct a story in which, short of a miraculous peacebroker's intervention, the cycle of violence will continue. Speaking with an authoritative narrator's voice, Koppel constructs a story of cyclical violence through carefully ordered plot and character development, overall narrative movement, choices of narrative segmentation, and planned and prerecorded stimulus segments.

Conclusion

In exploring the stories told by competing parties to explain and justify actions surrounding the *intifadeh*, *Nightline*'s "This Week in the Holy Land" provides a classic media example of White's narrativizing discourse. Koppel introduces a week of stories told by the participants in which he is the detached mediator and his correspondents provide balanced background reports. He offers stories to clarify the context of a confusing situation. We are given a sense that this will be news in depth, the news behind the news; but the stories that follow are clarified not by an in-depth analysis but by an overarching, simplifying plotline. The conflicting stories of the week are manipulated through careful ordering of stories and stimuli, segmentation of discussion moments, and characterization of participants. These stories become a larger familiar story. Complex multifaceted truths are reshaped into an American Truth.

Three anthologies of stories are interpreted and reinterpreted by the various parties. The anthology of victimage stories, already familiar to the world, are linked to national beginnings and national defense. With holocaust, diaspora, and terrorism plotlines, both sides claim the role of victim. The anthology of self and other develops characterization of the conflict participants through plotlines about the intransigent other, the political reality, and attributions of Goliath behavior to the other. Land claim stories form a third prominent anthology.

The stories reflect a sharing of concerns and experiences by the participants. Both groups have a deep love of land; both feel strong ties to this specific historical piece of earth; both have suffered separation from the land; both have had their needs ignored by a larger world; both have fought for their rights against great odds; both feel their side has not been heard. Superficially, these similarities should lay a groundwork for understanding, but for these two groups each is a major villain in the stories of the other. Each is a cause of the other's suffering. Each is not to be trusted by the other. These grounds for misunderstanding undermine the mutuality shared stories might encourage. Koppel's deconstruction of the stories of the conflict through story emphasis and story placement exacerbates the problem. We are led to expect more because he has assumed the role of narrator as peacebroker. At least we expect Koppel to search for common ground in the rhetoric each group offers.

Beginning with the admonition, "fairness and objectivity in this part of the world are very much in the eyes of the beholder" (*Nightline*, I, p. 2), Koppel leads his audience and subjects into a trap constructed by the requirements of journalistic objectivity: the posture of objectivity mandates a "balance" in taped stories, but that same "balance" fosters participant dichotomy. It focuses attention on polarizing difference. Balance in the documentary coverage of a controversy necessitates presenting both sides of the conflict. Such balance thus may encourage a simplification of a much more complex problem into a two-sided issue. This fits neatly with the familiar good guy-bad guy story line; implicitly there are only two sides even when we, the audience, aren't sure who is good and who is bad.

Further, the quest for balance is itself undermined by the tools used to frame the coherent story. The thousands of hours of raw footage with no editing, and no narrative explanation or intervention, might produce an objective story of conflict; but even then some potential readings of that story would be privileged by the order in which the footage was viewed. Constraints of time, interest, and comprehensibility, requirements of the popular commercial medium, prevent such marathon presentations. The balanced documentary would seem to be a myth of the objective reporter.

In the Israeli-Palestinian conflict story, even narrative similarity becomes a source of argument rather than reconciliation. Koppel recognizes and seeks to escape the "rather obvious paradox" (*Nightline*, I, p. 10) of this situation explained by shared stories. The Town Meeting is introduced with an example of what Koppel terms "a dialogue of violence" (*Nightline*, II, p. 2) between Israelis and Palestinians, as spokespeople for each side exhibit their rhetorical extremism. Koppel expresses a hope for "a more productive kind of dialogue" (*Nightline*, II, p. 2); but before the evening is over the early movements toward a dramatic break in the stalemate through Koppel's intervention are replaced with a strong focus on the cycle of violence story. The story stimuli and sharp questions that foster lively discussion also break that discussion, hampering resolution and preventing an uninterrupted explanation of even one participant's version of truth in the conflict. The story is not allowed to tell itself. Consistently, the basic elements of news structure—narrative segmentation, temporality, editing, character creation, and story placement—work against objectivity, leaving it a postured delusion and crystallizing the inevitability of Koppel's cycle of violence story.

Replacing the deafening conflicting stories with his own story, Koppel leads us, with the participants, from the confusion of contradiction to frustration as we recognize the apparent inevitability of continued conflict. Seeking the quick and easy "the-news-should-be-wrapped-up-in-a-few-days" solution, encouraged by an American preference for immediacy, the American story cannot live with the paradox of shared but mutually contradictory plotlines. Such paradox is irrational. In a region where both cultures claim an ethnic tie to the land through the same religious story, where both cultures claim their forebear was the son taken to be sacrificed by Abraham, narrative paradox is not irrational but a fact of daily life, however disconcerting. The easy story for the old conflict is not a story of resolution. Such resolution merely hides the discomfort inherent in living with the paradox of sharing the same story with reverse casting.

The Town Meeting panel participants seem ready to explore the shared values in those stories. The clearest statement comes from an Israeli:

> They will analyze and they will try to say that they are right. We
> will try to analyze history and we will try to claim that we are right.

> Maybe each of the sides will be 100 percent right but both of us will
> be 100 percent dead. The question is not who is right according to
> history. The question is how now both of us are going to live together,
> how we compromise. They have to give up part of their dreams about
> Jaffa and Jerusalem and Haifa, and we have to give up part of our
> dreams about Nablus, about Ramallah. This is the only way to live
> together. (*Nightline*, II, p. 9)

Here there is a recognition of validity within paradox, of hope for understanding within conflicting stories. Koppel, however, from an American
rational perspective, seems unable to see beyond the conflict to explore
the underlying mutuality that might be the basis for peace. The cycle
of violence story is a tighter package for television; it is more comprehensible for a Western audience. This is the ultimate disappointment
of the program. Rather than letting the rhetoric of the two parties evolve,
rather than asking the American viewing audience to let the two parties
work through the conflict at their own pace, the Koppel/ABC story leads
the audience to dismiss the warring parties as a people unable to
reasonably resolve their differences, to accept the inevitability of
continued violence.

Koppel reminds us that "the same events are remembered in different
ways" and that "it is precisely the ancient and not-so-ancient stories,
told and retold, that are used to justify this repetition" of the historical
cycle of violence in the Holy Land. The inevitability of the East we can
live with, paradox we cannot.

Koppel ends by acknowledging, "Television does distort the message"
(*Nightline*, V, p. 9), but he assures us that this week of coverage has
set no agendas, for "Those whom we cover out here have an agenda.
They had it before we came, and they'll have it after we leave." Certainly
those participant agendas exist, but equally certainly Koppel's coverage
is not inconsequential. It forefronts another agenda by encouraging the
American audience to retain belief in the inevitable cycle of violence
in the Middle East.

The "objective" standards of "responsible" journalism become the
tool by which narrative "truth" becomes anything but objective. Is the
conditioned journalistic employment of postured objectivity useful? Can
the objective standard be met, or does narrative structuring inevitably
make even an honest attempt at objectivity a mere posture?

Koppel began with an objective perspective, and to the casual viewer
he probably ended maintaining that same professional stance. But a
closer reading of the text shows the stance destroyed by the normal tools
of the medium and the "balance" obligations of the objective stance
itself. Whether Koppel's story was imposed intentionally or
unintentionally is irrelevant. A reading based on a structuralist approach
to narrative theory suggests an inherent weakness in the normative
documentary form.

Note

¹ This refers to the first of the five *Nightline* episodes. All citations to *Nightline* use this format.

References

Barkin, S., & Gurevitch, M. (1987). Out of work and on the air: Television news of unemployment. *Critical Studies in Mass Communication, 4,* 1-20.

Bennett, W., & Edelman, M. (1985). Toward a new political narrative. *Journal of Communication, 35,* 156-171.

Bennett, W., Gressett, L, & Haltom, W. (1985). Repairing the news: A case study of the news paradigm. *Journal of Communication, 35,* 50-68.

Chatman, S. (1978). *Story and discourse: Narrative structures in fiction and film.* Ithaca: Cornell University Press.

Edelman, M. (1988). *Constructing the political spectacle.* Chicago: University of Chicago Press.

Eliasoph, N. (1988). Routines and the making of oppositional news. *Critical Studies in Mass Communication, 5,* 313-334.

Flapan, S. (1987). *The birth of Israel: Myths and realities.* New York: Pantheon Books.

Gans, S. (1979). *Deciding what's news.* New York: Pantheon Books.

Genette, G. (1983). *Narrative discourse: An essay in method.* Ithaca: Cornell University Press.

Glasgow University Media Group. (1976). *Bad news.* London: Routledge & Kegan Paul.

Glasgow University Media Group. (1980). *More bad news.* London: Routledge & Kegan Paul.

Glasgow University Media Group. (1982). *Really bad news.* London: Writers and Readers.

Koppel, T. (Narr.) & Kaplan, R. (Exec. prod.). (1988, April 25-29). This week in the Holy land. Transc. *Nightline,* I-V.

Rimmon-Kenan, S. (1983). *Narrative fiction: Contemporary poetics.* London: Methuen.

Scholes, R. (1976). *Structuralism in Literature* (rev. ed.). New Haven: Yale University Press.

Sigman, S., & Fry, D. (1985). Differential ideology and language use: Reader's reconstructions and descriptions of news events. *Critical Studies in Mass Communication, 2,* 307-322.

Trew, T. (1979). Theory and ideology at work. In R. Fowler, B. Hodge, G. Kress, & T. Trew (Eds.), *Language and control* (pp. 94-116). London: Routledge & Kegan Paul.

Tuchman, G. (1978). *Making News.* New York: Free Press.

van Dijk, T. (1988). *News as discourse.* Hillsdale, NJ: Lawrence Erlbaum.

White, H. (1987). *The content of the form.* Baltimore: Johns Hopkins University Press.

The Rhetorical Power of a Compelling Story
A Critique of a "Toughlove" Parental Support Group

Thomas A. Hollihan and Patricia Riley

> It has recently been said that almost the bitterest and most hopeless tragedies of all are the tragedies of parents with bad children. The tragedy of children with bad parents is no less acute. . . .
>
> R. Cowell, *Cicero and the Roman Republic*, 1967, p. 298.

Families through the ages have been troubled by misbehaving and, at times, delinquent children. In 49 B.C., Cicero blamed his brother for his nephew Quintus' treacheries saying: "His father has always spoilt him but his indulgence is not responsible for his being untruthful or grasping or wanting in affection for his family, though it perhaps does make him headstrong and self-willed as well as aggressive" (Cicero, cited in Cowell, 1967, p. 299). Twenty centuries later, contemporary researchers, practitioners, and theorists continue to investigate the exceedingly complex interaction of parental actions, societal and cultural pressures, genetic predispositions, and children's behavioral choices that too often culminate in disaster or despair. Such studies still reflect Cicero's penchant for locating blame for juvenile delinquency in parental actions: e.g., parents who drink too much (Morehouse and Richards, 1982); parental relationships characterized by a great deal of conflict (Emery, 1982); parents who are lax in discipline (Fischer, 1983); abusive parents (Paperny and Deisher, 1983); or parents who fail to provide good nutritious food for their children (Stasiak, 1982).

Rather than suffer the disparagement of neighbors and relatives, or the accusations of teachers and counseling professionals, many parents try to cope with their problem children alone (Nemy, 1982). Recently, a program called "Toughlove" has begun to provide parents of delinquent

From *Communication Quarterly*, 35 (Winter 1987), 13–25. Used by permission of the Eastern Communication Association and the authors.

children with emotional support and hope for solutions to their common problems. "Toughlove" proselytizes that it is not the parents who are failing, it is their children. Founded by Phyllis and David York, the Toughlove groups promote highly disciplined child rearing practices in an attempt to stop unruly teenagers from controlling households, to rid parents of guilt feelings, and to enable parents and non-problem children to lead a normal family life (Nemy, 1982).

The Toughlove approach has attracted a great deal of national attention. It was endorsed by Ann Landers (1981), reported in *Time* ("Getting Tough," 1981), *People* ("David and Phyllis," 1981), *Ms.* (Wohl, 1985), and the *New York Times* (Nemy, 1982), and was featured on the "Phil Donohue Show" and ABC's "20-20." Partially as a result of this publicity, there are currently more than four-hundred Toughlove groups in the United States and Canada (Nemy, 1982).

A recent Gallup Poll reported that 37 percent of the respondents felt that the main problem with parents today was that they did not give their children sufficient discipline (cited in Wohl, 1985). The increased popularity of the Toughlove program has undoubtedly been a response to these sentiments. Toughlove has been credited with having sparked a series of books advising parents on how to discipline their children (Wohl, 1985; Bodenhamer, 1984; Sanderson, 1983; and Bartocci, 1984).

Toughlove, like Alcoholics Anonymous, operates primarily through a system of self-help groups that attempt to better people's lives, help them cope with crises, and teach them their own limitations (Alibrandi, 1982; Pattison, 1982; and Pomerleau, 1982). A rhetorical study of Toughlove should give insight into the appeal of this group and into the process that similar self-help groups use to become support systems. More importantly, the study of Toughlove will permit researchers to focus on how members are acculturated into the Toughlove philosophy, and how this philosophy guides their lives.

This study involved the observation of a series of Toughlove group meetings and an analysis of the flow of messages during these meetings. The form of these messages can best be described as the telling of individual stories, and ultimately the development of a shared group story. The study is grounded in the notion that these shared stories give insight into the group members' beliefs, actions, and worldviews, and into the process through which they attempt to change their lives. This perspective is best explicated in Walter R. Fisher's (1984) notion of the "narrative paradigm."

In developing the "narrative paradigm," Fisher (1984) asserted that human beings were essentially storytelling creatures and that the dominant mode of human decision making involved the sharing of these stories. Such stories contained "good reasons" which provided insight into the proper courses of human action. According to this perspective, the world consists of a set of stories from which people must choose. People are thus constantly engaged in storytelling and in evaluating the stories they are told (Fisher, 1984, pp. 7-8).

Where the rational world paradigm would expect individuals (advocates) to possess knowledge of subject matter and of the requirements of argumentative form—thereby creating experts with a capability for argument beyond that possessed by naive advocates—the narrative paradigm presumes that all persons have the capacity to be rational. Rationality is thus a function of the "narrative probability" and "narrative fidelity" of a given story—the degree to which stories hang together, their ability to make sense of encountered experience, and whether they corroborate previously accepted stories (Fisher, 1984).

Shared stories play an important role in the lives of those who tell them, for they are a way for people to capture and relate their experiences in the world. These stories respond to people's sense of reason and emotion, to their intellects and imagination, to the facts as they perceive them, and to their values. People search for stories which justify their efforts and resolve the tensions and problems in their lives, and desire stories that resolve their dissonance and are psychologically satisfying.

Those who do not share in the storytelling—those whose life experiences demand different types of stories—might view particular stories as mere rationalization, but this is to miss the very nature of the storytelling process. In this framework, one person's life story is another's rationalization, but if a story serves a useful purpose to those who tell it or listen to it, that story likely will be retold in the generative process of narrative understanding.

This study has three major goals: (1) to operationalize Fisher's narrative paradigm through actual observations; (2) to identify the Toughlove story; and (3) to critique the appeal of that story and discuss its possible consequences.

Method

A Toughlove group in a Los Angeles suburb was observed during four consecutive, three hour meetings. Two researchers attended the meetings and took extensive notes, each attempting to copy down as many of the participants' comments as possible in order to capture the essence of the discussion. We were not allowed to tape record the sessions because the group leaders feared that the presence of taping equipment might "chill" the participants and prevent them from talking in detail about their problems.

The group leaders (two women who founded the group after experiencing difficulties with their own children) were briefed about the nature of the study prior to the first observation. One of the leaders introduced us before our first meeting with the group and asked if anyone objected to our presence. No one objected. We explained to the group that we were interested in watching real-life groups as a part of a small group research project underway at a local university. After each meeting, the Toughlove group leaders were asked if the group's participants had behaved differently due to our presence. On each occasion, the leaders indicated that there appeared to be no differences in the group members' interactions. After the last observation we conducted interviews with several randomly selected group members. Each interviewee was asked if they felt the observation affected the group in any way. Again, no differences were reported.

Following the final observation, each observer's notes were prepared for analysis. While it would have been preferable to have access to complete transcripts of the group meetings, we discovered that our written notes were quite detailed and provided us with a great deal of rhetoric for analysis. We proceeded by first, comparing our notes and eliminating issues of disagreement, and second, sub-dividing the information into actual remarks made by group members and our own comments about the group's process. We next sub-divided the group members' statements into three categories that emerged from the notes: (1) story-lines ("Story-lines have beginnings, middles, and ends which give individual actions meanings, provide unity and self-definition to individual lives . . ." (Frentz, 1985, p. 5); (2) questions or comments to other parents; and (3) procedural issues (mainly leader comments).

Our approach is similar to a "mini-ethnography" where the observers are also the message analysts (Knapp, 1979). This perspective ensures that the highly emotional tone of the meeting, together with the dramatic nature of narrative fiction, are captured in the analysis. After the study was completed, the group as a whole was debriefed.

The Group

The group had been in existence for just over one year when the observations took place. While the group had a nucleus of eight parents who always attended the meetings, the group's size increased significantly during the observation period. Twelve persons attended the first observed meeting, but by the fourth meeting there were more than thirty parents. The growing attendance may have resulted from a story on the group which appeared in a local newspaper. Following the last observed meeting the group split into two smaller groups in order to maintain the close personal atmosphere necessary for the highly emotional, self-disclosive discussions. All of the participating parents had experienced, or were in the midst of experiencing, a family crisis precipitated by their child's (or children's) behavior.

Parents came from a variety of occupational and socio-cultural backgrounds, but they were predominantly from middle-class, blue collar families. They were also primarily Caucasian (one Hispanic couple attended, but no Blacks or Asians). Several couples attended, but most of the members were women. Many were single parents—mothers and fathers—and the vast majority of the women worked outside of the home.

The problems faced by these parents were generally quite serious, including simple acts of rebellion, physical assaults, and threats of murder. The most common problems were drug and alcohol abuse. To illustrate the kinds of behavioral problems discussed by the group, a description of some of the children follows (all names are fictitious):

> Ellen—A 13 year old female who skips school, steals from her parents, and during the time of the observation had run away from home.
>
> Bill—A 15 year old male who struck his father's head against the headboard of his bed while he was asleep.
>
> Mark—An 18 year old male who had been arrested for theft, breaking and entering, assault, and selling drugs. At the time of the observations, he was serving a one year sentence in a juvenile correction facility.
>
> Angie—A 15 year old female who carried a knife, had physical altercations with her mother, threatened her father by describing a dream in which she murders him, and was involved in a youth gang.
>
> John—A 16 year old male who had beaten his mother with a baseball bat, assaulted her with a knife, and painted "fuck the fat ugly bitch" on their living room wall.
>
> Maria—A 12 year old female who had run away from home and who was, during the time of observation, a prostitute.
>
> Keith—A 24 year old male who had no job, refused to leave home, and who threatened to beat his mother because she refused to allow him to smoke marijuana in their living room.

Analysis of the parents' stories showed drug or alcohol abuse to be present in slightly more than two-thirds of the cases. The remainder of the cases seemed to reflect either problems of general disobedience or psychological/emotional disturbances. It was not uncommon for parents to come to group meetings with blackened eyes or other visible bruises from violent confrontations with their children. Many parents reported that they were terrified of their own children and, in several cases, parents claimed that their children had threatened them with violence merely because they planned to attend the Toughlove meeting.

The Sharing of the Toughlove Story

In each meeting, individual tales of fear and helplessness were transformed into hope and perseverance as these stories were woven into shared narrative fiction. If parents truly loved their children, they could not let them destroy themselves or their families; they had to be tough—this was the Toughlove story.

The meetings can best be described as extended storytelling sessions where the members, together, created a powerful, compelling, and cohesive story. Numerous sagas of their children's triumphs over drugs or alcohol were often repeated as part of the "ritual" acculturation of the new members. This was far more than imparting information to the newcomers; the retelling was always a highly emotional experience for the parents, often tearful at the start, ending in the quiet determination that they had regained control over their lives. Through the storytelling, the parents transformed their lives into a moral drama, suffused with righteousness, that absolved them of their guilt and restored orderliness and discipline to their lives. The retelling of these stories provided examples that Toughlove parents could survive and even conquer crises, kept members involved in the day-to-day life of the group, and preserved a sense of community among the members.

The Toughlove story promised a new beginning. The group's regular members described their desperation before they discovered Toughlove, and contrasted these feelings with the solace they felt once they embraced the Toughlove way of life. Although new members initially may have been reticent to tell their tales in the presence of strangers, their need to talk to someone was apparent as they blurted out their stories in a torrent of emotions.

In this drama, the parents left forever their roles as weak victimized players whose offspring tyrannized them and wreaked havoc on society. The Toughlove narrative empowered them to take charge of their families and demand the respect due them as elders. They would never again be failures, for only their children could lose in the Toughlove story. As one parent declared: "You have not failed—it is your children who are failing. Kids have to learn the consequences of their own actions." Still another added: "We made it easy for them, we covered the sharp edges so they would not bump into things when they learned to walk. We made it too easy—they never had to fight—we went to battle for them. Now they know how to push buttons and use us." Thus if their children were delinquent, they *chose* to be that way, and there are times when there is nothing that parents can do to modify their children's behavior. One group member asserted: "Sometimes you have to realize that your kid is a loser and that there isn't a damn thing that you can do about it." Group members nodded their assent.

Thematic Analysis

The narrative fiction created by this Toughlove group contained several key themes. First, individual tales were interwoven to explain the "good reasons" for abandoning the predominant rival story—the modern approach to child-rearing. In their drama, the old-fashioned values, characterized by strict discipline, were purported to be superior to today's methods of raising children. The group members often blamed "TLC" (tender loving care) for the problems they had with their children. One father observed: "While TLC works for some kids it is a bust with others." Another father chimed in, "The best way to raise kids is with discipline—strict discipline—that's how our parents did it and we sure didn't cause them these kinds of problems." Several group members claimed that they had tried to use the modern approach in raising their own children but that it had failed. These same parents expressed pride that they now had the courage to condemn these modern approaches. As one mother adamantly claimed: "Everything we are learning here in Toughlove is contrary to Dr. Spock." The other members readily agreed.

This call for a return to traditional values had fidelity because it resonated with stories from the parents' youth, and because the loss of the old ways accounted for the traumas they had experienced. In this sense, the Toughlove narrative was one of historical renewal, a promise that the past could be recreated and the security and comfort of a bygone era recaptured (Bass, 1983). Parents frequently told stories from their own childhood—about how it felt to "go to the woodshed." They commented that they had feared their own parents at times, but they also respected them. Their own children, they sadly agreed, neither feared nor respected them. As one mother noted: "We raised our kids like they did on TV and not the way we were raised. It always worked on TV. It sure didn't work in my house."

These parents believed they were good people who had been misled. The Toughlove narrative was appealing because it confirmed their self-perceptions and absolved them of their failures. They may have been too kind, too lenient, not tough enough, but it was their children who had really failed because they took advantage of their parents' kindness.

A second major theme of the Toughlove narrative was the parents' disdain for the child service professionals. The professionals became villains in the story for two primary reasons. First, the parents claimed these professionals were too quick to blame them for the failures of their offspring. Virtually all of the parents attending the meetings complained that they had been told by counselors, teachers, principals, and others that they were responsible for their children's behavioral problems.

Second, these professionals were condemned as highly vocal proponents of the "modern" approaches to child-rearing. Thus they were spokespersons for the dominant rival story—a story which, for the parents, lacked narrative coherence and fidelity, and a story which reflected an unrealistic approach to raising children. Accounts of visits to counselors were always a central part of an evening's storytelling. These "experts" were portrayed as naive—"book smart" but "experience dumb"—and many group members related tales of their children "snowing" or "hoodwinking" the experts and bragging about it on their way home. Thus the professionals were depicted as part of the problem rather than as part of the solution.

Toughlove parents viewed the child care professionals' rival story as detrimental because it suggested that parents and children shared the responsibility for the problems in the home. The parents believed that this story gave their children an excuse to continue misbehaving. As adherents to the Toughlove narrative, the parents discounted the possibility that they were partially to blame for the problems in their homes. Several parents recalled that counselors had mentioned their drinking problems or marital difficulties as potential causes for their children's misdeeds, but they claimed that it was "just a cop out" for kids to blame their parents for these problems. The Toughlove story, however, allowed parents to blame their children for their own problems, and doing so did not seem to make this story any less probable. On several occasions parents asserted: "This problem with my son is destroying my marriage." Or, "My daughter's behavior is causing me to drink too much."

In their role as experts on juvenile problems, supplanting the professionals, Toughlove parents placed most of the blame on their children and external factors. The enemies in the drama became the professionals, the media, the permissiveness of society, their children's friends, the lack of discipline in the schools, or modern approaches to child-rearing. If they as parents could be faulted at all, it was only that they had relied on the rival story and in so doing had become estranged from the "old-fashioned" values with which they had been raised.

The third central theme of the Toughlove narrative was that the system is pro-child, and that they could best cope with their problem children by depending on, and supporting, each other. The Toughlove group meeting was exalted as the one place where parents knew there would be people willing to listen to their problems without judging them. Group members consistently reported that the social service agencies, the schools, the police and the juvenile courts were of little help. The consensus of the group members was that "the laws protect kids, but it is parents who need protection."

The parents agreed that neither teachers nor police were helpful. The consistent story-line was that the schools did not teach, teachers could not control their students, and students were permitted to use drugs right on the school grounds. The police refused to come then they were called, and if they did come, they generally took the teenager's side in the dispute. One woman recalled that after her daughter was arrested for selling drugs the police picked her up to take her to a juvenile facility. On the way the officer was kind enough to stop by a friend's house so the girl could pick up her hairdryer.

The tales which recounted the utter helplessness these parents felt in coping with their past crises played an important part in the development of the group's shared story. If parents could not trust "the system" to resolve their problems, then they were all the more dependent on their fellow group members.

In this narrative fiction, the police and the juvenile system were both materially and symbolically anti-parent. The group members discussed how important it was to learn to protect themselves from the law. Several parents explained that their children had filed complaints against them, alleging child neglect or abuse, while their offspring were in fact destroying all harmony in the home and terrorizing their families. The group also discussed in great detail their responsibilities in providing for minor children. One woman insisted: "All parents are required by law to provide is a roof over their head and minimally sufficient clothing." Another mother told the group how she left home to escape from her son, leaving him only a loaf of bread and a jar of peanut butter to eat. The common thread running through most of these stories was the declaration that the police and the courts did not take these complaints seriously and failed to realize that these children represented a genuine threat to their parents and siblings. One angry mother related how the police told her that they could do nothing even though her son, whom she had thrown out, had returned to steal her possessions and destroy her furniture. The police refused to act because her house was still considered the boy's home, and, according to the officer, "A kid can't steal from himself, and can destroy his own house if he wants to."

Consistent with this theme, group members jointly developed language strategies to convince the police to arrest their children the next time they were called to the house. Several parents explained that the police would not take a teenager away the first, second, or even the third time they were summoned, but after that, if you labeled your child "incorrigible" you will have "hit upon the right legal mumbo-jumbo" to get him/her arrested. Other valuable information was given via stories—one mother explained that parents can report their kid missing after he leaves the house, "then after the police find him and bring him to the station you can refuse to pick him up, not accept custody. Then they have no choice, they have to put him somewhere else. That's what I did.'' She was upset because her son had been selling drugs in her house.

In contrast to the lack of help available from more conventional sources, the Toughlove narrative dramatized that if parents needed assistance they could always call upon another group member. As one of the group leaders recalled: ''Crises don't happen between 8 AM and 5 PM when the social workers are willing to help. But if you are having trouble with your kid, even if it is midnight, you can call another Toughlove mom or dad. We will come by. These folks have come to my house when I needed help. And I've gone to theirs.'' Another member declared: ''Kids have always had gangs. Now we have one too.'' Thus the Toughlove narrative encouraged parents to take heart—they had formed their own social services system, a support group that could circumvent or beat the system if necessary.

The fourth, and last, prominent theme in the narrative called for parents to put Toughlove into action by setting ''bottom lines'' for their children. These were the rules their children had to obey if they wanted to live with their family. The key to this strategy was that parents had to enforce their bottom lines, no matter what. The bottom lines set by individual parents were frequently discussed during the meetings. They included: you will not drink, you will not use drugs, you will attend school, you will meet this curfew, you will clean up after yourself, you will not entertain someone of the opposite sex in your bedroom, etc. By spelling out the behaviors appropriate for each of their children, and enforcing them, the Toughlove parents reinforced the shared group story that strict discipline was the answer to their troubles. Youths who did not meet their bottom lines were told they could no longer live at home. Although ejecting a son/daughter from the house was to occur only as a last resort, several parents in this group had forced their children to leave home even though they had nowhere else to go. Two other parents managed to have their children detained in Juvenile Hall, a county detention facility, and one had committed her son to a private detoxification center. The group's leader said the message contained in these stories was a simple one: ''Set rules for your kids. If they don't follow them, tell them, 'don't let the door hit you on your way out.''' The Toughlove story thus characterized even these very unhappy outcomes as positive developments. It was presumed better to be rid of these problem children than it was to have to endure the profound disruptions that they caused in the home.

Newcomers were warned that instituting the bottom lines was no easy task, as the group leaders and regulars related anecdotes regarding their children's initial difficulties when the new rules were set. One woman recalled that her daughter kept breaking the rules, so she refused to prepare her meals. Since her daughter could not even find the can opener in the kitchen, the mother found that she gained the girl's cooperation fairly quickly. One father told the group that his daughter's bottom line was to do well in school. To make up for lost time, she had to attend classes regularly, go straight home after school and not have visitors, do her homework, and also help keep the house clean. He discovered that all she did was talk on the phone all afternoon, so he removed the phones from his home every morning and locked them in the trunk of his car so that she could not contact her friends during the day. New Toughlove members quickly understood that they were being prepared for a different type of battle than they were accustomed to, but one that they could hope to win.

During each meeting the group went through the reinforcing ritual of calling upon individual parents and asking them to describe what happened in their homes during the past week. Parents were asked to list the bottom lines they had set, and report whether or not their children had lived up to these rules. If a parent reported that one or more of the rules had been violated, the other group members cross-examined him/her to determine if the offending child had been suitably punished. Parents who showed signs of weakness were criticized, and parents who claimed they had been tough in enforcing the rules were praised by the other group members. This "grilling" of the parents allowed the Toughlove oldtimers to give encouragement to parents who were not used to standing firm. The Toughlove narrative left little room for "extenuating circumstances."

During this segment of storytelling, numerous parents exclaimed that their children were now behaving very differently as a result of the Toughlove program. Several expressed the conviction that they had finally managed to "win the respect" of their children—now that they could no longer be pushed around. These parents, furthermore, noted that while their children initially rebelled against the rules, they ultimately accepted them, because "children want and need discipline." The narrative was additionally strengthened when several parents commented that their children were happy that they had found Toughlove.

Most parents would leave the meeting after the story-telling/testimonial session, appearing more relaxed than when they arrived, imbued with the Toughlove spirit, and vowing to spread the word. Others, battered by recent crises, would remain to exchange sorrows, advice, hugs, and telephone numbers before braving the trip home.

Implications of the Toughlove Story

The Toughlove narrative proved to be comforting, engaging, predictable, and persuasive. Parents joined the group during times of crisis, many feeling as if they had failed because they had been unable to instill socially appropriate values and attitudes in their children. Shamed by the reactions of friends, relatives, and child care experts, and resentful of a system that could not help and only blamed them for allowing such a disgraceful state of affairs to exist, they readily embraced the Toughlove narrative as an alternative for their problems.

Human communication works by identification, and these parents discovered that no one else understood life with delinquent children except other parents in similar circumstances. The rational world, with its scientific notions of child-psychology and "Dr. Spock type experts," could not "speak" to them. The experts' story, which blamed them for their children's conduct, denied their own experiences and did not contain the formal or substantive features necessary for adherence. The Toughlove narrative met their needs and fulfilled the requirements for a good story, narrative probability—what constitutes a coherent story— and narrative fidelity—that a story rings true with a hearer's experience (Fisher, 1984). The story was probable because it was based on old-fashioned values, it restored the social order, and it placed blame where it belonged, on the shoulders of their disobedient and abusive offspring. The rival story which placed at least partial blame on the parents for their children's conduct was viewed as less probable. The story met the test of narrative fidelity because it resonated with their own feelings that they were essentially good people whose only failing had been that they were too permissive and not as tough as their own parents had been.

The Toughlove story was compelling because it so completely absolved parents of their guilt and relieved their sense of failure. The story also provided parents with a course of action that, at best, showed their children who was in charge and established rules they had to follow to remain part of the family, and at worst, allowed the remainder of the household to lead normal lives after the delinquent youth was "shown the door."

Despite the obvious appeal of these new "tough" approaches to child-rearing, however, they are not without risk. The dimension of the Toughlove story which holds that children who do not adhere to their bottom lines should be ejected from the house is especially controversial. There is, of course, great danger that the ejected child may be unprepared to face life on his/her own and may in fact become a real threat to him/herself and to society. For instance, John Hinckley's parents were following the Toughlove philosophy when they insisted that their son become financially independent by March 20, 1982, precisely the day that he shot President Reagan and three other men ("Hinckley's Family," 1984).

Hinckley's father has since embarked on a national speaking tour to warn parents of the dangers in the Toughlove approach, declaring: "For heaven's sake don't kick somebody out of the house when they can't cope. But I'd never heard that before, and it (kicking John out of the house) seemed to me to make a lot of sense at the time" ("Hinckley's Family," 1984, p. 12). Hinckley's parents now urge other parents who are told to eject their children from home to be sure to seek the advice of those experts they had been told could not be trusted ("Hinckley's Family," 1984). This warning seems reasonable enough: parents should not take drastic steps when a more conservative means for disciplining children might work equally well—they should always proceed with caution.

Before this or any other rival story is likely to capture the trust and attention of the Toughlove parents, however, it needs to accommodate them as the hopeful, newly self-confident, bearers of old-fashioned values which they have become. If a rival story cannot capture people's self-conceptions, it does not matter whether or not it is "fact." Fisher noted that, "Any story, any form of rhetorical communication, not only says something about the world, it also implies an audience, persons who conceive of themselves in very specific ways" (Fisher, 1984, p. 14). Parents who do not have "problem children" may find the Toughlove story objectionable, but to those parents in the midst of a crisis the story has obvious appeal. The advocates of any rival story can win adherents only by "telling stories that do not negate the self-conceptions people hold of themselves" (Fisher, 1984, p. 14).

The other great danger in the Toughlove story is that it can be readily adapted to fit all children and all situations. For example, during our observation we noted that if parents told the group that they did not believe drugs or alcohol were responsible for their children's bizarre behavior, they were given a lecture on how to substantiate these abuses. Other potential reasons for their children's erratic or destructive behavior, including emotional or psychological disturbances, were dismissed without consideration. The Toughlove story thus proved quite elastic and was easily stretched to permit the conclusion that "bad drugs" or a "bad crowd" caused all behavior problems and, therefore, all required the same remedy.

The pressure to enact the Toughlove story was great; all parents had to play the "enforcer" role that ritualistically proved their faith and imbued them with the credibility and unquestioned support granted only to other Toughlove moms and dads. While the group leaders seemed to be aware of the danger that parents might seek to get a quick-fix to their problems by ejecting their children from the house when far less drastic actions would be more appropriate, the potential danger from such decisions (as characterized by the Hinckley example) never appeared as imminent to the Toughlove parents as was the impending end to the chaos in their lives.

The truth or falsity of the Toughlove story is not really at issue in this study. What is important is that through an analysis we can come to understand the appeal of stories and perhaps even learn how to avoid the creation of stories which might precipitate harmful consequences. Perhaps the most useful outcome of such study is that child care professionals and social service agencies can learn how to create better stories—stories which affirm parents' self-worth, but also help them to deal with the crises in their homes without the risk of worsening those crises by reacting without careful deliberation.

References

Alibrandi, L. A. (1982). The Fellowship of Alcoholics Anonymous. In E. M. Pattison & E. Kaufman (Eds.), *Encyclopedic handbook of alcoholism* (pp. 979–986). New York: Gardner Press.

Bartocci, B. (1984). *My angry son: Sometimes love is not enough.* New York: Donald I. Fine.

Bass, J. D. (1983). Becoming the past: The rationale of renewal and the annulment of history. In D. Zarefsky, M. Sillars & J. Rhodes (Eds.), *Argument in transition: Proceedings of the Third Summer Conference on Argumentation* (pp. 305–318). Annandale, VA: Speech Communication Association.

Bodenhamer, G. (1984). *Back in control: How to get your children to behave.* Englewood Cliffs: Prentice-Hall.

Cowell, F. R. (1967). *Cicero and the Roman Republic* (4th ed.). Baltimore: Penguin Books.

David and Phyllis York treat problem teenagers with a stiff dose of "Toughlove." (1981, November 16). *People*, p. 101.

Emery, R. E. (1982). Intraparental conflict and the children of discord and divorce. *Psychological Bulletin, 92,* 310–330.

Fischer, D. G. (1983). Parental supervision and delinquency. *Perceptual and Motor Skills, 56,* 635–640.

Fisher, W. R. (1984). Narration as a human communication paradigm: The case of public moral argument. *Communication Monographs, 51,* 1–22.

Frentz, T. S. (1985). Rhetorical conversation, time, and moral action. *Quarterly Journal of Speech, 71,* 1–18.

Getting tough with teens. (1981, June 8). *Time*, p. 47.

Hinckley, J. & Hinckley, J. A. (1985). *Breaking Points.* Grand Rapids, MI: Zondervan.

Hinckleys: Family on a crusade. (1984, February 23). *Los Angeles Times*, p. 12.

Knapp, M. S. (1979). Ethnographic contributions to evaluation research: The experimental schools program evaluation and some alternatives. In T. D. Cook & C. S. Reichardt (Eds.), *Qualitative and quantitative methods in evaluation research* (pp. 118–139). Beverly Hills: Sage.

Landers, A. (1981, November). Giving kids "Tough" love. *Family Circle*, p. 34.

Loeber, R. & Dishion, T. (1983). Early predictors of male delinquency: A review. *Psychological Bulletin, 94*, 68–99.

Morehouse, E. & Richards, T. (1982). An examination of dysfunctional latency age children of alcoholic parents and problems in intervention. *Journal of Children in Contemporary Society, 15*, 21–33.

Nemy, E. (1982, April 26). For problem teen-agers: Love, toughness. *New York Times*, p. B12.

Paperny, D. M. & Deisher, R. W. (1983). Maltreatment of adolescents: The relationship to a predisposition toward violent behavior and delinquency. *Adolescence, 18*, 499–506.

Pattison, E. M. (1982). A systems approach to alcoholism treatment. In E. M. Pattison & E. Kaufman (Eds.), *Encyclopedic handbook of alcoholism* (pp. 1080–1108). New York: Gardner Press.

Pomerleau, O. F. (1982). Current behavioral theories in the treatment of alcoholism. In E. M. Pattison & E. Kaufman (Eds.), *Encyclopedic handbook of alcoholism* (pp. 1054–1067). New York: Gardner Press.

Sanderson, J. (1983). *How to raise your kids to stand on their own two feet*. New York: Congdon & Weed.

Stasiak, E. A. (1982). Nutritional approaches to altering criminal behavior. *Corrective and Social Psychiatry and the Journal of Behavioral Technology, Methods and Therapy, 28*, 110–115.

Wohl, L. C. (1985, May). The parent-training game—from "Toughlove" to perfect manners. *Ms.*, p. 40.

York, P. & York, D. (1980). *Toughlove*. Sellersville, PA: Community Service Foundation.

Stories in the Making about the Information Highway
A View from *Mademoiselle*

Linda Cooper Berdayes

A new technology currently is being introduced into our culture—that of the information highway, a high-speed digital information technology infrastructure. New technological devices that provide the means for the creation of this telecommunication infrastructure include the telephone, the personal computer, and television, all of which will be used, many experts suggest, to provide virtually unlimited services in all aspects of our lives.

The implications of technological systems often are not known until long after a technology has been implemented in daily life. Examination of the discourse around a technology such as the information highway at the time of its introduction into society provides one way of foreseeing such implications, allowing us to speculate about its effects and, more important, to alter the nature of the discourse and thus the technology if we so choose. As Raymond Williams (1974) asserts, without an understanding of the assumptions that lie at the heart of our discourse about technology, "much of the working analysis will be naive, or will at least be limited to the unexamined conventions of its culture" (p. 19).

In this essay, I will examine a small part of the discourse surrounding the information superhighway in an effort to discover the assumptions and values that characterize the discourse. I have chosen as my data an article by Julian Dibbell, "Easy Living on the Digital Planet," which appeared in the October, 1993, issue of *Mademoiselle*. In this article, Dibbell suggests that he is eagerly anticipating the services readers can expect to encounter in the future on the information highway. His view is that his readers never will have to leave the comfort of their armchairs to experience these services. He takes readers on a tour of the information highway, acting as a guide, as he presents nine sites to which readers will have access via the information highway—sites that include school, the mall, the hangout, the sex club, and the office.

This essay was written as part of the initial analysis of data for Linda Cooper Berdayes' doctoral dissertation, "Stories in the Making: The Information Highway in Public Discourse," Ohio State University, 1995. Used by permission of the author.

I selected this article for analysis because I am particularly interested in the discourse around the information superhighway that is directed at groups of people who often are not participants in the worlds of business and technology, where much of the discourse occurs, and who are not generally believed to be among those who will have input into or make significant use of the information highway. This article, because of where it was published, is directed at young women who presumably would not be in positions of power where they would have a great deal of influence on or access to the development of the information highway. It thus provides an opportunity to examine the nature of the discourse surrounding the information highway outside of the areas of business and technology—to include groups usually ignored or excluded and the assumptions held about the nature of their participation in the information highway.

I have chosen to analyze this article using as my units of analysis features of narratives. With its capacity to shed light on how those involved in the development and description of the information highway order and present the new world, a focus on narrative seems particularly appropriate as a means to understand the vision of the information highway that is being created. Such an analysis should suggest how the narrative constructed directs interpretations of the highway and functions to gain adherence for the perspective it presents concerning the role of women in the new technologies.

Significant Features of the Narrative

I began my analysis of this article by explicating many features of the narrative, including the settings, characters, narrator, events, temporal relations, causal relations, audience, and themes; I examined both the text and the accompanying illustration to construct the narrative presented by the article. Of the many features of the narrative I studied, four features seemed most significant in providing clues to the nature of the worldview presented around young women's participation in the information highway—setting, characters, narrator, and events.

Setting

The narrative depicts two primary settings. One is an armchair in the home, in which a young woman is shown sitting, holding a telephone to her ear with one hand and a remote control with her other. A lap-top computer rests on her lap, and she is looking at a television set positioned on a small table in front of her chair. The home is transformed, then, into a place of high technology, with multiple outlets that allow access to the information highway.

The second setting of the narrative is the electronic superhighway, which is described as a "fast-lane communications system" that will "blanket the nation" within a few years. The highway gives instant access to entertainment, information, and a variety of services to people in the home. It is composed of new technological devices—"super machines"—that combine the functions of the telephone, personal computer, and television. This highway is possible because of two technological processes—"fiber-optics," "hair-thin glass strands" that carry 65,000 times more information than copper phone lines, and "digitalization," a process in which sounds and images are translated into 1's and 0's, allowing the digits to "move through the fiber-optic cables." The result of these processes is reflected in the author's description of the information highway as a "superhighway," characterized by "high speed," which provides "instant access" and allows for "working, playing and living at the speed of electricity."

The setting of the electronic superhighway is elaborated in detail as a multiple setting of nine sites to which individuals can be linked via the information highway. The verbal text describes these sites largely in terms of the activities that would be done at each site. Four of the sites depicted concern professional activities. In the *school* setting, people are studying "with professors across thousands of miles" and accessing "library resources"; in the *media center*, creative materials are being produced and distributed without the need for film or music studios. The *office* is where "every office activity—from passing out memos to taking meetings to gossiping by the coffee maker—will be easily conducted from home." At the site of the *voting booth* is a voting network based in the home.

Four of the settings presented have to do with leisure and pleasure. One is the mall, where the individual can "order whatever you fancy." At the *hangout*, "people will feel closer to their digital 'communities' than to their geographic ones," and at the *multiplex*, movies are available on demand and video games can be played by people who are miles apart. The *sex club* is the site of "steamy get-togethers" and is "a couple of steps beyond phone sex." The final setting suggested is the *highway horizon*, the far future of the highway, where individuals can teleport themselves to other locations and "literally become digital information, our minds traveling down the electronic superhighway from one fabulous robot body to the next."

Characters

Two main characters populate this narrative: *you* and *experts*. The first character, you, is both a character in the narrative and the audience for the narrative. This character is presumed to be female because of the typical reader of this magazine and the visual depiction of the character in the article. The character is shown in the illustration as a woman who is young; thin; and wearing form-fitting, stylish clothing, her hair in a fashionable bob. She is busy juggling multiple tasks simultaneously, talking on the phone while using a lap-top computer and a remote control.

This woman is physically situated at home throughout the narrative. She stays in her armchair, where she actively participates in the information highway, in charge of her local technological universe. Her abundant activity is contradicted, however, by references to her passivity. She "can't drive a car" on the information highway, asserts Dibbell, who also portrays her as a passenger on the highway who must fasten her seat belt while she is transported along the highway. She is slow to adjust to changing times and prefers to react to circumstances rather than to affect or influence them, evidenced in the author's admonition to her that the electronic superhighway is coming "sooner than you think" and she had "better adjust."

The author's description of the young woman as someone who might "wear slippers to work" (and the visual illustration shows her wearing shoes in the style of ballet slippers) also suggests someone content to stay somewhat uninvolved—she isn't wearing the kinds of shoes necessary for active participation in the real world. In addition, slippers suggest this person is likely to be drowsy, dozy, and just emerging from sleep—preferring to snuggle down under the covers than face the world. She's not quite up to speed and ready to go in a way that would be necessary for active participation in the world. The one metaphor the narrator uses in the article reinforces this snoozy, uninvolved image of the woman as participant in the information highway. He refers to the highway as a communications system that will "blanket the nation," suggesting a highway that covers the participant, keeping her warm, and sheltering her from active involvement in the highway.

The second major character in the narrative is the expert. The expert enters the narrative when the author of the article cites the testimony of authorities to explain or support his claims about the information highway. One such expert is an unnamed scientist at Bellcore, who estimates that every American home will be hooked up to fiber-optic technology by the year 2015. Another is an administrator at the National Institute of Standards and Technologies, Roy G. Saltman, who expresses concern that electronic voting will facilitate undemocratic principles by denying technologically deprived citizens the right to vote. The third expert cited is Howard Rheingold, author of the book, *Virtual Reality*.

Narrator

The author or narrator, Julian Dibbell, is a part of the group of expert characters in the narrative. The overwhelming feature that marks his presence is his enthusiasm. The narrator's enthusiasm suggests he is someone who appreciates and enjoys technology and who is anxiously awaiting the arrival of the information highway. He is exuberant in his description of the information highway, suggesting it has virtually unlimited uses. "Garage bands will be able to put out their first singles without record labels," he asserts, and "[m]erchandising channels will multiply with everything from funky boutiques to department stores. . . ." He expresses only one reservation about the effects of the information highway, and it is voiced by the government expert regarding unequal access to voting networks.

The authority displayed by the narrator is the authority of an instructor, prophet, and advisor. He has information that most young women do not have, and he imparts it to them; he also advises them on how to make use of this information. Although he cites experts in the article, Dibbell reserves the role of ultimate expert for himself. The narrator's authority is further enhanced through his omnipresence; he has the ability to be in all sites on the information highway, regardless of space and time constraints.

Major Event

One primary event characterizes the narrative—the woman's "move" from her home to one or more of the other sites as a result of her connection to the information highway. She is not actually transported to the new site but rather is able to enjoy the benefits the site offers from her home. The major action, then, could be described as the accomplishing of activities in ways that make them faster and more efficient.

Women's Place in the Information Highway

The narrative told in the article in *Mademoiselle* contributes several assumptions to perceptions of the information highway, particularly as it pertains to young women and their role in it. This is a world in which women are portrayed as powerful in the home, but they are only passengers on the information highway. In the home, women are manipulating technology, working, creating, producing, and seemingly satisfying social needs, but once they move outside of the home, this power diminishes. They do not control technology but are the recipients of it. The information highway that comes into the home can provide women with "a professor teaching oceanography in Australia on your desktop" and sophisticated home-shopping experiences, but the important policy decisions are being made for them by others. Others, represented by the expert author of the article, teach them and provide the goods they purchase. The women at home adapt or acquiesce to these decisions and remain within the perimeters male experts have prescribed for them. Women are non-contributors, then, to the creation and development of the information highway.

The world of the information highway is a world in which the needs of business to gain profit and the forms of communication that business values—forms more often associated with the masculine in our culture—are emphasized over the communication needs and values most often associated with women. Speed and efficiency are emphasized at the expense of supportive, nurturing, emotional communication. Communication becomes the transmission of messages, not experiencing the intimate, emotional, rewarding presence of another human being. It is characterized by a fast pace, lots of action, and a focus on ends rather than on the processes used to accomplish those ends. Meandering; slowly taking in and appreciating one's environment; and enjoying the company of others, talking leisurely with close friends, have no place. The depiction of the sex club is a vivid example of the emphasis on speed and results at the expense of nurturing communication. The sex club is presented as a place not for the creation of intimacy, reciprocity, and mutuality but for sending "fast-paced prescriptions of what they're 'doing' to each other."

The worldview encapsulated by the narrative, then, suggests that young women will be staying home, consuming information and products that others have created for them. They are not helping to construct, develop, or control the information highway—such tasks are left to the experts. Women are excluded not only because they are offered no role in the development of the information highway but because that world seems to have no place for women's ways of knowing and being. No wonder the narrator is enthusiastic about the new world—it is his world, a masculine world, in which the expertise and the power belong to him and his colleagues.

Reference

Williams, R. (1974). Communication as cultural science. *Journal of Communication*, 24, 17–25.

Additional Samples

Narrative Criticism

Bass, Jeff. "The Appeal to Efficiency as Narrative Closure: Lyndon Johnson and the Dominican Crisis, 1965." *Southern Speech Communication Journal*, 50 (Winter 1985), 103–20.

Brown, William J. "The Persuasive Appeal of Mediated Terrorism: The Case of the TWA Flight 847 Hijacking." *Western Journal of Speech Communication*, 54 (Spring 1990), 219–36.

Burgchardt, Carl R. "Discovering Rhetorical Imprints: La Follette, 'Iago,' and the Melodramatic Scenario." *Quarterly Journal of Speech*, 71 (November 1985), 441–56.

Carlson, A. Cheree. "The Role of Character in Public Moral Argument: Henry Ward Beecher and the Brooklyn Scandal." *Quarterly Journal of Speech*, 77 (February 1991), 38–52.

Carpenter, Ronald H. "Admiral Mahan, 'Narrative Fidelity,' and the Japanese Attack on Pearl Harbor." *Quarterly Journal of Speech*, 72 (August 1986), 290–305.

Deming, Caren J. "*Hill Street Blues* as Narrative." *Critical Studies in Mass Communication*, 2 (March 1985), 1–22.

Dobkin, Bethami A. "Paper Tigers and Video Postcards: The Rhetorical Dimensions of Narrative Form in ABC News Coverage of Terrorism." *Western Journal of Communication*, 56 (Spring 1992), 143–60.

Fisher, Walter R. *Human Communication as Narration: Toward a Philosophy of Reason, Value, and Action*. Columbia: University of South Carolina Press, 1987, several essays, pp. 143–91.

Gerland, Oliver. "Brecht and the Courtroom: Alienating Evidence in the 'Rodney King' Trials." *Text and Performance Quarterly*, 14 (October 1994), 305–18.

Griffin, Charles J. G. "The Rhetoric of Form in Conversion Narratives." *Quarterly Journal of Speech*, 76 (May 1990), 152–63.

Gross, Daniel G. "A Teachers' Strike, Rival Stories and Narrative Agreement." *Nebraska Speech Communication Association Journal*, 31 (Spring/Summer 1992), 47–56.

Hollihan, Thomas A. "The Public Controversy Over the Panama Canal Treaties: An Analysis of American Foreign Policy Rhetoric." *Western Journal of Speech Communication*, 50 (Fall 1986), 368–87.

Jasinski, James. "(Re)constituting Community through Narrative Argument: Eros and Philia in *The Big Chill*." *Quarterly Journal of Speech*, 79 (November 1993), 467–86.

Katriel, Tamar, and Aliza Shenhar. "Tower and Stockade: Dialogic Narration in Israeli Settlement Ethos." *Quarterly Journal of Speech*, 76 (November 1990), 359–80.

Kirkwood, William G. "Storytelling and Self-Confrontation: Parables as Communication Strategies." *Quarterly Journal of Speech*, 69 (February 1983), 58–74.

Lewis, William F. "Telling America's Story: Narrative Form and the Reagan Presidency." *Quarterly Journal of Speech*, 73 (August 1987), 280–302.

Mandelbaum, Jennifer. "Couples Sharing Stories." *Communication Quarterly*, 35 (Spring 1987), 144–70.

Mumby, Dennis K. "The Political Function of Narrative in Organizations." *Communication Monographs*, 54 (June 1987), 113–27.

Olson, Scott R. "Meta-television: Popular Postmodernism." *Critical Studies in Mass Communication*, 4 (September 1987), 284–300.

Owen, A. Susan. "Oppositional Voices in *China Beach*: Narrative Configurations of Gender and War." In *Narrative and Social Control*, Ed. Dennis K. Mumby. Newbury Park, CA: Sage, 1993, pp. 207–31.

Peterson, Tarla Rai. "Telling the Farmers' Story: Competing Responses to Soil Conservation Rhetoric." *Quarterly Journal of Speech*, 77 (August 1991), 289–308.

Poulakos, Takis. "Isocrates's Use of Narrative in the *Evagoras*: Epideictic Rhetoric and Moral Action." *Quarterly Journal of Speech*, 73 (August 1987), 317–28.

Ritter, Kurt. "Drama and Legal Rhetoric: The Perjury Trials of Alger Hiss." *Western Journal of Speech Communication*, 49 (Spring 1985), 83–102.

Rosteck, Thomas. "Narrative in Martin Luther King's *I've Been to the Mountaintop*." *Southern Communication Journal*, 58 (Fall 1992), 22–32.

Rowland, Robert C., and Robert Strain. "Social Function, Polysemy and Narrative-Dramatic Form: A Case Study of *Do the Right Thing*." *Communication Quarterly*, 42 (Summer 1994), 213–28.

Rushing, Janice Hocker. "Mythic Evolution of 'The New Frontier' in Mass Mediated Rhetoric." *Critical Studies in Mass Communication*, 3 (September 1986), 265–96.

Rushing, Janice Hocker. "Ronald Reagan's 'Star Wars' Address: Mythic Containment of Technical Reasoning." *Quarterly Journal of Speech*, 72 (November 1986), 415–33.

Salvador, Michael. "The Rhetorical Genesis of Ralph Nader: A Functional Exploration of Narrative and Argument in Public Discourse." *Southern Communication Journal*, 59 (Spring 1994), 227–39.

Smith, Larry David. "Convention Oratory as Institutional Discourse: A Narrative Synthesis of the Democrats and Republicans of 1988." *Communication Studies*, 41 (Spring 1990), 19–34.

Smith, Larry David. "A Narrative Analysis of the Party Platforms: The Democrats and Republicans of 1984." *Communication Quarterly*, 37 (Spring 1989), 91–99.

Smith, Larry David. "Narrative Styles in Network Coverage of the 1984 Nominating Conventions." *Western Journal of Speech Communication*, 52 (Winter 1988), 63–74.

Solomon, Martha. "Autobiographies as Rhetorical Narratives: Elizabeth Cady Stanton and Anna Howard Shaw as 'New Women.'" *Communication Studies*, 42 (Winter 1991), 354–70.

Stuckey, Mary E. "Anecdotes and Conversations: The Narrational and Dialogic Styles of Modern Presidential Communication." *Communication Quarterly*, 40 (Winter 1992), 45–55.

Zelizer, Barbie. "Achieving Journalistic Authority through Narrative." *Critical Studies in Mass Communication*, 7 (December 1990), 366–76.

11

Pentadic Criticism

Pentadic criticism is rooted in the work and thinking of Kenneth Burke, who made significant contributions to our understanding of how and why human beings use rhetoric and to what effect. Although many of his ideas can be and have been used as units of analysis in criticism, in this chapter, the focus is on Burke's notion of the pentad and on pentadic criticism, derived from his theory of dramatism.

Dramatism is the label Burke gave to the study of human motivation through terms derived from the study of drama.[1] Two basic assumptions underlie dramatism. One assumption at the heart of dramatism is that language use constitutes action, not motion. Motion corresponds to the biological or animal aspect of the human being, which is concerned with bodily processes such as growth, digestion, respiration, and the requirements for the maintenance of these processes such as food, shelter, and rest. This level does not involve the use of symbols and thus is non-symbolic.

In contrast, action corresponds to the symbolic or neurological aspect of the human being, which Burke defined as the ability of an organism to acquire language or a symbol system. This, then, is the realm of action or the symbolic. Some of our motives are derived from our animality—as when we seek food in order to sustain our bodies, but others originate in our symbolicity. When we strive to reach goals in areas such as education, politics, religion, commerce, or finance, for example, we are motivated by our symbolicity. To be motivated to act in these areas requires a symbol system that creates the possibility for such desires in the first place.[2]

Burke elaborated on his notion of action at the heart of dramatism by establishing three conditions for action. First, it must involve freedom or choice. If we cannot make a choice, we are not acting but rather are being moved, like a ball hit with a racket—we are behaving mechanically. Of course, we never can be completely free, but implicit in the idea of action is some choice. A second condition necessary for an act is purpose or will. Either consciously or unconsciously, we must select or will a choice—we must choose one option over others. Finally, action requires motion. While motion can exist without action (as when an object falls, through the force of gravity, to the ground), action cannot exist without motion. Symbolic activity, or action, is grounded in the realm of the non-symbolic, although action cannot be reduced to motion.[3]

This distinction between motion and action is largely a conceptual or theoretical one, for once organisms acquire a symbol system, we are virtually unable to do anything purely in the realm of motion. Once we have a symbol system, everything we do is interpreted through that system. To cook a meal, for example, may be considered motion since it involves the biological need for food. Yet, creating a meal is impossible without the involvement of our symbolic conceptions of eating; the process, which has a biological basis, quickly becomes an action.

A second assumption of dramatism is that humans develop and present messages in much the same way that a play is presented. We use rhetoric to constitute and present a particular view of our situation, just as the presentation of a play creates a certain world or situation inhabited by characters who engage in actions in a setting. Through rhetoric, we size up situations and name their structure and outstanding ingredients. How we describe a situation indicates how we are perceiving it, the choices we see available to us, and the action we are likely to take in that situtation. Our language, then, provides a clue to our motive or why we do what we do. A rhetor who perceives that one person is the cause of a particular problem, for example, will use rhetoric that names that perception. She will describe the situation in such a way as to feature that person's characteristics and to downplay other elements that may be contributing to the problem. Once a critic knows how a rhetor has described a situation, the critic is able to discover that rhetor's motive for action in the situation.[4]

As rhetors describe their situations, they do so using the five basic elements of a drama—*act, agent, agency, scene,* and *purpose.* These five terms constitute what Burke called the *pentad,* and they are used as principles or a "grammar" for describing any symbolic act fully: "you must have some word that names the *act* (names what took place, in thought or deed), and another that names the *scene* (the background of the act, the situation in which it occurred); also you must indicate what person or kind of person (*agent*) performed the act, what means or instruments he used (*agency*), and the *purpose.*"[5] For those who are acquainted with journalistic writing, these elements will be recognized as the five questions a journalist must answer to write an adequate story about an act or event: who? (agent), what? (act), why? (purpose), when? and where? (scene). The agency is concerned with how the act was done.

In addition to terms for act, scene, agent, agency, and purpose, Burke sometimes included attitude as an element to be considered in the analysis of motivation. *Attitude,* in this case, designates the manner in which particular means are employed. The act of cultivating a garden is done through specific agencies such as seeds, plants, and water. To cultivate with extraordinary diligence and care, however, involves an attitude or a "how." Burke stated that "on later occasions I have regretted that I had not turned the pentad into a hexad, with "attitude as the sixth term,"[6] but saw attitude as part of agent: "But in its character as a state of mind that may or may not lead to an act, it is quite clearly to be classed under the head of agent."[7]

Procedures

The critic who chooses to use pentadic criticism as the source for units of analysis approaches an artifact in four steps: (1) formulating a research question and selecting an artifact; (2) selecting a unit of analysis; (3) analyzing the artifact; and (4) writing the critical essay.

Formulating a Research Question and Selecting an Artifact

The first step in the process of rhetorical criticism is to develop a research question to ask about rhetoric and to select a rhetorical artifact to analyze that provides an initial answer to the question. Because pentadic criticism provides a means to understand the way in which a rhetor encompasses a situation through rhetoric—through the selection and highlighting of particular terms—it is particularly useful for answering questions about rhetors' motives or their attempts to structure audiences' perceptions of situations.

Selecting a Unit of Analysis

The critic's next step is to select a unit of analysis that can help the critic answer the research question. The unit of analysis is that aspect of the artifact to which the critic attends in the analysis. The units of analysis offered in pentadic criticism are the five terms of the pentad—act, agent, agency, scene, and purpose.

Analyzing the Artifact

In criticism in which the terms of the pentad are used as units of analysis, two operations are performed by the critic: (1) labeling the five terms of agent, act, scene, purpose, and agency in the artifact: and (2) identifying the dominant term.

Labeling of Terms. The first step in a pentadic analysis is to identify the five terms in the rhetorical artifact from the perspective of the rhetor. Identification of the *agent* involves naming the group or individual who is the protagonist or main character of the situation as it is presented by the rhetor.[8] The agent could be the rhetor him- or herself or another person or group. In a presentation to the jury at a murder trial, for example, a lawyer—the rhetor—could choose as the agent the murderer, the murder victim, or the victim's family. In a speech by a president of the United States, the agent is the person, group, or institution that is the primary subject of the speech—perhaps Congress, the CIA, or the president's mother. The naming of the agent also may involve descriptions of what the agent is like—for example, *kind, vicious, unscrupulous, dangerous,* or *generous.*

The *act* is the rhetor's presentation of the major action taken by the protagonist or agent.[9] The critic who is studying the speeches of a United States president, for example, may find that the act is the effort to accomplish health-care reform, with the president serving as the agent. In a speech honoring someone for her community service, the act might be the creation of a literacy program by the person being honored. If the artifact being studied is the work of an artist, the critic may find that in a particular painting, the act is bathing a child, with the agent the woman who is featured as the subject of the work.

The means the rhetor says are used to perform the act or the instruments used to accomplish it are labeled the *agency*.[10] In a speech about health-care reform, for example, a president might depict the agency as hard work, careful compromise, or futile attempts to gain the cooperation of the opposing party. In a song about love gone wrong, the agency for the lover's departure might be portrayed as callous disregard for the protagonist's feelings and needs.

Scene is the ground, location, or situation in which the rhetor says the act takes place—the kind of stage the rhetor sets when describing physical conditions, social and cultural influences, or historical causes.[11] In a presidential inaugural address, for example, the new president might describe a scene of division and hatred among Americans. In an environmentalist's testimony before a city council on the impact a particular policy has on the local environment, the advocate might describe a scene of abundant nature in harmony and balance.

The purpose of the act is what the rhetor suggests the agent intends to accomplish by performing the act.[12] It is the rhetor's account of the protagonist's intentions, feelings, and values. The purpose for a Native American's protest speech at a Columbus Day celebration, for example, might be to gain recognition for Native Americans' primary role in the creation of American civilization and culture. The purpose attributed to a community volunteer's actions might be to repay the support she received from others early in her life. Purpose is not synonymous with motive; purpose is the reason for action that is specified by the rhetor for the agent, while motive is the explanation for the rhetor's action, manifest in the rhetorical artifact as a whole.

Identification of the five pentadic terms results in an overview of the rhetor's view of a particular situation. The critic may discover, for example, that a hijacker's statement to the FBI reveals these five terms: the agent is the United States, the act is the United States' imprisonment of her friend for a crime he did not commit; the agency is denial of basic rights to an American citizen; the purpose is to publicize her friend's imprisonment; and the scene is conditions of injustice and cover-up. Such a naming of the situation helps explain the hijacking by pointing to the hijacker's conception of the situation. This same hijacker, of course, has virtually an unlimited number of options she can use to describe her situation, and each description constitutes a different vocabulary of motives. She could name, for example, the agent as herself; the act as a heroic act of desperation she took only after she had exhausted all legal options; the agency as bravery and heroism; her purpose of saving her innocent friend from life in prison; and the scene as one of battle and perhaps martyrdom.

Identification of Dominant Term. The naming of the five terms of the pentad is the first step in the use of pentadic units of analysis. The next step is to discover which of the five elements identified dominates the rhetoric or is featured by the rhetor. Discovery of the dominant term provides insight into what dimension of the situation the rhetor privileges or sees as most important.

One way to discover the dominant pentadic element is to use what Burke called *ratios*. A ratio is a pairing of two of the elements in the pentad in order to discover the relationship between them and the effect that each has on the other. Each of the five elements, then, may be put together with each of the others to form these ratios: scene-act, scene-agent, scene-agency, scene-purpose, act-scene, act-agent, act-agency, act-purpose, agent-scene, agent-act, agent-agency, agent-purpose, agency-scene, agency-act, agency-agent, agency-purpose, purpose-scene, purpose-act, purpose-agent, and purpose-agency.

To use the ratios, the critic pairs two terms from those identified in the pentad. There is no right order with which to begin this process; the critic simply dives in and begins pairing various elements of the five named. With each ratio, the critic looks for the relationship between these two terms in the rhetor's description of the situation, trying to discover whether the first term influences the nature of the second term.

The critic may begin, for example, by putting together scene and act in a scene-act ratio. The critic's explanation of this ratio involves asking whether the nature of the scene, as described by the rhetor, affects the nature of the act the rhetor describes. (An act-scene ratio, in contrast, would explore whether the nature of the act dominates—whether the way the act is described takes precedence over the nature of the scene.) The critic may discover that there is a significant relationship between the two terms in a ratio or may find that the first term in the ratio has little impact or effect on the second. Let's say the rhetor describes the scene as a country in which oppressive and dangerous conditions exist, freedom is being repressed, and citizens are being denied the opportunity for self-determination; the act is described as the heroic invasion of that country. In a scene-act ratio, the scene is portrayed by the rhetor as the precipitating event that generates the act of heroism; there would be no need to perform acts of heroism without the dangerous scene. Thus, the scene dominates over act in this ratio.

If the critic discovers, on the other hand, that the rhetor describes a scene in which people are content and benefit from a country's political structure and names as the act the invasion of the country by the United States, the outcome of an exploration of the scene-act ratio would be different. In this case, the scene seems to have little influence on the act, but neither does the act have much effect on the scene. The critic probably would find, after investigating other ratios, that the dominant term of the rhetoric is something other than scene or act—perhaps agent (the nature of the United States as a domineering, imperialist power) or purpose (the United States' goal is to impose its will on other countries to bolster its own control and influence in the world).

The critic continues to pair terms in ratios, then, to discover if one term seems to affect the nature and character of another. Review of several of the ratios will produce a pattern in which the critic discovers that one term (or sometimes more than one) is the central, controlling term and defines the other terms in the pentad. This process of experimenting with the ratios to discover which term influences the others is not included in the essay of criticism the critic produces. This is work the critic does behind the scenes and prior to the writing of the essay. What the critic does in the essay is to identify the featured or dominant term and provide support for it. This support usually takes the form of a discussion of how this particular term influences the other elements of the rhetor's description of the situation.

Burke provided a suggestion for gaining a more in-depth view of a rhetor's definition of a situation once the critic has discovered the dominant term of the pentad. Once the critic discovers the dominant term, it can be used to identify the philosophical system to which it corresponds, with that system generating ideas about the definition of a situation, its meaning for rhetors and audiences, and its possible consequences. If the act is featured in the pentad, Burke suggested, the philosophy that corresponds is realism, the doctrine that universal principles are more real than objects as sensed. This philosophical position is opposite that of nominalism, the doctrine that abstract concepts, general terms, or universals have no objective reference but exist only as names. If the scene is featured, the philosophy that corresponds is materialism, the system that regards all facts and reality as explainable in terms of matter and motion or physical laws. If the agent is featured, the corresponding philosophy is idealism, the system that views the mind or spirit as each person experiences it as fundamentally real, and the totality of the universe is believed to be mind or spirit in its essence. If the means or agency is featured, the pragmatic philosophy corresponds. Pragmatism is the means necessary to the attainment of a goal—instrumentalism or concern with consequences, function, and what something is "good for." In this doctrine, the meaning of a proposition or course of action lies in its observable consequences, and the sum of these consequences constitutes its meaning. If the purpose is featured, the corresponding philosophy is mysticism. In mysticism, the element of unity is emphasized to the point that individuality disappears. Identification often becomes so strong that the individual is unified with some cosmic or universal purpose.[13]

In a speech by an anti-abortion advocate on the appropriateness of killing doctors who perform abortions, for example, the rhetor may describe the agent—himself—as a heroic savior, the act as stopping murder, the agency as any means necessary to stop murder, the purpose as saving innocent lives, and the scene as one of desperation in which legal tactics to stop murder have been unsuccessful. The critic may discover, as a result of application of the ratios, that the dominant term is purpose—to save innocent lives—suggesting that those who are persuaded by his argument accept a definition of the situation as focused on purpose. The corresponding philosophy is mysticism, which features identification with a cosmic or universal purpose. The critic then could speculate that the motivating force for the rhetor and those who share his definition of the situation is a belief that they are representatives of divine will, doing on earth God's work of honoring human life. The sacredness of this mission allows whatever acts are necessary to fulfill it.

Writing the Critical Essay

The critic who chooses to use the pentad as the unit of analysis writes an essay that includes five major components: (1) an introduction, in which the research question, its contribution to rhetorical theory, and its significance are discussed; (2) description of the artifact and its context; (3) description of the unit of analysis, the pentadic terms; (4) report of the findings of the analysis, in which the critic identifies the five pentadic terms and suggests which one is dominant; and (5) discussion of the contribution the analysis makes to answering the research question.

Sample Essays

Following are three sample essays in which the pentad has been used as the unit of analysis to discover the ways in which rhetors have chosen to describe their situations. The critics use these descriptions to understand various aspects of rhetoric. David A. Ling uses the terms of the pentad to explore and evaluate Edward Kennedy's efforts to persuade an audience to see him as the victim of rather than responsible for an accident. The research question that guides Ling's analysis is, "What types of definitions of situations are effective in enabling rhetors to maintain or regain their credibility?" In her pentadic analysis of a novel by Abigail Scott Duniway, Jean M. Ward seeks to answer the question, "How can rhetors define situations in ways that empower audiences?" In the third sample, Diana Brown Sheridan uses pentadic elements as units of analysis to explore an act of protest, guided by the research questions, "How are personal symbols used in public protests? What characteristics of the symbols make their use effective?"

Notes

[1] For a discussion of dramatism, see: Kenneth Burke, *Language as Symbolic Action: Essays on Life, Literature, and Method* (Berkeley: University of California Press, 1966), p. 54; Kenneth Burke, *The Philosophy of Literary Form* (1941; rpt. Berkeley: University of California Press, 1973), p. 103; Kenneth Burke, *A Grammar of Motives* (1945; rpt. Berkeley: University of California Press, 1969), pp. xxii, 60; Kenneth Burke, "The Five Master Terms: Their Place in a 'Dramatistic' Grammar of Motives," *View*, 2 (June 1943), 50–52; Kenneth Burke, "Dramatism," in *International Encyclopedia of the Social Sciences*, ed. David L. Sills ([New York]: Macmillan/Free Press, 1968), VII, 445–52; and Kenneth Burke, "Rhetoric, Poetics, and Philosophy," in *Rhetoric, Philosophy, and Literature: An Exploration*, ed. Don M. Burks (West Lafayette: Purdue University Press, 1978), pp. 32–33. The dramatistic approach is not limited to the work of Kenneth Burke. One good example of work by others in this area is James E. Combs and Michael W. Mansfield, eds., *Drama in Life: The Uses of Communication in Society* (New York: Hastings, 1976).

[2] The distinction between action and motion is discussed in: Burke, "Dramatism," p. 445; Kenneth Burke, *Permanence and Change: An Anatomy of Purpose* (1954; rpt. Indianapolis: Bobbs-Merrill, 1965), pp. 162, 215; Burke, *Language as Symbolic Action*, pp. 28, 53, 63, 67, 482; and Kenneth Burke, *The Rhetoric of Religion: Studies in Logology* (Berkeley: University of California Press, 1970), pp. 16, 274.

[3] Burke discusses conditions required for action in: *The Rhetoric of Religion*, pp. 39, 188, 281; *A Grammar of Motives*, pp. 14, 276; *The Philosophy of Literary Form*, p. xvi; and "Dramatism," p. 447.

[4] For more on the process of sizing up a situation through rhetoric, see Burke, *The Philosophy of Literary Form*, pp. 1, 6, 109, 298, 304.

[5] Burke, *A Grammar of Motives*, p. xv.

[6] Kenneth Burke, *Dramatism and Development* (Barre, Massachusetts: Clark University Press, 1972), p. 23.

[7] Burke, *A Grammar of Motives*, p. 20.

[8] For a discussion of agent, see Burke, *A Grammar of Motives*, pp. 20, 171–226.

[9] For a discussion of act, see Burke, *A Grammar of Motives*, pp. 227–74.

[10] Agency is discussed in Burke, *A Grammar of Motives*, pp. 275–320.

[11] Scene is discussed in: Burke, *A Grammar of Motives*, pp. xvi, 12, 77, 84, 85, 90; Burke, *The Rhetoric of Religion*, p. 26; and Burke, *Language as Symbolic Action*, p. 360.

[12] For a discussion of purpose, see Burke, *A Grammar of Motives*, pp. 275–320.

[13] Burke, *A Grammar of Motives*, pp. 128–30.

A Pentadic Analysis of
Senator Edward Kennedy's
Address to the People
of Massachusetts
July 25, 1969

David A. Ling

On July 25, 1969 Senator Edward Kennedy addressed the people of the state of Massachusetts for the purpose of describing the events surrounding the death of Miss Mary Jo Kopechne. The broadcasting networks provided prime time coverage of Senator Kennedy's address, and a national audience listened as Kennedy recounted the events of the previous week. The impact of that incident and Kennedy's subsequent explanation have been a subject of continuing comment ever since.

This paper will examine some of the rhetorical choices Kennedy made either consciously or unconsciously in his address of July 25th. It will then speculate on the possible impact that those choices may have on audience response to the speech. The principal tool used for this investigation will be the "Dramatistic Pentad" found in the writings of Kenneth Burke.

The Pentad and Human Motivation

The pentad evolved out of Burke's attempts to understand the bases of human conduct and motivation. Burke argues that "human conduct being in the realm of action and end . . . is most directly discussible in dramatistic terms."[1] He maintains that, in a broad sense, history can be viewed as a play, and, just as there are a limited number of basic plots available to the author, so also there are a limited number of situations that occur to man. It, therefore, seems appropriate to talk about situations that occur to man in the language of the stage. As man sees these similar situations (or dramas) occurring, he develops strategies to explain what

From *Central States Speech Journal*, 21 (Summer 1970), 81-86. Used by permission of the Central States Speech Association and the author.

is happening. When man uses language, according to Burke, he indicates his strategies for dealing with these situations. That is, as man speaks he indicates how he perceives the world around him.

Burke argues that whenever a man describes a situation he provides answers to five questions: "What was done (act), when or where it was done (scene), who did it (agent), how he did it (agency), and why (purpose)."[2] Act, scene, agent, agency, and purpose are the five terms that constitute the "Dramatistic Pentad." As man describes the situation around him, he orders these five elements to reflect his view of that situation.

Perhaps the clearest way to explain how the pentad functions is to examine Burke's own use of the concept in *The Grammar of Motives*.[3] In that work, Burke argues that various philosophical schools feature different elements of the human situation. For example, the materialist school adopts a vocabulary that focuses on the scene as the central element in any situation. The agent, act, agency and purpose are viewed as functions of the scene. On the other hand, the idealist school views the agent (or individual) as central and subordinates the other elements to the agent. Thus, both the materialist and the idealist, looking at the same situation, would describe the same five elements as existing in that situation. However, each views a different element as central and controlling. In Burke's own analysis he further suggests philosophical schools that relate to the other three elements of the pentad: the act, agency and purpose. What is important in this analysis is not which philosophical schools are related to the featuring of each element. What is important is that as one describes a situation his ordering of the five elements will suggest which of the several different views of that situation he has, depending on which element he describes as controlling.

This use of the pentad suggests two conclusions. First, the pentad functions as a tool for content analysis. The five terms provide a method of determining how a speaker views the world. Indeed, this is what Burke means when he says that the pentad provides "a synoptic way to talk about their [man's] talk-about [his world]."[4]

A second conclusion that results from this analysis is that man's description of a situation reveals what he regards as the appropriate response to various human situations. For example, the speaker who views the agent as the cause of a problem will reflect by his language not only what Burke would call an idealist philosophy, but he will be limited to proposing solutions that attempt to limit the actions of the agent or to remove the agent completely. The speaker who finds the agent to be the victim of the scene not only reflects a materialist philosophy but will propose solutions that would change the scene. Thus, an individual who describes the problem of slums as largely a matter of man's unwillingness to change his environment will propose self-help as the answer to the problem. The person who, looking at the same situation, describes man as a victim of his environment will propose that the slums be razed and its inhabitants be relocated into a more conducive environment. The way in which a speaker describes a situation reflects his perception of reality and indicates what choices of action are available to him.

The Pentad and Rhetorical Criticism

But what has all this to do with rhetoric? If persuasion is viewed as the attempt of one man to get another to accept his view of reality as the correct one, then the pentad can be used as a means of examining how the persuader has attempted to achieve the restructuring of the audience's view of reality. Burke suggests how such an analysis might take place when he says in *The Grammar:* "Indeed, though our concern here is with the Grammar of Motives, we may note a related resource of Rhetoric: one may deflect attention from scenic matters by situating the motives of an act in the agent (as were one to account for wars purely on the basis of a "warlike instinct" in people): or conversely, one may deflect attention from criticism of personal motives by deriving an act or attitude not from traits of the agent but from the nature of the situation."[5]

Thus beginning with the language of the stage, the Pentad, it is possible to examine a speaker's discourse to determine what view of the world he would have an audience accept. One may then make a judgment as to both the appropriateness and adequacy of the description the speaker has presented.

Edward Kennedy's July 25th Address

Having suggested the methodology we now turn to a consideration of Senator Edward Kennedy's address of July 25th to the people of Massachusetts. The analysis will attempt to establish two conclusions. First, the speech functioned to minimize Kennedy's responsibility for his actions after the death of Miss Kopechne. Second, the speech was also intended to place responsibility for Kennedy's future on the shoulders of the people of Massachusetts. These conclusions are the direct antithesis of statements made by Kennedy during the speech. Halfway through the presentation, Kennedy commented: "I do not seek to escape responsibility for my actions by placing blame either on the physical, emotional trauma brought on by the accident or on anyone else. I regard as indefensible the fact that I did not report the accident to the police immediately."[6] Late in the speech, in discussing the decision on whether or not to remain in the Senate, Kennedy stated that "this is a decision that I will have finally to make on my own." These statements indicated that Kennedy accepted both the blame for the events of that evening and the responsibility for the decision regarding his future. However, the description of reality presented by Kennedy in this speech forced the audience to reject these two conclusions.

Edward Kennedy—Victim of the Scene

The speech can best be examined in two parts. The first is the narrative in which Kennedy explained what occurred on the evening of July 18th. The second part of the speech involved Kennedy's concern over remaining in the U.S. Senate.

In Kennedy's statement concerning the events of July 18th we can identify these elements:

> The scene (the events surrounding the death of Miss Kopechne)
>
> The agent (Kennedy)
>
> The act (Kennedy's failure to report immediately the accident)
>
> The agency (whatever methods were available to make such a report)
>
> The purpose (To fulfill his legal and moral responsibilities)

In describing this situation, Kennedy ordered the elements of the situation in such a way that the scene became controlling. In Kennedy's description of the events of that evening, he began with statements that were, in essence, simple denials of any illicit relationship between Miss Kopechne and himself. "There is no truth, no truth whatever to the widely circulated suspicions of immoral conduct that have been leveled at my behavior and hers regarding that night. There has never been a private relationship between us of any kind." Kennedy further denied that he was "driving under the influence of liquor." These statements function rhetorically to minimize his role as agent in this situation. That is, the statements suggest an agent whose actions were both moral and rational prior to the accident. Kennedy then turned to a description of the accident itself: "Little over a mile away the car that I was driving on an *unlit* road went off a *narrow bridge* which had *no guard rails* and was built on a *left angle* to the road. The car overturned into a *deep pond* and immediately filled with water." (Emphasis mine) Such a statement placed Kennedy in the position of an agent caught in a situation not of his own making. It suggests the scene as the controlling element.

Even in Kennedy's description of his escape from the car, there is the implicit assumption that his survival was more a result of chance or fate than of his own actions. He commented: "I remember thinking as the cold water rushed in around my head that I was for certain drowning. Then water entered my lungs and I actually felt the sensation of drowning. But somehow I struggled to the surface alive." The suggestion in Kennedy's statement was that he was in fact at the mercy of the situation and that his survival was not the result of his own calculated actions. As an agent he was not in control of the scene, but rather its helpless victim.

After reaching the surface of the pond, Kennedy said that he "made repeated efforts to save Mary Jo." However, the "strong" and "murky" tide not only prevented him from accomplishing the rescue, but only succeeded in "increasing [his] state of utter exhaustion and alarm." The situation described is, then, one of an agent totally at the mercy of a scene that he cannot control. Added to this was Kennedy's statement that his physicians verified a cerebral concussion. If the audience accepted this entire description, it cannot conclude that Kennedy's actions during the next few hours were "indefensible." The audience rather must conclude that Kennedy was the victim of a tragic set of circumstances.

At this point in the speech Senator Kennedy commented on the confused and irrational nature of his thoughts, thoughts which he "would not have seriously entertained under normal circumstances." But, as Kennedy described them, these were not normal circumstances, and this was *not* a situation over which he had control.

Kennedy provided an even broader context for viewing him as the victim when he expressed the concern that "some awful curse did actually hang over the Kennedys." What greater justification could be provided for concluding that an agent is not responsible for his acts than to suggest that the agent is, in fact, the victim of some tragic fate.

Thus, in spite of his conclusion that his actions were "indefensible," the description of reality presented by Kennedy suggested that he, as agent, was the victim of a situation (the scene) over which he had no control.

Kennedy's Senate Seat: In the Hands of the People

In the second part and much shorter development of the speech, the situation changes. Here we can identify the following elements:

The scene (current reaction to the events of July 18th)

The agent (the people of Massachusetts)

The act (Kennedy's decision on whether to resign)

The agency (statement of resignation)

The purpose (to remove Kennedy from office)

Here, again, Kennedy described himself as having little control over the situation. However, it was not the scene that was controlling, but rather it was agents other than Kennedy. That is, Kennedy's decision on whether or not he will continue in the Senate was not to be based on the "whispers" and "innuendo" that constitute the scene. Rather, his decision would be based on whether or not the people of Massachusetts believed those whispers.

Kennedy commented: "If at any time the citizens of Massachusetts should lack confidence in their senator's character or his ability, with or without justification, he could not, in my opinion, adequately perform his duties and should not continue in office." Thus, were Kennedy to decide not to remain in the Senate it would be because the people of Massachusetts had lost confidence in him; responsibility in the situation rests with agents other than Kennedy.

This analysis suggests that Kennedy presented descriptions of reality which, if accepted, would lead the audience to two conclusions:

1. Kennedy was a tragic victim of a scene he could not control.
2. His future depended, not on his own decision, but on whether or not the people of Massachusetts accepted the whispers and innuendo that constituted the immediate scene.

Acceptance of the first conclusion would, in essence, constitute a rejection of any real guilt on the part of Kennedy. Acceptance of the second conclusion meant that responsibility for Kennedy's future was dependent on whether or not the people of Massachusetts believed Kennedy's description of what happened on the evening of July 18th, or if they would believe "whispers and innuendo."

Rhetorical Choice and Audience Response

If this analysis is correct, then it suggests some tentative implications concerning the effect of the speech. First, the positive response of the people of Massachusetts was virtually assured. During the next few days thousands of letters of support poured into Kennedy's office. The overwhelming endorsement was as much an act of purification for the people of that state as it was of Kennedy. That is, the citizenry was saying, "We choose not to believe whispers and innuendo. Therefore, there is no reason for Ted Kennedy to resign." Support also indicated that the audience accepted his description of reality rather than his conclusion that he was responsible for his actions. Guilt has, therefore, shifted from Kennedy to the people of Massachusetts. Having presented a description of the events of July 18th which restricts his responsibility for those events, Kennedy suggested that the real 'sin' would be for the people to believe that the "whispers and innuendoes" were true. As James Reston has commented, "What he [Kennedy] has really asked the people of Massachusetts is whether they want to kick a man when he is down, and clearly they are not going to do that to this doom-ridden and battered family."[7] The act of writing a letter of support becomes the means by which the people "absolve" themselves of guilt. The speech functioned to place responsibility for Kennedy's future as a Senator in the hands of the people and then provided a description that limited them to only one realistic alternative.

While the speech seemed to secure, at least temporarily, Kennedy's Senate seat, its effect on his national future appeared negligible, if not detrimental. There are three reasons for this conclusion. First, Kennedy's description of the events of July 18th presented him as a normal agent who was overcome by an extraordinary scene. However, the myth that has always surrounded the office of the President is that it must be held by an agent who can make clear, rational decisions in an extraordinary scene. Kennedy, in this speech was, at least in part, conceding that he may not be able to handle such situations. This may explain why 57 percent of those who responded to a CBS poll were still favorably impressed by Kennedy after his speech, but 87 percent thought his chances of becoming President had been hurt by the incident.[8]

A second reason why the speech may not have had a positive influence on Kennedy's national future was the way in which the speech was prepared. Prior to the presentation of Kennedy's speech, important Kennedy advisers were summoned to Hyannis Port, among them Robert McNamara and Theodore Sorensen. It was common knowledge that these advisers played an important role in the preparation of that presentation. Such an approach to the formulation was rhetorically inconsistent with the description of reality Kennedy presented. If Kennedy was the simple victim of the scene he could not control, then, in the minds of the audience that should be a simple matter to convey. However, the vision of professionals "manipulating" the speech suggested in the minds of his audience that Kennedy may have been hiding his true role as agent. Here was an instance of an agent trying to control the scene. But given Kennedy's description of what occurred on July 18th such "manipulation" appeared unnecessary and inappropriate. The result was a credibility gap between Kennedy and his audience.

A third factor that may have mitigated against the success of this speech was the lack of detail in Kennedy's description. A number of questions relating to the incident were left unanswered: Why the wrong turn? What was the purpose of the trip, etc.? These were questions that had been voiced in the media and by the general public during the week preceding Senator Kennedy's address. Kennedy's failure to mention these details raised the speculation in the minds of some columnists and citizens that Kennedy may, in fact, have been responsible for the situation having occurred: the agent may have determined the scene. If this was not the case, then Kennedy's lack of important detail may have been a mistake rhetorically. Thus, while Kennedy's speech resulted in the kind of immediate and overt response necessary to secure his seat in the Senate, the speech and the conditions under which it was prepared appear to have done little to enhance Kennedy's chances for the Presidency.

Conclusion

Much of the analysis of the effect of this speech has been speculative. Judging the response of an audience to a speech is a difficult matter; judging the reasons for that response is even more precarious. The methodology employed here has suggested two conclusions. First, in spite of his statements to the contrary, Kennedy's presentation portrayed him, in the first instance, as a victim of the scene and in the second, the possible victim of other agents. Second, the pentad, in suggesting that only five elements exist in the description of a situation, indicated what alternative descriptions were available to Kennedy. Given those choices, an attempt was made to suggest some of the possible implications of the choices Kennedy made.

Notes

[1] Kenneth Burke, *Permanence and Change* (Los Altos, California: Hermes Publications, 1954), p. 274.

[2] Kenneth Burke, *A Grammar of Motives and a Rhetoric of Motives* (Cleveland: The World Publishing Company, 1962), p. xvii.

[3] *Ibid.*, pp. 127–320.

[4] *Ibid.*, p. 56.

[5] *Ibid.*, p. 17.

[6] This and all subsequent references to the text of Senator Edward Kennedy's speech of July 25, 1969 are taken from *The New York Times*, CXVII (July 26, 1969), p. 10.

[7] James Reston, "Senator Kennedy's Impossible Question," *The New York Times*, CXVII (July 27, 1969), section 4, p. 24.

[8] "C.B.S. Evening News," C.B.S. Telecast, July 31, 1969.

A Pentadic Analysis of Abigail Scott Duniway's *The Happy Home; or, The Husband's Triumph*

Jean M. Ward

The Happy Home; or, The Husband's Triumph was the fourth of 17 serialized novels written by Abigail Scott Duniway (1834–1915) for the *New Northwest*, her "human rights" newspaper published weekly in Portland, Oregon, between 1871 and 1887. The popular novel appeared in 26 installments between 1874 and 1875 and was designed by Duniway to show that the "aristocracy of sex," which privileged men and disadvantaged women, should be replaced by equality of the sexes. To convince her readers of the need for social change, Duniway combined an argument from justice with an argument from expediency: Structural changes in unjust, inherently flawed, socially constructed systems will improve the human condition—woman's good is also man's good.

Duniway, who achieved regional and national prominence as an advocate for women's rights and equal suffrage, believed in the power of the "realistic novel" to inform, teach, persuade, and give pleasure—a combination of the rhetorical elements of verisimilitude, didacticism, advocacy, and entertainment. Over the course of 46 years, she published a total of 22 novels, all set in the Pacific Northwest. Her first novel, *Captain Gray's Company; or, Crossing the Plains and Living in Oregon* (1859), later was serialized in the *New Northwest*. Seventeen novels were written specifically for the *New Northwest*, and three other serialized novels appeared in the Portland *Pacific Empire* from 1895 through 1897. Duniway's last novel, *From the West to the West; Across the Plains to Oregon*, was published in 1905 by A. C. McClurg of Chicago.

The Happy Home is representative of Duniway's basic serial story of a woman who struggles to cope with adversity in a male-dominated world, and, like most of Duniway's serials, the novel has a happy conclusion. Mattie Armstrong, the central character, achieves a state of "honest independence" and chooses to participate in mutually beneficial social relationships with her sisters and brothers; new friends; and the doctor who becomes her husband, Amos Harding.

This essay was written while Jean M. Ward was a student in Sonja K. Foss' rhetorical criticism class at the University of Oregon in 1988. Used by permission of the author.

The novel is divided into two parts, which are bridged by the turning point when Armstrong becomes self-reliant and achieves independence from the male system that has dominated her life. In Part I, Duniway presents a graphic picture of the individual anguish and social disharmony that result from the oppression of women. As the eldest of Isaac Armstrong's 12 children, Armstrong appears to be trapped in Stonehenge—her father's cold, neglected, and loveless home. She has watched her mother die of overwork and successive pregnancies, and her young and feeble stepmother is "dying from apathy, the natural result of deferred hopes and crushed ambitions." Life at Stonehenge is characterized by circumscribed communication, patriarchal control of all goods and services, and abusive relationships. Finally, with the encouragement of Harding, Duniway's spokesperson for the unborn "law of woman" and redefined gender relations, Armstrong secures management of Stonehenge from her father, who has been worn down by her constant challenges to his authority.

In Part II, Duniway presents a contrasting vision of the individual accomplishments and social harmony that result from independent womanhood. Under Armstrong's hand, Stonehenge is transformed into a "human paradise" and "an acme of bliss." Equality for all, regardless of sex or age, characterizes the new "republic" of Stonehenge.

My purpose in this essay is to analyze Duniway's novel using as units of analysis the pentadic elements of act, agent, agency, scene, and purpose. As a result, I hope to suggest how an artifact's structure affects understanding of the need for social change and encourages readers to act in ways that facilitate that change. In other words, I will explore how the overall description of a situation, built on a featuring of particular elements, facilitates individual and societal transformation.

The progressive form of *The Happy Home* involves two related sets of pentadic elements. Set I is the pentad for the first half of the novel, when Armstrong seeks a state of independence by defying law and custom for women. Set II is the pentad for the second half of the novel, when Armstrong uses her newly found independence to create and sustain an appropriate setting for kin-keeping and other positive social relationships. Thus, the gains of Set II are linked to the achievement of Armstrong's independence in Set I. The two sets are outlined below.

Set I

 Act: defiance of law and custom for women
 Scene: the old Stonehenge—a bleak and oppressive house and grounds

Agent: oppressed woman (Mattie Armstrong), attitude of growing
         defiance

Agency: rejects dependency in marriage, reorganizes family life,
         assumes financial responsibility for siblings and self,
         works to fulfill responsibilities

Purpose: to reach a state of "honest independence" and autonomy
         as a woman

Set II

Act: creation of a "human paradise" of attractive social spaces

Scene: a new Stonehenge—an example of "thrift, taste,
         adaptation, and comfort"

Agent: independent woman (Mattie Armstrong), attitude of
         determination and compassion for others

Agency: physical work and planning with an eye to beauty, the
         exercise of "a molding power"

Purpose: to facilitate positive social relationships, including
         kin-keeping

My ratio pairings of the terms in Set I showed that the major term is the act—defiance of law and custom for women. The act is related strongly to the oppressed condition and defiant attitude of the agent, to the agency or means she uses, and to her purpose. Armstrong achieves the autonomy she desires by acting against the male paradigm that makes women the dependent property of men. Her act is not one of flight or escape from the life she "can't endure"—the circumstances of her oppression at Stonehenge. Instead, her act is one of challenge and defiance.

The featuring of act as the major term in Set I provides insight into Duniway's definition of women's situation in the first half of her novel. Burke found a correspondence between featuring of the act and the philosophy of realism, the doctrine that universal principles are more real than objects sensed. With an emphasis on realism, Duniway argues that universals of oppression and freedom—injustice and justice—are real and exist outside the mind or perception of the individual. Duniway's featuring of act in Set I is to point out what is wrong with law and custom and thereby convince readers that they must act to establish and sustain principles of independence and full personhood for women. In a didactic manner, Duniway uses the story of Armstrong's rebellious act to develop a progressive syllogistic form: Those who seek the principle of full personhood for humankind must take action against oppressive systems and forces. The success of Armstrong's action provides support for Duniway's argument.

Although the act is the major term in Set I, my ratio pairings showed that the major term for Set II is the scene—a new Stonehenge that is "an example of thrift, taste, adaptation, and comfort." The scene is related strongly to the independence, determination, and compassion of the agent—Armstrong; to the agency of her physical work and planning; to her act of creating a "human paradise"; and to her purpose of facilitating social relationships, including kin-keeping. After Armstrong's independence is achieved at the end of the first half of the story (Set I), the novel progresses to an emphasis on marked qualitative changes in the tone of social spaces and social relations at the new Stonehenge. These changes of beauty, comfort, caring, and love contrast with the bleakness, austerity, and coldness of the old Stonehenge. The emphasis on scene in Set II corresponds to what Burke has identified as the philosophy of materialism, a regard for facts and reality as explainable in terms of matter and motion or physical laws. Duniway shows that, once Armstrong is a free and creative agent, the world around her flourishes.

Undoubtedly, Duniway wanted to show her readers the "rightness" of the qualitative material changes at Stonehenge and thereby convince them that independent women could change the world for the better. Throughout her writings and speeches, Duniway pointed to the desirability of "self-reliant womanhood," and she wrote that the "general aim" of all her novels was to prove that "woman's greatest freedom leads to man's highest good" (New Northwest, August 21, 1884).

I find, however, a more specific function for the structure of terms in Set II. It points to an interactive effect between social spaces and social relations. The pentad and controlling element (scene) of Set II reveal this interaction: Attractive social spaces—"beautiful surroundings"— contribute to positive social relationships; positive—"loving"—social relationships contribute to attractive social spaces. Conversely, as seen in the old Stonehenge of Part I, ugly social spaces contribute to destructive social relationships, and destructive social relationships contribute to ugly social spaces.

My earlier readings of The Happy Home had led me to consider the agent, Armstrong, as the central element throughout the novel. Surely, I thought, a novel written by a woman about a woman would feature the woman character/agent. Conditioned to identify the agents in women's fiction as the controlling sources for identification/consubstantiation, I had overlooked the possibility of other powerful major elements. The process of pentadic analysis, however, revealed that the act in Set I and the scene in Set II are the controlling elements. This is not to say that Duniway's readers could not identify with the agent but rather that Duniway's worldview involved an emphasis on action to achieve changed circumstances for *all* women.

Duniway's structure in *The Happy Home* has implications for the study of rhetors' attempts at the empowerment of their audiences. To empower and not merely convince her readers, Duniway developed two complementary structures or sets of terms. She showed in Set I that women's acts of defiance against oppression are both desirable *and* possible, even in the most difficult of circumstances. Despite the overwhelming constraints of life at old Stonehenge, Armstrong refused to be a victim; literally armed herself as a strong, self-reliant woman; and successfully challenged male authority. In Set II, Duniway shared her vision of desirable *and* achievable social change—a world transformed by sexual equality. Rather than simply suggesting to readers that a strongly armed, independent woman such as Armstrong might improve the human condition, Duniway focused on particulars of Armstrong's creation of the new Stonehenge—an interactive scene of positive relationships and pleasant surroundings. Through the combination of these complementary pentads, Duniway sought to empower her audience with the knowledge that self-reliant womanhood and societal transformation are linked, needed, *and* attainable.

Teddy Bears at Greenham Common

Diana Brown Sheridan

At Greenham Common Royal Air Force Base in Newbury, Great Britain, nine miles of chain-link fence divide two worlds. The fence straddles what was once an idyllic English park, Greenham Common, purchased in 1938 for the enjoyment of local people. On one side are the wildflowers, gorse, heather, and silver birches of the park; on the other is an air base, jointly constructed by the United States and Great Britain. The base contains silos built from enormous mounds of concrete and movable offensive launching vehicles that can roam the countryside with cruise missiles of incomprehensible destruction.

In response to the construction of this military complex, 40 Women for Life on Earth walked the 110 miles from South Wales to this new base in August of 1981. Balking at society's enactment of military power and its incursions on the well-being of the human race, these women started the protest that came to be known as the Women's Peace Camp at Greenham Common, a 12-year testimony to women's commitment to waging peace. Although the Camp closed in 1993 with the end of the Cold War, the legacy of the women's life-affirming visions continues to affect the consciousness of those who work for peace around the world.

The fence, separating the protest and military groups, enshrouds a plethora of intense symbols that reflect the protesting women's intentions to soften the hard and sharp contours and angles that represent the unwavering persistence of military power. Over the years, women decorated, painted, encircled, climbed over, and cut through the fence in an effort to transform it into a celebration of life and beauty in contrast to its intended pronouncement of sterility and fear. They attached balloons, posters, baby clothes, stuffed animals, and photographs of children and loved ones. Weaving yarn, string, and ribbon in and out of the links in the fence, the women tried to revise the concept of the fence as an imprisoning chain, reformulating an image of repression into multiple webs, representing women's interconnectedness with all of life.

My purpose in this essay is to examine one personal form of expression that appeared on the fence in order to determine how personal symbols operate rhetorically in public protest action. I have chosen as my rhetorical artifact a pair of small, dark, furry-looking teddy bears

This essay was written while Diana Brown Sheridan was a student in Sonja K. Foss' rhetorical criticism class at the University of Oregon in 1988. Used by permission of the author.

adorning the fence. One is perched a bit higher on the fence than the other and has a small bow around its neck, arms hanging by its side, and ears bent forward slightly. The other is wearing a pair of light-colored overalls, has white hands and eyes, and its ears are perked up.

In a pentadic criticism of the pair of teddy bears, I have identified as the five terms:

Act: Hanging objects on the fence at Greenham Common

Scene: Fence surrounding the missile base at Greenham Common

Agent: Protesting women at Greenham Common

Agency: Pair of teddy bears that are soft, cuddly, lovable, and endearing

Purpose: To protest the placement of missiles at Greenham Common

After examining the ratios, I suggest that *agency*—the teddy bears' soft, enduring, and human qualities—stands out as the most significant element in the pentad. The bears' soft, cub-like characteristics serve to transform the *scene* of the fence from a hardened barrier to an animated playground of action. The snugly qualities of the bears make the protest *act* of hanging bears a reminder of motherly devotion to the often-playful nurturing of children, a nurturing that well might cease if the missiles are ever put into action. The lovable qualities of the bears determine that the Greenham women, as *agents*, are imbued with the same essence of softness and life-affirming affection that distinguishes the teddy bears, in contrast to the hardness and lack of emotionality that define weaponry. The distinctiveness of the bears alters the women's *purpose* by turning a commonly shared feeling—fondness for a favorite childhood memory—into a humanizing and personal element in their protest against an apparently inhuman and brute military force.

An emphasis on agency leads me to conclude that the symbol of the teddy bears on the fence creates a new vision of the slogan, "the personal is political." By using beloved teddy bears, the women are tapping into a commonly shared and cherished memory of childhood that they transfer from the private arena of home to the public setting of anti-militarist protest. They use a gentle toy of childhood to show the folly of such grown-up and fearful toys as missiles. The bears are cuddly, reminiscent of the human condition; they are innocent, signifying an untainted world; and they are endearing and lasting, epitomizing the continuity of the human experience.

In full view of patrolling soldiers and protesting women, a pair of tiny teddy bears becomes the humanized symbol for the kind of armor required to protect the human race. Qualities such as endearing softness are needed, according to the women, to replace the oppressive and hard characteristics of huge weapons capable of destroying the earth. In addition, the teddy bears personify the connectedness of shared childhood, making the women's action one of inclusiveness, in contrast to the exclusiveness of an impersonal weapon system.

The function of the teddy bears on the fence, revealed in a pentadic analysis, suggests that when a personal symbol of humanity and connectedness is made public, the political no longer remains beyond the scope of everyday life for most people. What is personal becomes political—as a means of action, a new form of armor, and a context for creating a changed reality. The observable consequence of absorbing the teddy bears' qualities, therefore, becomes a pragmatic one in which new meaning is constituted through the women's protest action. The qualities of the personal symbol are brought into the public sphere, providing a source of power for action for those who previously felt they lacked agency and power in that sphere.

Additional Samples
Pentadic Criticism

Appel, Edward C. "The Perfected Drama of Reverend Jerry Falwell." *Communication Quarterly*, 35 (Winter 1987), 26–38.

Birdsell, David S. "Ronald Reagan on Lebanon and Grenada: Flexibility and Interpretation in the Application of Kenneth Burke's Pentad." *Quarterly Journal of Speech*, 73 (August 1987), 267–79.

Blankenship, Jane, Marlene G. Fine, and Leslie K. Davis. "The 1980 Republican Primary Debates: The Transformation of Actor to Scene." *Quarterly Journal of Speech*, 69 (February 1983), 25–36.

Brown, Janet. "Kenneth Burke and *The Mod Donna*: The Dramatistic Method Applied to Feminist Criticism." *Central States Speech Journal*, 29 (Summer 1978), 138–46.

Brummett, Barry. "A Pentadic Analysis of Ideologies in Two Gay Rights Controversies." *Central States Speech Journal*, 30 (Fall 1979), 250–61.

Cali, Dennis D. "Chiara Lubich's 1977 Templeton Prize Acceptance Speech: Case Study in the Mystical Narrative." *Communication Studies*, 44 (Summer 1993), 132–43.

Carlson, A. Cheree. "Narrative as the Philosopher's Stone: How Russell H. Conwell Changed Lead into Diamonds." *Western Journal of Speech Communication*, 53 (Fall 1989), 342–55.

Cooks, Leda, and David Descutner. "Different Paths from Powerlessness to Empowerment: A Dramatistic Analysis of Two Eating Disorder Therapies." *Western Journal of Communication*, 57 (Fall 1993), 494–514.

Fisher, Jeanne Y. "A Burkean Analysis of the Rhetorical Dimensions of a Multiple Murder and Suicide." *Quarterly Journal of Speech*, 60 (April 1974), 175–89.

Hahn, Dan F. and Anne Morlando. "A Burkean Analysis of Lincoln's Second Inaugural Address." *Presidential Studies Quarterly*, 9 (Fall 1979), 376–89.

Ivie, Robert L. "Presidential Motives for War." *Quarterly Journal of Speech*, 60 (October 1974), 337–45.

Kelley, Colleen E. "The 1984 Campaign Rhetoric of Representative George Hansen: A Pentadic Analysis." *Western Journal of Speech Communication*, 51 (Spring 1987), 204–17.

Nelson, Jeffrey, and Mary Ann Flannery. "The Sanctuary Movement: A Study in Religious Confrontation." *Southern Communication Journal*, 55 (Summer 1990), 372–87.

Peterson, Tarla Rai. "The Will to Conservation: A Burkeian Analysis of Dust Bowl Rhetoric and American Farming Motives." *Southern Speech Communication Journal*, 52 (Fall 1986), 1–21.

Procter, David E. "The Rescue Mission: Assigning Guilt to a Chaotic Scene." *Western Journal of Speech Communication*, 51 (Summer 1987), 245–55.

Rushing, Janice Hocker. "Mythic Evolution of 'The New Frontier' in Mass
   Mediated Rhetoric." *Critical Studies in Mass Communication*, 3 (September
   1986), 265–96.
Rushing, Janice Hocker. "Ronald Reagan's 'Star Wars' Address: Mythic
   Containment of Technical Reasoning." *Quarterly Journal of Speech*, 72
   (November 1986), 415–33.
Stewart, Charles J. "The Internal Rhetoric of the Knights of Labor."
   Communication Studies, 42 (Spring 1991), 67–82.
Tonn, Mari Boor, Valerie A. Endress, and John N. Diamond. "Hunting and
   Heritage on Trial: A Dramatistic Debate Over Tragedy, Tradition, and
   Territory." *Quarterly Journal of Speech*, 79 (May 1993), 165–81.
Yingling, Julie. "Women's Advocacy: Pragmatic Feminism in the YWCA."
   Women's Studies in Communication, 6 (Spring 1983), 1–11.
Zulick, Margaret D. "The Agon of Jeremiah: On the Dialogic Invention of
   Prophetic Ethos." *Quarterly Journal of Speech*, 78 (May 1992), 125–48.

12

Generative Criticism

One of the most important steps in the process of rhetorical criticism is the critic's selection of a unit of analysis to answer the research question. This is the unit the critic uses as the vehicle or lens for examining the artifact, and it directs the critic to focus on some aspects of the artifact rather than others.

One source for units of analysis is formal methods of criticism that have been developed by rhetorical critics and theorists; this is the source for units of analysis offered in the preceding chapters of this book. Methods of criticism such as narrative criticism or fantasy-theme criticism are used, in these chapters, as sources for units of analysis such as characters and settings, fantasy themes and rhetorical visions. As useful as these units of analysis are for answering some research questions, they do not always provide the critic with the units of analysis that best enable the critic to answer a research question.

In many cases, the critic asks a research question where the units of analysis of formal methods of criticism are not the vehicles the critic needs to get at what is interesting and significant in the artifact. They do not provide a satisfactory way of understanding the artifact and answering the research question. In such cases, the critic needs to generate or create units of analysis—ones not found in formal methods of criticism. The process by which such units of analysis are generated is the focus of this chapter. This kind of criticism is *generative* in that the critic generates units of analysis rather than selecting them from previously developed, formal methods of criticism.

Procedures

As in other types of criticism, the critic who engages in generative criticism analyzes an artifact in a four-step process: (1) formulating a research question and selecting an artifact; (2) selecting a unit of analysis; (3) analyzing the artifact; and (4) writing the critical essay.

Formulating a Research Question and Selecting an Artifact

The first step in the process of rhetorical criticism is to develop a research question to ask about rhetoric and to select a rhetorical artifact to analyze that will provide an initial answer to the question.

Selecting a Unit of Analysis

In criticism in which the unit of analysis is not derived from formal methods of criticism, two primary methods of generating units of analysis are possible: (1) creation of units of analysis from concepts or theories; and (2) creation of units of analysis from the research question.

Development of Units of Analysis from Concepts or Theories. Concepts or theories frequently are used for the development of units of analysis in criticism. These concepts and theories may be drawn from the communication discipline or from other disciplines. They are selected because they seem to explain significant features of the artifact and provide useful insights into it that answer the research question. A critic, for example, may discover that concepts such as accommodation, the ideograph,[1] identification,[2] the comic frame,[3] dialectic, masquerade, parody, irony, *ethos*, mystery, and performance are useful as units of analysis. Suppose the critic wants to examine how inconsistencies in arguments function—what happens when a rhetor offers arguments or perspectives that are internally inconsistent. The critic could use concepts such as paradox, dissociation,[4] or perspective by incongruity[5] to analyze a rhetor's discourse to answer the research question.

Theories, philosophies, or perspectives may function as units of analysis just as concepts do. The major components of Michel Foucault's theory of the discursive formation,[6] for example, may serve as units of analysis. Zen Buddhism, Karlyn Kohrs Campbell's theory of a feminine rhetorical style,[7] Starhawk's theory of a rhetoric of inherent value,[8] Perennial philosophy,[9] and spectatorship[10] are other examples of theories that could be used by a critic as sources for units of analysis. One approach to generating a unit of analysis, then, is to create it from a construct or theory.

Development of Units of Analysis from the Research Question. Yet another source for the development of units of analysis is the research question itself. In many instances, the wording of the research question almost automatically suggests the appropriate unit of analysis. A critic whose research question is, "How does a subculture that challenges the dominant culture (such as punk music) resist the dominant culture's efforts to legitimize and co-opt it?," for example, is led to the unit of analysis by the question. The research question suggests as the unit of analysis strategies of rhetorical resistance, so the critic would examine the artifact for ways in which punk musicians resist legitimacy and co-optation. Similarly, if the critic's research question is, "How do rhetors who are members of an oppressed group establish credibility and authority when communicating with their oppressors?," the unit of analysis suggested by the research question is strategies of enhancing authority—the various ways in which the rhetors establish their influence and credibility. The research question itself, then, often directs the critic to a particular unit of analysis.

Analyzing the Artifact

Analysis Using a Concept or Theory as the Unit of Analysis. In criticism in which a unit of analysis is generated from a concept, the critic begins by defining it, outlining its history if that is important, identifying its features, and discussing its relevance to the research question. If the concept generated to serve as the unit of analysis is the oxymoron, for example, the critic defines *oxymoron* and explains that it is a rhetorical device that involves the juxtaposition of contradictions; explains how it works; and suggests why the oxymoron, as a unit of analysis, will provide insights that will help answer the research question. Following an explanation of the concept, the critic applies it to the artifact, using the various features or dimensions of the concept to explore the workings of the artifact. If oxymoron is the unit of analysis, the critic identifies the contradictory concepts that are juxtaposed and explains how that juxtaposition functions in the artifact.

When a theory, philosophy, or perspective is used as the unit of analysis, the critic begins by providing an overview of the theory, including an explanation of its origins, assumptions, and basic tenets. The critic also, of course, explains why the theory, philosophy, or perspective is relevant to the research question—how the units of analysis it provides will help the critic answer the research question. Following the explanation of the concept or theory, the critic uses its various variables or components as the means for analyzing the artifact. Not all of the components of the theory have to be used in this process— they all may not be relevant to answering the critic's research question. Those components that generate insights into the artifact are used to examine and explore the artifact. If, for example, Karlyn Kohrs Campbell's theory of a feminine rhetorical style[11] is selected as the source for the unit of analysis, the various components that comprise this style are used to analyze the artifact. The critic looks in the artifact for the features of a feminine rhetorical style—a personal tone; use of personal experience, anecdote, and examples as evidence; an inductive structure; audience participation; and identification between speaker and audience.

Analysis Using the Research Question as the Source for the Unit of Analysis.   In criticism in which the unit of analysis is developed from the critic's research question, the analysis involves one primary process—carefully and thoroughly examining the artifact for any traces or evidence of the phenomenon suggested by the unit of analysis. In this inductive process, a concept or theory is not applied to the artifact; rather, the insights gleaned emerge from the artifact itself, guided by the research question. The unit of analysis suggests what to look for in the artifact but does not say anything about the form it will assume. If the critic's research question, for example, concerns how subcultures resist legitimation and co-optation, the form the strategies of resistance assume is not specified. The critic looks for traces of resistance, whatever form they take, and develops the traces discovered into the rhetorical strategies that are reported in the essay.

Writing the Critical Essay

After completion of the analysis, the critic writes an essay that includes five major components: (1) an introduction, in which the research question, its contribution to rhetorical theory, and its significance are discussed; (2) description of the artifact and its context; (3) description of the unit of analysis, derived from a concept, theory, or the research question; (4) report of the findings of the analysis, in which the critic reveals the insights gained from exploration of the artifact using the unit of analysis generated; and (5) discussion of the contribution the analysis makes to answering the research question.

Sample Essays

The three sample essays that follow demonstrate the two primary routes to generating a unit of analysis when it is not derived from formal methods of criticism—developing a unit of analysis from a concept or theory and developing it from the research question. The first two essays illustrate the first route—development of a unit of analysis from a concept or theory. In their essay on the controversy surrounding the Environmental Protection Agency during President Ronald Reagan's administration, Robert C. Rowland and Thea Rademacher use as their unit of analysis the concept of the passive style to answer the research question, "How do rhetors dissipate crises and thereby avoid losing support?" Robert E. Terrill's essay on the movie, *Batman*, provides an example of a theory used as the source for units of analysis. He uses the psychological theory of Carl G. Jung in his analysis of the film in order to answer the general research question, "What is the rhetorical function performed by the projection of the psyche of the audience into cultural products?" In particular, he seeks to answer the question, "How does such a projection work to explain the appeal of *Batman*?"

Tarla Rai Peterson's analysis of a Senate subcommittee hearing on wilderness legislation is an example of the second route for generating a unit of analysis—its development from the research question. Peterson's impetus for the analysis is the research question, "What rhetorical strategies are used to construct institutional authority?" This research question is the source for her unit of analysis—the strategies by which participants reproduce authority.

Notes

[1] The ideograph is a notion developed by Michael Calvin McGee. See, for example, Michael Calvin McGee, "The 'Ideograph': A Link Between Rhetoric and Ideology," *Quarterly Journal of Speech*, 66 (February 1980), 1–16.

[2] Identification as a communication concept is associated with Kenneth Burke. See, for example: Kenneth Burke, *A Rhetoric of Motives* (1950; rpt. Berkeley: University of California Press, 1969), pp. xiv, 21, 24, 46, 55; and Kenneth Burke, *Language as Symbolic Action: Essays on Life, Literature, and Method* (Berkeley: University of California Press, 1966), p. 301.

[3] The comic frame is a concept developed by Kenneth Burke. See, for example, Kenneth Burke, *Attitudes Toward History* (1937; rpt. Berkeley: University of California Press, 1984), pp. 39–44.

[4] Dissociation is discussed by Chaim Perelman and L. Olbrechts-Tyteca in *The New Rhetoric: A Treatise on Argumentation* (Notre Dame: University of Notre Dame Press, 1969), pp. 411–59.

[5] Perspective by incongruity is a concept Kenneth Burke discusses in *Attitudes Toward History*, pp. 308–14.

[6] Foucault defines the discursive formation in *The Archaeology of Knowledge*, trans. A. M. Sheridan Smith (New York: Pantheon, 1972), pp. 38, 191; and *The Order of Things: An Archaeology of the Human Sciences* (New York: Pantheon, 1970), p. xx.

[7] Karlyn Kohrs Campbell, *Man Cannot Speak for Her: A Critical Study of Early Feminist Rhetoric*, Vol. 1 (New York: Greenwood, 1989), pp. 12–15.

[8] For a summary of the rhetorical theory derived from the work of Starhawk, see Sonja K. Foss and Cindy L. Griffin, "A Feminist Perspective on Rhetorical Theory: Toward a Clarification of Boundaries," *Western Journal of Communication*, 56 (Fall 1992), 330–49. Starhawk's works include: *Truth or Dare: Encounters with Power, Authority, and Mystery* (San Francisco: Harper & Row, 1987); and *Dreaming the Dark: Magic, Sex and Politics* (1982; rpt. Boston: Beacon, 1988).

[9] Among those who have contributed to the development of Perennial philosophy is Aldous Huxley in *The Perennial Philosophy* (New York: Harper & Row, 1970). For an example of the use of Perennial philosophy in criticism, see Janice Hocker Rushing, "E.T. as Rhetorical Transcendence," *Quarterly Journal of Speech*, 71 (May 1985), 188–203.

[10] For an overview of the concept of spectatorship, see Judith Mayne, *Cinema and Spectatorship* (New York: Routledge, 1993).

[11] Campbell.

The Passive Style of Rhetorical Crisis Management
A Case Study of the Superfund Controversy

Robert C. Rowland and Thea Rademacher

There is a growing perception that few issues of real importance receive the consideration they deserve.[1] In this view, which is typified in a recent essay by Donald Kaul,[2] public attention tends to focus on scandals and trivia, not on serious problems. Kaul illustrates the point by juxtaposing the vast public interest in the Pete Rose betting scandal with almost total lack of concern for the greenhouse effect. He somewhat cynically concludes: "The best thing to do about the greenhouse effect is to forget it and hope that you die before the air runs out."[3]

The failure of the public adequately to confront hard issues such as the greenhouse effect, ozone depletion, acid rain, and the budget deficit obviously should be of great concern to students of public rhetoric. Since Aristotle, rhetoric has been justified as a means of facilitating rational and just decision making (Rhetoric 1355 a21–22).[4] If issues of real importance cannot adequately be considered in the public arena, then this situation suggests serious problems in the functioning of the public, the discourse that is presented to the public, or both.

In recent years no phrase better seems to reflect both public apathy toward the issues and the danger that discourse may be used to evade those issues than "Teflon presidency."[5] Through the first six years of his presidency, Ronald Reagan seemed to live a charmed life. He was the "great communicator,"[6] "a man with a golden political touch, whom crisis never marred and adversity never defeated."[7] No matter what happened—the decision to go to Bitburg, the bombing of the marine barracks in Lebanon, the space shuttle explosion, or David Stockman's comments about the budget process—the people didn't seem to care. In these events and others, Reagan seemed immune from public scrutiny. No matter how serious the issue, he appeared able to wave his rhetorical magic wand and make it disappear.

From Communication Studies, 41 (Winter 1990), 327–42. Used by permission of the Central States Communication Association and the authors.

It would seem, therefore, that a consideration of how Reagan created his rhetorical Teflon coating is an appropriate way to get at larger questions concerning the quality of political discourse and the capacity of the public rationally to evaluate that discourse.

While there have been any number of analyses of the various rhetorical strategies upon which Reagan relied, almost without exception these analyses have focused on how he generated support and not on the rhetorical means he used to dissipate crises and thereby avoid losing support. Recent essays have focused on Reagan's use of value-laden commonplaces and transcendent terms,[8] metaphorical depictions of the Soviets as savages,[9] social narrative and myth,[10] a heroic persona,[11] the role of faith healer in response to economic ills,[12] and a combination of mythic, value-laden, and narrative strategies similar to the oral tradition found in preliterate cultures.[13] Despite differences in detail, these analyses reveal general agreement that much of Reagan's rhetorical success can be traced to a reliance on value affirmation via language strategies, especially metaphor, social narrative, and myth, and a description of the characters in his stories as well as his own persona as generally heroic. We have a good idea of how Reagan used rhetoric to energize the public; what we are less clear about is the recipe Reagan used to create the Teflon coating in which he sealed that public support.

We believe one of the keys to understanding both the state of public discourse and the Teflon effect lies in a consideration of what Murray Edelman has referred to as the "passive style" of rhetorical crisis management. In the passive style, the leader avoids "firm positions on controversial subjects"[14] while expressing strong value commitments to end the crisis. The leader resolves the crisis "through publicized action on noncontroversial policies or on trivia, and through a dramaturgical performance emphasizing the traits popularly associated with leadership."[15] In this essay we use a case study of Reagan's response to the Superfund scandal first to define more precisely the rhetorical dimensions of the passive style and then to illustrate how Reagan so successfully resolved political crises for six years. In the final section, we identify differences between the Superfund and Iran-Contra incidents that largely explain the very different results and argue that the efficacy of the passive style seriously diminishes the capacity of the public to make informed and rational decisions on many issues of great import to the nation.

The Superfund Controversy

Shortly after Reagan's inauguration, the Environmental Protection Agency (EPA) sharply curtailed its enforcement of various environmental protection laws.[16] According to Brock Evans, the enforcers at the EPA looked "for every possible reason to grant industry's request to relax standards."[17]

The change in environmental policies led to a "storm of protest"[18] from environmentalists but little reaction from the general public. What had been an issue of concern primarily to environmentalists, however, became a crisis for the Reagan administration in the winter of 1983 when accusations of corruption were made regarding the EPA's enforcement of toxic waste control legislation. Initially, investigations revealed that Rita Lavelle, the chief administrator of the Superfund program, had significant contact with several industries she was assigned to regulate,[19] creating the impression that the EPA was "in bed with polluters."[20] By February 1983, the scandal reached the point that Reagan had no choice but to fire Lavelle.[21]

Shortly after Lavelle was fired, the EPA admitted that it had destroyed "excess copies" of documents that had been subpoenaed by a House subcommittee.[22] It soon became clear that "the shredders are used in the absence of guidelines"[23] and that a variety of other important evidence also had disappeared.[24]

To make matters worse, the Reagan administration was criticized for its decision to invoke executive privilege in withholding information from Congress.[25] The dispute was magnified at a presidential press conference when Reagan announced, "I can no longer insist on executive privilege if there's a suspicion in the minds of the people that maybe it is being used to cover some wrongdoing."[26] A spokesperson later "clarified" Reagan's statement by insisting that the claim of executive privilege remained in force.

The crisis came to a head after the Justice Department refused to continue representing the head of the EPA, Anne Burford, because it feared a "conflict of interest."[27] Within a week Burford had resigned and Reagan had given up the claim of executive privilege.[28]

The problems posed by the EPA crisis were especially troublesome to Reagan because of a general perception that he "was too close to business and indifferent to environmental issues."[29] Public support for strong environmental policies[30] made the scandal still more important. One senior official described the situation as akin to "carrying a vial of nitroglycerin down a rocky road."[31]

Consequently, it appeared that the environment might provide the Democrats with the issue they needed in 1984. Senators Howard Baker and Paul Laxalt were quoted as saying that the scandal at the EPA "may soon be a political liability"[32] for the 1984 campaign. The crisis seemed so important that the *New York Times* referred to it as a "watershed for environmentalism."[33]

To make matters worse, the EPA crisis created a general perception of corruption. For some, the scandal had "eerie tones of Watergate, or 'Sewergate.'"[34] House Republican leader Robert Michel's comment "where there is so much smoke there is surely a little fire"[35] illustrates that Republicans were aware of the importance of the issue. The scandal at the EPA was especially serious because it had the potential of touching Reagan directly. The decision to withhold documents from Congress was a "terrible blunder"[36] because it created the impression that Reagan was involved directly. And Reagan's apparent flip-flop on executive privilege[37] could only raise doubts about his leadership.[38] In the crisis at the EPA, Reagan was "playing with political dynamite."[39]

Clearly, Reagan defused the crisis. Despite Walter Mondale's attempts to focus on the environmental issue (he claimed the Reagan administration had "the lousiest environmental record in the nation's history"[40]), the environment did not become a major issue in the 1984 campaign. In fact, Reagan's image on the environment improved so dramatically before the November election that one major news magazine reported that the President was "breathing fresh air into his environmental policies."[41] And as Reagan's image improved, the power of environmentalists declined; "the days of wine and roses" were over. Environmental groups saw a "dwindling of the growth in memberships and donations."[42]

That Reagan somehow eliminated the environment as a major issue seems inexplicable. After the resignations of Burford and Lavelle at the EPA and also James Watt at the Interior Department, he did appoint William Ruckelshaus and William Clark as the new chiefs of the two agencies. Clark and especially Ruckelshaus were far more popular with the environmental movement than their predecessors, yet their appointments seem an inadequate explanation for the rapid end to the scandal: While Ruckelshaus and Clark were more palatable to many environmentalists, the basic policies of the administration did not change.[43] Shabecoff cited the conclusion of environmental activists that "there has been no basic change in . . . the Administration's anti-environmental policies."[44]

If the end to the crisis cannot be attributed to policy change, one plausible assumption might be to attribute it to Reagan's rhetorical skill. Reagan took no significant actions to appease the environmental movement. Yet the crisis dissipated. Given his great rhetorical successes in other areas, it is reasonable to conduct a close analysis of his environmental rhetoric in order to determine whether that rhetoric might be the primary factor that explains the end of the Superfund crisis.

The Passive Style

On first glance Reagan's apparent success in dealing with the crisis at the EPA is surprising. In argumentative terms, Reagan's response seems clearly inadequate. In the press conferences and two speeches in which he directly confronted the problems at the EPA, Reagan largely ignored the specific charges that had been leveled against the EPA and officials like Burford. Rather, he generally praised the EPA and its environmental policies. For example, in a press conference on February 16, 1983, Reagan characterized the record of the EPA as "splendid," argued that much progress had been made in settling Superfund disputes with industry, and claimed that the agency's accomplishments had been overlooked in a "flurry of accusations."[45] While Reagan made a number of other general defenses of the EPA, he left the specific charges essentially unanswered.

Instead, Reagan combined the general praise of Burford and the EPA with attacks on those who criticized the agency. In the press conference shortly after the resignation of Burford, Reagan blamed the controversy on those who had attacked her: "I don't think that the people who were attacking her were concerned about the environment."[46] He also focused on his personal commitment to the environment, especially as it had been reflected in his actions as Governor of California.[47]

While it is clear that Reagan somehow defused the controversy over the Superfund, a first inspection of his speeches and policy actions is not revealing. Reagan largely ignored the specifics of the charges against Lavelle and Burford as well as the attacks on their policies. Instead, he emphasized his personal commitment to the environment by citing his record in California, a device that must have seemed completely irrelevant to environmentalists who were concerned with what Reagan was doing as President in 1983, not what he had been doing in California in 1966. And yet, the crisis was resolved. We suggest that Reagan dealt with the Superfund controversy not primarily with argument but by relying on the passive style as a means of deadening (as opposed to confronting) public reaction.

The first step in understanding the passive style is to consider the role "issues" play in influencing public opinion. At one time most political commentators believed issues had little import for the general public. It was images, party, and family background that made the difference. In The Symbolic Uses of Politics, Edelman summarizes this view: "the voting behavior studies have shown that issues are a minor determinant of how people cast their ballots, most voters being quite ignorant of what the issues are and of which party stands for what position."[48] However, research conducted in the 1960s and 1970s gradually revealed that the description of the public as ignorant and apathetic was too simplistic. Beginning with the work of V. O. Key, who argues that "voters are not fools," and continuing with works such as *The Changing American Voter*,[49] it became clear that the issues do matter. Surely, the Vietnam war illustrated the capacity of certain issues to arouse public opinion.

However, while issues clearly influence public opinion, they do not play quite the role a rationalistic model would predict. Few people carefully read competing policy positions and make their choice based on the evidence and argument.[50] The public is concerned with the issues, but only when they directly or symbolically affect their lives. As Edelman explains:

> The mass public does not study and analyze detailed data about secondary boycotts, provision for stock ownership and control in a proposed space communication corporation, or missile installations in Cuba. It ignores these things until political actions and speeches make them symbolically threatening or reassuring.[51]

In general, issues become important when one of two situations occurs: (1) the issue touches a large segment of the public directly or (2) the issue casts doubt on the competence or integrity of a political leader. It is this second situation that concerned Reagan in the controversy over the Superfund. Edelman argues persuasively that one effective way to resolve political crises concerning issues such as the Superfund controversy is to rely on a "passive leadership style." While not specifically dealing with rhetorical strategy, Edelman's conception of the passive style as one in which the political leader avoids specific policy positions in favor of dramatic performances and general statements of concern for the problem is a useful starting point for identifying the characteristics that define a passive rhetorical style.

Elements of the Passive Style

Building on Edelman, we suggest that the passive style possesses three related elements, each of which is important for symbolically resolving a crisis. First, in the passive style, the focus is on personal value commitments rather than specific issues. One way to understand this strategy is to consider the different functions served by deliberative and epideictic rhetoric. In the *Rhetoric*, Aristotle distinguishes between deliberative or policy rhetoric, which is aimed at "establishing the expediency or harmfulness of a course of action" (1358b 22–23), and epideictic or ceremonial rhetoric, which "either praises or censures" (1358b 12). While the aim of deliberative rhetoric is to establish the worth of a given policy, epideictic rhetoric serves a different function. Through praise and blame, a speaker reaffirms basic values and establishes his or her personal quality in relation to those values.

Previously, most rhetorical theorists focused on how affirmation of shared values may be used to energize the mass public. For example, Perelman and Olbrechts-Tyteca argue that epideictic "strengthens the disposition toward action by increasing adherence to the values it lauds."[52] Oravec notes that epideictic may "serve as advice upon the future action of the audience."[53] Crable and Vibbert demonstrate that Mobil used epideictic to reinforce support for values in order to allow its "deliberative discourse (via corporate advocacy) to flourish."[54] In these analyses, epideictic serves a prepolicy function. It is used to "pump up" support for values that later will be drawn upon in deliberative rhetoric. As we noted earlier, a number of commentators have described how Reagan relied on this strategy.

What has not been recognized in the previous analyses, however, is that epideictic may be used not only to energize public reaction but also to prevent it. In such an instance the rhetor's focus is not on reaffirming a public value in order to create support for some policy action, but rather in stating a personal commitment to that value in order to reinforce personal standing with the audience and avoid the necessity of acting on the value. Here the hope is that the personal commitment will satisfy the public and prevent the value from being used to energize a public policy reaction. If reaffirmation of values can pump up their power, which then can be tapped in deliberative rhetoric, then statements of personal commitment may have the opposite effect. Unlike the typical epideictic situation, in the passive style, value reaffirmation is used to deaden, not to produce, audience reaction.

A second and closely related strategy is to displace blame on subordinates. Here the rhetor claims that he or she was not responsible for whatever event had occurred; it was a subordinate who made the mistake. Often this blame displacement occurs implicitly rather than explicitly and relies upon the media to complete the message. In this situation the subordinate is forced to resign and by assuming the role of scapegoat seems to prove the innocence of his or her boss. At the same time the political leader can deny having forced the subordinate to resign and therefore prove his or her loyalty. Through blame displacement, the political leader can distance him- or herself from the crisis and prove that he or she really does care about the issue under dispute.

Finally, in the passive style, actions are not designed to alter fundamentally the policy environment but merely to symbolically resolve the crisis. In a number of works, Edelman demonstrates that one of the most potent means of creating political quiescence is through symbolic action in which political actors express support for a general goal but then fail to implement specific policies to carry out that goal.[55] Symbolic acts are important as rhetorical symbols, but not necessarily as public policy. For example, Edelman argues that independent regulatory agencies reassure the public that they are being protected even though such agencies actually aid industry.[56] Symbolic action "strengthens reassuring beliefs regardless of their validity and discourages skeptical inquiry about disturbing issues."[57] Edelman cites Harold Lasswell, who notes that politicians often seek "a magical solution which changes nothing . ... and which merely permits the community tó distract its attention to another set of equally irrelevant symbols."[58]

Superfund Strategies and the Passive Style

At this point, Reagan's response to the Superfund controversy becomes intelligible. First, Reagan clearly acted in the epideictic mode by emphasizing his personal commitment to the environment as opposed to advocating a particular set of policies. In this context, Reagan's references to his environmental protection efforts while Governor of California become understandable. With these comments, Reagan was not attempting to answer the charges of the critics. Rather, he was trying to reassure the audience about his general value commitment to the environment. For example, he claimed that "we [in California] led the Federal Government in environmental protection. We were the forerunner of the whole movement."[59] In his speech announcing the nomination of Ruckelshaus, Reagan claimed that during his term as Governor, California discovered "for the whole Nation, what caused smog."[60] The discussion of his experience in California apparently was irrelevant. The public should have been concerned with the policies of the Reagan administration, not California more than a decade before. However, by focusing on his record in California, Reagan was able both to avoid a defense of the details of his current policies and also to reaffirm his support for general environmental goals.

Reagan found a variety of other means to affirm commitment to environmental values as well. For example, he claimed that his philosophy always had been "to enforce the laws and to use common sense in doing this."[61] In addition, Reagan used the swearing-in ceremony for Ruckelshaus as a means of marking his commitment to the environment. The majority of that speech consisted of Reagan listing four areas of immediate concern (acid rain, toxic wastes, coordination of governmental cleanup programs, and enforcement) that he wanted Ruckelshaus to "address as quickly as possible in your new post."[62] Thus, Reagan symbolically committed himself to environmental goals and proved his personal concern for the environment, while in fact not significantly altering the policies of the administration.[63] Reagan used claims that he personally valued the environment to undercut support for public policies protecting the environment. He praised his commitment to the environment so that he would not have to demonstrate it.

And what of blame? Reagan's second strategy was to displace the blame for the problem on subordinates. Here Reagan wanted and got it both ways. By forcing Lavelle and Burford to leave, Reagan again showed his commitment to the environment and clearly placed the blame for problems elsewhere. At the same time, he continued to praise Burford as a way to prove his loyalty and leadership ability.

Reagan began this process of rhetorical distancing by calling on the Department of Justice to investigate the scandal.[64] This act seemed to prove Reagan's personal innocence while also separating him from the staff at EPA. On February 23, he somewhat awkwardly reiterated this point, noting that he hadn't found "much substantiation accompanying those [allegations]—but any of those are immediately turned over to the Justice Department, and the FBI is investigating and tracking down every charge that's been made."[65] Clearly, Reagan wanted to distance himself from any perceived wrongdoing.

When the crisis deepened, Burford was forced to resign,[66] thus serving the rhetorical function of further distancing Reagan from the scandal. While Reagan separated himself from the act, he also appeared to defend his staff. After her resignation, Reagan defended Burford's performance on environmental protection as one of which "this administration can be very proud," praised her for reducing "waste and extravagance," and denied that she had made politically based decisions.[67] He went on to explain his personal commitment to Burford by noting that when he had "faith in the individual, I am not going to yield to the first attack and run for cover and throw somebody off the sleigh."[68] Of course, the irony was that Reagan had done precisely what he denied doing.

From the beginning of the crisis, Reagan effectively displaced blame on his subordinates while still playing the role of loyal boss. In this instance, Reagan's actions, especially in establishing the FBI probe, firing Lavelle, and pushing Burford out, served rhetorical more than policy-making functions. These actions did not fundamentally change the environmental policy of the Reagan administration. What they did do, however, was insulate Reagan from the crisis. Thus, Reagan could be loyal while in effect blaming Burford and others for the problem.

Reagan's use of displacement also is interesting when juxtaposed with the one issue in the crisis on which he was specific, his own role in releasing documents to the press. Reagan made quite a detailed defense of his decision on executive privilege. He insisted that he was responsible for the decision, which was one of the "prerogatives of the institution," noted that he had made more than 800,000 documents available to

Congress, and claimed that he was willing to give Congress access to the remaining documents in a "kind of controlled way."[69] Reagan was far more specific when defending his own role in the controversy than elsewhere.

Finally, Reagan relied on symbolic action first to contain the crisis and eventually to bring it to a close. In this regard, the FBI investigation functioned not only to insulate Reagan from the crisis but also to symbolize Reagan's commitment to the environment. More fundamentally, Reagan used the nomination of Ruckelshaus to prove symbolically that his administration was environmentally conscious. In his address announcing the nomination of Ruckelshaus, Reagan noted Ruckelshaus's qualifications, especially focusing on his work as the first administrator of the EPA. Reagan claimed that during Ruckelshaus's tenure at the EPA "he played a critical role in shaping and launching the Agency. He is staunchly committed to protecting the Nation's air and water and land."[70] Reagan recalled his days as Governor of California and cited his experience with Ruckelshaus. According to Reagan, Ruckelshaus "deeply impressed me. He was tough, fair, and highly competent."[71] Reagan followed very similar strategies in his speech at the swearing-in ceremony for Ruckelshaus. Initially, he praised Ruckelshaus: "I can't imagine anyone who's more qualified or better suited to be at the helm once again than 'Mr. Clean,' Bill Ruckelshaus."[72] Reagan also discussed in some detail Ruckelshaus's accomplishments as the first EPA administrator, crediting him with setting "this nation on a course we still follow today—a course that has brought many tangible signs of progress."[73]

Clearly, Reagan relied upon Ruckelshaus's reputation as "Mr. Clean" to end the crisis. Jay Hair of the National Wildlife Federation responded to the Ruckelshaus nomination: "Not only is Ruckelshaus the best choice anyone could hope for from the administration, he would be an excellent choice in any administration."[74] Reagan also used the Ruckelshaus nomination as another way to stress his personal commitment to the environment. We noted earlier that the Ruckelshaus nomination did not resolve the crisis in any logical sense. His appointment did not eliminate the wrongdoing of Burford and Lavelle or, as it turned out, alter the basic environmental goals of the administration, but symbolically it was a masterful stroke. Edelman explains that it is "the political function of public officials to attract blame or praise." He adds that the "catharsis of praising or ousting a leader can readily divert demands for abandoning the policies that failed."[75] In appointing Ruckelshaus after firing Burford and Lavelle, Reagan symbolically disposed of the evil subordinates by sending in the white knight. The Ruckelshaus nomination was an exercise in image building through which Reagan symbolically resolved the dispute.

At this point it could be argued that few in the public would have been exposed to much of Reagan's rhetoric on the crisis and that therefore it is implausible that the end of the crisis can be traced to that rhetoric. Such an argument, however, actually points to the power behind the passive style. If the public had followed the details of the controversy carefully, they would have been aware of the failure of the administration to change its basic policies. Reagan's reliance on the passive style, however, did not require full access to his speeches on the question. Reagan's use of the passive style was effective because his three-part strategy so easily could be reduced to brief sound bites. The public did not need to be exposed to all of Reagan's rhetoric. All they needed to do was see Reagan fire Burford and appoint Ruckelshaus and hear him talk earnestly about his commitment to the environment. The basics of his strategy were apparent in these acts, which were far more important rhetorically than they were as indicators of policy change, and the brief clips from his speeches that went with these acts.

In sum, Reagan's strategies were well adapted to resolving the Superfund problem. Despite strong public support for the environment in general, there was little concern with specific issues such as acid rain. Acid rain involves complicated technical issues about which the public possesses little knowledge, and acid rain is not a highly visible problem. This explains why environmental activists had so little success in arousing public ire, both before and after the Superfund scandal. The public was concerned about the environment, but this concern easily could be controlled through symbolic actions expressing commitment to environmental protection. It was only when the issue shifted from environmental protection to one of corruption that the mass public was aroused.

The Success and Failure of Reagan's Rhetoric

Passive Strategies as Characteristic Rhetoric

The foregoing analysis clarifies the means Reagan used to produce the Teflon coating that seemed to surround his presidency and insulate him from scandal. We suggest that Reagan consistently relied on the three strategies we have identified to minimize the effect political scandal could have on his administration.

First, Reagan acted as an epideictic speaker who consistently stated personal values that his administration in fact did not support. Thus, Reagan could emphasize his own commitment to the environment or a balanced budget while avoiding policies that would protect the environment or balance the budget. In handling a rhetorical crisis, Reagan shifted his approach to values from one of drawing upon traditional values (to energize the public) to one of reaffirmation of personal values (to deaden public reaction).

Second, Reagan consistently placed the blame either directly or indirectly (via the media) on subordinates. No matter the problem, it always seemed that Reagan was not aware of the details. It was someone on his staff who must take the blame. When David Stockman criticized the economic policies of the administration, Reagan took him to the woodshed and Stockman admitted his mistake.

In the aftermath of the Tower Commission report, Reagan's management style was criticized because it resulted in his delegating much of the control of policy to subordinates. At the same time, Reagan's management style, his distancing from actual policy-making, provided significant rhetorical advantages. His role was that of the cheerleader whose job it was to create public support for the administration. In this context, a focus on specific issues could only damage his effectiveness. Reagan was more than willing to claim credit for the successes of the administration, as he did in Grenada, but when the administration was attacked it was important that he avoid the controversy. If he were dragged into a discussion of the details of policy on the environment or some other issue, it could only expose his lack of familiarity with those details. His management style allowed Reagan to stick to a general discussion of the values of the administration while both avoiding the specifics of the particular controversy and distancing himself from those involved.

Finally, Reagan relied upon symbolic action to quiesce the general public. He symbolically committed the administration to general values that in fact the administration did not support. Again his support for a balanced budget amendment is a good illustration of this process. Examples from education, civil rights, and a host of other areas also might be cited. These symbolic commitments had the effect of reassuring all but the most politically aware.

While these strategies commonly are used by politicians and others, both the degree to which Reagan relied upon them and also their use in combination are distinctive. Few recent political leaders have been as willing as Reagan to place responsibility on subordinates. Presidents, in particular, tend to take a "the buck stops here" attitude. Eisenhower, for instance, allowed a summit meeting to collapse rather than deny responsibility for sending a U2 reconnaissance mission over the Soviet Union. While Reagan occasionally mouthed such sentiments, his normal practice was to deny responsibility. Similarly, few politicians have relied as heavily as Reagan on value affirmation and symbolic policy actions. Reagan's unwillingness (or inability) to deal with the complexities of public policy has been a theme repeated in any number of White House memoirs. Yet as persuasive devices, Reagan's refusal to focus on issues, his emphasis on personal values, and his tendency to utilize symbolic action served him well.

Passive Style and the Iran-Contra Scandal

It is clear that Reagan attempted to use similar strategies in resolving the Iran-Contra scandal. Initially, he relied on displacement (the ongoing investigation to "get to the bottom" of the charges) to justify his refusal to comment on the details of the controversy. In the Tower Commission address, he explained, "I felt it was improper to come to you with sketchy reports or possibly even erroneous statements."[76] Since it was his aides who had acted without his knowledge, he had to wait until the Tower board had completed its investigation.

As in the Superfund scandal, Reagan attempted to have it both ways in terms of displacing responsibility. In a long passage in the Tower Commission address, Reagan appeared to take responsibility for the actions of his subordinates while in fact doing the opposite. According to Reagan:

> First, let me say I take full responsibility for my own actions and for those of my Administration. As angry as I may be about activities undertaken without my knowledge, I am still accountable for those activities. As disappointed as I may be in some who served me, I am still the one who must answer to the American people for this behavior. And as personally distasteful as I find secret bank accounts and diverted funds, as the Navy would say, this happened on my watch.

Here Reagan played the role of the brave and loyal commander taking responsibility for the actions of his subordinates, but his message made it clear that it wasn't actually his fault.

At other times during the Iran-Contra affair, Reagan distanced himself from his subordinates while continuing to praise them personally. In this context, Reagan's praise of Oliver North becomes intelligible. To many it made no sense that Reagan could force North to resign and yet continue to refer to him as a hero. However, from the perspective of the passive style, Reagan's actions made very good sense. Again, Reagan wanted it both ways. He wanted to distance himself from North but still take advantage of any positive attitudes toward North. Thus, he forced North out but proved his loyalty by praising him personally.

In his response to the Iran-Contra scandal, Reagan also relied on value affirmation. For example, in the Tower Commission address he began by reinforcing traditional patriotic values. In the opening paragraph he claimed that presidential power lies not within the Oval Office but "in you the American people, and in your trust." Later, he explained his actions in trading arms for hostages based on his "personal concern for the hostages." He seemed to be saying that while the policy may have been wrong, surely his values were good. This strategy also is found in the second half of the speech where he endorsed a policy on covert operations "in compliance with American values." Finally, through a variety of acts, beginning with the appointment of the Tower Commission itself, Reagan used symbolic acts in an attempt to bring the crisis to a close. The second half of the Tower Commission speech is essentially a list of all the symbolic changes he had made in his administration, including the appointments of Howard Baker, Frank Carlucci, and William Webster to positions of trust and alterations in the basic operating procedures of the National Security Council. These actions in no way denied wrongdoing in the affair; they were symbolic acts that Reagan used in an attempt to deaden public reaction.

Limits of the Passive Style

In confronting the Iran-Contra affair, however, the symbolic action, distancing, and value reaffirmation were not enough precisely because for the first time it was Reagan's competence and honesty that were primarily at issue. While many praised Reagan's Tower Commission speech,[77] the public response was less favorable, as reflected in his approval rating.[78] Reagan did regain some of his support, but he never reached the heights of 1981–1986.

It was not that Reagan was any less skillful but that his normal strategies were no longer appropriate. The Iran-Contra scandal cast doubt upon Reagan's competence itself. Distancing himself from his aides could only add to public concern that the President was not in charge. Nor could reaffirmation of a personal commitment to basic values or symbolic action resolve the problem. Here the issue was not a question of policy that briefly had caught the attention of the public. If the issue had been merely the wisdom of selling arms to Iran, Reagan's strategies undoubtedly would have succeeded. Here the issue was Reagan's competence itself, and reliance on rhetorical distancing, affirmation of personal support for basic values, and symbolic action could not resolve this problem. It was excusable for the President not to know all the details of EPA enforcement policies, but lack of knowledge about two major covert foreign policy initiatives was not acceptable. In this case, Reagan needed a completely different response. For once he needed to focus on the details of the issues, at least as they affected him, not because the details were important to most of the public, but because only by focusing on those details could he reassure the people of his competence.

In the Superfund controversy Reagan seemed to realize that any issue that touched on the competence or honesty of the President merited a different type of rhetorical response. Thus, he presented a detailed defense of his decision to invoke executive privilege. He needed to make a similar defense to resolve the Iran-Contra affair.

Said another way, the rhetorical recipe for Reagan's Teflon coating was composed of a management style that allowed him to distance himself from his staff, an emphasis on epideictic speaking through which he could reaffirm a personal commitment to basic values, and a reliance on symbolic action to resolve crises. The Iran-Contra affair cut deep into the public trust in Reagan himself. In this situation, use of the passive style could only increase public doubts about the competence and honesty of the President. Put differently, the Iran-Contra affair scratched Reagan's rhetorical Teflon coating and exposed the weaknesses in the passive style. Once a Teflon-coated pan is scratched, it becomes worthless; a cook has no alternative but to replace the pan. The Iran-Contra affair put Reagan in the position of the cook who must replace the pan. The strategies that he had relied upon to such great effect no longer would work.

The Status of Public Discourse: A Final Conclusion

The foregoing analysis bears not only on an understanding of the passive style as a general approach for dealing with rhetorical crises and on Reagan's rhetoric, but also suggests two important conclusions for the status of public discourse itself. First, Reagan's success with the passive style indicates that those defending the present system possess an important strategic advantage that is explained not by the conservative nature of the public nor by an argumentative presumption against change, but by the rhetorical strategies available to the opponent of change. Through the three components of the passive style, a politician can appear to commit him- or herself to reform of the system while in practice opposing that reform. Such a strategy, as the Superfund controversy indicates, will satisfy all but the most ideologically committed among the general public.

The power of the passive style to satisfy the public does not mean that rhetorical practices inevitably favor the conservative. It is easy to imagine a liberal Democrat using the passive style to satisfy opponents of social programs. While liberals have not been nearly as adept as conservatives at using the passive style, ideology is not inherent to the strategy.

Of course the advocate of change always faces difficulties. Since the classical era, it has been a commonplace view that there should be a presumption for the maintenance of the present system. The power of the passive style, however, does not relate to argumentative burdens inherent to advocacy, but rather to strategic strengths, *regardless* of the argumentative merit of the particular case. The conclusion is that opponents of change (whether in defense of liberal or conservative programs) possess built-in rhetorical advantages in comparison to proponents of change. This may in part explain the difficulty Congress and the President have had in dealing with intractable political problems such as the budget deficit. Purely symbolic action, 1990's new budget compromise for instance, was enough to satisfy the people, and thus fundamental change does not occur.

Second, the analysis of the strategies defining the passive style suggests that on certain types of issues it will be extremely difficult to mobilize public opinion. The power of the passive style comes from personal value affirmation, blame displacement, and symbolic action. Clearly, it will be easier to overcome these strategies on some issues than on others. The passive style will be weakest in cases that directly relate to strong societal values that already have been activated and that have relatively clear policy implications. It also will lack power if it is difficult for the political leader involved to displace responsibility and if dramatic events have occurred that involve the people directly. On the other hand, in cases in which the issue is not tied to widely shared values, or is overly complex, or lacks a dramatic component, or on which there is a readily available scapegoat, sustained public interest will be difficult or impossible to maintain. Unfortunately, many of the most important issues of our time lack the characteristics that facilitate public discussion. Questions involving the environment, technology development, and even defense policy tend to be highly complex, without personal drama, and with a host of potential scapegoats.

The foregoing suggests that much of the consideration of a crisis in the public sphere has been misstated. As we noted earlier, until the mid-sixties the conventional wisdom among political scientists was that "voters are fools." Others, notably Farrell and Goodnight, argue that the problems lie not with the public but with manipulation of the public by the media and/or the technocratic elites.[79]

The view we have developed is more complex. The public often is concerned with issues, but that concern generally is limited to cases that directly affect them, suggest political corruption, or possess characteristics negating the passive style (thus making it easier to activate the audience). As a result, for example, there has been far more public concern with the few hundred children who have been stolen from their parents in childnapping cases than with depletion of the ozone layer, although the ozone question poses an infinitely greater potential threat for society than the childnapping issue. The childnapping issue can be condensed into a personal, visual, dramatic package on television, in magazine stories, and even on the back of milk cartons or on bulletin boards. Ozone depletion, however, does not possess the characteristics that invite public concern; it is an extremely complex scientific issue not clearly related to a breakdown of societal values, with little or no dramatic or visual component.

Thus, the rhetorical strength of the passive style suggests the chance for societal gridlock on potentially crucial issues such as the greenhouse effect or acid rain. The importance of these problems is widely accepted, yet action may be difficult or impossible to produce. Past treatments of the state of the public sphere have focused on the capacity for public rationality or the dangers associated with technocratic control. While both concerns are important, the more crucial problem may relate to the way the passive style makes action difficult on some of the most important issues of the day.

Notes

[1] See, for instance, John B. Judis, "Running for Cover," rev. of *See How They Run: Electing a President in an Age of Mediaocracy*, by Paul Taylor, *New Republic*, 29 October 1990, 39–41; "Beating the System," *New Republic*, 5 November 1990, 7–9.

[2] Donald Kaul, "Pete Rose Has Made a Mockery of All Our Hopes and Ambitions," *Kansas City Times*, 1 July 1989, p. A25.

[3] Kaul, p. A25.

[4] Aristotle, *Rhetoric*. In *The Basic Works of Aristotle*. Trans. W. Rhys Roberts, Ed. Richard McKeon (New York: Random House, 1941).

[5] See, for instance, Austin Ranney, *The American Elections of 1984* (Durham: Duke University Press, 1985), 29; Mark Green, "Amiable Dunce or Chronic Liar?" *Mother Jones*, June/July 1987, 9.

[6] See, for instance, Paul D. Erickson, *Reagan Speaks, The Making of an American Myth* (New York: New York University Press, 1985), 1.

[7] R. W. Apple, "In a Spirit of Contrition," *New York Times*, 5 March 1987, p. A1.

[8] Martin J. Medhurst, "Postponing the Social Agenda: Reagan's Strategy and Tactics," *Western Journal of Speech Communication* 48 (1984): 262–276; Henry Z. Scheele, "Ronald Reagan's 1980 Acceptance Address," *Western Journal of Speech Communication* 48 (1984): 51–61.

[9] Robert L. Ivie, "Speaking 'Common Sense' About the Soviet Threat," *Western Journal of Speech Communication* 48 (1984): 46.

[10] William F. Lewis, "Telling America's Story: Narrative Form and the Reagan Presidency," *Quarterly Journal of Speech* 73 (1987): 280–302.

[11] Walter R. Fisher, "Romantic Democracy, Ronald Reagan, and Presidential Heroes," *Western Journal of Speech Communication* 46 (1982): 299–310; Amos Kiewe and David W. Houck, "The Rhetoric of Reaganomics: A Redemptive Vision," *Communication Studies* 40 (1989): 107.

[12] Richard E. Crable and Steven L. Vibbert, "Argumentative Stance and Political Faith Healing: 'The Dream Will Come True,'" *Quarterly Journal of Speech* 69 (1983): 290–301.

[13] Ellen Reid Gold, "Ronald Reagan and the Oral Tradition," *Central States Speech Journal* 39 (1988): 159–176.

[14] Murray Edelman, *The Symbolic Uses of Politics* (Urbana: University of Illinois Press, 1964), 80.

[15] Edelman, *The Symbolic Uses of Politics*, 81.

[16] Brock Evans, "No Ordinary Scandal," *Audubon*, May 1983, 46, 48.

[17] Evans, 48.

[18] See Evans, 44.

[19] Stuart Taylor, Jr., "Dingell Says He Has Evidence of EPA Criminal Conduct," *New York Times*, 2 March 1983, p. A22; Philip Shabecoff, "Dismissed Official Faults EPA Chief," *New York Times*, 24 February 1983, p. B14.

[20] Evans, 44.

[21] David Burnham, "Reagan Dismisses High EPA Official," *New York Times*, 8 February 1983, p. A1.

[22] Leslie Maitland, "EPA Says It Shredded Duplicate Documents," *New York Times*, 11 February 1983, p. A1.

[23] Maitland, p. A17.

[24] Maitland, p. A17; Raymond Bonner, "EPA Officials Say Inquiry Data Have Been Erased or Are Missing," *New York Times*, 20 February 1983, p. A1.

[25] Jonathan Lash, Katherine Gilman, and David Sheridan, *A Season of Spoils: The Reagan Administration's Attack on the Environment* (New York: Pantheon, 1984), 75.

[26] Reagan is quoted in Philip Shabecoff, "Reagan Ends Fight to Withhold Data in Dispute on EPA," *New York Times*, 17 February 1983, p. A1.

[27] Philip Shabecoff, "EPA Chief Urges Opening of Files to Quash Dispute," *New York Times*, 4 March 1983, p. A1.

[28] "Texts of Mrs. Burford's Letter of Resignation and the President's Acceptance," *New York Times*, 10 March 1983, p. B12.

[29] Steven R. Weisman, "EPA Issue for Reagan," *New York Times*, 26 February 1983, p. A9.

[30] See Lash, Gilman, and Sheridan, 29; Philip Shabecoff, "Environmental Agency, Deep and Persisting Woes." *New York Times*, 6 March 1983, p. A38.

[31] Melinda Beck, "The Toxic Tar Baby at Reagan's EPA," *Newsweek*, 28 February 1983, 14.

[32] "The Political Pain of Sewergate," *Business Week*, 7 March 1983, 119.

[33] Philip Shabecoff, "Politics and the EPA Crisis: Environment Emerges as a Mainstream Issue," *New York Times*, 29 April 1983, p. B5.

[34] Melinda Beck, "Reagan's Toxic Turmoil," *Newsweek*, 21 February 1983, 22.

[35] Michael Reese, "Storm Over the Environment," *Newsweek*, 7 March 1983, 17.

[36] Francis Clines, "White House Seeks to Peer Beyond EPA Smoke," *New York Times*, 11 March 1983, p. A18.

[37] Stuart Taylor, Jr., "Reagan Asserting Claim of Privilege on Files of EPA," *New York Times*, 18 February 1983, p. A1.

[38] Hedrick Smith, "Reagan's EPA Retreat: Democrats Get An Edge," *New York Times*, 10 March 1983, p. B12.

[39] John McLaughlin, "The EPA Debacle," *National Review*, 18 March 1983, 304.

[40] See Bernard Weinraug, "Mondale Renews Attack on Reagan's Record," *New York Times*, 30 July 1984, p. A13.

[41] Ronald A. Taylor, "Environment: A New Leaf For Reagan?" *U.S. News and World Report*, 27 February 1984, 59.

[42] Philip Shabecoff, "Earth, Wind, and Loss of Momentum," *New York Times*, 28 April 1984, p. A9.

[43] See Ronald A. Taylor, "For Reagan, No Truce in Battle Over Ecology," *U.S. News and World Report*, 20 August 1984, 40; Melinda Beck, "EPA: Ruckelshaus Bows Out," *Newsweek*, 10 December 1984, 39.

[44] Phillip Shabecoff, "Environment Shrinks as a Political Issue," *New York Times*, 8 July 1984, p. D4.

[45] Ronald Reagan, "The President's News Conference of February 16, 1983," *Weekly Compilation of Presidential Documents*, 16 February 1983, 244.

[46] Ronald Reagan, "Domestic and Foreign Issues," *Weekly Compilation of Presidential Documents*, 11 March 1983, 393.

[47] Reagan, "Domestic and Foreign Issues," 393.

[48] Edelman, *The Symbolic Uses of Politics*, 2–3; also see Angus Campbell, Philip E. Converse, Warren E. Miller, and Donald E. Stokes, *The American Voter* (New York: Wiley, 1960); Bernard R. Berelson, Paul F. Lazarsfeld, and William N. McPhee, *Voting* (Chicago: University of Chicago Press, 1954).

[49] See V. O. Key, Jr., *The Responsible Electorate* (Cambridge: Harvard University Press, 1966); also see Norman H. Nie, Sidney Verba, and John R. Petrocik, *The Changing American Voter*, enlarged edition (Cambridge: Harvard University Press, 1979), and Gerald M. Pomper, *Voters' Choice: Varieties of American Electoral Behavior* (New York: Harper & Row, 1975).

[50] Murray Edelman, *Political Language: Words That Succeed and Policies That Fail* (New York: Academic Press, 1977), 50.

[51] Edelman, *The Symbolic Uses of Politics*, 172.

[52] Chaim Perelman and L. Olbrechts-Tyteca, *The New Rhetoric: A Treatise on Argumentation*, trans. John Wilkinson and Purcell Weaver (Notre Dame: University of Notre Dame Press, 1969), 50.

[53] Christine Oravec, "'Observation' in Aristotle's Theory of Epideictic," *Philosophy & Rhetoric* 9 (1976): 170. Condit also notes that epideictic may on occasion serve what is essentially a prepolicy role. See Celeste Michelle Condit, "The Function of Epideictic: The Boston Massacre Orations as Exemplar," *Communication Quarterly* 33 (1985): 284–298.

[54] Richard E. Crable and Steven L. Vibbert, "Mobil's Epideictic Advocacy: 'Observations' of Prometheus-Bound," *Communication Monographs* 50 (1983): 394.

[55] Murray Edelman, *Politics as Symbolic Action: Mass Arousal and Quiescence* (Chicago: Markham, 1971), 180.

[56] Edelman, *Political Language*, 148.

[57] Edelman, *Political Language*, 3.

[58] Edelman, *The Symbolic Uses of Politics*, 38.

[59] Reagan, "Domestic and Foreign Issues," 393.

[60] Ronald Reagan, "Environmental Protection Agency," *Weekly Compilation of Presidential Documents*, 21 March 1983, 430.

[61] Reagan, "Environmental Protection Agency," 429.

[62] Ronald Reagan, "Environmental Protection Agency," *Weekly Compilation of Presidential Documents*, 18 May 1983, 742.

[63] See Taylor, "For Reagan, No Truce in Battle Over Ecology," 40; Beck, "EPA: Ruckelshaus Bows Out," 39; Shabecoff, "Environment Shrinks as a Political Issue," p. D4.

[64] Reagan, "The President's News Conference," 244.

[65] Ronald Reagan, "Domestic and Foreign Issues," *Weekly Compilation of Presidential Documents*, 23 February 1983, 280–281.

[66] See Philip Shabecoff, "Mrs. Burford Says She Decided to Quit Before President Yielded to Congress," *New York Times*, 11 March 1989, p. A18; Smith, pp. A1, B12.

[67] Reagan, "Domestic and Foreign Issues," 392.

[68] Reagan, "Domestic and Foreign Issues," 393.

[69] Reagan, "Domestic and Foreign Issues," 393.

[70] Reagan, "Environmental Protection Agency," 428.

[71] Reagan, "Environmental Protection Agency," 428.

[72] Reagan, "Environmental Protection Agency," 741.

[73] Reagan, "Environmental Protection Agency," 742.

[74] "Chapter Two: Ruckelshaus Wades Into EPA," *Time*, 30 May 1983, 18.

[75] Edelman, *Political Language*, 151.

76 All references to the Tower Commission address are to Ronald Reagan, "Text of the President's Address to the Nation on the Iran Arms Controversy," *New York Times*, 5 March 1987, p. A18.

77 See Gerald M. Boyd, "President Asserts He is Moving Away From Iran Affair," *New York Times*, 6 March 1987, pp. A1, A10; Larry Martz, "The Long Road Back," *Newsweek*, 16 March 1987, 18–20; Jacob V. Lamar, Jr., "Trying a Comeback," *Time*, 16 March 1987, 18–23.

78 See Phil Galley and Robin Tower, "Reagan and Iran Controversy: Reactions Are Mixed in Akron and Nashville," *New York Times*, 10 March 1987, p. A14; "President Reagan's Speech Helped Him, But only Slightly," *Newsweek*, 16 March 1987, 20; Fred Barnes, "Life After Death," *New Republic*, 10 and 17 August 1987, 12–13; Tom Morganthau, "Still No Smoking Gun," *Newsweek*, 10 August 1987, 12–13; "Opinion Outlook: Views on Presidential Performance," *National Journal*, 4 July 1987, 1744.

79 See Thomas B. Farrell and G. Thomas Goodnight, "Accidental Rhetoric: The Root Metaphors of Three Mile Island," *Communication Monographs* 48 (1981): 271–300; G. Thomas Goodnight, "The Personal, Technical, and Public Spheres of Argument: A Speculative Inquiry Into the Art of Public Deliberation," *Journal of the American Forensics Association* 18 (1982): 214–227.

Put On a Happy Face
Batman as Schizophrenic Savior

Robert E. Terrill

Batman, the 1989 movie, made a lot of money. *The Economist* (1989,
p. 73) called it "the most financially successful film in the most successful summer in Hollywood's history." The movie recouped its $35 million
production costs in the first weekend, sold over $100 million worth of
tickets in its first ten days, and earned two spots in the *Guinness Book
of Records*—for the highest one-day and opening-day grosses. Hundreds
of *Batman* toys and games flooded the market, and the president of
Warner Brothers' advertising and publicity called the public's response
to the licensed products a "feeding frenzy" (Barol, 1989, p. 73). *Motor
Trend* reviewed the Batmobile, Ralston Purina created Batman cereal,
and one distributor described the Bat-fever as "bigger than the California
Raisins" (Barol, p. 70).

The success was somewhat surprising, and not just because 30-year-
old director Timothy Burton's only other commercially released movies
were the quirky pair *Pee Wee's Big Adventure* and *Beetlejuice*. First,
the *Wall Street Journal* reported in November, 1988, that thousands of
Bat-fans were protesting the casting of Michael Keaton as Batman.
Warner Brothers became so concerned about the film's success that they
cut a trailer months ahead of schedule, hoping to drum up interest by
showing it during the Christmas season (Barol, 1989). Second, the movie
itself was a gloomy exception to typically sunny mid-summer box office
releases. Gotham City is left the same shadowy, dingy place that it is
in the opening shots; the hero is increasingly unstable; and the central
romance reaches no satisfactory resolution. Further, the action sequences
are sluggishly paced and the special effects are far less sophisticated than
a contemporary, post-*Star Wars* audience might be expected to tolerate.
Why, then, did the public respond so overwhelmingly to the most recent
manifestation of this 50-year-old superhero?

Actress Kim Basinger, who plays Vicki Vale, provides a useful insight:
"The film is emphasizing that wonderful psychological story of three

From *Quarterly Journal of Speech*, 79 (August 1993), 319–335. Used by permission of
the Speech Communication Association and the author.

people who, I guess, live in all of us" (de Vries, 1989, p. 11). This essay will argue that there are actually four "people" in the film who warrant examination, but the idea that much of the film's popularity stems from the projection onto the screen of the psyche of the audience is one central assertion of this analysis.

Davies, Farrell, and Matthews (1982, p. 327) argue that application of psychological theory to film analysis might not only "point to otherwise unnoticed images and structures within a film" but also "offer insight into the relationship between the film and the viewer, and can suggest the relevance of the film . . . to the society in which it arises." There is a growing body of criticism of contemporary rhetorical discourse that exploits this psychological and symptomatic connection between film and society. Many such analyses focus either on the psychic integration of the hero as a prescription for society or on the tendency of popular film to ameliorate life's unpleasantness, as in the following three examples.

Rushing and Frentz (1980) explore the changes in the psyches of the young warriors in *The Deer Hunter* and note that Michael alone of the three main characters successfully integrates into his psyche the shadows conjured by the horrors of war. As a result, Michael becomes a more powerful, effective leader: "By being psychologically prepared, Michael experienced war sacredly, and, in so doing, reaffirmed the mythic qualities in himself and his community" (p. 404). Martha Solomon (1983) suggests that *Chariots of Fire* presents a "soothing" conflict between two opposing myths of the American Dream in which "each myth has validity" (p. 277) and neither is vanquished by the other. The film was successful, therefore, because it "creates an optimistic, humanistic view of life" (p. 281). David Payne (1989) sees the annual spring television screening of *The Wizard of Oz* as a contemporary "media ritual" that speaks to "typical audience problems and situations" (p. 29). Specifically, Dorothy's adventure of maturation may be "therapeutic for those who continue to search and to question the basic values of self and society" (p. 37).

Other rhetorical criticisms of film chart either the disintegration of the hero or the failure of the unification of the vying mythic stances within the film. Davies et al. (1983) point out that in *The Shining*, Jack Torrance's "excessive concern over his image" produces the insanity which eventually destroys him and almost destroys his family (p. 340); thus, the film "cautioned that extensive looking outward . . . brings the tumultuous consequences of a neglected *inner* life" (p. 341). Rasmussen and Downey (1989) describe "dialectical disorientation" as a set of "diametrically opposed perspectives within a *discourse*" (p. 69), which "demands its audience acknowledge life's dilemmas by proclaiming the inevitability of disquieting tension in life" (p. 67). They use this model in a criticism of *Agnes of God*, in which both a "linear" and a "holistic" orientation are presented as explanatory frameworks for the narrative. Neither framework can account for all the evidence within the film, so "choosing one explanation over the other is at best a temporary respite, at worst, impossible" (p. 81). Rasmussen and Downey (1991) extend the concept of "dialectical disorientation" in exploring the warrior myth as it is presented in a certain cluster of Vietnam films. This myth entails a "tension between the devastating killer and the humane individual, between the *militaristic* and the *moralistic*" (p. 180). In *The Deer Hunter*, *Apocalypse Now*, *Platoon*, and *Full Metal Jacket*, they argue that the two sides of this myth are played against one another until "confrontation between militarism and moralism shatters the myth" (p. 180). These Vietnam films create "uncertainty and ambiguity because the form destroys the myth's principles and values, questions its foundations, and provides no substitution for its ruin" (p. 190).

  Batman, like other films that chart disintegration, fails to unify a number of psychic/mythic elements. However, in *Batman* there exists a tension between an apparent movement toward integration and the actions of the hero that furiously oppose it. This tension precipitates the manifestation of a more complex psychic process of disintegration than those suggested in the above analyses. Like Jack Torrance, Wayne/ Batman's psyche is progressively splintered until he is clearly insane; but instead of becoming an axe-wielding menace, Batman becomes Gotham City's savior. As in *Agnes of God*, mythic stances are not integrated; but rather than indicating a "concomitant need to accept resolution through embracing disquieting uncertainty" (Rasmussen & Downey, 1989, p. 69), *Batman* suggests that maintaining the *status* quo requires violent suppression of uncertainty and thus continued psychic chaos. And, as in the Vietnam films, a myth is destroyed through disintegration from within; however, *Batman* not only destroys the myth of a unified savior but further suggests that such a savior is an impossibility for the contemporary psyche. Ironically, this bleak denouement is responsible for much of the film's remarkable popularity. For if Gotham City is a recognizable depiction of the unbalanced American psyche, then it may be a strangely attractive proposition that Batman, a schizophrenic savior, exists to shield us from the disturbing work of attempted psychic integration.

  Because much of my analysis is grounded in the psychological theories of Carl G. Jung, I will begin by outlining relevant aspects of that theory. Then I suggest that Gotham City is a dream world, a representative projection of image-centered dreams. Within the framework of Jung's model, I show the principal characters to be archetypal manifestations that erupt from Gotham's unconscious. Wayne/Batman is a splintered

manifestation of a potential whole; his condition represents the schizophrenia required of a hero dedicated to the preservation of the fractured
psyche of Gotham.

The Model of the Psyche

Jung describes the psyche as composed of three layers: consciousness,
the personal unconscious, and the collective unconscious. "The personal
unconscious consists firstly of all those contents that became
unconscious either because they lost their intensity and were forgotten
or because consciousness was withdrawn from them (repression), and
second of contents . . . which never had sufficient intensity to reach
consciousness but have somehow entered the psyche" (Jung, 1971, p.
38). The contents of the collective unconscious "consist of mythological
motifs or primordial images," elements which are all the more powerful
and potentially dangerous because they are common to all people,
elements which Jung has termed *archetypes* (1971, p. 39). These
archetypes of the collective unconscious manifest themselves in dreams.
Four archetypes—the *Self*, the *shadow*, the *wise old man*, and the
anima—are manifested within the dream world of Gotham City.

Especially in his later writings, Jung "distinguished between the
archetype as form and the culturally influenced archetypal images which
are expressed in motifs that allude to an underlying form" (Young-
Eisendrath & Wiedemann, 1987, p. 36). For example, Jung writes: "The
archetype in itself is empty and purely formal . . . a possibility of
representation which is given *a priori*" (1959a, p. 79). Wayne/Batman,
Napier/Joker, Alfred the butler, and Vicki Vale are culture-specific
archetypal images, but they may resonate cross-culturally as a function
of underlying archetypal forms.

Jung (1971, pp. 121–122) believes that the positive goal of individual
self-knowledge involves an assimilation of the contents of the unconscious into consciousness, a process he calls *individuation*. The ego will
necessarily resist individuation because the integration of the
unconscious entails a loss of the dominion of consciousness. One
manifestation of resisting the assimilation of the unconscious is excessive
attention to building the *persona*, which Jung describes as the identity
or mask that is constructed and presented to the world. The persona is
"designed on the one hand to make a definite impression upon others,
and, on the other, to conceal the true nature of the individual" (Jung,
1983, p. 94). Continued repression of the contents of the unconscious,
as occurs in Gotham City, only increases the likelihood that these
archetypal contents will attempt to invade consciousness.

Jung (1971, pp. 111–121) describes two possible negative outcomes of this invasion by the unconscious, "regressive restoration of the persona" and "identification with the collective psyche." Regressive restoration results in a regression to a childlike state, a retreat to an earlier stage of development to save face—to restore the persona. In identification, consciousness is overwhelmed by the contents of the unconscious, and psychosis or schizophrenia results. Jung explains (1971, p. 122): "In the former case the self retires into the background and gives place to social recognition; in the latter, to the auto-suggestive meaning of a primordial image. In both cases the collective has the upper hand" and the individual is lost. *Batman* displays both these reactions to invading unconscious elements.

The Psyche of the City

Jung (1971, p. 478) believed that the cinema, because it "enables us to experience without danger to ourselves all the excitements, passions, and fantasies which have to be repressed in a humanistic age," can present cultural dreams analogous to the dreams of individuals. Thus, film provides a propitious environment for the manifestation of culturally repressed archetypes. Also, Davies et al. (1983, p. 333) suggest that because film is a subjective representation of objective reality, it "is able to create a stylized reality, a juxtaposition of the 'real' and the 'fantastic' that can reflect the conscious-unconscious interplay described by Jung." In other words, film entails real objects (consciousness) shown through a fantastic, fictionalizing lens (unconsciousness). Gotham City, because it is mostly "fantastic," is a visualization of the dark world of the unconscious: a dream.

Because dreams are products and representations of the unconscious, they are largely unaffected by the linear, ordering influence of consciousness. Jung (1959a, p. 276) notes that dreams often present themselves "in fairly chaotic and unsystematic form. Dreams . . . show no apparent order and no tendency to systematization." While *Batman*'s plot may skip "from tableau to tableau [like a comic book] rather than progressing by any of the more accepted routes" (Billson, 1991, p. 32), it is the foundation of the plot, the setting, which is most oddly ambiguous. Specifically, it is impossible to place the movie in any particular time. A subtitle labels the first view as "Gotham City," but does not include the date that generations of movie audiences have been conditioned to expect. The young family mugged in the early scenes is wearing clothing of the 1930s and trying to flag down taxis that belong on a contemporary urban street; a few moments later, a police lieutenant dressed like Philip Marlowe oversees the loading of muggers into thoroughly modern ambulances. Gotham's unsettling hodgepodge of architectural styles is in the gray-scale monochromatism of a black-and-white film, but certain elements (the ambulances, the Joker, the party scene in Wayne's mansion) splash the screen with 1990s color. According to Anton Furst, who designed the production, the lack of continuity was intentional: "I took an almost Dadaist approach and augmented it as much as I possibly could, so that we have a kind of potpourri, an incredible mixture of styles . . . every camera angle will confuse you. Is it now? Was it then? Or is it maybe a few years in the future?" (Nightingale, 1989, p. 16). The various destabilizing techniques invite the audience to experience the city as a dream, as both a darkly fantastic and disturbingly realistic projection of their psyches.

Jung's model of the psyche reflects a vertical metaphor. He describes elements moving up into consciousness, down into the personal unconscious, and down further still into the collective unconscious. Gotham City, as a manifestation of this model of the psyche, enacts a corresponding vertical metaphor. Consciousness is the highest level, represented by the sky. Because Gotham City is a dream world, a mostly unconscious world, there is very little sky to be seen. The sunless streets of Gotham, crowded canyons crushed beneath buildings that cantilever out over the sidewalks, are a visual metaphor for the collective unconscious; these ornate and overbuilt structures are themselves representations of the city's concern for its image and seem to pin the sidewalks to the earth. It is at street level that the criminals enjoy their greatest power, where muggers attack both the young family of the opening scene and Wayne's own parents. When Batman is on the streets, even if in his Batmobile, he is reduced to fleeing. At the level of the rooftops, between consciousness and the collective, is the personal unconscious. For reasons to be discussed, this is the level at which Batman is most effective; it is at this level that he thrashes the two muggers, and it is from this level that he drops Jack Napier into the vat of acid.

The Joker hints at another aspect of this vertically stratified dream world when he asks: "Can somebody tell me what kind of a world we live in where a man dressed up as a bat gets all of my press?" He later answers his own question when he reminds Vicki Vale "how concerned people are about appearances these days." Gotham City is a world that assures a man dressed in a funny suit plenty of press because it is a world where appearances count above all else. Psychologically, a society such as Gotham focuses only on the conscious, surface aspects of reality and ignores the unconscious. In Jungian terms, Gotham City is *persona*-possessed. Gotham has run out of money for the celebration of its 200th birthday, an element of the plot that at first appears to have little to do with the story. Rather than being a throwaway, or a loose end left dangling by the writers' strike that hit Hollywood as *Batman* went into production, the Mayor's obsession with the festival is the key to the psyche of the city. He tells District Attorney Harvey Dent: "We are going to have a festival if I have to get a shotgun and get people there myself." The mayor doesn't care if the people of Gotham are actually celebrative or not, as long as they *look* like they're having a good time. The scene just prior to the Mayor's threat of forced revelry opens with makeup artists improving the appearance of two newscasters who immediately report the death of two fashion models. Later, the newscasters look horrible; they have gone without their cosmetics because the Joker has tainted them with deadly Smylex. The newscasters tell the audience that "Gotham City goes on a forced fast," thus metaphorically elevating makeup to the level of a basic need, food.

Threatening to force people to party at gunpoint and equating cosmetics to nourishment are certainly indications of an excessive attention to the persona, an attempt to keep the unconscious contents from becoming conscious. When questioned by the reporter Alexander Knox about Batman, Dent tells him that "we have enough problems in this city without worrying about ghosts and goblins." This statement is ironic, since it is precisely the ghosts and goblins of Gotham's neglected unconscious to which Dent and the others should be paying attention. As Jung points out (1983, p. 225), the archetypal contents of the collective unconscious will not tolerate repression indefinitely and will eventually force themselves into consciousness. Davies et al. (1981, p. 342) note that Jung believed "the modern world errs, and induces the psychological consequences of neuroses and compulsions, through the rational assumption that consciousness is the totality of the psyche." Thus, Gotham is a dark reflection of this sort of American psyche, engaged in frantic persona-building despite its need to acknowledge and integrate the contents of its collective unconscious. Such a personality is unlikely to avoid the dire psychological consequences of which Jung warns and is ripe for the eruption of archetypal images.

The Manifestation of the Archetypes

In Jung's model, archetypal images manifest themselves in an unbalanced psyche, like Gotham's, because these archetypes represent aspects of the psyche that have been ignored and must be reassimilated; their function is *compensatory* (Jung, 1983, p. 184). The four most important characters in the film can be discussed in terms of four basic and powerful archetypes of the collective unconscious: the *Self*, the *shadow*, the *wise old man*, and the *anima*. Together, they represent the *quaternity* described by Jung as "the fourfold basis of wholeness" (1959b, p. 159). These four characters represent four aspects of the personality whose integration would precipitate the process of the city's individuation, the healing of Gotham.

The first and most important of these archetypal images to emerge is, of course, Wayne/Batman. The trauma of witnessing his parents' murder, and his subsequent repression of that trauma, provokes a division in his psyche. In a flashback, the young Master Bruce and his parents are shown leaving the Monarch Theater, the butterfly a symbol of the metamorphosis that is about to occur within the boy. The family walks in step, underscoring the order and linearity of consciousness governing Wayne's world. Silently, a 1959 "batwing" Chevy cruises past as two muggers follow the Waynes into a dark alley. The murder scene contains a slow-motion shot of Wayne's mother's pearls dropping to the street as the young Jack Napier kills her; it is disclosed later that the scene takes place on Pearl Street. The destruction of the ordered circle of pearls parallels the disruption of ego-consciousness caused by his parents' murder, the tipping toward darkness that eventually results in the emergence of Batman. Thus, the manifestation of Batman separates Wayne's personality into two parts—one light, one dark.

Following the convention of denoting the Self archetype with a capital "S" to differentiate it from the more common meaning as a synonym for "ego" (Whitmont, 1969, p. 218; Young-Eisendrath & Wiedemann, 1987, p. 39), I suggest that Wayne/Batman is an imperfect, or *potential*, manifestation of the Self of the city. Jung describes the Self as representing "a nuptial union of opposite halves" (1959, p. 64) and "the sum total of . . . conscious and unconscious contents" (1989, p. 242). As such, the Self is both an archetype of wholeness and the driving force which guides an individual toward achieving this wholeness (Whitmont, 1969, pp. 218–219). But, Wayne/Batman does not display the unity generally associated with this archetype. As a manifestation of the Self of the city, the split in his own psyche mirrors the split in the city's psyche; he contains opposing psychic aspects, but they are held separate within him.

The dualistic nature of Wayne/Batman is highlighted throughout the film. Vicki Vale points out that he gives money for humanitarian aid (as Bruce Wayne) but collects the costumes of war (costumes similar to the Batsuit). She also elicits his comment about his house that "some of it is very much me, some of it isn't." In Vale's apartment when he is attempting to tell her he is Batman, Wayne explains that "people have different sides to their personality." This is an understatement in Wayne's case, for he and Batman are a study in contrasts. Batman is first shown as a confident figure, making all the right moves as he subdues two muggers on the dark rooftops of Gotham. Holding one thief out over the edge of the building, he identifies himself, somewhat redundantly: "I'm Batman." He wants the mugger to tell all his friends that Batman is there. The first appearance of Wayne's name, on the other hand, is to indicate he is *absent* from Harvey Dent's inaugural news conference. The darker identity has more presence, establishing a pattern continued when Wayne seems lost and unsure of himself even though he is the host of the well-lit party; he asks his guests how much more champagne to open, and needs Alfred's help in finding the door. It is clear that Wayne/Batman represents an unintegrated, split psyche, and that the darker part, Batman, is more powerful than the light half, Wayne. As is true in Gotham's psyche, continued repression is forcing dark unconsciousness to usurp the whole.

Wayne/Batman's relationship to the city is more intricate than a mirroring of psychological splits. According to Jung, manifestations of the Self, because they represent a unity of opposites, the totality of human experience, are often perceived as saviors. For example, Jung sees Christ as a flawed savior because he contains only the light, or conscious, side of the Self archetype (1959b, p. 44). Gotham City is in need of a savior. The cathedral in which Batman and the Joker stage their final showdown is, as designer Furst notes, "closed and allowed to rot because God left the city long ago and no one goes to church anymore" (Nightingale, 1989, p. 16). Just as Jung suggests that cultures do when they are severely unbalanced and need a new savior (1959c), Gotham learns to produce its Batman. After Vicki Vale has discovered his identity, she asks Wayne why he does "all this," presumably meaning dressing like a bat and picking fist fights with bad guys. Wayne's answer: "Because nobody else can." Only the city's savior can protect it from the manifestation of its shadow.

When Wayne witnesses his parents' murder he is confronted with the shadow archetype, but he is not overwhelmed by this element of the collective unconscious. This is evidenced by his ability to enter and leave the Batcave at will; the position of the Batcave within the vertical metaphor of Gotham City and its identification as the place where Wayne becomes Batman reflect its function as a point of contact with the collective unconscious, but Wayne is not trapped by this contact. Therefore, Wayne's reaction to his confrontation with the shadow archetype was a *partial* "identification with the collective" (Jung, 1971, p. 111) in which part of his psyche—the dark part that would someday emerge as Batman—became "the fortunate possessor of the great truth which was only waiting to be discovered, of the eschatological knowledge which spells the healing of the nations" (Jung, 1971, p. 118). As will be shown, though, Batman is an ironic savior who labors not to heal Gotham but rather to preserve Gotham's psychosis.

Batman and the Joker have a complex and curiously dichotic relationship: they are essentially similar yet almost completely opposite. The Joker is a manifestation of the *shadow* archetype, displaying the characteristics of this archetype as described by Edward C. Whitmont:

> The shadow is projected in two forms: individually, in the shape of the people to whom we ascribe all the evil; and collectively, in its most general form, as the Enemy, the personification of evil. Its mythological representations are the devil, archenemy, tempter, fiend or double; or the dark or evil one of a pair of brothers or sisters. (1969, p. 163)

The Joker, as a particularly potent manifestation of the shadow, embodies both its individual and collective forms. As Batman's individual shadow, the Joker must function as *doppelgänger*, or dark double. The similarities of the two characters are emphasized throughout the film and symbolized in the Bat-logo, which the camera explores behind the opening credits as if it were a landscape. So much of Warner's advertising focused on this symbol that the *New York Times* (1989) ran a brief editorial complaining that "it's impossible to go anywhere without seeing the logo," even though "some people misread it, seeing a mouthful of gold teeth rather than a bat against a gold field." The logo is simultaneously an image of Batman and the garish smile of the Joker, and seeing only one or the other is an illusion. Like Batman and the Joker, the black bat and the golden grin are opposing parts of the same whole.

An indication of their essential similarity is the "psychological profile" of Napier that Wayne reads: "violent mood swings, highly intelligent, emotionally unstable; aptitudes include science, chemistry, and art." This same profile could be used to describe Wayne/Batman. His mood swings are controlled, but are evident in the transformation from the mild-mannered Wayne into the vigilante Batman. His ability to decode the Joker's chemical tampering with Gotham's cosmetics shows that he, too, must have an aptitude for science and chemistry— and, of course, the decor of his home indicates he values art. In characteristically opposite fashion, the Joker's mood swings are uncontrolled, he uses his scientific aptitude for destruction, and he literally devalues the art in the museum.

The two figures are similarly attracted to Vicki Vale, who elicits statements that reveal both characters to share equally idealistic but opposite goals. Vale notes that Wayne/Batman seeks a perfect world, a world without evil, and that he is willing to sacrifice himself to that end. By keeping his identity a secret, he cannot take credit for his good deeds. The Joker, on the other hand, seeks a perfectly corrupt world and hopes to advance his own interests in doing so. When Vale asks him what he wants, he tells her: "My face on the one-dollar bill."

The confrontation between Batman and the Joker in the final scenes of the film further highlights this reflective relationship. When Batman tells the Joker, "I'm going to kill you," the Joker replies, "You idiot, you made me!" Batman returns: "You killed my parents. I made you— you made me first." These two characters are responsible for each other's existence, and it is logical that one of them must be responsible for the other's destruction. The Joker is eventually destroyed, but their battle first stalls in a near draw with Batman clinging to the same ledge that is crumbling under the Joker's feet. Batman gains the decisive advantage only by roping the Joker's leg to the heavy, bat-winged gargoyle that pulls him to his death. Thus, the similarity of these two characters extends even to their potency. Their mirror-image opposition is reinforced when Batman is *saved* from falling to his death by hooking a rope into another gargoyle.

As a manifestation of the collective shadow of Gotham City, the Joker displays "the 'negative' side of the [collective] personality, the sum of all those unpleasant qualities we like to hide" (Jung, 1983, p. 87). Gotham is attempting to hide its crime problem by focusing on the creation of a socially acceptable persona; thus, crime becomes associated with the city's shadow. Jack Napier's first act as the Joker is to take control of Gotham's organized crime by killing the current boss, Grissom. When Grissom warns Napier that killing him would make his life worthless, Napier explains that he has been dead once already and "found it liberating." Carnivalesque music plays as the Joker, liberated as he is from the constraints of anything resembling an acceptable persona, laughs and cavorts and empties his gun into Grissom. The Joker soon kills all remaining Gotham crime bosses and usurps leadership; he becomes a super-criminal, the symbol and incarnation of the city's crime problem and therefore an "adverse representative of the dark chthonic [under-] world" of the city, its collective shadow (Jung, 1959b, p. 34).

Like the city that spawned him, the Joker is concerned primarily with appearances. Even as Jack Napier, he is first seen in a room decorated with oversized fashion prints and in the company of Alicia, whose face graces the cover of a *Vogue* magazine on the table. As he is gazing at himself in a mirror, Alicia assures him: "You look fine." Napier tells her he didn't ask. When he and Batman initially meet face to face, Napier's first comment is "Nice suit." Then, Batman drops him into the vat of acid, symbolically down to the street-level of the collective unconscious. In fact, the Joker has plunged even below the street, down through the sewers and into Gotham's polluted river; he has drowned in the collective. These sewers are actually at the level of the Batcave, that point of contact with the collective so important to Batman. Unlike

Wayne/Batman, however, Napier does not retain the ability to exit this level of Gotham's vertical metaphor. "Beautiful Dreamer" becomes the Joker's theme song, signifying his unconsciousness.

The acid strips off the persona that Napier has admired so much and replaces it with the death-grin of the shadow—another archetypal image is born in Gotham. A neon sign flashes "SHOW" outside the basement where the plastic surgeon slowly removes the bandages around Napier's head. Napier, eager to be shown his new self, struggles out of the remaining bandages and demands a mirror; he shatters it when he sees his now-hideous image. He laughs wildly, breaks a light bulb, and climbs the stairs out of the darkened basement. In Jungian terms, the Joker has contacted the collective and has been overwhelmed by the shadow archetype. His reaction to this experience is a "regressive restoration of the persona" (Jung, 1971, p. 111). The regressed, childlike state symptomatic of this condition is evidenced here by the Joker's hysterical laughter; later he kills a man with a high-voltage joy-buzzer, and still later he wonders where Batman gets "all those wonderful toys."

That he requests and then shatters the mirror indicates that Napier, now the Joker, is still fixated on the persona but now on destroying instead of maintaining it. His Smylex poison not only kills but also transforms its victims, replacing their persona with a copy of the Joker's own grin, and the first two victims are models: image symbols. The Joker also destroys Alicia's face and squirts acid from his lapel flower in an attempt to do the same to Vicki Vale. The Joker first sees Vale in a photograph, while cutting up a huge pile of photos, and the first thing he does after commenting on Vale's beauty is to cut up her picture, too. In the museum (where one goes to look at things), after he and his men have defaced the canon of Western art, the Joker describes himself as "the world's first, fully-functioning homicidal artist." Art is traditionally an act of creation, but the Joker is enjoying an art of destruction; he is destroying Gotham's persona.

As noted earlier, excessive attention to the persona is one defense against the unconscious becoming conscious. With the city's persona, its device of repression, replaced by the Joker's own grin—and the Mayor's persona-festival replaced with a celebration of the shadow—the Joker could invade the consciousness of the city more easily. Indeed, the parade balloons filled with Smylex gas are an attempt to destroy the persona of the entire population. Significantly, the Joker enacts the "tempter" aspect of the collective shadow by luring the Gothamites to their death with the promise of "free money."

So, the Joker functions as shadow at two levels, both as Batman's personal shadow and as Gotham City's collective shadow. Jung points out that a personality might survive an encounter with the shadow of the personal unconscious, but the archetypal shadow of the collective is infinitely more powerful (Jung, 1959b, p. 10). When the Joker is destroyed, a mechanical device in his pocket allows him the last laugh; as the eerie nighttime press conference indicates, Gotham remains a dark, shadowy place. Batman has prevented the shadow from flying his helicopter into consciousness, but the sky is none the brighter. The collective shadow, a force that Batman cannot vanquish, still controls the city.

These two archetypal images, the Self and the shadow, constitute two poles of the four-sided quaternity described by Jung. Their appearance is a symptom of Gotham City's fixation with persona and inattention to the contents of the unconscious. The two other archetypes that round out the quaternity are drawn to this polarization of opposites and represent additional aspects of the psyche that must be integrated for individuation to occur. The first of these other two archetypes to appear is Alfred, the *wise old man*. He has been with Wayne since "young Master Bruce" was a child, apparently taking the role of guardian upon the murder of Wayne's parents. Jung (1983, p. 126) suggests that the wise old man archetype "always appears in a situation where insight, understanding, good advice, determination, planning, etc., are needed but cannot be mustered on one's own resources." Bruce Wayne's troubled mind cannot be expected to muster consistently good judgment, and Alfred provides this judgment for him. For example, Alfred perceives the importance of Vicki Vale as the necessary catalyst to help Wayne begin the healing of his psyche. Alfred advises Wayne accordingly several times, each time more vehemently. At first he points out that "there's a certain weight [repression] that lifts when she's here." He next offers the insight that Wayne's "present course of action [not returning her calls] will only strengthen her resolve" and suggests that she is "special" enough for Wayne to tell her the truth about Batman. Wayne fails to do this, and Alfred further urges him to begin the process of integration by informing him, tersely, that he has "no wish to fill my few remaining years grieving for the loss of old friends—or their son." When Wayne still seems unable to confront Vale directly, Alfred simply brings her to him in the Batcave. The final scenes of the movie show Alfred again bringing Vale to Wayne.

Wayne is attracted to Vale, but is also hesitant in his relationship with her. At the benefit party where they first meet she asks him "which one of these guys is Bruce Wayne?" "I'm not sure," he answers, but later introduces himself in the war-costume room. "Are you sure?" she asks; "Yeah, this time." Bruce Wayne actively pursues her but fails to reveal Batman, while Batman both saves her from the clutches of the Joker and works to keep Bruce Wayne hidden. The simultaneous attraction and uneasiness with which Wayne/Batman reacts to Vale is indicative of a male's confrontation with the *anima* archetype: a female figure, a guide to the unconscious (Jung, 1983, p. 103). "In Jung's descriptions, the anima image exerts a powerful and ambivalent pull on men" (Wehr, 1987, p. 55); "'she' is the psychic entity that seduces, lures, attracts, and even imperils a man" (p. 66). Because the anima will lead the man to the contents of his unconscious, she represents both the source of his sanity and the dissolution of his present state of mind.

Vale's name, as a homonym of "veil," describes her relationship to Wayne/Batman in at least three ways. She is capable of removing the veil from Wayne's eyes, exposing him to information essential to his integration; her true importance is hidden from Wayne behind the veil of his preoccupation with the Joker; and the veil is removed from her own eyes when Alfred brings her to Wayne in the Batcave. That her name describes Vicki Vale only in terms of her relationship to Wayne/Batman is telling, for her character is defined only through that relationship. She is introduced as an object when the reporter Knox first greets her: "Hello, legs." When asked why she is in Gotham—asked to justify her existence in the narrative—her answer is simply, "I like bats." She is there because Batman is there; if he did not exist then neither would she.

Vale's character is simple, but her relationship to Wayne/Batman is well-developed. Jung (1983, p. 106) further describes the anima figure as "a source of information about things for which a man has no eyes," so it is significant that Vale is a photographer of whom Wayne says "you have a good eye." Knox first recognizes her as a fashion photographer from "*Vogue* and *Cosmo*," but she points out to him that her most recent subjects are corpses, victims of some sort of civil strife on the fictional island of Corto Maltese. This shift toward darkness and away from the persona-world of high fashion indicates that she is a guide qualified to lead Wayne/Batman toward the darkness of his unconscious.

The Joker is also attracted to Vicki Vale, so three of the four elements of the archetypal quaternity are involved in a rather bizarre love-triangle. This tension fuels much of the plot and is parallel to Jung's formulation that the anima should be a solitary element within the male psyche as opposed to the multiple male *animus*-images within the female psyche (Wehr, 1987, p. 67). It is tempting, then, to suggest that Wayne/Batman and the Joker represent Vale's multiple animus images, the keys to her psychological growth. However, Vale shows no inclination toward such growth. Thus, Vale is not complex enough to support analysis under any of the several extended theoretical frameworks being developed by feminist Jungian scholars (Lauter, 1984; Wehr, 1987; Young-Eisendrath & Wiedemann, 1987). Vale's characterization is limited by her perfunctory role in the narrative as a traditional Jungian anima figure who leads the male personality toward the necessary unconscious elements.

Vale's entire presence within the psyche of Gotham is as an object toward which the principal combatants are drawn. For instance, it is in pursuit of her that the savior and the shadow meet in a pivotal scene in her apartment. The black-and-white, circle-and-square motifs on Vale's apartment door suggest a *mandala*, an archetypal symbol which Jung says emerges "in conditions of psychic dissociation or disorientation" (1983, p. 236). The shape of the mandala, generally a "*squaring of the circle*, taking the form of a circle in a square or vice versa" (1959a, p. 361), not only calls attention to a splintered psyche, but the combination of opposing colors and shapes in a single figure symbolizes the integration of opposites required to mend it. Vale's entire apartment, with its stark black-and-white color scheme and rounded windows enclosing the exaggerated linearity of the furniture, represents a "walk-in" mandala. Wayne and the Joker respond similarly to this room, both voicing the same line when they enter: "Nice place; lots of space." Wayne has come with the intention of telling Vale about Batman, but can't seem to say the words. The Joker presumably has come to take Vicki Vale away, but, as Pauline Kael notes, he "trots off without his prize" (1989, p. 83). Wayne threatens the Joker with a fireplace poker and the Joker fires a shot at Wayne, but neither is hurt. This mandala-room in which neither can injure the other, and in which each is in the presence of anima-image Vale, would seem to encourage integration. The conflict is unresolved because, as I will suggest, the very existence of Batman would be imperiled by its resolution.

The archetypes these four characters represent—the *Self*, the *shadow*, the *wise old man*, and the *anima*—must become one if Wayne/Batman's splintered psyche is to heal. Because Wayne/Batman and the Joker represent the city's collective Self and collective shadow respectively, the healing of the city also depends on the integration of these divided elements. In the collective psyche represented by Gotham City, however, neither problem can be solved.

The Failure of the Integration

The logo Batman wears on his chest is the round shape of a mandala, but because it is dominated by a split between two opposing shapes, one light and one dark, it is what Jung describes as "neurotically disturbed" (1959a, p. 379). This logo symbolizes extreme psychic unbalance, but instead of working toward the integration necessary if Wayne/Batman (and Gotham) is to achieve wholeness and sanity, this schizophrenic savior prevents it.

Jung (1959b, p. 22) points out that "the integration of the shadow, or the realization of the personal unconscious, marks the first stage in the analytic process." Wayne appears to realize this when he tells Alfred that he "can't go on with [my relationship to Vale] right now" and instead focuses all his attention on the Joker. However, Batman wants to destroy, not assimilate, the shadow. Similarly, Wayne's attraction to Vale indicates that he recognizes her as an anima figure, but he resists her attempts at integration. "I just got to know," she asks Batman near the end of the film, "are we going to try to love each other?" His reply: "I'd like to, but he's out there right now and I've got to go to work." To become whole, Wayne would have to integrate his shadow and accept Vale's advances. By refusing to do either, Wayne dooms his psyche to an eternal split.

Wayne tells Vale that "Alfred is my family" and that "I couldn't find my socks without him," and Wayne does *attempt* to follow Alfred's advice to "tell her [Vale] the truth." If the qualities of the wise old man were fully integrated into Wayne's psyche, then of course there would no longer be a need for their manifestation as Alfred. However, Wayne's willingness to accept some of Alfred's advice (even if he cannot act on it) suggests that the archetype indicated by Alfred is at least on the path toward integration. This is in contrast to Wayne/Batman's contact with Vale, which leaves him unchanged.

Wayne sleeps with Vale, but he refuses to allow this sexual encounter to make any changes in his psyche. As the evening progresses, the two move from opposite ends of an absurdly long table to a cozy kitchen where they sit close together, and they then make a romantic assent up a long flight of stairs to Wayne's bedroom. Both the symbolic coming together of the Self and the anima and the exploitation of Gotham City's vertical metaphor suggest that this scene is ripe for integration and attainment of a higher level of consciousness. Instead, Wayne is troubled and gets out of bed to hang upside down from his exercise equipment, like a bat. The experience has affected him, but has not altered him. Vale is an unsuccessful anima figure, then, because Wayne is successful at avoiding integration and maintaining his splintered personality. He is also preventing the individuation of Gotham City and therefore maintaining its persona-possessed psychosis.

"There's a 'Rosebud' to [Wayne's] character," explains Sam Hamm, the movie's principal scriptwriter, "and it erupts as 'Batman.' That is the psychological thrust of the plot" (de Vries, 1989, p. 19). Hamm's use of the verb "erupt" suggests Jung's belief that if the contents of the unconscious are actively ignored they will eventually rupture into consciousness. As discussed earlier, there are several possible results of this invasion of the contents of the unconscious into consciousness, one of which is schizophrenia. Jung defines the simplest form of schizophrenia, paranoia, as a "simple doubling of the personality"

(1983, p. 40). A schizophrenic may seem normal at one moment, displaying a socially acceptable persona, but may career into insanity a moment later:

> The patient strikes us at first as completely normal; he may hold office, be in a lucrative position, we suspect nothing. We converse normally with him, and at some point we let fall the word "Freemason." Suddenly the jovial face before us changes, a piercing look full of abysmal mistrust and inhuman fanaticism meets us from his eye. (Jung, 1983, p. 41)

For Wayne, the word probably would be "Joker," and not "Freemason," but otherwise the characterization seems consonant. Wayne is indeed "in a lucrative position," apparently holding untold wealth. Confronting the Joker in Vale's apartment he exhibits a particularly violent mood swing. He is reciting a short history of Jack Napier's life, his voice a studied calm. Suddenly, he explodes into a rage, smashes a vase, shouts "Let's get nuts," and brandishes a fireplace poker. Wayne/Batman represents the splintered Self of the schizophrenic. One of Wayne's two sides is socially acceptable and one is not; all of the most important people of Gotham attend Wayne's benefit party, but the *Gotham Globe* refers to Batman as a "winged freak." He actively cultivates this split between the accepted and the rejected aspects of his personality.

Bruce Wayne dons the Batsuit, always at night, to find his way (like a bat) through the dark, crime-ridden world of the repressed unconscious of Gotham City. In putting on the mask and cape, Wayne assumes the identity of an archetype—specifically, the shadow. This he must do, for to battle the Joker he must trod the Joker's turf. However, Batman's costume only empowers him as far down as the rooftops of the personal unconscious; he cannot plumb the depths of the collective because Batman is a denizen of Wayne's personal unconscious, not of the collective unconscious of Gotham. Before Batman fights Napier, Napier must climb up the stairs of the Axis chemical plant; before Batman fights the Joker, the Joker must climb the long flight of stairs inside the cathedral. Vale's penthouse apartment renders Wayne and the Joker equipotent to the extent that neither harms the other and equally impotent in that neither achieves his goal. But at the top of the cathedral, dressed in the Batsuit, Batman does gain the upper hand. He cannot fight the Joker at street level (when they meet in the street-level museum, Batman flees), but he can meet him on the rooftops and stop the Joker from ascending any higher. This is why Batman is unable to hit the Joker, standing in the middle of the street, with the laser-guided fire-power of his Batwing.

The Joker's culturally acceptable mask has been burned off and the archetypal grin of the shadow permanently etched into his face. Several times in the movie the Joker covers his white skin with flesh-tone makeup, but he cannot cover the grin. Unlike Batman, the Joker cannot re-enter the conscious realm simply by removing his mask. His bid to rise into consciousness, which began as he climbed up the stairs out of that darkened basement operating room, is doomed to failure. Batman *can* remove his mask, become Wayne again, and re-enter the conscious world. He assumes the identity of the archetype but does not fully *identify* with it; if he did he would be consumed (as the Joker was) and lose touch with consciousness.

Batman remains insane and disintegrated at the end. The Joker has been cast back into the collective unconscious with such force that he is actually embedded into the pavement. No hope for integration there. The final scenes show Alfred and Vale both separated from Batman, and both at the level of the street, while Batman gazes upward at the Batsignal from the rooftops of Gotham. He has successfully defended the high ground of consciousness but has sacrificed his psyche. Similarly, he has successfully saved the city from the Joker but has thwarted any chance of communal integration.

Implications

The fissured world of Gotham City requires a madman to keep the repressed contents of the collective unconscious from erupting into consciousness, and Wayne/Batman must protect his splintered psyche to maintain the psychosis of the city. He spurns the opportunity for integration presented by Vale, Alfred, and the Joker, and thus he retains his ability to become temporarily engulfed by the personal unconscious. He can meet the shadow halfway, and when the Joker attempts to erupt into consciousness, Batman can successfully drop him from the rooftops. It is ironic that the relationship between Batman and Gotham is such that the sanity of its savior would result in the destruction of the city and that the psychological growth of the city would mean the destruction of its hero. The Batsignal only works at night, and only against a cloudy sky; if Gotham's skies were to become clear and bright, not only would the city not *need* to invoke its savior, it *couldn't*. The film seems to imply, then, that a city like Gotham, which is unwilling to do the hard work of confronting the shadow that lurks in its darkest alleys, can maintain order only through the efforts of a lunatic.

Reading the cultural psyche from this dark and brooding film is tempting, and I will to some degree succumb to the temptation. Such a reading is not without risk, however, precisely because of the prodigious hype that presaged *Batman*'s release. Time-Warner, as Eileen

Meehan (1991) points out, is "the predominant media conglomerate in the world" and was in a unique position both to orchestrate and profit from a *Batman* fad: its holdings include DC Comics, where Batman was born in 1939, and the Warner Brothers film unit (p. 49). Meehan concedes, however, that "where people are the prime purchasers, revenues can not be completely shielded from the direct responses of consumers" (p. 60). Therefore, after the initial premiere, "the summer-long success of *Batman* at the box office would depend on the film itself, its ability to resonate with our experiences and visions, and to tap into the conflicting ideologies through which we make sense of social life" (p. 61). That *Batman* did remain successful for the remainder of the summer, eventually earned a total box office of nearly $300 million, and became one of the top five highest-grossing films of all time indicates that audiences were responding to more than Time-Warner's advertising campaign. As Jim Collins (1991) and John Parsons (1991) suggest, the film must connect with audiences at a deeper level than the political economist's thesis will allow.

As I stated earlier, there exists a growing body of rhetorical criticism that explores the psychological connection between film and society. These studies delineate a variety of ways in which contemporary film acquires rhetorical potency. Rushing & Frentz (1980) ascribe the rhetorical force of *The Deer Hunter* to its "aestheticizing of war as a universal ritual" (p. 405). By inviting the audience to perceive the Vietnam war as the arena for a generalized initiation rite, the politics of this specific war are mostly ignored and war itself may be valorized as a site of potential personal maturation. Solomon (1983) argues "that the rhetorical force of 'Chariots [of Fire]' derives from its manipulation and reaffirmation of both myths of the American Dream" (p. 275). These two myths, according to Fisher (1973), are rhetorically robust because they cohabit and define the American psyche. *The Wizard of Oz* (Payne, 1989) attains its rhetorical force through the enactment of a mythic maturation: "a rhetoric that orients and exhorts the audience toward particular values and behaviors" (p. 33). The rhetorical potency of *Batman*, I believe, emanates from a more subtle and intimate connection between artifact and audience.

I have suggested that "dialectical disorientation," which describes certain Vietnam films fracturing the warrior myth from within (Rasmussen & Downey, 1991), bears some resemblance to the destruction of the myth of the unified savior in *Batman*. The mechanism that amplifies the rhetorical impact of this film, however, is the scenic representation of the psyche itself. Davies et al. (1982) describe the Overlook Hotel as a representation of the psyche in their discussion of *The Shining*, but do not pursue the rhetorical implications: the projection onto the screen of the psyche of the audience provides a particularly potent opportunity for identification with the text. With Gotham City as psychic-scenic "container" and the archetypal images of Batman, Joker, Alfred, and Vale as mythic agents "contained," the audience is invited to experience the narrative as unfolding within the confines of their own heads. Rather than merely identifying with a character in the story and thereby projecting themselves into the film, the audience members may experience the film as a projection of themselves. Burke (1945, p. 7) reminds us that "there is implicit in the quality of a scene the quality of the action that is to take place within it," and that scene and agent enjoy a similarly "synecdochic relation." Because Gotham City is a projection of the psyche of the audience, the audience is disposed to experience Gotham's inhabitants as manifestations within that psyche. The rhetorical power of archetypal images is therefore enhanced in films like Batman that invite the audience to identify psyche as scene.

But Gotham City is persona-possessed, and the overwhelming enthusiasm with which audiences reacted not only to the movie but also to all the post-release Bat products suggests that audiences had little difficulty accepting such a persona-possessed world as a projection of their own psyches. This portrayal of the audience as psychotic would seem more likely to distress and alienate the masses than to enthrall them. After all, when the Joker urges Gotham to "Put on a happy face!" he is referring to the terrifying effects of paying too much attention to consciousness and not enough to the unconscious. Unless the encroaching collective shadow is confronted and accepted, the persona that has been the subject of so much care will be destroyed. Precisely because it does not allow competing myths to coexist, this stance is far more bleak than Rasmussen and Downey's "dialectical disorientation." And, replacing the unified savior with a schizophrenic vigilante may be more disturbing than failing to replace it at all. Rather than to account for the film's success, then, this reading of Batman seems to outline a formula for box-office failure.

Batman was a success because there is a comforting difference between Gotham City and the psyche it represents: Gotham has its Batman. At the end of the movie, during that peculiar nighttime news conference, Harvey Dent reads a letter from Gotham's newborn savior. In it, Batman promises that "if the forces of evil should rise again to cast a shadow on the heart of the city," the people of Gotham need merely shine the golden Bat-mandala into the night sky and he will duly knock the shadows back into the abyss. Gotham will never have to change, never have to give up the persona it has been frantically working to build, never have to do the hard work of facing the contents of its unconscious, as long as Batman is only a light-switch away. But within those of us on this side of the screen, there is no Batman. There is no one to save us from the shadows that are threatening to erupt into our consciousness at every turn. The many woes of the postmodern age threaten to overflow the distant landfills of our collective unconscious and overwhelm us, disintegrating the image we have so carefully crafted. This is a frightening thing indeed—frightening, at least, until we experience Gotham's psyche as a projection of our own and thus Batman as within ourselves. Perhaps the movie was so popular because it offers an attractive, if Faustian, bargain: if we accept ourselves as terminally unbalanced, psychologically disintegrated individuals, then we can happily and indefinitely continue to build our personas, repress our shadows, and avoid the hard work that psychic maturity demands. We, like the citizens of Gotham, can comfortably drift off into an empty, dreamless sleep.

References

Barol, B. (1989, June 26). Batmania: A summer struggle for the dark soul of a mythic American hero—and a boom in bat-products [Rev. of *Batman*]. *Newsweek* pp. 70–74.

Batman busters [Editorial]. (1989, June 30). *New York Times*, sec. 1, p. 28.

Batman continues to dominate movie box office. (1989, July 4). *New York Times*, sec. 3, p. 14.

The batmogul and the abyss. (1989, August 26). [Rev. of *Batman*]. *The Economist*, p. 73.

Billson, A. (1991, July 26). Blade runner [Rev. of *Edward Scissorhands*]. *New Statesman & Society*, p. 32.

Bingham, P. & Hoffman, B. J. (1989, July). The batmobile. *Motor Trend*, pp. 56–58.

Burke, K. (1945). *A grammar of motives*. New York: Prentice-Hall.

Collins, J. (1991). Batman: The movie, Narrative: The hyperconscious. In R. E. Pearson & W. Uricchio (Eds.), *The many lives of the Batman* (pp. 164–181). New York: Routledge.

Davies, R. A, Farrell, J. M., & Matthews, S. S. (1983). The dream world of film: A Jungian perspective on cinematic communication. *Western Journal of Speech Communication*, 46, 326–343.

de Vries, H. (1989, February 5). *Batman* battles for big money. *New York Times*, sec. 2, pp. 11, 19.

Fisher, W. R. (1973). Reaffirmation and subversion of the American dream. *Quarterly Journal of Speech*, 59, 160–167.

Jung, C. G. (1959a). *Collected works of C. G. Jung, Vol. 9, Pt. 1: The archetypes and the collective unconscious*. H. Read, M. Fordham, & G. Adler (Eds.) and R. F. C. Hull (Trans.). Princeton: Princeton University Press.

Jung, C. G. (1959b). *Collected works of C. G. Jung, Vol. 9, Pt. 2: Aion, researches into the phenomenology of the self*. H. Read, M. Fordham, & G. Adler (Eds.) and R. F. C. Hull (Trans.). Princeton: Princeton University Press.

Jung, C. G. (1959c). Flying saucers: A modern myth. In H. Read, M. Fordham, & C. Adler (Eds.) and R. F. C. Hull (Trans.), *Collected works of C. G. Jung, Vol. 10: Civilization in Transition* (pp. 309–433). Princeton: Princeton University Press.

Jung, C. G. (1971). *The portable Jung* (J. Campbell, Ed.). New York: Viking Penguin. (Original works published 1927–1951).

Jung, C. G. (1983). *The essential Jung* (A. Storr, Ed.). Princeton: Princeton University Press. (Original works published 1927–1951).

Kael, P. (1989, July). The current cinema: The city gone psycho [Rev. of *Batman*]. *The New Yorker*, pp. 83–85.

Lauter, E. (1984). *Women as mythmakers: Poetry and visual art by twentieth-century women.* Bloomington: Indiana University Press.

Meehan, E. R. (1991). "Holy commodity fetish, Batman!": The political economy of a commercial intertext. In R. E. Pearson & W. Uricchio (Eds.), *The many lives of the Batman* (pp. 47–65). New York: Routledge.

Nightingale, B. (1989, June 18). Batman prowls a Gotham drawn from the absurd. *New York Times*, sec. 2, p. 1.

Parsons, P. (1991). Batman and his audience: The dialectic of a culture. In R. E. Pearson & W. Uricchio (Eds.), *The many lives of the Batman* (pp. 47–65). New York: Routledge.

Payne, D. (1989). *The Wizard of Oz*: Therapeutic rhetoric in a contemporary media ritual. *Quarterly Journal of Speech, 75,* 25–39.

Rasmussen, K. & Downey, S. D. (1989). Dialectical disorientation in *Agnes of God. Western Journal of Speech Communication, 53,* 66–84.

Rasmussen, K. & Downey, S. D. (1991). Dialectical disorientation in Vietnam war films: Subversion of the mythology of war. *Quarterly Journal of Speech, 77,* 176–195.

Rushing, J. H. & Frentz, T. S. (1980). "The Deer Hunter": Rhetoric of the warrior. *Quarterly Journal of Speech, 66,* 392–406.

Solomon, M. (1989). Villainless quest: Myth, metaphor, and dream in "Chariots of Fire." *Communication Quarterly, 31,* 274–281.

Wehr, D. S. (1987). *Jung & feminism: Liberating archetypes.* Boston: Beacon Press.

Whitmont, E. C. (1969). *The symbolic quest: Basic concepts of analytical psychology.* Princeton: Princeton University Press.

Young-Eisendrath, P. & Wiedemann, F. (1987). *Female authority: Empowering women through psychotherapy.* New York: Guilford Press.

The Rhetorical Construction of Institutional Authority in a Senate Subcommittee Hearing on Wilderness Legislation

Tarla Rai Peterson

Research on organizational culture focuses attention on the symbolic processes through which social reality is created and sustained within various institutional structures (Conrad, 1985; McPhee and Tompkins, 1985; Pacanowsky and O'Donnell-Trujillo, 1983; Pondy, Frost, Morgan, & Dandridge, 1983; Putnam and Pacanowsky, 1983). Although this research enables us to view "organization" as a form of human expression rather than as an instrument or mechanism (Smircich, 1983), it has rarely focused on the dynamic interplay between participants' assumptions and their symbolic enactments. Structuration theory, which focuses on understanding human agency as it interacts with social institutions, offers such an approach (Giddens, 1979; 1984, p. xvii, pp. 1-9). Giddens (1984) claims that actors constantly recreate structures of signification, domination, and legitimization. Organizations construct structural properties rather than *have* structures, and "structure" arises from resources recursively implicated in social reproduction. These resources are of two kinds: authoritative ones derive from coordinating the activity of human agents, and allocative structures derive from control of material objects. Organizational stability depends upon the mobilization of both (pp. 31-33; 258-262). Riley (1983) demonstrates the potential value of studying structuration in her analysis of symbol systems that constitute both authoritative and allocative structures of signification, legitimization, and domination.

In this essay I argue that rhetorical strategies provide organizational participants with a comprehensive means of mobilizing authoritative resources. These strategies enable human agents to draw upon structural properties that constitute relations of domination. Giddens (1984) argues

From *Western Journal of Speech Communication*, 52 (Fall 1988), 259-76. Used by permission of the Western States Communication Association and the author.

that "we should not conceive of the structures of domination built into social institutions as in some way grinding out 'docile bodies' who behave like automata. . . ." Even as social systems presume relations of autonomy and dependence between actors, they also "offer some resources whereby those who are subordinate can influence the activities of their superiors. This is what I call the *dialectic of control* . . ." (p. 16). By focusing on rhetorical strategies used to mobilize resources of authority it is possible to explore Giddens' dialectic of control.

I examined discourse from a Senate subcommittee hearing in order to explore this routine constitution of institutional authority. The analysis revealed three major communicative strategies that participants in the hearing used to reproduce authority: position markers, pseudo-requests, and images of order. These strategies were recurrently enacted through a number of tactics. Use of these strategies both reconfirmed hierarchical domination and contributed to the success or failure of individual participants. Ironically, one participant's alienation and resulting "failure" to achieve his goals further legitimized structures of domination in both the subcommittee hearing and the social system which constituted its context.

Studying the relationship between rhetorical strategies and authority means examining how discourse produces and reproduces hierarchy. As Burke (1969) has argued, hierarchic mystery is grounded in the nature of language and reinforced by social institutions (pp. 141, 279). He presumes that the hierarchic principle is inevitable, but not that any specific hierarchy is inherently preferable. Riley (1983) points out that symbolic systems create and reproduce organizational structure, and are constrained by that structure (see also Giddens, 1979, pp. 69–95; Giddens, 1984, pp. 179–180, 199–206). The rhetorical configuration of hierarchy is fundamental to an organization's structure of authority.

For purposes of this essay, authority is considered a property of symbol systems that is created through discursive transactions (Burke, 1959, pp. 329–336; Sennett 1980; Winch, 1986). My purpose is to explain how discourse in a Senate subcommittee hearing continually reproduced configurations of meaning that constituted authority.

The Strategic Construction of Authority

Text for Analysis

The Senate hearing occurred in the Subcommittee on Public Lands and Reserved Water of the Committee on Energy and Natural Resources. The proposed bill (S 842) was presented to the first session of the 97th

Congress, and was discussed in committee on April 22, April 23, and June 17, 1981. It would have released for nonwilderness use certain lands studied for possible wilderness designation. The bill represented a reaction against the 96th Congress, which had allocated huge acreages of new wilderness in 1980. Senators from several Western states, who wanted a final deposition of lands studied for possible wilderness designation, co-sponsored the bill. It failed to pass, however, and after more than twenty years of studies and numerous congressional hearings, the fate of much of this land still remains undecided.

The hearing drew representatives from most major corporations interested in primary resource use such as oil, timber, and gas companies. Conservation groups such as Audubon, Sierra, and the Wilderness Society also sent representatives. Thus, some panels supported commercial use, others preservation. The committee chair, McClure (of Idaho), co-sponsored the bill, while the subcommittee chair, Wallop (of Wyoming), was technically neutral. Both represented states with land under consideration in this bill. Other participants represented groups that either supported or opposed the bill. This analysis focuses on interactions between the two chairs and the two most vocal opponents. Rupert Cutler, who represented the National Audubon Society, had served as Assistant Secretary of Agriculture in the Carter administration. William Turnage represented the Wilderness Society and had held no analogous political positions.

I selected this discourse for three reasons. First, a hearing provides an opportunity for groups to frame a situation around their own interests. Thus, subcultures of self-interest emerging as political undercurrents in any organization assume paramount significance. Political performances socially reaffirm hierarchy, maintaining the authority's "right" to control and other members' "duty" to comply (Trujillo, 1985, pp. 208–210). Although publicizing their groups' views was the panelists' avowed purpose, a more basic goal also existed. The sponsor and those representing groups favoring the bill obviously wanted it passed, whereas those panelists representing groups opposing the bill wanted it to fail. To these ends, participants attempted to influence each other to adopt, or at least validate, their opposing points of view. Thus, this incident provides a context which brings competing interests explicitly into focus.

Second, conservation is an increasingly volatile political issue that speech communication researchers have largely ignored (exceptions include Oravec, 1981, 1984; and Peterson, 1986). Preservationism has traditionally generated dramatic social controversy, and environmental impact must now be explained and justified by organizations promoting agricultural, recreational, retail, manufacturing, social and other goals. Oravec (1984) argues that "to advocate a policy of preservationism was to espouse . . . radically un-American values in form and content to the public view" (pp. 454–455; see also Worster, 1979). Wilderness designation, the topic considered during this hearing, promotes intense conflict, for in preferring wilderness one implies its superiority over the fruits of progressive democracy. Thus, analysis of the language used by participants in the hearings focuses attention on the negotiation of authority when symbolic hierarchies clash.

My third reason for selecting this discourse is to respond to Deetz and Kersten's (1983) suggestion that it is valuable to explore organizational communication "in the context of society as a whole" rather than limiting analysis to specific organizations or organizational types. Organizations should be critically examined in their role as part of total social development (pp. 154–155). The hearing's fluid nature facilitates such an interactive focus. For example, participants attempted to justify otherwise incongruous behavior by explicitly referring to outside affiliations. In fact, those affiliations justified most members' very presence. Thus, simultaneous membership in multiple organizations, some of which have conflicting goals, became an important factor in the dynamics of these Senate hearings.

Rhetorical Strategies

Participants in the hearing consistently used three rhetorical strategies to mystify institutional authority: *position markers, pseudo-requests*, and *images of order*. These legitimization strategies were enacted through several tactics and were rarely performed separately. Typically, individual utterances served multiple functions simultaneously. For example, when Wallop asked if panelists "could tone down your overreaction," he was using a position marker by asserting his right to determine appropriate behavior for others, a pseudo-request by commanding people to act without overtly stating the command, and an image of order that signaled an institutional preoccupation with stability and calm. These strategies created a supportive atmosphere for institutional authority by inviting people to affirm the principles of faith on which organizational hierarchy depends.

Position Markers

Giddens (1984) claims that "social identities, and the position-practice relations associated with them . . . are associated with normative rights, obligations and sanctions which, within specific collectivities, form roles" (p. 282). Participants in the hearing strategically used these markers to contextualize themselves within the system. Position markers labeled people both according to their insider/outsider status and according to their hierarchical level within the organization.

Direct Naming.   Name conventions provide organizational members an opportunity to demonstrate their assessment of both interpersonal relationships and the formality of the situation (Fowler & Kress, 1979a, p. 200). The hearing's relative formality required that all members be referred to by title plus last name. Hierarchical divisions were articulated despite this limitation, for the two senators referred to each other as "Mr. Chairman," doubling the use of title and deleting the personal name. When referring to other participants they (and everyone else) used a single title with a personal name. Although other participants referred to each other by name, they never directly addressed either chair. Such routinized avoidance further reified implicit assumptions regarding hierarchical division. Authority gains legitimacy by representing hierarchical perfection, or the culmination of hierarchic principles (Burke, 1969, p. 141). Names of "perfect" persons or concepts (such as deity) are inappropriate for casual conversation. Participants in the hearing helped shroud organizational leaders in mystery by offering them the respect traditionally reserved for perfection.

Special Vocabularies.   Participants unobtrusively vested the hearing with additional mystery by calling the proposed bill "S 842" and referring to the Second Roadless Area Review and Evaluation report as "RARE II." This marked them as insiders, for presumably one does not use an abbreviation unless one is familiar with the term and uses it often enough that an abbreviation provides utility or efficiency. Evered (1983) points out that "in" words not only differentiate a group from other groups but also mark the status or role of group members. Relabeling therefore manifests control through one-way flow of knowledge whereby insiders can decide whether to pass information on to outsiders. Fowler and Kress (1979b, p. 33) claim that such control is more powerful than that exercised in commands, for one cannot evade a new terminology without withdrawal.

Members also teach and learn from each other the vocabulary needed to behave as competent organizational participants. Senator Wallop illustrated the teaching role's potential for control when utilizing the abbreviation "CRS." At first, he simply said:

> According to a preliminary report from the Congressional Research Service . . . (S 842, p. 66)

Next, he asked:

> This is a CRS figure that you're quoting. Congressional Research Service? (S 842, p. 66)

Finally, he used only the abbreviation:

> . . . well, the CRS report says despite industrial urging . . . (S 842,
> p. 67)

Wallop provided an opportunity for panelists new to the organization to learn some organizational jargon, a skill that enabled them more completely to embody elements of hierarchical perfection.

Teaching presupposes a knower of appropriate behavior who must transmit knowledge to others. By acting as an organizational mouthpiece, Wallop further legitimized his own authority as subcommittee chair. Accepting such knowledge constitutes agreement with hierarchical role-relationships. Teacher/student transactions reify organizational hierarchy by emphasizing its accessibility. Teaching directs attention to the smooth operation of organizational rules and away from questions regarding their appropriateness. Since it provides subordinates with ample opportunity to learn proper behaviors, those who choose not to so behave must bear the guilt for their resulting alienation.

Displays of Deference. Participants also directly marked themselves as subordinate. For example, Wallop's authority was substantiated each time panelists began speaking. Although participants were neither physically restrained nor called out of order for speaking without Wallop's recognition, their language demonstrated cognizance that such behavior was unacceptable. During a relatively informal inquiry a person whom Wallop had not formally recognized entered the discussion. Although his statement was completely topical, he apologized for his intrusion: "Along that line, it is too bad we cannot explore in the wilderness area. Pardon me, my name is Neal Williams, . . ." (S 842, p. 136). In another instance, Turnage attempted to legitimize unauthorized entrance into the interrogation of Cutler with: "I'd like to respond to that" (S 842, p. 127). Such displays of deference toward Wallop identified the new speaker as a legitimate participant in organizational hierarchy. They provided panelists with a structure within which they could circumvent convention without endangering hierarchical relations.

Transcendent Positions. Organizational leaders also emphasized their ability to transcend individual agendas. Their transcendent positions were created by an illusion of independence, or "a strength of calmness and above-the-storm which [made] telling others what to do seem natural" (Sennett, 1980, p. 86). They saw beyond the immediate scene, because their thinking was uncontaminated by sectional interests. McClure used his roles as Senator and chair of the larger Committee on Energy and Natural Resources to help create this image. For example, he emphasized his position as representative of a unit which had greater institutional legitimacy than any panel at the hearing when saying, "I go into my State . . ." (S 842, p. 124). Relabeling Idaho as "my State" contextualized McClure among both people and environmental resources dependent on this bill.

McClure's situational power supported attempts to negotiate with Cutler, a vice president for the National Audubon Society, as illustrated in the following interaction:

McClure: As I recall our conversations in your earlier—you suggested that RARE II was designed to bring about a final solution and as I recall those conversations when I was defending you against the forest industry—

Cutler: I appreciated it.

McClure: I thought you needed it. But you were suggesting that we'll get the RARE II done and then we'll come to a final conclusion of this issue . . . (S 842, p. 121)

McClure could have much more efficiently moved directly from "RARE II was designed to bring about a final solution" (in his first utterance), to "of this issue" (in the second utterance); resulting in the following sentence: "RARE II was designed to bring about a final solution of this issue." However, the insertion created a display of obligation reminding Cutler that he owed McClure a favor and was relatively powerless in the current situation. This position marker sequence could also be interpreted as an attempt to begin the process of building an unlikely alliance through the reminder that Cutler and McClure had a common purpose transcending this particular hearing.

Cutler's acquiescence to existing authority structures translated into acceptable negotiation strategies. Although he opposed the bill, Dr. Cutler was a professional forester who had served as Assistant Secretary of Agriculture under the Carter administration. He unobtrusively called attention to his status by prefacing answers with indirect references to his recognized environmental expertise and experience such as, "When I testified before this committee in my previous incarnation on the subject . . ." (S 842, p. 122). He suggested the value of his recommendation by beginning another answer with, "I will recommend to the committee a document . . ." (S 842, p. 124).

These strategies adjusted thematic priorities, contextualizing Cutler more deeply in organizational functions. He obscured conflicts between his current position and those of the committee chairs by emphasizing his historical involvement in environmental politics. For example, rather than responding to questions by referring directly to S 842, Cutler focused on the ongoing RARE II process. Affiliations outside the context of this hearing led Senator McClure and Dr. Cutler to use the same strategy to accomplish different goals. McClure's discourse presented

S 842 as a transcendent solution to a problematic situation, whereas Cutler's discourse presented the bill as a simplistic response to a transcendent process.

Pseudo-Requests

Transactions involving pseudo-requests, or unobtrusive commands, also contributed to the construction of institutional authority. Pseudo-requests perpetuate institutional domination because they are predicated on the myth of autonomy. Sennett (1980) argues that "autonomy removes the necessity of dealing with other people openly and mutually. There is an imbalance" (p. 86). Autonomous authorities need no justificatory grounds, for they simply have the right to command others. By making and responding to pseudo-requests, participants treated the subcommittee system as a "real" order of relationships. Such transactions are intimately linked to authority, for accepting an organizational hierarchy as "real" constitutes its foundation as an expression of domination.

Turn Taking Behaviors. Pfeffer (1982) claims that groups pressure individuals to conform to central attitudes in return for acceptance into the group. To the extent that organizational members accept organizational premises and customs, they are socialized to accept the reigning authority structure. Senator Wallop eased this process through the nature of his turn taking assignments. He phrased orders to begin speaking as questions, and orders to stop speaking as ritualized thanks. For example, "Thank you, Mr. Maddock. And Mr. Craine, if you're ready, please proceed with your statement" (S 842, p. 60). When a new panel began speaking Wallop greeted panel members with statements such as:

> The next panel is. . . Would you proceed, Mr. Cutler? (S 842, p. 70)
>
> Welcome. It's nice to see you. I would ask you to proceed . . . (S 842, p. 130)

And the properly enculturated members immediately did so. These polite commands painlessly inculcated the principle of obedience into organization members' behavior. Since Wallop commanded them to do that which they wished, obedience occurred almost automatically. Wallop also reified his own authority each time he assigned a panelist to speak. His use of pseudo-requests to determine who spoke at what time accentuated his controlling role in the proceedings.

Polite Reproval. Wallop's unusual transition at the conclusion of Cutler's testimony illustrates variation within strategies. Cutler had presented a lengthy testimony on behalf of the National Audubon Society after all panelists had been requested to keep their oral remarks as brief as possible. Wallop handled the changeover as follows:

> Thank you Mr. Cutler. I would remind the remaining witnesses on this panel that others have seen fit to summarize their statements and there are a lot of people. I think it is only fair to indulge in the same summary as those who preceded you went through. So with that, will Mr. Turnage please proceed. (S 842, p. 86)

This pseudo-request preserved and emphasized hierarchic distinction between Wallop and Cutler, as well as between Wallop and other panelists. Rather than "telling" future presenters anything, Wallop simply "reminded" them of facts. Instead of referring to requests for brevity, he stated that given these facts, "others have seen fit to" behave appropriately. Thus, he represented their actions as resulting from individual choice. Appeals to abstract values such as fairness further justified his remarks.

Wallop's depersonalized scolding technique and his demonstrated ability to make a total judgment of members' actions helped constitute and represent his autonomous authority. His structural power as subcommittee chair contributed to his success in using such implied commands, and panelists' prompt acquiescence further legitimized existing structure. Thus, polite transactions, rather than any individual's utterances, reinforced system constraints (Goffman, 1981, p. 25).

Information Probes.   Wallop's position also facilitated other indirect commands, as illustrated when he asked, "I wonder if you could comment on the legitimacy of their position" (S 840, p. 127). The first panelist to reply indicated acceptance of this pseudo-request as a command by commenting on his understanding of that position. Hodge and Fowler (1979, pp. 17–21) claim that requests that delete the command form mystify control:

> Anyone who can give orders without even acknowledging this in the surface of his utterance has access to an insidiously powerful form of command. The person who obeys accepts the reality of a power that has not been claimed, which has been completely mystified into the form of an apparently neutral, factual observation. (p. 18)

Both McClure's and Wallop's commands perpetuated internally inconsistent power relationships through such obfuscation.

Senator McClure also displayed personal power when requesting information. Jacobs and Jackson (1983) state that "relations of authority and obligation between speaker and hearer . . . may be so obvious as to establish strong pre-set expectations that a request is or is not intended" (p. 289). McClure's status as committee chair encouraged pseudo-quests to function as commands in several situations. In one instance he said, "If you'd like to submit it for the record later, I would appreciate having it" (S 842, p. 126). This "request" was taken as a command to submit information.

Another example comes from an exchange between Senators McClure and Wallop:

> McClure: . . . and again I hope, Mr. Chairman, we can get that for the record.
>
> Wallop: I'll direct the staff to supply that. (S 842, p. 126)

This exchange furthered hierarchical domination. When McClure commanded Wallop to procure information he indicated respect by naming him. Although direct naming by subordinates might indicate undesirable familiarity between hierarchical levels, direct naming by one's superior offers the potential for personal affirmation through closer identification with organizational structure. The doubled title used to address Wallop further contextualized him, for his name's meaning depended completely on organizational existence.

Wallop's reply to this command obscured hierarchical contradictions, for while assuring McClure that the information he sought would be obtained, Wallop separated himself from that subservient task by depersonalization. He created the illusion of self control by transforming the proscribed behavior into another party's action. Distinctions were additionally obscured by labeling that party as the faceless "staff." Wallop further attenuated his potential action by distancing himself from the staff's future act. Rather than ensuring that it would supply the information, he would simply "direct" it to do so. Thus, Wallop and McClure cooperatively structured command/response strategies that constituted and represented organizational hierarchy.

Images of Order

Farrell (1982) argues that "the whole point of authority has always been to overcome, to transcend, to 'stop' history" (p. 139). Giddens (1984) adds that "in the enactment of routines agents sustain a sense of ontological security" (p. 282). As an interpretative process that disguises power as stability and order, authority is founded on the illusion that such an existence is possible (Sennett, 1980, pp. 18–20, p. 104). Senators McClure and Wallop used the root metaphor of "order" or "stability" to legitimize authority, suggesting "order" as a means of transcending individual versions of perfection (for a discussion of root metaphor see Pepper, 1982).

Lakoff and Johnson (1981) claim that metaphors define reality by highlighting some features and hiding others. When accepting a metaphor, one chooses to focus on those aspects of reality it highlights (p. 322). Burke (1984, pp. 255–261) argues that metaphor provides resources whereby people are labeled and hierarchically positioned. While metaphors suggest ways of acting, they also eliminate the legitimacy of other actions (Deetz & Mumby, 1985; Smith and Eisenberg, 1987). Sennett (1980, p. 80) adds that metaphor simplifies complexity.

Unobtrusive Images of Domination. Senator McClure's pronoun usage deemphasized his individuality, emphasizing instead his paternalistic role as a facilitator. Sennett (1981) defines paternalism as "power exercised for the good of others. . . . The care of others is the authority's gift" (p. 84). McClure used utterances beginning with the word "I" for supportive statements such as "I understand," and he rarely expressed disagreement with the referent "I." He also responded positively to differing opinions with statements such as: "That is really what we're trying to do in legislation here" (S 842, p. 124). This usage exemplified what Fowler and Kress (1979a, p. 203) call "the most threatening form" of the inclusive pronoun, wherein a single voice "speaking for a large group is fused with the power-laden 'we' in the pronouncements of those with state-power." McClure invited others to participate in hierarchical legitimization by joining in the corporate "we."

The committee chair assiduously avoided the individualizing "I" when disagreeing. His strongest opening disagreement was phrased as: "Not necessarily so" (S 842, p. 125). This contrasts sharply with opening disagreements made by others. For example, Wallop said, "I would take some exception to that" (S 842, p. 124). Cutler registered his disagreement with "I don't think that . . ." (S 842, p. 127). These statements still display tactful disagreement. However, Turnage, who ultimately became alienated from other participants, typically began his utterances with direct disagreements. Thus, strategic pronoun usage validated the metaphor of domination by presenting McClure as an authority figure who ruled in order to serve.

After members of the second panel had presented their statements, McClure structurally insinuated his role as an appropriate arbitrator for the two opposing platforms with such utterances as: "Sometimes I despair at the polarization. . . . The truth lies somewhere between. . . . Perhaps you're right" (S 842, p. 121). His attempts to structure alliances among members provided them an opportunity to transcend individual differences by identifying as a group with organizational goals. Sennett (1980, pp. 78–79) claims that the emotional unity achieved by such unobtrusive domination enables authority figures to influence organization members by defining a "comforting image of strength"

(p. 19). Conrad and Ryan (1985) add that, when persons "manipulate the meaning of action, they can manipulate the identities of other humans. If they can manipulate identities, they can control the power and solidarity of others" (p. 247). Thus McClure's claims that he understands opposing points of view, as well as his compromise suggestions, legitimized organizational hierarchy by proposing solutions to all potential conflict from within the existing framework.

Images of Order Through Cooperation.   Both McClure and Wallop used "horse" metaphors to describe opponents' unruly behavior. When Turnage, executive director of the Wilderness Society, claimed that legislation might be needed in the future, but not currently, McClure replied, "You know, lock the barn door after the horse is out. This horse has been trying to get out for 16 years" (S 842, p. 128). After questioning members of the panel representing groups formally opposed to the bill, Wallop pleaded, "It would be my hope that you would as the panel before you and anybody else that is going to testify, climb off the high horses and see if there isn't some way to resolve this" (S 842, p. 130). McClure's and Wallop's metaphors relabeled those opposing the bill, creating a simplistic dichotomy between those who cooperate with human efforts to control a headstrong animal and those who identify with the animal. McClure's metaphorical construction emphasized the bill's value as a controlling measure. Wallop focused on panelists presenting arguments opposing the bill who rode "high horses" and encouraged disarray of hierarchical relationships. Their illegitimate behavior threatened existing order, the destruction of which would be chaotic and generally detrimental to all members (Burke, 1984; Deetz & Kersten, 1983, pp. 163–165).

Wallop further illustrated metaphorical simplification when he dramatized the hearing as a choreographed activity in which all players must participate:

> Part of the problem appears to be that both sides come at this thing from rather extreme perspectives. Somehow or other, we have to dance around in the middle and try to put some reason on what we heard from both sides. Part of the problem appears to be that there is a perceived challenge to everything. (S 842, p. 127)

The dance metaphor suggests stylized cooperative action as a means of resolving the dispute. Dancers must perform the appropriate movements as determined by the leader. The inclusive "we" in Wallop's pseudo-request strengthened this attempt at hierarchical validation by implicating listeners in the content of Wallop's discourse, thus increasing the potential for intimacy and solidarity (Fowler & Kress, 1979a, p. 202).

The dance metaphor provides a perspective for mystifying principles underlying organizational hierarchy. Such mystification reverses values, celebrating the skill with which participants perform subordinate roles: those who dance well are rewarded, and moderation is strongly preferred. Thus subordinates' actions are ennobled by showing that in their subordination to hierarchical principles they become equal to the elite, who are powerful only because they too subordinate themselves to those same principles (Burke, 1957, pp. 422–424). This inversion provides an ironic equality across organizational levels, while confirming the "naturalness" of existing hierarchical division. In presenting the hearing as a dance, Wallop intimated that those who chose not to follow his commands were engaged in self-destruction, for they threatened the very existence of a hearing which provided the sole medium through which their goals could be achieved. Ultimately, Wallop's request invited a feeling of communion among participants. Those who retained their group identification confirmed the hierarchy's sanctity by acquiescing to such requests from its leaders.

When Strategies Fail: Alienation Through Rejection

Position Markers that Failed

Turnage, who represented the Wilderness Society, chose to rebel against both Wallop's and McClure's authority. This led to certain unintended consequences. The relative failure of his attempts to mark himself as a powerful player emphasizes how rhetorical structuration is context dependent. Turnage followed McClure's lead in attempting to enhance personal power by using pronouns emphasizing his representative role. When either "I" or "we" would have been equally appropriate he employed "we" far more often than did other participants. For example, he answered questions with statements such as:

> What we're saying here is that we don't think this legislation is necessary. (S 842, p. 127)
>
> We have a very deep stake in resolving this issue. (S 842, p. 129)
>
> What we're saying is that we don't believe we need legislation to resolve it. . . . We believe the process is working. (S 842, p. 129)

Cutler responded to similar questions with answers such as:

> I still believe that if we proceed . . . [we will] be pretty well complete. (S 842, p. 121)
>
> I still have reservations about it. (S 842, p. 123)

I don't think that, see that an emergency exists. (S 842, p. 124)

I feel somewhat differently about it. (S 842, p. 125)

Fowler and Kress (1979a, p. 202) argue that because the inclusive "we" implicates addressees in the content of discourse it is potentially "more intimate and solidary" than the singular form, or "I." But Turnage's status as an outsider, as well as his rejection of enculturation attempts, negated the potential impact of this strategy.

Turnage also attempted to invoke power as an official representative of a large group of people, claiming:

I have to think about my job here . . . I think I would probably be able to retain my job if we agreed on legislation that . . . made permanent wilderness out of all the wilderness and future planning areas. (S 842, p. 129)

However, Turnage's situational power did not support this appeal. In a Senate hearing, the Wilderness Society does not share equivalent legitimacy with any of the fifty states, and the agreement he suggested was so unacceptable that his group was further delegitimized.

Rejecting Pseudo-Requests

Interactions such as the following between Senator McClure and Turnage communicated the expectation that participants would learn and conform to organizational goals:

McClure: You didn't make a very balanced offer.

Turnage: Well, it's the beginning of a negotiation.

McClure: I understand too that you get organization memberships by protecting people against things and not by agreeing. (S 842, p. 129)

McClure's pseudo-request implied that within the context of this hearing, legitimate offers must be "balanced." The emphasis on balance further sustains organizational preoccupation with stability, for unbalanced structures tend to topple.

McClure's request also illustrates the power of non-commands. He could have said, "I command you to make a more balanced offer." However, his pseudo-request more effectively supported hierarchical relationships. The command structure left Turnage two choices. He could have flagrantly disobeyed a respected leader, or he could have obeyed a non-command. Such obedience insidiously reifies organizational hierarchy, for the obedient member essentially offers a leader control which s/he has not requested. When Turnage resisted this enculturation attempt, McClure directly attacked his identification as a legitimate hearing participant by accusing him of using the hearing to build a competing organization. Thus, Turnage was accused of entertaining motives that ran counter to the organizational goal of deciding whether the proposed bill was needed and beneficial.

Pseudo-Requests as Position Markers

Turnage's attempt to justify otherwise unacceptable behavior as responsible leadership failed, partially because it dramatized his "outsider" status. By emphasizing precommitment to a separate organizational hierarchy, Turnage exposed himself to accusations that he was motivated by inappropriate organizational goals and that this conflict of interest prevented his cooperation. Turnage attempted to realign the perception of his motives by emphasizing that he (like all Americans) wanted to buy a house, which led him to understand timber harvesters. Senator Wallop's reply to this realignment attempt further emphasized his authority as autonomous observer:

> In line with that statement, let me say this. That if you say S 842 is an overreaction, perhaps you all at this table could tone down your overreaction and we could settle the business and get on with what you just said. All of us have a big stake. (S 842, p. 129)

Wallop thus relabeled the hearing as "business" that can be settled only by the group as a whole. The single hindrance to group process came when individuals overreacted, preventing reasonable solutions. Wallop's own pseudo-request, his interaction with McClure, and other members' responses to his commands, created an image of an autonomous authority who capably judges all organizational behavior. This image legitimized the implied threat of alienation for Turnage and anyone else who "overreacts," while the implied threat further reified Wallop's authority as subcommittee chair. Wallop's pronoun usage further dramatized the potential for alienation. Those who overreacted were separated from the group by the referent "you," while those who could "settle the business" were joined with the corporate "we."

Rejecting Images of Order

Turnage undermined his group identification by additional unenculturated displays. For example, rather than accepting Wallop's invitation to become a cooperative group member he replied, "I will absolutely promise to drop the rhetoric and not any longer overreact if you will agree to drop the bill" (S 842, p. 129). At this point, Turnage had destroyed his own credibility. His alienation was emphasized by

Wallop's denigrating reply: "I mean lets [sic] do be serious about this" (S 842, p. 129). When a person is unable to accept the reasonableness of the reigning authority, that individual is threatened with alienation, or "driven into a corner" (Burke, 1959, pp. 216–224). Turnage ignored several cues suggesting that his behavior violated organizational norms. As a guest, Turnage was *allowed* to present his views. When he refused to participate cooperatively in the constitution of authority, his presence became undesirable.

Wallop further characterized Turnage as a disorderly member when responding to Turnage's offer "to drop the rhetoric . . . if you will agree to drop the bill." Wallop stated, "I have no position on this bill right now, one way or the other, but I'm inclined to take one when I see people getting on the outside edges and hammering on it as though there were no reasonable process" (S 842, p. 129). Turnage's reply to this threat contained the first (and only) direct gesture of agreement he made during the entire proceedings: "I agree absolutely" (S 842, p. 129).

Turnage's threat to organizational stability may have invited this uncharacteristically hostile statement. By refusing to follow the organization's guide for conduct, Turnage raised the spectre of an alternate course of action, which violated the sanctity of the hearing. This complicated the process of justifying the group's existence and disproportionate power in the social community. Complicating the group's agenda threatened its symbols of authority, for their very existence depends on the perception that the hearing simplifies complexity. Thus, in becoming alienated from organizational hierarchy, Turnage directly threatened Wallop.

Turnage selected his problematic strategies for articulating disagreement from a variety of options. Cutler chose other options, and his disagreements with the bill were handled more smoothly. Cutler's ability and willingness to adapt to cultural norms facilitated dialogue. As a result, although he opposed the bill, more negotiation occurred between the chair and Cutler than between the chair and Turnage. Cutler's rhetorical strategies depersonalized his answers, mystifying the source of his authority. Significantly, the very strategies Cutler used for presenting disagreements while maintaining group identification perpetuated the system which necessitated their use. By agreeing to, and taking advantage of hierarchical relationships, he reconstituted their authority.

Turnage, on the other hand, used position markers to highlight his status in a marginal organization rather than to contextualize himself within the larger environmental planning community. He contributed to increased alienation by making pseudo-requests that further emphasized his outsider position. His refusal to comply with images of order suggested by McClure and Wallop created a hostile environment for his suggestions. As a fully enculturated member, Cutler retained his identification with both the Audubon Society and with organizational hierarchy, whereas Turnage was estranged from the hearing as well as from individual members. In this way, organizational constraint operated through Turnage's choice to emphasize his involvement in a separate organization rather than to contextualize himself within the hearing.

Conclusion

Analysis of this hearing has revealed three rhetorical strategies whereby participants constituted and legitimized institutional authority. Position markers enabled members to identify more closely within various organizational niches; pseudo-requests made by organizational leaders and followed by panelists reified hierarchical structure; and images of order enabled participants to redefine problematic contradictions within the hearing. These rhetorical strategies masked authority's coercive power by creating situations wherein subordinates voluntarily complied with their leaders. The dialectic of control operating throughout the hearing can be seen in the repertoire of tactics developed by participants to articulate structural dimensions and adapt that structure to their individual agendas. One panelist (Turnage) rejected these opportunities for identification and became alienated. His alienation did not result in freedom. Instead, his statements became instruments fashioned for use against organizational authority rather than contributing to constructive alternatives.

Although he rejected institutional authority, Turnage remained tied to its mystery. Mystification is grounded in the desire for simplification, and it enables participants to imagine the achievement of order and stability. McClure's and Wallop's rhetorical strategies invited panelists to join them in reproducing a hierarchical structure that would simplify complexity, provide efficiency, and create order out of chaos. To the extent that panelists accepted this invitation, they reified existing structures. Because society typically rejects coercion as a legitimate means of control, we use rhetorical strategies to remind people of the structure within which their agendas must fit. Mystery grows as people acquiesce to these strategies of unobtrusive control.

The same process functions in other organizational settings—for instance, when women legitimize patriarchally structured religious institutions by participating in church sponsored service clubs. Political systems also augment legitimacy when urging citizens to exercise their liberty by voting for political candidates. High voter turn-out then reifies both the system and the winning candidate. Thus, by manipulating identity and rationalizing action, authority figures legitimize hierarchical relationships (Conrad and Ryan, 1985, p. 247–248).

Identification with particular levels of the hierarchy, however, always creates the potential for alienation. Sennett (1980) observes that "we have a freedom to disbelieve in authority, and more importantly to declare our disbelief" (p. 119). Such rejection results in alienation, which leads to distrust of the fundamental processes whereby deprivation occurs. Ironically, alienated members are not freed from organizational constraints. Rather, their motives become suspect, and their status is diminished until they become non-persons. Turnage lost his credibility as a "serious" participant. Similarly, patriarchally administered churches are no longer responsible for the salvation of those women who become alienated by oppressive rules. In the political arena, citizens who refuse to vote lose the "right" to dissent. Personal alienation thus releases the organization from any responsibilities it may have had toward individual members.[1]

Mystifying organizational hierarchy encourages compliance with prevailing domination patterns. The present analysis attempts to identify the strategic nature of such compliance. Because it is grounded in the context provided by a specific Senate hearing, the strategies and tactics identified do not constitute all possible means of structuring hierarchy. However, they do illustrate how the dialectic of control affects institutional authority. Burke (1969, p. 31) suggests that when acquiescing to authority, persons adopt the belief structure of the authority figure. Hearing participants embraced the organization's beliefs and values by deferring to leaders. Such displays of deference embedded the notion of respectful obedience in the mundane order of organizational life. Authority thereafter exercised by both McClure and Wallop was "more complete than coercion because in its routine appearance it [was] protected from challenges and examinations" (Deetz & Kersten, 1983, p. 164). By accepting and reinforcing hierarchical division, members consummated their identification with institutional authority. Thus, rhetorical strategies reconstituted power relationships.

Sennett (1980) argues that while "domination is a necessary disease the social organism suffers, . . . we can fight against it" (p. 189). Rhetorical analysis of dominance and displacement enables the researcher to ground such an agenda in Burke's (1984) "activist concept of resignation . . . [wherein one resigns] oneself to struggle" (p. 271). Although the ironical consequence of Turnage's alienation in the restricted context of the hearing was to perpetuate institutional forms, such reproduction could have turned out differently. For example, his constituency could have become physically violent, or Cutler could have joined him in attempting to negate the hearing's orderly image. Although the hearing buttressed McClure's image as a "reasonable" man, the bill did not pass. Cutler, who was subordinate to McClure and Wallop, made use of resources available within the system to influence the outcome of the hearing. While his rhetorical strategies reproduced existing authority relationships, his behavior also legitimized his constituency as a potential participant in future wilderness decision making. Choices made by these agents led to constant transformation of the hearing's structure. Potential for change increases as organizational members penetrate vulnerable points of any hierarchy. Thus, although domination remains an inherent condition of human organization, perceptive participation may render its character more pliant.

Note

[1] Peter d'Errico. (1986, November), *Corporate personality and the commoditization of persons*. This paper presented at the American Legal Studies Association Meeting, Philadelphia, the interaction of personal alienation, or estrangement, and judicial decision making regarding corporate organizations. d'Errico argues that the construct of corporate personality has provided corporations with legal protection from individuals who have become estranged from the corporation.

References

Burke, K. (1957). *The philosophy of literary form: Studies in symbolic action.* NY: Vintage Books.

_____. (1959). *Attitudes toward history.* Los Altos, CA: Hermes Publications.

_____. (1969). *A rhetoric of motives* (Rev. ed.). Berkeley: University of California Press.

_____. (1984). *Permanence and change—an anatomy of purpose* (Rev. ed.). Berkeley: University of California Press.

Conrad, C. (1985). Chrysanthemums and swords: A reading of contemporary organizational communication theory and research. *The Southern Speech Communication Journal, 50,* 189–200.

Conrad, C. & Ryan, M. (1985). Power, praxis, and self in organizational communication theory. In R. D. McPhee & P. K. Tompkins (Eds.), *Organizational communication: Traditional themes and new directions* (pp. 235–258). Beverly Hills: Sage.

Deetz, S. A. & Kersten, A. (1983). Critical models of interpretive research. In L. L. Putnam & M. E. Pacanowsky (Eds.), *Communication and organizations: An interpretive approach* (pp. 147–172). Beverly Hills: Sage.

Deetz, S., & Mumby, D. (1985). Metaphors, information, and power. *Information and Behavior, 1,* 369–386.

d'Errico, P. (1986, November), *Corporate personality and the commoditization of persons.* Paper presented at the American Legal Studies Association Meeting, Philadelphia.

Evered, R. (1983). The language of organizations: The case of the Navy. In L. R. Pondy, P. J. Frost, G. Morgan, & T. C. Dandridge (Eds.), *Organizational symbolism* (pp. 125–143). Greenwich, CT: JAI Press.

Farrell, T. B. (1982). Knowledge in time: Toward an extension of rhetorical form. In J. R. Cox & C. A. Willard (Eds.). *Advances in argumentation theory and research* (pp. 123–153). Carbondale: Southern Illinois University Press.

Fowler, R. & Kress, G. (1979a). Critical linguistics. In R. Fowler, B. Hodge, G. Kress, & T. Trew (Eds.), *Language and control* (pp. 185–213). London: Routledge & Kegan Paul.

———. (1979b). Rules and regulations. In R. Fowler, B. Hodge, G. Kress, & T. Trew (Eds.), *Language and control* (pp. 26–45). London: Routledge & Kegan Paul.

Giddens, A. (1979). *Central problems in social theory: Action, structure and contraction in social analysis.* Berkeley: University of California Press.

———. (1984). *The constitution of society: Outline of the theory of structuration.* Berkeley: University of California Press.

Goffman, E. (1981). *Forms of talk.* Philadelphia: University of Pennsylvania Press.

Hodge, B. & Fowler, R. (1979). Orwellian linguistics. In R. Fowler, B. Hodge, G. Kress, & T. Trew (Eds.), *Language and control* (pp. 6–25). London: Routledge & Kegan Paul.

Jacobs, S. & Jackson, S. (1983). Strategy and structure in conversational influence attempts. *Communication Monographs, 50,* 285–304.

Lakoff, G. & Johnson, M. (1981). Conceptual metaphor in everyday language. In M. Johnson (Ed.), *Philosophical perspectives on metaphor* (pp. 286–328). Minneapolis: University of Minnesota Press.

McPhee, R. D. & Tompkins, P. K. (Eds.). (1985). *Organizational communication: Traditional themes and new directions.* Beverly Hills: Sage.

Oravec, C. (1981). John Muir, Yosemite, and the sublime response: A study in the rhetoric of preservationism. *Quarterly Journal of Speech, 67,* 245–258.

———. (1984). Conservationism vs. preservationism: The "public interest" in the Hetch Hetchy controversy. *Quarterly Journal of Speech, 70,* 444–458.

Pacanowsky, M. E. & O'Donnell-Trujillo, N. (1983). Organizational communication as cultural performance. *Communication Monographs, 50,* 126–147.

Pepper, S. (1982). Metaphor in philosophy. *The Journal of Mind and Behavior, 3,* 197–205.

Peterson, T. R. (1986). The will to conservation: A Burkeian analysis of dust bowl rhetoric and American farming motives. *The Southern Speech Communication Journal, 52,* 1–21.

Pfeffer, J. (1982). *Organizations and organization theory.* Boston: Pitman.

Pondy, L. R., Frost, P. J., Morgan, G., & Dandridge, T. C. (Eds.). (1983). *Organizational symbolism.* Greenwich, CT: JAI Press.

Putnam, L. L. & Pacanowsky, M. E. (Eds.). (1983). *Communication and organizations: An interpretive approach.* Beverly Hills: Sage.

Riley, P. (1983). A structurationist account of political culture. *Administrative Science Quarterly, 28,* 414–437.

Senate Hearing of S. 842 (Ap. 22, 23, Jn. 17, 1981). Subcommittee on Public Lands and Reserved Water of the Committee on Energy and Natural Resources. 97th Congress, 1st Session.

Sennett, R. (1980). *Authority*. New York: Knopf.

Smircich, L. (1983). Concepts of culture and organizational analysis. *Administrative Science Quarterly*, 28, 339–358.

Smith, R. C. & Eisenberg, E. M. (1987). Conflict at Disneyland: A root-metaphor analysis. *Communication Monographs*, 54, pp. 367–380.

Trujillo, N. (1985). Organizational communication as cultural performance: Some managerial considerations. *Southern Speech Communication Journal*, 50, 201–224.

Winch, M. G. (1986, November). *Authority and Organization: A Burkeian Perspective on Organizational Persuasion*. Paper presented at the Speech Communication Association Convention, Chicago.

Worster, D. (1979). *Dust bowl: The southern plains in the 1930s*. New York: Oxford University Press.

Additional Samples

Generative Criticism

Concepts or Theories as the Source for Units of Analysis

Browne, Stephen. "'Like Gory Spectres': Representing Evil in Theodore Weld's *American Slavery as It Is*." *Quarterly Journal of Speech*, 80 (August 1994), 277–92.

Burkholder, Thomas R. "Kansas Populism, Woman Suffrage, and the Agrarian Myth: A Case Study in the Limits of Mythic Transcendence." *Communication Studies*, 40 (Winter 1989), 292–307.

Collins, Catherine Ann, and Jeanne E. Clark. "Jim Wright's Resignation Speech: De-Legitimization or Redemption?" *Southern Communication Journal*, 58 (Fall 1992), 67–75.

Fabj, Valeria. "Motherhood as Political Voice: The Rhetoric of the Mothers of Plaza de Mayo." *Communication Studies*, 44 (Spring 1993), 1–18.

Glynn, Kevin. "Reading Supermarket Tabloids as Menippean Satire." *Communication Studies*, 44 (Spring 1993), 19–37.

Gonzalez, Alberto, and John J. Makay. "Rhetorical Ascription and the Gospel According to Dylan." *Quarterly Journal of Speech*, 69 (February 1983), 1–14.

Killingsworth, M. Jimmie, and Jacqueline S. Palmer. "The Discourse of 'Environmentalist Hysteria.'" *Quarterly Journal of Speech*, 81 (February 1995), 1–19.

King, Andrew, and Kenneth Petress. "Universal Public Argument and the Failure of Nuclear Freeze." *Southern Communication Journal*, 55 (Winter 1990), 162–74.

Mackey-Kallis, Susan, and Dan F. Hahn. "Questions of Public Will and Private Action: The Power of the Negative in the Reagans' 'Just Say No' Morality Campaign." *Communication Quarterly*, 39 (Winter 1991), 1–17.

Mackey-Kallis, Susan, and Dan Hahn. "Who's to Blame for America's Drug Problem?: The Search for Scapegoats in the 'War on Drugs.'" *Communication Quarterly*, 42 (Winter 1994), 1–20.

Medhurst, Martin J. "The Rhetorical Structure of Oliver Stone's *JFK*." *Critical Studies in Mass Communication*, 10 (June 1993), 128–43.

Moore, Mark P. "Life, Liberty, and the Handgun: The Function of Synecdoche in the Brady Bill Debate." *Communication Quarterly*, 42 (Fall 1994), 434–47.

Murphy, John M. "Civic Republicanism in the Modern Age: Adlai Stevenson in the 1952 Presidential Campaign." *Quarterly Journal of Speech*, 80 (August 1994), 313–28.

Murphy, John M. "Epideictic and Deliberative Strategies in Opposition to War: The Paradox of Honor and Expediency." *Communication Studies*, 43 (Summer 1992), 65–78.

Rasmussen, Karen, and Sharon D. Downey. "Dialectical Disorientation in Vietnam War Films: Subversion of the Mythology of War." *Quarterly Journal of Speech*, 77 (May 1991), 176–95.

Rushing, Janice Hocker. "E.T. as Rhetorical Transcendence." *Quarterly Journal of Speech*, 71 (May 1985), 188–203.

Sellnow, Deanna D., and Timothy L. Sellnow. "John Corigliano's 'Symphony No. 1' as a Communicative Medium for the AIDS Crisis." *Communication Studies*, 44 (Summer 1993), 87–101.

Stuckey, Mary E., and Frederick J. Antczak. "The Battle of Issues and Images: Establishing Interpretive Dominance." *Communication Quarterly*, 42 (Spring 1994), 120–32.

Wendt, Ronald F., and Gail T. Fairhurst. "Looking for 'The Vision Thing': The Rhetoric of Leadership in the 1992 Presidential Election." *Communication Quarterly*, 42 (Spring 1994), 180–95.

Research Question as the Source for Units of Analysis

Benson, James A. "Crisis Revisited: An Analysis of Strategies Used by Tylenol in the Second Tampering Episode." *Central States Speech Journal*, 39 (Spring 1988), 49–66.

Browne, Stephen H. "Samuel Danforth's *Errand into the Wilderness* and the Discourse of Arrival in Early American Culture." *Communication Quarterly*, 40 (Spring 1992), 91–101.

Dionisopoulos, George N., and Richard E. Crable. "Definitional Hegemony as a Public Relations Strategy: The Rhetoric of the Nuclear Power Industry After Three Mile Island." *Central States Speech Journal*, 39 (Summer 1988), 134–45.

Dionisopoulos, George N., and Steven R. Goldzwig. "'The Meaning of Vietnam': Political Rhetoric as Revisionist Cultural History." *Quarterly Journal of Speech*, 78 (February 1992), 61–79.

Foss, Sonja K., and Karen A. Foss. "The Construction of Feminine Spectatorship in Garrison Keillor's Radio Monologues." *Quarterly Journal of Speech*, 80 (November 1994), 410–26.

Gow, Joe. "Mood and Meaning in Music Video: The Dynamics of AudioVisual Synergy." *Southern Communication Journal*, 59 (Spring 1994), 255–61.

Jorgensen-Earp, Cheryl R. "The Lady, The Whore, and The Spinster: The Rhetorical Use of Victorian Images of Women." *Western Journal of Speech Communication*, 54 (Winter 1990), 82–98.

Logue, Cal M. "Coping with Defeat Rhetorically: Sherman's March through Georgia." *Southern Communication Journal*, 58 (Fall 1992), 55–66.

Logue, Cal M. "The Rhetorical Complicity Indigenous to Winning the North Georgia Campaign." *Communication Studies*, 43 (Summer 1992), 124–31.

Salvador, Michael. "The Rhetorical Subversion of Cultural Boundaries: The National Consumers' League." *Southern Communication Journal*, 59 (Summer 1994), 318–32.